LEARNING
FOUNDATION

An Active Learning Approach

Business
Decision Analysis

D0569519

LEEDS BECKETT UNIVERSITY
LIBRARY
DISCARDED

LEEDS BECKETT UNIVERSITY
LIBRARY
DISCARDED

Leeds Metropolitan University

17 0527514 X

LEEDS BECKETT UNIVERSITY

THE
OPEN
LEARNING
FOUNDATION

An Active Learning Approach

BUSINESS DECISION ANALYSIS

**Graham Hackett and
Peter Luffrum**

BLACKWELL
Business

Copyright © Open Learning Foundation Enterprises Ltd, 1999

This edition © Blackwell Publishers Ltd, 1999

First published 1999

Blackwell Publishers Ltd
108 Cowley Road
Oxford OX4 1JF
UK

Blackwell Publishers Inc
Commerce Place
350 Main Street
Malden, MA 02148
USA

All rights reserved. Except for the quotation of short passages for the
purposes of criticism and review, no part of this publication may be reproduced,
stored in a retrieval system, or transmitted, in any form or by any means, electronic,
mechanical, photocopying, recording or otherwise, without the prior permission
of the publisher.

Except in the United States of America, this book is sold subject to the condition
that it shall not, by way of trade or otherwise, be lent, resold, hired out or otherwise
circulated without the publisher's prior consent in any form of binding or cover
other than that in which it is published and without a similar condition
including this condition being imposed on the subsequent purchaser.

British Library Cataloguing in Publication Data

A CIP catalogue record for this book is available from the British Library

Library of Congress Cataloging-in-Publication Data

Library of Congress data has been applied for.

The ISBN for this title is 0631 201 769

This book is printed on acid-free paper

LEEDS METROPOLITAN
UNIVERSITY
LIBRARY

1705525 S14X
BSQB
BV-HG-371
80.6.07
658.3054 MAC
LEEDS BECKETT UNIVERSITY

Acknowledgements

For the Open Learning Foundation

Martin Gibson (University of Central Lancashire), *Series Editor*

Tim Gutteridge, *Copy Editor and Open Learning Editor*

George Rawlings (University of Central Lancashire), *Reviewer*

Leslie Mapp, *Director of Programmes*

Stephen Moulds (DSM Partnership), *Production Manager*

Caroline Pelletier, *Publishing Manager*

Julia Peart, *Programmes Assistant*

Copyright acknowledgements

Every effort has been made to contact copyright holders, but if any have been inadvertently overlooked, the Open Learning Foundation will be pleased to make the necessary arrangements at the first opportunity.

Contents

Unit 4   Regression Analysis   277

Appendix 1 Drawing charts with *Microsoft Excel*

Appendix 2 Installing the regression tool

GUIDE FOR STUDENTS

Course introduction

Welcome to *Business Decision Analysis*. The objectives of this guide are:

- to explain why it is important for you to study business decision analysis as part of your degree

- to give you an outline of the subject of business decision analysis

- to describe the nature of the material on which this workbook is based

- to outline the programme which you will be following

- to offer practical hints and advice on how to study business decision analysis using the open learning approach

- to point out some of the advantages to you of studying business decision analysis by the method used in this book.

Why study Business Decision Analysis?

For those involved in business, particularly for those in managerial positions, the ability to make effective decisions or to contribute to the decision-making process is of vital importance. The ability to use mathematical techniques is becoming an increasingly important part of the manager's 'tool kit', especially as low cost and more powerful information technology becomes accessible and enables more sophisticated techniques to be utilised. Even for those who are not themselves primarily involved in the use of mathematical techniques to improve business decision-making, the ability to interpret quantitative information and to understand the strengths and limitations of the techniques being used are often important aspects of the managerial role.

The examples and activities utilised within the module will provide some clues as to the range of applications to which BDA can be put. Throughout the text you will have the opportunity to work on problems relating to investment decisions, marketing and distribution, and product development. By working through the exercises you will begin to understand the potential which BDA can bring to improving decisions in areas as diverse as organisational planning and forecasting, human resource management and manufacturing.

As well as acquiring specific techniques which can be used to support effective decision making, the study of BDA also provides some important underpinning skills which have a more general application. So, for example, the module emphasises the importance of carefully defining problems before solutions are sought, of specifying the criteria which will be used in reaching acceptable solutions, of identifying the resource constraints which influence what the business can achieve and so on. These are important skills to acquire whether one intends to work in specialist decision support roles or in more generalist positions.

City Campus Library
Self Issue
Leeds Metropolitan University

Customer name: Garrido, Dinay . (Miss)
Customer ID: 0333478173

Title: Business decision analysis : an active
learning approach
ID: 170527514X
Due: 21/3/2013,23:59

Title: Quantitative approaches in business
studies
ID: 1704341402
Due: 21/3/2013,23:59

Total items: 2
07/03/2013 11:51
Checked out: 2
Overdue: 0
Hold requests: 0
Ready for pickup: 0

Student Survey Season -
Have your say!
Chance to win an iPad, iPod Touch
or £50 iTunes voucher
To take part log in to X-Stream

What is in this workbook?

Business Decision Analysis presents an introductory overview of the study of the quantitative analysis of business problems and decisions. It covers material one would normally expect to encounter in the second year of an undergraduate business studies degree.

The module is intended to be largely free-standing, although it does build on some of the material contained in *Quantitative Methods*, one of the other modules in the Active Learning series.

The workbook is divided into six study units. These have been written specifically for undergraduate business students by authors who are experienced in teaching such courses. *Business Decision Analysis* is designed as part of a series of interactive texts designed to cover the entire curriculum of an undergraduate Business Studies degree. It can be used by itself or in conjunction with the other volumes in the series.

This module is particularly useful for students who may be following a course in which an 'open learning' approach is being used. The features which make it particularly suitable for open learning include:

- very careful sequencing of the materials so that there is a clear and logical progression

- a step-by-step approach so that you will be able to understand each new point thoroughly before proceeding to the next one

- a very clear layout with relatively short sections and paragraphs

- numerous activities and examples which help to illustrate the ideas and provide opportunities for analysis and developing understanding

- lots of opportunities for you to check that you understand what you have just read.

Students on more conventional courses will also find that the workbook provides a useful supplement to other text books which they may have been recommended.

Although the workbook is designed to be complete in itself, your understanding of the subject will be improved by wider reading. Each unit therefore has a list of recommended reading to guide you towards the more important and useful literature.

Unit structure

Unit 1 considers the theoretical nature of the material which is developed later in the module and provides an overview of the theory and practice of BDA. You will then consider the kind of business problems that the BDA specialist can work on and the different stages of the BDA approach. The unit develops the idea of mathematical model building and explains the ways in which mathematical models can be used for exploring business situations and attempting to predict the behaviour of business systems. Unit 2 considers decision-making under conditions of risk and uncertainty and examines a range of techniques for decision-analysis in these circumstances. Unit 3 considers linear programming as a basis for decision-making which is designed to maximise (or minimise) business objectives. We also explore some of the extensions of the technique and some of its limitations.

Unit 4 introduces the technique of regression analysis which enables us to model key variables in a business situation, variables such as costs or sales volumes for example, and to predict how these variables might behave in the future. In Unit 5 we examine a number of techniques for analysing time-series data such as information on sales, output and profits over successive periods of time. We also consider how such analysis can be used as the basis for forecasting future values of the variables concerned. Finally in Unit 6 we consider the use of simulation methods for building working models of the dynamics of business and for understanding issues such as cash flow and inventory control. As with the techniques explored in some of the other units, considerable use will be made of Microsoft Excel.

Using the workbook

You will probably find it most effective to work through the units in sequence. You should begin by noting the points which the unit outline identifies as the crucial aspects of the material. This will put the contents of the units into context and guide you through them.

Each unit is based around a number of activities. All of these are intended to be attempted by you as they arise and should be completed before you move on. The suggested solutions to each activity and the commentaries about them are given immediately after each activity.

The activities are intended to give you practice and the opportunity to reinforce your knowledge and understanding. Avoid the temptation to skip through the activities quickly. They are there to assist you in developing your knowledge and understanding and your confidence with the material. Often the activities are included in order to develop important learning points and the commentaries which follow them provide an important basis for discussing the ideas and techniques being covered. Rather like a question and answer session in a tutorial they are included to help you learn and not just to test your understanding.

Some of the activities will only take you a few minutes to deal with. By contrast, others may take considerably longer to complete. It is important that you discipline yourself to complete each activity before you refer to the answer provided.

During the module you will be exploring a number of computer-based techniques. In order to complete many of the activities, therefore, you will need access to a computer with *Microsoft Excel* (version 5 or later) installed. The module contains all the instructions you need to work with *Excel*. If you have previously read *Business Skills*, one of the other modules in the Active Learning series, will find that *Business Decision Analysis* reinforces and develops some of the IT skills covered in that volume.

Avoid rote learning

You should avoid any attempt at rote learning the material in this workbook. You should aim to understand the underlying logic in the ideas presented by working carefully through all the activities. Simply trying to learn and remember the techniques is inappropriate and insufficient. Rather, you should attempt to understand the principles behind the ideas and models, and understand the thinking behind the particular techniques presented.

Set time aside for your studies

At the start of the study period you will not know how long it will take to do the necessary work. It is sensible, therefore, to make a start on the work at an early stage in the study period. Try to discipline yourself to set aside particular times in the week to study, though not necessarily the same times each week. Experiment with different ways of studying the material to find the one which suits you. Try skimming each unit to get a grasp of the ideas covered before you go through it in detail. Alternatively, try reading the unit objectives and the summaries before you settle down to study the unit in any depth. Try to find the most suitable time to study when your concentration is at its highest and interruptions are at a minimum. And do set aside sufficient time to complete all the activities – they are a crucial part of the learning process.

UNIT 1
AN INTRODUCTION TO BUSINESS DECISION ANALYSIS

Introduction

This unit provides an introduction to the very practical subject of **business decision analysis** (BDA). Throughout the course, you will be learning how to define business problems and how to use different techniques to obtain solutions to these problems. It will be all too easy to lose sight of the important matters of scientific, philosophical and mathematical theory which underpin the methods you will be studying. The main aims of this introductory unit, therefore, are to allow you to develop a general perspective on the subject of BDA and to give you some insight into its theoretical background.

In this unit we will be studying themes which we will revisit as we make progress through the module. We will also be investigating what BDA is, and what sort of problems it attempts to solve. We will then look at model building in general, prior to undertaking a more detailed analysis of mathematical models in particular. We will study the ways in which the different factors in a problem may vary, and we will also consider the effect of such variability on the decision-making process.

Objectives

By the end of this unit you should be able to:

- define the meaning of **business decision analysis** (BDA)
- list the various stages in the BDA process
- describe some typical problems amenable to BDA
- differentiate between **physical, analogue** and **mathematical models**
- list the various stages of the model-building process
- define the terms **deterministic** and **stochastic** as used in BDA
- explain the difference between **single-attribute** and **multi-attribute decision models**
- explain what is meant by **sensitivity analysis.**

SECTION 1

What is Business Decision Analysis?

Introduction

In this module, you will be learning about the subject we call **business decision analysis**, sometimes called simply BDA for short. It is therefore useful to reflect on the wider environment in which BDA is used. Perhaps it is not very helpful to think of BDA as a subject at all. Sometimes it seems more like a ragbag of techniques searching for uses, while many of the writers, academics and practitioners working in this area cannot even agree on a single name to give to it. You will sometimes also hear it referred to as **management science**, and sometimes by the name of **operational research** (OR). In order to avoid confusion, we will normally use the term **business decision analysis** or the abbreviation BDA.

In this section we will look firstly at what BDA actually does, and then at the special role of **quantitative analysis** within it. This aim will be achieved by considering some practical problems of the type encountered by the analyst.

By the end of this section you should be able to define the meaning of BDA, list the various stages in the BDA process and describe some typical problems amenable to BDA.

1.1 A definition of BDA

One definition of the activity carried out by practitioners in the area of BDA is given here.

"BDA combines scientific method and the tools of quantitative analysis to:

- define business problems
- assess the criteria for listing acceptable solutions to these problems
- investigate the resources and limitations which constrain the decision-maker's choices between the different solutions
- choose the best possible solution to the problem."

So the definition of problems is an important early goal of the decision-maker. It does not follow that the decision-maker will find it easy to define the problem (or problems), nor is it always the case that he or she will be aware that there is a problem at all. Even when a problem is recognised, it does not follow that adoption of a suitable problem-solving strategy is an easy matter. Decision-makers do not have a free hand in the choice of solution, for some decision alternatives will not be possible given the constraints of human resources, materials and finance found in any business situation. If several solutions are possible, the problem of selecting the best one arises, together with the concomitant task of deciding exactly what 'best' means in any given situation. BDA can help the decision-maker by using a body of quantitative techniques to search for possible solutions to a problem and evaluate them critically.

1.2 Management and quantitative analysis

The practice of management is often portrayed as an essentially qualitative process, with heavy emphasis placed on individual managerial judgement and the use of creativity and intuition. While these are certainly essential business skills, unless managers can couple their creative visions with some quantitative analysis, there is a danger that their ideas will come to nothing.

Fortunately, the application of analytical tools to management has gained greatly from the development and diffusion of computing technology. Many BDA techniques require substantial amounts of complicated calculations. The change from large mainframes towards networked systems of microcomputers means that a modern manager can now expect to have personal hands-on access to both the software and the hardware required to perform such calculations.

While the results of such universal access have in general been beneficial, a cautionary note must always be attached to the use of analytical tools. Such tools should be used to support managerial judgement, not to supplant it. They can provide information which will aid the decision-making process, but they cannot make the decision themselves.

1.3 Some typical problems encountered in BDA

What sort of problems might typically be encountered in BDA? Here are some simple examples. Do not attempt to solve them just now: they are merely provided here as illustrative examples of BDA problems. You will be asked to solve them later, as you work your way through Units 2 to 6.

Case Study: the dockland corporation

A dockland corporation has received approval for the construction of a marina, which will require an investment of £2.5 million. The required funds will come from a debenture issue and loans from two merchant banks. (**Debentures** are loans at fixed interest raised by issuing bonds to the general public.) Underwriters have informed the corporation that they will be unable to sell more than £1 million in debentures at the proposed rate of 12 per cent. Two merchant bankers are involved, *Strider* and *Gelthorn*. *Strider* will loan up to £2 million at an interest rate of 14 per cent but insists that the amount of debenture debt plus the amount owed to *Gelthorn* will be no more than twice the amount owed to itself. *Gelthorn* will loan an amount up to the amount loaned by *Strider* but at a rate of 16 per cent. The dockland corporation must decide how to raise its funds.

Case Study: the machine tool manufacturer

A manufacturing company would like to develop a method for forecasting sales of machine tools in Britain. The company has monthly data concerning sales performance in the recent past. It also has some reliable data on advertising expenditure for machine tools, and some data about the general level of economic activity in Britain. The company must decide how to go about choosing a suitable method for forecasting product sales for the period ahead. The company also needs to know if its forecasting system works.

Case Study: the distribution problem

A business anxious to keep its costs to a minimum is considering how to transport products from its three manufacturing plants (Ternville, Doveton and Kempside) to each of three distribution warehouses (Ampleside, Beerside and Cheapside). Ternville has a production capacity of 150 units compared with 450 each for Doveton and Kempside. Ampleside needs 450 units while Beerside and Cheapside both need 300 units. Per unit it costs Ternville £7.50 to supply Ampleside, £3.00 to supply Beerside and £4.50 to supply Cheapside. Unit shipping cost for Doveton is £12.00 to Ampleside, £6.00 to Beerside and £4.50 to Cheapside. To ship from Kempside costs £13.50 per unit to Ampleside, £10.50 to Beerside and £7.00 to Cheapside. The company needs to plan its transportation.

Case Study: the builders' merchants

A tiling firm is considering the marketing of a new roofing tile which would be sold in lots of 1,000, at a provisional selling price of £255 per lot. Costs may vary from week to week. For example, unit cost could be anything between £155 and £195 per lot, while fixed cost might be any value between £5,250 and £5,950 per week. Sales volume could be any value between 70 and 150 lots per week, but it is thought that these values are unlikely and that the most likely weekly sales volume is 110 lots. The firm needs to calculate the weekly distribution of profits likely to result from this data. It then needs to decide whether to proceed with the new product.

Case Study: prospecting for oil

An oil company recently purchased an area of land, together with testing and drilling rights. The company believes that there is a 55 per cent chance of finding oil in sufficient quantities to exploit. If the company drills and finds oil, returns are estimated at £100 million over and above the cost of the land. If no oil is found the company will be able to sell the land but for an estimated £40 million less than the original price. If the company does not wish to take on the risk of drilling, it can dispose of the land and all rights on the open market for a return of £45 million, but only before any test drillings have been undertaken.

A preliminary geological survey is a possibility. If oil is present, the survey has a 77 per cent chance of detecting it. If oil is not present then it has an 83 per cent chance of making a correct survey decision. If the preliminary test shows a positive result then the land can be disposed of on the open market for £70 million. If the test is negative, then a sale of the land rights will yield only £15 million. This preliminary survey costs £500,000. The oil company must decide what to do with the land.

Before we begin examining the above problems in a little more detail, try the following activity.

ACTIVITY 1

Without looking back to Section 1.1, complete the following sentence to provide a definition of BDA.

BDA combines scientific method and the tools of quantitative analysis to:

define ...

assess ...

investigate ...

choose ...

Compare your answer to the definition given in Section 1.1.

1.4 The BDA problems revisited

We will now consider the problems in a little more detail.

THE DOCKLAND CORPORATION

ACTIVITY 2

Reread the definition of BDA in Section 1 and then look back at the problem involving the dockland corporation.

1. What is the corporation's problem?

2. Is there more than one possible solution to the problem?

3. What limitations prevent the corporation from choosing any solution it likes?

4. What criteria do you think it might adopt in preferring one solution to another?

1. The corporation's problem is to carry out the investment proposal. It has to borrow money in order to do this and we can assume that the corporation would like to make a high return from this investment by keeping borrowing costs low.

2. Since the company can borrow the money by issuing bonds and by borrowing from two different bankers in differing proportions, there is a range of possible solutions to the problem. Even if the company aims to attain the highest possible return on its investment, there may still be different ways of achieving this. However, some of the possible solutions to the problem may be ruled out because of limited resources or other restrictions.

3. Both banks have lending restrictions. *Strider* requires that money obtained from other sources (debentures and *Gelthorn*) is no more than twice the amount loaned by *Strider* itself (which is subject to 14 per cent interest and an upper limit of £2 million). *Gelthorn* will restrict the amount it will advance to a maximum figure matching the *Strider* loan, but at the higher rate of 16 per cent.

4. If there are no other limitations on the choice exercised by the corporation, the decision-maker will need to borrow money from all three sources in such a way as to:

   ● minimise the cost of borrowing **and**

   ● stay within the £1 million debenture limit **and**

   ● satisfy the lending requirements of the two merchant bankers.

In the event, a quantitative tool called **linear programming** is at the disposal of decision-makers. It has been specifically devised to assist in the analysis of such problems as that of the dockland corporation. It is a substantial and important part of the business decision analyst's toolkit and Unit 3 is devoted to it.

THE MACHINE TOOL MANUFACTURER

There are two problems facing the machine tool manufacturer: to construct a forecasting system (designed specifically to use the data they have), and to measure the extent to which this forecasting system delivers accurate forecasts.

These two problems raise a number of subsidiary issues which need to be addressed. We must first decide whether the sales data possessed by the company is the only pertinent information it has to hand. If the answer to this question is 'yes', we will identify whether the sales data contains any patterns which will assist in the task of forecasting. Such a measurement of a single variable over time is described as a **time series** and there are established procedures available to deal with its analysis.

However, there may be other relevant data (such as amount spent on advertising, economic activity levels and so forth). If this is the case, there are other techniques available which we can use to analyse such data in order to generate predictions. Once we have identified the data available and an appropriate technique for analysing it, we still have to decide whether the technique selected is the best available both now and in the future. In short, we have to develop a good forecasting system. But as we have seen, deciding what 'good' means in the context of forecasting may be difficult.

The problem of forecasting is a matter you will learn considerably more about in the units on **regression analysis** (Unit 4) and **time series analysis** (Unit 5).

THE DISTRIBUTION PROBLEM

The problem here is how to decide the amount to be shipped from each of the manufacturing units to each of the warehousing depots in such a way as to minimise the costs of the activity. You will probably have spotted that it is not possible to just suggest always shipping the required amounts by the cheapest route, attractive though that proposition might be. There are the obvious limitations of the supply available at each manufacturing unit. Also (although it is not mentioned in this problem), there may be problems of limited capacity on some routes, which might conflict with the route's desirability in terms of low cost. Again, we have a problem which can be stated in terms of achieving some clear objective (in this case, minimum cost) complicated by the need to balance possible limitations on our freedom of action.

You may well have spotted a similarity between this problem and that of the dockland corporation and, in fact, a solution may be obtained using the same techniques. However, this particular set of circumstances is an example of such a large sub-group of linear programming problems that a special technique called the **transportation algorithm** has been developed to deal with them. You will be studying this topic in the unit on **linear programming** (Unit 3).

THE BUILDERS' MERCHANTS

At first sight there may seem to be no obvious problem here. However, since the firm has yet to decide whether or not to launch the new roofing tile, we could define the problem as one of viability. Is the estimated profit from the product likely to be sufficient to justify production?

What makes this type of problem different from an orthodox accounting problem of breakeven points and profit calculation is the uncertainty surrounding the behaviour of fixed costs, unit costs and sales volume. In such circumstances, an accountant might ask questions about the financial situation such as 'what if sales volume were X, fixed costs were Y and unit costs were Z?'.

Although the technique of asking 'what if' questions in financial (and other) analysis is a powerful one and not to be disparaged, it only gives part of the picture here. Since costs and volume are uncertain, an equally pertinent question is 'how likely is it that a particular outcome will happen?'.

There are many such cases in BDA where, although some of the factors in a business problem are under the control of the decision-maker, others are subject to the laws of chance. There is a technique called **simulation,** which makes it possible to discern an underlying structure in problems which might otherwise seem to be at the whim of chance. You will be studying simulation in Unit 6.

PROSPECTING FOR OIL

ACTIVITY 3

Now take another look at the problem entitled **prospecting for oil** in Section 1.3. Identify:

1. The possible company objectives.

2. The possible solutions to the problem.

3. The factors which limit the choice of a possible solution.

---

1. The company might wish to maximise the potential return connected with the land it has purchased. Alternatively, the company may try to minimise its potential losses. Since we are dealing with a situation where probability is a key feature, the company might also wish to take the decision which has the least risk.

2. The company must firstly consider whether to sell the land or to keep it and drill for oil. If it sells the land that is the end of the matter, but if the company has made the wrong decision it will have lost the opportunity (if oil is later found) to make rich returns. Of course, if it has made the right decision then it will have saved itself from making a potential loss. If the company decides to retain the land, then the matter is not over. It must then decide whether or not to commission a special geological survey which, unfortunately, does not have a 100 per cent success rate at detecting oil. So if the survey reports a positive or negative result, the company still has to decide whether or not to go ahead with full exploration.

3. The restriction affecting the choice of decision is the lack of information if any given course of action is chosen. We know that a number of outcomes are possible but have no idea which one. Even if we are able to obtain information, for example by undertaking a geological survey, the knowledge gained will be less than perfect and cannot, therefore, remove the element of risk.

This kind of problem is typical of many where the laws of chance are operative:

- we have to take one of several possible decisions
- each decision has one of a number of possible outcomes
- we cannot know in advance which outcome will occur
- some of these outcomes will result in a profit, and some in a loss.

However, while we seem to be at the mercy of uncertainty, we have some monetary amounts (profits or losses) and some probability figures which might allow us to assess the degree of risk attached to each decision. In the unit on **decision analysis** (Unit 2) we shall be studying some ways in which we might use this kind of information to clarify decision alternatives.

Summary

In this section we began by looking at a definition of BDA, and discussed the contribution of quantitative analysis to the subject. In particular, we emphasised the importance of defining the problem clearly, the need to state explicitly which criteria should be used when choosing an acceptable solution, and the kinds of resource limitations which might restrict such a choice. Finally, in order to clarify the kinds of problems which might be amenable to the analytical techniques studied in this course, we considered a number of case studies and provided an initial definition of the problems of each.

In the next section we look at the process of model building.

Section 2
Model Building in Business Decision Analysis

Introduction

Business decision analysts rarely study a problem by taking a wait-and-see approach: that is, by taking a decision and then observing what occurs. Even if such an approach were possible, it would be too costly. Instead, analysts often study problems by building a **model** of the situation first, and observing how the model behaves.

An economic or business model is an attempt to describe and capture the key characteristics of some activity or process. For example, we may be interested in the behaviour of sales over a period of time, or the way in which profit reacts to changes in other factors such as prices and costs. We can assume that the decision-maker would like some information about the likely behaviour of sales and profits before taking any decisions which might affect them. A theory or model which purported to explain and predict this behaviour would be an invaluable aid to the decision-making process. In this section we will be looking at two types of model, physical models and mathematical models.

By the end of this section you should be able to differentiate between physical, analogue and mathematical models.

2.1 Physical models

Many people studying BDA for the first time find the concept of a model in the business and economic domain difficult to grasp. A useful introduction to business modelling is via the much more familiar notion of a physical model. For example, a scale model of an aircraft or a ship is a physical model or representation of a real aircraft or ship. Such models are sometimes called **iconic** models, and their purpose has long been understood in the world of engineering.

ACTIVITY 4

1. What kind of useful information do you think an engineer might gain from building a scale model of an aircraft or ship?

2. How would the model allow the engineer to study the behaviour of the aircraft or ship?

LEEDS METROPOLITAN UNIVERSITY LIBRARY

1. The type of information which would be useful at the design stage would be the effect of various kinds of stresses and resistance on the fuselage of the aircraft, or the hull of the ship.

2. The engineer could study the behaviour of a scale model of an aircraft in a wind tunnel, or a ship in a flotation tank. The behaviour of the real aircraft or ship under various conditions could be simulated by the model, thus possibly avoiding costly design errors which might be impossible to correct after building the full-sized prototype. Of course, the laboratory tests will only be strictly true for the scale model, rather than the full-sized version. Even so, if the model successfully incorporates the features of the real version, the outcome of the lab experiments will be invaluable.

An extension of the physical model is the **analogue** model. These models are physical in form but do not have the same appearance as the object being studied. For example, the height of the fluid in a thermometer is an analogue of the behaviour of temperature. An interesting example of an analogue model is the old Treasury model of the UK economy. In this model, now regarded as something of a museum piece, the behaviour of the flows of cash, credit, income, imports and exports and so forth was modelled by an elaborate system of water flows, weights and counterweights.

2.2 Mathematical models

In the area of economic and business systems, physical and analogue models are of little use. The business analyst usually wishes to know how some complex variable, such as profits or consumer demand, is likely to behave given hypothetical changes in certain circumstances. Moreover, while the engineer using physical models usually has the advantage of dealing with scientific laws, in the economic environment there are many different forces at work, in conditions which are not always precisely definable.

For these reasons, we will have to simulate real business conditions not by building physical models but by theorising about what is, and what is not, important. We will often need to represent a problem by using a system of symbols to represent various components of it and by defining the relationships between these different components. Of course, it would be possible to define these relationships in a verbal or graphical way, but it is usually much clearer and more concise to use mathematical reasoning. Such a set of symbols and relationships is known as a mathematical model, and the study of such models is a very important element of this course. It may be useful at this stage to refer to a simple example of a mathematical model.

Case Study: **a profit problem**

A business finds that total profit is related to the quantity of the product it places on sale. The current selling price is £1.50, the fixed costs of the operation are £10,000 and unit costs are £0.50. (**Fixed costs** do not vary, whatever the level of production, while **unit costs** are the additional cost of producing each unit of product.)

If we use the symbol N to represent the quantity produced, then total revenue R will be:

$$R = 1.50N$$

And total costs TC will be equal to total unit costs plus fixed costs or:

$$TC = 0.50N + 10,000$$

Consequently, a mathematical expression for profit P will be revenue less total costs, or:

$$P = R - TC$$

$$= 1.50N - (0.50N + 10,000)$$

$$= 1.50N - 0.50N - 10,000$$

$$= N - 10,000$$

We have developed a model (albeit a simple one) to explain the behaviour of profit.

ACTIVITY 5

1. Try manipulating the above model of profit for yourself. What would the model predict the profit level would be if the business produced:

- 15,000 units of the product
- 25,000 units of the product?

2. An ability to be critical of a model is perhaps even more important than the ability to manipulate it. Can you suggest any ways in which the above model might be over-simplistic as an explanation of the behaviour of profit?

---

1. If 15,000 units were produced (N = 15,000), then profit would be:

$$P = N - 10,000$$

$$= 15,000 - 10,000$$

$$= £5,000$$

If 25,000 units were produced (N = 25,000), then profit would be:

$$P = N - 10,000$$

$$= 25,000 - 10,000$$

$$= £15,000$$

2. There are many factors which make this model over-simplistic. For a start, it is unlikely that costs will remain fixed (as the model implicitly assumes). Greater production quantities often create economies of scale, which result in lower unit costs. Similarly, the model assumes that price does not respond to supply.

In reality, it is unlikely that the company could continue to offload all of the increasing quantity of goods it makes without making a downward adjustment in price. This model acknowledges none of these complications.

You should not be unnecessarily troubled by the apparent naivety of the model described above. All mathematical models used in BDA begin life in a very simple form. They gradually become more complex as the analyst tries to make them more realistic.

Case Study

Consider the example of a retailer receiving deliveries of two products, one being supplied from Birmingham and the other from Leeds. Because of different transport costs, goods bought from Birmingham cost £0.40 per unit while those coming from Leeds cost £0.45. We need to calculate the size and cost of the total shipment of the products.

As in any mathematical model, we use symbols to represent the main elements of this situation. In this instance, let us use the symbols x and y, where x equals the amount of the product shipped from Birmingham and y equals the amount of the product shipped from Leeds.

Then the total amount of goods received by the retailer is:

$x + y$

Since each unit from Birmingham costs £0.40, then the total costs of x units from that source amounts to:

£0.40x

And the total cost of shipments from Leeds is:

£0.45y

Consequently, the total cost C of the retailer's stock is:

$C = £0.40x + £0.45y$

ACTIVITY 6

Now you can try your hand at manipulating this model.

Suppose that during the period under consideration, the retailer sells an unknown amount of each product. The retailer is able to sell the product from Birmingham at £0.50 per unit, and the product from Leeds at £0.55 per unit.

Develop an expression for the total amount of profit made during the period from these two products. (Assume that there are no other costs than those already mentioned.)

Hint: you will need to define some new mathematical symbols.

As well as the shipments received from Birmingham and Leeds (represented by the symbols (x and y), we now have to deal with the amount actually sold by the retailer, which we cannot assume to be exactly the same as the amount in stock.

We need to define two new symbols to represent sales, because there are two products, selling at different prices. Let us proceed by using the symbols a and b where a equals sales of the Birmingham product and b equals sales of the Leeds product. Since the former sells at £0.50 per unit and the latter at £0.55 per unit, then total revenue R will be:

$$R = 0.50a + 0.55b$$

Profit P is calculated as revenue minus cost, and we already know that cost C is equal to:

$$C = 0.40x + 0.45y$$

This means that the profit made by the retailer during the period can be modeled by the expression:

$$P = R - C$$

$$= (0.50a + 0.55b) - (0.40x + 0.45y)$$

There are, of course, alternative (but equivalent) ways of stating this.

This model is still fairly unsophisticated. Even so, it is more complex than the previous one since it uses the notion of supply and demand as well as revenue and cost. There are ways of making this model more realistic still. For instance, if supply was less than demand, this might place an upward pressure on price. Similarly, if supply was greater than demand, this might exert a downward pressure on price. A more sophisticated model could try to incorporate this by making price reflect the balance between supply and demand.

This is often how mathematical models progress from their initial beginnings in the imagination and the researches of the analyst through to operational usefulness in a fully fledged BDA project. They may begin as very unsophisticated first approximations to events, but gain in their sophistication and similarity to reality (and also, unfortunately, in complexity) as they develop.

Summary

This section has been concerned with the notion of a model as it is used in BDA. We began by considering the importance of gaining information about the possible consequences of any decision we may be considering. The best way to do this is to build a model of the situation we are dealing with, and study how this model reacts when we make changes to it. Next, we considered a typology of models, rejecting the physical and analogue models in favour of the mathematical model. This type of model proceeds by using mathematical symbols, operations and relationships in order to represent the real world of business. Finally, we considered two very simple models for relatively unsophisticated scenarios. We saw, however, that a model can be gradually increased in complexity if required.

In Section 3, we will examine the process of developing mathematical models in more detail.

SECTION 3

The Components of a Mathematical Model

Introduction

In Section 2 we looked at examples of two mathematical models, one for calculating profits, the other for calculating shipment costs. The process of building these models is, as yet, far from complete. We still have some way to go, in that we have only formulated mathematical statements to describe the way in which the various factors in the model might behave. This is, of course, essential to any development of a business model, but we must also have some idea as to the **objectives** which the decision-maker wishes to achieve. Perhaps the retailer in the last example has the simple objective of wishing to obtain the maximum possible profit. Can we represent such a business objective in mathematical form?

In addition, there are usually factors which place limits on the decision-maker's freedom to achieve his or her objectives. Any mathematical model must include such restrictions. In the previous example, the retailer's wish to maximise profits would probably be restricted by limitations on the amounts that could be supplied by Birmingham and Leeds. There would probably also be a point at which consumer demand for these products fell off.

In this section we examine the factors which, typically, any mathematical model will incorporate, often called the **inputs** and **outputs** of a model.

By the end of this section you should be able to list the various stages of the model-building process.

3.1 The objective

Any business problem will have an objective (or several different objectives). If there is a single objective, it is usually expressed as the wish to obtain an **optimum** solution. Economists and others are very fond of using the term **optimising** to describe certain types of goal-seeking behaviour on the part of individuals or businesses. Very often, optimising means trying to find the combination of events which brings some factor to a **minimum** or **maximum**.

Examples of this might be:

- maximising the profit made from sales of a product
- maximising the sales revenue made by a product
- maximising the number of potential consumers reached by an advertising campaign
- minimising the cost needed in order to achieve a given production plan
- minimising the materials needed in order to achieve a given production plan.

The mathematical expression which describes the decision-maker's objective is sometimes called the **objective function**, and is an important element of any mathematical model.

3.2 Constraints

There are limitations on the pursuit of the objective. These are referred to as constraints, and must be represented in the mathematical model. If there were no constraints in any given situation, then no business problem would exist. For example, if the objective of a business is to maximise the profit to be made from the production and sale of some commodity, then it is a common situation for this aim to be restricted by resource constraints. The production process may use raw materials which are in short supply, or there may be some government licensing law which restricts the amount which can be produced. These are examples of constraints which place upper limits on something: you cannot produce any more of a product than available materials will allow. Constraints can also create lower limits. For example, we may have to produce more than a certain quantity of a product because of contractual obligations we have already entered into.

3.3 Constants and variables

CONSTANTS

A **constant** (or **given**) is something which is assumed not to be subject to change, at least during the operation of our model. This does not mean that it can never change: it simply means that such factors remain fixed during the period to which we are applying the model.

VARIABLES

Variables are the factors in a model which change, either over time or when influenced by events. A complicating factor in our discussion of variables is that some of them are under the direct control of the decision-maker: they are variable factors because we choose to make them so. For example, in the profit model that we constructed in Section 2.2, we may decide that the price we charge for the product is a factor which we want to include within our model. Our own prices are under the direct control of the decision-maker. The fact that such variables are controllable by the decision-maker has earned them the alternative name of **control** or **decision variables**.

Other factors may be variable but not within our control. They vary as a result of changes in conditions which are outside the immediate influence of the decision-maker. For example, in the profit model we may decide that competitor prices are another factor which we want to include within our model. Whilst our own prices might be controllable by the decision-maker, competitor prices are definitely not. For this reason we refer to such factors as **uncontrollable variables**.

You may find some of this difficult to understand, and it is certainly true that correct identification of the various factors of a problem as either constants or controllable or uncontrollable variables can be difficult. We will have more to say about constants and variables during the module.

3.4 The model statement

The model itself is the formal definition of symbols representing the inputs described above, together with the collection of mathematical expressions which describes the relationships between them. The mathematical expressions may refer to objectives, constraints and the behaviour of variables.

3.5 Model output

When the variables, whether controllable or uncontrollable, have been specified, and the model has been formulated, the analyst may then proceed to the next stage. This usually involves evaluating the objective function for given values of the variables. This is the **output** of the model. There is nothing to prevent the analyst from continually re-evaluating the model with different specifications for the variables and thus obtaining lengthy and complex output. It is exactly this quality of repeatability which gives mathematical models their analytical advantages. We shall now apply these concepts to solving a practical problem.

ACTIVITY 7

A decision-maker is struggling with a problem and decides to use a mathematical model. He must decide how many units of a product to make in order to maximise profit. We will use the symbol x to represent the number of units made and sold.

The product sells for £180, generating a profit of £20, so that total profit can be represented by the expression:

$$P = 20x$$

Each unit of the product made uses 4 hours of labour and there are only 48 hours per week available. Therefore the number of labour hours used cannot exceed 48, so that:

$$4x \leq 48$$

Also, the business must make a profit of at least £160 per week. This can be stated as:

$$20x \geq 160$$

1. What is the objective of the decision-maker?

2. What are the constants in this problem?

3. What are the controllable variables in this problem?

4. Are there any uncontrollable variables in this problem?

5. Write out, in symbolic terms, the complete mathematical model.

6. What would be the output from the model? Illustrate by assuming a production level of 4 units.

---

1. In this problem, the objective of the decision-maker was explicitly stated as the achievement of maximum profit.

2. The constants of the situation are the product price, unit labour requirements, total labour resources and minimum profit requirement. Notice that none of these are constant in an absolute sense: they are invariate only for this particular model, and may well be variable in other situations.

3. The number of units of labour to be used is a controllable variable as it is under the control of the decision-maker.

4. There are no uncontrollable variables in this problem.

5. A full statement of the mathematical model would be:

$$P = 20x \text{ (objective)}$$

$$4x \leq 48 \text{ (labour constraint)}$$

$$20x \geq 160 \text{ (profit constraint)}$$

We need to find a value of x which maximises profit, whilst remaining within the boundaries imposed by the constraints.

6. Output from the model would be, for any give value of x, the profit achieved and the amount of labour used. For a production level of 4 units, x equals 4, so profit would be:

$$P = 20x = 80$$

As you will see in Activity 8, this solution remains within the labour constraint but breaks the profit constraint.

An alternative way of viewing the profit problem in Activity 7 is shown in Figure 1.

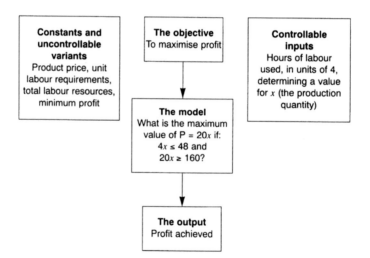

Figure 1: Decision model for the profit problem

3.6 Solving the model

Once the model has been stated, the variables and constants have been defined, and the nature of the output has been decided, the decision-maker can move to the solution stage. In the case of the problem described in Activity 7 there is only one objective: to find the production level which generates the highest profit level. One possible procedure is to use a trial-and-error procedure. That is to say, we start with a production of 1 unit, calculate the profits generated by this level, check that this is within the constraints stated in the model, and then try the same procedure with a production level of 2 units and so on, until we reach our desired objective. The next activity requires you to try just such a procedure with the profit model.

ACTIVITY 8

Reread the details of the profit problem discussed in Activity 7, and then fill in the details in the table below. (The first line has been completed for you.) How much should the company produce, and what profit level does this generate?

Amount to produce	Resulting profit (£)	Amount of labour used	Is labour constraint breached?	Is minimum profit achieved?	Is this a possible solution?	Is this an optimal solution?
1	20	4	No	No	No	No
2						
4						
6						
8						
10						
12						
14						
16						

You should be able to see from Table 1 that a solution which is both possible and optimal is to produce 12 units, making a profit of £240.

Amount to produce	Resulting profit (£)	Amount of labour used	Is labour constraint breached?	Is minimum profit achieved?	Is this a possible solution?	Is this an optimal solution?
1	20	4	No	No	No	No
2	40	8	No	No	No	No
4	80	16	No	No	No	No
6	120	24	No	No	No	No
8	160	32	No	Yes	Yes	No
10	200	40	No	Yes	Yes	No
12	240	48	No	Yes	Yes	Yes
14	280	56	Yes	Yes	No	No
16	320	64	Yes	Yes	No	No

Table 1: Completed table for the profit problem

The trial-and-error method shown in Table 1 is often called an **iterative process** in BDA terminology. 'Iteration' means that a process is continually repeated with just one small alteration at each repetition until some desired state is reached. In the case of the profit model of Activity 8, at each stage the level of production is altered and profit and labour usage recalculated. This process is continued until we reach the highest possible profit level, subject to staying within the labour constraint. As a problem-solving method, iteration can be costly in terms of the analyst's time, although the use of computers goes some way to alleviating this problem.

Summary

In this section we further developed the idea of a mathematical model. Each business problem has its own unique characteristics, which means that there is no single model which we can apply to all cases. Nevertheless, there are some stages of model development which occur frequently, and we have dealt with them in Section 3. In particular, we learned the importance of formulating objectives, listing constraints, and incorporating these features into a set of mathematical statements. In so doing, we formulated working definitions of variables and constants, and learned that some variables are under the control of the decision-maker whilst others are not. Finally, we examined the kind of output which a model generates and the solution process which is used to obtain such output.

In the next section we will continue this development of mathematical modelling by examining what happens when some of the variables used in a model are subject to chance variation.

SECTION 4

Deterministic and Stochastic Models

Introduction

In Section 3 we looked at the different components of a mathematical model. In Section 4 we look at two types of mathematical model: **deterministic** models and **stochastic** models. In Section 4.1 we provide a brief overview of the differences between these two types of model. In Section 4.2 we use a case study to look in more depth at an example of a stochastic model.

By the end of this section you should be able to define the terms deterministic and stochastic as used in BDA.

4.1 An overview of deterministic and stochastic models

So far we have discussed models where, although there are inputs which are not under the control of the decision-maker, these are nevertheless known with certainty and either cannot vary at all, if they are constants, or can only vary according to known rules, if they are variables. So, in the example in Activity 7, the labour usage per unit and the product price are known with certainty. Such a model is said to be **deterministic**. In practical terms, once we define the values of the main variables and constants, deterministic models will always result in the same outcome every time they are run.

However, there are many circumstances where the uncontrollable inputs are subject to uncertainty. Such models are referred to as **probabilistic** or **stochastic**. For example, in the profit problem of Activity 7 it might well be the case that price is not fixed but, instead, changes in response to fluctuations in supply and demand. Since supply and demand conditions are unlikely to be known with certainty, price will therefore be subject to chance. A more realistic model might try to incorporate this chance element. Although this will produce more realism, it must be recognised that stochastic models are more difficult to analyse and interpret than deterministic ones.

4.2 An example of a stochastic model

Because stochastic models are such an important part of business analysis, you will find it useful to read through a rather longer and more complicated problem than we have so far encountered.

Case Study: Bike Inc

Bike Inc, a bicycle manufacturer, is considering a new addition to its range. The company needs to decide whether forecast profits for this new product will justify going into production. The product in question is a mountain bike called the *Demon*. *Bike Inc*'s managing director needs to be convinced that the *Demon* has a high probability of an overall three-year return of at least £70,000 and very little chance of losses. The company has the following information about the various factors which need to be considered.

Potential total market size

The company has estimates compiled by six different trade journals indicating the likely size of the potential market for products like the *Demon*. These estimates are as shown in Table 2.

Potential market size	Journal
60,000	(Mountain Racer)
75,000	(Bike Trader)
100,000	(Power Bike)
110,000	(Racing Bike)
125,000	(Outdoor Sports)
140,000	(The Roadster)

Table 2: Potential market size for mountain bikes

As it is not clear which of these figures is likely to be most accurate, it has been decided to weight all of the estimates equally.

Overall market share and percentage sales

The marketing campaign would be designed to ensure that the *Demon* captures something between 7.5 and 10.5 per cent of the total market within a three-year review period. The company does not envisage taking all of this share in the first year alone but would build up to it by the end of the third year. The first year should bring in anything between 10 and 30 per cent: a best guess would be 20 per cent. The second year should bring in between 20 and 45 per cent: probably around 35 per cent. The third year should pull in the balance. These figures, subject to variation as they are, are not just wild guesses, but are from a survey of potential carried out by the company accountants.

Price

The price of the *Demon* will initially be £399 but, if sales are below 1,500 units in Year 1, it will be reduced by £50. If total cumulative sales at the end of Year 2 are less than 5,000 units, price will be reduced by a further £40 in order to achieve the planned 7.5 to 10.5 per cent market share by the end of Year 3. *Bike Inc* is aware that product demand is slightly price-elastic: a 1 per cent reduction in price would be likely to lead to a 1.5 per cent increase in sales during the year the change takes place.

Unit cost

Unit cost of the *Demon* is volume sensitive. Table 3 shows the relationship between yearly production and unit cost. The minimum viable order is 100.

Yearly quantity	Unit cost
100 – 239	£225
240 – 1,199	£220
1,200 – 2,999	£215
3,000 and above	£205

Table 3: Unit costs for production of bicycles by Bike Inc

Freight cost
Freight cost is fixed at 10 per cent of product cost.

Sales commission
Sales commission is fixed at 10 per cent of sales revenues.

Overheads
Overheads are easily predictable, with around £80,000 in the first year, increasing by 2 per cent in the second year and by another 3 per cent in the third year.

Marketing costs
Bike Inc has little idea about marketing costs at present, but believes they will be any value between £40,000 and £60,000 per annum, with equal likelihood.

ACTIVITY 9

Take another look at the data contained in the case. For each of the factors or inputs, say whether it is a constant or a variable. If it is a variable, say whether it is controllable or uncontrollable and whether its variation is random or non-random (stochastic or deterministic, to use the terminology introduced earlier).

The inputs to the problem are listed below.

Potential total market size is an uncontrollable variable subject to random or stochastic variation. It could be any one of six figures between 60,000 and 140,000 with equal probability.

Overall market share is the company's share of the total market. Like potential total market size, it is an uncontrollable variable and is subject to random or stochastic variation. It could be any figure between 7.5 and 10.5 per cent with equal probability.

Percentage sales in Year 1 is the portion of overall market share which the company expects to achieve in Year 1. It is, therefore, another uncontrollable variable input, subject to random or stochastic variation. Note that in this case not all possibilities are equally likely. The share could be anything between 10 and 30 per cent, but the most likely outcome is that percentage sales will be 20 per cent.

Percentage sales in Year 2 is the portion of overall market share which the company expects to achieve in Year 2. As for percentage sales for Year 1, it is an uncontrollable variable input, subject to random or stochastic variation. Once again, not all possibilities are equally likely: the share could be anything between 25 and 45 per cent, but the most likely outcome is 35 per cent.

Percentage sales in Year 3 is the portion of overall market share which the company expects to achieve in Year 3. Since the Year 1 and 2 percentage sales are themselves uncontrollable random variables, then the Year 3 percentage will also be an uncontrollable random variable.

Price is a controllable variable. Its level during Year 1 is fixed at £399 but it could be altered in Years 2 and 3 as a result of events in Year 1.

Unit cost is determined by the level of production. However, the level of production is an uncontrollable random variable, dependent upon market size and market share. Unit cost is also, therefore, an uncontrollable random variable.

Freight cost and **sales commission** are constants as they remain at 10 per cent whatever the situation. It is, of course, true that the actual monetary amounts of commission and freight will vary, as production varies. However, as these amounts are determined entirely by the level of production, we do not treat them as variables.

Overheads are a constant.

Marketing costs are subject to chance variation.

The investigation of the effect of chance on the inputs to and outputs from a business problem is of great importance. In most cases the factors relating to a particular problem cannot be known exactly. You may have read simplistic descriptions of the behaviour of market price, in which it appears that factors such as income and supply and demand are predetermined quantities. Similarly, you may have undertaken studies in accounting which involve calculating breakeven production quantities. Such accounts often give the impression that crucial quantities such as fixed and unit costs can be known exactly. In fact, if these costs relate to future production, it is very unlikely that an analyst will have a precise idea as to their size.

ACTIVITY 10

The main problem encountered by *Bike Inc* is how to investigate the possible profit earned by the *Demon* given the number of unknown or partly known factors.

Think very carefully. Is there anything at all definite that can be calculated with respect to profit, given the facts in the case? Would this information be of much use to *Bike Inc*?

Given the number of chance variables in the *Bike Inc* case study, it may seem surprising that anything can be known for certain. However, it is possible to calculate the best possible and worst possible profit positions. This can be done by assuming the most favourable and least favourable demand, market share and cost situations, and calculating the resulting profit (or loss). This would be of some use to *Bike Inc*, in that it would establish the outside limits on profit. However, we would have no idea as to how likely it is that these best and worst possible scenarios would occur in practice.

We shall have to deal with situations where some factors are subject to chance. You may have assumed, as a result of Activity 10, that nothing useful can be done with models which incorporate such factors. However, although their presence complicates matters, even if some of the inputs to a problem are subject to random chance, this does not necessarily prevent us from carrying out useful analysis. In statistics, the expression **random** does not mean 'without pattern' as it often does when used by the layman. Random variables may demonstrate patterns of behaviour because they are subject to the laws of probability, and they may often follow known probability distributions. If you toss a coin 100 times, although the outcome of each toss is a random event, the most likely overall outcome is a similar number of heads and tails. Consequently, we are not in a hopeless situation whenever we depart from the strict relationships of a deterministic model. In fact, deliberately incorporating a random element into a model will often allow us to make it much more realistic. Great advances have been made in the analysis of random models since the popularisation of computers. Chance events can be modelled by comparing them to the outcome of the throw of a dice, the spin of a coin or the roll of a roulette wheel. For this reason, the analytical methods used on stochastic models are often collectively known as **Monte Carlo methods**.

Summary

In Section 4 we briefly defined the meaning of the terms **deterministic** and **stochastic** as they occur in the practice of mathematical modelling. The complicating effect of chance variation was examined through a case study where many of the factors could not be known with any certainty. We saw that such factors could only be represented within a mathematical model by using probability statements. However, we concluded by observing that, even though factors may be subject to chance variation, this does not rule out useful analysis. Even in the apparently random output from a stochastic model, we may still be able to detect patterns and trends.

In Section 5 we further extend the mathematical model by looking at the difference between single-attribute and multi-attribute problems.

SECTION 5
Single-Attribute and Multi-Attribute Problems

Introduction

One of the important stages in building a model is the formulation of the criteria which will be used to evaluate the alternative decisions. There are many problems in which only one attribute of a decision process is important. For example, we may wish to find the decision which maximises profit. In this case we have a **single-attribute problem** (sometimes also called a **single-criterion problem**). However, there are also many situations in which we need to assess decisions in the light of several different criteria. For example, consider the task of deciding between several different job offers. It is unlikely that we would evaluate each job purely on salary alone. We might make a decision by referring to the criteria of starting salary, job potential, geographical situation and job satisfaction. In such cases, we have a **multi-attribute (or multi-criteria) problem**.

Methods such as **decision analysis** and **linear programming** (discussed in Units 2 and 3) are traditionally based on single-attribute models. Other more flexible techniques, such as **simulation** (discussed in Unit 6), allow the possibility of exploration of multiple objectives. This course will mainly be concerned with the single-attribute problem. However, it is essential that you are aware of the multi-attribute approach.

By the end of this section you should be able to explain the difference between single-attribute and multi-attribute decision models.

5.1 Multi-attribute problems

An example of a problem involving more than one decision criteria will help us understand how such problems are formulated.

Case Study: a multi-attribute production problem

A company produces two products, industrial lubricant and engineering oil. To produce these commodities it operates a process which blends three raw materials. A tonne of industrial lubricant needs 0.5 tonnes of material A, 0.1 tonnes of material B and 0.4 tonnes of material C. A tonne of engineering oil uses 0.4 tonnes ·of material A and 0.6 tonnes of material B.

The company has available 40 tonnes of material A, 10 tonnes of material B and 42 tonnes of material C.

The company has two goals which it wishes to achieve:

- to make at least 60 tonnes of industrial lubricant (goal 1)
- to make at least 30 tonnes of engineering oil (goal 2).

It is quite clear that we now have a multi-attribute problem involving the achievement of two different goals. This will present us with problems quite different from the single-attribute case. It may not be possible to attain both goals. Another problem concerns the degree of priority which we attach to each goal: it is quite likely that a business will regard some objectives as being more important than others.

ACTIVITY 11

1. Suppose that goal 1 (to produce at least 60 tonnes of industrial lubricant) has absolute priority. Is it possible to achieve both goals? If not, then what can be achieved?

2. Suppose that the situation is reversed, and that goal 2 (to produce at least 30 tonnes of engineering oil) has absolute priority. What is it possible to achieve now?

---

1. If goal 1 has the highest priority and cannot be compromised, then we must make at least 60 tonnes of lubricant. This would use:

   $60 \times 0.5 = 30$ tonnes of material A (leaving 10 tonnes for goal 2)

   $60 \times 0.1 = 6$ tonnes of material B (leaving 4 tonnes for goal 2)

   $60 \times 0.4 = 24$ tonnes of material C (goal 2 does not require this material)

It is easy to see that goal 2 cannot be met. The most that can be made of engineering oil is 6.67 tonnes (this is the amount which exhausts material B, which is in the shortest supply). Clearly, goal 2 falls short of target.

2. If goal 2 has the highest priority, then we must make at least 30 tonnes of engineering oil and cannot compromise this target. This would use:

$30 \times 0.4 = 12$ tonnes of material A (leaving 28 tonnes for goal 1)

$30 \times 0.6 = 18$ tonnes of material B (but we only have 10 tonnes of this material)

goal 2 does not use material C.

Clearly, goal 2 cannot be achieved even if we accord it absolute priority. In fact, the maximum amount of engineering oil we can produce is only 16.67 tonnes.

In the situation described in Activity 11, the decision is easy to analyse. In such a case, a goal is described as having **pre-emptive priority** because it has priority over other goals and we cannot compromise achieving it in favour of other goals.

5.2 Goal programming and the analytic hierarchy process

In the previous section we examined a simple two-attribute problem, and looked at the situation when one of the goals had absolute priority over the other. However, if both goals have equal priority, then we clearly have a different kind of problem. If we cannot achieve all goals, which targets do we allow to fall short? It may be that we would like to consider an even more complex situation. For example, what if we decide that goal 1 should have 65 per cent priority and goal 2 should have 35 per cent priority? Such a situation might easily occur if we had several different objectives and had to decide on the relative degree of importance of each of them. This could also be a highly subjective process, since different decision-makers will have different priorities. How can we solve a decision problem which not only incorporates a number of possible objectives but also attaches different levels of priority to them?

One procedure, used in a method called **goal programming**, is to introduce other factors into the problem (called **deficiency variables**), which represent the degree to which our achievements fall short of target. Thus, in the problem in Activity 11 there would be two deficiency variables, one for each goal. We would then need to find a solution which would stay within the constraints and also reduce these deficiency variables to their smallest possible size.

Algorithms for solving multiple goal problems exist, and these allow the analyst to attach different weights to each goal (it is not essential for goals to have equal weights). There is also a technique called the **analytic hierarchy process** which assists the decision-maker in allotting priorities to goals by using a system of ranked preferences. Although this technique is outside the scope of this module, it is useful to have some understanding of it as it will help you to place single-attribute models in a wider context.

ACTIVITY 12

Suppose a customer is considering the purchase of a new computer but is unsure about which to choose from a list of three possibilities. We shall call these three possibilities computers A, B and C. Now suppose that, rather than having just one criterion to satisfy, the buyer has several. In particular, she has identified **after-sales service, speed of processor, size of memory** and **packaged software** as criteria to satisfy when buying. It should be possible to numerically measure, or rate, the computers for each of these criteria.

The use of the analytical hierarchy process in developing a model to aid us in the choice of a computer might begin to resemble the process in the following diagram. Complete the diagram by filling in the blank boxes.

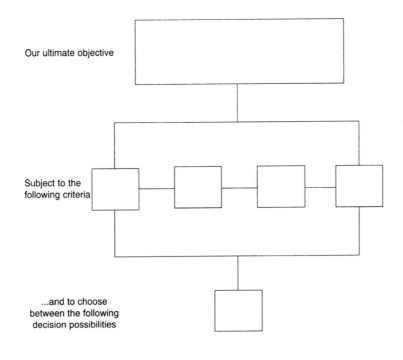

The answer to Activity 12 is shown in Figure 2.

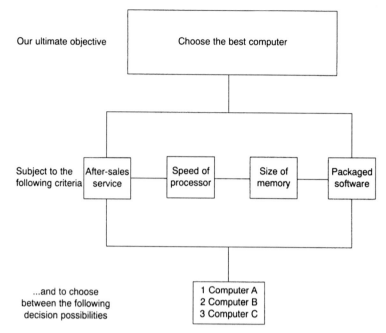

Figure 2: The analytic hierarchy process

You may have spotted that some of the criteria used for evaluating a decision will already be numeric (speed of processor, size of memory), while others (after-sales service and packaged software) will not be measurable in their current form. Part of the analytical hierarchy process will consist of developing ways of rating the decision alternatives for each of these criteria. This is necessary if we are to establish priorities for each alternative.

One method used is to develop a preference scale and use it to make **pairwise** comparisons between the decision alternatives. For example, we might use a five-point scale for rating alternative X against alternative Y, as follows:

1 = neutral between the two alternatives

2 = moderate preference for X over Y

3 = strong preference for X over Y

4 = very strong preference for X over Y

5 = extreme preference for X over Y

Of course, the preferences obtained from this scale as expressed by a particular decision-maker will be highly subjective.

The next stage is to obtain a pairwise comparison matrix for each of the decision criteria. We do this by getting the decision-maker to evaluate the three computers in terms of each of the evaluation criteria using the five-point scale. For example, if we select after-sales service as the criterion, then we might end up with a matrix such as the one shown in Table 4.

	Computer A	Computer B	Computer C
Computer A		2	4
Computer B			3
Computer C			

Table 4: Pairwise comparison matrix for after-sales service

This table shows that, considering the criterion of after-sales service, computer A is moderately preferred to computer B but is very strongly preferred to computer C. Computer B is strongly preferred to computer C. This procedure is continued so that a matrix similar to Table 4 is obtained for each of the decision criteria.

The process is still not complete, for we must now get the decision-maker to list the four criteria in order of importance for each of the three computers. A complex procedure exists for reducing this information to a single number for each computer. Only then will it be possible to choose a computer which satisfies the preferred multiple criteria.

So it is possible to produce a BDA model which incorporates multiple goals, although the procedure for doing this is quite complex and is beyond the scope of this module. Throughout, we will be able to manage by assuming that the decision-maker has just one criterion to use as the means of selecting a decision. However, the analyst should always be aware of the possibilities open to him or her if this assumption ceases to be true.

Summary

In Section 5 we relaxed the assumption of a single criterion (such as maximising profit or minimising cost) and examined what might happen if we assumed that there were multiple criteria to satisfy. We looked at an example involving two criteria. We then discussed the situation where one of the goals had absolute, or pre-emptive, priority over the others, before looking at what happened when none of the goals had pre-emptive priority, but they could be ranked in order of importance. Finally, we discussed the use of the analytical hierarchy process as a way of attaching numerical significance to each decision choice for each of the characteristics used in the selection process.

In Section 6 we look at how models respond to changes to the inputs. This is known as **sensitivity analysis**.

SECTION 6
Sensitivity Analysis and Model Building

Introduction

Having looked at multi-attribute decision-making in the previous section, we now return to the single-attribute models discussed in Sections 2 to 4. In this section we shall examine the effect on single-attribute models of changes to the inputs to such models.

By the end of this section you should be able to explain what is meant by sensitivity analysis.

6.1 What is sensitivity analysis?

An important part of model building is an activity called **sensitivity analysis**. In constructing any business model we will probably have to deal with a large number of factors, which may be variables or constants (whether controllable or uncontrollable, deterministic or stochastic). We will also have to make working estimates of the values of these factors. What would be the effect of changing these values?

In some cases, we may find that even very small changes in the value of a factor can cause a change in the decision suggested by the model. The solution is said to be **sensitive** to changes in the factor and such factors are therefore described as **critical**.

In other cases, we may find that changing the factor by even a relatively large amount will not cause a change in the decision recommended by the model. Such factors are described as **non-critical**.

Sensitivity analysis can provide an appraisal of the original formulation of the problem. When a model is first being formulated, it is not always clear which factors are critical and which are non-critical, but it is essential to have this information. That is why sensitivity analysis is so important. You may have heard of **'what-if' analysis**: this is just another term for sensitivity analysis. The next activity gives you something of the flavour of sensitivity analysis.

ACTIVITY 13

Take another look at the profit problem in Activity 7. You obtained a solution for this in Activity 8. In that problem, minimum profit and labour usage were important factors. Recalculate the decision recommended by the model in the light of the following changes. For each, state what conclusions can be drawn about the sensitivity of the model to the relevant factor (minimum profit or labour usage).

1. Currently, the business must make a profit of at least £160 per week. What would happen to the decision recommended by the model if this figure changed to £200?

2. What would happen to the decision if the minimum weekly profit figure changed to £250?

3. What would happen to the decision if labour input changed from the current 4 hours per unit to 6?

---

1. If you take another look at the response to Activity 8 you should be able to see that changing the minimum profit to £200 does not affect the solution obtained at that stage. The optimum profit is still £240, achieved by producing 12 units. The model is insensitive to this change in the minimum profit restriction.

2. However, it does not follow that the model would be insensitive to any change in minimum profit, no matter how large. If, for example, we altered the minimum profit to £250, we would have to produce at least 13 units to achieve this.

   Unfortunately, we cannot produce 13 units because it would demand 52 hours of labour, and we only have 48 hours available. Changing the minimum profit to £250 has dramatically altered the model. It now has no possible solution. This demonstrates that a model may be insensitive to changes in some variables, but only within limits.

3. The solution to the model is immediately sensitive to any alteration in labour input. For example, if we now require 6 hours of labour per unit instead of 4 (without any change in the available total of 48 hours), we find that we can only produce 8 units of the product. This would yield a total profit of £160. This solution is possible, since it reaches the minimum profit figure.

6.2 The advantages of sensitivity analysis

We have seen that large changes in some variables may leave a solution to a model unaltered, while even quite small alterations to others cause dramatic changes. There are several advantages in exploring the sensitivity of the model to changes in the inputs.

1. It concentrates the mind of the decision-maker on the most critical areas of the problem. He or she may not need to be concerned about changes to inputs to which the model is insensitive.

2. It enhances the process of model building. It is not enough for operating staff to merely concentrate on particular aspects of a problem in which they happen to be interested: they also need to be aware of each and every critical factor which can influence a decision. This encourages them to co-operate with other personnel involved in the decision-making process.

3. It familiarises operating personnel with the most critical areas of a decision model at an early stage.

4. It encourages management co-operation and dynamic decision-making because it sets outer limits beyond which the critical factors may not go without endangering the achievement of the final objective.

6.3 Some applications of sensitivity analysis

Sensitivity analysis is used in many areas of model building. The following list gives some examples.

1. In **linear programming**, sensitivity analysis is the study of how changes in the mathematical expressions for constraints in a linear programming problem will affect the solution. Because this is a rather technical explanation, an example might be useful. Suppose the objective of a builder making two different kinds of door from wood and glass is to maximise his profit. He wishes to know how many of each door to produce to achieve this end. Calculations are made to find the best production plan and a solution seems to have been reached. What would be effect on production plans if there were a reduction of 5 per cent in the quantity of glass available?

2. In **decision analysis** and **simulation**, sensitivity analysis is a study of how changes in the probability estimates for the states of nature affect the decision chosen. This will be of crucial importance in stochastic models, where we may be compelled to make subjective estimates as to the likelihood of various valuations of such key factors as price, demand, cost and so forth. For example, suppose that a manufacturer is contemplating whether or not to build a new plant. There are three options: to build a large plant, to build a small plant or to build no plant at all. The states of nature are the various levels of future demand for the product made by the plant. On the assumption of varying likelihood for demand, a decision is arrived at. However, the manufacturer has assumed a 55 per cent probability of a high demand. How would the decision be affected if an estimate of 60 per cent seemed more reasonable?

3. In **forecasting**, sensitivity analysis is a study of how changes in the forecasting parameters affect the accuracy of forecast results. Many sales forecasts are made up from averages of sales achieved in past periods. If we give different periods extra weight (that is, more importance) in the calculation of this average, then we can obtain different forecasts by altering these weights.

4. There are many other areas of management science where sensitivity analysis is used, for example in **project planning** and **investment appraisal**.

6.4 Some limitations of sensitivity analysis

Although sensitivity analysis is an important part of the analyst's toolbox, it has limitations. There will be many occasions when it will lack precision, or even exaggerate or underestimate the sensitivity of a model to a particular input. This may occur because management has to use past relationships to predict a future environment. Estimates of critical factors may also be subjective. Moreover, the decision-maker often concentrates on analysing the deviation to decision objectives caused by variation in just one critical factor alone. It is not always easy to analyse the effect of changes occurring in several critical factors simultaneously.

Summary

This section of the unit addressed the question of sensitivity analysis. First, we defined sensitivity analysis as a study of the degree to which the solution to a model is affected by changes in the inputs. We then gave a number of examples of the application of sensitivity analysis to the areas of linear programming, simulation, forecasting and decision analysis. We then went on to identify the advantages and applications of sensitivity analysis before pointing out some of its limitations.

Unit Summary

This first unit of the course has been largely concerned with explaining the theoretical background to the material you are to study later. The material in this unit has not only set the scene for the more detailed studies you will encounter in Units 2 to 6, but should provide you with some kind of structural overview of the theory and practice of BDA as a whole.

We began by discussing the nature of the material that BDA specialists work with, and the kinds of problems they are likely to encounter. We then introduced the key concept of the business model and the practice of constructing such models, a matter which we shall be returning to frequently as you work your way through this course. After this brief introduction to the subject of model building, we anticipated another important future area of study: the effect that random variables have on the analysis of business problems. We also indicated the importance of studying how solutions to problems can be sensitive even to slight changes in the inputs to the problem.

Before you start any new unit, you may find it useful to return to Unit 1 and reread the parts of it which relate to the new area of study.

Recommended Reading

Anderson, J, Sweeney, D R and Williams, T A (1994) *An Introduction to Management Science*, West Publishing, Minneapolis, USA.

This is an excellent general textbook intended for MBA students. The authors are major authorities in the field of quantitative methods as applied to business. The many case studies are mostly based on US experience, but are still pertinent to the issues discussed in this module. The book is a general guide to the techniques used in BDA, and Chapter 1 in particular provides a good overview of the subject area of modelling.

Hillier, F S and Liebermann, G J (1995) *Introduction to Operational Research*, McGraw-Hill, New York, USA.

This is a good introductory text for business students. It has been selected for extra reading here because it provides a little more of the mathematical underpinning for the subject of BDA. An extra recommendation is that it comes with a software pack of routines for constructing many kinds of models. Chapters 1 and 2 cover the same ground as Unit 1 of this module.

Rivett, P (1986) *The Craft of Model Building*, John Wiley, New York, USA.

This book covers in great detail all of the material dealt with in Unit 1 of this module. It is a superb and exhaustive account of the process of model building and deals particularly well with the philosophical issues and with the problem of the analysis and interpretation of output.

UNIT 2
DECISION ANALYSIS

Introduction

Business decision-making usually involves some level of uncertainty. But business organisations or public sector organisations still have to take decisions, and therefore have to adopt strategies to cope with this lack of certainty. In the absence of such certainty, there are two possibilities. Either the decision-maker has probabilistic information available, based upon past experience or personal belief: this situation is termed one of **risk**. Alternatively there is a complete absence of any probabilistic information: this situation is termed one of **uncertainty**.

This unit is concerned with how we arrive at decisions given conditions of risk or uncertainty. In Section 1 we look at two ways of representing decision problems: through the use of decision trees, and through the use of payoff matrices. In Section 2 we look in more detail at decision-making under conditions of uncertainty while in Section 3 we look at decision-making under conditions of risk. In Section 4 we look at multi-stage decision problems while in Section 5 we address the issue of revising the probabilities in a decision-making problem. Finally, in Section 6, we look at some extensions to the approaches introduced in Sections 1 to 5.

Objectives

By the end of this unit you should be able to:

- construct a payoff matrix
- construct a decision tree
- distinguish between conditions of risk and uncertainty, and determine what decision models are appropriate to each
- use a range of different approaches to decision-making under uncertainty
- calculate expected values
- use expected monetary value and expected opportunity loss to choose between alternative courses of action
- determine the value of perfect information
- evaluate a decision tree
- revise probabilities using incomplete information
- determine the value of imperfect information
- distinguish between single- and multi-attribute decision-making
- use pairwise comparisons and attribute scaling in the resolution of simple multi-attribute problems
- calculate and use the variance of a set of payoffs as a measure of risk
- explain the relevance of utility to decision-making.

SECTION 1
Decision Trees
and Payoff Matrices

Introduction

In Section 1.1 we introduce a case study where a decision has to be made under conditions of risk. In Sections 1.2 and 1.3 we analyse the choices or strategies available and display these in two ways: as a decision tree, and as a payoff matrix.

By the end of this section you should be able to construct a payoff matrix and construct a decision tree.

1.1 Making a decision under conditions of risk

Case Study: the wheat problem

The owner of a 50-acre farm must decide which of four varieties of wheat to grow. (For convenience, we shall name the four varieties A, B, C and D.) Each variety will produce varying yields depending upon the level of rainfall experienced during the growing season. The annual profit is therefore dependent upon the rainfall (classified as low, medium or high) and the variety of wheat which the farmer has selected. The rainfall level cannot be predicted with certainty. We refer to the various possible levels of rainfall as **states of nature**. The decision-maker cannot control or influence such states of nature. Despite this lack of certainty as to which state of nature will prevail, the decision-maker must choose between the four varieties of wheat. We shall refer to these choices as **strategies**. The resulting annual profit will then depend upon the strategy chosen and the state of nature that prevails. The outcomes that result from each chosen strategy and prevailing state of nature are termed **payoffs**. In our example, there are four strategies and three states of nature. There are therefore 12 different possible payoffs.

1.2 Tree diagram representation of a decision problem

Suppose that, based upon past data, the decision-maker is able to estimate these 12 possible payoffs. This information can then be presented as either a **decision tree** or a **payoff matrix**. Figure 1 shows a decision tree for this problem.

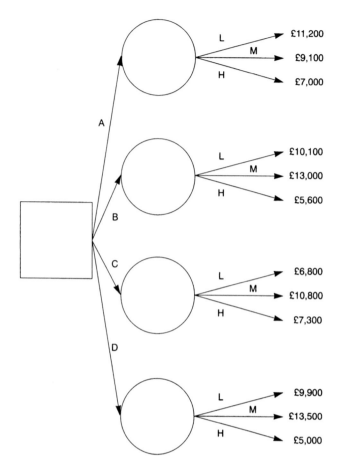

Figure 1: Decision tree for the wheat problem

The figures on the right are the estimated payoffs. A, B, C and D denote the four varieties of wheat respectively, and L, M and H denote the three levels of rainfall (low, medium and high).

Notice that the tree has 12 final branches, each branch corresponding to a payoff. There are two types of branching point. Squares represent **decision points**. At these points in the tree the decision-maker has to choose one of a set of strategies. Hence, at these points one branch is required for each strategy. Circles represent **event points**. Events are the different states of nature and we require one branch for each of these.

Reading left to right across the tree, the complete set of branches represents all possible sequences of strategies and states of nature. For example, the uppermost sequence in Figure 1 is the decision to choose variety A, followed by the event of rainfall being low.

1.3 Matrix representation of a decision problem

This information can also be shown as a payoff matrix, as in Table 1.

	Low	Medium	High
Variety A	11,200	9,100	7,000
Variety B	10,100	13,000	5,600
Variety C	6,800	10,800	7,300
Variety D	9,900	13,500	5,000

Table 1: Payoff matrix for the wheat problem

States of nature form the columns of the matrix, and strategies form the rows. So if, for example, variety A is chosen and low rainfall occurs then the payoff is £11,200.

Payoff matrices have the limitation that they can only be used to represent problems for which a single decision is required. Under such circumstances they are probably superior to a representation using a decision tree. However, if a decision problem is multi-staged (that is, a staged sequence of related decisions are required) then this can only be represented by use of a tree.

Summary

In this section we looked at a decision problem in which we had to choose between a number of different options or strategies. We saw that each strategy can give rise to one of several outcomes or payoffs depending upon the prevailing conditions or states of nature. We then looked at two ways of representing a decision problem: as a decision tree, and as a payoff matrix.

In Section 2 we look we look in more detail at decision-making under conditions of uncertainty.

state of Nature coloune —

Strategjee

SECTION 2

Decision-Making under Conditions of Uncertainty

Introduction

In this section we examine decision-making in situations characterised by complete **uncertainty**: that is, in circumstances where no probabilities can be attached to the states of nature that have a bearing upon the problem. We then look at different ways of responding to this uncertainty, depending on whether the decision-maker is interested primarily in minimising the worst possible outcome or maximising the best possible outcome. We then explore the decision-making process in more detail by considering the notion of **regret** and by discussing the implications of an assumption that all states of nature are equally likely to occur. Finally we draw on **game theory** to introduce a problem known as 'the prisoner's dilemma'. This allows us to consider the fact that other decision-makers form an important part of the environment in which we operate.

By the end of this section you should be able to use a range of different approaches to decision-making under uncertainty.

2.1 The maximin criterion

We start with what is probably the most common approach to decision-making under uncertainty.

ACTIVITY 1

Consider the payoff matrix for the wheat problem in Table 1 in Section 1.3. Suppose that you are the decision-maker. Further suppose that what most concerns you is the worst outcome that might result from any given choice of strategy.

1. If you choose variety A, what is the worst thing that could happen?

2. And if you choose varieties B, C or D?

3. So if your dominant concern is with minimising the worst thing that could happen, what strategy do you choose?

1. If you choose variety A, the worst thing that can happen (if high rainfall occurs) is that you obtain an annual profit of £7,000.

2. For varieties B, C and D, the worst outcomes are respectively £5,600, £6,800 and £5,000.

3. Hence, if your dominant concern is with the worst outcomes that can happen, you will choose variety A. This guarantees that the payoff cannot be less than £7,000.

In this approach to the decision problem, first the **minimum** payoff is established for each strategy and then the strategy with the highest (the **maximum**) of these minimum payoffs is chosen. Our aim, in other words, is to **maximise** our minimum payoff. This approach is therefore called the **maximin** criterion. It represents a pessimistic solution to the problem.

2.2 The maximax criterion

Let us now suppose that what concerns you is the best outcome that can result from a given strategy.

ACTIVITY 2

What do you now decide?

For varieties A, B, C and D the best outcomes are respectively £11,200, £13,000, £10,800 and £13,500.

Choice of variety D ensures that the highest payoff is not precluded. It does not, however, guarantee that it will be obtained.

In this approach to the decision problem, first the **maximum** payoff is established for each strategy and then the strategy with the highest (the **maximum**) of these maximum payoffs is chosen. Our aim, in other words, is to **maximise** our maximum payoff. This approach is therefore called the **maximax** criterion. It represents an optimistic solution to the problem.

2.3 The minimax regret criterion

The maximin and maximax criteria represent extreme approaches to the problem of decision-making under uncertainty. We now explore an alternative and somewhat less restrictive approach.

Again, consider the payoff matrix in Table 1. Suppose that you choose variety A and that subsequently low rainfall occurs. Then, after the event, it is clear that you made the best choice. Accordingly, you are said to have no **regret**. However, if you chose variety B and low rainfall occurred, you would regret not having chosen variety A. We can calculate this regret as a monetary value. It is the difference between the profit which would have resulted from the best strategy available and the profit resulting from the strategy actually chosen. The best strategy available (choosing variety A) would have yielded a profit of £11,200. The strategy actually chosen yielded a profit of only £10,100. So the monetary value of our regret is £1,100.

ACTIVITY 3

1. Suppose you choose varieties C or D and low rainfall actually occurs. What will be your regrets?

2. By considering each state of nature in turn, construct a matrix showing all possible regrets.

3. On the assumption that you would wish to minimise potential regret, which strategy will you choose?

---

1. If variety C is chosen and low rainfall actually occurs, then the regret is:

   11,200 – 6,800 = £4,400

   If variety D is chosen and low rainfall actually occurs, then the regret is:

   11,200 – 9,900 = £1,300

2. You should have obtained the following regret matrix:

Strategy	Low	Medium	High
A	0	4,400	300
B	1,100	500	1,700
C	4,400	2,700	0
D	1,300	0	2,300

Table 2: Regret matrix for the wheat problem

What concerns us now is the maximum regret that can result from a given choice of strategy. These maximum regrets are shown in Table 3.

Strategy	Maximum regret
A	4,400
B	1,700
C	4,400
D	2,300

Table 3: Maximum regrets for the wheat problem

3. So, if we wish to minimise potential regret, we should choose variety B. This guarantees that the regret cannot exceed £1,700.

In this approach to the decision problem, first the **regret matrix** is established and then, for each strategy, the **maximum regret** is determined. Finally the strategy with the **minimum** of these **maximum regrets** is chosen. Our aim, in other words, is to **minimise** our **maximum regret**. This approach is therefore called the **minimax regret** criterion. Following this approach protects the decision-maker from the worst consequences of what may have been an inappropriate choice of strategy.

2.4 The principle of insufficient reason

Another possible response to uncertainty is to assume that all consequences are equally likely. We are now bringing some notion of probability into the discussion, but in a very weak form. This is known as the **principle of insufficient reason**.

Applying this to the wheat problem, we will assume that low, medium and high rainfall are equally likely. We now need to interpret the notion of 'equal likelihood'. Since there are three states of nature, we are saying that there is a one-in-three probability of each of the three states of nature occurring.

Suppose that variety A is chosen. Having assumed that the £11,200, £9,100 and £7,000 payoffs (from low, medium and high rainfall respectively) are equally likely, we can calculate the average payoff for this strategy as:

$$\frac{11,200 + 9,100 + 7,000}{3}$$

$$= \frac{27,000}{3}$$

$$= £9,100$$

Similarly for the remaining strategies the average payoffs are:

$$\frac{10,100 + 13,000 + 5,600}{3} = £9,567 \text{ (variety B)}$$

$$\frac{6,800 + 10,800 + 7,300}{3} = £8,300 \text{ (variety C)}$$

$$\frac{9,900 + 13,500 + 5,000}{3} = £9,467 \text{ (variety D)}$$

Since choice of variety B yields the highest average payoff, it would seem to be preferable.

You should now check your understanding of the concepts and methods that have been introduced in this section by working through the following activity.

ACTIVITY 4

A dairy company wishes to set up a number of regional plants to act as centres for the collection, processing, bottling and daily distribution of milk. The major unknown factor in the analysis is the future cost of fuel. Three strategies have been proposed and the net monthly payoff (in £000s) for each strategy has been estimated for different petrol costs as follows:

	Cost of petrol		
	High	Medium	Low
Strategy A	5	10	15
Strategy B	-5	20	50
Strategy C	-20	15	100

The company is unable to attach any probabilities to the three states of nature (petrol costs being high, medium or low). For each of the criteria listed below, recommend which strategy the company should adopt. Where appropriate, construct a table of payoffs or a regret matrix.

1. Maximin.

2. Maximax.

3. Minimax regret.

4. Insufficient reason.

---

1. For the maximin approach, you should have constructed a table of minimum payoffs as shown.

Strategy	Minimum payoff
A	5,000
B	–5,000
C	–20,000

Table 4: Minimum payoffs for the milk problem

On this criterion, strategy A is preferable as a payoff of at least £5,000 per month is guaranteed. Remember that, in this approach, the decision-maker assumes that the worst might happen and chooses accordingly.

2. For the maximax approach, you should have constructed a table of maximum payoffs as shown.

Strategy	Maximum payoff
A	15,000
B	50,000
C	100,000

Table 5: Maximum payoff matrix for the milk problem

On this criterion, strategy C is preferable. By choosing this variety, we don't preclude the chance of obtaining a £100,000 payoff. Any other choice reduces the maximum possible payoff. Remember that this approach, while keeping open the possibility of a maximum payoff, may also leave the decision-maker open to substantial losses. For this reason it is not normally adopted.

3. For the minimax regret approach, you should have constructed a regret matrix identifying the maximum regrets as shown:

	High	Medium	Low	Maximum regret
A	0	10	85	85
B	10	0	50	50
C	25	5	0	25

Table 6: Regret matrix and maximum regrets for the milk problem

So the appropriate choice is strategy C because, if the wrong decision is proved to have been made, strategy C entails the lowest potential regret.

4. In the insufficient reason approach, you should have calculated the average payoffs for each strategy. Here we assume that all states of nature are equally likely. In this case, since there are three possibilities for petrol costs, we assume that each has a probability of one third. So the average payoffs are:

$$\frac{5,000 + 10,000 + 15,000}{3} = £10,000 \text{ (strategy A)}$$

$$\frac{-5,000 + 20,000 + 50,000}{3} = £21,667 \text{ (strategy B)}$$

$$\frac{-20,000 + 15,000 + 100,000}{3} = £31,667 \text{ (strategy C)}$$

On this basis, strategy C would be recommended.

We have explored a number of criteria that may be employed for decision-making under uncertainty. What can we conclude from this investigation?

Firstly, that there is no such thing as a 'best' criterion. The choice of approach depends upon the attitude of the decision-maker. Secondly, that all these criteria assume that the decision-maker is unable to provide probabilistic information regarding states of nature. If any such information is available then, in general, these criteria should be abandoned in favour of other approaches. And finally, that all the criteria are for decision-making when 'nature' is the opponent. However, in many situations, decision-making under uncertainty involves two or more intelligent opponents. Analysis of this requires a different approach.

2.5 The prisoner's dilemma

The problem that follows is known as 'the prisoner's dilemma'. It is drawn from a wider set of problems studied as part of **game theory**.

Suppose that you and a companion have both been arrested by the police and placed into separate cells. It is impossible for you to communicate with each other, either directly or via a third party. A policeman enters your cell and tells you that you are charged with committing two offences. The more serious carries 20 years imprisonment if guilty, whilst the lesser offence carries only three years. He tells you that they have certain proof that you and your companion have committed the less serious offence. Although the police also believe that you both committed the more serious one, they don't possess the same overwhelming evidence. The policeman offers you the following deal regarding the serious offence:

- if you confess and your companion also confesses, then you will each get ten years

- if you confess and your companion does not, then you will walk free and your companion will get 20 years

- if you don't confess and your companion does, then you are the one who will get the 20 years, whilst your companion will walk free

- if neither of you confess to the serious offence, then both of you will get three years for the lesser one.

This is summarised in Table 7. In each case the first figure within the bracket applies to you and the second to your companion.

		Your companion	
		Confess	Not Confess
You	Confess	(10, 10)	(0, 20)
	Not Confess	(20, 0)	(3, 3)

Table 7: Prisoner's dilemma

ACTIVITY 5

Your problem is this: what strategy is in your best interests?

Think carefully before you decide. Your companion has already made a decision. Assume for the purposes of the activity that you are certain the policeman is trustworthy.

Before deciding what strategy to choose, you have to decide what interests you most, minimising the worst possible outcome or maximising your chances of achieving the best possible outcome.

If you confess there are two possible outcomes: either your companion has also confessed, in which case you face a ten-year sentence; or your companion has not confessed, in which case you will walk free. In other words, the worst possible outcome of confessing is a ten-year sentence and the best is obviously that you go free.

If you do not confess, there are also two possible outcomes: either your companion has confessed, in which case you face a 20-year sentence; or your companion has also not confessed, in which case you will get three years.

So, if you wish to ensure that you receive the least bad of the worst possible outcomes (maximin), you will confess in order to avoid the possibility of a 20-year sentence. If you wish to maximise the chances of achieving the best possible outcome (maximax), you will also confess. The possibility of walking free is not then precluded.

Both maximin and maximax approaches yield the same conclusion. You confess to the serious offence. Even if you knew for certain what your companion would do, your best choice would still be to confess.

Only if your companion is with you in the same cell and you both answer 'not confess' when jointly asked the question, does the dilemma not exist. This is precisely the reason why you are being kept in separate cells!

The problem is that your companion has gone through the same process of reasoning. In consequence the outcome is that you are jointly worse off: both go to prison for ten years. The paradox is that if each person follows self-interest, both will suffer.

This particular problem is somewhat artificial but it does mirror many real situations. For example, we all make decisions as to whether to consume certain goods and services on the basis of a personal calculation of gain and loss. What we individually don't take into account is the impact of these decisions upon others. During this century the use of the private motor vehicle has led to a substantial extension of personal freedom. However, each car driver ignores the consequences for others (traffic congestion, impact upon the environment, emission of greenhouse gases and so forth, what the economist calls **externalities**). Sooner or later unbridled self-interest has to be constrained, if necessary by governmental action, in order to secure the general good.

Such dilemmas can, and do, easily occur in a business context. For example, consider the decision faced by any enterprise as to whether (and to what degree) it should invest in pure, as distinct from applied, research and development. It is clearly true that it would be wise for any enterprise to keep abreast of technical and scientific developments that might impinge upon its future profitability and this might well entail expenditure on developments that can be patented, so ensuring that the commercial rewards are reserved for the patentee. However, the potential returns from undertaking pure research are much more problematic and it may be very difficult, or even impossible, to ensure that the fruits of any success are not dissipated to the wider marketplace.

But, if most business enterprises reason in this way, then there will be an under-investment in pure research. The gains that this might generate for all will not then be realised, unless some third party (probably the government) steps in to redress the situation.

If you have thought through this problem carefully, then you might find the outcome rather surprising. After all we have been taught since Adam Smith that the pursuit of self-interest is the vehicle via which the general good is obtained. Yet, in the prisoner's dilemma, if both parties pursue their own self-interest they are jointly worse off.

There are a number of means by which such dilemmas might be solved or mitigated. For example, if the prisoner's dilemma is posed repeatedly then a point soon arises at which both 'players' (having learned from experience) decide not to confess to the serious offence. However, there is always a temptation to revert back to confessing. Despite this qualification, this suggests that experiential learning is one way in which decision-makers can learn to obtain their joint advantage.

Another approach, ruled out in the prisoner's dilemma by isolating the prisoners in separate cells, is to resort to collusive behaviour. In business, if there is uncertainty about the consequences of decisions made by one's competitors, then a possible solution is to jointly agree upon matters such as prices and market shares. However, such anti-competitive behaviour is usually illegal and the law may be successful in preventing such overt collusion.

You might care to examine how the outcome of the problem would be affected if both you and your companion behave in an altruistic way. This time your decision is determined by a concern for your companion's interests. If you reason it through, you will find that now your decision (and that of your companion) will be to not confess. In this case, altruistic behaviour leads to the joint good of both.

Finally, solutions at a macro level may require governmental intervention either by regulation or by changes in taxation. For example, the traffic congestion and pollution problems briefly discussed earlier might be mitigated by a combination of tax changes (such as annual increases in the tax on motor fuel) and regulation (such as curbs on the provision of city-centre car parking). However, these issues are taking us a long way from decision analysis and will not be pursued any further in this unit.

Summary

In this section of the unit we have considered decision-making under uncertainty. Here the decision-maker is unable, or unwilling, to associate probabilities with the various states of nature that have a bearing upon the decision.

We investigated a number of approaches that a decision-maker might adopt. Maximin places the stress upon the worst outcome that might result from each choice of strategy. Using this approach, the strategy with the highest of these minimum outcomes should be selected. By comparison, a maximax approach identifies the best outcome for each strategy. In this case the decision-maker will select the strategy which has the largest of these maximum outcomes. Minimax regret stresses the potential losses that might result from an incorrect choice of strategy. Following this approach the decision-maker will choose that strategy which minimises such potential losses. Finally, it may be sensible to treat all states of nature as being equally likely and choose between them by comparing their average outcomes.

It was stressed that there are no rules that state that one or other of these approaches must be adopted. Instead which criterion is followed is dependent upon the views and attitudes of the decision-maker. The section ended with a discussion of 'the prisoner's dilemma'.

In Section 3 we look at decision-making under conditions of risk.

SECTION 3
Decision-Making under Conditions of Risk

Introduction

In this section we examine decision-making in situations where the decision-maker is able to attach probabilities to the various payoffs relating to any given choice of strategy. We revise the notion of the expected value of a probability distribution and show that it can be understood as a long-run average. Since payoffs are usually monetary, we define **expected monetary value** and show that, when choosing between competing strategies, it is appropriate to select the one which maximises expected monetary value.

The concept of regret, which was introduced in Section 2, is reinterpreted as an opportunity loss. We then show that minimising opportunity loss and maximising expected monetary value are equivalent. In some situations, additional information may be available which accurately predicts what state of nature will occur. Such perfect information has a value to the decision-maker and we show how this may be determined.

Finally we return to payoff matrices (which were introduced in Section 1 as a convenient way of representing a decision problem) and show how they are constructed and used in decision-making.

By the end of this section you should be able to distinguish between conditions of **risk** and **uncertainty**, and determine what decision models are appropriate to each. You should also be able to calculate **expected values**, and use **expected monetary value** and **expected opportunity loss** to choose between alternative courses of action. You should also be able to determine the value of perfect information.

3.1 Expected monetary value

We now explore decision-making under risk by examining the concept of **expected monetary value**. For the wheat problem that we studied in Sections 1 and 2 of this unit, it seems highly likely that there would be some data available relating to previous rainfall levels for the locality. Such data could be employed to attach probabilities to the three rainfall outcomes. If such probabilities are available, the problem becomes one of decision-making under risk.

To see how such information might be used we start by defining the concept of **expected value**. In statistics, an expected value is defined as the **mean** value for a probability distribution. To see what is meant by this, consider the information given in Table 8, which lists the probabilities for obtaining 0, 1, 2, 3 and 4 heads in four tosses of a coin.

X (number of heads)	Probability (X)
0	1/16
1	4/16
2	6/16
3	4/16
4	1/16

Table 8: Probability distribution for the number of heads in four tosses of a coin

Notice that, since it is a certainty that the number of heads must take one of these five values, then the probabilities must sum to 1. For the purpose of this unit you do not need to know how we have arrived at these probabilities. However, you may recognise from your previous studies that the results are obtained by using the binomial distribution.

The expected or mean value for this distribution is equal to:

$$(0 \times 1/16) + (1 \times 4/16) + (2 \times 6/16) + (3 \times 4/16) + (4 \times 1/16)$$

$$= 0 + 4/16 + 12/16 + 12/16 + 4/16$$

$$= 2$$

In other words, if on a number of occasions we tossed a coin four times, we would **on average** expect to obtain 2 heads. This does not mean that, if the coin is tossed four times, we will necessarily obtain 2 heads. In fact, a glance at Table 8 shows it to be more likely that we will not obtain 2 heads. However, suppose the experiment is repeated a large number of times. The greater the number of repetitions of the four tosses, the closer the mean number of heads will approximate to 2. So the expected value can be understood as the long-run mean number of heads obtained from repeated four tosses of the coin.

As another example, look at Table 9, which shows the likely annual UK sales by *Chaos Ltd.*

Sales (£million)	Probability
2.4	0.15
2.7	0.30
3.0	0.35
3.3	0.15
3.6	0.05

Table 9: Probability distribution for Chaos Ltd'sales

Chaos Ltd believes that annual sales could take any one of the five listed values. A table such as this is termed a probability distribution and gives, for each value of the variable (in this case, sales), the probability that it will occur. We then obtain the average sales by multiplying each value by its probability and adding the resultant values together, as follows:

$$(0.15 \times 2.4) + (0.3 \times 2.7) + (0.35 \times 3) + (0.15 \times 3.3) + (0.05 \times 3.6)$$
$$= £2.895 \text{ million}$$

Averaging a probability distribution in this way yields its expected value. Since, in this case, the sales levels are monetary sums, we refer to the **expected monetary value** (EMV). But what does this mean? It is not saying that, in any one year, *Chaos Ltd's* sales will be equal to £2.895 million, since the only possible outcomes are those listed in Table 9. Rather, it is saying that, over a sequence of years, annual sales will on average amount to £2.895 million. Of course, this interpretation rests upon the assumption that both the sales levels and the probabilities recorded in Table 9 will continue to hold over a period of years.

To check that you have understood how to calculate an expected value, try Activity 6.

ACTIVITY 6

Chaos Ltd has been advised as to the likely annual cost of utilising its new warehouse capacity. (See the table below.)

Cost (£s)	Probability
200,000	0.2
230,000	0.4
250,000	0.3
270,000	0.1

What is the expected value of the cost for this proposal?

The expected value is:

$$(0.2 \times 200,000) + (0.4 \times 230,000) + (0.3 \times 250,000) + (0.1 \times 270,000)$$
$$= £234,000$$

Now that we have determined how to use probabilities, we can return to the wheat problem.

ACTIVITY 7

1. Establish the expected monetary value for each of the four strategies. Use the probabilities for low, medium and high rainfall given in the table below and the outcomes contained in the payoff matrix in Table 1 in Section 1.3 of this unit.

Probability that rainfall will be low	0.2
Probability that rainfall will be medium	0.5
Probability that rainfall will be high	0.3
Total probabilities	1.0

2. Which strategy would you now choose?

---

1. Remember that we obtain an expected value by multiplying each possible outcome by its respective probability and then adding the products. For example, the choice of variety A yields £11,200 when rainfall is low, £9,100 when rainfall is moderate and £7,000 when rainfall is high. Since the probabilities for the three levels of rainfall are 0.2, 0.5 and 0.3, then the expected monetary value for this strategy is:

$$(0.2 \times 11,200) + (0.5 \times 9,100) + (0.3 \times 7,000) = £8,890$$

Calculating the expected monetary value for the other three strategies similarly gives:

Strategy	EMV (£)
A	8,890
B	10,200
C	8,950
D	10,230

Table 10: Expected monetary values for the wheat problem

2. Clearly it makes sense to choose the strategy with the highest expected monetary value. So variety D will be the appropriate choice.

Having arrived at this conclusion, it may have struck you that we are overlooking something. We have established that the expected monetary value is the long-run average payoff. So, suppose that our decision-maker is proposing to grow wheat for one season only. Does it still make sense to use expected monetary value as the decision-making criterion? After all, if variety D was chosen and rainfall proved to be high, then the resulting profit (for that single year) would be the lowest of all the 12 possible payoffs.

The point is a serious one. If the decision-maker intends to grow wheat over a number of years then (on present information regarding probabilities) choice of variety D is clearly optimal, since taking one year with the next this should maximise the average annual payoff. But this implies that the use of expected monetary value would not necessarily be appropriate for a single, one-off decision. There are two possible responses to this. The decision-maker may, indeed, choose to use another approach (for example, the maximin or minimax regret approaches outlined in Section 2 of this unit). Alternatively, the decision-maker may be prepared to use EMV for one-off decisions provided that, in choosing between strategies, the spread around the expected values is also allowed for. How this might be achieved is explored in Section 6.2 of this unit.

To end this section we will use expected monetary value to analyse a typical business problem.

Case Study: marketing methods

A company is considering which of two methods of marketing it should use, direct mailing or newspaper advertisements. It regards these forms of marketing as mutually exclusive. It has a budget for marketing expenditure of £200,000.

Direct mailing costs £0.25 for each mailshot. The company is unsure as to what response rate to expect and has decided to assume possible responses of 6 per cent, 8 per cent and 12 per cent. The probabilities of these rates occurring are estimated to be 0.15, 0.65 and 0.2 respectively. Newspaper advertisements have been used in the past and these also produce varying response rates. The company's budget would allow it to run a campaign of weekly insertions in Sunday newspapers, the total number of insertions being 52. Response rates are assumed to be 700, 1,400 or 2,000 per insertion. The probabilities of these rates occurring are estimated at 0.2, 0.55 and 0.25 respectively. Experience has shown that, for both forms of marketing, only 40 per cent of the responses can be expected to produce a sale. Each sale generates a net income of £10.

Let us start by determining the expected monetary value for the direct mailing strategy. Since the advertising budget is £200,000 then, at a cost of £0.25 per shot, 800,000 shots can be carried out. Remember that, in each case, only 40 per cent of the responses are likely to lead to a sale. So with 800,000 shots, a 6 per cent response rate yields 48,000 responses, 40 per cent of which (that is 19,200) are likely sales. Each sale generates a net income of £10, yielding £192,000 in total. The probability of this occurring is 0.15.

This leaves the net income from the other two response rates. You are asked to establish these as part of Activity 8.

ACTIVITY 8

1. Determine the net income from direct mailing when the response rates are 8 per cent and 12 per cent.

2. So what is the expected monetary value of the direct mailing strategy?

---

1. Your calculations should agree with those given in Table 11.

Response rate	Number	Sales	Net income
8%	64,000	25,600	256,000
12%	96,000	38,400	384,000

Table 11: Payoffs from direct mailing

2. The expected monetary value from direct mailing is given by the sum of each payoff multiplied by its corresponding probability. That is:

$$(0.15 \times 192,000) + (0.65 \times 256,000) + (0.2 \times 384,000) = £272,000$$

We now need to compare this outcome with the expected monetary value from using newspaper advertisements. Remember that there are 52 insertions and so, for example, a response rate of 700 per insertion is equivalent to 36,400 responses over a year. Only 40 per cent of these (14,560) are expected to lead to sales, giving a net income of £145,600. This will occur with a probability of 0.2.

ACTIVITY 9

1. What is the net annual income from newspaper advertisements at response rates of 1,400 and 2,000 per insertion?

2. What is the expected monetary value of the newspaper strategy?

3. Which strategy should the company adopt?

---

1. Your calculations should agree with those in Table 12.

Response rate per advert	Response rate per annum	Sales per annum (£)	Net income (£)
1,400	72,800	29,120	291,200
2,000	104,000	41,600	416,000

Table 12: Payoffs from newspaper advertisements

2. So the expected monetary value from newspaper advertising is:

$$(0.2 \times 145,600) + (0.55 \times 291,200) + (0.25 \times 416,000) = £293,280$$

3. As you will remember from Activity 8, the expected monetary value from direct mailing was £272,000. Our advice to the company would be to use newspaper advertising.

3.2 Expected opportunity loss

An alternative, but related, way of using probabilities is to consider the expected opportunity loss resulting from each choice of strategy. To do this, we shall return to the wheat problem. The regret matrix for that problem is shown in Table 13.

	Low	Medium	High
A	0	4,400	300
B	1,100	500	1,700
C	4,400	2,700	0
D	1,300	0	2,300

Table 13: Regret matrix for the wheat problem

As you may recall, the probability of rainfall being low was rated at 0.2, the probability of rainfall being medium was rated at 0.5, and the probability of rainfall being high was rated at 0.3.

The first row of the matrix shows the regrets associated with choice of variety A. If rainfall proves to be low, then variety A is the best choice and so the regret is zero. However, if rainfall is either medium or high, then the regrets are £4,400 and £300 respectively. Averaging these outcomes (using the probabilities for the three rainfall levels) yields an expected regret of:

$$(0 \times 0.2) + (4,400 \times 0.5) + (300 \times 0.3) = £2,290$$

Since a regret measures the potential loss from an incorrect choice of strategy, it is also referred to as an **opportunity loss**. So, the expected regret of £2,290 from choice of variety A is termed the **expected opportunity loss**. For the decision-maker, it is a way of measuring the consequence of any given choice of strategy.

ACTIVITY 10

1. Using the probabilities for low, medium and high rainfall, determine the expected opportunity loss for the remaining three strategies (choice of variety B, C or D).

2. On the assumption that the decision-maker wishes to minimise expected opportunity loss, what is the best strategy?

3. Compare your answer with that for Activity 7. What do you notice?

---

1. The expected opportunity loss if variety B is chosen is:

$$(1,100 \times 0.2) + (500 \times 0.5) + (1,700 \times 0.3) = £980$$

Continuing in the same way for the remaining two strategies gives:

Strategy	Expected opportunity loss (£)
A	2,290
B	980
C	2,230
D	950

Table 14: Expected opportunity losses for the wheat problem

2. Hence, if the objective is to minimise the expected opportunity loss, then the best choice would be variety D.

3. Comparing this result with that in Activity 7, you should have noticed that the criteria 'maximise expected monetary value' and 'minimise expected opportunity loss' yield the same choice, namely variety D. This is not an accident. You can get a feel of why this should be the case after you have studied Section 3.3.

3.3 Perfect information

For the wheat problem, the hypothetical probabilities that we have been using are assumed to be derived from past data. Now suppose that additional information, regarding rainfall levels in each coming year, is obtainable from a local weather forecaster. Furthermore, suppose that this forecaster is totally reliable.

The question that now arises is 'what is the maximum price which our decision-maker should be prepared to pay to acquire such perfect information?'. We can establish this by asking the slightly different question 'what is the expected value of perfect information to our decision-maker?'.

If the (correct) forecast were for low rainfall, then the optimal strategy for that year would be to choose variety A, with a payoff of £11,200. For a forecast of medium rainfall the optimal choice would be variety D, with a payoff of £13,500. And, for a forecast of high rainfall, the optimal choice would be variety C, with a payoff of £7,300.

Now, over some future sequence of years, low rainfall can be expected to occur for one fifth of the years, medium rainfall for half of the years and high rainfall for the remaining three tenths of the years. Suppose that we consider a ten-year sequence. In two of these years we expect the forecast to be for low rainfall, in which case variety A is chosen, with a payoff of £11,200 in each year. In five of the years we expect the forecast to be for medium rainfall, in which case variety D is chosen, with a payoff of £13,500 in each year. Finally, in the remaining three years we expect the forecast to be for high rainfall, in which case variety C is chosen, with a payoff of £7,300 in each year. So, over the ten years the expected payoff is:

$$(11,200 \times 2) + (13,500 \times 5) + (7,300 \times 3) = £111,800$$

That is, an annual average of £11,180.

We call this the **expected payoff using perfect information**. You may have noticed that we can obtain it more directly by multiplying each payoff by its probability, giving:

$$(11,200 \times 0.2) + (13,500 \times 0.5) + (7,300 \times 0.3) = £11,180$$

We can now determine the value to the decision-maker of acquiring such perfect information.

Look back at the commentary on Activity 7. Without perfect information, the optimal strategy would be to choose variety D. The expected monetary value of this strategy is £10,230.

It follows that the expected value of perfect information can be calculated by subtracting the expected monetary value of the optimal strategy without perfect information from the expected annual payoff using perfect information. This gives:

$$11,180 - 10,230 = £950$$

Therefore, the maximum price that our decision-maker should be prepared to pay (each year) to acquire perfect information is £950.

To check that you have understood how to determine the value of perfect information, you should work through the following activity.

ACTIVITY 11

A pension fund manager wishes to invest in a portfolio of shares, but she only has sufficient funds to buy either portfolio A, portfolio B or portfolio C. The performance of each of the portfolios will depend upon the level of economic activity in the future. We possess the following information about the likely behaviour of the economy and the resultant payoffs (in £000s) for each of the portfolios:

Portfolio	Level of economic activity		
	Expansion	Stability	Contraction
A	100	50	–50
B	50	100	–25
C	–50	0	180

We also possess the following information regarding the estimated probabilities of each level of economic activity occurring:

State of the economy	Probability
Expansion	0.1
Stability	0.4
Contraction	0.5

1. Calculate the expected monetary value for each portfolio. What is the best strategy?
2. If perfect information as to the state of the economy were available to the manager, what is the maximum sum that she should pay to acquire it?

---

1. We need the expected monetary value for each strategy (that is, for each choice of portfolio). Remember that this is obtained by multiplying each payoff by its associated probability and then adding the products. So, for portfolio A, the expected monetary value is:

$$(100 \times 0.1) + (50 \times 0.4) - (50 \times 0.5) = £5,000$$

The full set of outcomes is shown in Table 15.

Portfolio	EMV
A	5,000
B	32,500
C	85,000

Table 15: Expected monetary values for the investment problem

So portfolio C would be selected.

2. The expected annual payoff using perfect information is obtained by multiplying the optimal choice for each state of nature by its probability and adding the products. This gives:

$$(100 \times 0.1) + (100 \times 0.4) + (180 \times 0.5) = £140,000$$

It follows that the maximum sum that should be paid to acquire such information is given by the expected monetary value with perfect information less the expected monetary value without such information. This is:

$$140,000 - 85,000 = £55,000$$

We now return to the issue that was raised after Activity 10. As we saw, the criteria 'maximise expected monetary value' and 'minimise expected opportunity loss' yielded the same choice of optimal strategy. It's now time to establish why this is always the case.

ACTIVITY 12

For the wheat problem, compare the £950 expected value of perfect information with the expected opportunity losses that you worked out in Activity 10. What do you notice? Can you account for this?

The expected value of perfect information is equal to the expected opportunity loss from the (optimal) choice of variety D.

Why should this be? Well, if variety D is grown each year, then, on average, the decision-maker will lose £950 per annum, relative to what would have been the best choice of variety for each year (as given by that year's rainfall). So, if the decision-maker has the opportunity to acquire accurate information as to each year's rainfall then this opportunity loss can be avoided. So the value of such perfect information must be the same as this opportunity loss, namely £950.

3.4 Constructing a payoff matrix

For the decision problems studied so far in this section, there was no need to formally construct a payoff matrix. However, in most cases constructing a payoff matrix is a useful way of sorting the problem out. An example will make clear how this is done.

Suppose that the secretary of a Premier League football club has sought your advice regarding the number of programmes to be printed for each game. Using a local printer, the cost of producing and printing programmes for each game amounts to £1,000 for typesetting (fixed costs) plus £0.80 per copy (variable costs). This quotation is based on print runs of 10,000 or multiples thereof, and also requires that the same number of programmes be printed for each game during the season. The advertising space in the programmes has already been sold for the whole season and the revenue from this source will amount to £2,400 per game (irrespective of how many programmes are printed and sold). Programmes are sold for £2.00 each. Programmes not sold at any game can be disposed of as waste paper, at £0.10 per copy. A review of last season's programme sales shows the following pattern.

Number of programmes sold	Number of games
10,000	2
20,000	8
30,000	6
40,000	4

Table 16: Probability distribution for programme sales

It is expected that this pattern will be repeated during the coming season of 20 home games. The club secretary's view is that, for the coming season, 20,000 programmes should be ordered per home game because that is the most likely sales figure.

ACTIVITY 13

1. How many strategies are there? What are they?

2. How many states of nature are there? What are they?

3. How many payoffs do we need to calculate?

---

1. The strategies are the four different programme order levels, namely 10,000, 20,000, 30,000 and 40,000.

2. The states of nature are the four possible levels of sales, again 10,000, 20,000, 30,000 and 40,000.

3. For each strategy and each state of nature there will be a payoff, giving 16 in total.

We need to establish what these payoffs are. Suppose that 10,000 copies are ordered and printed per game.

ACTIVITY 14

What do we know about the likely programme sales if 10,000 copies are printed for each game?

Last season the minimum programme sale was 10,000. (Assume for the sake of simplicity that everyone will buy a programme.) Hence, if the same pattern is repeated during the coming season, we can always be certain of selling all 10,000 programmes. It is true that in 18 of the coming games the club would be able to sell more than 10,000 programmes. But this is neither here nor there: it merely means that for those games the demand for programmes will exceed the supply. The 10,000 programmes printed will always get sold.

So for each of the four states of nature the payoff will be exactly the same, namely the net proceeds (per game) from the production and sale of 10,000 copies. For each game the costs (fixed and variable) amount to:

$$1,000 + (0.80 \times 10,000)$$

$$= 1,000 + 8,000$$

$$= £9,000$$

The revenue per game, allowing for the advertising and programme sales, will be:

$$2,400 + (2.00 \times 10,000) = £22,400$$

So, for regular match sales of 10,000, the payoff per game is:

$$22,400 - 9,000 = £13,400$$

If 20,000 copies are printed per game, then more care is required in establishing the payoffs. If potential sales are 20,000 or more then clearly all copies will be sold. However, if only 10,000 copies are sold then the remainder will have to be disposed of as waste paper. We need to consider these two cases separately.

Firstly, let us consider what happens if all copies are sold. This should happen in 18 out of 20 games, that is, with a probability of 0.9 per game. The payoff per game will be:

Receipts from Sales + Advertising – Fixed Costs – Variable Costs

$$= (2.00 \times 20,000) + 2,400 - 1,000 - (0.80 \times 20,000)$$

$$= \pounds25,400$$

This payoff will accrue for the three states of nature with potential sales of at least 20,000.

Now let us consider what happens if only 10,000 copies are sold, the remaining 10,000 being disposed of as waste paper. This will happen in two out of 20 games, that is with a probability of 0.1 per game. The payoff per game will be:

Receipts from Sales + Advertising + Sales to Scrap – Fixed Costs – Variable Costs

$$= (2.00 \times 10,000) + 2,400 + (0.10 \times 10,000) - 1,000 - (0.80 \times 20,000)$$

$$= \pounds6,400$$

It is convenient to record these outcomes in a **payoff matrix** as shown in Table 17.

Sales per game	Copies produced per game			
	10,000	20,000	30,000	40,000
10,000	13,400	6,400		
20,000	13,400	25,400		
30,000	13,400	25,400		
40,000	13,400	25,400		

Table 17: Payoff matrix for the football programmes problem

The first column of the matrix shows that, if 10,000 programmes are printed the payoff per game is £13,400 irrespective of the potential sales.

The second column of the matrix shows that, when 20,000 copies are printed but only 10,000 are sold, the payoff is £6,400. If all 20,000 copies are sold, the payoff is £25,400.

If 30,000 copies are printed, sales will be 10,000, 20,000 or 30,000. Similarly, if 40,000 copies are printed, sales will be 10,000, 20,000, 30,000 or 40,000.

ACTIVITY 15

1. Determine the payoffs that result from 30,000 programmes printed per game.

2. Determine the payoffs resulting from a decision to print 40,000 copies per game.

3. Complete the payoff matrix in Table 17.

---

1. If 30,000 programmes are printed per game then the payoff for sales of 10,000 will be:

   Receipts + Advertising + Sales to Scrap − Fixed Costs − Variable Costs

   $= (2.00 \times 10{,}000) + 2{,}400 + (0.10 \times 20{,}000) - 1{,}000 - (0.80 \times 30{,}000)$

   $= -£600$

   For sales of 20,000, the payoff will be:

   $(2.00 \times 20{,}000) + 2{,}400 + (0.10 \times 10{,}000) - 1{,}000 - (0.80 \times 30{,}000)$
   $= £18{,}400$

   For sales of 30,000, the payoff will be:

   $(2.00 \times 30{,}000) + 2{,}400 + 0 - 1{,}000 - (0.80 \times 30{,}000) = £37{,}400$

2. If 40,000 programmes are printed per game then the payoff for sales of 10,000 will be:

   $(2.00 \times 10{,}000) + 2{,}400 + (0.10 \times 30{,}000) - 1{,}000 - (0.80 \times 40{,}000)$
   $= -£7{,}600$

   For sales of 20,000, the payoff will be:

   $(2.00 \times 20{,}000) + 2{,}400 + (0.10 \times 20{,}000) - 1{,}000 - (0.80 \times 40{,}000)$
   $= £11{,}400$

   For sales of 30,000, the payoff will be:

   $(2.00 \times 30{,}000) + 2{,}400 + (0.10 \times 10{,}000) - 1{,}000 - (0.80 \times 40{,}000)$
   $= £30{,}400$

   And, for sales of 40,000, the payoff will be:

   $(2.00 \times 40{,}000) + 2{,}400 + 0 - 1{,}000 - (0.80 \times 40{,}000) = £49{,}400$

3. The completed payoff matrix is shown in Table 18.

		Copies produced per game			
		10,000	20,000	30,000	40,000
Sales	10,000	13,400	6,400	−600	−7,600
per	20,000	13,400	25,400	18,400	11,400
game	30,000	13,400	25,400	37,400	30,400
	40,000	13,400	25,400	37,400	49,400

Table 18: Completed payoff matrix for the football programmes problem

We now distinguish between the **conditional payoff** (that is, the payoff before allowing for its probability), and the **expected payoff** (that is, the payoff after allowing for its probability). The expected payoff is calculated by multiplying the conditional payoff by its probability of occurrence.

Table 19 shows the complete situation for our football programme problem. The second column shows the probabilities for each of the four levels of sales (states of nature). CP and EP denote the conditional and expected payoff respectively.

		Number of programmes printed							
Sales	Prob.	10,000		20,000		30,000		40,000	
		CP	EP	CP	EP	CP	EP	CP	EP
10,000	0.1	13,400	1,340	6,400	640	−600	−60	−7,600	−760
20,000	0.4	13,400	5,360	25,400	10,160	18,400	7,360	11,400	4,560
30,000	0.3	13,400	4,020	25,400	7,620	37,400	11,220	30,400	9,120
40,000	0.2	13,400	2,680	25,400	5,080	37,400	7,480	49,400	9,880
			13,400		23,500		26,000		22,800

Table 19: Calculations for the football programmes problem

The expected monetary value for each strategy is then obtained by adding each of the EP columns. For example, if 40,000 copies are printed then the conditional payoffs are −£7,600, £11,400, £30,400 and £49,400. These will arise with probabilities of 0.1, 0.4, 0.3 and 0.2 respectively. The expected payoffs are then:

$$(0.1 \times -7,600) = -£760$$

$$(0.4 \times 11,400) = £4,560$$

$$(0.3 \times 30,400) = £9,120$$

$$(0.2 \times 49,400) = £9,880$$

The sum of these expected payoffs is £22,800. This is the expected monetary value for this strategy.

ACTIVITY 16

How many programmes should the secretary order per game? On average, how much will this earn for the club per game?

The maximum expected monetary value is obtained from the strategy of always ordering 30,000 programmes per game. This will earn the club an average of £26,000 per game.

Now suppose that the club secretary has a further source of information concerning programme sales. A local market research firm indicates that it can accurately predict the actual programme sales for each game during the coming season.

ACTIVITY 17

Why would the information about programme sales for the coming season be of value to the club?

If the club can obtain advance knowledge of the attendance for each game then it can adjust its weekly print order accordingly.

The local printing firm requires an annual fee of £20,000 as a condition of agreeing to a variable print order. To justify printing a variable number of programmes, the average payoff per game must be greater than the expected monetary value of £26,000 obtained from a constant print order of 30,000. Moreover, this increase in the average payoff will have to be sufficient to offset the £20,000 additional annual cost. The next activity asks you to identify the benefits of printing variable numbers of programmes, given perfect information about levels of sales. You are then asked to use this information to calculate the value of the perfect information.

ACTIVITY 18

Determine the maximum annual sum which the secretary should be prepared to pay for such perfect information. You should start by calculating the expected payoff (per game) with perfect information.

What is the expected payoff using perfect information? Look at the figures shown in Table 19. Since the club will know for certain how many programmes can be sold per game then, when sales are predicted to be 10,000, the club will print 10,000 and the conditional payoff will be £13,400. When the prediction is for sales of 20,000 then that is the number that will be printed, with a payoff of £25,400. Similarly when the prediction is for sales of 30,000 or 40,000 then that number will be printed with payoffs of £37,400 and £49,400 respectively.

Using the probabilities for the four levels of sales, this gives the expected payoff using perfect information as:

$$(0.1 \times 13{,}400) + (0.4 \times 25{,}400) + (0.3 \times 37{,}400) + (0.2 \times 49{,}400)$$
$$= £32{,}600$$

The expected value of perfect information (per game) is given by subtracting the expected monetary value without perfect information from the expected monetary value using perfect information. This is:

32,600 – 26,000 = £6,600

Hence, over the whole season (consisting of 20 home games), perfect information is worth:

20 × 6,600 = £132,000

Allowing for the additional £20,000 fee required by the printers, the club should, therefore, be willing to spend no more than £112,000 to acquire the market research information (£132,000 minus £20,000).

Now try the following problem.

ACTIVITY 19

A canteen is supplied daily with cream cakes by a local bakery. The cakes cost £0.30 to buy and are sold for £0.50. Cakes which are left over at the end of the day are sold to the canteen staff for £0.20 each.

From past experience, the daily demand for cream cakes has the following probability distribution:

Cakes demanded	Probability
10	0.1
20	0.4
30	0.3
40	0.2

1. Calculate the expected monetary values for the different daily order sizes and display your results in a table.

2. How many cream cakes should the canteen manager order each day?

3. Assuming that the canteen manager orders this number of cream cakes, what is the minimum price that the canteen can charge such that over the year it will break even?

1. There are four strategies: these are to order 10, 20, 30 or 40 cream cakes per day. There are also four states of nature, given by the potential daily sales of 10, 20, 30 or 40 cakes. Hence, there are 16 payoffs. Your calculations should agree with those shown in Table 20.

Sales	Prob.	Cakes ordered							
		10		20		30		40	
		CP	EP	CP	EP	CP	EP	CP	EP
10	0.1	2	0.2	1	0.1	0	0.0	−1	−0.1
20	0.4	2	0.8	4	1.6	3	1.2	2	0.8
30	0.3	2	0.6	4	1.2	6	1.8	5	1.5
40	0.2	2	0.4	4	0.8	6	1.2	8	1.6
			2.0		3.7		4.2		3.8

Table 20: Calculations for the cream cake problem

2. As the highest expected monetary value results from ordering 30 cream cakes per day, this is the number which the canteen manager should order.

3. Firstly, since 30 cakes a day are being ordered at a price of £0.30 per cake, the cost of the daily order is £9 (0.3 × 30). In order to break even over the year, the expected daily revenue needs to be £9.

To progress, we need to determine the expected daily revenue. Let x equal the refectory price. With 30 cakes, on sale there are three possibilities.

Either only 10 cakes are sold, the other 20 being leftover sales. The resulting revenue will be $10x + (0.2 \times 20)$. This will occur with a probability of 0.1

Or, exactly 20 cakes are sold, the remaining 10 being leftover sales. The resulting revenue will be $20x + (0.2 \times 10)$. This will occur with a probability of 0.4.

Or, all 30 cakes are sold. The resulting revenue will be $30x$. This will occur with a probability of 0.5. (If you thought that this probability figure should be 0.3 then you were wrong. 0.3 is the probability that exactly 30 cakes are demanded. But all 30 cakes can also be sold on those days when in fact the demand is for 40. Hence, the required probability is 0.3 plus 0.2.)

The expected daily revenue is then:

$$\{10x + (0.2 \times 20)\}0.1 + \{20x + (0.2 \times 10)\}0.4 + \{30x\}0.5$$

$$= x + 0.4 + 8x + 0.8 + 15x$$

$$= 24x + 1.2$$

If we want to break even, we must ensure that expected daily revenue is equal to daily cost. As daily cost is £9, daily revenue of $24x + 1.2$ must equal 9. So:

$$24x + 1.2 = 9$$

$$24x = 7.8$$

$$x = 0.325$$

The minimum price for canteen sales is therefore £0.325.

Summary

In this section of the unit, we have considered decision-making under risk. Here the decision-maker is able to associate probabilities with the various states of nature that have a bearing upon the decision. We showed that an optimal strategy can be determined using expected monetary value. However, there is a danger in using this criterion for decision-making. Since an expected value is best interpreted as a long-run average then, in general, it is only safe to use EMVs alone to choose between alternative strategies when the events to which they refer are being repeated. However, it may be appropriate to use EMVs in the investigation of one-off decisions if the spread around the expected values is also taken into account.

We also showed how certain kinds of business problem can be investigated by the construction of a payoff matrix. This records the strategies, states of nature and payoffs relevant to the problem, and can be used to determine that strategy which has the optimal expected monetary value.

In Section 4 we look at multi-stage decision problems.

SECTION 4

Multi-Stage Decision Problems

Introduction

Section 1 of this unit showed how a decision tree could be used to represent a decision problem. In this section we examine how such trees should be constructed so as to correctly represent the historical and logical order in which decisions required are to be taken. We then show how expected monetary values are used to determine the optimal strategy at each decision point on the decision tree. Often the data and probabilities for a decision problem are subject to some error or doubt. We therefore end the section by showing how **sensitivity analysis** can be employed to investigate how decisions react to changes in the parameters.

By the end of this section you should be able to evaluate a decision tree.

4.1 Using a decision tree to solve a decision problem

Case Study: renovate or replace?

A company operates an incineration plant which is becoming outdated. Three separate proposals have been put forward for either its renovation or complete replacement. The decision as to which proposal should be adopted depends primarily on expected future levels of demand. The company plans ten years ahead.

Proposal A is to renovate the existing plant now, at a cost of £9 million, with an option to enlarge the plant after five years at an estimated further cost of £7 million. Proposal B is to demolish the existing plant, redevelop the land and build a new plant at a cost of £23 million. There is an option to extend the plant after five years at a further cost of £3 million. Proposal C is to demolish the existing plant, redevelop the land and build a new plant at a cost of £30 million. This size of plant is expected to be sufficient to cope with any future increase in demand and would not require any extension for at least ten years.

As a first step in constructing any decision tree, it is essential to determine what decisions are required and in what order they need to be made.

ACTIVITY 20

What decisions does the company need to take with relation to this problem, and when does it need to take them?

The company needs to take two different decisions. Firstly, it needs to decide what to do now. Should it choose proposal A, B or C? Secondly, if it chooses A or B now, it will need to take another decision in five years' time.

As Activity 20 shows, the problem is multi-staged. This is because the company needs to decide now which of the three proposals it will choose. Then, if either proposal A or proposal B is chosen, the company will need to decide in five years' time whether or not it needs to extend the plant.

The decisions are heavily influenced by the likely future levels of demand. These have been estimated to be as shown in Table 21.

State of demand		Probability
Years 1 to 5	Years 6 to 10	
High	High	0.48
High	Low	0.12
Low	High	0.12
Low	Low	0.28

Table 21: Probability distribution for demand for the incineration plant problem

The costs of running the various plants are fixed and are estimated to be as shown in Table 22. Costs are given in millions of pounds per annum.

		High demand	Low demand
Proposal A	without extension	11	8
	with extension	8	9
Proposal B	without extension	7	5
	with extension	5	6
Proposal C		5	5

Table 22: Estimates of running costs for the incineration plant problem

We need to determine the company's optimal strategy: namely, what it should do now; and what it should do in five years' time if it opts for either proposal A or B now. We start by constructing a decision tree for this problem. To do this we need to abide by two rules.

1. A decision tree must be drawn and read from left to right and the tree must be constructed so that decision points occur in the right order. If, for example, decision Y cannot be made until the outcomes from decision X have occurred, then decision X must come before decision Y in the tree. It is, therefore, essential to sort out the order in which decisions occur before starting to draw the tree.

2. Decision points must be distinguished from event points (see Section 2 of this unit). At every decision point there must be a separate branch for each strategy that might be adopted. Similarly, at each event point there must be a separate branch for each of the possible states of nature (in this case, the levels of demand).

ACTIVITY 21

Draw the decision tree for the incineration plant problem. For the moment, don't try to insert any information regarding either costs or probabilities: that will come later.

You should build up a decision tree such as this step by step. Begin at the extreme left of the tree (see Figure 2). The starting point must be the decision whether to opt for proposal A, B or C. Notice that the running costs for proposal C are independent of the level of demand. There is, therefore, no need to allow for the different states of nature with regard to this option.

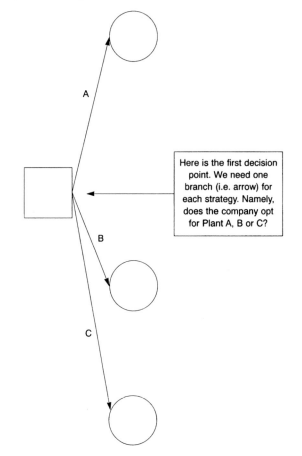

Here is the first decision point. We need one branch (i.e. arrow) for each strategy. Namely, does the company opt for Plant A, B or C?

Figure 2: Decision tree for the incineration plant problem – step one

Now suppose that proposal A is chosen: in the first five years demand will be either high or low. So, following a decision in favour of proposal A, there are two states of nature. Either demand is high during years 1 to 5 or it is low. Exactly the same states of nature result from a decision in favour of proposal B. However, in the case of proposal C running costs are independent of the state of demand.

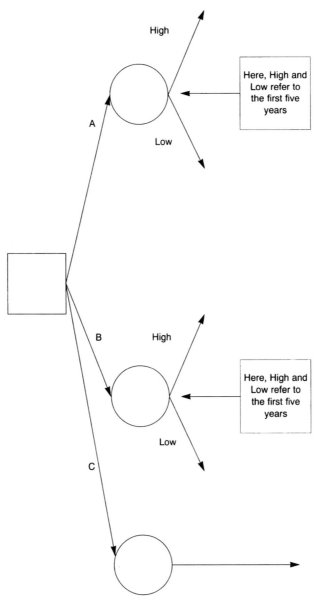

High

Here, High and
Low refer to
the first five
years

A

Low

B   High

Here, High and
Low refer to
the first five
years

Low

C

Figure 3: Decision tree for the incineration plant problem – step two

Now suppose that proposal A is chosen and demand is high during the first five years. The company now needs to decide whether or not to enlarge the plant. Exactly the same decision arises if demand is low during years 1 to 5. Of course, if the plant is enlarged then demand will either be high or be low in the remaining five years. Again the same two states of nature will result if the plant is not enlarged. As a result, the expanded tree will now be as in Figure 4.

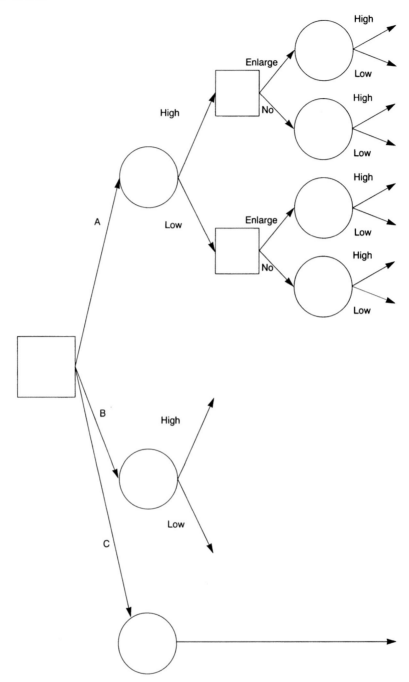

Figure 4: Decision tree for the incineration plant problem – step three

Finally, a similar set of decisions and states of nature will arise with respect to an initial decision to opt for proposal B. Hence, the completed decision tree is as shown in Figure 5. Your tree should be in agreement with this. Although you may well have the branches in a different order from that in Figure 5, your tree must include the same set.

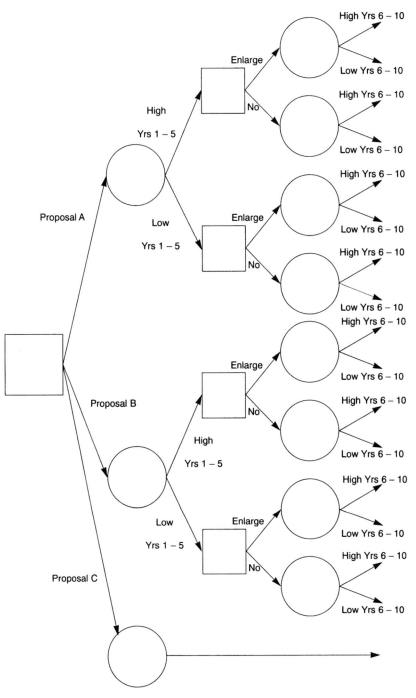

Figure 5: Completed decision tree for the incineration plant problem

Now that we have constructed the tree, the next step is to insert the relevant information. This will be of two kinds.

Firstly, we need to insert the costs (**capital costs** and **operating costs**) that result from each choice of strategy and resulting state of nature. These values must be inserted at the correct points on the tree. For example, suppose that proposal A is chosen and is followed by high demand for the first five years. A decision must then be taken as to whether the plant should be enlarged. The only costs relevant to that decision are those that will arise as a consequence of it, namely:

- if the plant is enlarged, a capital cost of £7 million and annual running costs of £8 or £9 million depending upon whether demand proves to be high or low
- if the plant is not enlarged, an annual running cost of £11 or £8 million, again depending upon whether demand is high or low.

Any costs that have already been incurred prior to this point are irrelevant to the decision as to whether the plant should be enlarged or not.

Secondly, we require the probabilities for each state of nature. Remember that these relate to events which are outside the control of the decision-maker, but for which we have probabilistic information.

Activity 22

For the first five years, demand will be either high or low. Given the information in Table 21, determine the probabilities for these two events.

Although there are four distinct possibilities for the behaviour of demand over the whole ten years, in two of these cases demand will be high during the first five years. So the probability that demand will be high in years 1 to 5 will be the sum of the probabilities for these two cases, that is:

$$0.48 + 0.12 = 0.6$$

Conversely, the probability that demand will be low in years 1 to 5 is:

$$0.12 + 0.28 = 0.4$$

We now need to evaluate the probabilities for demand being either high or low over the last five years (that is years 6 to 10). This is decidedly more tricky.

Activity 23

Look at the decision tree for this problem, shown as Figure 5.

Consider the branch that runs:

> Proposal ➡ High demand ➡ Enlarge ➡ High demand
> A   in years 1 to 5   in years 6 to 10

We know, from Activity 22, that the probability of demand being high in years 1 to 5 is 0.6. Will the probability of demand being high in years 6 to10, given that it was high in years 1 to 5, also be 0.6?

Hint: you are being asked for a **conditional probability**.

Look at Table 21. High demand in years 1 to 5 is either followed by high demand in years 6 to 10, with a probability of 0.48, or is followed by low demand in years 6 to 10, with a probability of 0.12.

So the chance of a known high demand in years 1 to 5 being followed by high demand in years 6 to 10 is:

$$\frac{0.48}{0.48 + 0.12} = 0.8$$

We can also use a formula to obtain this result. Let X and Y denote any two events. Then we let:

> $Pr(X)$ denote the probability that event X occurs
>
> $Pr(Y)$ denote the probability that event Y occurs
>
> $Pr(X \cap Y)$ denote the joint probability that both X and Y occur
>
> $Pr(Y/X)$ denote the conditional probability that Y occurs, given that X has occurred

Then, by the **multiplication rule of probability**:

> $Pr(X \cap Y) = Pr(X) \times Pr(Y/X)$

In other words, the probability that both X and Y occur is equal to the probability of X occurring multiplied by the probability of Y occurring given that X has occurred.

Rearranging this rule gives:

$$Pr(Y/X) = \frac{Pr(X \cap Y)}{Pr(X)}$$

From Table 21, we know that the probability that demand is high throughout the ten years (that is, $Pr(X \cap Y)$) is 0.48.

From Activity 22 we know that the probability that demand is high in years 1 to 5 (that is, $Pr(X)$) is 0.6.

So let X be the event that 'demand is high in years 1 to 5', and Y be the event that 'demand is high in years 6 to 10'. Then:

$$Pr(Y/X) = \frac{Pr(X \cap Y)}{Pr(X)} = \frac{0.48}{0.6} = 0.8$$

ACTIVITY 24

Determine the remaining conditional probabilities. You will need to establish:

Pr(demand low in years 6 to 10/demand high in years 1 to 5)

Pr(demand low in years 6 to 10/demand low in years 1 to 5)

Pr(demand high in years 6 to 10/demand low in years 1 to 5)

Firstly, high demand in years 1 to 5 can only be followed by either high or low demand in years 6 to 10. But from Activity 23 we know that the probability of high demand in years 1 to 5 being followed by high demand in years 6 to 10 is 0.8. Therefore, it must be the case that the probability that demand is low in years 6 to 10, given that it was high in the previous five years, is 0.2.

Now suppose that demand is low in years 1 to 5. Then using, the information in Table 21 and the results from Activity 22, we have that:

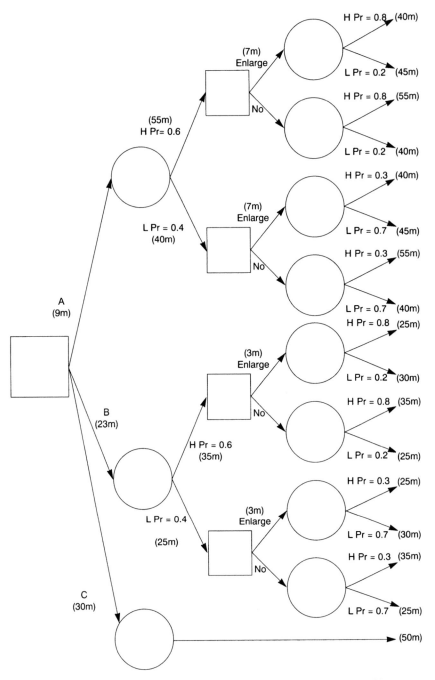

Figure 6: Costs and probabilities for the incineration plant problem

$$\text{Pr}\left(\frac{\text{demand is low in years 6 to10}}{\text{demand is low in years 1 to 5}}\right)$$

$$= \frac{\text{Pr (demand is low over the whole period)}}{\text{Pr (demand is low in year 1 to 5)}}$$

$$= \frac{0.28}{0.4}$$

$$= 0.7$$

To complete the picture, it follows that:

$$\text{Pr}\left(\frac{\text{demand is high in years 6 to 10}}{\text{demand is low in years 1to 5}}\right) = 0.3$$

Now that we have obtained all the required probabilities, we can insert these, along with the other information, at the appropriate points on the decision tree (see Figure 6 opposite). Since all the monetary sums are negative, we have followed the accounting convention of enclosing them within brackets. On the tree, H denotes high demand and L denotes low demand.

To see how the data has been entered onto the tree, consider the top four branches. Figure 7 shows the required calculations. Using Table 22, you should now check that you agree with the data recorded on the other branches in the full tree shown in Figure 6.

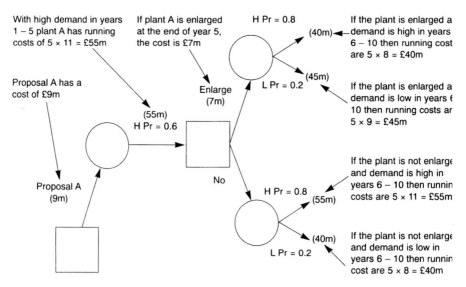

Figure 7: Calculations for the incineration plant problem decision tree

Having drawn the decision tree and inserted all the relevant information, the final step is to evaluate it. As you know, construction of a decision tree has to follow various rules. The same is true when you evaluate a decision tree. So what are these rules?

1. The decision criterion that we are employing is expected monetary value. If the expected monetary values are, say, expected profits or contributions, then we choose between strategies so as to maximise expected monetary value. If, as is the case in our current problem, the expected monetary values are expected costs, then clearly we seek the strategy that will minimise expected monetary value.

2. At each decision point the expected monetary value for each strategy must be determined. The optimal strategy for that decision point will then be the one with the best expected monetary value. All other strategies, at that decision point, can then be ruled out.

3. To evaluate the decision tree we have to proceed from right to left (in the opposite direction from that in which the tree was constructed). This is usually referred to as 'rolling back the tree'.

So let us evaluate the tree for the incinerator problem. We will start with the top four branches, as shown in Figure 7. Suppose that proposal A is chosen at the outset, and demand proves to be high over the first five years. We need to establish whether the plant should be enlarged or not. Remember that in making this decision we only take into account those costs that are contingent upon it.

ACTIVITY 25

1. What is the expected cost from enlarging the plant?
2. What is the expected cost from not enlarging the plant?
3. What is the optimal decision?

---

1. If the plant is enlarged, the operating cost for years 6 to 10 will be £40 million if demand is high (the probability of this is 0.8); and the operating cost for years 6 to 10 will be £45 million if demand is low (the probability of this is 0.2). The capital outlay will be £7 million.

   So the expected cost is:

   $(40 \times 0.8) + (45 \times 0.2) + 7 = £48$ million

2. If the plant is not enlarged, the operating cost for years 6 to 10 will be £55 million if demand is high (the probability of this is 0.8); and the operating

cost for years 6 to 10 will be £40 million if demand is low (the probability of this is 0.2).

So the expected cost is:

$$(55 \times 0.8) + (40 \times 0.2) = £52 \text{ million}$$

3. Since the objective here is to minimise costs, then at this point on the tree the optimal decision would be to enlarge the plant.

We now record the outcomes from Activity 25, on the tree (see Figure 8). Having decided that it would be optimal to enlarge the plant, we show this by inserting a double line (//) across the branch for not enlarging it. So far as we are concerned, that branch has no further relevance. The optimal expected monetary value (that is, a cost of £48m) is inserted in the square for that decision point.

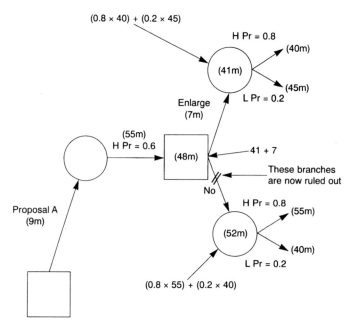

Figure 8: Evaluation of first decision point

ACTIVITY 26

Now suppose that proposal A is chosen, but demand is low over the first five years. Would it still be optimal to enlarge the plant? To establish this you should proceed in exactly the same way as in Activity 25.

The relevant portion of the tree is as shown in Figure 9. Remember that we must only take into account those costs that are contingent upon the decision of whether or not to enlarge the plant.

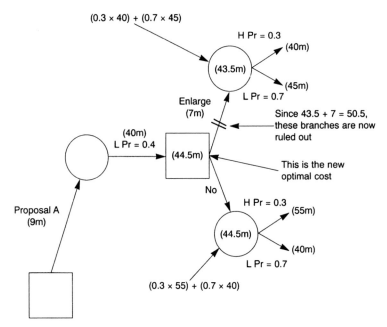

Figure 9: Evaluation of second decision point

The expected cost if the plant is enlarged is:

$$(40 \times 0.3) + (45 \times 0.7) + 7 = \text{£}50.5 \text{ million}$$

However, if the plant is not enlarged then the expected cost is:

$$(55 \times 0.3) + (40 \times 0.7) = \text{£}44.5 \text{ million}$$

Hence, the optimal decision is to not enlarge the plant.

Up to this point we have determined that if proposal A is chosen and demand is high over the first five years the optimal strategy is to enlarge the plant. And, if demand is low over the first five years the optimal strategy is not to enlarge it. Figure 10 summarises the position.

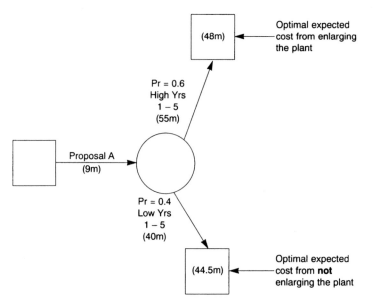

Figure 10: Optimal decisions following from choice of proposal A

Now that these branches have been rolled back, as shown in Figure 10, we can determine the expected cost of a decision to choose proposal A. Following an initial outlay of £9m, there is a 0.6 probability of the running cost being £55m in years 1 to 5, followed by an expected cost of £48m consequent upon the optimal decision to enlarge the plant. On the other hand, there is a 0.4 probability of demand being low in years 1 to 5, in which case the running costs will be £40m in those years, followed by a further expected £44.5m resulting from the optimal decision not to enlarge the plant.

ACTIVITY 27

So what is the expected cost of choosing proposal A?

Look at Figure 10. Suppose that demand is high in years 1 to 5. Then the operating costs for these years will total £55m, followed by an expected cost of £48m consequent upon the optimal decision to enlarge the plant. So there is a 0.6 probability of costs totalling £103 million if the decision is taken to select proposal A (£55 million + £48 million).

Conversely, if demand is low in years 1 to 5, then costs will total £40 million for the first five years, followed by an expected cost of £44.5 million, given the optimal decision not to enlarge the plant. So there is a 0.4 probability of costs amounting to £84.5 million (£40 million + £44.5 million).

1Finally we must allow for the £9 million capital cost of proposal A. Therefore, the expected cost of proposal A is:

$$(103 \times 0.6) + (84.5 \times 0.4) + 9 = £104.6 \text{ million}$$

We now need to compare this with the expected costs of proposals B and C. It will be a good test of your understanding of how to evaluate a decision tree for you to determine these for yourself.

ACTIVITY 28

1. Determine the expected cost of proposal B. You should follow the same approach as that employed for proposal A, that is you must start by evaluating the two decision points at the end of the first five years.

2. Determine the expected cost of proposal C.

---

1. To start, we need to evaluate the two decision points at the end of year 5. Firstly, suppose that demand is high in years 1 to 5. Then, the expected cost from extending the plant is:

    $$(25 \times 0.8) + (30 \times 0.2) + 3 = £29 \text{ million}$$

    And the expected cost from not extending the plant is:

    $$(35 \times 0.8) + (25 \times 0.2) = £33 \text{ million}$$

    Hence, the optimal decision is to extend the plant.

    Secondly, suppose that demand is low in years 1 to 5. Then the expected cost from extending the plant is:

    $$(25 \times 0.3) + (30 \times 0.7) + 3 = £31.5 \text{ million}$$

    And the expected cost from not extending the plant is:

    $$(35 \times 0.3) + (25 \times 0.7) = £28 \text{ million}$$

    For this decision point the optimal choice is not to extend the plant.

    Putting all of this together (see Figure 11) gives the expected cost of proposal B as:

    $$0.6(35 + 29) + 0.4(25 + 28) + 23$$
    $$= 21 + 17.4 + 10 + 11.2 + 23$$
    $$= £82.6 \text{ million}$$

Figure 11 shows the outcome for proposal B.

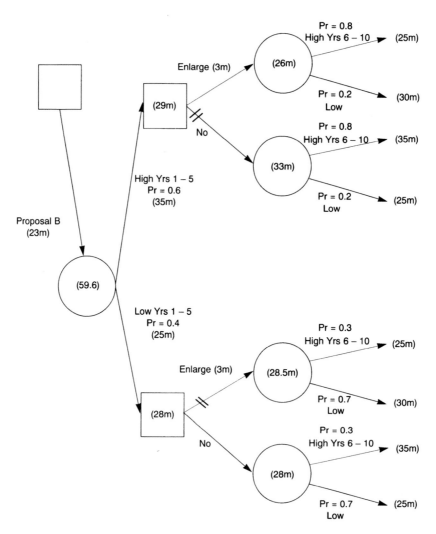

Figure 11: Optimal Decisions following from choice of proposal B

2. Thankfully, obtaining the expected cost for proposal C is a good deal more straightforward! Look at the completed decision tree in Figure 6. All we have is a capital outlay of £30 million and a certain running cost of £50 million (that is £5 million a year for ten years). So the certain cost of proposal C is:

30 + 50 = £80 million

Now that we have determined the expected costs for each of the three strategies (that is, choice of proposal) we are in a position to choose between them.

ACTIVITY 29

What is our recommendation to the company?

Table 23 summarises our conclusions regarding the three proposals. Costs are given in millions of pounds.

Proposal	Expected cost
A	104.6
B	82.6
C	80.0

Table 23: Expected costs for the three proposals

Since the objective here is to minimise the expected cost, then we recommend adoption of proposal C.

Now let's look at another problem.

Case Study: a marketing problem

A surgical appliance firm is about to launch a new product and needs to establish its optimal strategy. A market research survey costing £50,000 will establish whether or not the product has the potential for success. The company estimates that there is a 60 per cent chance of the market research survey showing that the new product has potential. If the results of the survey are negative, the firm will cut its losses and sell its rights in the product for £20,000.

If the survey shows that the product has potential, the company has the opportunity to undertake a test marketing operation at a cost of £100,000. Should evaluation of this test marketing be very favourable, a large-scale launch of the product involving capital expenditure of £1.5 million will be undertaken. If the product is successful, it will yield an expected contribution to profit of £3 million over its lifetime. If the product is a failure, it will yield only £500,000.

Should the test marketing result be only moderately favourable, a relatively small-scale launch involving capital expenditure of only £500,000 will be undertaken. This smaller project is estimated to yield a contribution to profit of £1 million, if the product is successful, but only £200,000 if it is a failure. An unfavourable test marketing result would lead to the firm selling all its rights in the product, but now receiving only £5,000, due to the adverse publicity.

Given its past experience in the launch of new products, the company believes that there is a 70 per cent chance of the test marketing result indicating that the product is a real winner. with a 20 per cent chance that it shows only a moderately favourable result. If the large-scale launch takes place there is an estimated 80 per cent chance of success, whilst that of the more modest launch is 90 per cent.

The company could choose not to undertake a test marketing operation, but instead go direct to a national launch (provided that the market research survey shows that the product has potential). In the absence of a test marketing operation, the probability of the large-scale launch being a success is estimated at 60 per cent. However. contributions to profits would be as before.

ACTIVITY 30

Construct a decision tree for this problem. For the moment do not insert any data or probabilities.

You should have a tree similar to that shown in Figure 12 (opposite).

Reading across the tree from left to right, the starting point (1) is the decision to carry out a market research survey.

Event point (2) shows the outcomes for the survey showing potential or otherwise. If no potential is revealed, then the only strategy is to sell the rights. If the survey reveals potential, a choice must be made at decision point (3) between the alternatives of a test marketing operation or an immediate national launch.

If a decision is taken to go direct to a national launch, then the only outcomes (4) are that it proves to be a success or a failure. Conversely, if the test marketing operation is chosen, then event point (5) lists the outcomes.

Tracing down the remaining branches, at decision point (8) a large-scale launch will be chosen, with event point (9) listing the outcomes. If the test marketing is only moderately favourable (6), then event point (7) gives the outcomes.

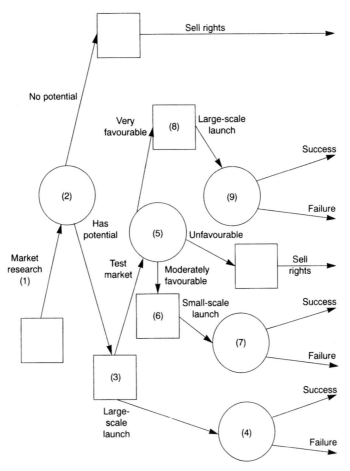

Figure 12: Decision tree for the marketing problem

As you probably discovered when working through the previous activity, it is essential to sort out the logical order in which decisions must be taken before you attempt to draw the tree. Moreover, for anything other than a very trivial problem, getting this order and the resulting tree fully correct usually requires more than one attempt. Because of this, you must always check any tree against the problem, amending and redrawing it as necessary until you are certain that you have correctly allowed for all decision and event points.

For the current problem, having drawn the decision tree, the final step is to insert the data and probabilities and roll it back. You will do this in the next activity.

ACTIVITY 31

Insert the data and probabilities on the decision tree shown in Figure 12. Determine the expected monetary values at each of the event points and the optimal decisions where appropriate. Recommend a course of action to the company.

Your evaluated decision tree should agree with that shown in Figure 13.

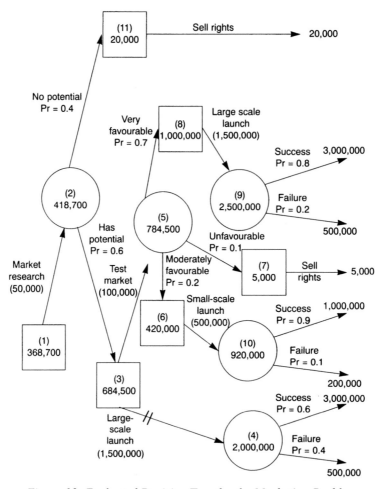

Figure 13: Evaluated Decision Tree for the Marketing Problem

Working backwards across the tree the calculations at the various event and decision points are as shown below.

Event (9):

$$(0.8 \times 3,000,000) + (0.2 \times 500,000) = £2,500,000$$

Decision Point (8) (allowing for the cost of the large-scale launch):

$$2,500,000 - 1,500,000 = £1,000,000$$

Event (10):

$$(0.9 \times 1,000,000) + (0.1 \times 200,000) = £920,000$$

Decision Point (6) (allowing for the cost of the small-scale launch):

$$920,000 - 5000,000 = £420,000$$

Event (5) (expected value):

$$(0.7 \times 1,000,000) + (0.1 \times 5,000) + (0.2 \times 420,000) = £784,500$$

Event (4):

$$(0.6 \times 3,000,000) + (0.4 \times 500,000) = £2,000,000$$

Decision Point (3)

The expected return from an immediate national launch:

$$2,000,000 - 1,500,000 = £500,000$$

And the expected return from choosing a test marketing operation is:

$$784,500 - 100,000 = £684,500$$

So the optimal decision is to run the test marketing operation and rule out the immediate national launch. Hence, £684,500 is inserted into the square at (3).

Event (2). Since the return if the survey shows no potential is a certain 20,000, then the expected value at this point is:

$$(0.4 \times 20,000) + (0.6 \times 684,500) = £418,700$$

Decision Point (1):

$$418,700 - 50,000 = £368,700$$

This is the expected return from the new product.

We therefore conclude that, provided the market research demonstrates potential, the company should carry out the test marketing operation and not go to an immediate national launch.

It may have struck you that one complication has been overlooked when evaluating the decision trees that we have seen up to this point. For example, in the case of the tree shown in Figure 13 we have made the assumption that income or expenditure which arises in the future has the same value to the company as income or expenditure which arises now. As an illustration of this, if the product is launched nationally then an investment of £1.5 million will lead to returns of £3 million if the launch is successful, but of only £500,000 otherwise. However, these returns will occur over the future life of the product, whereas the investment cost arises in the present. It follows that, in a business context, when evaluating a decision tree where any monetary sums occur over time, it is essential to discount all EMVs to present value. However, this will not be pursued in this unit.

4.2 Sensitivity analysis

Once a decision tree has been constructed and evaluated it is usually sensible to undertake some **sensitivity analysis** on the results. As well as obtaining a recommendation, as a consequence of rolling back the tree, it is important to know how sensitive the conclusions are to changes in the data. Such analysis enables the decision-maker to determine how robust the recommendations are in the face of changes to the parameters of the problem.

To explore this, consider the following problem.

Case Study: celtic suppliers

Recent research has highlighted the potential dangers for asthma sufferers from the use of certain types of chalk in the classroom. As a result *Celtic Suppliers*, a supplier of educational resources, needs to investigate whether there might be any allergy-inducing components in its products. The company has approached the *University of Brumford* with a view to conducting trials, in the hope of establishing that its products are safe when used as intended. From past experience, the probability that the products will be found not to be allergy-inducing is thought to be approximately 0.85.

Celtic Suppliers has already been considering the use of alternative constituents for the products: these have been fully tested and are known not to be allergy-inducing. In the company's view, if given time to respond (rather than being rushed into it), the required changes at the manufacturing plant would cost approximately £250,000. However, if public disquiet forces an immediate response, the cost to the company of such an abrupt change is likely to be of the order of £750,000. At a recent board meeting there was a strong voice in favour of not making a precipitate response, in the expectation that the university would be almost certain to report that the allergy fears were ill-founded. Of course, if this were to be the case then there would be no need to make any changes to the manufacturing process and, in consequence, no extra costs would arise.

One dissident board member argued that this would be a misguided decision since, if the university were to find that the fears were actually justified, then not only would the company be forced to adopt the product changes but would also lose up to £2 million in lost sales.

ACTIVITY 32

Draw the decision tree for this problem and use it to recommend what *Celtic Suppliers* should do.

The tree for this problem is shown in Figure 14.

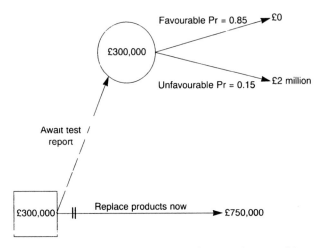

Figure 14: Decision tree for the celtic suppliers problem

Replacing the products now will cost £750,000, whereas the expected cost of a decision to await the test report is:

$$(0.85 \times 0) + (0.15 \times 2,000,000) = £300,000$$

So the recommendation would be that the company should wait for the report on the tests.

However, suppose that there is doubt at to whether the 0.85 probability will actually apply in this case. Clearly, the lower the probability that the university will find the product to be safe, the greater the risk of waiting for the report rather than replacing the product now. The question that then arises is 'how low would this probability need to be before the recommendation arrived at in Activity 32 should be changed?'.

Look at Figure 14. If the probability of a favourable report is 0.85, then the expected cost from awaiting the report is less than the £750,000 cost of replacing the product now. Our recommendation to the company will only change if the expected cost from waiting becomes at least equal to this sum. To find out the point at which this occurs we proceed as follows.

Let p equal the probability of a favourable report. Then the expected cost of waiting for the report is $(1 - p) \times £2$ million.

For example, if p falls as low as 0.5 then the expected cost is:

$$(1-p)2,000,000 = 0.5 \times 2,000,000 = £1,000,000$$

Remember that if the product is cleared then no costs will be incurred.

To continue with the current recommendation, we require that at worst:

$$(1 - p)2,000,000 = £750,000$$

This rearranges to give:

$$1 - p = \frac{750,000}{2,000,000} = 0.375$$

And so:

$$p = 1 - 0.375 = 0.625$$

For any lower value of p it would be preferable to replace the product now and not wait for the outcome of the report.

The probability of the report being favourable is not the only aspect of the problem which has a bearing on the decision. Whether the company should await the report also depends upon the costs that will result if the university concludes that the product is allergy-inducing. Here, we are interested in the sensitivity of the recommendation to changes in these costs. You will explore this in the final activity for this section.

ACTIVITY 33

Suppose that the probability of the university issuing a favourable report remains at 0.85. At present the costs resulting from an adverse report are thought to be £2 million.

By how much can these costs increase before the recommendation to await the report, rather than take immediate action, is changed? You should follow the same approach as used above.

Our recommendation would change if the expected cost from awaiting the report exceeds £750,000. So let the cost consequent to an unfavourable report equal £x.

The expected cost from waiting is:

$$(0.85 \times 0) + 0.15x = 0.15x$$

Again, remember that no costs arise if the report is favourable.

Then we require that:

$$0.15x = £750,000$$

And so:

$$x = \frac{750,000}{0.15} = £5 \text{ million}$$

For any figure higher than £5 million, it would be preferable to replace the product now.

Summary

In this section of the unit we have explored the use of **decision trees** in the evaluation of multi-stage decision problems. A decision tree must be constructed so as to allow for all relevant sequences of decisions and states of nature. Although it is drawn across the page from left to right, it is **evaluated** (or **rolled back**) in the reverse direction. At each decision event the optimal strategy is determined, using only those costs and returns that arise subsequent to that point.

Finally, we saw how determining the optimal set of decisions is not the end of the analyst's work. It is important to see how robust these conclusions are in the face of any changes in the parameters of a problem. Sensitivity analysis is as relevant here as it is for any activity within business decision analysis.

In the next section we look at the issue of revising probabilities.

SECTION 5
Revising Probabilities

Introduction

We have already looked at the importance to the decision-maker of information. In particular, in Section 3, we looked at how much the decision-maker should be prepared to pay to obtain perfect information. In this section we look at information which is not perfect. While such information is not 100 per cent reliable, it is still potentially valuable to the decision-maker. This is because it can be used to revise the probability of any given event occurring.

We use a case study to explore the use of imperfect information to revise such probabilities. We then look at the effect of such information on the decision-making process and calculate its value to the decision-maker by offsetting the cost of the information against the benefits which it brings.

By the end of this section you should be able to revise probabilities using incomplete information. You should also be able to determine the value of imperfect information.

5.1 Prior and posterior probabilities

We will start by looking at a case study.

Case Study: Cambrian TV
Cambrian TV is considering producing a new drama series for networking within the UK and for overseas distribution. This is a new departure for *Cambrian TV* and the company is concerned about the potential viewing audience. *Cambrian TV* predicts that the series will either be a success, with gross receipts of £2,350,000, or a failure, in which case the gross receipts will be only £750,000.

Cambrian TV is faced with an immediate decision. It must choose between two possible strategies: to produce and market the series immediately or to undertake an in-house market survey at a cost of £80,000 before deciding whether to go ahead.

The production costs of the series are estimated at £1,125,000. If the market survey is carried out, the results will be classified as either favourable or unfavourable and *Cambrian TV* will have to decide whether to produce or drop the series. *Cambrian TV*'s initial view, based on the experience of other television companies, is that there is a 50 per cent chance that the new series will be a success. The company's previous experience indicates that its in-house surveys are 80 per cent reliable when a series is a success and are 70 per cent reliable when a series is a failure.

ACTIVITY 34

Draw the decision tree for this problem. For the moment ignore all the costs, receipts and probabilities.

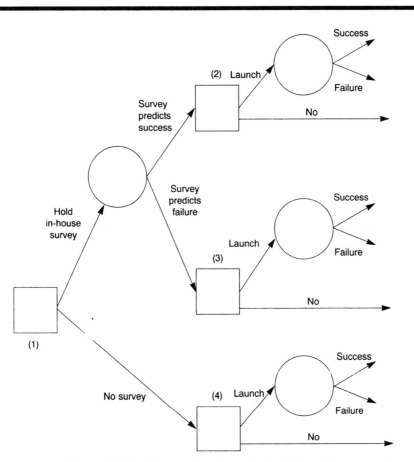

Figure 15: Decision tree for the cambrian TV problem

Decision point (1) is whether or not to run the in-house survey. If the answer to this is 'yes', then the survey may predict either success or failure. Either way, a decision must be made as to whether to launch the series (decision points (2) and (3)). If the series is launched, it may turn out to be either a success or a failure.

If the answer at decision point (1) is 'no', then a decision must still be made as to whether to launch the series (decision point (4)). Again, if the series is launched, it may turn out to be either a success or a failure.

Having constructed the tree, the next step is to insert the relevant information. Let us start with what we already know.

We know the estimated gross receipts and the production costs. We calculate net receipts by subtracting production costs from gross receipts. So if the series is a success, then net receipts are:

2,350,000 – 1,125,000 = £1,225,000

And if the series is a failure, then net receipts are:

750,000 – 1,125,000 = –£375,000

We know the cost of the in-house survey. It is £80,000.

We know the probability of the series being a success as assessed by *Cambrian TV*, prior to any in-house survey. *Cambrian TV* considers this to be 0.5.

We have information on the reliability of in-house surveys previously conducted by *Cambrian TV*. They are 80 per cent reliable when a series is a success and are 70 per cent reliable when a series is a failure.

Therefore, we have enough information to roll back that part of the tree which starts with a decision not to undertake the in-house survey.

ACTIVITY 35

1. Roll back that part of the tree which starts with a decision not to undertake the in-house survey.

2. Showing the data and probabilities, what expected monetary value results from a decision not to undertake an in-house survey?

---

1. The part of the tree starting with a decision not to undertake the in-house survey is shown in Figure 16.

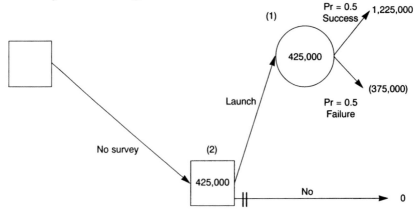

Figure 16: Rolled back tree for the Cambrian TV problem – step one

2. At the event point labelled (1), the expected monetary value from a decision to launch is:

$$(0.5 \times 1,225,000) - (0.5 \times 375,000) = £425,000$$

So, if no in-house survey is undertaken, the optimal policy (at decision point (2)) is to launch rather than abandon, with an expected monetary value of £425,000.

Having completed Activity 35 and evaluated the lower part of the tree, we now seem to be stuck. If you check the tree (see Figure 15) you will see that, to make any further progress, we need to know:

- the probability that an in-house survey declares the series likely to be a success (or failure)
- the conditional probability for the series being a success (or failure) given that the in-house survey predicts success
- the conditional probability for the series being a success (or failure) given that the in-house survey predicts failure.

All that we have at our disposal is:

- a pre-survey probability of success (or failure)
- statements about the past reliability of in-house surveys.

Somehow or other we need to use the probabilities that we do know, to establish those that we require for the tree.

Before working out how to do this, some notation will help. Let:

S = the series is a success

F = the series is a failure

Y = the in-house survey predicts the series will be a success

N = the in-house survey predicts the series will be a failure

We will also need to refer to conditional and joint events. Conventionally a conditional event is indicated by a forward slash (/). So, for example, the notation Y/S is the event that the in-house survey predicts the series to be a success, **given that** the series is a success.

Joint events are indicated using the intersection symbol (∩). So, for example, Y∩S is the event that the in-house survey predicts the series to be a success, **and** the series is a success.

Using this notation, what do we know? We know the probabilities of success or failure prior to conducting an in-house survey. So we have that:

Event	Probability
Success (S)	0.5
Failure (F)	0.5

Table 24: Prior probabilities of success or failure

These are referred to as **prior probabilities**.

However, past in-house surveys have not been 100 per cent reliable. Of successful series, only 80 per cent were predicted to be successes by the in-house surveys: so the other 20 per cent were predicted to be failures. So for any single series that actually proves successful, there is only a 0.8 probability that the survey correctly predicted this. It follows that if the new series were to be proved successful then any survey report on it would only have a 0.8 probability of correctly predicting this.

In other words, the probability of Y (the survey predicting success) **conditional upon** the series actually being a success is 0.8. Using the notation, we can express this as:

$Pr(Y/S) = 0.8$

ACTIVITY 36

What then would be the probability of N (the survey predicting failure) **conditional upon** the series actually being a success? In other words, what is the value of $Pr(N/S)$?

If in-house surveys are 80 per cent reliable when a series is a success, then it follows that on the remaining 20 per cent of occasions when a series is a success, the survey has incorrectly predicted failure. We can express this as a probability of 0.2. Using the notation, we can therefore say that:

$Pr(N/S) = 0.2$

There are only two possibilities here; a successful series being preceded by an accurate or an inaccurate prediction. Therefore, the two probabilities must together add up to 1 (that is, one of the two possibilities must occur). Using our notation we can therefore say that:

$Pr(Y/S) + Pr(N/S) = 1$

Once we have calculated one of the probabilities we can obtain the other by subtracting the known probability from 1. We could have obtained the answer for the preceding activity using this means. Our calculation, knowing that Pr(N/S) = 0.2, would have been as follows:

$$Pr(Y/S) + Pr(N/S) = 1$$

$$Pr(Y/S) + 0.2 = 1$$

$$Pr(Y/S) = 1 - 0.2$$

$$Pr(Y/S) = 0.8$$

We also know that, of those previous series which have failed, 30 per cent of them were incorrectly predicted as being successes. So applying this result to the new series we have that:

$$Pr(Y/F) = 0.3$$

ACTIVITY 37

What then would be Pr(N/F)?

$$Pr(Y/F) + Pr(N/F) \text{ must equal } 1, \text{ and so:}$$

$$Pr(N/F) = 1 - 0.3 = 0.7$$

Collecting all of these results together, Table 25 shows the probabilities that we already know.

Even	Probability	Description
S	0.5	Pre-survey probability that the series is a success
F	0.5	Pre-survey probability that the series is a failure
Y/S	0.8	Probability survey predicts success, given that series is successful
N/S	0.2	Probability survey predicts failure, given that series is successful
Y/F	0.3	Probability survey predicts success, given that series is a failure
N/F	0.7	Probability survey predicts failure, given that series is a failure

Table 25: The known probabilities for the Cambrian TV decision problem

The first two of these, namely Pr(S) and Pr(F), are known as the **prior probabilities**. The remaining four are **conditional probabilities**.

Checking back to the decision tree for this problem (see Figure 15) what we need to establish are the probabilities shown in Table 26.

Event	Probability	Description
Y		In-house survey predicts series will be successful
N		In-house survey predicts series will be a failure
S/Y		Series is successful, given that survey predicted success
F/Y		Series is not successful, given that the survey predicted success
S/N		Series is successful, given that the survey predicted failure
F/N		Series is not successful, given that the survey predicted failure

Table 26: The unknown probabilities for the Cambrian TV decision problem

Of the events in Table 26, the conditional probabilities for the bottom four are known as the **posterior probabilities**. This is the additional (imperfect) information that results from undertaking the in-house survey. The question will be whether the benefit of such information is sufficient to justify its cost.

The first step in obtaining these probabilities is to construct what is called a **reverse tree** (see Figure 17). We have recorded, on this reverse tree, the probabilities that we already know. Reading from right to left, the starting branches are the events that the series is a success or failure with prior probabilities of 0.5 for each case. The two branches at point (1) are the events that the survey predicts either success or failure, given that the series is a success.

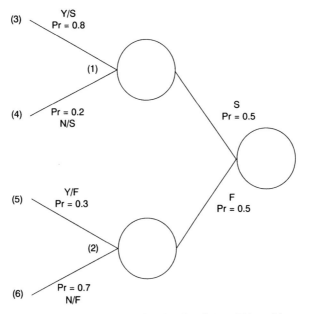

Figure 17: Reverse tree for the Cambrian TV problem

Now consider point (3) on this reverse tree. Let this represent the joint event that the survey predicts success **and** the series actually is successful. Using our previously defined notation, this is the event Y∩S, where the intersection symbol ∩ simply means 'and'. Using the multiplication rule of probability, we have that:

$$Pr(Y∩S) = Pr(S) \times Pr(Y/S) = 0.5 \times 0.8 = 0.4$$

Now check that you have understood this, by establishing the other three joint probabilities.

ACTIVITY 38

The remaining joint events are N∩S, Y∩F and N∩F.

Explain, in words, the meaning of these joint events, and determine their respective probabilities.

N∩S is the event that the survey predicts failure **and** the series is a success. Using the multiplication rule, its probability is:

$$0.5 \times 0.2 = 0.1$$

Y∩F is the event that the survey predicts success **and** the series is a failure. Its probability is:

0.5 × 0.3 = 0.15

N∩F is the event that the survey predicts failure **and** the series is a failure. Its probability is:

0.5 × 0.7 = 0.35

Figure 18 shows these outcomes entered onto the reverse tree.

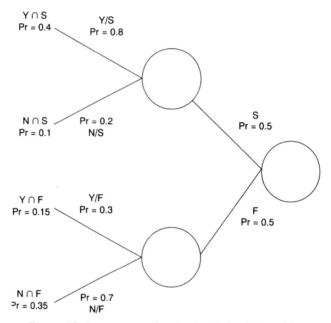

Figure 18: Reverse tree for the Cambrian TV problem

Notice that the four joint probabilities sum to 1: this is not fortuitous and so is a useful check upon your calculations. Having completed the reverse tree we can now start the process of obtaining the probabilities that we need (see Table 26).

ACTIVITY 39

Look at the joint probabilities in Figure 18. What are Pr(Y) and Pr(N)?

Remember that the four joint probabilities are for the events:

$Y \cap S$ = survey predicts success and series is a success

$N \cap S$ = survey predicts failure but series is a success

$Y \cap F$ = survey predicts success but series is a failure

$N \cap F$ = survey predicts failure and series is a failure

Of these joint events, two include the survey predicting a success. So:

$$Pr(Y) = Pr(Y \cap S) + Pr(Y \cap F) = 0.40 + 0.15 = 0.55$$

Similarly:

$$Pr(N) = Pr(N \cap S) + Pr(N \cap F) = 0.10 + 0.35 = 0.45$$

Since the only possibilities for the in-house survey are a predicted success or a predicted failure, the two probabilities should sum to 1 and, as you can see, they do.

We are now in a position to obtain the posterior probabilities. Let us start by obtaining the probability that the series is a success, given that the in-house survey predicts a success. To do this we need to use the multiplication rule of probability. Using our notation, this gives us:

$$Pr(Y \cap S) = Pr(Y) \times Pr(S/Y)$$

In words, this states that 'the probability that a series is a success **and** the survey correctly predicts this' is given by the probability that the survey predicts success multiplied by the probability that the series is a success given this prediction. We know that $Pr(Y) = 0.55$ and we have established that $Pr(Y \cap S) = 0.4$. Using these results:

$$0.4 = 0.55 \times Pr(S/Y)$$

$$Pr(S/Y) = 0.4/0.55 \approx 0.727$$

(The symbol $\approx$ stands for 'is approximately equal to'. In the calculation above, the answer has been rounded to three decimal places.)

To check that you have understood this, Activity 40 asks you to determine the remaining three posterior probabilities.

ACTIVITY 40

The remaining three posterior probabilities are $Pr(F/Y)$, $Pr(S/N)$ and $Pr(F/N)$.

State their meaning (in words), and establish their values.

Firstly, let us consider Pr(F/Y): that is, the probability of the series being a failure given an in-house survey predicting success.

Since a favourable survey can only be followed by either a success or a failure, then it must be the case that:

$$Pr(F/Y) + Pr(S/Y) = 1$$

Since we have already established that Pr(S/Y) is approximately 0.727, then it follows that:

$$Pr(F/Y) \approx 1 - 0.727 = 0.273$$

Secondly, Pr(S/N) is the probability that the series is a success, even though it was predicted to be a failure. Using the multiplication rule:

$$\frac{Pr(N \cap S)}{Pr(N)} = \frac{0.10}{0.45} \approx 0.222$$

Finally, Pr(F/N) is the probability that the series is a failure given that it was predicted to be a failure.

Since it must be the case that Pr(F/N) + Pr(S/N) = 1, then:

$$Pr(F/N) \approx 1 - 0.222 = 0.778$$

If an in-house survey is not conducted, then we are informed that the **prior probability** of the series being successful (that is Pr(S)) is 0.5.

Now, using the additional (imperfect) information, the revised probabilities of success are 0.727 if the in-house survey predicts success (Pr(S/Y)), and 0.222 if the in-house survey predicts failure (Pr(S/N)).

However, what we have yet to establish is whether it is worth paying £80,000 to acquire these revised probabilities. To determine this, we need to complete the rolling back of the decision tree. So far (see Activity 35 and Figure 16) we have dealt just with the outcomes that flow from a decision not to undertake an in-house survey.

ACTIVITY 41

1. Finish rolling back the tree for the *Cambrian TV* problem. To do this you will need to:

   ● insert all data and probabilities onto the tree

   ● calculate the expected monetary values for the alternative strategies at each event point

● determine and carry forward the optimal choice at each decision point.

2. What do you recommend *Cambrian TV* should do?

---

1. Figure 19 shows the completed tree: below it is a review of the required calculations.

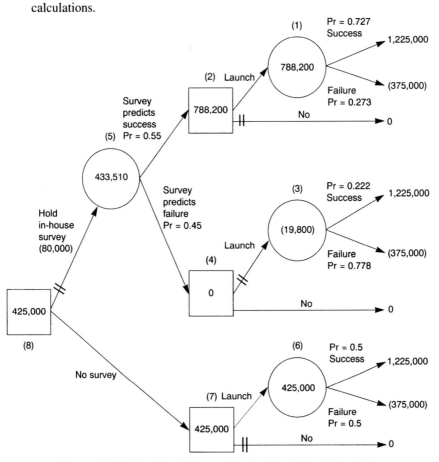

Figure 19: Rolling back the tree for the Cambrian TV problem

The calculations at each point on the tree are as follows.

Event (1). The probabilities on the two branches are for the series being a success or a failure, given that the survey predicts success. Then:

$$(0.727 \times 1,225,000) - (0.273 \times 375,000) = £788,200$$

This value is inserted at this event point.

Decision (2). Since launching the series yields an expected return of £788,200, whilst not launching it yields £0, then the optimal choice is to launch.

Event (3). At this event point, the two probabilities are for the series being a success or a failure given that the survey predicts failure. Then:

$$(0.222 \times 1{,}225{,}000) - (0.778 \times 375{,}000) = -£19{,}800$$

This value is inserted at this point.

Decision (4). It follows that the optimal decision at this point is not to launch the series.

Event (5). At this event point:

$$(0.55 \times 788{,}200) + (0.45 \times 0) = £433{,}510$$

This value is inserted here.

Event (6)/Decision (7). As previously established:

$$(0.5 \times 1{,}225{,}000) - (0.5 \times 375{,}000) = £425{,}000$$

Decision (8). Since £433,510 minus £80,000 is smaller than the expected return from not undertaking a survey, the optimal decision is not to have a survey.

2. We therefore recommend that *Cambrian TV* should go direct to a launch of the series, without undertaking a survey.

In this case the improved information resulting from the in-house survey is insufficient to compensate for the costs involved in acquiring it. You are now asked to establish whether this is true for the oil prospecting case study which you first encountered in Unit 1.

Case Study: prospecting for oil

An oil company has recently acquired rights to test and drill for oil in a certain area. The likelihood of oil being found in the area in sufficient amounts to exploit is estimated as about 0.55. If the company finds oil, the returns are estimated as £100 million. If no oil is found, then a loss of £40 million is likely. The company can dispose of the rights on the open market, for a return of £45 million before any test drillings have been undertaken.

It is possible to undertake a preliminary geological survey to establish whether oil is present. The survey is not 100 per cent certain to make the right prediction but, if oil is present, then it has a 0.77 chance of correctly saying so. If oil is not present then it has a 0.83 chance of making the correct prediction. If this preliminary test shows a positive result then the rights to the land can be disposed of for £70 million. If the test proves negative, a sale of the land rights will yield only £15 million. This preliminary survey will cost £500,000.

ACTIVITY 42

1. Calculate the simple and conditional probabilities for the various events. (Do not calculate any joint probabilities at this stage.)

2. Draw a decision tree for the oil company and enter the probabilities onto it.

3. Draw a reverse tree and use it to help establish the probabilities for the four possible joint events.

4. Establish the posterior probabilities required to evaluate the decision tree for this problem.

5. Roll back the whole decision tree using the probabilities to calculate expected monetary values for the various possible events and decisions.

6. What course of action do you recommend that the oil company should take?

---

1. We use the following notation:

O = oil is found

D = oil not found

F = survey predicts oil

U = survey does not predict oil

The probabilities are shown in Table 27.

Notice that, since we are told that $Pr(F/O) = 0.77$, then it follows that:

$Pr(U/O) = 1 - 0.77 = 0.23$

Similarly, since $Pr(U/D) = 0.83$, then:

$Pr(F/D) = 1 - 0.83 = 0.17$

Event	Probability	Description
O	0.55	Pre-survey probability that oil will be found
D	0.45	Pre-survey probability that oil will not be found
F/O	0.77	Probability survey predicts oil, given that oil is found
U/O	0.23	Probability survey does not predict oil, given that oil is found
F/D	0.17	Probability survey predicts oil, given that oil is not found
U/D	0.83	Probability survey does not predict oil, given that oil is not found

Table 27: The known probabilities for the oil survey problem

2. Figure 20 gives the decision tree for this problem. Its structure is the same as that for the problem that faced *Cambrian TV*.

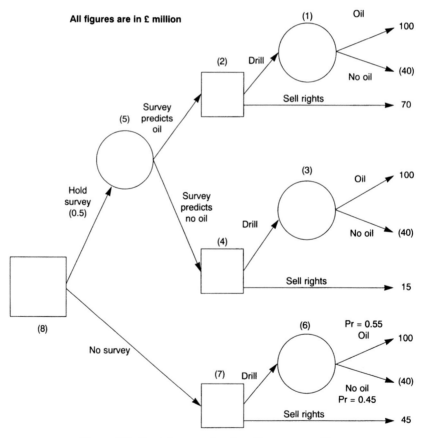

Figure 20: Decision tree for the oil survey problem

3. To establish the other probabilities that we need, we set up a reverse tree as in Figure 21.

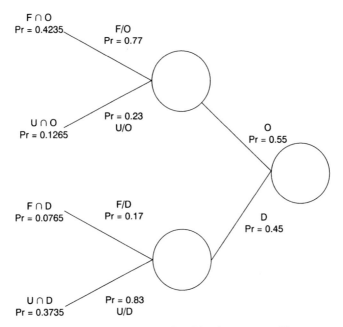

Figure 21: Reverse tree for the oil survey problem

The probability that the survey predicts oil, and oil is subsequently found is:

$$Pr(F \cap O) = Pr(F/O) \times Pr(O) = 0.77 \times 0.55 = 0.4235$$

The probability that the survey does not predict oil, and oil is subsequently found is:

$$Pr(U \cap O) = Pr(U/O) \times Pr(O) = 0.23 \times 0.55 = 0.1265$$

The probability that the survey predicts oil and oil is subsequently not found is:

$$Pr(F \cap D) = Pr(F/D) \times Pr(D) = 0.17 \times 0.45 = 0.0765$$

The probability that the survey does not predict oil and oil is subsequently not found is:

$$Pr(U \cap D) = Pr(U/D) \times Pr(D) = 0.83 \times 0.45 = 0.3735$$

Using these joint probabilities we obtain:

$$Pr(F) = 0.4235 + 0.0765 = 0.5$$

$$Pr(U) = 0.1265 + 0.3735 = 0.5$$

4. Using these results, gives the posterior probabilities as:

$$Pr(O/F) = \frac{Pr(F \cap O)}{Pr(F)} = \frac{0.4235}{0.5} = 0.847, \text{ and so,}$$

$$Pr(D/F) = 1 - 0.847 = 0.153$$

$$Pr(O/U) = \frac{Pr(U \cap O)}{Pr(U)} = \frac{0.1265}{0.5} = 0.253, \text{ and so,}$$

$$Pr(D/U) = 1 - 0.253 = 0.747$$

5. Once the revised probabilities have been inserted onto the tree it can be fully rolled back, as in Figure 22.

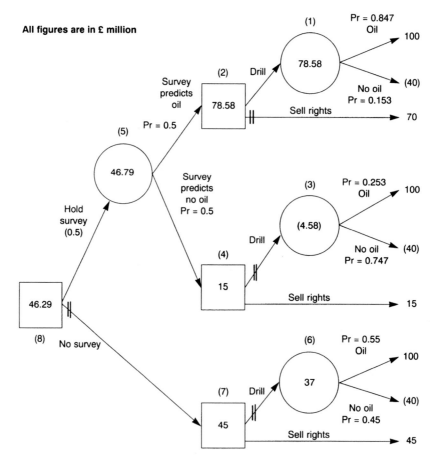

Figure 22: Rolled back decision tree for the oil survey problem

The calculations at the various points on the tree are:

Event (1).

$$(0.847 \times 100) - (0.153 \times 40) = 78.58$$

Decision (2). Since the expected return from drilling (that is £78.58 million) exceeds the return from selling the rights, then the optimal decision is to drill.

Event (3).

$$(0.253 \times 100) - (0.747 \times 40) = -4.58$$

Decision (4). At this point the optimal decision is to sell the rights.

Event (5).

$$(0.5 \times 78.58) + (0.5 \times 15) = 46.79$$

Event (6).

$$(0.55 \times 100) - (0.45 \times 40) = 37$$

Decision (7). The optimal decision here is to sell the rights.

Decision (8). Since $46.79 - 0.5 = 46.29$, then the optimal decision is to undertake the survey.

6. We recommend that the company should undertake the survey. If the survey predicts that the oil is present in economic quantities, the company should undertake drilling. Otherwise, the company should sell the rights.

5.2 The value of imperfect information

The approach that we followed in the previous section of the unit was to determine whether the benefits of revised probabilities outweighed the costs of acquiring this additional information. When, in Section 3, we examined the concept of perfect information, the question we raised was, what sum a decision-maker would be prepared to pay for information that was 100 per cent reliable. An analogous question can be posed for the acquisition of imperfect information, and you will explore this in the final activity for this section of the unit.

ACTIVITY 43

A company is required to choose between two mutually exclusive investments. The returns are dependent upon the future state of demand in the economy and are estimated as:

Project	Return
Project 1	£12 million if demand is high
	–£3 million if demand is low
Project 2	£6 million if demand is high
	£3 million if demand is low

The company's marketing department considers that the probability that demand will be high over the life of the projects is 0.4. They have the opportunity of seeking a market intelligence report from *Glamorgan Consultants*. Investigation shows that past reports from the consultants made correct predictions in 80 per cent of the occasions when demand in fact was high. However, they also made incorrect predictions on 30 per cent of the occasions when demand turned out to be low.

Now solve the problem in the following stages.

1. Define some appropriate notation.

2. Draw up a table of the known probabilities.

3. Calculate the posterior probabilities.

4. Draw the decision tree and insert the data and probabilities.

5. Establish the expected monetary values for the alternative strategies at each event point and at each decision point determine, and carry forward the optimal choice.

6. Compare the expected monetary values resulting from decisions either to obtain or not to obtain an intelligence report, in order to establish the maximum amount that the company should be willing to pay.

---

1. It is always helpful to fix some suitable notation before starting work on a decision tree. Let:

   H = sales are high

   L = sales are low

   F = the outcome that the survey predicts high sales

   U = the outcome that the survey predicts low sales

   C = the cost of obtaining a report from *Glamorgan Consultants*

2. We have the following information on probabilities, as shown in Table 28.

Event	Probability	Description
H	0.4	Pre-report probability that sales will turn out to be high
L	0.6	Pre-report probability that sales will turn out to be low
F/H	0.8	Probability survey predicts high sales and sales are high
U/H	0.2	Probability survey predicts low sales and sales are high
F/L	0.3	Probability survey predicts high sales and resulting sales are low
U/L	0.7	Probability survey predicts low sales and resulting sales are low

Table 28: The known probabilities

3. We can calculate the following conditional probabilities:

$$Pr(F \cap H) = Pr(H) \times Pr(F/H) = 0.4 \times 0.8 = 0.32$$

$$Pr(U \cap H) = Pr(H) \times Pr(U/H) = 0.4 \times 0.2 = 0.08$$

$$Pr(F \cap L) = Pr(L) \times Pr(F/L) = 0.6 \times 0.3 = 0.18$$

$$Pr(U \cap L) = Pr(L) \times Pr(U/L) = 0.6 \times 0.7 = 0.42$$

It is helpful to check that these four probabilities sum to 1, as they should. They do here, as you can confirm.

From these results, we have that:

$$Pr(F) = 0.32 + 0.18 = 0.5$$

So $Pr(U)$ also $= 0.5$.

The required posterior probabilities are, therefore:

$$Pr(H/F) = \frac{Pr(F \cap H)}{Pr(F)} = \frac{0.32}{0.5} = 0.64$$

$$Pr(H/U) = \frac{Pr(U \cap H)}{Pr(U)} = \frac{0.08}{0.5} = 0.16$$

It follows that:

$$Pr(L/F) = 1 - 0.64 = 0.36$$

$$Pr(L/U) = 1 - 0.16 = 0.84$$

4. Now that we have obtained the full set of probabilities, we can continue with the decision tree (see Figure 23 below). To proceed, we assume that the survey is free and work out the expected monetary values. Having done that,

we then establish the maximum sum worth paying. Below the tree is a review of the required calculations.

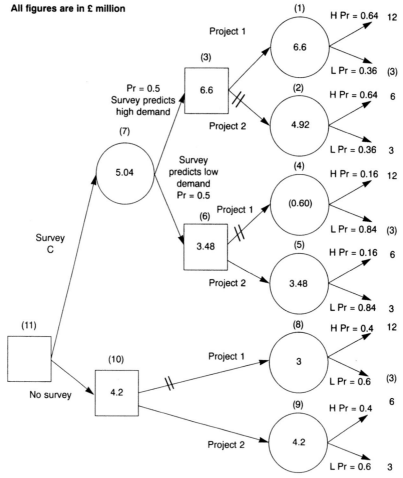

Figure 23: Decision tree for the investment problem

5. The expected monetary values (in £ millions) are given below.

Event (1).

$$(0.64 \times 12) - (0.36 \times 3) = 6.6$$

Event (2).

$$(0.64 \times 6) + (0.36 \times 3) = 4.92$$

Decision (3). At this decision point the optimum choice is for project 1.

Event (4).

$$(0.16 \times 12) - (0.84 \times 3) = -0.6$$

Event (5).

$$(0.16 \times 6) + (0.84 \times 3) = 3.48$$

Decision (6). At this decision point the optimum choice is for project 2.

Event (7).

$$(0.5 \times 6.6) + (0.5 \times 3.48) = 5.04$$

Event (8).

$$(0.4 \times 12) - (0.6 \times 3) = 3$$

Event (9).

$$(0.4 \times 6) + (0.6 \times 3) = 4.2$$

Decision (10). At this decision point the optimum choice is project 2.

6. If C equals the cost of the survey report, to find the maximum sum worth paying we let:

$$5.04 - C = 4.2$$

This solves to yield a value for C of 0.84: that is, £840,000. So that is the maximum sum that should be paid to *Glamorgan Consultants*.

Summary

In this section of the unit we have examined problems in which the decision-maker has the opportunity to acquire additional, albeit imperfect, information. This necessitated using those probabilities that are already known (the prior probabilities) to determine the new set of probabilities generated by this extra information (the posterior probabilities). A reverse tree was drawn to facilitate these calculations.

At issue is the value to the decision-maker of any additional information which has a bearing upon the decision problem. Such information has value only if the benefits resulting from its use exceed the costs of acquiring it. The section ended by showing how the value of additional information can be established.

In the next section we look at some extensions to the approaches to decision analysis explored in Sections 1 to 5.

SECTION 6

Extensions

Introduction

The final section of this unit will explore some extensions to the approaches to decision-making that we have examined up to this point.

We start, in Section 6.1, by contrasting decision problems characterised by a single objective (or **attribute**) with those in which the decision-maker needs to take into account a number of possibly conflicting objectives.

In Section 6.2 we revise the concept of the variance of a probability distribution and explain how it can be interpreted as a measure of risk. We then show that the variance, in conjunction with the expected value, provides the decision-maker with the tool for choosing between strategies when the decision is not subject to repetition.

Finally, in Section 6.3, we introduce the notion of expected utility and use it to demonstrate why decision-makers are invariably **risk adverse**.

By the end of this section you should be able to distinguish between **single-** and **multi-attribute decision-making**. You should be able to use **pairwise comparisons** and **attribute scaling** in the resolution of simple multi-attribute problems. You should also be able to calculate and use the **variance** of a set of payoffs as a measure of risk and you should be able to explain the relevance of **utility** to decision-making.

6.1 Multi-attribute decision-making

All the decision problems that we have explored up to this point have been one-dimensional, in the sense that the decision-maker has had a single objective in mind in coming to a decision. For example, this might be to choose that strategy which maximises some expected measure (such as profit, revenue or the net return on an investment), or to choose that strategy which minimises potential regret. This is known as **single-attribute decision-making**. However, many of the problems that arise in business are not one-dimensional. As an example, consider the decision facing a departmental manager who requires to select which of five applicants should be recommended for promotion. In choosing between them, a number of possibly conflicting objectives might be relevant, such as years of experience, qualifications and the ability to work with others. Problems of this sort are said to be multi-attribute and we thus refer to **multi-attribute decision-making**.

Once two or more attributes are deemed relevant, some form of aggregation is normally required. For the promotion problem referred to above, suppose that data has been collected on the qualifications of the five applicants, their number of years of appropriate experience, and their ability to work with others. This last attribute has been measured on a scale from 1 to 10 (the higher the value, the better the team-working ability), using agreed criteria. Table 29 gives the details.

Candidate	Qualifications	Experience	Team ability
Rajiv	A Level	15	8
Jane	Degree	5	7
Stefan	Degree	10	6
Selena	A Level	8	4
Morris	None	25	9

Table 29: Attribute table for five candidates for promotion

One of these five must be selected, and as a first step we can look to see whether any of them can be eliminated, using all three attributes.

ACTIVITY 44

In the role of the decision-maker, can you immediately reject any of the candidates?

Looking at Table 29, it is clear that Rajiv ranks either superior or equal to Selena on all three attributes. We can, therefore, certainly rule Selena out.

In this case, one of the candidates (our 'strategies') is dominated by at least one other. Of course, it may be true that in some situations one strategy dominates the rest on all the attributes, in which case the decision problem is trivial. However, the greater the number of attributes, the less likely this is. Clearly it is not the case for this problem, as you can check.

So how should we identify the best candidate from the remaining four? There are a number of fairly straightforward approaches that we can resort to. Since this section is simply intended to introduce you to these ideas, just one will be explored here, namely the **pairwise comparison** approach.

Suppose we look at each pair of candidates, taking each attribute in turn. For example, consider Rajiv by comparison with Jane. For qualifications Rajiv ranks lower than Jane, but he outperforms her on the other two attributes. We can show this in Table 30 below. The 'XX' shows that Rajiv dominates on that attribute, whereas the '– –' shows that Jane dominates.

Pair of candidates	Qualification	Experience	Team ability
Rajiv and Jane	– –	XX	XX

Table 30: Pairwise comparisons for Rajiv and Jane

We need to determine the outcomes for the remaining pairs.

ACTIVITY 45

Complete the table below. In each case you are recording the outcome from the perspective of the first name in the pair. If, the pair are equally ranked then record this using a single 'X'.

Pair of candidates	Qualifications	Experience	Team ability
Rajiv and Jane	– –	XX	XX
Rajiv and Stefan			
Rajiv and Morris			
Jane and Rajiv			
Jane and Stefan			
Jane and Morris			
Stefan and Rajiv			
Stefan and Jane			
Stefan and Morris			
Morris and Rajiv			
Morris and Jane			
Morris and Stefan			

Your results should agree with those in Table 31.

Pair of candidates	Qualifications	Experience	Team ability
Rajiv and Jane	– –	XX	XX
Rajiv and Stefan	– –	XX	XX
Rajiv and Morris	XX	– –	– –
Jane and Rajiv	XX	– –	– –
Jane and Stefan	X	– –	XX
Jane and Morris	XX	– –	– –
Stefan and Rajiv	XX	– –	– –
Stefan and Jane	X	XX	– –
Stefan and Morris	XX	– –	– –
Morris and Rajiv	– –	XX	XX
Morris and Jane	– –	XX	XX
Morris and Stefan	– –	XX	XX

Table 31: Pairwise comparisons of candidates over all three attributes

We now add up the number of 'XX's (that is, pairwise dominant rankings) for each candidate. As you can check, Rajiv has five, Jane has three, Stefan has three, and Morris has six. Since Morris has the greater number of pairwise dominances, we may well decide in favour of him. However, in coming to this conclusion we have implicitly assumed that each of the three attributes should be given equal weighting and this may well not be the case.

This suggests that a different approach should be taken by the decision-maker. Firstly, a decision has to be made about the relative value of the attributes. Suppose that, for the present problem, it is agreed that the attributes 'qualifications', 'experience' and 'team ability' should have weightings of 0.5, 0.2 and 0.3 respectively. Notice that, since these are the only attributes deemed relevant to the decision, the weightings must sum to 1.

Secondly, the ratings for each attribute must be converted to a value scale. We will use one running from 0 to 1, for each attribute. This is straightforward for team ability, since the coded values merely require division by 10. However, problems immediately arise for the other two. Consider years of experience. We might choose to assume that each extra year adds equally to the candidate's worth. On the other hand, it might seem more plausible to suggest that experience is subject to diminishing returns. We will adopt the simpler view here, for the sake of arithmetical convenience. Since the maximum years are 25, then dividing all the values by this figure will scale them from 0 to 1.

We are left with the need to scale the remaining attribute. This must be done by the decision-maker, on the basis of prior experience of the relative value of alternative qualifications to the organisation. In this case suppose that 'A level' is scaled at 0.4 and 'degree' at 1.0.

Table 32 shows the adjusted ratings for the four remaining candidates. Remember that Selena has already been eliminated.

Candidate	Qualifications (0.5)	Experience (0.2)	Team ability (0.3)
Rajiv	0.4	0.6	0.8
Jane	1.0	0.2	0.7
Stefan	1.0	0.4	0.6
Morris	0.0	1.0	0.9

Table 32: Adjusted attribute table

Given this information, an aggregate score can be obtained for each of the four candidates. For example, consider Rajiv. His individual scores for 'qualifications', 'experience' and 'team ability' are 0.4, 0.6 and 0.8 respectively. We can then define his aggregate score as being the weighted average of these individual scores. Since the weights are 0.5 (qualifications), 0.2 (experience) and 0.3 (team ability), the weighted average is:

$$(0.5 \times 0.4) + (0.2 \times 0.6) + (0.3 \times 0.8) = 0.56$$

We obtain an aggregate score by multiplying each attribute score by its weight and summing the products. Activity 46 below asks you to carry out the same calculations for Jane, Stefan and Morris.

ACTIVITY 46

1. Obtain the aggregate score for Jane, Stefan and Morris.

2. On this basis, who is the best candidate?

---

1. The calculations are:

   Rajiv:

   $$(0.5 \times 0.4) + (0.2 \times 0.6) + (0.3 \times 0.8) = 0.56$$

   Jane:

   $$(1 \times 0.5) + (0.2 \times 0.2) + (0.7 \times 0.3) = 0.75$$

   Stefan:

   $$(1 \times 0.5) + (0.4 \times 0.2) + (0.6 \times 0.3) = 0.76$$

   Morris:

   $$(0 \times 0.5) + (1 \times 0.2) + (0.9 \times 0.3) = 0.47$$

2. On the basis of the aggregate scores, the decision should go in favour of Stefan. However, as there is only 0.01 of a difference between Jane and Stefan's scores, the decision-maker will almost certainly want to carry out further comparison.

This example highlights the clear distinction between multi-attribute and single-attribute decision-making. Faced with a choice between strategies using the single objective of, say, maximising expected monetary value, all decision-makers will arrive at the same solution (provided that they are in agreement on the size of payoffs and the relevant probabilities). This will not be the case when decision-makers confront multiple attributes, since any aggregation procedure is necessarily dependent upon judgements of relative worth.

However, this should not be seen as simply opening the floodgates to subjectivity. Any aggregation process, such as the one above, forces the decision-maker to determine and justify both which attributes are considered to be relevant in any given decision problem and the relative value to be placed upon them. It then becomes clear why particular decisions have been arrived at and also acts to promote consistency.

6.2 Variance as a measure of risk

In Section 3.1 of this unit we developed the use of expected monetary value as an approach for choosing between alternative strategies. However, we acknowledged some problems in applying this approach to one-off events. In these cases, it may still be sensible to compare alternative strategies using expected monetary values, provided that the decision-maker also looks at their **variances**. The latter can be viewed as measures of the degree of risk attached to each strategy.

For example, consider the following decision problem. Choice of strategy A generates a certain return equal to £217,000, whereas if strategy B is chosen then the possible returns are as given in Table 33.

Return (£s)	Probability
320,000	0.1
250,000	0.4
190,000	0.3
140,000	0.2

Table 33: Probability distribution of returns from strategy B

Since the return from strategy A is a certainty, we need only establish the expected monetary value for strategy B. Multiplying each possibility by its respective probability yields an expected monetary value of:

$$(0.1 \times 320,000) + (0.4 \times 250,000) + (0.3 \times 190,000) + (0.2 \times 140,000)$$
$$= £217,000$$

So we have a choice between strategy A, which yields a certain £217,000, and strategy B for which the expected monetary value is exactly the same. Of course, if strategy B is chosen then the actual return will be either in excess of, or below, its expected value. We can then think of the spread of possibilities around the expected value as a measure of the degree of risk entailed in that choice. Since, in general, most decision-makers are risk averse (see Section 6.3 below) then strategy A would normally be selected.

This approach needs to be formalised. For any probability distribution, we can determine its variance, in addition to its mean or expected value. For the distribution in Table 33, we have already calculated the mean (or expected value) to be £217,000.

Let us now obtain its variance. Table 34 shows the calculation. For each value ('X') of the variable we calculate the difference between 'X' and the mean ('X – mean') and square the outcome. Multiplying this by the probability for that 'X' value and summing the products yields the variance. All calculations are in £000s.

Cost(X)	Mean	(X–mean)	(X–mean)^2	Pr(X)	(X–mean)^2 × Pr(X)
320	217	103	10,609	0.1	1,060.9
250	217	33	1,089	0.4	435.6
190	217	–27	729	0.3	218.7
140	217	–77	5,929	0.2	1,185.8
					2,901.0

*Table 34: Calculation of the variance of the
distribution of returns from strategy B*

Since the variance has been obtained by the operation of squaring the sum 2,901 represents units of (£000)^2. It is, therefore, easier to work with the standard deviation, which is defined as the square root of the variance. For this case it is:

$$\sqrt{2,901} \approx 53.861$$

That is £53,861.

You should now check that you have understood how to obtain a variance and standard deviation, by working through Activity 47.

ACTIVITY 47

The probability distribution for the cost of installing a new computer based information system into a small company is as shown.

Cost (£s)	Probability
110,000	0.3
120,000	0.4
130,000	0.2
140,000	0.1

Determine the expected value and standard deviation for this probability distribution. You should use the approach that was followed in Table 34 and work in £000s.

The mean or expected value is equal to:

$$(0.3 \times 110,000) + (0.4 \times 120,000) + (0.2 \times 130,000) + (0.1 \times 140,000)$$
$$= £121,000$$

Your calculation of the variance should be in agreement with Table 35. All figures are in £000s, but remember that the variance is in $(£000s)^2$.

Cost(X)	Mean	(X–mean)	$(X-mean)^2$	Pr(X)	$(X-mean)^2 \times Pr(X)$
110	121	−11	121	0.3	36.3
120	121	−1	1	0.4	0.4
130	121	9	81	0.2	16.2
140	121	19	361	0.1	36.1
					89.0

*Table 35: Calculation of the variance of the
distribution for information system costs*

So the variance is £89 million and the standard deviation is the square root of this. So the standard deviation is £9,434.

Using this approach, choosing between two or more strategies entails comparing their expected monetary values and their variances. For example, consider the following portion of a decision tree, shown in Figure 24.

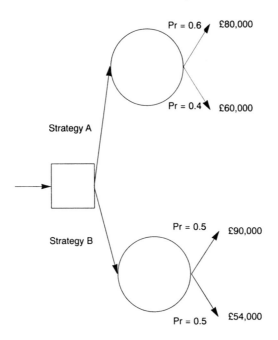

Figure 24: Decision tree for choosing between two strategies

ACTIVITY 48

Determine the expected monetary value and standard deviation for strategies A and B in Figure 24 and, hence, decide which is preferable. In calculating the standard deviations you should follow the approach used in Tables 34 and 35.

For strategy A, the expected monetary value is:

$$(0.6 \times 80{,}000) + (0.4 \times 60{,}000) = £72{,}000$$

For strategy B, the expected monetary value is:

$$(0.5 \times 90{,}000) + (0.5 \times 54{,}000) = £72{,}000$$

Tables 36 and 37 show the calculation of the respective variances. (Figures are in £000s.)

Cost(X)	Mean	(X–mean)	(X–mean)^2	Pr(X)	(X-mean)^2 × Pr(X)
80	72	8	64	0.6	38.4
60	72	–12	144	0.4	57.6
					96.0

Table 36: Calculation of the variance for srategy A

So the standard deviation for strategy A is:

$$\sqrt{96} = £9{,}798$$

Cost(X)	Mean	(X–mean)	(X–mean)^2	Pr(X)	(X–mean)^2 × Pr(X)
90	72	18	324	0.5	162
54	72	–18	324	0.5	162
					324

Table 37: Calculation of the variance for strategy B

So the standard deviation for strategy B is:

$$\sqrt{324} = £18{,}000$$

Since both strategies have the same expected value and given that the standard deviation is a measure of risk, most decision-makers would take the view that strategy A is preferable.

Choosing between strategies A and B in Activity 48 presented little difficulty, given that both had the same expected value. The problem comes when the strategies being compared differ with respect to both their expected values and standard deviations. In such cases the decision-maker may be prepared to trade off increased risk for a greater expected monetary value.

To operationalise such an approach to decision-making, the analyst will need to establish the decision-maker's attitude to risk. There are ways in which this can be done, but to explore this further in this unit would not be appropriate.

6.3 Expected utility

In choosing between strategies using expected monetary values, a crucial assumption is that the value of each monetary unit to the decision-maker is the same, regardless of the amounts that are involved. For example, suppose that choice of a particular strategy generates two possible outcomes, depending upon which of two states of nature occur. In one case, the consequence is a yield of £1 million and in the other a yield of £100,000. Suppose that the probability for the first is 0.25 and for the second is 0.75. Then the resulting expected monetary value is given by:

$$(0.25 \times 1,000,000) + (0.75 \times 100,000) = £325,000$$

Now suppose that the decision-maker is required to spend £325,000 as a condition of choosing this strategy. You can think of this as a gamble. For an outlay of £325,000, the returns are either £1 million, with a probability of 0.25, or £100,000, with a probability of 0.75. The question that now arises is whether a decision-maker would be willing to make this bet. If the value that the decision-maker places upon each pound decreases, as the return increases, then the gamble will be rejected. At issue here is the distinction between a monetary sum and the value placed upon it. This latter is called its **utility**. For this approach, expected utility and not expected monetary value is the appropriate vehicle for decision-making.

Ranking strategies in terms of their expected monetary values rests upon the assumption that, for a decision-maker, the value of each pound (in any given payoff) is independent of the number of pounds that are involved. If this assumption holds, then a decision-maker is said to be **risk neutral**. However, there are good grounds for taking the view that most decision-making does not take place under conditions of risk neutrality.

Economists use the term **utility** to denote the satisfaction derived from consumption of goods and services. Marginal utility is then the incremental gain in satisfaction resulting from a marginal increase in consumption. A well-known proposition, the law of diminishing marginal utility, asserts that these incremental utility gains decrease in size, as more of a product is consumed. For example, somebody who already owns ten pairs of jeans will get less satisfaction from acquiring an additional pair than somebody who only owns one pair and who then acquires a second one.

Suppose that a decision-maker takes a similar view, with respect to the utility derived from increasing monetary payoffs. The situation would then be as in Figure

25, with a utility scale on the vertical axis and the monetary payoff on the horizontal one.

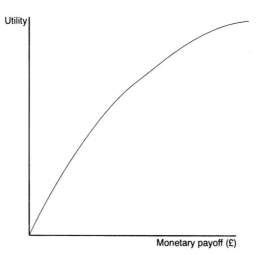

Figure 25: Assumed utility curve for a decision-maker

Notice that although utility increases with the monetary payoff, it does so at a decreasing rate. Now suppose that the decision-maker is required to choose between two alternative strategies. The first has a certain payoff of £100, whilst for the second there is a 0.5 probability that the payoff is £150 and a 0.5 chance that it will be only £50. A quick check will confirm that the expected monetary value for the second strategy is £100, the same as that for the certain outcome. Using the assumed shape of the decision-maker's utility curve, the choice problem is shown in Figure 26. 'U(50)', 'U(100)' and 'U(150)' are respectively the utilities associated with monetary payoffs of £50, £100 and £150.

Then the utility derived from the choice of a certain £100 is clearly 'U(100)'. Now consider the expected utility resulting from choice of the alternative strategy. Since the two outcomes (£50 and £150) are equally likely, then the expected utility is given by:

$$\{0.5 \times U(50)\} + \{0.5 \times U(150)\}$$

Consulting Figure 26, it is clear that the point '$\{0.5 \times U(50)\} + \{0.5 \times U(150)\}$' must lie half way along the line 'ab'. It then follows that the expected utility from the uncertain outcome is less than that from the certain outcome, even though the expected monetary value from the alternative strategy is £100. Situations such as this are referred to as **fair bets** because, in the long run, choosing the second strategy rather than the first one will not leave the decision-maker worse off in monetary terms.

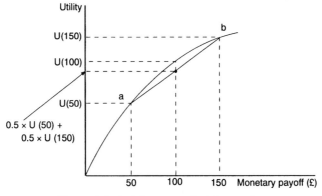

Figure 26: A risk-averse decision-maker

Yet our conclusion is that, in this situation, the fair bet will always be turned down, in favour of the certain outcome. When this occurs, the decision-maker is said to be **risk averse**.

ACTIVITY 49

What shape would the curve relating utility to the monetary payoff need to be for a decision-maker to be risk neutral?

For a decision-maker to be risk neutral, the curve would need to be linear. Then equal increments to the monetary payoff generate equal increments of utility.

To incorporate utility into decision analysis requires a mechanism via which a decision-maker's utility curve can be precisely determined. Methods for doing this exist, one of which revolves around obtaining the decision-maker's responses to hypothetical gaming problems. This is something that you might wish to explore if you intend to investigate decision analysis further. However, it is not a topic that we are able to pursue within the confines of this unit.

Summary

In this section we introduced some extensions to the decision-making models that had been explored up to this point. We started by contrasting multi-attribute decision-making with single criterion decision-making. The method of pairwise comparison selects as optimal the strategy which possesses the largest number of pairwise dominances. However, we showed that this approach assumes that attributes are of equal concern. If the decision-maker is unhappy with this assumption, then the outcomes for each attribute require aggregation and we showed how this might be achieved.

We revised the concept of the variance of a probability distribution and interpreted it as a measure of risk. Given that decision-makers are usually risk adverse, we showed that, as between strategies with the same expected monetary values, the one with the lowest variance would normally be chosen. Decision-makers might well be prepared to accept increased risk in return for a higher expected monetary value. However, the precise terms of such trade-offs would be dependent upon attitudes to risk.

Choosing between strategies using expected monetary value rests on the assumption that incremental rises in money sums always have equal value to a decision-maker. The unit ended by contrasting this with utility approaches to decision-making, which allow the possibility that, at some point, increments to monetary payoffs have a declining extra value to the decision-maker.

Unit Summary

This unit has examined decision-making under conditions of risk and uncertainty. If decision-makers are unable or unwilling to attach probabilities to the outcomes that might result from alternative strategies, the situation is referred to as one of uncertainty. When probabilities can be determined the decision problem is one of risk.

In Section 1, the terms **strategy**, **payoff** and **state of nature** were defined. Strategies are the choices open to the decision-maker, payoffs are the outcomes that might result from any given choice of strategy, and states of nature are the differing scenarios that are outside of the decision-maker's control. We then showed how a decision problem can be represented using either a decision tree or a payoff matrix.

In Section 2 we explored a number of approaches to decision-making under uncertainty: maximin, maximax, minimax regret and the principle of insufficient reason. There is no single, correct way of allowing for uncertainty. Instead, the approach adopted is dependent upon the attitudes of the decision-maker.

Section 3 revised the notion of the expected value of a probability distribution. The payoffs flowing from a choice of strategy are usually monetary and so we defined the expected monetary value for a strategy as being the sum of each payoff multiplied by its respective probability. An alternative, average value for a strategy is its expected opportunity loss, defined as the sum of each regret (opportunity loss) multiplied by its probability. We showed that ranking strategies by expected monetary value and by expected opportunity loss is exactly equivalent. Additional perfect information may also be available to a decision-maker, and we established how its value can be calculated. Finally, we showed how a payoff matrix can be constructed to solve simple single-decision problems.

In Section 4 we examined how to construct and evaluate a decision tree. Decision trees are drawn from left to right and reflect all possible sequences of decisions and events: they are evaluated by being rolled back in the opposite direction. At each decision point the optimal strategy is determined using expected monetary value and the remaining branches are discarded. As in other areas of BDA, it is essential to determine how sensitive the optimal strategies are to changes in both data and probabilities.

Section 5 showed how the decision-maker's prior probabilities can be amended using additional imperfect information. Use of a reverse tree enables posterior probabilities to be calculated. The value of any imperfect information can also be established.

Finally, in Section 6 a number of extensions to the basic decision analysis models were discussed. Many decision problems involve multiple objectives or attributes. We explored the use of pairwise comparisons as a means of solving such problems. We also addressed the issue of how to weight different objectives through a process of aggregation.

We then returned to the issue of how decisions might be arrived at for non-repetitive events. In Section 6 we revised the notion of the **variance** as a measure of the **spread** of a probability distribution and stated that it can be interpreted as the degree of risk attached to any given strategy. Choosing between strategies using both the expected monetary value and the variance then offers a way of handling events that are unique. Section 6 concluded with a brief consideration of the use of utility in decision-making. If a decision-maker is risk adverse, then choosing between strategies according to their expected monetary values would not be optimal.

In the next unit we look at **linear programming**.

Recommended Reading

All textbooks in management science and operations research contain one or more chapters covering decision analysis. Their content will broadly follow that in this unit, although some of them give more extended treatment to the role of utility and also make explicit reference to the use of Bayes' theorem in the revision of probabilities. They also differ in their level of mathematical sophistication.

The following two texts are good places to start.

Dennis, T L and Dennis, L B (1991) *Management Science*, West Publishing, Minneapolis, USA

Chapter 13 covers decision analysis. It is particularly useful for its discussion of utility and will also extend your understanding of the process of revising probabilities.

Oberstone, J (1990) *Management Science*, West Publishing, Minneapolis, USA

Chapters 1 to 3 cover decision analysis, including an approach to multi-attribute decision-making using utility methods. It is somewhat more technically sophisticated than the text by Dennis and Dennis, although it should be quite accessible once you have completed this unit.

If you wish to extend your understanding of decision analysis (including multi-attribute analysis and the use of utility) then the following text is an appropriate starting point. Although it utilises a greater range of mathematical tools, none of these should be beyond your understanding given that you have mastered the contents of this unit.

Lindley, D V (1994) *Making Decisions*, John Wiley, New York, USA

UNIT 3
LINEAR PROGRAMMING

Introduction

Linear programming is concerned with making decisions so as to maximise outcomes such as profit or sales revenue, or to minimise outcomes such as cost or distance travelled. Such decisions are taken within the context of constraints such as restrictions on production capacity or on supplies of raw materials.

Section 1 of this unit looks at how we formulate problems in linear programming. Section 2 goes on to look at solving such problems using graphical methods. Section 3 covers the issue of how solutions to problems react to changes to the input: this is known as **sensitivity analysis**. Section 4 goes on to look at the use of computer software to solve linear programming problems.

Section 5 looks at a particular class of problem, known as the transportation problem. This, as the name suggests, deals with the issue of transporting goods and components between locations. Section 6 looks at another class of problem, known as the assignment problem. This deals with the issue of assigning tasks in such a way as to make the most efficient use of resources. Finally, in Section 7, we identify some of the limitations of this approach to decision-making and indicate how they may be remedied.

To complete this unit, you will need some graph paper and a pencil and ruler. **You will also need a computer with *Microsoft Excel* (including the *Solver* add-in). If you do not have *Solver* installed as part of *Microsoft Excel*, you will need to install it before completing this unit. You should be able to do this from your original setup disks.**

Objectives

By the end of this unit you should be able to:

- formulate linear programming problems involving two or more decision variables

- use the graphical method to solve linear programming problems involving two decision variables

- use an appropriate software package to solve linear programming problems involving two or more decision variables

- perform a sensitivity analysis on the solution, using relevant software

- employ two special types of linear programming models, the assignment model and the transportation model

- determine when it would be appropriate to use other mathematical programming approaches as an alternative to linear programming.

Formulating a Linear Programming Problem

Introduction

Any linear programming problem consists of three components: decision variables, an objective and a set of constraints. **Decision variables** are those factors that can be determined by the decision-maker and for which optimal values are sought. The **objective** is a mathematical statement of the goal which the decision-maker wishes to achieve. **Constraints**, which must also be stated mathematically, are the restrictions within which the decision-maker must pursue his or her goal.

In Section 1.1, we introduce a case study of a furniture manufacturer to demonstrate how linear programming problems are formulated. In Section 1.2, we identify the decision-maker's objective and we then go on, in Sections 1.3 and 1.4, to define the constraints within which this objective must be achieved.

By the end of this section, you should be able to formulate linear programming problems involving two or more decision variables.

1.1 A linear programming problem

We start by using a case study to introduce a simple linear programming problem.

Case Study: RIP Upholsterers

RIP Upholsterers is a small firm which produces upholstered chairs, largely for the export market. The company produces two types of chair: the *Ambassador*, which has leather upholstery, and the *Diplomat*, which is covered in Dralon. *RIP Upholsterers* is organised in three departments: a joinery department, an upholstery department and a packaging department. Both types of chair can be handled within the joinery and packaging departments, but the upholstery department is divided into separate sections for leather and Dralon.

Given the capacity available in the joinery department, a maximum of either 300 *Ambassadors* or 450 *Diplomats* (or a pro rata production of both: for example, 150 *Ambassadors* and 225 *Diplomats*) can be constructed per week. The packaging department can handle a maximum of either 400 *Ambassadors* or 400 *Diplomats* (or pro rata) per week. In the upholstery department, the leather section can handle up to 150 *Ambassadors* per week and the Dralon section can handle up to 375 *Diplomats* per week.

RIP Upholsterers has established that the contribution to profit per *Ambassador* is £660 while the contribution to profit per *Diplomat* is £540. Market intelligence suggests that there is a ready market for all the *Ambassadors* and *Diplomats* that the company might be able to manufacture. *RIP Upholsterers'* problem is to establish the best or optimum weekly output of *Ambassadors* and *Diplomats*.

1.2 Identifying the objective function

With any linear programming problem, it is essential to start by identifying exactly what decisions need to be made.

ACTIVITY 1

What decisions does *RIP Upholsterers* need to make?

Since *RIP Upholsterers'* problem is to establish the optimum weekly output of the two types of chairs, then the two decisions that the company needs to make are how many *Ambassador* chairs to produce each week and how many *Diplomat* chairs to produce each week.

We call these the **decision variables.** In every linear programming problem, identifying the decision variables is always the crucial first step. It would be helpful to define *RIP Upholsterers'* decision variables formally so let:

A = the weekly output of *Ambassadors*

D = the weekly output of *Diplomats*

RIP Upholsterers seeks the optimum weekly production levels of the two types of chair. To establish this optimum, we need a criterion to enable us to choose between different production possibilities. We call this the **objective**. A key assumption in linear programming is that decision-making problems are characterised by a single objective.

ACTIVITY 2

Suggest an appropriate objective for *RIP Upholsterers'* decision problem.

Since *RIP Upholsterers* is a commercial concern, an appropriate objective would be to maximise profits. Another way of putting this is that the company wishes to manufacture that number of *Ambassadors* and *Diplomats* per week so as to maximise their contribution to profit.

With A as the number of *Ambassadors* and D as the number of *Diplomats*, the weekly contribution to profit is given by:

Contribution = 660A + 540D

For example, if *RIP Upholsterers* was to manufacture 100 chairs of each type then weekly contribution to profit would be:

$(660 \times 100) + (540 \times 100) = £120,000$

So far, we have established that a suitable objective for *RIP Upholsterers* is to fix its weekly outputs of *Ambassadors* and *Diplomats* so as to obtain the maximum possible weekly contribution. We call this the **objective function**. Formally, the decision problem is to determine values for A and D, such as will maximise Contribution = 660A + 540D.

1.3 Defining the constraints

ACTIVITY 3

However, *RIP Upholsterers* cannot choose any values that it likes for A and D. Why not?

In setting its weekly production levels, *RIP Upholsterers* must keep within the limitations currently set by the capacity limits of its three departments (joinery, upholstery and packaging). We refer to these limitations as **constraints**. In the current case, they are capacity constraints. If there were no such constraints, the problem would have no solution, as the company would be able to produce an infinite number of chairs.

So what exactly are these constraints? Consider the upholstery department. It's split into separate sections for leather and Dralon and so it has two capacity limitations, one for each type of chair. Let us start by determining the constraint for the leather upholstery section. It is helpful to begin the process by trying out some values.

ACTIVITY 4

Can the leather upholstery section deal with 50 *Ambassadors* per week? What about 100 or 150 or 200?

So what exactly is the constraint? If A is the weekly output of *Ambassadors*, what values can A take?

We are told that the leather upholstery section can manufacture up to 150 *Ambassadors* per week. So it can certainly produce 50 or 100 or 150 per week, but not 200. So the constraint is that it can produce any amount up to and including 150, but no more.

Given that A is the weekly output of *Ambassadors*, the constraint is that A cannot exceed 150.

We can write this constraint more concisely as:

$$A \le 150$$

A statement like this is called an **inequality**.

We now require a constraint for the Dralon upholstery section.

ACTIVITY 5

Can you write down a similar constraint for the Dralon upholstery section?

Well, this must be the inequality:

$$D \le 375$$

This states that D (the number of *Diplomats*) must take a value less than or equal to 375.

So far we have established that the constraints imposed by the upholstery department are:

$$A \le 150$$

$$D \le 375$$

Now consider the packaging department. It can handle a maximum of 400 *Ambassadors* or 400 *Diplomats* or proportionate numbers of both per week. We need to reduce this to a compact statement, similar to those above.

We are told that packaging can handle up to 400 *Ambassadors* or up to 400 *Diplomats* per week, so in the time it takes to package one *Ambassador* chair it could have packaged one *Diplomat*. It follows that it can package any combination of the two types of chair, provided that the total does not exceed 400. This gives as the constraint:

$$A + D \le 400$$

Remember that this is simply a shorthand way of stating that the overall production of chairs cannot exceed 400 per week.

That leaves us with the joinery department. Establishing this constraint is slightly trickier, and will involve us in somewhat more work. Checking back, the joinery department can handle a maximum of either 300 *Ambassadors* or 450 *Diplomats* or proportionate numbers of both, per week. We need to formalise this into a constraint, using A and D for the two variables.

We know the department can handle up to 300 *Ambassadors* only, or up to 450 *Diplomats* only. So in the time that it takes to output one *Ambassador* it could have output 1.5 *Diplomats* ($450 \div 300 = 1.5$). So, if it produces just 200 *Ambassadors* it would still have the capacity to produce 150 *Diplomats* (100×1.5).

ACTIVITY 6

1. If the joinery department produces just 150 *Ambassadors*, how many *Diplomats* can it output?

2. And if it produces 100 *Ambassadors*?

---

1. In the time taken to produce one *Ambassador*, the joinery department can manufacture 1.5 *Diplomats*. So, if it produces only 150 *Ambassadors* (which is less than the maximum number of 300), then in the remaining time it could produce 225 *Diplomats* (150×1.5).

2. If it produces only 100 *Ambassadors*, then it can also produce 300 *Diplomats* (200×1.5).

So what is the joinery department constraint? Well let us try out some possibilities. We will start with $A + D \le 300$.

Will this work? No it will not. Suppose that no *Diplomats* are produced, then D is 0.

It follows that A has a maximum of 300, which does not break the constraint. But now suppose that no *Ambassadors* are produced. Then A is 0, in which case D has a maximum value of 300, which is wrong.

Is the formulation A + D ≤ 450 any better? Unfortunately, this will not work either. Suppose we set A at 0, then the inequality states that D has a maximum value of 450, which is correct. However, setting D at 0, the inequality states that A has a maximum value of 450, and this is not correct.

ACTIVITY 7

Now try writing down the correct formulation for this constraint.

Hint: Start with the formulation ?A + D ≤ 450. You must get the result that when no *Ambassadors* are produced, no more than 450 *Diplomats* can be dealt with by the joinery department. Also when no *Diplomats* are produced no more than 300 *Ambassadors* can be produced.

The correct formulation is:

$$1.5A + D \leq 450$$

Or, on multiplying throughout by 2, to remove the decimal fraction:

$$3A + 2D \leq 900$$

Firstly, let us check that this works. Setting A as 0 gives a maximum value for 2D of 900 and, hence, a maximum value of 450 for D. That is correct. Then, setting D as 0 gives a maximum value for 3A of 900 and, hence, a maximum value of 300 for A. That is also correct. So the inequality does work.

Secondly, how do you go about establishing this correct formulation? Well you might try trial and error, but a better approach is to use some reasoning.

Suppose we start with ?A + D ≤ 450. We know that, on setting A to 0, this works for D. So we need a coefficient for A such that, when D is 0, the maximum value for A is 300. Now, since 300 is 2/3 of 450 the coefficient 3/2 (that is, 1.5) will work. If D is 0, then setting 1.5A to be less than or equal to 450, gives A as less than or equal to 450 × 2/3, which is what we want.

1.4 Non-negativity conditions

We have now established the objective function for *RIP Upholsterers'* decision problem, along with the four constraints set by its existing capacity. There remains one further qualification.

ACTIVITY 8

There are clearly upper limits on the quantities of the two chairs that can be produced. Are there any lower limits? If so, what are they?

Hopefully, you agree that there are lower limits on the weekly production of the two chairs. Clearly the minimum output for either type of chair is 0! This may appear to be obvious, but it does need to be explicitly stated.

So it must be the case that:

$$A \geq 0$$

$$D \geq 0$$

These are shorthand ways of stating that neither A nor D can take negative values. We refer to them as **non-negativity conditions**.

At this point we can give a concise statement of the decision problem facing *RIP Upholsterers*:

Determine values for A (number of *Ambassadors*) and D (number of *Diplomats*) that will:

Maximise Contribution = 660A + 540D

Subject to the constraints:

3A	+	2D	≤	900
A	+	D	≤	400
A			≤	150
		D	≤	375

Non-negativity conditions

A		≥	0
	D	≥	0

All linear programming problems have this structure: namely, objective function, constraints and non-negativity conditions.

Sorting *RIP Upholsterers'* problem into this structure is termed 'formulating the problem'. In any linear programming problem, this is the crucial first stage and it requires a high degree of care. If the problem is formulated incorrectly then the solution will also be incorrect. The acronym GIGO (garbage in, garbage out) applies!

Summary

In this section of the unit, we used the *RIP Upholsterers* case study to investigate how to formulate a linear programming problem. We saw that any problem has three components: decision variables, an objective function and a set of constraints.

Decision variables are those factors within the control of the decision-maker and for which optimal values are sought. The objective function summarises the objective that we wish to optimise: this might be to maximise or minimise some variable, such as contribution to profit or costs of production. Pursuit of any objective is rarely unrestricted, so the third component of any problem is to set up the constraints which have to be adhered to. In the *RIP Upholsterers* case these constraints were set by productive capacity. In addition, for a problem to make economic sense, it is usually necessary that the decision variables do not take negative values.

In the next section we look at how to solve linear programming problems using graphical methods.

SECTION 2

Solving Linear Programming Problems Using a Graphical Method

Introduction

In Section 1, we looked at how to formulate a linear programming problem. In this section, we shall look at how to solve such problems through the use of graphs.

We start, in Section 2.1, by obtaining a solution to the *RIP Upholsterers* problem from Section 1. We then go on to look at a similar problem in Section 2.2. In Section 2.3, we look at a minimisation problem through a case study of a small mining company. Finally, in Section 2.4, we formulate and solve three more problems.

By the end of this section you should be able to use the graphical method to solve linear programming problems involving two decision variables.

2.1 Solving a formulated problem

We left our review of the upholstery problem in Section 1 at the point where it had been fully formulated. We now proceed to solve the *RIP Upholsterers* problem. The formulated problem is:

Determine values for A (number of *Ambassadors*) and D (number of *Diplomats*) that will:

Maximise contribution = 660A + 540D

Subject to the constraints:

$$3A + 2D \leq 900$$
$$A + D \leq 400$$
$$A \leq 150$$
$$D \leq 375$$
$$A \geq 0$$
$$D \geq 0$$

We start by plotting the constraints on a graph. Initially we will graph each one separately. Consider the constraint 3A + 2D ≤ 900, which relates to the joinery department. Look at Figure 1.

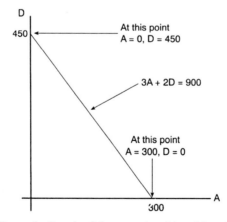

Figure 1: Graph of the equation 3A + 2D = 900

The number of *Ambassadors* (A) is plotted along the horizontal axis and the number of *Diplomats* (D) is plotted along the vertical axis. Since A and D cannot have negative values, we can confine our graph to the positive quadrant (the top right-hand corner).

To graph an inequality we always begin by graphing the equation part of the constraint. In this case, we need to graph the equation $3A + 2D = 900$. This is best done by determining the points at which the graph of the equation cuts the two axes. To do this we proceed as follows.

Suppose that $A = 0$. Then:

$$3A + 2D = (3 \times 0) + 2D = 2D = 900$$

And so $D = 450$.

Suppose that $D = 0$. Then:

$$3A + 2D = 3A + (2 \times 0) = 3A = 900$$

And so $A = 300$.

Since the equation $3A + 2D = 900$ is linear, we obtain its graph by joining these two points with a straight line.

Perhaps you are uncertain about the statement that the equation $3A + 2D = 900$ is linear. In general, any equation of the form $aX + bY = c$, where X and Y are variables and a, b and c are constant numbers, is linear. This is a standard result, which we simply make use of in linear programming.

Now consider any point that lies below the graph of the equation $3A + 2D = 900$. For example, look at the point ($A = 100$, $D = 100$) shown in Figure 2.

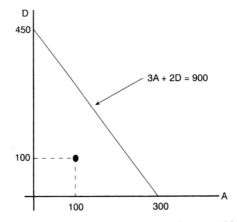

Figure 2: Example point (A = 100, D = 100)

At this point:

$$3A + 2D = (3 \times 100) + (2 \times 100) = 500$$

This is clearly less than 900. So the combination of 100 *Ambassadors* and 100 *Diplomats* lies inside the inequality $3A + 2D \leq 900$. We now need to consider points that lie to the right of the graph of the equation $3A + 2D = 900$. Figure 3 shows one such point, defined by the coordinates (A = 300, D = 300).

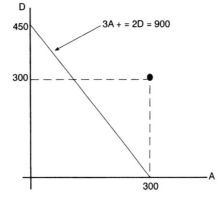

Figure 3: Example point (A = 300, D = 300)

ACTIVITY 9

Consider the point (A = 300, D = 300), shown in Figure 3. Does this point lie within the inequality $3A + 2D \leq 900$?

In this case:

$$3A + 2B = (3 \times 300) + (2 \times 300) = 1,500$$

This is greater than 900. So the combination of 300 chairs of each type does not lie within the inequality $3A + 2D \leq 900$.

We can make some generalisations from these results. For any point that is below the line, $3A + 2D$ will be less than 900. Conversely, for any point that is above the line, $3A + 2D$ will be greater than 900.

So the inequality $3A + 2D \leq 900$ is the shaded area shown in Figure 4. It shows all combinations of the two types of chair that are within the capacity of the joinery department.

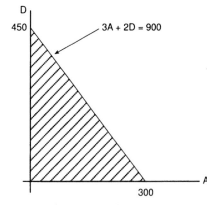

Figure 4: The joinery department constraint

Notice that this area is bounded by the two axes (this is due to the two non-negativity restrictions) and the line $3A + 2D = 900$.

Let us now turn to the second constraint.

ACTIVITY 10

Graph the inequality $A + D \leq 400$. You should start by graphing the equation $A + D = 400$.

Your graph should agree with that shown in Figure 5. It shows all combinations of *Ambassadors* and *Diplomats* that are within the capacity of the packaging department.

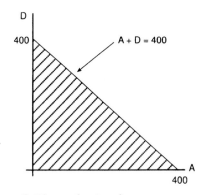

Figure 5: The packaging department constraint

To obtain the graph of the equation $A + D = 400$, we note that $A = 0$ implies that $D = 400$ and conversely $D = 0$ implies that $A = 400$.

All points below the line satisfy the inequality A + D ≤ 400. You can establish this by checking any point that lies below the line. For example, using the origin as a check point, when A and D are both 0 then A + D = 0, which is clearly less than 400.

We now have the upholstery constraints to consider. The constraint for the Dralon section is shown in Figure 6. Remember the constraint is D ≤ 375. You should interpret the graph of the inequality as saying that, no matter what value A has, D cannot exceed 375.

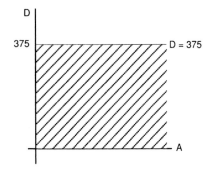

Figure 6: The Dralon upholstery constraint

ACTIVITY 11

Graph the leather upholstery constraint: that is, A ≤ 150.

Your graph should agree with that in Figure 7.

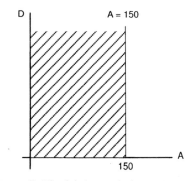

Figure 7: The leather upholstery constraint

Of course *RIP Upholsterers'* production levels must abide by all four constraints. We therefore require a single graph that shows all four inequalities.

Look at Figure 8. The shaded area is the region of the graph common to all four constraints. It consists of all points that simultaneously lie below the lines 3A + 2D = 900, A + D = 400 and D = 375 and to the left of the line A = 150.

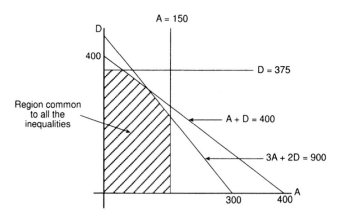

Figure 8: The region common to the four constraints

The region common to all the inequalities shows all possible output combinations (per week) of *Ambassadors* and *Diplomats*, that abide by the capacity constraints set by the joinery, upholstery and packaging departments. The area common to the inequalities is called the **feasible region**. The region is feasible because all the production combinations contained within it are feasible, given the capacity constraints. Any production combination outside the region is **infeasible**, since it breaks at least one of these constraints.

Notice that the feasible region has the shape of an irregular polygon. That is, it is bounded by a series of straight lines and, therefore, has a number of corners (or vertices). Later in this section we will show that these corners are crucial for the solution of a linear programming problem.

Remember that *RIP Upholsterers* seeks the optimal weekly production of *Ambassadors* and *Diplomats*: that is, the combination that maximises contribution to weekly profits. Furthermore, this optimal combination must be within the feasible region. So the question is 'what combination of *Ambassadors* and *Diplomats*, within the feasible region, will maximise contribution?'. To establish this we need to make use of the objective function.

The objective function for this problem is:

Maximise Contribution = 660A + 540D

As it stands, this equation cannot be graphed unless we give contribution some particular value. For example, if we set contribution to be equal to £118,800 then we can graph the equation.

ACTIVITY 12

Graph the equation $118,800 = 660A + 540D$.

Your graph of the equation should be as in Figure 9. The intersection points at the two axes are obtained as follows:

$$A = 0 \Rightarrow (660 \times 0) + 540D = 540D = 118,800$$

And so $D = 220$.

$$D = 0 \Rightarrow 660A + (540 \times 0) = 660A = 118,800$$

And so $A = 180$.

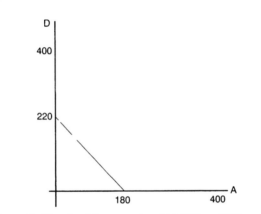

Figure 9: Graph of the equation 118,800 = 660A + 540D

It is essential to interpret this graph with care. What it shows is all production combinations that yield a weekly contribution to profit of £118,800, ranging from 220 *Diplomats* and 0 *Ambassadors*, to 180 *Ambassadors* and 0 *Diplomats*.

ACTIVITY 13

1. On the same graph as above, sketch the lines for contribution levels of £59,400 and £237,600.

2. How do the three lines relate to each other?

1. Your sketch should be as shown in Figure 10.

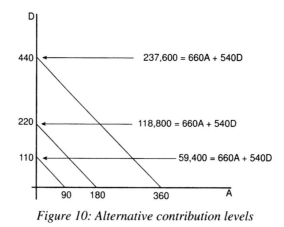

Figure 10: Alternative contribution levels

2. The lines that you have drawn should all be parallel.

Activity 13 should have convinced you that we can graph the objective function as a set of parallel lines, such that each line shows all production combinations (of *Ambassadors* and *Diplomats*) yielding the same level of contribution, and the further we move north-east from the origin, the higher the level of contribution.

Figure 11 shows the feasible region and the objective function line for a contribution of £59,400. It is conventional to show the objective function as a dashed line.

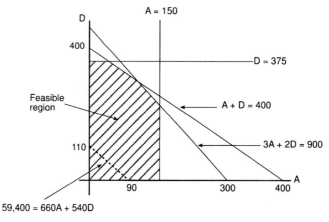

Figure 11: Contribution of £59,400

The line $59,400 = 660A + 540D$ shows all possible output combinations of *Ambassadors* and *Diplomats* that yield a weekly contribution to profit of £59,400.

ACTIVITY 14

Are the production combinations along this line feasible?

Yes they are. All combinations of *Ambassadors* and *Diplomats* along the line 59,400 = 660A + 540D are within the feasible region. Producing at any point along this line will not break *RIP Upholsterers'* capacity constraints. So *RIP Upholsterers* are guaranteed a weekly contribution of £59,400.

However, the question is can they do better than this? The answer is 'yes'. Checking Figure 11, there are combinations of production quantities of the two chairs that are feasible (that is, that are in the feasible region), and lie to the right of the line for £59,400 (and, therefore, must earn a greater contribution).

Now consider the objective function line 118,800 = 660A + 540D, as shown in Figure 12.

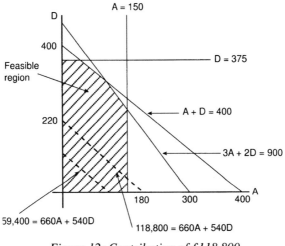

Figure 12: Contribution of £118,800

ACTIVITY 15

1. Is it possible for *RIP Upholsterers* to earn a contribution of £118,800 per week?

2. Can the company do even better than this?

1. *RIP Upholsterers* can earn a contribution to profit of £118,800 per week. How do we know this? Well, some of the combinations along the line 118,800 = 660A + 540D lie within the feasible region. It is also true that some of them do not, but that does not concern us. As long as there are combinations along the line that are within the feasible region, then this is all that matters. For example, the combination of 220 *Diplomats* and 0 *Ambassadors* is perfectly feasible and will yield a weekly contribution of £118,800.

2. There are still feasible combinations that lie to the right of this line and which, therefore, must earn more contribution. So long as this remains the case, the contribution can be increased.

Think of the process as being one of shifting the objective function line to the right (while keeping it parallel to the original line). The further to the right the line can be shifted, the higher the weekly contribution. Of course the line can only be shifted any further to the right if there are still feasible combinations that can be reached.

ACTIVITY 16

How far to the right can the line be shifted? Where in the feasible region is the resulting optimal point?

Figure 13 shows the position of the optimal point within the feasible region.

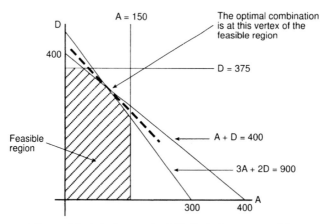

Figure 13: Solution to the RIP Upholsterers problem

If you are not certain why this is the case, then study the following argument carefully.

The objective function line can be moved outwards from the origin (keeping it parallel to the original line) until it just touches (that is, is a tangent to) the feasible region. This point gives the optimal solution. In the present case, this is at one of the corners of the feasible region.

It can be shown that the solution to any linear programming problem is always at one of the corners to the feasible region. This makes the process of finding a solution very straightforward, since (provided the feasible region has been correctly determined) the optimum value of the objective function can always be found by a careful check of all its corners.

We can now complete the *RIP Upholsterers* problem. Since the solution is at the corner shown, its coordinates (which give the A and D values) can be read off the graph, provided it has been drawn with care. Alternatively, since we know the equations of the two lines that form the corner, we can obtain an accurate solution by solving them simultaneously.

Look again at Figure 13. The two lines forming the corner are $A + D = 400$ and $3A + 2D = 900$.

Normally, the best way of solving a pair of simultaneous equations is to use **row operations**. In this method, one (or sometimes both) of the equations is multiplied throughout by some number, to yield the outcome that the coefficient for one of the variables is the same in both equations.

In the present example it would be convenient if the coefficient for the D variable in the equation $A + D = 400$ could be increased to 2. Then, subtracting the modified equation from the equation $3A + 2D = 900$ will leave a single equation in which A is the only unknown. Here are the steps that we follow:

$$(1) \quad A \quad + \quad D \quad = \quad 400$$

$$(2) \quad 3A \quad + \quad 2D \quad = \quad 900$$

Multiplying equation (1) throughout by 2 gives:

$$(3) \quad 2A \quad + \quad 2D \quad = \quad 800$$

So we now have as our two equations:

$$(2) \quad 3A \quad + \quad 2D \quad = \quad 900$$

$$(3) \quad 2A \quad + \quad 2D \quad = \quad 800$$

Then, subtracting equation (3) from equation (2) gives:

$$3A - 2A + 2D - 2D = 900 - 800$$

And so $A = 100$. Therefore, from equation (1), $D = 300$.

So we have determined that *RIP Upholsterers'* optimal weekly production is 100 *Ambassadors* and 300 *Diplomats*. This yields a weekly contribution to profit of:

$$(660 \times 100) + (540 \times 300) = £228,000$$

Let us summarise the procedure that we followed to obtain this solution. We solved *RIP Upholsterers'* problem using the following steps.

1. Decide upon the decision variables.
2. Determine the objective function.
3. Identify the constraints.
4. Graph the constraints and, hence, locate the feasible region.
5. Graph the objective function. Choose a suitable value that places the line on the middle of your graph.
6. Shift the objective function line outwards from the origin (keeping it parallel to the original line) to find the optimal solution.
7. Read off the optimal solution from the graph, or obtain it more accurately using simultaneous equations.

Now see whether you can formulate and solve a two-variable linear programming problem.

2.2 Formulating and solving a maximisation problem

We now use a case study to explore how to formulate and solve a maximisation problem.

Case Study: Haven Manufacturing

Haven Manufacturing produces bicycle frames for the quality end of the cycle market. In recent years the company has reduced the number of frames in its range, to the point where it only manufactures two: the *Workhorse* (which is intended for urban cycling) and the *Bentley* (which caters for mountain bikers).

Production of each type of frame involves two processes, which we will call process I and process II. The number of hours currently required for each production process is as shown in Table 1.

	Hours used per *Workhorse*	Hours used per *Bentley*
Process I	2	4
Process II	1	3

Table 1: Requirements of bicycle frame production

The firm considers that it has available no more than 2,000 manufacturing hours for process I and 1,200 manufacturing hours for process II per week.

Past experience suggests that sales of *Workhorses* are unlikely to exceed 900 per week. Finally, each *Workhorse* sold earns a contribution to profit of £40 and each *Bentley* earns a contribution of £90.

ACTIVITY 17

What are the decision variables? Define them formally.

Haven Manufacturing has to decide the weekly output of the two products: *Workhorses* and *Bentleys*. These decision variables need to be defined formally, so let:

W = the number of *Workhorses* manufactured per week

And let:

B = the number of *Bentleys* manufactured per week

We now need to determine the constraints on the weekly outputs of the two products. There are two types of constraint in this problem: constraints on production and constraints on sales. Manufacture of both types of frame requires the running of processes I and II. But the number of hours of manufacturing time for each process is limited. This gives two production constraints: one for each process. There are also limitations on the sales of *Workhorses*. This gives one further constraint. So there are three constraints in total.

We know (see Table 1) that to produce each *Workhorse* requires 2 hours of process I, whereas each *Bentley* requires 4 hours. So, using W and B to denote the quantities of *Workhorses* and *Bentleys* produced, the firm will require 2W + 4B hours of process I. Similarly it requires W + 3B hours of process II.

Clearly *Haven Manufacturing* cannot use more process hours per week than are currently available.

ACTIVITY 18

Formally state the constraints on production in the *Haven Manufacturing* case.

The important point is that the firm cannot use more process hours per week than it has available.

Stated mathematically, this means that the number of hours used must be less than or equal to the number of hours available. So, for process I:

$$2W + 4B \leq 2{,}000$$

Similarly, for process II:

$$W + 3B \leq 1{,}200$$

There is, of course, another constraint: the constraint on sales. We know that sales of *Workhorses* are unlikely to exceed 900 per week. (They could, of course, be less than this figure.) We can state this formally as:

$$W \leq 900$$

So far we have as constraints:

$$2W + 4B \leq 2{,}000$$
$$W + 3B \leq 1{,}200$$
$$W \leq 900$$

ACTIVITY 19

To make the problem economically meaningful, what else must we state about W and B?

Although it would seem obvious, we must state that W and B cannot take negative values. Hence, in the formulated problem, we must include the non-negativity constraints. We can state these formally as:

$W \geq 0$

$B \geq 0$

Having established the constraints, we now need to determine the objective function. We know that each *Workhorse* earns a contribution of £40, and each *Bentley* earns a contribution of £90.

ACTIVITY 20

What is the objective function for this problem?

The objective function is:

Maximise Contribution = 40W + 90B

Putting all the bits and pieces together, the formulated linear programming problem is:

Determine values for W and B that will:

Maximise Contribution = 40W + 90B

Subject to:

2W	+	4B	$\leq$	2,000
W	+	3B	$\leq$	1,200
W			$\leq$	900
W			$\geq$	0
		B	$\geq$	0

ACTIVITY 21

Solve this problem, using an appropriate graph. In order to do this, you will need to establish the optimum weekly output of *Workhorses* and *Bentleys* and the resulting weekly contribution to profit.

Figure 14 shows the feasible region for this problem and the optimal solution. Remember that the feasible region (the shaded area in the figure) is the area common to all the constraints. In this case it is bounded by the two axes and the three lines 2W + 4B = 2,000, W + 3B = 1,200 and W = 900.

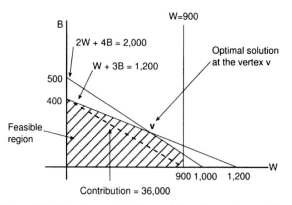

Figure 14: Solution to the Haven Manufacturing problem

The objective function line for Contribution = 36,000 lies wholly within the feasible region, so all combinations of W and B along this line are feasible. However, there are (W, B) combinations that lie to the right of this line which are also in the feasible region and which, therefore, will yield a higher contribution.

Moving the line out north-east from the origin, keeping it parallel, until there are no further feasible (W, B) combinations that are to the right of it, yields the solution at the point where the objective function just touches (that is, is a tangent to) the feasible region at the corner labelled v in Figure 14.

We can now read off the solution, which is given by the coordinates of this corner. Alternatively, and more accurately, we can obtain the solution by using simultaneous equations.

At the corner v we have that:

$$\text{(1) } 2W + 4B = 2,000$$

$$\text{(2) } W + 3B = 1,200$$

Multiplying equation (2) throughout by 2 gives:

$$\text{(3) } 2W + 6B = 2,400$$

Then, equation (3) minus equation (1) is:

$$(2W + 6B) - (2W + 4B) = 2,400 - 2,000$$

$$2W + 6B - 2W - 4B = 400$$

$$2B = 400$$

$$B = 200$$

Then, using equation (2), we can find the value of W:

$$W + 3B = 1,200$$

$$W = 600$$

You should always check these calculations against the graph, to make certain that they are correct and that you have not made an error when manipulating the simultaneous equations.

Finally, using the objective function, we establish that:

$$\text{Contribution} = (40 \times 600) + (90 \times 200) = £42,000$$

So we have solved the *Haven Manufacturing* problem and we recommend that the company manufactures 600 *Workhorses* and 200 *Bentleys* per week, for a contribution to profit of £42,000.

The two linear programming problems that we have investigated so far both involved maximising some objective function. We now turn to a problem where the objective is to **minimise** the objective function.

2.3 Formulating and solving a minimisation problem

Case Study: Myfanwy Mining Ltd

Myfanwy Mining Ltd is a small mining company that currently works two coal seams and produces three grades of coal. It costs £100 an hour to work the *Morgan* seam, obtaining in that time 10 tonnes of anthracite (a type of coal), 50 tonnes of best quality coal and 20 tonnes of ordinary coal. The *Davies* seam is more expensive to work, at a cost of £150 per hour, but it yields in that time 40 tonnes of anthracite, 60 tonnes of best coal and 10 tonnes of ordinary coal. Existing contracts require *Myfanwy Mining Ltd* to produce at least 80 tonnes of anthracite, 300 tonnes of best coal and 80 tonnes of ordinary coal each day. The colliery owner wishes to determine the number of hours per day that each seam should be worked so as to meet daily requirements as cheaply as possible.

ACTIVITY 22

What are the decision variables for this problem?

From the statement of *Myfanwy Mining Ltd's* problem, it should be obvious that the two decision variables are the number of hours per day that each of the two seams should be worked.

Formally we let M equal the number of hours per day that the *Morgan* seam is worked, and we let D equal the number of hours per day that the *Davies* seam is worked.

Myfanwy Mining Ltd's objective is to choose values for M and D that minimise the cost of meeting the daily coal requirements.

ACTIVITY 23

What is the objective function?

From the statement of the problem, it is clear that the objective is to minimise cost. Hence, the objective function is:

Minimise Cost = 100M + 150D

We now need to consider the constraints. *Myfanwy Mining Ltd* must extract enough coal each day to meet daily requirements. There are three types of coal, and this suggests that there are three constraints.

Firstly, consider anthracite. The daily requirement is for at least 80 tonnes. So the daily output can be more than this, but cannot be less. How much anthracite can be extracted each day? If the *Morgan* seam is worked for one hour, 10 tonnes can be obtained. If the *Davies* seam is worked for one hour, 40 tonnes can be obtained. So, if the *Morgan* seam is worked for M hours per day and the *Davies* seam for D hours per day, a total of 10M + 40D tonnes of anthracite can be extracted per day.

So the constraint is that:

$$10M + 40D \geq 80$$

ACTIVITY 24

Now formulate the constraints for best quality coal and ordinary coal.

You should have the additional constraints:

$50M + 60D \geq 300$ (best quality coal)

$20M + 10D \geq 80$ (ordinary coal)

As well as formulating the objective function and the constraints, we need to ensure that the solution values for M and D are meaningful.

ACTIVITY 25

What further restrictions must we place upon M and D?

We must specify that neither M nor D can take negative values. These are the usual non-negativity conditions.

We have now completed our formulation of the *Myfanwy Mining Ltd* decision problem. It is:

Determine values for M and D that will

Minimise Cost $= 100M + 150D$

Subject to:

10M	+	40D	$\geq$	80
50M	+	60D	$\geq$	300
20M	+	10D	$\geq$	80
M			$\geq$	0
		D	$\geq$	0

ACTIVITY 26

Solve the *Myfanwy Mining Ltd* problem. The objective here is to minimise cost, so you will need to shift the objective function line inwards towards the origin as far as possible.

Figure 15 shows the feasible region for this problem. Notice that the constraints are of the 'greater than or equal to' type, which explains its shape. For example, consider the anthracite constraint $10M + 40D \geq 80$. Any combination of M and D that lies below the line $10M + 40D = 80$ will not produce the required minimum 80 tonnes. The same applies to the other two constraints. So, to be feasible, combinations of M and D must simultaneously lie on or above the three lines $10M + 40D = 80$, $50M + 60D = 300$ and $20M + 10D = 80$.

In a minimisation problem the objective is to move the objective function line as far in towards the origin as possible. In this case the solution is at the corner of the feasible region labelled as *v*.

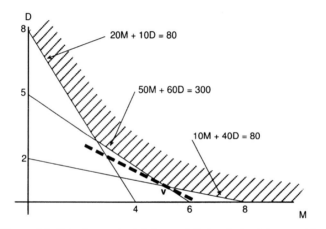

Figure 15: Solution to the Myfanwy Mining Ltd mining problem

At this solution corner *v*, we have that:

$$(1) \quad 10M + 40D = 80$$

$$(2) \quad 50M + 60D = 300$$

Multiplying equation (1) by 5 gives:

$$(3) \quad 50M + 200D = 400$$

Subtracting equation (2) from equation (3) gives:

$$(50M + 200D) - (50M + 60D) \quad = \quad 400 - 300$$

$$50M + 200D - 50M - 60D \quad = \quad 100$$

$$140D \quad = \quad 100$$

$$D = 100/400 = 5/7$$

So D = 5/7 hours: that is, approximately 43 minutes. Therefore, M = 36/7 hours: that is, approximately 5 hours 9 minutes. Hence the minimum cost is £621 per day.

In many linear programming problems, the decision variables are constrained to take only integer (that is, whole number) values. This was certainly the case for the *RIP Upholsterers* problem, as it is not possible to produce fractional chairs!

In the solution to the *Myfanwy Mining Ltd* problem (Activity 26) we established that the optimal values for M and D were 36/7 and 5/7 hours respectively. However, suppose that *Myfanwy Mining Ltd* can only work each seam for a whole number of hours. We now require an integer solution to the problem.

To obtain this we cannot just round the two values downwards. If we round down our optimal values for M and D, we have an integer value for M of 5 hours, and for D of 0 hours. However, this is outside the feasible region. This is because, with a value for M of 5, and a value for D of 0, the output of best quality coal is:

$$50M + 60D = (50 \times 5) + (60 \times 0) = 250$$

This is well below the minimum daily requirement of 300 tonnes so does not represent a feasible solution. There are, therefore, just three possibilities to consider.

Either we round both solution values upwards. (This must be a feasible solution, but it might not be the cheapest.) Or we round M up and round D down. (This must be cheaper than rounding both values upwards, but it may not be feasible.) Or we round M down and round D up. (Again, this must be cheaper than rounding both values upwards, but it may not be feasible.)

ACTIVITY 27

Which of the three possibilities listed above gives the best integer solution to *Myfanwy Mining Ltd's* problem?

If we round both M and D up, our new values will be M = 6 and D = 1. As already stated, this is a feasible solution. The daily cost is:

$$(100 \times 6) + (150 \times 1) = £750$$

If we round M up and round D down, our new values will be M = 6 and D = 0. We need to test if this is feasible. Remember that the production of coal is defined by the formulae 10M + 40D for anthracite, 50M + 60D for best quality coal, and 20M + 10D for ordinary coal. Replacing M with the value 6 and replacing D with the value 0 gives us the following outputs.

For anthracite:

$$(10 \times 6) + (40 \times 0) = 60 + 0 = 60$$

For best quality coal:

$$(50 \times 6) + (60 \times 0) = 300 + 0 = 300$$

For ordinary coal:

$$(20 \times 6) + (10 \times 0) = 120 + 0 = 120$$

This means that the solution is infeasible as it fails to produce enough anthracite to meet the minimum requirement for 80 tonnes.

If we round M down and round D up, our new values will be M = 5 and D = 1. Again, we need to test if this is feasible. Replacing M with the value 5 and replacing D with the value 1 gives us the following outputs.

For anthracite:

$$(10 \times 5) + (40 \times 1) = 50 + 40 = 90$$

For best quality coal:

$$(50 \times 5) + (60 \times 1) = 250 + 60 = 310$$

For ordinary coal:

$$(20 \times 5) + (10 \times 1) = 100 + 10 = 110$$

This means that the solution is feasible as it meets the minimum requirements for all three types of coal. The daily cost is:

$$(100 \times 5) + (150 \times 1) = £650$$

So this solution is cheaper than rounding both M and D up. Therefore, the company should work the *Morgan* seam for 5 hours per day and the *Davies* seam for 1 hour.

From working through the activities that you have met in this section, it should have become apparent that formulating problems is the key skill in linear programming. While every linear programming model consists of the same components (decision variables, objective function and constraints), the circumstances of each problem will be different. This is amply demonstrated by the range of examples that you are asked to investigate in the final part of this section.

2.4 Other problems

Now try the problems in the next three activities.

ACTIVITY 28

A livestock farmer feeds his animals on a blend of two types of feed: F_1 and F_2. He wants to establish what mixture of F_1 and F_2 to purchase to provide the least expensive blend that will satisfy the minimum daily requirements of the animals.

The table below gives the minimum daily requirement of four ingredients (I_1, I_2, I_3 and I_4), and the amount of each ingredient provided by F_1 and F_2 (expressed as a percentage of weight).

The costs of the two types of feed are £2 per kg for F_1 and £3 per kg for F_2.

Ingredients	% of ingredient in each type of feed		Minimum daily requirement (kg)
	F_1	F_2	
I_1	20	15	2.0
I_2	0	25	1.0
I_3	25	0	1.5
I_4	20	30	3.0

1. Formulate the problem.

2. Solve the problem.

To formulate the problem, you will need to identify the decision variables, define the objective function, and define the constraints.

To solve the problem, you will need to draw a graph of the problem, and identify the optimal solution by using the graph and/or by solving the simultaneous equations. You should note that the amount of each ingredient contained in F_1 and F_2 is expressed as a percentage.

1. Although there are four ingredients and two types of feed, there are only two variables. This is because the quantities of the ingredients depend upon the quantities of the two types of feed. Varying the amounts of F_1 and F_2 purchased per day will automatically vary the amounts obtained of the four ingredients. So the two variables are the quantities of F_1 and F_2. We will let X equal the number of kg of F_1 purchased, and we will let Y equal the number of kg of F_2 purchased.

The objective function is:

   Minimise Cost $= 2X + 3Y$

For each ingredient there is a single constraint. For example, consider ingredient I_1. 20 per cent of F_1 is ingredient I_1. In other words, for every kg purchased of F_1, there will be 0.2 kg of I_1. So, if X kg of F_1 are purchased, this will contain 0.2X kg of I_1. Similarly, 15 per cent of F_2 is ingredient I_1. So every kg purchased of F_2 yields 0.15 kg of I_1. Hence, if Y kg of F_2 are purchased, this will contain 0.15Y kg of I_1. Therefore, if X kg of F_1 and Y kg of F_2 are purchased, then the feed will contain $0.2X + 0.15Y$ kg of ingredient I_1. Remember that the constraint is that the blend of the two types of feed must contain a minimum of 2 kg of this ingredient. This gives:

   $0.2X + 0.15Y \geq 2$

Similar reasoning yields the remaining three constraints:

   $0.25Y \geq 1 \ (I_2)$

   $0.25X \geq 1.5 \ (I_3)$

   $0.2X + 0.3Y \geq 3 \ (I_4)$

So the formulated problem is:

Determine values for X and Y that will:			
Minimise Cost $= 2X + 3Y$			
Subject to:			
0.20X +	0.15Y $\geq$		2
	0.25Y $\geq$		1
0.25X		$\geq$	1.5
0.20X +	0.30Y $\geq$		3

Notice that it is already the case, from the second and third constraints, that X and Y must both be non-negative.

2. The graph for this problem is shown in Figure 16. Since the constraints are of the 'greater than or equal to' type, the feasible region is the area above and to the right of the three lines $0.25X = 1.5$, $0.25Y = 1$ and $0.2X + 0.3Y = 3$.

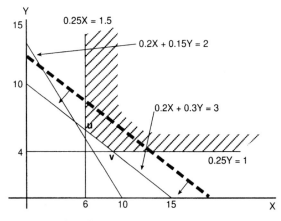

Figure 16: Solution to the livestock feed problem

Notice that the objective function line is parallel to the boundary of the constraint for I_4 (that is, the equation $0.2X + 0.3Y = 3$). Consequently, the optimal solution is not unique. So the solution is given by corners u and v, and any point between them.

The solution for corner u is given by the equations $X = 6$ and $0.2X + 0.3Y = 3$. Since we know that $X = 6$, we can calculate Y as follows:

$$0.3Y = 3 - 0.2X = 3 - (0.2 \times 6) = 1.8$$

And so $Y = 6$.

Cost is given by the formula Cost = $2X + 3Y$, and so will be £30 per day.

The solution for corner v is given by the equations $Y = 4$ and $0.2X + 0.3Y = 3$. Since we know that $Y = 4$, we can calculate X as follows:

$$0.2X = 3 - 0.3Y = 3 - (0.3 \times 4) = 1.8$$

And so $X = 9$. Again the cost will be £30 per day.

Multiple solutions are unusual in practice (especially in situations with more than two decision variables), but you should always look out for them.

The next activity will give you further practice in formulating and solving a maximisation problem. It also asks you to determine whether a change in the objective leads to a change in the optimal solution.

ACTIVITY 29

A workshop manufactures two types of doll: the *Cindy Lou* doll, with a selling price of £20 and variable costs of £8; and the *Sue Ellen* (moving mouth) doll, with a selling price of £32 and variable costs of £12.

The workshop has the capacity to produce 2,000 *Cindy Lou* dolls per day or 1,000 *Sue Ellen* dolls per day. The supply of plastic is just sufficient to produce 1,500 dolls of either type each day. The *Sue Ellen* requires a special mechanism to make its mouth move, and there are only 600 of these available per day.

1. Formulate and solve the problem, assuming that the workshop wishes to maximise daily contribution to profit.

2. Would this solution change if the workshop wanted to maximise sales revenue instead?

---

1. For the decision variables for this problem, let:

    X = the daily output of *Cindy Lou* dolls

    And let:

    Y = the daily output of *Sue Ellen* dolls

    The objective function is:

    Maximise Contribution = $12X + 20Y$

    (Remember that contribution is defined as revenue less variable costs.)

    As constraints we note the limitations upon workshop capacity, the supply of plastic and the supply of mouth mechanisms.

    The latter two constraints are:

    $X + Y \leq 1500$ (plastic limitation)

    $Y \leq 600$ (mouth mechanisms limitation)

    So far as production capacity is concerned, the workshop can produce either 2,000 *Cindy Lou* dolls or 1,000 *Sue Ellen* dolls or proportionate quantities of each per day.

    This gives as the constraint:

    $X + 2Y \leq 2,000$

    So, if $Y = 0$, then X has a maximum value of 2,000, and if $X = 0$, then Y has a maximum value of 1,000. Hence, the formulated problem is

Determine values for X and Y that will:

Maximise Contribution = 12X + 20Y

Subject to:

$$X \quad + \quad Y \quad \leq \quad 1{,}500$$
$$X \quad + \quad 2Y \quad \leq \quad 2{,}000$$
$$Y \quad \leq \quad 600$$
$$X \quad \quad \geq \quad 0$$
$$Y \quad \geq \quad 0$$

Figure 17 shows the graph for this problem, with the solution at the corner of the feasible region labelled as *v*.

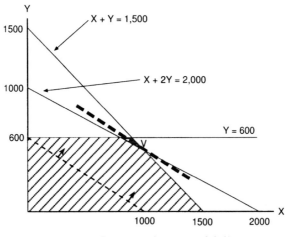

Figure 17: Optimal output of dolls

At the corner labelled *v*:

(1) X + 2Y = 2,000
(2) X + Y = 1,500

So, subtracting equation (2) from equation (1):

$$(X + 2Y) - (X + Y) \quad = \quad 2{,}000 - 1{,}500$$
$$X + 2Y - X - Y \quad = \quad 500$$

And so Y = 500 and X = 1,000.

As the contribution to profit is £12 per *Cindy Lou* doll (X) and £20 per *Sue Ellen* doll (Y), this yields a total daily contribution to profit of:

$$12X + 20Y = £22{,}000$$

2. If the workshop seeks to maximise revenue instead of maximising daily contribution, the objective function will be:

Maximise Revenue = 20X + 32Y

The constraints remain the same.

If we graph the objective function for Revenue = 20,000 = 20X + 32Y, we find that the line will be from (X = 1,000, Y=0) to (X = 0, Y ≈ 630). This is slightly steeper than the original objective function (see Figure 17). However, the solution corner remains unchanged.

Now try the remaining problem in this section.

ACTIVITY 30

Suppose that, by law, a certain type of slimming food must contain at least 3 per cent Vitamin A and at least 7 per cent Vitamin B. A manufacturer can obtain stocks of two compounds (*FIFO* and *LIFO*) with the following vitamin content:

	Vitamin A	Vitamin B
FIFO	2%	10%
LIFO	5%	6%

The intention is to blend *LIFO* and *FIFO* to make a new product called *VitaMagic*, which meets the minimum vitamin requirements. Initially the manufacturer considers that sales of *VitaMagic* are likely to be at least 120 kg per day. *FIFO* costs £4 per kg and *LIFO* £5 per kg.

Assume that the manufacturer wishes to minimise cost.

1. Formulate the problem.

2. Solve the problem to find the optimum proportions in which the two compounds should be blended.

---

1. This problem is rather more tricky to formulate correctly. Quantities of *LIFO* and *FIFO* have to be mixed to obtain VitaMagic. Hence, the decision variables are the number of kg of *FIFO* per day and the number of kg of *LIFO* per day. We shall call these X and Y respectively.

The objective function is:

Minimise Cost = 4X + 5Y

There are two constraints relating to minimum contents of Vitamin A and Vitamin B, and there is also a sales constraint, giving three constraints in total.

The sales constraint is comparatively straightforward. Daily sales of *VitaMagic*, we are told, will be greater than or equal to 120 kg. Now, *VitaMagic* simply consists of *LIFO* plus *FIFO*. So the number of kg of *VitaMagic* equals the number of kg of *FIFO* plus the number of kg of *LIFO* which is simply X + Y. So the constraint is:

$$X + Y \geq 120$$

More care is needed to sort out the constraints that relate to the two vitamins. Let us start with the Vitamin A requirement. *FIFO* contains 2 per cent Vitamin A and *LIFO* contains 5 per cent. *VitaMagic* must contain at least 3 per cent Vitamin A.

If X kg of *FIFO* are used, then it will contain 0.02X kg of Vitamin A. If Y kg of *LIFO* are used it will contain 0.05Y kg of Vitamin A. So, if X kg of *FIFO* are blended with Y kg of *LIFO*, there will be 0.02X + 0.05Y kg of Vitamin A in the mix. Hence, the proportion of Vitamin A in the blend will be:

$$\frac{0.02X + 0.05Y}{X + Y}$$

This has to be at least 0.03, so the Vitamin A constraint is:

$$\frac{0.02X + 0.05Y}{X + Y} \geq 0.03$$

Multiplying both sides by (X + Y) gives:

$$0.02X + 0.05Y \geq 0.03(X + Y)$$

$$0.02X + 0.05Y \geq 0.03X + 0.03Y$$

$$0.02X + 0.05Y - 0.03X - 0.03Y \geq 0$$

$$-0.01X + 0.02Y \geq 0$$

And finally, on multiplying throughout by 100:

$$-X + 2Y \geq 0$$

By similar reasoning, the Vitamin B constraint is given by:

$$\frac{0.1X + 0.06Y}{X + Y} \geq 0.07$$

$$0.1X + 0.06Y \geq 0.07 (X + Y)$$

$$0.1X + 0.06Y - 0.07X - 0.07Y \geq 0$$

$$0.03X - 0.01Y \geq 0$$

$$3X - Y \geq 0$$

So the formulated problem is:

> Determine values for X (kg of *FIFO*) and Y (kg of *LIFO*) that will:
>
>   Minimise Cost = 4X + 5Y
>
> Subject to:
>
> | | | | | |
> |---:|:--:|:---:|:--:|:--:|
> | X | + | Y | ≥ | 120 |
> | − X | + | 2Y | ≥ | 0 |
> | 3X | − | Y | ≥ | 0 |
> | X | | | ≥ | 0 |
> | | | Y | ≥ | 0 |

2. Figure 18 shows the graph for this problem.

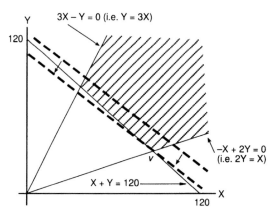

Figure 18: Solution to the VitaMagic blending problem

Some care is required when graphing the second and third constraints. Consider the constraint for Vitamin A, namely −X + 2Y ≥ 0.

It can be rearranged as 2Y ≥ X. (Move the −X across to the other side of the inequality and change its sign.)

Consider the graph of the equation 2Y = X (see Figure 18).

$$Y = 0 \Rightarrow X = (2 \times 0) = 0$$

So the graph must start from the origin.

Since the equation is linear, we require just one further point in order to draw the line. For example:

$$Y = 10 \Rightarrow X = (2 \times 10) = 20$$

We now need to determine the side of the line for which 2Y is greater than X. We can establish this by checking any point that does not lie along the line. An obvious point to choose is (X = 120, Y = 0). Clearly 120 is not less than '2 × 0'! Look again at Figure 18. The point we just explored lies below the line 2Y = X. It follows that the constraint is the area above or on the line 2Y = X.

Similarly the constraint $3X - Y \geq 0$ is the area below or on the line Y = 3X. Since the remaining constraint is $X + Y \geq 120$, the feasible region is the area above the line X + Y = 120 that is bounded by the lines Y = 3X and 2Y = X.

The solution is at the corner of the feasible region labelled as *v*. At this corner:

(1) $-X + 2Y = 0$

(2) $X + Y = 120$

Adding equation (1) and equation (2) gives:

$3Y = 120$

$Y = 40$

$X = 80$

In other words, to produce 120 kg of *VitaMagic,* the optimum blend is 80 kg of *FIFO* to 40 kg of *LIFO*. However, the proportions of the blend are independent of the level of sales. Why is this the case? The blend simply represents the cheapest way of producing *VitaMagic* while meeting the vitamin content constraints. Therefore we can say that the optimum blend is two parts of *FIFO* to one part of *LIFO*.

Summary

In this section of the unit, we have seen how to formulate and solve a two-variable linear programming problem using a graphical method. This consisted, firstly, of graphing the inequalities that constitute the constraints of a problem. We then identified the feasible region as the area common to these inequalities. Having graphed the objective function for one particular value, we then either moved the line out from the origin (for a maximisation problem) or in towards the origin (if the objective was to be minimised) until it was tangential to the feasible region. Apart from multiple solutions, the resulting optimal point was always at a corner of the feasible region. For a carefully drawn graph the solution can be obtained by reading off the coordinates at this point. However, a more satisfactory approach is to identify those lines that form this corner and to solve the corresponding equations simultaneously.

SECTION 3
Sensitivity Analysis of Solutions

Introduction

In Section 2, we considered how to solve linear programming problems through the use of graphs. In Section 3, we look at how these solutions react to changes to the input. This is sometimes referred to as **what-if analysis**. However, in the context of linear programming it is usually known as **sensitivity analysis**.

We start, in Section 3.1, by introducing the concept of **shadow prices** in the context of the doll manufacturing problem introduced in Section 2. In Section 3.2, we investigate the effect of changes to the constraints. Specifically, we examine how our solution to the doll manufacturing problem reacts to increases and reductions in the production capacity of the workshop. Finally, in Section 3.3, we look at the effect of changes to the objective function. For example, in the doll manufacturing problem our solution is based on certain assumptions about the contribution to profit per doll. In Section 3.3 we explore the effect of changing these assumptions.

By the end of this section you should be able to perform a sensitivity analysis on the solution to a linear programming problem.

3.1 Shadow prices

In any linear programming problem, we optimise an objective function (by maximising or minimising it), subject to a set of constraints. Since this optimum is always to be found at a corner of the feasible region, it follows that it must occur at a point where one or more of the constraints are exactly satisfied. For example, in the *RIP Upholsterers* problem (see Section 2.1 and in particular Figure 13) the constraints that were exactly satisfied at the optimal solution were those for the joinery and packaging departments. In the case of *Haven Manufacturing* (see Section 2.2 and in particular Figure 14) it was the two process constraints.

When a constraint is exactly satisfied it is said to be **binding**. By contrast, if at the optimal solution a constraint is not binding there will be some **slack** (when the constraint is of the 'less than or equal to' type), or some **surplus** (when it is of the 'greater than or equal to' type). For example, in the case of *RIP Upholsterers* neither the Dralon nor the leather upholstery constraints were binding (see Figure 13). Their slacks (or shortfalls) were that they could upholster an extra 75 *Diplomats* and 50 *Ambassadors* respectively per week. For *Myfanwy Mining Ltd* (see Section 2.3 and in particular Figure 15) the constraint for ordinary coal was not binding. Consequently more than the required 80 tonnes per day were to be extracted.

ACTIVITY 31

Look back to the doll manufacturing problem in Activity 29. (The solution is given in Figure 17.)

1. Which constraints are binding?

2. For the **non-binding** constraint(s), what is the size of the slack?

---

1. See Figure 17. The binding constraints are those for the workshop capacity and the supply of plastic.

2. Only the limitation on the number of mouth mechanisms is not binding at the solution. Since 600 mechanisms are available but only 500 are required (the output of *Sue Ellen* dolls) the slack is 100.

When a constraint is binding, a change in its right-hand side must impact upon the optimal value of the objective function. For example, consider the doll manufacturing problem in Section 2.4. With X as the daily output of *Cindy Lou* dolls, and Y as the daily output of *Sue Ellen* dolls, the formulated problem is:

Determine values for X and Y that will:

$$\text{Maximise Contribution} = 12X + 20Y$$

Subject to:

X + Y	$\leq$	1,500	(plastic constraint)
X + 2Y	$\leq$	2,000	(workshop capacity constraint)
Y	$\leq$	600	(moving mouth constraint)
X	$\geq$	0	
Y	$\geq$	0	

The solution is shown in Figure 19. At the optimal corner *v*, X (the number of *Cindy Lou* dolls) equals 1,000, and Y (the number of *Sue Ellen* dolls) equals 500. The resulting maximum daily contribution is:

$$(12 \times 1,000) + (20 \times 500) = £22,000$$

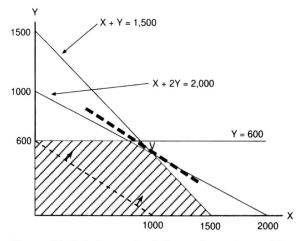

Figure 19: Solution to the doll manufacturing problem

As we saw in Activity 31, the supply of plastic is a binding constraint. It is given by:

$$X + Y \leq 1,500$$

Now suppose that we increase the right-hand side from 1,500 to 1,501. In other words, the supply of plastic is now sufficient to manufacture 1,501 dolls in total. Look at Figure 19. It is clear that the optimal solution will still be at the corner formed by the intersection of the lines $X + 2Y = 2,000$ (equation 1) and $X + Y = 1,501$ (equation 2).

We can solve the two equations simultaneously by subtracting equation (2) from equation (1):

$$(X + 2Y) - (X + Y) = 2,000 - 1,501$$

$$X + 2Y - X - Y = 499$$

$$Y = 499$$

Substituting 499 for Y in equation (2) gives:

$$X + 499 = 1,501$$

$$X = 1,501 - 499$$

$$X = 1,002$$

The resulting optimal contribution to profit is:

$$12X + 20Y = (12 \times 1,002) + (20 \times 499) = 12,024 + 9,980 = £22,004$$

So, increasing the supply of plastic by 1 unit has raised contribution by:

$$22,004 - 22,000 = £4$$

We refer to this additional contribution as the **shadow price** for this constraint.

The other binding constraint for the doll manufacturing problem is that for the workshop capacity.

ACTIVITY 32

For the doll manufacturing problem, determine the shadow price for the constraint set by workshop capacity. You should follow the same method as that used above. Be careful to return the right-hand side for the plastic constraint to its original value of 1,500.

This time we add 1 unit to the right-hand side of the workshop capacity constraint so that it becomes $X + 2Y \leq 2,001$.

Look at Figure 19 again. It is clear that the solution corner will be at the intersection of the lines:

$$(1) \quad X \quad + \ 2Y \ = \ 2,001$$
$$(2) \quad X \quad + \ \ Y \ = \ 1,500$$

Subtracting equation (2) from equation (1) gives a value of 501 for Y and, therefore, a value of 999 for X.

Contribution is now:

$$(12 \times 999) + (20 \times 501) = £22,008$$

This is an increase of £8. So the shadow price for the workshop capacity constraint is £8.

Let us summarise the procedure that we have followed to determine the shadow price for a binding constraint:

- increase the right-hand side of the constraint by 1 unit
- obtain the solution to the problem using the revised constraint
- calculate the resulting change in the objective function.

ACTIVITY 33

Suppose a constraint is not binding at the optimal solution. What will be its shadow price?

It must be 0. Since the constraint is not binding, a 1 unit increase in its right-hand side will leave the optimal value of the objective function unchanged.

For the doll manufacturing problem, the mouth mechanism constraint is not binding. Since mouth mechanisms are not being fully utilised, obtaining an extra one will add nothing to the optimal contribution.

This result should not be surprising as a key principle of economic theory is that scarcity generates value. It turns out that the solution to any linear programming problem always imputes the optimal value of the objective function wholly to the binding constraints.

To see that this is the case, consider the two shadow prices that we have obtained above. Multiplying each shadow price by the constraint availability (the right-hand side) gives:

(plastic shadow price × plastic availability) + (workshop capacity shadow price × workshop capacity available)

$$= (4 \times 1,500) + (8 \times 2,000) = £22,000$$

= the optimal contribution

This result always holds true (this is known as the **duality theorem**). However, we will not pursue it further here.

Why should a decision-maker be interested in the shadow prices for the binding constraints? Perhaps the following activity will provide an answer.

ACTIVITY 34

Suppose that, in the case of the doll manufacturing problem, additional quantities of plastic can be obtained at a cost of £2.50 per unit. What should be the response to this offer?

We know that (before allowing for the £2.50 per unit cost) each extra unit of plastic will add £4 to the optimal contribution. So, allowing for the extra cost, the gain to overall contribution will be £1.50 per extra unit. This suggests that the offer should be accepted.

In general, it must be beneficial to increase the amount used of a binding constraint if the incremental cost (if any) from so doing is less than its shadow price. However, this conclusion needs to be qualified. If the availability (the right-hand side quantity) of such a constraint is increased, there must come a point at which it will cease to be binding. It then becomes essential to determine when this will occur.

3.2 Sensitivity analysis of right-hand side range

Additional quantities of a constraint remain valuable (that is, have a positive shadow price) only so long as the constraint remains binding. Conversely, if the right-hand side of a constraint is reduced, a point may arise at which increasing scarcity generates an increase in the shadow price.

For example, in the doll manufacturing problem a sufficient increase in workshop capacity will eventually cause the shadow price for this constraint to fall from £8 per unit to £0. On the other hand, if workshop capacity were to be reduced then at some point the shadow price may well rise, reflecting this greater scarcity.

It is, therefore, important to determine the range of variation for the right-hand side of a constraint such that the shadow price remains unchanged. We refer to this as a sensitivity analysis of the right-hand side range.

In the case of the doll manufacturing problem, let us determine the right-hand side range for the workshop capacity constraint. Firstly, by how much can workshop capacity be increased before it ceases to be scarce? Remember that this constraint is given by $X + 2Y \leq 2,000$. So, if the right-hand side is increased, then the boundary equation will successively change to $X + 2Y = 2,001$, $X + 2Y = 2,002$ and so on. So the graph for this boundary equation will steadily shift to the right, staying parallel to the original line. Suppose it moves to the right until it cuts through the point labelled a in Figure 20.

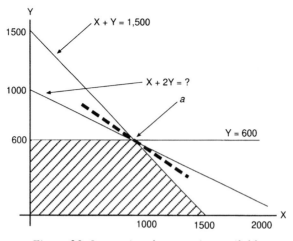

Figure 20: Increasing the capacity available

The feasible region will now be as shown in Figure 20 with the optimal corner being at *a*. Notice that this corner is now formed by the intersection of all three constraints. Now suppose that workshop capacity is increased still more. Then the boundary equation shifts further to the right and the workshop capacity ceases to be scarce. So we need to determine the value of the right-hand side of the constraint at the point at which the boundary equation cuts through the point *a*.

We know that the lines $Y = 600$ and $X + Y = 1{,}500$ intersect at the point *a*. Solving these two equations simultaneously gives a value of 600 for Y, and a value of 900 for X. We require that the boundary of the workshop capacity constraint passes through this point and so (see Figure 20) we must have:

$$X + 2Y = 900 + (2 \times 600) = 2{,}100$$

This represents a rise of 100 on the current availability. We conclude that the shadow price of £8 will hold only for a right-hand side increase up to this amount.

So far we have determined the upper limit to the right-hand side range such that the shadow price remains unchanged. We now need to investigate the lower limit (if one exists). Let us suppose that workshop capacity is reduced from the original quantity of 2,000. Then the boundary of the constraint shifts to the left, still staying parallel.

ACTIVITY 35

Is there a point at which the shadow price for the workshop capacity constraint becomes greater than £8 per unit?

If the answer is 'yes', when does this occur and what does the shadow price become?

There is a point at which the shadow price increases. To see why this is the case, let us reduce the workshop capacity to 1,500. Look at Figure 21: the constraint will now be $X + 2Y \leq 1{,}500$. The shaded area shows the new feasible region, with the corner labelled *b* being the optimal solution. At this point X equals 1,500 and Y equals 0.

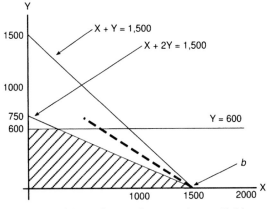

Figure 21: Reducing the capacity available

For successive reductions in workshop capacity from 2,000 down to 1,500, the optimal corner of the feasible region is still at the intersection of the plastic and workshop capacity constraints, and the shadow price remains at £8 per unit. Now suppose that workshop capacity is reduced further. The boundary of the workshop capacity constraint shifts to the left and in consequence the plastic constraint (its boundary is the line $X + Y = 1,500$) ceases to be binding. Since the moving mouth constraint is also not binding at the solution point *b* (none of the *Sue Ellen* dolls are being produced), it follows that only workshop capacity is scarce.

If the workshop capacity is reduced by a further unit, the boundary becomes $X + 2Y = 1,499$, and at the solution point X is now equal to 1,499. One less *Cindy Lou* doll will be manufactured and so contribution falls by £12. So if the workshop capacity falls below 1,500, the shadow price increases to £12.

We have established that the right-hand side range for the workshop capacity constraint is as shown in Table 2.

Constraint	Lower limit	Right-hand side	Upper limit
Capacity	1,500	2,000	2,100

Table 2: The right-hand side range for the capacity constraint

It is essential to determine the right-hand side range for a constraint. Knowledge of its shadow price is of little value without also knowing the range within which it remains unchanged. Working through the next activity will check that you have understood this.

ACTIVITY 36

The workshop has the opportunity to expand its workshop capacity by up to 200 units. It will then be able to produce either 2,200 *Cindy Lou* dolls, or 1,100 *Sue Ellen* dolls, or proportionate quantities of each, per day.

1. What is the new workshop capacity constraint?

2. Advise the workshop as to what action it should take.

---

1. The new workshop capacity constraint is $X + 2Y \leq 2,200$. When Y equals 0, then X (the number of *Cindy Lou* dolls) has a maximum of 2,200. Conversely, when X equals 0, then Y (the number of *Sue Ellen* dolls) has a maximum of 1,100.

2. The right-hand side for the workshop capacity constraint is now 2,200, an increase of 200 on its current value. However, from Table 2, it is clear that each unit rise above 100 will add nothing further to contribution because the shadow price will fall to 0.

   So our advice is that the workshop should expand capacity by only 100 of the 200 units available. Weekly contribution to profit will then increase by:

   $(8 \times 100) = £800$

So far we have considered the impact upon the optimal solution to a linear programming problem of any change in (and therefore any uncertainty regarding) the right-hand side values for the constraints. We now turn our attention to similar uncertainties with respect to the coefficients occurring in the objective function.

3.3 Sensitivity analysis of objective function coefficients

In the doll manufacturing problem, we needed to maximise the objective function $12X + 20Y$, in which the **coefficients** were the £12 and £20 per doll contribution to profit from dolls of each type. We now suppose that these coefficients either change, or are subject to error or uncertainty, and we explore the consequences by carrying out a sensitivity analysis.

Remember that the optimal solution to any linear programming problem is always established by shifting the graph of the objective function until it is tangential to the feasible region. (If we are dealing with a maximisation problem, we shift the graph outwards from the origin, and if we are dealing with a minimisation problem, we shift the graph inwards towards the origin.)

It follows that the solution will be found at one of the corners of the feasible region. Of course the objective function might be parallel to one of the constraints (the livestock feed problem in Section 2.4 was an example of this), but even then the multiple solutions will include corners of the feasible region. A key implication of this conclusion is that some variation in the coefficients of the objective function can take place and the optimal solution will remain unchanged.

For example, look at the formulation of the doll manufacturing problem. Suppose the contribution per *Cindy Lou* doll is increased from £12 to £14, everything else remaining unchanged. The objective function is now Maximise Contribution = 14X + 20Y.

We now pose the question 'will this change in the X coefficient be sufficient to alter the solution to the doll manufacturing problem?'. To answer this, we must start by determining how this change affects the graph of the objective function.

ACTIVITY 37

Graph both the original and revised objective functions for a contribution level of £16,800. How do the graphs compare?

Figure 22 shows the lines 12X + 20Y = 16,800 (the original objective function) and 14X + 20Y = 16,800 (the revised objective function).

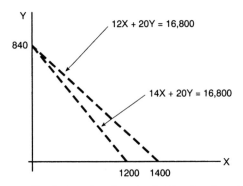

Figure 22: Original and revised objective functions

Comparing the two, we see that the revised objective function is steeper than the original. This simply reflects the fact that, because the X coefficient (the contribution per *Cindy Lou* doll) has increased, the same overall contribution level can be obtained by producing fewer dolls of this type.

Having established that the objective function becomes steeper, we now need to determine whether or not this will cause the solution to change. Look at Figure 23. As the objective function becomes steeper so the solution initially remains at the corner labelled *v*.

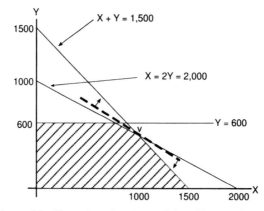

Figure 23: Changing the slope of the objective function

However, at some point the gradient of the objective function becomes the same as that for the line X + Y = 1,500. If the gradient increases further, the solution will jump to the corner labelled *w* in Figure 24. This is because a steeper objective function line will now cut through the feasible region at the point v, rather than be tangential to it. Not surprisingly, on comparing the new solution corner with the original, more will now be produced of that product whose objective function coefficient has increased. In this case, that product is the *Cindy Lou* dolls, represented by the variable X.

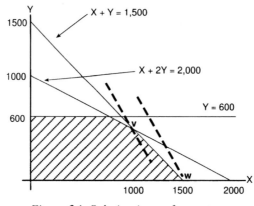

Figure 24: Solution jumps from v to w

ACTIVITY 38

Look at Figure 24 again. Write the objective function as Maximise Contribution = $pX + 20Y$. Determine the value of p (the X coefficient) at which the solution jumps from the corner labelled v to that labelled w.

You should have determined that the solution jumps to the corner w for values of p greater than £20.

For the solutions v and w to be equally optimal, the objective function must have the same gradient as the constraint boundary line $X + Y = 1,500$. For this to hold, the coefficients in the objective function must have the same 1:1 ratio. Since we know the Y coefficient to be 20, then the same must be true for the X coefficient.

So when p equals £20, the corners v and w yield the same level of contribution. For any value of p greater than this, the solution moves to the corner w.

At this point we have established that, for the solution to the doll manufacturing problem to remain unchanged, the coefficient on the X variable must be no greater than 20. In other words, the contribution per *Cindy Lou* doll must not exceed this figure. We obtained this result by:

- determining how the gradient of the objective function changes given increases in the X variable coefficient
- setting the gradient of the objective function equal to that of the constraint forming the feasible region boundary line between the original and the new optimal solution.

That leaves the lower limit for the X coefficient to be established.

ACTIVITY 39

Currently the contribution per *Cindy Lou* doll is £12. Using the method above, determine the minimum contribution per doll such that the solution remains at the corner v (see Figure 23).

Firstly, a decrease in the X coefficient (the contribution per *Cindy Lou* doll) causes the objective function to become less steep. A sufficient reduction will, therefore, jump the solution from the initial corner v to the point u (see Figure 25). This is because the less steep objective function will now cut through the feasible region at the point v. The tangent point will now be at u.

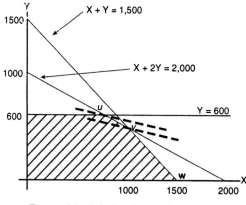

Figure 25: Solution jumps from v to u

Secondly, the solution will move from *v* to *u* when the gradient of the objective function becomes less steep than the constraint boundary line $X + 2Y = 2,000$.

For the solutions *v* and *u* to be equally optimal, the objective function must have the same gradient as the constraint boundary line $X + 2Y = 2,000$. For this to hold, the coefficients in the objective function must have the same 1:2 ratio. Since we know the Y coefficient to be 20, then the X coefficient must be 10. So the minimum contribution per *Cindy Lou* doll such that the solution remains at the corner *v* is £10.

Our conclusions regarding the X coefficient in the objective function can be summarised as follows: the optimal solution remains unchanged so long as the contribution per *Cindy Lou* doll is no lower than £10 and no higher than £20.

You should take care over the interpretation of such an analysis. What remains unchanged, so long as the X coefficient stays within these limits, is the optimal values for X and Y, the output of each type of doll. The overall contribution to profit will clearly not stay the same.

Summary

In this section we considered the role that sensitivity analysis plays in linear programming. It should now be clear that it is never sufficient simply to quote the solution to a linear programming problem, without some understanding as to how robust that solution is. Sensitivity analysis is a key part of the business decision analyst's toolbox. Any recommendations that are based upon a solution to a linear programming problem must always be tempered by a knowledge of how dependent such solutions may be upon the original data.

You may well have found this section of the unit relatively difficult. However, it is essential that you understand sensitivity analysis before you use computer software to generate solutions. Without such an understanding, you will not be able to interpret the results which the computer generates. In the next section of this unit, you will use computer software both to solve linear programming problems and to carry out sensitivity analysis on the solutions.

SECTION 4

Computer Solution of Linear Programming Problems

Introduction

In Sections 2 and 3, we used graphical methods to solve problems and to carry out a sensitivity analysis of the model. However, such methods cease to be usable as soon as a linear programming problem involves three or more decision variables.

Fortunately, there is a wide range of computer software available for use in such situations. In the rest of this unit you will be using one of the tools available in *Microsoft Excel*, called *Solver*. Although not as efficient as dedicated software, *Solver* will handle the size of problem that we are investigating very comfortably.

You may also have heard of an algorithm (that is, a computational procedure) called *Simplex*. This is used in dedicated linear programming software. Commercial software which utilises this algorithm is widely available and will run on any standard personal computer. In any more complex use of linear programming, such dedicated linear programming software is essential.

In Section 4.1 we study how to use *Solver* to produce solutions to a two-variable linear programming problem, and how to interpret the information which *Solver* generates. In Section 4.2 we look at a three-variable problem and also show how to use *Solver* to obtain an integer or 'whole number' solution. It is at this point that the value of using software really becomes apparent. Finally, in Section 4.3, we provide further practice in using software to solve decision problems by looking at three more multi-variable linear programming problems.

By the end of this section, you should be able to use *Microsoft Excel* and *Solver* to solve linear programming problems involving two or more decision variables. You should also be able to use *Microsoft Excel* and *Solver* to perform a sensitivity analysis on the solution.

Please note that, if you do not have *Solver* installed, you will need to install it before completing this section. You should be able to do this from your original set-up disks.

4.1 Using Solver

To show how to use *Solver*, and interpret the output that it generates, we will return to the *RIP Upholsterers* decision problem. You may well remember that the formulated problem (with A as the weekly output of *Ambassadors* and D as the weekly output of *Diplomats*) was:

Determine values for A and D that will:

> Maximise Contribution = 660A + 540D

Subject to:

$$3A + 2D \leq 900 \quad \text{(joinery constraint)}$$
$$A + D \leq 400 \quad \text{(packaging constraint)}$$
$$A \leq 150 \quad \text{(leather upholstery constraint)}$$
$$D \leq 375 \quad \text{(Dralon upholstery constraint)}$$
$$A \geq 0$$
$$D \geq 0$$

Open a new worksheet in *Microsoft Excel*. Enter the information as given in Table 3. Make sure that you enter the information in the correct cells, as shown in the table (you will need to widen the first column). Save your worksheet as **Rip.xls**.

	A
1	**RIP UPHOLSTERY PROBLEM**
2	
3	**Objective Function – Maximise Contribution**
4	
5	**Decision Variables**
6	Weekly Output of *Ambassador* Chairs (A)
7	Weekly Output of *Diplomat* Chairs (D)
8	
9	**Constraints**
10	Joinery Department
11	Packaging Department
12	Leather Upholstery
13	Dralon Upholstery
14	Non-Negativity *Ambassadors*
15	Non-Negativity *Diplomats*

Table 3: Spreadsheet for the RIP Upholsterers problem

To use *Solver* correctly, you need to ensure you set up the linear programming problem properly. The following instructions guide you through the process of completing the worksheet.

1. Cell B3 will hold the value for the contribution. *Solver* optimises (in this case maximises) the contents of this cell, subject to the constraints that we input.

   The objective function for this problem is:

   > Maximise Contribution = 660A + 540D

On your worksheet, cell B6 holds the value of A (weekly output of *Ambassadors*) and cell B7 holds the value of D (weekly output of *Diplomats*). So, in cell B3 enter the formula:

=660*B6+540*B7

Cell B3 will, for the moment, show the value 0.

2. Enter the value **0** into cells B6 and B7.

3. In cells C10 to C13 enter the right-hand side values for each of the four constraints. So:

in cell C10 enter **900**

in cell C11 enter **400**

in cell C12 enter **150**

in cell C13 enter **375**

4. In cells C14 and C15 enter the right-hand side for each of the non-negativity requirements.

So:

in cell C14 enter **0**

in cell C15 enter **0**

5. In cells B10 to B13 enter formulae for the left-hand side of each of the constraints.

We will start with the joinery constraint. This is $3A + 2D \le 900$. The left-hand side of this constraint is $3A + 2D$, and the value of A is contained in cell B6 while the value of D is contained in cell B7. So the formula to enter into cell B10 is:

=3*B6+2*B7

(Remember that, in *Excel*, a formula must always start with an '='.)

For the packaging constraint $A + D \le 400$, the formula to enter into cell B11 is:

=B6+B7

For the leather upholstery constraint $A \le 150$, the formula to enter into cell B12 is:

=B6

For the Dralon upholstery constraint $A \le 150$, the formula to enter into cell B13 is:

=B7

6. In cells B14 and B15 enter formulae for the left-hand side of the two non-negativity requirements. So, in cell B14 enter:

=B6

And in cell B15 enter:

=B7

That completes the first step in setting out the problem on your worksheet. We now need to call up *Solver* and provide it with further information.

From the *Microsoft Excel* menu bar, click on **Tools** and then on *Solver.* You will obtain a dialogue box similar to that shown in Figure 26.

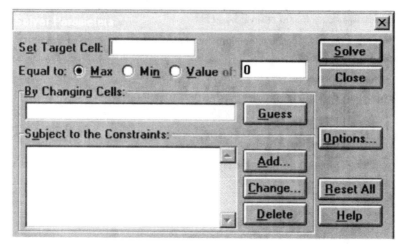

Figure 26: Solver Parameters dialogue screen

1. In the box entitled **Set Target Cell:**, enter the reference for the cell which you wish to optimise. For the current problem it is cell **B3**.

2. For **Equal to:**, the default setting is **Max**, which is correct for this problem. (You use **Min** for a minimisation problem.)

3. In the box entitled **By Changing Cells:**, enter the range for the cells that contain the decision variables. For the current problem it is the range **B6:B7**.

4. Click on the **Add** button, next to the box entitled **Subject to the Constraints:**. You obtain a dialogue window which you should complete as shown in Figure 27.

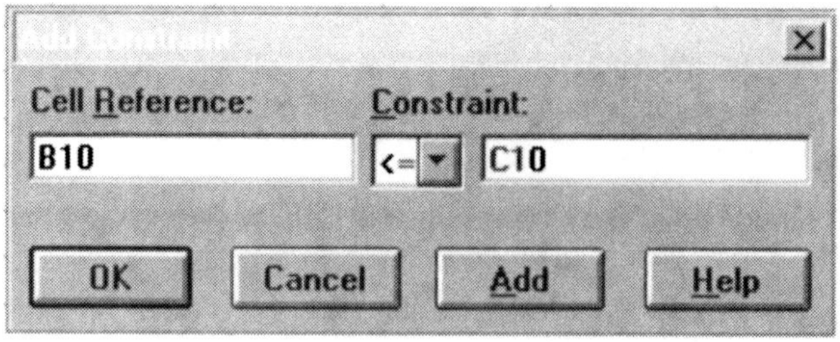

Figure 27: Completed Solver Parameters constraints addition box

Consider the first constraint in our problem, $3A + 2D \leq 900$.

The *Excel* formula for the left-hand side of this constraint is '=3*B6+2*B7'. This is contained in cell B10. The right-hand side of this constraint is 900. This value is contained in cell C10. We need to tell *Solver* that B10 ≤ C10. So complete the dialogue window by:

1. Entering the cell reference **B10** in the **Cell Reference** box.
2. Leaving the constraint at ≤ (Excel shows this as '<=').
3. Entering the cell reference **C10** in the narrow box on the right-hand side of the window.

Your dialogue window should now look similar to that shown in Figure 27 above.

Now enter the remaining constraints, namely:

B11 ≤ C11

B12 ≤ C12

B13 ≤ C13

B14 ≥ C14

B15 ≥ C15

Click on **Add** after entering each constraint, and then click **OK** when all the constraints have been entered. Take care: you need '≤' for the first three constraints and '≥' for the non-negativity conditions.

At this point your screen should be as shown in Figure 28.

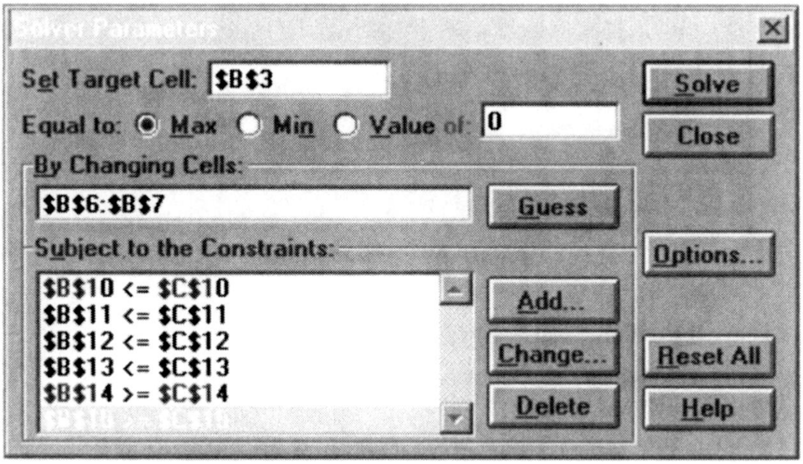

Figure 28: Completed Solver Parameters dialogue screen

Now click on **Options**. You obtain the *Solver* Options dialogue box shown in Figure 29.

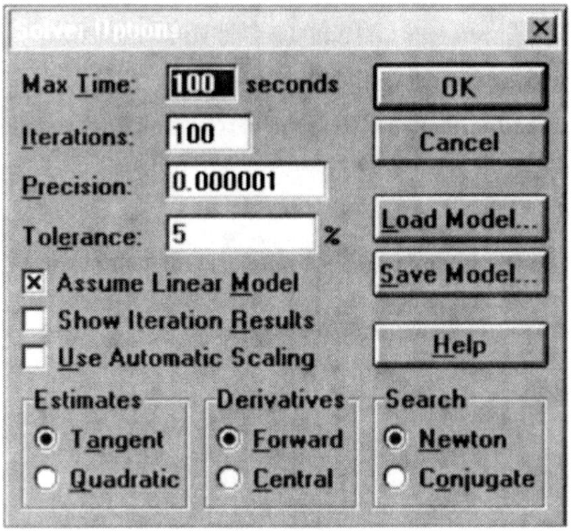

Figure 29: Solver Options dialogue box

Make sure that the **Assume Linear Model** box is checked. Otherwise, leave the dialogue box unaltered. Click on **OK** to leave *Solver* **Options** and return to the completed *Solver* **Parameters** window as shown in Figure 28 above.

To run *Solver*, click on **Solve**. Once *Solver* has found a solution, it will produce the dialogue box shown in Figure 30.

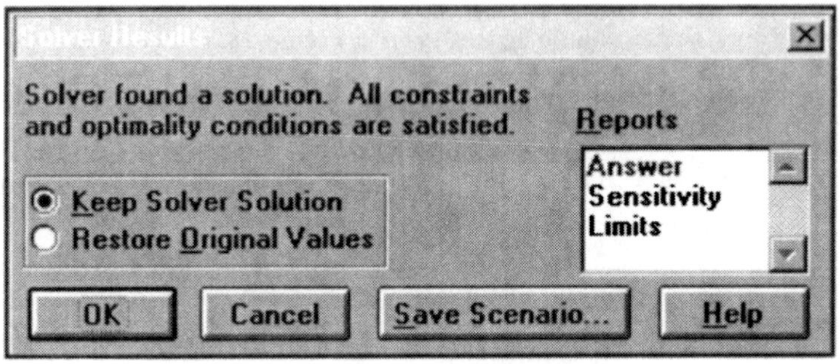

Figure 30: Solver Results

1. Leave the option **Keep Solver Solution** selected.

2. In the window entitled **Reports**, select all three options ('Answer', 'Sensitivity' and 'Limits').

3. Click on **OK** at the bottom left-hand corner of the dialogue box.

Solver produces four types of output. These are as follows: **solution values** for the problem, an 'Answer Report', a 'Sensitivity Report' and a 'Limits Report'.

The solution values are output onto your original worksheet. For the current problem you will find these values in cell B3, cells B6 to B7, and cells B10 to B15. These values are explained below.

The three reports are output as separate worksheets, entitled 'Answer Report', 'Sensitivity Report' and 'Limits Report'.

We will start with the solution values. These are shown in Table 4.

	A	B	C
1	**RIP UPHOLSTERY PROBLEM**		
2			
3	**Objective Function – Maximise Contribution**	228000	
4			
5	**Decision Variables**		
6	Weekly Output of *Ambassador* Chairs (A)	100	
7	Weekly Output of *Diplomat* Chairs (D)	300	
8			
9	**Constraints**		
10	Joinery Department	900	900
11	Packaging Department	400	400
12	Leather Upholstery	100	150
13	Dralon Upholstery	300	375
14	Non-Negativity *Ambassadors*	100	0
15	Non-Negativity *Diplomats*	300	0

Table 4: Solution values for the RIP Upholsterers problem

Cell B3 gives the maximum contribution as £228,000. Cells B6 and B7 give the optimal outputs as 100 *Ambassadors* and 300 *Diplomats*. These values are repeated in cells B14 and B15.

Cells B10 to B13 give the total amount of the resource that is used up. So cells B10 and B11 show that there is no **slack** or unused capacity in either the joinery or packaging departments. In other words, these constraints are binding. However, there is unused capacity in both the upholstery sections. The leather section could handle another 50 chairs and the Dralon section another 75.

We now turn to the 'Answer Report'. Click on the worksheet tab to obtain the 'Answer Report' sheet. A quick check tells you that this does not provide any information that is additional to what we already know from the solution values, and so we will not discuss it any further here.

The 'Limits Report' also does not add much to what we now know, and can be ignored.

Much more useful is the 'Sensitivity Report'. Click on the worksheet tab for this sheet. You obtain the output shown in Table 5.

Changing Cells						
Cell	Name	Final Value	Reduced Cost	Objective Coefficient	Allowable Increase	Allowable Decrease
$B$6	Weekly Output of Ambassador Chairs (A)	100	0	660	150	120
$B$7	Weekly Output of Diplomat Chairs (D)	300	0	540	120	100
Constraints						
Cell	Name	Final Value	Shadow Price	Constraint R.H. Side	Allowable Increase	Allowable Decrease
$B$10	Joinery Department	900	120	900	50	75
$B$11	Packaging Department	400	300	400	25	25
$B$12	Leather Upholstery	100	0	150	1E+30	50
$B$13	Dralon Upholstery	300	0	375	1E+30	75
$B$14	Non-Negativity Ambassadors	100	0	0	100	1E+30
$B$15	Non-Negativity Diplomats	300	0	0	300	1E+30

Table 5: 'Sensitivity Report' for the RIP Upholsterers problem

The output for the **Constraints** at the bottom of the table gives the **Shadow Price** for each constraint and the **Allowable Increase** and the **Allowable Decrease** for the right-hand side of each constraint. (Note that *Microsoft Excel* outputs what it calls shadow prices for the two non-negativity conditions. This makes no sense and should be ignored. Similarly, ignore the allowable increase and the allowable decrease for the non-negativity conditions.)

For the joinery constraint, the £120 per unit shadow price holds for a right-hand side range from 825 up to 950. That is, the original right-hand side constraint of 900 can be increased by up to 50 or decreased by up to 75 without affecting the shadow price. For the packaging constraint, the £300 shadow price holds for a right-hand side range from 375 to 425.

We saw in Table 4 that there was unused capacity in the leather upholstery department and so the shadow price for this constraint is 0. This situation will obviously remain unchanged for any increase to the capacity of this department (that is, to the right-hand side of this constraint). The entry in the 'Allowable Increase' column for this department, namely 1E+30, is scientific notation for 10^{30}. This is the highest number that *Solver* is able to output! It simply states that the zero shadow price holds for any increase beyond a capacity of 150. The entry for the Dralon upholstery department in this column has the same interpretation. Remember that you should ignore the entries relating to the non-negativity conditions.

The output for what *Microsoft Excel* calls the **Changing Cells** relates to our decision variables: the weekly output of *Ambassadors* and *Diplomats*. As you should remember, the objective coefficient is the contribution to profit per chair produced. So our 'Sensitivity Report' tells us that for *Ambassadors* the contribution to profit could be any value between £540 and £810 without affecting the solution value of 100 *Ambassadors* and 300 *Diplomats* produced per week. And for *Diplomats* the contribution to profit could be any value between £440 and £660 without affecting the solution values.

The solutions obtained from the 'Sensitivity Report' are based on the assumption that all other elements of the problem remain unchanged. That is, we can only vary one element (objective coefficient of *Ambassadors*, shadow price of packaging constraint and so forth) at a time. Ignore the column headed 'Reduced Cost'. We will not be investigating this in this unit.

So *Solver* gives us all the information that we need: the optimal values for the decision variables and the objective function, and a full sensitivity analysis. Of course, in the case of the *RIP Upholsterers* problem we could easily find the solution by graphical means. However, *Solver* comes into its own as soon as we turn to more realistic linear programming problems with more than two decision variables, since in these cases graphs cannot be used. Solving the problem facing *Peach Electronics* (see Section 4.2 below) will demonstrate this.

4.2 Solving a problem with three decision variables

Peach Electronics is expanding its plant in south Wales. The company plans to add to its existing products by manufacturing a range of recordable compact discs to be used for the long-term storage of computer data. Currently, three types of CD are contemplated, each with a different storage capacity. Details are given in Table 6.

CD type	Capacity
A	950 MB
B	800 MB
C	650 MB

Table 6: CD product range

Compact disc manufacture requires specialised equipment, and *Peach Electronics* expects to spend £743,750 before production can start. As a business decision analyst consulted by *Peach Electronics*, you have been commissioned to determine how many of each type of disk *Peach Electronics* would need to produce to recoup this initial outlay, with a minimal additional expenditure on variable costs. Relevant information supplied by the accounts department is summarised in Table 7.

CD type	Variable cost per CD (£s)	Selling price per CD (£s)
A	6.60	10.50
B	5.89	8.99
C	5.30	7.99

Table 7: Variable costs and selling prices of CDs

Peach Electronics' market research suggests that, at these prices, it could sell at least 25,000 type A discs, 80,000 type B discs, and 90,000 type C discs. The company also expects sales of type C discs to be at least equal to the combined sales of discs of type A and type B.

Peach Electronics' production director has stressed that it is unlikely that more than 250,000 CDs in total can be manufactured, given the investment that *Peach Electronics* has made in its plant. Also, various logistical problems on the shop floor lead to the conclusion that the number of type B CDs manufactured is unlikely to exceed 110,000.

To start we need to formulate the problem. Only then can we use *Solver* to obtain the solution.

ACTIVITY 40

What are the decision variables for this problem?

This is usually the most straightforward step in formulating any linear programming problem. Here it is clear that the decision variables are the quantities of each type of compact disc. We will let:

A = the number of CDs of type A

B = the number of CDs of type B

C = the number of CDs of type C

Having identified the decision variables, the next step is to specify the objective function.

ACTIVITY 41

What is the objective function?

The objective is to minimise variable production costs. So the objective function is:

Minimise Variable Cost = 6.6A + 5.89B + 5.3C

We now need to sort out the constraints. These are of three types:

- those that result from the market research that *Peach Electronics* has undertaken
- those that result from limitations upon production of the discs
- the requirement to break even.

ACTIVITY 42

Write down the four constraints that result from the market research.

According to the market research department, *Peach Electronics* can expect to sell at least 25,000 type A discs, 80,000 type B discs, and 90,000 type C discs. So formally we have that:

$A \geq 25,000$

$B \geq 80,000$

$C \geq 90,000$

In addition, we are told that the company expects sales of type C discs to be at least equal to the combined sales of discs of types A and B. So we can write that:

$C \geq A + B$

However, in order to use *Solver*, this inequality has to be arranged into the following expression:

$-A - B + C \geq 0$

This is because *Solver* requires that all constraints only have a coefficient on the right-hand side.

ACTIVITY 43

Write down the constraints that result from the limitations on production.

There are two production constraints. Firstly, the production director has stated that it is unlikely that more than 250,000 CDs in total can be manufactured from the existing plant. Total production is A + B + C and so the constraint is:

$$A + B + C \leq 250{,}000$$

There are also reasons why the output of type B discs cannot exceed 110,000 which gives:

$$B \leq 110{,}000$$

That leaves the final constraint to be considered.

ACTIVITY 44

Formulate the constraint which relates to the need to break even. This must be when the contribution to profit, from manufacturing and selling the discs, is sufficient to cover the initial outlay of £743,750.

Breakeven will occur when contribution $\geq$ fixed costs. The contribution per disc (that is, the selling price minus the variable cost) for each type is as follows:

$$\text{Type A} = 10.50 - 6.60 = 3.90$$

$$\text{Type B} = 8.99 - 5.89 = 3.10$$

$$\text{Type C} = 7.99 - 5.30 = 2.69$$

So breakeven occurs when:

$$3.9A + 3.1B + 2.69C \geq 743{,}750$$

The fully formulated problem is:

Determine values for A, B and C that will:

Minimise Variable Cost = 6.6A + 5.89B + 5.3C

Subject to:

3.9A	+ 3.1B	+ 2.69C		≥	743,750
A				≥	25,000
		B		≥	80,000
			C	≥	90,00
−A	− B	+	C	≥	0
A	+ B	+	C	≤	250,000
		B		≤	110,000

(Notice that, because of the sales constraints upon A, B and C, it is already the case that the three decision variables must be non-negative, so we have no need to explicitly state this.)

Since this problem has three decision variables, it cannot be solved graphically and so we need to make use of *Solver*. Start by setting up a worksheet containing the information shown in Table 8, including the figures in cells B6 to B8. Save your worksheet as **Peach.xls**.

	A	B	C
1	**PEACH ELECTRONICS PROBLEM**		
2			
3	**Objective Function – Minimise Variable Costs**		
4			
5	**Decision Variables**		
6	Output of Type A CDs	0	
7	Output of Type B CDs	0	
8	Output of Type C CDs	0	
9			
10	**Constraints**		
11	Breakeven requirement		
12	Minimum Production Type A		
13	Minimum Production Type B		
14	Minimum Production Type C		
15	Market Research re Sales of Type C		
16	Overall limit on Production		
17	Production limit for Type B		

Table 8: Worksheet for Peach Electronics

ACTIVITY 45

Complete the worksheet as follows.

    1. Enter a formula for the objective function in B3.

    2. Enter the right-hand side values of the constraints in cells C11 to C17.

    3. Enter formulae for the left-hand side of the constraints in cells B11 to B17.

---

    1. In cell B3 you should have entered the formula:

        =6.6*B6+5.89*B7+5.3*B8

    2. In cells C11 to C17 you should have entered the following values:

        743750 (in cell C11)

        25000 (in cell C12)

        80000 (in cell C13)

        90000 (in cell C14)

        0 (in cell C15)

        250000 (in cell C16)

        110000 (in cell C17)

    3. In cells B11 to B17 you should have entered the following formulae:

        =3.9*B6+3.1*B7+2.69*B8 (in cell B11)

        =B6 (in cell B12)

        =B7 (in cell B13)

        =B8 (in cell B14)

        =–B6–B7+B8 (in cell B15)

        =B6+B7+B8 (in cell B16)

        =B7 (in cell B17)

ACTIVITY 46

Now call up *Solver* and complete the problem input. Do not obtain a report yet. We will do that later.

Care is needed when entering the constraints. You should have the following *Solver Parameters* dialogue box when you have entered all the constraints.

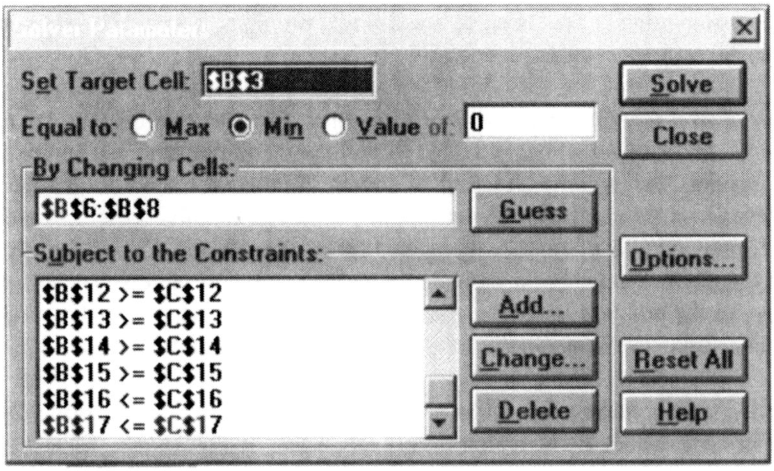

Figure 31: Completed Solver Parameters dialogue box for Peach Electronics

Now that you have input the problem, you can obtain the solution.

Click on **Options** to check that **Assume Linear Model** has been selected. Then click on **Solve**, to obtain the solution to this problem. Do not ask for the three reports.

You should obtain the solution shown in Table 9.

	A	B	C
1	**PEACH ELECTRONICS PROBLEM**		
2			
3	**Objective Function – Minimise Variable Costs**	1401808	
4			
5	**Decision Variables**		
6	Output of Type A CDs	42572.08	
7	Output of Type B CDs	80000	
8	Output of Type C CDs	122572.1	
9			
10	**Constraints**		
11	Breakeven requirement	743750	743750
12	Minimum Production Type A	42572.08	25000
13	Minimum Production Type B	80000	80000
14	Minimum Production Type C	122572.1	90000
15	Market Research re Sales of Type C	0	0
16	Overall limit on Production	245144.2	250000
17	Production limit for Type B	80000	110000

Table 9: Solution values for the Peach Electronics problem

Examining cells B6 to B8 we notice that this is not an integer (or 'whole number') solution. Although the problem facing *Peach Electronics* is a very simple one, there is no reason why we should expect to obtain integer outcomes. Certainly, when linear programming is used to solve a real-world problem, it would be very unusual for it to generate nice whole numbers!

There are two ways in which we can respond to this situation. Firstly, we could ignore the fact that *Solver* has provided a continuous solution, and just approximate these results. Our recommendation to *Peach Electronics* would then be that breakeven can be reached with minimum additional variable cost if it were to manufacture 42,572 of type A discs, 80,000 of type B and 122,572 of type C. However, there are potential dangers in making the assumption that an integer solution to the problem is always close to the continuous solution. It is probably a reasonable thing to assume in this case, but it is not always true.

Secondly, we can make a few minor additions to our problem, thus requiring *Solver* to generate a whole number solution. Look back at Figure 31. As additional constraints, we now want the output in cells B6 to B8 to be integers and so we need to include this within the *Solver* parameters. To do this, reopen *Solver* and click **Add** (to add additional constraints). You will see the **Add Constraint** dialogue box as shown in Figure 32.

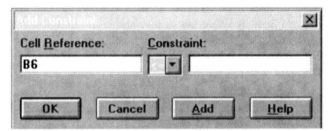

Figure 32: Add Constraint - Specifying an Integer Constraint

Type **B6** in the **Cell Reference:** window. Click on the down arrow below the heading **Constraint:**, and select **Int**.

Click **Add** and repeat this for cells B7 and B8.

Then click on **OK** followed by Solve to obtain the output shown in Table 10.

	A	B	C
1	**PEACH ELECTRONICS PROBLEM**		
2			
3	**Objective Function – Minimise Variable Costs**	1401819	
4			
5	**Decision Variables**		
6	Output of Type A CDs	42573	
7	Output of Type B CDs	80000	
8	Output of Type C CDs	122573	
9			
10	**Constraints**		
11	Breakeven requirement	743756.1	743750
12	Minimum Production Type A	42573	25000
13	Minimum Production Type B	80000	80000
14	Minimum Production Type C	122573	90000
15	Market Research re Sales of Type C	0	0
16	Overall limit on Production	245146	250000
17	Production limit for Type B	80000	110000

Table 10: Revised integer solution for Peach Electronics

Comparing this with the solution shown in Table 9, the differences are marginal.

Section 4.3 asks you to solve some more problems.

4.3 Other problems

We have seen that *Solver* allows us to solve problems with more than two variables, that it can provide us with sensitivity analyses of our results, and that it allows us to readjust models to take account of the requirement to produce integer or 'whole number' outcomes. In this section you will gain further practice in applying *Solver* to a range of linear programming problems.

ACTIVITY 47

The investment manager of the *Wessex Pension Fund* has £1,500,000, which she wishes to invest in fixed interest securities. She is aware that such investments carry a varying degree of risk and, whilst seeking to achieve the maximum return for the fund, needs to observe some caution. From a range of possibilities, she has narrowed down her interest to five particular securities, which we will call A, B, C, D and E. The table below shows the current yield for each security, per £100 invested.

Security	Yield (%)
A	10
B	8
C	6
D	5
E	4

Yields on securities A, B, D and E are expected to remain unchanged over the coming year, but there is some doubt as to whether the current modest yield on security C is sustainable.

The manager has decided that the total amount invested in securities A and B be no more than 50 per cent of that invested in securities C, D and E. Furthermore, for every £1 invested in security A at least £3 must be invested in either D or E.

1. Advise her as to the investments that should be made. To do this, you will need to formulate and solve the problem. (Enter the data into a worksheet and save it as **Pension.xls**.)

2. If the yield on security C were to fall to 5.5 per cent, would your advice remain the same? Use the 'Sensitivity Report' to help you decide.

---

1. We will start by formulating the problem. The decision variables are:

   A = £s invested in security A

   B = £s invested in security B

   C = £s invested in security C

   D = £s invested in security D

   E = £s invested in security E

   Total return is calculated by summing the yield from investment in each of the securities. This can be expressed as:

   $0.1A + 0.08B + 0.06C + 0.05D + 0.04E$

   The investment manager's objective is to maximise return, so the objective function is to:

   Maximise $0.1A + 0.08B + 0.06C + 0.05D + 0.04E$

   The constraint on the total investment is:

   $A + B + C + D + E = 1,500,000$

In addition, the total sum invested in securities A and B must be no more than 50 per cent of that invested in securities C, D and E. So:

$$A + B \leq 0.5(C + D + E)$$

$$A + B \leq 0.5C + 0.5D + 0.5E$$

$$A + B - 0.5C - 0.5D - 0.5E \leq 0$$

That leaves the specific restriction on investment in security A: every £1 invested in this security must be matched by at least £3 invested in either D or E. This gives:

$$A \leq \frac{(D + E)}{3}$$

$$3A \leq D + E$$

$$3A - D - E \leq 0$$

Hence the formulated problem is as follows.

Determine values for A, B, C, D and E that will:

Maximise Return $= 0.1A + 0.08B + 0.06C + 0.05D + 0.04E$

Subject to:

A + B	+	C +	D	+	E	=	1,500,000
A + B	−	0.5C −	0.5D	−	0.5E	≥	0
3A		−	D	−	E	≤	0
A						≥	0
	B					≥	0
		C				≥	0
			D			≥	0
					E	≥	0

Since there are five decision variables, we need to use *Solver*. Table 11 shows the solution that it generates.

	A	B	C
1	**Wessex Pensions Fund**		
2			
3	**Objective Function – Maximise Return**	100000	
4			
5	**Decision Variables**		
6	Investment in Security A (A)	0	
7	Investment in Security B (B)	500000	
8	Investment in Security C (C)	1000000	
9	Investment in Security D (D)	0	
10	Investment in Security E (E)	0	
11			
12	**Constraints**		
13	Total Investment	1500000	1500000
14	Limitation on Investment in A and B	0	0
15	Limitation on Investment in A	0	0
16	Non-Negativity A	0	0
17	Non-Negativity B	500000	0
18	Non-Negativity C	1000000	0
19	Non-Negativity D	0	0
20	Non-Negativity E	0	0

Table 11: Solution values for the Wessex Pension Fund problem

Our advice would be to invest £500,000 in security B and £1,000,000 in security C.

2. To determine whether our advice would remain the same if the yield on security C were to fall to 5.5 per cent, you need to look at the 'Sensitivity Report' that *Solver* generates. An extract from this report is shown in Table 12.

Name	Final Value	Reduced Cost	Objective Coefficient	Allowable Increase	Allowable Decrease
Investment in Security A (A)	0	0	0.1	0.01	0.02
Investment in Security B (B)	500000	0	0.08	0.02	0.01
Investment in Security C (C)	1000000	0	0.06	0.02	0.003333333
Investment in Security D (D)	0	0	0.05	0.003333333	1E+30
Investment in Security E (E)	0	0	0.04	0.013333333	1E+30

Table 12: Extract from the Sensitivity Report for the Wessex Pensions Fund problem

In this problem, the objective coefficient is the percentage yield per investment. The information we are interested in is contained in the columns headed 'Allowable Increase' and 'Allowable Decrease'. So our 'Sensitivity Report' tells us that, for security C the yield could be any value between approximately 5.7 per cent and 8 per cent without affecting the solution values of an investment of £500,000 in security B and an investment of £1,000,000 in security C. For security B the yield could be any value between 7 per cent and 10 per cent without affecting the solution values. As before, the solutions obtained from the 'Sensitivity Report' are based on the assumption of all other elements of the problem remaining unchanged.

It follows that our advice would not remain the same if the yield on security C fell to 5.5 per cent. This is because 5.7 per cent is the lowest value for the yield on security C for which our solution values remain unchanged.

You may well find the next activity rather more difficult. The key skill in linear programming is sorting out the problem and formulating it correctly. Once that has been done, the process of solution is quite straightforward. The questions that you should always ask yourself are:

- what are the decision variables?
- what is the objective?
- what factors are constraining pursuit of this objective?

In working through the next activity, you should keep these three questions firmly in mind.

ACTIVITY 48

Peterson Builders has just acquired a 40-acre site on which it intends to erect residential dwellings. Three types of house are under consideration. Since the company is undecided as to what names to use for these houses, they are for the moment referred to as types *Alpha, Beta* and *Gamma: Alpha* houses are detached luxury four-bedroom houses; *Beta* houses are detached three-bedroom houses; and *Gamma* houses are semi-detached three-bedroom houses.

Peterson Builders has planning permission to erect homes on the site, provided that the average density of houses does not exceed 8 per acre. *Alpha* houses are to be built to a density of 4 per acre, and will make a contribution to profit of £30,000 per house. *Beta* houses are to be built to a density of 6 per acre, and will make a contribution to profit of £20,000 per house. Finally, *Gamma* houses are to be built to a density of 12 per acre, and will make a contribution to profit of £12,000 per house.

On the basis of some market research, *Peterson Builders* has decided that the number of *Gammas* should be no more than four times the number of *Alphas*.

1. Formulate the problem.

2. Use *Microsoft Excel* and *Solver* to solve the problem to decide how many houses *Peterson Builders* should build. (Enter the data into a worksheet and save it as **Peterson.xls.**)

---

1. The decision variables are the quantities of the three types of houses. So we will let:

A = the number of *Alphas*

B = the number of *Betas*

G = the number of *Gammas*

The aim of the decision-maker is to generate the maximum contribution to profit by building the three types of house. Each *Alpha* makes a contribution to profit of £30,000, each *Beta* makes a contribution to profit of £20,000, and each *Gamma* makes a contribution to profit of £12,000. So the total contribution to profit of the three types of house is:

30,000A + 20,000B + 12,000G

So the objective function for this situation is to:

Maximise 30,000A + 20,000B + 12,000G

Usually it is the formulation of the constraints that causes problems. There are three constraints for this problem. Let us take them in turn.

Planning permission has been given for the site, on condition that the average density of houses is no more than 8 per acre. The total number of houses built must be equal to A + B + G and, since there are 40 acres available, this constraint specifies that:

$$\frac{A + B + G}{40} \leq 8$$
$$A + B + G \leq 320$$

Peterson Builders also has its own density requirements for each type of house. These are 4 per acre for *Alphas*, 6 per acre for *Betas* and 12 per acre for *Gammas*. These are additional to the planning permission restriction.

You may have thought that these requirements generate three constraints, but that is wrong. Acres used up to build *Alphas*, for example, mean that fewer *Betas* and *Gammas* can be erected and so the three house types cannot be considered separately. Suppose that *Peterson Builders* builds 80 *Alphas*, then this will use up 20 acres (80 ÷ 4). So if it builds A *Alphas*, then A/4 acres will be used. Similarly, if it builds B *Betas*, then B/6 acres will be used up.

Likewise, G *Gammas* will use G/12 acres. This can be stated in a single formula as follows:

Total Acreage Used = A/4 + B/6 + G/12

The restriction is that *Peterson Builders* only has 40 acres available. This gives us the following constraint:

A/4 + B/6 + G/12 ≤ 40

On multiplying throughout by 12, this gives us:

3A + 2B + G ≤ 480

Finally, we need to take note of the market research information. We are told that, on the basis of this, *Peterson Builders* has decided that the number of Gammas be no more than four times the number of *Alphas*. We can immediately write down this constraint as it stands, namely:

G ≤ 4A

Rearranging this to meet *Solver* requirements gives as the third constraint:

− 4A + G ≤ 0

The formulated problem is, therefore:

Determine values for A, B and G that will:

Maximise 30,000A + 20,000B + 12,000G

Subject to:

	A	+	B	+	G	≤	320
	3A	+	2B	+	G	≤	480
	−4A			+	G	≤	0
	A					≥	0
			B			≥	0
					G	≥	0

---

2. Using *Solver*, the solution to this problem is shown in Table 13.

	A	B	C
1	*Peterson Builders*		
2			
3	**Objective Function – Maximise Contribution**	5280000	
4			
5	**Decision Variables**		
6	Number of type *Alpha* Houses (A)	80	
7	Number of type *Beta* Houses (B)	0	
8	Number of type *Gamma* Houses (G)	240	
9			
10	**Constraints**		
11	Overall Site Density	320	320
12	Density Requirement for each House Type	480	480
13	Market Research	–80	0
14			
15	**Non-Negativity Requirements**		
16	Type *Alpha* Houses	80	0
17	Type *Beta* Houses	0	0
18	Type *Gamma* Houses	240	0

Table 13: Solution values for the Peterson Builders problem

Our advice to *Peterson Builders* is, therefore, to erect 80 houses of type *Alpha* and 240 of type *Gamma*, for an optimal contribution to profit of £5,280,000.

Notice that in this optimal solution, *Peterson Builders* should not build any houses of type *Beta*. However, if the contribution figure per house (of this type) were to increase, there would come a point at which our advice would change. To discover by how much the contribution per *Beta* would have to increase, we can check the Sensitivity Report. An extract from this is shown in Table 14.

Changing Cells						
Cell	Name	Final Value	Reduced Cost	Objective Coefficient	Allowable Increase	Allowable Decrease
$B$6	Number of type Alpha Houses (A)	80	0	30000	6000	2000
$B$7	Number of type Beta Houses (B)	0	0	20000	1000	1E+30
$B$8	Number of type Gamma Houses (G)	240	0	12000	18000	2000

Table 14: Extract from the Sensitivity Report for the Peterson Builders problem

The second row in Table 14 shows that the objective function coefficient for B would have to rise by 1,000 before the solution would change. So, for a contribution figure per house in excess of £21,000 it becomes optimal for *Beta* houses to be built on the site. (This assumes that all other elements of the problem are unchanged.)

Now attempt the remaining activity in this section: it illustrates the use of linear programming to solve a scheduling problem.

ACTIVITY 49

Vigilant Security Services has a contract to provide 24-hour security for the *East Midshire Hospital Trust*. The number of security staff required for each duty period is shown in the table below.

Duty period	Time	Staff required
1	02.00 – 06.00	8
2	06.00 – 10.00	20
3	10.00 – 14.00	40
4	14.00 – 18.00	30
5	18.00 – 22.00	20
6	22.00 – 02.00	10

All security staff employed by *Vigilant Security Services* are required to work for two consecutive duty periods, for example from 06.00 to 14.00 hours. Staff can be asked to report for duty at the start of any of the duty periods.

Formulate and solve the problem to decide the minimum number of security staff *Vigilant Security Services* must employ in order to provide 24-hour cover. Save the data on a worksheet with the name **Vigilant.xls**.

As always we need to start by identifying the decision variables. So what are they here? Well we are told that staff can be asked to report for duty at the start of any of the six duty periods. So the six decision variables are the number of staff required to commence work at the beginning of each of these duty periods. Formally, we will let:

X_1 = the number starting at 02.00

X_2 = the number starting at 06.00

X_3 = the number starting at 10.00

X_4 = the number starting at 14.00

X_5 = the number starting at 18.00

X_6 = the number starting at 22.00

The total number of staff employed is given by the formula:

Staff Numbers $= X_1 + X_2 + X_3 + X_4 + X_5 + X_6$

Vigilant Security Services's objective is to minimise the number of security staff employed. Hence the objective function is:

Minimise $X_1 + X_2 + X_3 + X_4 + X_5 + X_6$

Now we need to formulate the constraints. Consider the 02.00 to 06.00 duty period. Eight security staff must be in place during that period. For this to be the case, they must either have started at 22.00 on the previous evening or at 02.00 at the start of this duty period. It follows that the number of staff on duty from 02.00 to 06.00 must be equal to the sum of X_1 and X_6. To guarantee that the staffing constraint is met, we must have that:

$X_1 + X_6 \geq 8$

By the same reasoning, the constraints for the remaining five duty periods are:

$X_1 + X_2 \geq 20$

$X_2 + X_3 \geq 40$

$X_3 + X_4 \geq 30$

$X_4 + X_5 \geq 20$

$X_5 + X_6 \geq 10$

Therefore, the formulated problem is:

Determine values for X_1 X_2 X_3 X_4 X_5 and X_6 that will:		
Minimise $X_1 + X_2 + X_3 + X_4 + X_5 + X_6$		
Subject to:		
$X_1 + X_6$	$\geq$	8
$X_1 + X_2$	$\geq$	20
$X_2 + X_3$	$\geq$	40
$X_3 + X_4$	$\geq$	30
$X_4 + X_5$	$\geq$	20
$X_5 + X_6$	$\geq$	10
$X_1, X_2, X_3, X_4, X_5, X_6$	$\geq$	0

Using *Solver* generates the solution shown in Table 15.

	A	B	C
1	*Vigilant Security Services*		
2			
3	**Objective Function – Minimise Staff Numbers**	68	
4			
5	**Decision Variables**		
6	Staff starting at 2.00 (X_1)	8	
7	Staff starting at 6.00 (X_2)	20	
8	Staff starting at 10.00 (X_3)	20	
9	Staff starting at 14.00 (X_4)	10	
10	Staff starting at 18.00 (X_5)	10	
11	Staff starting at 21.00 (X_6)	0	
12			
13	**Constraints**		
14	Requirement 2.00–6.00	8	8
15	Requirement 6.00–10.00	28	20
16	Requirement 10.00–14.00	40	40
17	Requirement 14.00–18.00	30	30
18	Requirement 18.00–22.00	20	20
19	Requirement 22.00–2.00	10	10
20			
21	**Non-Negativity**		
22	X_1	8	0
23	X_2	20	0
24	X_3	20	0
25	X_4	10	0
26	X_5	10	0
27	X_6	0	0

Table 15: Solution values for the Vigilant Security Services problem

The minimum number of security staff that Vigilant Security Services should employ is 68.

Summary

In this section of the unit we used the *Solver* utility in *Microsoft Excel* to obtain solutions to linear programming problems with two or more decision variables. Although two-variable problems can be correctly solved quite easily by graphical means, the use of computer-based approaches such as *Solver* (which, in addition to generating a solution, also provides a full sensitivity analysis) will produce results more quickly and with greater reliability. For problems with three or more variables, computer-based approaches will provide us with solutions which would be difficult to achieve by other means.

In Sections 4.1 and 4.2 we showed how to implement the *Solver* utility and used it to solve problems with two or more variables. Sometimes it is essential that solutions take only integer (or 'whole number') values, and we showed how such restrictions could be allowed for. In Section 4.3 of this unit, we gained further practice in applying *Solver* to a range of linear programming problems.

In the next section of this unit we look at a class of linear programming problems known as transportation problems.

SECTION 5
The Transportation Problem

Introduction

This section looks at a particular class of problem known as the **transportation problem.** This, as the name suggests, deals with the issue of transporting goods and components between locations. Businesses always need to supply their customers, and in many commercial operations the production side of the business is geographically separate from the storage and warehousing side. In such cases, if there are many sources of supply (producers) and many sources of demand (customers or storage warehouses) then the problem of transportation will arise. The transportation model provides techniques designed to solve such problems.

In Section 5.1 we use a case study of a supplier of personal computers to identify the main elements of a transportation problem. In Section 5.2 we provide a formal definition of the transportation problem and identify two ways in which it may be displayed: through the use of a diagram called a **network flow diagram** and through the use of a table or **matrix**. We then go on to provide an initial solution of the case study problem. In Section 5.3 we apply computer-based linear programming techniques to our case study from Section 5.1 and to another example of a transportation problem. Finally, in Section 5.4, we look at some possible complications to the transportation problem and explore ways of dealing with these complications.

By the end of this section you should be able to formulate and solve transportation problems using the appropriate linear programming techniques.

5.1 The main elements of a transportation problem

In this section we use a case study of a supplier of personal computers to identify the main elements of a transportation problem.

Case Study: Hercules Computers

Hercules Computers supplies desktop personal computers (PCs) to business customers. Rather than producing its own parts, the company buys sets of parts from two main suppliers, one based in Birmingham, the other based in Hull.

Hercules Computers has four plants. These assemble the parts bought in from Birmingham and Hull, and also serve as despatch points for the company's own customers. These plants are in Watford, Cardiff, Manchester and Durham.

Sets of parts can be shipped from either of the two suppliers to any of the four *Hercules Computers* plants. However, transportation costs vary widely depending upon the location of the supplier and the plant. *Hercules Computers* is very keen to ensure that these costs are kept to a minimum.

Per set of parts, the schedule of transportation costs is as follows:

Hull to Watford	£3.00
Hull to Cardiff	£9.00
Hull to Manchester	£9.00
Hull to Durham	£3.00
Birmingham to Watford	£1.50
Birmingham to Cardiff	£3.00
Birmingham to Manchester	£7.50
Birmingham to Durham	£10.50

Each of the *Hercules Computers* plants has a known demand for parts. During the period in question, Watford requires 1,400 sets, Cardiff requires 3,200 sets, Manchester requires 2,000 sets and Durham requires 1,400 sets. However, there are restrictions on the quantities of parts available. During the period in question, Hull is able to supply a maximum of 5,000 sets and Birmingham is able to supply a maximum of 3,000 sets.

Hopefully, you will be able to spot that we have the makings of an optimisation problem here. *Hercules Computers* wishes to send sets of PC parts from two possible sources of supply to its four assembly plants. In doing so, the company needs to keep a close eye on the capacity of its suppliers, and the demand requirements of its own customers. In linear programming language, anything the company does must be **feasible**. Additionally, the company wishes to schedule the movement of parts at the lowest possible cost to itself. In other words, the company wants an **optimal** solution.

ACTIVITY 50

1. What are the decision variables for *Hercules Computers?* How many such decision variables are there?

2. In devising an objective function for this problem, what is *Hercules Computers'* objective?

3. What are the constraints of the problem?

There is no need to express your answers mathematically at this stage, just write them down in words.

---

1. As with any linear programming problem, the decision variables are the factors whose variation causes changes in profit, costs, revenue and so forth (whatever is being maximised or minimised). You should be able to see that the amounts transported over each route are the important variables here. Consequently, there will be eight decision variables, one for each of the routes between the two suppliers and the four assembly plants.

2. *Hercules Computers'* objective is to minimise cost.

3. The constraints for this problem are of two types: the actual physical amounts available from each supplier and the requirements of each of the *Hercules Computers* assembly plants.

You might have spotted that the supply from the two suppliers exactly matches the demand from *Hercules Computers.* We refer to situations such as this as being balanced. Also, we assume that all of the eight transportation routes are available to us.

5.2 Displaying the transportation problem

We now have an informal definition of the transportation problem. The next step is to devise a formal method for displaying the relevant data, as opposed to the informal method adopted at the beginning of this section.

We will start by drawing a **network flow diagram** for the data. A network flow diagram consists of circles, referred to as **nodes**. One set of nodes represents sources, whilst the other set represents destinations. **Lines**, representing transportation routes, are drawn between the nodes, and it is usual to write numbers representing the appropriate demand, supply and transport cost data on to the diagram.

The network flow diagram for the *Hercules Computers* problem is shown as Figure 33.

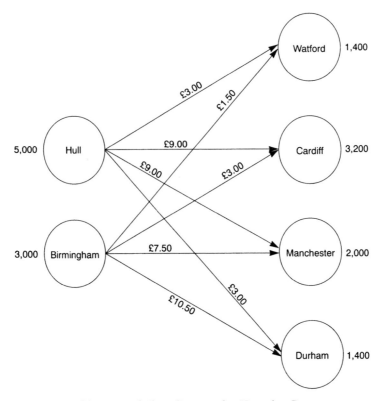

Figure 33: Network flow diagram for Hercules Computers

The number to the left of each source node shows the supply available, and the number to the right of each destination node shows the amounts demanded. Lines are drawn between each supplier and each destination. Because there are two suppliers and four buyers, there are eight such lines, each one representing a possible route by which goods could be shipped. Finally, the cost of transporting one unit on each route is shown on the line representing that route.

Network flow diagrams are a useful way of showing the structure of a particular transportation problem though, as you can probably imagine, they become very cumbersome when the number of sources and destinations grows larger. Instead of drawing a network flow diagram, a clearer and more concise way to display the data for a problem is via a table or **matrix**.

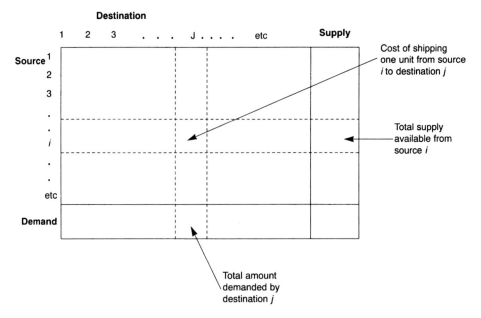

Figure 34: Tabular display for a transportation problem

The rows of the table usually represent the sources of the goods, while the columns represent the destinations. The amount demanded by each destination is recorded as a column total, while the amount available at each source is shown as a row total. The cost of transporting a unit between source *i* and destination *j* is entered in cell *ij* in the table. The next activity asks you to represent the *Hercules Computers* information in this way.

ACTIVITY 51

Fill in the table below for the *Hercules Computers* problem. The first entry has been made for you.

	Watford	Cardiff	Manchester	Durham	Supply
Hull	£3.00				
Birmingham					
Demand					

The completed table is shown below.

	Watford	Cardiff	Manchester	Durham	Supply
Hull	£3.00	£9.00	£9.00	£3.00	5000
Birmingham	£1.50	£3.00	£7.50	£10.50	3000
Demand	1400	3200	2000	1400	

Table 16: Completed table for Hercules Computers supply problem

Remember that a solution to a transportation problem must be **feasible** (it must meet the required demand and not exceed supply) and **optimal** (it must be at the lowest possible cost).

To explore this we will start by investigating one possible transportation plan.

ACTIVITY 52

You should use the information in Table 16 for this activity.

Suppose that *Hercules Computers* adopts the following transportation plan:

> 1,400 shipped from Hull to Watford
>
> 3,200 shipped from Hull to Cardiff
>
> 400 shipped from Hull to Manchester
>
> 1,600 shipped from Birmingham to Manchester
>
> 1,400 shipped from Birmingham to Durham

1. Is this solution feasible?

2. What is the cost of this solution?

3. Can you say, without further calculation, whether this solution is optimal?

---

1. To decide whether this solution is feasible, we check to see if any of the constraints are breached by this solution. We will start by checking to see if all of the demand requirements are met:

   Amount shipped to Watford = 1,400

   Amount shipped to Cardiff = 3,200

   Amount shipped to Manchester = 400 + 1,600 = 2,000

   Amount shipped to Durham = 1,400

   This clearly meets the demand requirements for each of the four assembly plants.

   Now we will check to see if the solution stays within the supply limits:

   Amount shipped from Hull = 5,000

   Amount shipped from Birmingham = 3,000

   So the schedule stays within the supply limits for each manufacturer. Therefore, the solution is certainly feasible.

2. Itemising each route, the cost of this solution is:

   1,400 units from Hull to Watford at £3.00 per unit = £4,200

   3,200 units from Hull to Cardiff at £9.00 per unit = £28,800

400 units from Hull to Manchester at £9.00 per unit = £3,600

1,600 units from Birmingham to Manchester at £7.50 per unit = £12,000

1,400 units from Birmingham to Durham at £10.50 per unit = £14,700

In total, this amounts to £63,300.

3. Unless we try out all feasible possibilities, we have no way of knowing whether this solution is optimal.

5.3 Linear programming and transportation problems

Before we can proceed with our discussion of transportation problems, we need to provide formal definitions of some of the terms we have been using.

Source: the point where goods are shipped from. This is usually a supplier or a warehouse.

Destination: the point to which goods are shipped. This is usually a customer.

Route: a channel of communication (usually for distribution of goods) between any source and any destination.

We also need to introduce some notation. If there are i sources and j destinations, then there will be ij routes ($i \times j$). A quantity of goods will be sent along each route, and it is standard practice to call this (as yet unknown) amount of goods X_{ij}. The subscript letters ij after the X refer to the transportation route from source i to destination j. So, for example, the quantity X_{12} is shorthand for 'the amount shipped from source 1 to destination 2'. You should note that this is read as 'X one-two' and not as 'X twelve'!

ACTIVITY 53

Suppose that in the *Hercules Computers* problem we decide to code the sources as 1 for Hull and 2 for Birmingham. Similarly, we code the destinations as 1 for Watford, 2 for Cardiff, 3 for Manchester, and 4 for Durham.

Write, in words, the meaning of the following:

$$X_{11}, X_{12}, X_{13}, X_{14}, X_{21}, X_{22}, X_{23}, X_{24}$$

The meaning of the notations is as follows:

X_{11} stands for the amount shipped from Hull to Watford

X_{12} stands for the amount shipped from Hull to Cardiff

X_{13} stands for the amount shipped from Hull to Manchester

X_{14} stands for the amount shipped from Hull to Durham

X_{21} stands for the amount shipped from Birmingham to Watford

X_{22} stands for the amount shipped from Birmingham to Cardiff

X_{23} stands for the amount shipped from Birmingham to Manchester

X_{24} stands for the amount shipped from Birmingham to Durham

If all routes are available, and supply and demand are equal, then the number of decision variables in a transportation problem will be equal to the number of sources multiplied by the number of destinations. So in the *Hercules Computers* case there are eight such variables (2 × 4). You can readily imagine that a problem with a sizeable number of sources and destinations can generate a very large linear programming model.

If we are to solve transportation problems using linear programming, then we will need to set up an objective function. We already know that *Hercules Computers* wishes to solve its transportation problem at the lowest possible cost. This means that the objective function will be an algebraic statement of the total cost of shipping goods from all sources to all destinations.

As a start to this process of formulating the objective cost function, let X_{11} be the number of units shipped from Hull to Watford. Now since it costs £3.00 to ship 1 unit between these towns, it follows that the cost of shipping X_{11} units will be £3.00X_{11}. Similar cost statements can be made for each transport route.

ACTIVITY 54

Continuing the process started above, formulate an objective function for the *Hercules Computers* transportation problem.

Multiplying each decision variable by the appropriate shipping cost per unit, and then adding, we get:

$$3X_{11} + 9X_{12} + 9X_{13} + 3X_{14} + 1.50X_{21} + 3X_{22} + 7.5X_{23} + 10.5X_{24}$$

This constitutes the objective function for *Hercules Computers*. We need to plan the transportation schedule in such a way as to minimise it.

You now know how to formulate an objective function for a transportation problem. You may have been struck by the length of the function, compared with other problems elsewhere in this unit. This is quite typical of such problems. In a model with 10 sources and 10 destinations, there would be up to 100 coefficients in the cost function!

We can now move on to the second requirement of a linear programming problem: we need to decide what the constraints are, and then state them algebraically.

You may remember from Activity 50 that *Hercules Computers'* constraints are of two types: the amounts actually available at the two suppliers in Hull and Birmingham, and the supply requirements for each of its four plants in Watford, Cardiff, Manchester and Durham.

We will take just one of the supply figures, to show how a linear constraint is formulated in a transportation model.

Whatever else is true, we cannot ship more than 5,000 units out of Hull, because that source has only that quantity available. Continuing with our X_{ij} notation, where X_{ij} is the amount shipped from source i to destination j, we know that the sum of all the amounts which involve Hull must be less than or equal to 5,000.

The first subscript letter in the X_{ij} notation represents the source. So in this case we are only interested in those routes where i has the value 1. (Remember that Hull is represented by 1.) The total amount to be shipped out of Hull is given by:

$$X_{11} + X_{12} + X_{13} + X_{14}$$

Since this must be limited to 5,000, we end up with the following linear constraint:

$$X_{11} + X_{12} + X_{13} + X_{14} \leq 5,000 \text{ (Hull supply)}$$

ACTIVITY 55

You can now continue the process of formulating the linear constraints yourself. Write out all the constraints for the *Hercules Computers* problem in algebraic form. There is another supply constraint (for Birmingham), and there are four demand constraints (for Watford, Cardiff, Manchester and Durham).

You should have established that the remaining supply constraint is:

$$X_{21} + X_{22} + X_{23} + X_{24} \leq 3{,}000 \text{ (Birmingham supply)}$$

That leaves the demand constraints:

$$X_{11} + X_{21} = 1{,}400 \text{ (Watford demand)}$$

$$X_{12} + X_{22} = 3{,}200 \text{ (Cardiff demand)}$$

$$X_{13} + X_{23} = 2{,}000 \text{ (Manchester demand)}$$

$$X_{14} + X_{24} = 1{,}400 \text{ (Durham demand)}$$

We are now in a position to formulate the complete linear programming model for *Hercules Computers*. Remember that we need to state that none of the decision variables can take negative values. The model is:

Minimise $3X_{11} + 9X_{12} + 9X_{13} + 3X_{14} + 1.50X_{21} + 3X_{22} + 7.5X_{23} + 10.5X_{24}$

Subject to:

$$
\begin{array}{rcl}
X_{11} + X_{12} + X_{13} + X_{14} & \leq & 5{,}000 \\
X_{21} + X_{22} + X_{23} + X_{24} & \leq & 3{,}000 \\
X_{11} + X_{21} & = & 1{,}400 \\
X_{12} + X_{22} & = & 3{,}200 \\
X_{13} + X_{23} & = & 2{,}000 \\
X_{14} + X_{24} & = & 1{,}400 \\
X_{ij} & \geq & 0
\end{array}
$$

We can now proceed to solve this problem, using the *Solver* utility in *Microsoft Excel*. If you are unsure about how to use *Solver*, then look back at Section 4 of this unit. Enter the information for the *Hercules Computers* problem into a new worksheet as shown in Table 17. Save your worksheet as **Herctran.xls**.

	A	B	C
1	*Hercules* Computers		
2			
3	**Objective Function – Minimise Transport Cost**	0	
4			
5	**Decision Variables**		
6	Amount shipped from Hull to Watford (X_{11})	0	
7	Amount shipped from Hull to Cardiff (X_{12})	0	
8	Amount shipped from Hull to Manchester (X_{13})	0	
9	Amount shipped from Hull to Durham (X_{14})	0	
10	Amount shipped from Birmingham to Watford (X_{21})	0	
11	Amount shipped from Birmingham to Cardiff (X_{22})	0	
12	Amount shipped from Birmingham to Manchester (X_{23})	0	
13	Amount shipped from Birmingham to Durham (X_{24})	0	
14			
15	**Constraints**		
16	Hull supply	0	5000
17	Birmingham supply	0	3000
18	Watford demand	0	1400
19	Cardiff demand	0	3200
20	Manchester demand	0	2000
21	Durham demand	0	1400
22	Non-Negativity X_{11}	0	0
23	Non-Negativity X_{12}	0	0
24	Non-Negativity X_{13}	0	0
25	Non-Negativity X_{14}	0	0
26	Non-Negativity X_{21}	0	0
27	Non-Negativity X_{22}	0	0
28	Non-Negativity X_{23}	0	0
29	Non-Negativity X_{24}	0	0

Table 17: Spreadsheet for the Hercules Computers transport problem

ACTIVITY 56

You need to enter appropriate formulae into cells B3 and cells B16 to B29. What formulae should go into these cells?

Cell B3 holds the objective function, and so should contain the formula:

=3*B6+9*B7+9*B8+3*B9+1.5*B10+3*B11+7.5*B12+10.5*B13

For the remaining cells, your formulae should be as shown in Table 18.

Cell	Formula	Cell	Formula
B16	= B6+B7+B8+B9	B23	= B7
B17	= B10+B11+B12+B13	B24	= B8
B18	= B6+B10	B25	= B9
B19	= B7+B11	B26	= B10
B20	= B8+B12	B27	= B11
B21	= B9+B13	B28	= B12
B22	= B6	B29	= B13

Table 18: Formulae for the Hercules Computers transport problem

As you can imagine, transportation problems require extra care during data entry. Problems with a large number of sources and destinations produce quite substantial linear programming models and there is always a danger of error at the data input stage.

ACTIVITY 57

Call up *Solver* and complete the *Solver* **Parameters** screen. Set the **Target Cell** and the **Changing Cells** and enter the constraints. Take some care with this. Check back to the formulation of the problem to see what operation (that is '≥', '≤' or '=') you require for each constraint. For example, for the first constraint you need to state that **B16 ≤ C16**.

There is one further point to note. In any solution to this problem, all of the decision variables must have integer (or 'whole number') values. So, for example, you must state that B6 is integer and so on for the other decision variables. If you have forgotten how to do this, then check back to Section 4 of this unit.

When you have finished entering information into *Solver* **Parameters**, your screen should be as in Figure 35. Before clicking **Solve**, remember to click **Options** to check that it has been set for **Assume Linear Model**.

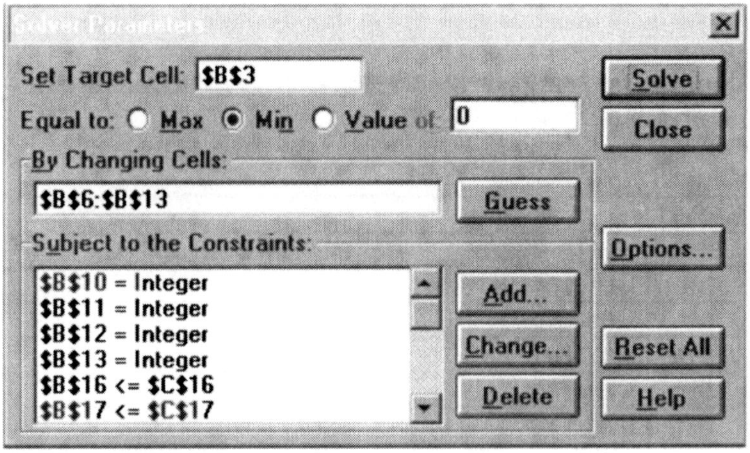

Figure 35: Solver Parameters for the Hercules Computers transport problem

You should now check that all entries are correct before proceeding.

ACTIVITY 58

Click **Solve** to obtain a solution. What is the optimal transportation schedule?

Your solution should agree with that shown in Table 19. If it does not, then you probably made an error in entering one or more of the constraints. You should check through them carefully. Also, did you enter the correct range for the changing cells and input the correct formula in cell B3?

In the *Hercules Computers* problem, 1,400 units are to be shipped from Hull to Watford, 200 units from Hull to Cardiff, 2,000 units from Hull to Manchester, 1,400 units from Hull to Durham and 3,000 units from Birmingham to Cardiff. This solution will have a minimum cost of £37,200 and will ensure both that demand requirements are met and that supply constraints are observed. Notice that some routes have not been used.

	A	B	C
1	*Hercules* Computers		
2			
3	**Objective Function – Minimise Transport Cost**	37200	
4			
5	**Decision Variables**		
6	Amount shipped from Hull to Watford (X_{11})	1400	
7	Amount shipped from Hull to Cardiff (X_{12})	200	
8	Amount shipped from Hull to Manchester (X_{13})	2000	
9	Amount shipped from Hull to Durham (X_{14})	1400	
10	Amount shipped from Birmingham to Watford (X_{21})	0	
11	Amount shipped from Birmingham to Cardiff (X_{22})	3000	
12	Amount shipped from Birmingham to Manchester (X_{23})	0	
13	Amount shipped from Birmingham to Durham (X_{24})	0	
14			
15	**Constraints**		
16	Hull supply	5000	5000
17	Birmingham supply	3000	3000
18	Watford demand	1400	1400
19	Cardiff demand	3200	3200
20	Manchester demand	2000	2000
21	Durham demand	1400	1400
22	Non-Negativity X_{11}	1400	0
23	Non-Negativity X_{12}	200	0
24	Non-Negativity X_{13}	2000	0
25	Non-Negativity X_{14}	1400	0
26	Non-Negativity X_{21}	0	0
27	Non-Negativity X_{22}	3000	0
28	Non-Negativity X_{23}	0	0
29	Non-Negativity X_{24}	0	0

Table 19: Solution values for the Hercules Computers transport problem

Now try the following problem.

ACTIVITY 59

Northern Manufacturers Ltd is currently considering how it should ship its product from the three manufacturing plants it owns (Ternville, Doveton and Kempside) to each of three warehouses used for distribution purposes (Ampleside, Beerside and Cheapside). Ternville has a capacity of 150 units while Doveton and Kempside are able to supply 450 units each. Ampleside requires 450 units and Beerside and Cheapside both require 300.

Per unit, it costs Ternville £7.50 to supply Ampleside, £3.00 to supply Beerside and £4.50 to supply Cheapside. Unit shipping costs for Doveton are £12.00 to Ampleside, £6.00 to Beerside and £4.50 to Cheapside. To ship from Kempside costs £13.50 per unit to Ampleside, £10.50 to Beerside and £7.00 to Cheapside.

The business wishes to minimise cost.

1. Draw a network flow diagram to illustrate this problem.

2. Summarise the costs, demand and supply in a suitable table.

3. Formulate the linear programming model for this problem.

4. Use the formulated problem to find the optimum transportation schedule for this firm. You will need to use *Solver*.

Hint: use your worksheet for the *Hercules Computers* problem as a template and amend it for the data of this new problem. Save the amended worksheet as **Northern.xls**.

---

1. A network flow diagram for this problem is shown in Figure 36.

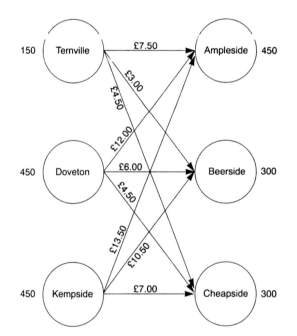

Figure 36: Network flow diagram for the Northern Manufacturers problem

2. You should notice that, as there are three sources and three destinations, there are nine different routes. This means that we require a linear programming model with nine decision variables. As with the previous problem, supply is equal to demand, and there are no restrictions on any of the routes.

Table 20 displays the same information in tabular form.

		Destinations			
		Ampleside	Beerside	Cheapside	Supply
	Ternville	£7.50	£3.00	£4.50	150
Sources	Doveton	£12.00	£6.00	£4.50	450
	Kempside	£13.50	£10.50	£7.00	450
Demand		450	300	300	

Table 20: Information in tabular form for the Northern Manufacturers problem

3. Using the X_{ij} coding for variables, Ternville is denoted by the number 1, Doveton by 2 and Kempside by 3. Likewise, for the destinations, Ampleside is denoted by the number 1, Beerside by 2 and Cheapside by 3.

Multiplying each decision variable by the unit cost, we have the following objective function:

$7.5X_{11} + 3X_{12} + 4.5X_{13} + 12X_{21} + 6X_{22} + 4.5X_{23} + 13.5X_{31} + 10.5X_{32} + 7X_{33}$

This is to be minimised, subject to linear constraints. We can now turn our attention to formulating these constraints. They are directly related to the supplies available and the amounts demanded. You should have established that:

$X_{11} + X_{12} + X_{13} \leq 150$ (Ternville supply)

$X_{21} + X_{22} + X_{23} \leq 450$ (Doveton supply)

$X_{31} + X_{32} + X_{33} \leq 450$ (Kempside supply)

$X_{11} + X_{21} + X_{31} = 450$ (Ampleside demand)

$X_{12} + X_{22} + X_{32} = 300$ (Beerside demand)

$X_{13} + X_{23} + X_{33} = 300$ (Cheapside demand)

Hence, the formulated problem is:

Minimise $7.5X_{11} + 3X_{12} + 4.5X_{13} + 12X_{21} + 6X_{22} + 4.5X_{23} + 13.5X_{31} + 10.5X_{32} + 7X_{33}$

Subject to:

$$X_{11} + X_{12} + X_{13} \leq 150$$
$$X_{21} + X_{22} + X_{23} \leq 450$$
$$X_{31} + X_{32} + X_{33} \leq 450$$
$$X_{11} + X_{21} + X_{31} = 450$$
$$X_{12} + X_{22} + X_{32} = 300$$
$$X_{13} + X_{23} + X_{33} = 300$$
$$X_{ij} \geq 0$$
$$X_{ij} = \text{Integer}$$

4. Having entered the problem into a *Microsoft Excel* worksheet, your screen should look like that shown in Table 21.

	A	B	C
1	*Northern Manufacturers*		
2			
3	**Objective Function – Minimise Transport Cost**	0	
4			
5	**Decision Variables**		
6	Amount shipped from Ternville to Ampleside (X_{11})	0	
7	Amount shipped from Ternville to Beerside (X_{12})	0	
8	Amount shipped from Ternville to Cheapside (X_{13})	0	
9	Amount shipped from Doveton to Ampleside (X_{21})	0	
10	Amount shipped from Doveton to Beerside (X_{22})	0	
11	Amount shipped from Doveton to Cheapside (X_{23})	0	
12	Amount shipped from Kempside to Ampleside (X_{31})	0	
13	Amount shipped from Kempside to Beerside (X_{32})	0	
14	Amount shipped from Kempside to Cheapside (X_{33})	0	
15			
16	**Constraints**		
17	Ternville supply	0	150
18	Doveton supply	0	450
19	Kempside supply	0	450
20	Ampleside demand	0	450
21	Beerside demand	0	300
22	Cheapside demand	0	300
23	Non-Negativity X_{11}	0	0
24	Non-Negativity X_{12}	0	0
25	Non-Negativity X_{13}	0	0
26	Non-Negativity X_{21}	0	0
27	Non-Negativity X_{22}	0	0
28	Non-Negativity X_{23}	0	0
29	Non-Negativity X_{31}	0	0
30	Non-Negativity X_{32}	0	0
31	Non-Negativity X_{33}	0	0

Table 21: Spreadsheet for the Northern Manufacturers problem

Cell B3 holds the objective function, and so should contain the formula:

=7.5*B6 + 3*B7 + 4.5*B8 + 12*B9 + 6*B10 + 4.5*B11 + 13.5*B12 + 10.5*B13 + 7*B14

For the remaining cells, your formulae should be as shown in Table 22.

Cell	Formula	Cell	Formula
B17	=B6+B7+B8	B25	=B8
B18	=B9+B10+B11	B26	=B9
B19	=B12+B13+B14	B27	=B10
B20	=B6+B9+B12	B28	=B11
B21	=B7+B10+B13	B29	=B12
B22	=B8+B11+B14	B30	=B13
B23	=B6	B31	=B14
B24	=B7		

Table 22: Formulae for the worksheet for the Northern Manufacturers problem

After completing all entries in the *Solver* **Parameters** screen, including the **Target Cell** (B3), the **Changing Cells** (B6:B14) and the constraints (inclusive of the integer requirement for cells B6 to B14) your screen should be similar to that shown in Figure 37.

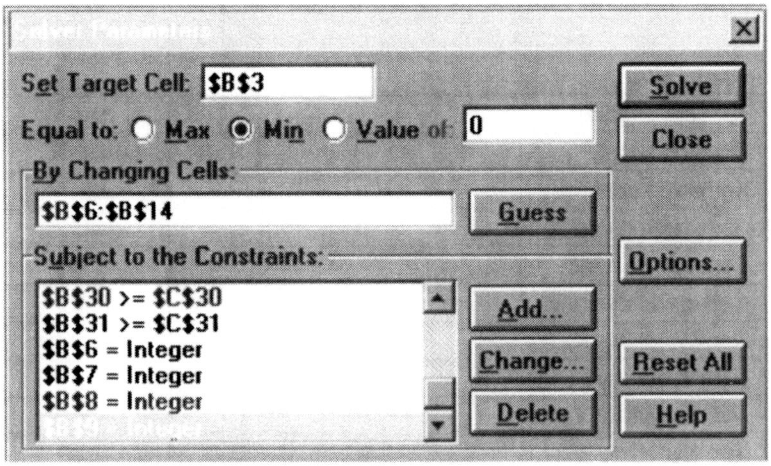

Figure 37: Solver Parameters for the Northern Manufacturers problem

Clicking **Solve** should generate the output shown in Table 23. Remember to use the **Options** button, to check that *Solver* has been set for **Assume Linear Model**.

	A	B	C
1	*Northern Manufacturers*		
2			
3	**Objective Function – Minimise Transport Cost**	8700	
4			
5	**Decision Variables**		
6	Amount shipped from Ternville to Ampleside (X_{11})	150	
7	Amount shipped from Ternville to Beerside (X_{12})	0	
8	Amount shipped from Ternville to Cheapside (X_{13})	0	
9	Amount shipped from Doveton to Ampleside (X_{21})	0	
10	Amount shipped from Doveton to Beerside (X_{22})	300	
11	Amount shipped from Doveton to Cheapside (X_{23})	150	
12	Amount shipped from Kempside to Ampleside (X_{31})	300	
13	Amount shipped from Kempside to Beerside (X_{32})	0	
14	Amount shipped from Kempside to Cheapside (X_{33})	150	
15			
16	**Constraints**		
17	Ternville supply	150	150
18	Doveton supply	450	450
19	Kempside supply	450	450
20	Ampleside demand	450	450
21	Beerside demand	300	300
22	Cheapside demand	300	300
23	Non-Negativity X_{11}	150	0
24	Non-Negativity X_{12}	0	0
25	Non-Negativity X_{13}	0	0
26	Non-Negativity X_{21}	0	0
27	Non-Negativity X_{22}	300	0
28	Non-Negativity X_{23}	150	0
29	Non-Negativity X_{31}	300	0
30	Non-Negativity X_{32}	0	0
31	Non-Negativity X_{33}	150	0

Table 23: Solution values for the Northern Manufacturers problem

We now have a solution to the problem.

150 units should be shipped from Ternville to Ampleside

0 units should be shipped from Ternville to Beerside

0 units should be shipped from Ternville to Cheapside

0 units should be shipped from Doveton to Ampleside

300 units should be shipped from Doveton to Beerside

150 units should be shipped from Doveton to Cheapside

300 units should be shipped from Kempside to Ampleside

0 units should be shipped from Kempside to Beerside

150 units should be shipped from Kempside to Cheapside

This arrangement yields a minimum cost of £8,700.

5.4 Coping with complications

Finally, to end this section of the unit, we examine four complications which may arise with the basic transportation model, namely:

- supply and demand do not match
- a particular route has a limited capacity, or a required minimum
- a particular route is unacceptable
- we wish to maximise profit rather than minimise cost.

SUPPLY AND DEMAND DO NOT MATCH

In the two examples used so far (*Hercules Computers* and *Northern Manufacturers Ltd*), it happened to be the case that supply and demand were equal. We cannot expect this to occur in every situation. Does it make any difference to the method of solution if demand does not equal supply?

In the case where supply is greater than demand there is no problem: the linear programming model is formulated as usual. If you are curious about this, then just try rerunning the *Hercules Computers* problem with an extra 50 units of supply given to Hull. All that will happen is that Hull is left with 50 units that are not shipped.

The situation where supply is less than demand is quite a different matter. If you try to formulate and solve the linear programming model for such a problem using the procedures that we have followed so far, you will find that no solution exists! In technical language, it is described as infeasible. How can we resolve this situation?

This problem can be dealt with by adding a new dummy source of supply. Since supply is less than demand, the dummy represents a transportation shortfall. This source, a dummy in the sense that it does not actually exist, will have a supply equal to the excess demand, and the costs of transporting any unit from it will be 0. It will add more decision variables to your linear programming model (there will be a new variable for each dummy-to-destination route) but this cannot be avoided.

Figure 38 shows how the network flow diagram for the *Northern Manufacturers* problem would change if each warehouse demanded an extra 20 units while supply remained unchanged.

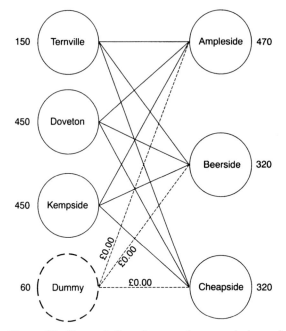

Figure 38: Network flow diagram for an unbalanced problem using a dummy source

Some of the detail on the diagram has been omitted to avoid unnecessary clutter. The dummy source is connected to each destination and has a notional supply of 60 (the amount of the excess demand), shipped at a unit cost of £0.00. No units will ever actually leave the dummy, and the use of zero cost in the objective function will ensure that our solution gives the cost of goods actually shipped. The solution values obtained for the dummy decision variables can be ignored: they only exist in order to make the problem feasible.

ACTIVITY 60

Look again at the solution to the transportation problem for *Northern Manufacturers Ltd* (see Activity 59).

1. On your worksheet **Northern.xls**, amend each warehouse demand figure upwards by an extra 20 units. Leave the supplies from Ternville, Doveton

and Kempside unchanged. Add the three dummy routes. You will need to amend existing constraints and add some new ones. Since there is no cost attached to the use of the dummy routes, there is no need to amend the objective function in cell B3.

2. Obtain the solution to this problem.

---

1. The reworked table accommodating the dummy is shown as Table 24.

		Destinations			
		Ampleside	Beerside	Cheapside	Supply
	Ternville	£7.50	£3.00	£4.50	150
Sources	Doveton	£12.00	£6.00	£4.50	450
	Kempside	£13.50	£10.50	£7.00	450
	Dummy	£0.00	£0.00	£0.00	60
Demand		470	320	320	

Table 24: Information in tabular form for the revised Northern Manufacturers problem

You should take careful note of the new row representing the dummy variable: shipping costs to each destination are set to zero, and it has a supply of 60 – the exact amount of the overall shortfall. Hence, the problem will now have three additional decision variables:

X_{41} (the route between the dummy and Ampleside)

X_{42} (the route between the dummy and Beerside)

X_{43} (the route between the dummy and Cheapside)

The revised objective function will be:

$$7.5X_{11} + 3X_{12} + 4.5X_{13} + 12X_{21} + 6X_{22} + 4.5X_{23} + 13.5X_{31} + 10.5X_{32} + 7X_{33} + 0X_{41} + 0X_{42} + 0X_{43}$$

The constraint list will alter as follows:

$X_{11} + X_{12} + X_{13} \leq 150$ (Ternville supply – unchanged)

$X_{21} + X_{22} + X_{23} \leq 450$ (Doveton supply – unchanged)

$X_{31} + X_{32} + X_{33} \leq 450$ (Kempside supply – unchanged)

$X_{41} + X_{42} + X_{43} \leq 60$ (Dummy supply – new constraint)

$X_{11} + X_{21} + X_{31} + X_{41} = 470$ (Ampleside demand – amended constraint)

$X_{12} + X_{22} + X_{32} + X_{42} = 320$ (Beerside demand – amended constraint)

$X_{13} + X_{23} + X_{33} + X_{43} = 320$ (Cheapside demand – amended constraint)

There is a new constraint, showing the notional supply held at the dummy source. Also, each of the demand constraints has been altered to allow for the theoretical new source.

2. We can now proceed with the solution to this problem. See Table 25.

	A	B	C
1	*Northern Manufacturers*		
2			
3	**Objective Function – Minimise Transport Cost**	8470	
4			
5	**Decision Variables**		
6	Amount shipped from Ternville to Ampleside (X_{11})	150	
7	Amount shipped from Ternville to Beerside (X_{12})	0	
8	Amount shipped from Ternville to Cheapside (X_{13})	0	
9	Amount shipped from Doveton to Ampleside (X_{21})	0	
10	Amount shipped from Doveton to Beerside (X_{22})	320	
11	Amount shipped from Doveton to Cheapside (X_{23})	130	
12	Amount shipped from Kempside to Ampleside (X_{31})	260	
13	Amount shipped from Kempside to Beerside (X_{32})	0	
14	Amount shipped from Kempside to Cheapside (X_{33})	190	
15	Amount shipped from Dummy to Ampleside (X_{41})	60	
16	Amount shipped from Dummy to Beerside (X_{42})	0	
17	Amount shipped from Dummy to Cheapside (X_{43})	0	
18			
19	**Constraints**		
20	Ternville supply	150	150
21	Doveton supply	450	450
22	Kempside supply	450	450
23	Dummy supply	60	60
24	Ampleside demand	470	470
25	Beerside demand	320	320
26	Cheapside demand	320	320
27	Non-Negativity X_{11}	150	0
28	Non-Negativity X_{12}	0	0
29	Non-Negativity X_{13}	0	0
30	Non-Negativity X_{21}	0	0
31	Non-Negativity X_{22}	320	0
32	Non-Negativity X_{23}	130	0
33	Non-Negativity X_{31}	260	0
34	Non-Negativity X_{32}	0	0
35	Non-Negativity X_{33}	190	0
36	Non-Negativity X_{41}	60	0
37	Non-Negativity X_{42}	0	0
38	Non-Negativity X_{43}	0	0

Table 25: Solution values for the revised Northern Manufacturers problem

Let's examine the worksheet in Table 25. The objective function formula in B3 is unchanged. Three new decision variables have been added (X_{41}, X_{42} and X_{43}) to allow for the three dummy routes. The formulae in cells B20 to B22 are unchanged. We have a new constraint for Dummy supply, with the formula **=B15+B16+B17** in cell B23. Since Ampleside, Beerside and Cheapside now have an additional supply source (Dummy), then the formulae in cells B24 to B26 require amendment to allow for this. Finally we must include non-negativity constraints for the three dummy routes.

Entering the new constraints into *Solver,* including specifying that cells B15 to B17 must be integer, generated the output shown in Table 25.

So the revised optimal solution is to ship:

150 units from Ternville to Ampleside

320 units from Doveton to Beerside

130 units from Doveton to Cheapside

260 units from Kempside to Ampleside

190 units from Kempside to Cheapside

The 60 units shown for decision variable X_{41} are the Dummy to Ampleside route. This quantity is not actually transported, and thus represents a shortfall for Ampleside. They require 470 units, but only succeed in obtaining 410. This solution is optimal at a cost of £8,470.

A PARTICULAR ROUTE HAS A LIMITED CAPACITY, OR A REQUIRED MINIMUM

Sometimes a particular route may have a limited capacity. For example, the vehicles used on this route might be limited in terms of load size. On some other routes there may be a minimum amount required, perhaps because the business has an inescapable commitment to supply that number to a particular destination. How do we change the model in order to incorporate such possibilities?

The answer to this is quite straightforward: we introduce another constraint which recognises the limit. Suppose that, in the *Northern Manufacturers Ltd* example, the Ternville to Ampleside route could only handle 70 units. We would then write:

$$X_{11} \leq 70$$

Or, if Doveton had guaranteed to send Beerside 50 units, we would write:

$$X_{22} \geq 50$$

We can, then, readily solve the changed linear programming model.

ACTIVITY 61

Use the revised *Northern Manufacturers Ltd* problem from Activity 60. Suppose that 220 units have to be sent from Kempside to Cheapside in order to meet a previous commitment.

1. Alter the linear programming model and solve it.

2. How does this prior commitment affect transportation cost?

---

1. Look back to your answer to Activity 60. The only change required in your worksheet (see Table 25) is to replace the non-negativity restriction on X_{33}, the Kempside to Cheapside route, with the restriction that $X_{33} \geq 220$.

   So amend cell C35 to read **220**. You should also change the wording in cell A35 to read, 'Kempside must send 220 units to Cheapside'.

   No changes are required to *Solver* **Parameters**, since we still need B35 to be greater than C35 (**B35 ≥ C35**).

   Solver yields as the solution:

   150 units from Ternville to Ampleside

   30 units from Doveton to Ampleside

   320 units from Doveton to Beerside

   100 units from Doveton to Cheapside

   230 units from Kempside to Ampleside

   220 units from Kempside to Cheapside

2. At this optimal solution the cost is £8,500. Comparing this with your answer to Activity 60, you will see that the effect of prioritising the Kempside to Cheapside route has been to increase cost by £30.

A PARTICULAR ROUTE IS UNACCEPTABLE

Sometimes it is not possible to establish a shipping route between every source and every destination. For example, if the Doveton to Appleside route were unavailable how would this affect the problem? In such a case we would simply remove the variable X_{21} from the objective function and constraints. The problem would then have eight decision variables instead of nine.

WE WISH TO MAXIMISE PROFIT RATHER THAN MINIMISE COST

It is perfectly possible to solve a transportation problem where the routes are itemised by profit (or revenue) per unit shipped rather than by cost. All that is necessary is to maximise the objective function rather than minimise it. The constraints will remain the same.

Summary

In this section of the unit we have studied the application of linear programming to a large class of problems known as transportation models. This entailed defining the transportation problem and displaying the problem both through the use of network flow diagrams and through the use of matrices. We then applied computer-based linear programming techniques to two examples of transportation problems. Finally, we looked at four possible complications to the transportation problem.

In the next section we look at another type of linear programming problem, the **assignment problem**.

SECTION 6
The Assignment Problem

Introduction

In this section of the unit, we take a look at another broad class of problems known collectively as **assignment problems**. They have much in common with transportation problems, and can also be analysed using the techniques of linear programming.

In many types of business problem, a decision-maker has to consider how different resources will be assigned to different tasks. For example, a sales manager may wish to assign sales representatives of differing skills to different sales territories. The sales manager may have the additional objective of achieving a given level of sales with the smallest number of customer calls.

In Section 6.1 we revisit the *Hercules Computers* case study from Section 5 and use it to identify the main elements of an assignment problem. In Section 6.2 we use a network flow diagram to define more precisely the objective and the constraints of the problem. In Section 6.3 we formulate the problem and solve it using computer-based linear programming techniques. Finally, in Section 6.4, we look at some variations to the standard assignment model.

By the end of this section you should be able to formulate and solve assignment problems using appropriate linear programming techniques.

6.1 The main elements of an assignment problem

In this section we use the *Hercules Computers* case study to introduce the main elements of an assignment problem.

Case Study: Hercules Computers revisited

You met *Hercules Computers* in the previous section of this unit, where the company was struggling with the problem of scheduling the delivery of computer parts from its two main suppliers to its four construction plants. *Hercules Computers* also supplies tailor-made systems programs to its corporate clients and in order to do this has a staff of three trained writers of program code: Henry Gibson, Mohammed Patel and Celia Johnson. Three customers currently require programs to be written for them. (We shall simply refer to them as customers 1, 2 and 3.) The head of corporate sales has made an assessment of how long each programmer would take to write the code required by each customer, based upon his knowledge of their respective abilities and the complexities of the tasks involved. This assessment is shown in Table 26 (all times are in days). So for example, the department head assesses that Gibson would take 15 days to complete the coding required by customer 1.

		Customer		
		(1)	(2)	(3)
	Gibson (1)	15	24	48
Programmer	Patel (2)	21	33	60
	Johnson (3)	33	36	51

Table 26: Customer time requirements per programmer

Each member of staff is to be allocated to be exclusively responsible for one (and only one) of the above projects.

ACTIVITY 62

Hercules Computers wishes to allocate staff so as to complete all three projects in the minimum time possible.

1. Write down, in words, what you think the objective function for this problem should be.

2. In how many different ways can programmers be assigned to projects?

3. Suppose that Gibson is to be assigned to customer 2, Patel to customer 3 and Johnson to customer 1. What would be the value of the objective function in this case? Are you able to say whether it is optimal or not?

---

1. A valid objective function would be to allocate programmers to tasks in such a way as to minimise the total time spent.

2. There are three different tasks and three different programmers to carry them out. Since each programmer can be allocated in three different ways, then in total there are nine different possible assignments.

3. Remember that the objective function sums the total amount of staff time used. Gibson will take an estimated 24 days to deal with customer 2, Patel will take 60 days to deal with customer 3, while Johnson is likely to take 33 days to deal with customer 1. In total, this will take up an estimated 117 days of staff time. We have no way of knowing whether this is an optimal assignment (that is, one that minimises total time) unless we go through every one of the nine possible assignment schedules. Although this would not be particularly arduous with the small *Hercules Computers* problem, it could become extremely tedious for larger problems. We therefore need a systematic method for finding the optimum assignment schedule.

6.2 Developing an assignment model

You should have been able to see, from the previous discussion, that we have the germ of an optimisation problem here:

- we have a clear objective to meet (in this case it is to complete the three projects in the minimum possible time)

- we have limited resources (in this case only three programmers)

- we have decision variables (three programmers to be allocated to the three projects).

It is a useful first step, in developing an assignment model, to use the network flow diagram approach introduced in the section on transportation. To do this, we will regard the programmers rather like the **sources** in a shipment problem, and the clients, or customers, as being similar to **destinations**. Just as we had to match up sources and destinations, we now have to match up programmers and customers. Figure 39 shows a network flow diagram for the *Hercules Computers* assignment problem.

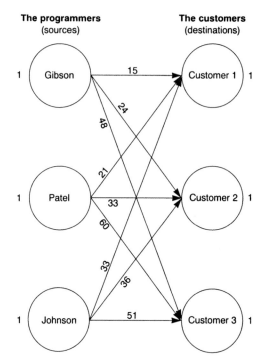

Figure 39: The Hercules Computers assignment problem

The programmers represent the supply or source nodes of the flow chart, and they supply their services to the demand or destination nodes. Notice that there is a number on each of the lines connecting programmers to clients. This number represents the length of time taken by the programmer to complete a particular project. For example, Johnson will take an estimated 36 days to complete the project for customer 2. Hence we write the number 36 on the line connecting these two nodes. So far, the network flow diagram for an assignment problem is remarkably similar to that for the transportation problem.

There is, however, one important difference. You will see that against each source and destination node is written the number 1. In a network flow diagram of a transportation problem, these numbers would correspond to the amount of supply and demand. However, in the *Hercules Computers* assignment problem we do not have multiple amounts of Johnsons, Patels or Gibsons: there is only one of each! Likewise there is only one customer 1 (or customer 2 or 3). Consequently, we must write a 1 against each node. It is important to remember that an assignment problem is very much like a transportation problem, **but with all the supplies and demands equal to 1**.

You may recall that in the transportation problem the objective was to decide which source-destination routes to use, in order to achieve some predetermined objective, such as minimisation of cost. In the *Hercules Computers* assignment case, we shall develop a similar objective function to decide which particular programmer-client schedule minimises time taken.

How shall we represent our decision variables in the new situation? You may remember that, in dealing with transportation, we used symbols such as X_{12} to denote the route from source 1 to destination 2. We can use the same approach to describe the decision variables in assignment problems.

ACTIVITY 63

1. Describe, in words, the decision variables of an assignment problem.

2. How many decision variables are there in the *Hercules Computers* assignment problem?

3. The symbol X_{12} could be used to represent one of the decision variables in the *Hercules Computers* problem. What does it mean in words?

4. Write down mathematical symbols to represent each of the decision variables in the *Hercules Computers* assignment problem, and describe what they mean in words.

---

1. Each of the programmer-client assignments constitutes a decision variable. For example, the assignment 'Gibson to customer 2' is one of the possible decision variables. This is a very similar arrangement to that used in transportation analysis, where each source-destination pairing was a decision variable.

2. In Activity 62 we saw that there were nine possible programmer-customer schedules. This means that there will be nine decision variables in the *Hercules Computers* assignment problem.

3. You should recall that the symbol X_{12} in transportation analysis referred to the route from source 1 to destination 2. Similarly, in assignment analysis X_{12} will refer to the pairing of programmer 1 (Gibson) with customer 2.

4. Using the same ordering of programmers and customers as used in the network diagram (Figure 39) and the table preceding it (Table 26), we would use the following symbols:

X_{11} to represent the assignment of Gibson to customer 1

X_{12} to represent the assignment of Gibson to customer 2

X_{13} to represent the assignment of Gibson to customer 3

X_{21} to represent the assignment of Patel to customer 1

X_{22} to represent the assignment of Patel to customer 2

X_{23} to represent the assignment of Patel to customer 3

X_{31} to represent the assignment of Johnson to customer 1

X_{32} to represent the assignment of Johnson to customer 2

X_{33} to represent the assignment of Johnson to customer 3

We now have a convenient symbolic system for representing our decision variables in the objective function. For example, X_{12} represents the assignment of programmer 1 (Gibson) to customer 2. It is an example of what is called a **0 – 1 variable,** also called a **binary** variable. That is, it can only take these two values. If it has the value 0, then this means that that particular assignment is not being used. Alternatively, if it has the value 1, then this means that the assignment of programmer 1 to customer 2 has been made. It will take programmer 1 an estimated 24 weeks to service customer 2, so the objective function would need to contain (among others) the expression $24X_{12}$.

ACTIVITY 64

Formulate the complete objective function for the *Hercules Computers* assignment problem.

Remember that our decision variables may only take the values 0 (when the assignment is not being used) or 1 (when the assignment is being used). You also need to remember that, in this case, the objective function represents the amount of time in staff days being used by the three assignments.

Each decision variable must be multiplied by the number of days taken up by that assignment. Consequently, the full objective function will be:

$$15X_{11} + 24X_{12} + 48X_{13} + 21X_{21} + 33X_{22} + 60X_{23} + 33X_{31} + 36X_{32} + 51X_{33}$$

(The coefficients are taken from Table 26.)

Activity 64 has shown you how to formulate an objective function for an assignment problem. As is the case with transportation problems, the length of the function can be sizeable. In the *Hercules Computers* case, our model had nine different decision variables and, therefore, nine coefficients in the objective function. You can easily imagine how the number of coefficients might rapidly get out of hand as the number of programmers and clients grows.

We now have to formulate, in mathematical terms, the constraints of a typical assignment problem.

ACTIVITY 65

Think about the *Hercules Computers* assignment problem for a moment. There are suppliers (programmers) and customers. Write down, in words, the constraints within which *Hercules Computers* must operate.

There are two kinds of constraints, some concerning programmers and some concerning customers.

Programmer constraints: programmers must not be assigned to work on more than one customer problem. In the *Hercules Computers* case, the number of customers and programmers is exactly matched (the problem is balanced), so that we could set such constraints to be exactly equal to 1, if we wished. However, in some problems, where there are more programmers than customers, some assignments may not be made. This would mean that some of these constraints might be 0.

Customer constraints: in the specification for this problem, it has been agreed that each customer must have one (and only one) programmer assigned to them. Consequently, however we formulate such constraints, we would set them equal to 1.

Let us deal firstly with the constraint which states that each programmer can only be assigned to (at most) one project. Let us take the example of Gibson (programmer 1). We are using the following notation:

X_{11} means 'assign programmer 1 to customer 1'

X_{12} means 'assign programmer 1 to customer 2'

X_{13} means 'assign programmer 1 to customer 3'

Remember that each X_{ij} can only have the value 1 (meaning that the assignment is used) or the value 0 (meaning that the assignment is not used). Since Gibson can only be allocated to a maximum of one project at a time, it follows that:

$$X_{11} + X_{12} + X_{13} \leq 1$$

(As stated in the response to Activity 65, we could, in this case, make all of these inequalities into equalities. This is because we have the same number of programmers as customers. However, there will be situations when there are more programmers than customers, which will mean some of the former will not be assigned. It is thus good practice to make these constraints the '$\leq$' type rather than '$=$'.)

ACTIVITY 66

Now see if you can complete this process. Formulate the linear constraints which relate to Patel and Johnson.

Patel is programmer 2, so in this case we require that:

$$X_{21} + X_{22} + X_{23} \leq 1$$

Similarly, Johnson is programmer 3, so we require that:

$$X_{31} + X_{32} + X_{33} \leq 1$$

The next group of constraints relate to each customer's need to have one, and only one, programmer allocated to their project. You can examine how this should be done in the next activity.

ACTIVITY 67

Write out in mathematical terms the constraints which relate to each of the three customers' need to have just one programmer assigned to them.

Hint: what are all the possible X_{ij} symbols which might be written down for customer 1?

It is the j part of the ij notation which refers to the customers. For example, X_{11} would represent the assignment of programmer 1 to customer 1, X_{21} represents programmer 2's assignment to customer 1 and, finally, X_{31} symbolises programmer 3's allocation to customer 1. Consequently, assignment of a programmer to customer 1 can be represented by the expression:

$$X_{11} + X_{21} + X_{31}$$

Also, since we have specified that each customer must have a programmer assigned to them, then we require that:

$$X_{11} + X_{21} + X_{31} = 1$$

By a similar process of reasoning, we can work out that the customer 2 and 3 constraints are:

$$X_{12} + X_{22} + X_{32} = 1$$

$$X_{13} + X_{23} + X_{33} = 1$$

By making each constraint equal to 1, we are representing the requirement that a customer must have an assignment made to them. So what happens if there are more customers than programmers? Clearly, in such a case there will be unsatisfied customers. We cannot solve this type of problem by replacing '=' with '≤', as we did with the programmer constraints. Instead, we would need to use more drastic methods. This will be discussed later in this section of the unit.

6.3 Solving the assignment problem

After working through the previous activity, we are now able to formulate the complete model for the *Hercules Computers* assignment problem.

Determine values for X_{11}, X_{12}, X_{13}, X_{21}, X_{22}, X_{23}, X_{31}, X_{32} and X_{33} that will:

$$\text{Minimise } 15X_{11} + 24X_{12} + 48X_{13} + 21X_{21} + 33X_{22} + 60X_{23} + 33X_{31} + 36X_{32} + 51X_{33}$$

subject to:

$$X_{11} + X_{12} + X_{13} \leq 1$$
$$X_{21} + X_{22} + X_{23} \leq 1$$
$$X_{31} + X_{32} + X_{33} \leq 1$$
$$X_{11} + X_{21} + X_{31} = 1$$
$$X_{12} + X_{22} + X_{32} = 1$$
$$X_{13} + X_{23} + X_{33} = 1$$

And all X_{ij} are 0 – 1 variables

Notice that because all the decision variables (the X_{ij}) are 0 – 1 variables (that is each of them can only take the value 0 or 1) then we have a linear programming problem quite unlike any that you have seen up to this point. Actually, it is an example of an **integer programming** problem and is one very important way in which the basic linear programming model can be extended, to allow for a richer set of possibilities. In Section 7 of this unit, we will briefly discuss the limitations of the basic linear programming model and the ways in which that model can be extended.

Commercial linear programming packages make special provision for integer problems (for example 0 – 1), and thus obviate the need for setting up the constraints required to ensure that a variable remains 0 – 1, as do later versions of

Microsoft Excel (from version 7). In this course we are using the *Solver* utility in *Microsoft Excel*, and if you are using an earlier version than version 7 you will need to worry about how to guarantee, in any solution to a problem, that all 0 – 1 variables remain exactly that.

ACTIVITY 68

In the formulation of the *Hercules Computers* assignment problem, all decision variables are required to be 0 – 1.

Consider the variable X_{11}. Write down a set of constraints that ensure that X_{11} will be a 0 – 1 variable.

Three conditions are required to ensure that X_{11} is 0 – 1, namely:

$X_{11} \geq 0$ (this states that X_{11} cannot take a value less than 0)

$X_{11} \leq 1$ (this states that X_{11} cannot take a value greater than 1)

X_{11} integer (this, together with the other two conditions, ensures that X_{11} can take only the values 0 and 1)

Remember that, when using *Solver*, the *Solver* **Parameters** screen enables you to constrain the contents of any cell to be integer. That leaves the other two constraints to be explicitly included in the *Microsoft Excel* worksheet for the problem. You must follow this procedure for every 0 – 1 decision variable in the model. However, if you are using *Microsoft Excel* version 7 then you should use the *Solver* **Parameters** screen to declare the contents of any cell to be **bin** (that is binary).

Let us proceed to solve the *Hercules Computers* assignment problem, using *Solver*. Complete a new worksheet as per Table 27. Save your worksheet as **Hercass.xls**. Please note that you only require the 0 – 1 constraints if you are not using *Microsoft Excel* version 7.

	A	B	C
1	*Hercules Computers*		
2			
3	**Objective Function – Minimise Days Taken**	0	
4			
5	**Decision Variables**		
6	Assign Gibson to Customer 1 (X_{11})	0	
7	Assign Gibson to Customer 2 (X_{12})	0	
8	Assign Gibson to Customer 3 (X_{13})	0	
9	Assign Patel to Customer 1 (X_{21})	0	
10	Assign Patel to Customer 2 (X_{22})	0	
11	Assign Patel to Customer 3 (X_{23})	0	
12	Assign Johnson to Customer 1 (X_{31})	0	
13	Assign Johnson to Customer 2 (X_{32})	0	
14	Assign Johnson to Customer 3 (X_{33})	0	
15			
16	**Constraints**		
17	Gibson's assignment	0	1
18	Patel's assignment	0	1
19	Johnson's assignment	0	1
20	Customer 1 served	0	1
21	Customer 2 served	0	1
22	Customer 3 served	0	1
23			
24	**0 – 1 Constraints**		
25	$X_{11} \geq 0$	0	0
26	$X_{11} \leq 1$	0	1
27	$X_{12} \geq 0$	0	0
28	$X_{12} \leq 1$	0	1
29	$X_{13} \geq 0$	0	0
30	$X_{13} \leq 1$	0	1
31	$X_{21} \geq 0$	0	0
32	$X_{21} \leq 1$	0	1
33	$X_{22} \geq 0$	0	0
34	$X_{22} \leq 1$	0	1
35	$X_{23} \geq 0$	0	0
36	$X_{23} \leq 1$	0	1
37	$X_{31} \geq 0$	0	0
38	$X_{31} \leq 1$	0	1
39	$X_{32} \geq 0$	0	0
40	$X_{32} \leq 1$	0	1
41	$X_{33} \geq 0$	0	0
42	$X_{33} \leq 1$	0	1

Table 27: Worksheet for the Hercules Computers assignment problem

In cell B3, you need the formula for the objective function. This is:

$$=15*B6+24*B7+48*B8+21*B9+33*B10+60*B11+33*B12+36*B13+51*B14$$

In cells B17 to B22 and B25 to B42, you should enter the formulae shown in Table 28. If you are using *Mircosoft Excel* version 7 you will not need to enter the formula given for cells B25 to B42.

Cell	Formula	Cell	Formula
B17	=B6+B7+B8	B31	=B9
B18	=B9+B10+B11	B32	=B9
B19	=B12+B13+B14	B33	=B10
B20	=B6+B9+B12	B34	=B10
B21	=B7+B10+B13	B35	=B11
B22	=B8+B11+B14	B36	=B11
B25	=B6	B37	=B12
B26	=B6	B38	=B12
B27	=B7	B39	=B13
B28	=B7	B40	=B13
B29	=B8	B41	=B14
B30	=B8	B42	=B14

Table 28: Formulae for the worksheet
for the Hercules Computers assignment problem

ACTIVITY 69

Call up *Solver*. You need to set B3 as the **Target Cell** and B6:B14 as the **Changing Cells**. Ensure that you have selected **Min** as the objective. Add the constraints. Remember that the programmer constraints are of the type '≤' and the customer constraints are of the type '='. In addition to the '≥' and '≤' constraints for each decision variable, you also need to specify that the contents of cells B6 to B14 are all integer. You should also declare the contents to be **bin** (binary) if you are using *Microsoft Excel* version 7. Before clicking **Solve**, check that all constraints have been entered correctly, and (on clicking **Options**) check that **Assume Linear Model** has been selected.

You should then obtain the output shown in Table 29.

	A	B	C
1	*Hercules Computers*		
2			
3	**Objective Function – Minimise Days Taken**	96	
4			
5	**Decision Variables**		
6	Assign Gibson to Customer 1 (X_{11})	0	
7	Assign Gibson to Customer 2 (X_{12})	1	
8	Assign Gibson to Customer 3 (X_{13})	0	
9	Assign Patel to Customer 1 (X_{21})	1	
10	Assign Patel to Customer 2 (X_{22})	0	
11	Assign Patel to Customer 3 (X_{23})	0	
12	Assign Johnson to Customer 1 (X_{31})	0	
13	Assign Johnson to Customer 2 (X_{32})	0	
14	Assign Johnson to Customer 3 (X_{33})	1	

Table 29: Solution values for the Hercules Computers assignment problem

The optimal assignment is to allocate Gibson to customer 2, Patel to customer 1 and Johnson to customer 3. This solution will result in all projects being completed in 96 days.

In the next activity you are asked to formulate and solve an assignment problem yourself.

ACTIVITY 70

Southern Fabrications plc has three current assembly jobs, all of which require the use of a particular machine. Luckily, it has three machines of this type, and each job must be assigned to one, and only one, machine. All three jobs must be scheduled to begin at the start of next day's shift, and the production scheduler is unsure as to how to allocate which job to which machine. Her problem is that each machine requires varying amounts of electricity to get the job done, and she wishes to schedule the jobs so as to use the minimum amount of power. She reckons that the usage of power by each machine, for each job, is as follows:

Job 1: Machine 1 needs 20 units of power, machine 2 requires 18 units and machine 3 will need 12 units of power

Job 2: Machine 1 needs 30 units of power, machine 2 requires 36 units and machine 3 will need 28 units of power

Job 3: Machine 1 needs 18 units of power, machine 2 requires 10 units and machine 3 will need 6 units of power

Advise the production scheduler as to how she should schedule machines to jobs.

Hint: since this is another 3 x 3 problem, you can use the *Hercules Computers* assignment problem as a template. Save your amended worksheet as **South1.xls**.

As usual with linear programming problems, we must first decide what we have to make decisions about, and what the decision variables are. If we compare the production scheduler's problem with the *Hercules Computers* case, we would need to regard the machines, like the programmers, as the suppliers of a service, and the jobs, like the *Hercules Computers* customers, as the receivers of the service. All assignment problems require us to schedule particular suppliers to provide for particular receivers. So, in this case, we need to make decisions about which machines will perform which jobs. There are three machines, and three jobs, so there are nine possible decision variables, each one representing a single machine-job assignment.

The next step is to decide what objective is to be met. The production scheduler is trying to match machines to jobs, so as to minimise the amount of electricity used. Using the notation that we have previously developed, X_{11} will represent the allocation of machine 1 to job 1, X_{12} the allocation of machine 1 to job 2, and so on. Then to obtain the objective function we multiply each X_{ij} by the amount of electricity used when machine i is allotted to job j. This will mean that our objective function is:

$$20X_{11} + 30X_{12} + 18X_{13} + 18X_{21} + 36X_{22} + 10X_{23} + 12X_{31} + 28X_{32} + 6X_{33}$$

If we regard the *Hercules Computers* problem as a template for this one, we can reason that there will be a number of constraints for representing that each job needs to be allocated to one machine. Since there are three jobs, then there will be three constraints of this type. There will also be three constraints (one for each machine) representing a machine's requirement to be allotted to no more than one job at a time.

So the formulated problem becomes:

Determine values for $X_{11}, X_{12}, X_{13}, X_{21}, X_{22}, X_{23}, X_{31}, X_{32}, X_{33}$ that will:

$$\text{Minimise } 20X_{11} + 30X_{12} + 18X_{13} + 18X_{21} + 36X_{22} + 10X_{23} + 12X_{31} + 28X_{32} + 6X_{33}$$

Subject to:

$$X_{11} + X_{12} + X_{13} \leq 1$$

$$X_{21} + X_{22} + X_{23} \leq 1$$

$$X_{31} + X_{32} + X_{33} \leq 1$$

$$X_{11} + X_{21} + X_{31} = 1$$

$$X_{12} + X_{22} + X_{32} = 1$$

$$X_{13} + X_{23} + X_{33} = 1$$

And all X_{ij} are $0 - 1$ variables

As you can quickly check, this is the same formulation as for the *Hercules Computers* problem apart from the difference in the objective function. So to solve it we can use the worksheet developed for the *Hercules Computers* case, remembering to change the formula in cell B3 to:

=20*B6+30*B7+18*B8+18*B9+36*B10+10*B11+12*B12+28*B13+6*B14

Running *Solver* gives as the solution:

	A	B
1	*Southern Fabrications plc*	
2		
3	**Objective Function – Minimise Power Used**	52
4		
5	**Decision Variables**	
6	Assign Machine 1 to Job 1 (X_{11})	0
7	Assign Machine 1 to Job 2 (X_{12})	1
8	Assign Machine 1 to Job 3 (X_{13})	0
9	Assign Machine 2 to Job 1 (X_{21})	0
10	Assign Machine 2 to Job 2 (X_{22})	0
11	Assign Machine 2 to Job 3 (X_{23})	1
12	Assign Machine 3 to Job 1 (X_{31})	1
13	Assign Machine 3 to Job 2 (X_{32})	0
14	Assign Machine 3 to Job 3 (X_{33})	0

Table 30: Solution to the Southern Fabrications plc assignment problem

We would, therefore, advise the production scheduler to allocate machine 1 to job 2, machine 2 to job 3 and machine 3 to job 1. This assignment will use an optimally minimum 52 units of electricity.

6.4 Variations to the standard assignment model

There are four variations to the assignment problem as set out above:

- the number of suppliers is more than the number of tasks
- the number of tasks is more than the number of suppliers
- the problem requires to be maximised rather than minimised
- it may be necessary to rule out some assignments altogether.

THE NUMBER OF SUPPLIERS IS MORE THAN THE NUMBER OF TASKS

Think about the case of *Southern Fabrications plc*. Suppose that the number of machines was not the same as the number of jobs to be undertaken. For example, suppose there were four machines available for the three jobs. Would this have any serious implications for setting up the model? The answer is 'no': the extra machine would remain unassigned to a job. Try it yourself in the following activity.

ACTIVITY 71

Suppose that in the *Southern Fabrications plc* problem there were a fourth machine which was estimated to use 18 units of electricity for job 1, 32 units for job 2 and 14 units for job 3. Reformulate the linear program for *Southern Fabrications plc*, incorporating this new information. What happens to the solution?

Hint: how would you alter the objective function and the constraints to accommodate this new situation?

Think about this for a moment. We have a new machine which might be assigned to any of the three jobs. Consequently, we have three new decision variables in the objective function. Continuing with the *ij* notation for the new machine 4, we would have:

X_{41} representing the assignment of machine 4 to job 1

X_{42} representing the assignment of machine 4 to job 2

X_{43} representing the assignment of machine 4 to job 3

Taking into account the amount of electricity used by machine 4, the objective function would now be:

$$20X_{11} + 30X_{12} + 18X_{13} + 18X_{21} + 36X_{22} + 10X_{23} + 12X_{31} + 28X_{32} + 6X_{33} + 18X_{41} + 32X_{42} + 14X_{43}$$

Existing constraints, relating to the requirement for each job to have a machine assigned to it, will also need amendment. For example, the constraint relating to job 1 becomes:

$$X_{11} + X_{21} + X_{31} + X_{41} = 1$$

In addition, there will be one wholly new constraint, concerning the assignment of machine 4 to a job. This would look as follows:

$$X_{41} + X_{42} + X_{43} \leq 1$$

You may now begin to appreciate the reason why we use the '$\leq$' symbol for the machine allocation assignments, rather than the straight equality '$=$'. Since there are more machines than jobs, one of these constraints must equal 0.

Including this new objective function, and the changes to the constraints, the revised formulation for the problem is:

Determine values for X_{11}, X_{12}, X_{13}, X_{21}, X_{22}, X_{23}, X_{31}, X_{32}, X_{33}, X_{41}, X_{42} and X_{43} that will:

$$\text{Minimise } 20X_{11} + 30X_{12} + 18X_{13} + 18X_{21} + 36X_{22} + 10X_{23} + 12X_{31}$$
$$+ 28X_{32} + 6X_{33} + 18X_{41} + 32X_{42} + 14X_{43}$$

Subject to:

$$X_{11} + X_{12} + X_{13} \leq 1 \quad \text{(Machine 1)}$$

$$X_{21} + X_{22} + X_{23} \leq 1 \quad \text{(Machine 2)}$$

$$X_{31} + X_{32} + X_{33} \leq 1 \quad \text{(Machine 3)}$$

$$X_{41} + X_{42} + X_{43} \leq 1 \quad \text{(Machine 4)}$$

$$X_{11} + X_{21} + X_{31} + X_{41} = 1 \quad \text{(Job 1)}$$

$$X_{12} + X_{22} + X_{32} + X_{42} = 1 \quad \text{(Job 2)}$$

$$X_{13} + X_{23} + X_{33} + X_{43} = 1 \quad \text{(Job 3)}$$

And where all X_{ij} are $0 - 1$ variables

To solve this problem, you can use the worksheet developed for Activity 70. You will need to:

- amend the formula in cell B3
- include the three new decision variables (use rows 15 to 17 for this)
- add the machine 4 allocation constraint (use row 23 for this, with the required formula in cell B23)
- add the '$\geq$' and '$\leq$' constraints for the three new $0 - 1$ variables.

Remember to declare the 12 variables to be binary if you are using Microsoft Excel version 7. Save your amended worksheet as **South2.xls**.

Calling up *Solver*, you need to:

- alter the range for the **Changing Cells**
- add the additional constraints (for machine 4 and for the three new 0 – 1 variables)
- specify that the contents of cells B15 to B17 are integer.

Hopefully you have noticed that *Solver* is dynamic, in that it automatically adjusts its cell references if you change the layout of your worksheet by, for example, adding extra rows. So do not change the existing settings.

Your solution should agree with that shown in Table 31.

	A	B
1	*Southern Fabrications plc*	
2		
3	**Objective Function – Minimise Power Used**	52
4		
5	**Decision Variables**	
6	Assign Machine 1 to Job 1 (X_{11})	0
7	Assign Machine 1 to Job 2 (X_{12})	1
8	Assign Machine 1 to Job 3 (X_{13})	0
9	Assign Machine 2 to Job 1 (X_{21})	0
10	Assign Machine 2 to Job 2 (X_{22})	0
11	Assign Machine 2 to Job 3 (X_{23})	1
12	Assign Machine 3 to Job 1 (X_{31})	1
13	Assign Machine 3 to Job 2 (X_{32})	0
14	Assign Machine 3 to Job 3 (X_{33})	0
15	Assign Machine 4 to Job 1 (X_{41})	0
16	Assign Machine 4 to Job 2 (X_{42})	0
17	Assign Machine 4 to Job 3 (X_{43})	0

Table 31: Solution values for revised Southern Fabrications assignment problem

Notice that the solution to this problem has not been altered by the addition of the fourth machine. The values X_{41}, X_{42} and X_{43} are all 0, which means that the new machine remains unassigned to a job.

THE NUMBER OF TASKS IS MORE THAN THE NUMBER OF SUPPLIERS

A more serious situation develops if there are more tasks to be done than there are suppliers to do them. This might happen in the *Southern Fabrications plc* case if there were four jobs to be done and only three machines. Under the limiting conditions facing the production scheduler (see Activity 70), where all jobs must start at the same time, and have one and only one machine assigned to them, then it will mean that the problem becomes, to use technical language, **infeasible**. This is serious: we cannot solve such a problem as it is presently constituted.

In dealing with this situation, you may well have remembered how we addressed this kind of difficulty in the transportation problem. When there was greater demand than supply, we simply invented a dummy source of supply. We can adopt a similar approach in the assignment problem. When we have more tasks to be done than suppliers to do them, we write in a dummy supplier for each extra task. In the *Southern Fabrications plc* case, this would be an extra dummy machine. The problem then becomes solvable.

This leads us to question whether the dummy variable has an effect on the objective function. The answer is that it does because, dummy or not, we have a new supplier and, therefore, new decision variables. They will be entered into the objective function, but will have a zero value, since they do not use any resources. A dummy machine, in the *Southern Fabrications plc* problem, will not use any electricity. New constraints will also be required to represent the allocation of the dummy supplier to tasks. When we interpret the solution, we will find that tasks will be allocated to the dummy variable, and this will mean that, in an optimum solution, those particular tasks cannot be assigned at the current time.

ACTIVITY 72

Here is the relevant data concerning the power requirements of each job.

	Power requirement of job		
Machine	1	2	3
1	20	30	18
2	18	36	10
3	12	28	6

Suppose that a fourth job exists. This will require an estimated 25 units of power if assigned to machine 1, 12 units if assigned to machine 2 and 10 units if assigned to machine 3. Reformulate the *Southern Fabrications plc* model, taking into account this new job, and obtain the new solution. Which jobs are allocated, and which job remains unassigned?

Hint: remember that you will need to introduce a dummy machine to make this problem feasible. How will the above table change? What amendments will you need to make to the objective function? What will your list of constraints look like?

We only have three machines to perform four jobs and, as has already been stated, left like this, the problem will be infeasible. We therefore introduce a dummy machine, which for convenience we will call machine 4. It is essential to keep clearly in your mind that no such machine actually exists: it is a logical construct and exists purely to turn an insoluble problem into a soluble one.

The new table showing the allocation of machines to jobs will look as follows:

Machine	Power requirement of job			
	1	2	3	4
1	20	30	18	25
2	18	36	10	12
3	12	28	6	10
Dummy	0	0	0	0

Table 32: Power requirements of Southern Fabrications plc jobs

Notice that there is an additional column to represent the new job, and the figures in this column give the power each machine is thought likely to need to perform this task. Machine 1 will require 25 power units, so we have a new decision variable X_{14} (machine 1 to job 4), which will appear as $25X_{14}$ in the revised objective function. Similarly, machine 2 to job 4 (requiring 12 units of power) can be represented as X_{24}, and the objective function will need to have $12X_{24}$ included in it. This process is repeated for X_{34}, the machine 3 to job 4 decision variable.

However, when we come to represent the allocation of the dummy machine 4 to jobs, we must remember that any such assignments will use zero power. Dummy machines cannot use power! Consequently, the assignments X_{41}, X_{42}, X_{43} and X_{44} (dummy to jobs 1 to 4) will all have a zero coefficient in the objective function, which can be written as:

$$20X_{11} + 30X_{12} + 18X_{13} + 25X_{14} + 18X_{21} + 36X_{22} + 10X_{23} + 12X_{24} + 12X_{31}$$
$$+ 28X_{32} + 6X_{33} + 10X_{34} + 0X_{41} + 0X_{42} + 0X_{43} + 0X_{44}$$

So we now have the updated objective function. It remains to consider how the constraints will change. Remember that there is a constraint needed to represent each machine's assignment to a job, even if it is only a dummy machine. So there will be an additional constraint for machine 4, namely:

$$X_{41} + X_{42} + X_{43} + X_{44} \leq 1$$

The formulation of the revised problem is:

Determine values for X_{11}, X_{12}, X_{13}, X_{14}, X_{21}, X_{22}, X_{23}, X_{24}, X_{31}, X_{32}, X_{33}, X_{34}, X_{41}, X_{42}, X_{43}, and X_{44} that will:

Minimise $20X_{11} + 30X_{12} + 18X_{13} + 25X_{14} + 18X_{21} + 36X_{22} + 10X_{23} + 12X_{24}$
$+ 12X_{31} + 28X_{32} + 6X_{33} + 10X_{34} + 0X_{41} + 0X_{42} + 0X_{43} + 0X_{44}$

Subject to:

$$X_{11} + X_{12} + X_{13} \leq 1 \quad \text{(Machine 1)}$$
$$X_{21} + X_{22} + X_{23} \leq 1 \quad \text{(Machine 2)}$$
$$X_{31} + X_{32} + X_{33} \leq 1 \quad \text{(Machine 3)}$$
$$X_{41} + X_{42} + X_{43} \leq 1 \quad \text{(Dummy)}$$
$$X_{11} + X_{21} + X_{31} + X_{41} = 1 \quad \text{(Job 1)}$$
$$X_{12} + X_{22} + X_{32} + X_{42} = 1 \quad \text{(Job 2)}$$
$$X_{13} + X_{23} + X_{33} + X_{43} = 1 \quad \text{(Job 3)}$$
$$X_{14} + X_{24} + X_{34} + X_{44} = 1 \quad \text{(Job 4)}$$

And where all X_{ij} are $0 - 1$ variables

If you have used *Solver* to obtain a solution to this problem then you should agree with the results shown in Table 33.

	A	B
1	*Southern Fabrications plc*	
2		
3	**Objective Function – Minimise Power Used**	38
4		
5	**Decision Variables**	
6	Assign Machine 1 to Job 1 (X_{11})	1
7	Assign Machine 1 to Job 2 (X_{12})	0
8	Assign Machine 1 to Job 3 (X_{13})	0
9	Assign Machine 1 to Job 4 (X_{14})	0
10	Assign Machine 2 to Job 1 (X_{21})	0
11	Assign Machine 2 to Job 2 (X_{22})	0
12	Assign Machine 2 to Job 3 (X_{23})	0
13	Assign Machine 2 to Job 4 (X_{24})	1
14	Assign Machine 3 to Job 1 (X_{31})	0
15	Assign Machine 3 to Job 2 (X_{32})	0
16	Assign Machine 3 to Job 3 (X_{33})	1
17	Assign Machine 3 to Job 4 (X_{34})	0
18	Assign Dummy Machine to Job 1 (X_{41})	0
19	Assign Dummy Machine to Job 2 (X_{42})	1
20	Assign Dummy Machine to Job 3 (X_{43})	0
21	Assign Dummy Machine to Job 4 (X_{44})	0

Table 33: Solution values for revised Southern Fabrications assignment problem with dummy machine

In this new optimal solution, machine 1 will perform job 1, machine 2 will be allotted job 4, and machine 3 is assigned job 3. Notice that machine 4 (the dummy) will be allocated to job 2. This is just another way of stating that job 2 will not be performed.

The optimal minimum electricity consumption is 38 units.

The Problem Requires to be Maximised Rather than Minimised

Many problems may be stated in terms of profits or revenue, or some other variable requiring to be maximised. This will only require that the objective function be altered. Other than that, no change in technique is required.

It May be Necessary to Rule Out Some Assignments Altogether

It may be the case that it is undesirable to make certain assignments. For example, in the case of *Southern Fabrications plc*, it may be that machine 1 cannot handle the electricity load for job 2. Restrictions such as this can be easily dealt with by simply omitting the decision variable (in this case X_{12}) from the linear programming formulation.

Summary

In this section of the unit we have studied the application of linear programming to a large class of problems known as assignment models. This entailed defining the assignment problem, and displaying the problem both through the use of network flow diagrams and through the use of matrices. We went through the process of formulating and solving assignment problems in which the number of agents was equal to the number of tasks to be performed. We then saw how this basic model needed to be modified, through the use of a dummy agent, in cases where this equality did not exist.

In the final section of this unit, we look at some of the limitations of the basic linear programming model. We also look at some of the ways in which these limitations can be overcome by extending the basic model.

SECTION 7
Linear Programming – Limitations and Extensions

Introduction

Although the basic linear programming model is a powerful tool for the solution of business problems, it does have a number of limitations. In this section of the unit we look at some of these limitations and at ways of extending linear programming models in order to deal with these limitations.

In Section 7.1 we address the limitations which come from the assumption that decision variables are continuous or **divisible**.

Another key assumption which underlies linear programming models is that of **linearity**. This rules out such common features of business life as price discounts on bulk orders and economies of scale. In Section 7.2 we examine ways of addressing this weakness through the use of **non-linear programming**.

The third key, limiting assumption behind linear programming is that there is only a single objective to be maximised or minimised. In the world of business, it is often the case that there are a number of objectives which may well be conflicting. In Section 7.3 we indicate that there are models that can be drawn upon in these circumstances but these are not pursued further in this unit.

By the end of this section you should be able to determine when it would be appropriate to use other mathematical programming approaches as an alternative to linear programming.

7.1 Divisibility

In the basic linear programming model, decision variables are assumed to be divisible or continuous. In many contexts, this is a perfectly reasonable thing to suppose and causes no problems. In other situations, however, the decision variables are either wholly or in part integer. For example, if a decision variable is the number of houses then an answer in the form 31.5 houses clearly makes no sense! Of course, an initial continuous solution could always be found using linear programming. We could then proceed by seeking an integer solution close to it. However, in situations that involve a large number of decision variables, this would be very inefficient, possibly very difficult and might generate a highly inaccurate solution. In practice, the remedy is to use another type of mathematical programming called **integer programming**. We have already made reference to this in Section 6 of this unit, where we defined the decision variables for the assignment model as being 0 – 1. This is a special case of integer programming.

We shall now contrast continuous and integer solutions to a linear programming problem.

ACTIVITY 73

Solve the following linear programming problem. Assume that the variables X and Y are continuous: a solution correct to two decimal places will suffice. You should use *Solver*. Save your worksheet as **Contin.xls**.

Determine values for X and Y as will:

$$\text{Maximise } 8X + 11Y$$

Subject to:9

$$3X + 2Y \leq 12$$
$$4X + 7Y \leq 28$$
$$X, Y \geq 0$$

	A	B	C
1	**Continuous versus Integer Programming**		
2			
3	**Objective Function**	47.69231	
4			
5	**Decision Variables**		
6	X variable	2.153846	
7	Y variable	2.769231	
8			
9	**Constraints**		
10	3X+2Y≤12	12	12
11	4X+7Y≤28	28	28
12	Non-negativity X	2.153846	0
13	Non-negativity Y	2.769231	0

Table 34: Continuous solution to a linear programming problem

Using *Solver* gives as the solution (correct to two decimal places):

$$X = 2.15$$

$$Y = 2.77$$

The optimal value of the objective function is 47.69.

We now modify the problem, by adding the further restriction that both X and Y should be integer. Suppose we seek the new solution by using our continuous solution as an approximation.

ACTIVITY 74

Since X and Y are now required to be integer, the only possible (X,Y) combinations that approximate the continuous solution are the following:

(3,3), (2,3), (3,2), (2,2)

Which of these is a feasible solution to our new integer programming problem?

It should be immediately clear, that, if (X = 2.15, Y = 2.77) is the continuous solution, then (X = 3, Y = 3) is not feasible, since it breaks both constraints. Nor is the solution (X = 2, Y = 3) feasible, since it breaks the second constraint. (X = 3, Y = 2) is also infeasible, since it breaks the first constraint. That leaves us with the final possibility (X = 2, Y = 2), which must be feasible and yields an objective function equal to 38.

We now have an integer solution which is feasible. However is it optimal?

ACTIVITY 75

Is (X = 2, Y = 2) the optimal solution to the integer programming problem?

As you should have discovered, the answer is 'no'. If you rerun *Solver,* adding as constraints that the two variables must be integer (remember that you do this in the *Solver* **Parameters** dialogue box), then you obtain the solution shown in Table 35.

	A	B	C
1	**Continuous versus Integer Programming**		
2			
3	**Objective Function**	44	
4			
5	**Decision Variables**		
6	X Variable	0	
7	Y Variable	4	
8			
9	**Constraints**		
10	$3X + 2Y \leq 12$	8	12
11	$4X + 7Y \leq 28$	28	28
12	Non-negativity X	0	0
13	Non-negativity Y	4	0

Table 35: Integer solution to a linear programming problem

As you can see, there is a substantial difference between this solution and the approximation obtained above. Now it is the case that (X = 0, Y = 4), with an optimal objective function value of 44.

This example is sufficient to demonstrate the important conclusion that using a continuous linear programming model to approximate an integer programming problem can lead to serious error. Therefore, if a formulated model requires variables (wholly or in part) to be integer (whether 0 – 1 or otherwise), it is essential either to use purpose-constructed integer programming computer software or, when using tools such as *Solver*, to carefully specify all of the integer restrictions.

Integer programming is outside the scope of this course and will not be pursued any further here. However, if you are interested in exploring this area further (it does not involve any difficult mathematics) then consult the recommendations for further reading at the end of this unit.

7.2 Linearity

As the name implies, a crucial assumption of linear programming, both in the objective function and the constraints, is that of linearity. The type of behaviour that this rules out is, for example:

- economies of scale (for example, the cost per unit of an input varying with the quantity used)
- price discounts on bulk orders.

To deal with features such as these we must have recourse to **non-linear programming**. To explore this approach in any depth requires the use of mathematical tools which go beyond those expected of students of business studies. However, some indication both of the types of problem that can be investigated and the methods of solution can be obtained from the following example.

Let us start with the simple two-variable problem shown below.

Determine values for X and Y that will:

      Maximise 3X + 2Y

Subject to:

$$X + 2Y \leq 12$$
$$2X + Y \leq 12$$
$$X \geq 0$$
$$Y \geq 0$$

This problem can be solved using the graphical approach that was investigated in Section 2 of this unit. Graphing the constraints yields the feasible region shown in Figure 40. Ignoring the origin, we know that the solution to the problem must be at one of its three remaining corners.

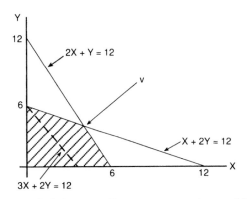

Figure 40: Solution to linear programming problem

To establish which of these corners is optimal, we graph the objective function and shift it outwards from the origin until we find the extreme point. It is straightforward to see that, for this objective function, the solution is to be found at corner *v*.

Using simultaneous equations, we find that at this corner (X = 4 and Y = 4). So the maximum value of the objective function is:

$$(3 \times 4) + (2 \times 4) = 20$$

Of course, if the gradient of the objective function is made either steeper or shallower, then there will be a point at which the solution will jump to the corners (6,0) and (0,6) respectively. We explored this in Section 3 of this unit **(sensitivity analysis)**.

So far we are still on very familiar territory. However, suppose that we amend the problem, by increasing the number of constraints, to the extent shown in Figure 41.

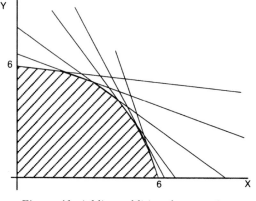

Figure 41: Adding additional constraints

Since there are now six constraints (plus the two axes) then, ignoring the origin, we have seven candidates for the solution corner. Some care would be required shifting out the objective function, but the optimal corner can still be found.

If we continue adding constraints in this way, then the resulting feasible region will approximate more and more to that shown in Figure 42.

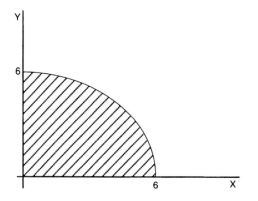

Figure 42: A non-linear feasible region

What we have done is to replace a feasible region shaped as a polygon (that is, a figure with straight edges) with one whose boundary (apart from the axes) is now a smooth, continuous curve.

We have moved from **linearity** to **non-linearity**, but in doing so we are still stating that all (X,Y) combinations within the confines of the curve and the axes (our familiar non-negativity requirement) are feasible.

Now suppose we still wish to maximise the objective function:

3X + 2Y

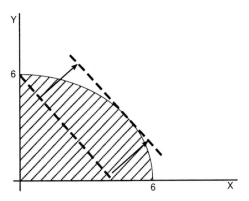

Figure 43: Non-linear optimisation

Then shifting it out to the right still generates the optimal solution as being the point where the objective function line is just tangential to the feasible region (see Figure 43). However, there is no corner at this point and, therefore, no obvious way of determining its (X,Y) coordinates. Let us state our non-linear problem more formally.

Determine values for X and Y as will:

Maximise 3X + 2Y

Subject to:

$$X^2 - 2X + 4Y \leq 24$$

$$X, Y \geq 0$$

Notice that the boundary of the constraint is the non-linear equation $X^2 - 2X + 4Y = 24$, which can be rearranged as $Y = -0.25X^2 + 0.5X + 6$. You may recognise this as a quadratic.

We have ended up with a simple example of a non-linear programming problem: it remains to find a solution.

A carefully drawn graph will yield a reasonably accurate solution. However, the only efficient way of solving this problem is to use some mathematics. Here is one way of doing this: it is not the mathematically most sophisticated approach although it does make some use of calculus. Look again at Figure 43. At the extreme point, the gradients of the objective function and the constraint are the same. Let us make use of this fact.

Firstly what is the gradient of the objective function? Remember that it graphs as a set of parallel lines: Figure 44 shows the outcome for a value of 12.

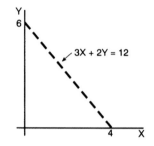

Figure 44: Graph of the objective function

The gradient of a straight line is given by the vertical change divided by the horizontal change, which in this case is:

$$-6/4 = -1.5$$

Notice that the line slopes down from left to right, and so the gradient is negative.

We now need the gradient of the (quadratic) equation $Y = -0.25X^2 + 0.5X + 6$. Since this is non-linear, the gradient is not constant, but instead it is a function of X. It can be established by differentiating the expression. If this is not something known to you, or you are unsure as to what this means, then just accept the result as giving the gradient at any given X value.

In this case, differentiating yields the gradient as $-0.5X + 0.5$. So, at the solution point for the problem we require that:

gradient of objective function $=$ gradient of constraint

$$-1.5 = -0.5X + 0.5$$

Solving this equation, we obtain $X = 4$. Then substituting 4 for X into $Y = -0.25X^2 + 0.5X + 6$, gives $Y = 4$.

So the solution to the problem is the point ($X = 4$, $Y = 4$) with an objective function value of 20. You might care to compare this with the linear programming problem, with which we started.

This is all that we have to say on the subject of non-linearity. Perhaps this limited discussion has whetted your appetite, in which case you might like to explore the area further by consulting the recommendations for further reading given at the end of this unit. However, you should be warned that you must expect to come across some quite demanding mathematics.

7.3 The existence of a single maximand

Linear programming rests on the crucial assumption that, in any problem, there is only a single objective to be either maximised or minimised. This might be to minimise cost, or to maximise contribution to profit. In effect, decision-makers are assumed to have a single, or perhaps a dominant, goal.

This can be a very restrictive assumption. A firm, for example, might have the objectives of:

- securing an adequate return for its shareholders
- achieving an adequate rate of growth
- demonstrating a concern for the environment.

Since such objectives might well be conflicting, they cannot be encompassed within the framework of linear programming. There is another branch of mathematical programming called **game programming** that can be employed to illuminate such problems, but it will not be considered here.

Summary

In this final section of the unit we noted that the basic linear programming model is subject to a number of limitations. Continuous solutions are not appropriate if the decision variables are required to take only integer values. Linearity of both constraints and objective function rules out the use of linear programming for certain types of business problem. Finally all linear programming models are predicated on the assumption that decision-makers are motivated by a single goal.

However, linear programming is only part of a wider approach to decision-making known as **mathematical programming**. We showed that the limitations of linear programming can be overcome by accessing this wider set of techniques. For example, if decision variables may take only integer values, then integer programming should be employed. If the assumption of linearity is too restrictive, then it should be dropped in favour of non-linear optimisation. Finally multiple goals can be accommodated in the approach known as goal programming. Unfortunately, however, recourse to these approaches usually requires much greater mathematical sophistication.

Unit Summary

In this unit we have investigated the operational research technique called linear programming. In Section 1 we showed how a linear programming problem is formulated. Any linear programming model consists of three components: decision variables, an objective function and a set of constraints. Decision variables are those factors in a problem for which a decision-maker seeks the optimal values. The objective function is a mathematical statement of the goal which the decision-maker wishes to achieve: it may be to maximise some quantity such as contribution to profit or sales revenue, or to minimise a quantity such as cost. Constraints are a mathematical statement of the limitations within which the decision variables are to be optimised.

Provided that a linear programming model has only two decision variables it can be solved by graphical means. Section 2 showed how this is done. For any problem, the constraints are represented by inequalities. To graph these, firstly the boundary linear equation is graphed, and then the side of the line representing the inequality is determined. The feasible region is the simultaneous solution to these constraint inequalities: it shows all combinations of the decision variables that are feasible given the constraints. Having graphed the objective function, it is shifted either outwards from the origin (for a maximisation problem) or inwards towards the origin (for a minimisation problem) until it is tangential to the feasible region. The optimal solution is always to be found at one of the corners of this region.

Having determined a solution to a linear programming problem, it is essential to investigate how robust this solution is in the face of any changes to the parameters on which it is based. Such parameters would include the right-hand side values for the constraints, and the coefficients for the decision variables in the objective function. In Section 3 we showed that, at the optimal solution, one or more of the constraints will be binding. We then examined how to determine the incremental change in the optimal value of the objective function resulting from a 1-unit change in the right-hand side of a binding constraint. This was defined as its shadow price. We then showed how to establish the right-hand side range for a constraint such that the shadow price remains unchanged. Of course, any change to the coefficient for a decision variable in the objective function might also perturb the solution to the problem. However, for this to occur the change must be sufficient to move the optimal solution to a neighbouring corner of the feasible region.

Graphical solution methods break down as soon as there are three or more decision variables. In Section 4 we used the *Solver* tool in *Microsoft Excel* to solve multi-variable linear programming problems. We saw that *Solver* also generates a full sensitivity analysis. Dedicated linear programming software is also available and would be employed for the analysis of what are often very large commercial problems.

Sections 5 and 6 introduced two refinements to the basic linear programming model: the transportation model and the assignment model. Transportation models seek the optimal routes for moving quantities from a number of sources to a number of destinations. Given that there are limits to both the amounts available from each source and the amounts required at each destination, then a typical transportation problem is to determine that set of routes which minimises cost. Assignment models are similar, except that sources and destinations have respectively an availability of and requirement for only 1 unit.

The basic linear programming model has a number of limitations: it rests on the assumption that decision variables are divisible, that both constraints and objective function are linear, and that decision-makers are motivated by a single goal. However, these limitations are not as restrictive as might first appear. Linear programming is only one of the approaches within the mathematical programming toolbox and the final section of the unit showed how such limitations can be overcome by resorting to integer, non-linear and goal programming.

Recommended Reading

Linear programming, and its extensions, is a topic in all the general textbooks on operational research and management science. In some cases the level is equivalent to that in this unit. In other instances a greater degree of mathematical sophistication is required. This is because, in any specialist treatment of linear programming, some understanding of matrices is required. The recommended reading is indicative of this spread of texts.

Dennis, T L and Dennis, L B (1991) *Management Science*, West Publishing, Minneapolis, USA

This text covers linear programming comprehensively and makes no great mathematical demands upon the reader. As well as dealing with graphical linear programming (Chapter 3), computer solutions to LP problems (Chapter 6) and transportation and assignment models (Chapter 7) it will extend your understanding in a number of directions. Firstly, Chapter 4 discusses the simplex algorithm: this is the basis for most commercial linear programming software. Secondly, Chapter 5 shows that, for any LP problem, there is a related problem know as the **dual**. Finally, Chapter 9 examines integer programming.

Anderson, J, Sweeney, D R and Williams, T A (1994) *An Introduction to Management Science*, West Publishing, Minneapolis, USA

Chapters 2 to 8 cover the same range of topics as Dennis and Dennis: the approach is not particularly mathematical. Chapter 5 is a very useful discussion of a range of linear programming applications. This includes some reference to the relatively new technique of data envelopment analysis, which is used to determine relative efficiency across a set of decision-making units, such as schools and hospitals. Chapter 15 has a discussion of goal programming which, since it uses only a graphical approach, should be completely accessible to the business studies student.

Taha, H A (1992) *Operations Research*, Oxford University Press, London

This text is indicative of those that provide a full mathematical grounding in linear programming. It demands an understanding of linear algebra, although there is a brief appendix that revises matrices and the required operations. Chapters 2 to 7 and Chapter 9 cover linear programming and its applications. There is an introduction to non-linear programming in Chapter 12, though you are warned that this is more mathematically demanding. Dynamic (multi-stage) programming is investigated in Chapter 10.

UNIT 4
REGRESSION ANALYSIS

Introduction

Regression analysis is an important quantitative technique which enables us to model the behaviour of key variables (such as sales or costs) and to predict how these variables will behave in the future. Although predicting the behaviour of business variables is an area about which much scepticism exists, it is also a task which is of vital importance in strategic planning and forecasting.

Section 1 of this unit looks at the nature of **functional relationships** between variables. Section 2 goes on to look at **causal models** involving two variables: these are known as **bivariate models**. Section 3 looks at the technique of **regression analysis**. Sections 4 to 6 introduce a variety of methods for testing the accuracy of the predictions which regression analysis produces. Section 4 deals with the predictive accuracy of regression models, Section 5 introduces a technique known as the analysis of **residuals**, while in Section 6 we estimate the likely scale of any errors produced by our predictions. This is done through the use of the concept of **confidence intervals**.

All of the material in Sections 1 to 6 refers to models with only two variables. In Section 7, we look at models with more than two variables: these are known as **multivariate models**. In Section 8 we look at ways of assessing the predictions produced by such models and in Section 9 we use this assessment to refine the model. Finally, in Section 10, we take a brief look at some more advanced techniques to allow regression analysis to be applied to **non-linear** relationships.

To complete this unit, you will need some graph paper and a pencil and ruler. **You will also need a computer with *Microsoft Excel* (including the *Regression* Add-in). If you do not have *Regression* installed as part of *Microsoft Excel*, you will need to install it before completing this unit. You should be able to do this with *Microsoft Excel* running. Click on Tools and select the Add-Ins sub-menu. Make sure the Analysis ToolPak box is checked and click on OK.**

Objectives

After working through this unit you should be able to:

- define the terms dependent, independent and explanatory as they are used in relation to variables
- distinguish between linear, exponential and logarithmic functions and express them using functional notation
- check for the strength and type of relationship between variables by analysing bivariate data using scatterplots and correlation
- construct a simple linear regression model for bivariate data
- make use of *Microsoft Excel* to obtain appropriate regression output

- use the analysis of R-Squared to analyse the performance of a regression model

- use residuals analysis to analyse the performance of a regression model

- use confidence intervals to estimate the likely scale of any errors produced by a regression model

- construct the general linear multivariate regression model

- use this model to make predictions

- use dummy variables to incorporate qualitative variables into a regression model

- use lagged variables in regression analysis

- recode and transform selected non-linear variables in order to use the technique of linear regression on them.

SECTION 1
Functional Relationships

Introduction

Section 1 of this unit looks at the nature of functional relationships between variables. In Section 1.1 we introduce functional notation as a means of describing functional relationships, and in Section 1.2 we distinguish between dependent and independent variables. In Sections 1.3 and 1.4 we examine the relationships which can exist between variables. Section 1.3 looks at linear relationships, while Section 1.4 looks at two types of non-linear relationship, those where the relationship is of an exponential nature and those where the relationship is logarithmic. By the end of this section, you should be able to define the terms **dependent, independent** and **explanatory** as they are used in relation to variables, and you should also be able to distinguish between linear, exponential and logarithmic functions and express them using functional notation.

1.1 Functional notation

Any mathematical model implies the existence of a set of two or more variables, and a set of functional relationships specified to hold between these variables. A functional relationship is one where one of the variables is dependent on one or more other variables. A common form of notation used when discussing functional relationships is as follows:

$$y = f(x)$$

The letter y represents the variable which depends upon the other variable, represented by the letter x. The letter f is an abbreviation for 'function'. A function is a kind of mathematical rule which precisely describes the nature of the relationship between the two variables. So we would read the whole expression as 'y is a function of x'. This is called functional notation, and it is a useful first step when building mathematical models.

ACTIVITY 1

Suppose that we wish to analyse the weekly demand for a certain consumer product. The most important influences on demand are supply and price. We start by defining the relevant variables as follows, where Q stands for 'quantity':

P = the price per unit of the product

Q_d = the demand for the product

Q_s = the supply of the product

Use functional notation to state the relationships between these variables.

This is what is known as the demand-supply relationship, and is a standard component of most economic theory.

There are two functional relationships:

$$Q_d = f(P)$$

$$Q_s = f(P)$$

$Q_d = f(P)$ is the demand function and states that quantity demanded is a function of price. $Q_s = f(P)$ is the supply function and states that quantity supplied is a function of price.

This can also be expressed in a single statement:

$$Q_d = f(P, Q_s)$$

This states that quantity demanded is a function of both price and quantity supplied. The full statement will also include a condition for equilibrium:

$$Q_s = Q_d$$

In other words, supply equals demand.

The process of describing functional relationships between variables is known as **mathematical modelling**.

1.2 Dependent and independent variables

In any functional relationship, some variables are described as **dependent** and some as **independent**. For example, we might be interested in constructing a model of how demand for a product is related to the size of the promotion budget for the product, the type of promotion used, and the price of the main competing product.

In this case we can say that demand is the dependent variable because we believe that it depends in some way on the other three variables, which are consequently described as independent. In any model, it is the analyst who decides whether a variable is described as dependent or independent. If we wish to analyse the behaviour of sales, then sales becomes the dependent variable and we must look for a set of independent variables which we believe exert some collective influence on sales. So, if a business analyst wishes to develop a model which will assist him or her in the prediction of some important variable, then this variable will be the dependent variable. An important step in the development of a good predictive model is the selection of a set of independent variables which can successfully predict or explain the behaviour of whatever variable is of interest to us. For this reason, the independent variables are also sometimes called **explanatory** variables.

ACTIVITY 2

Suppose that an estate agency wishes to develop a model to help predict the value of a house. In such a case, value is the dependent variable. Can you think of three other factors which could be used as independent or explanatory variables?

There are a very large number of potential explanatory variables for such a model. You may have suggested some of the following:

- age of property
- size of property
- parking facilities
- garden
- proximity of property to amenities
- condition of property.

In a search for explanatory variables to use in a model, it does not follow that all of the factors we might initially think to be good predictors of our dependent variable will be equally useful. As we shall see later, an important part of the process of model development is to include only the variables which we find useful and exclude those which tell us nothing useful about the behaviour we wish to predict.

A model which has two or more independent, or explanatory variables is called a **multivariate** model. A model with only one independent variable is called a **bivariate** model.

1.3 Linear relationships between variables

So far, we have explained how to use functional notation to describe relationships between variables and we have also differentiated between dependent and independent (or explanatory) variables. We know that the expression $y = f(x)$ is a shorthand way of saying 'y is a function of x'. But how exactly is y related to x? There are a number of possible functional relationships which can exist between two variables. For the moment, we will restrict ourselves to discussing linear relationships: in Section 1.4 we will discuss non-linear relationships.

As you should remember from Unit 3, two variables are linearly related if the graph illustrating the relationship is a straight line. Expressed more formally, if two variables (conventionally called X and Y) are exactly linearly related, then we can express this relationship as an algebraic equation. The general form of a linear equation, where α and β are **constants** is:

$$Y = \alpha + \beta X$$

The constant α (the Greek letter 'alpha') is called the Y intercept of the function because it represents the point where the graph of the function cuts through the vertical axis. The constant β (the Greek letter 'beta') represents the rate of change of the variable Y for a given unit change in X. It therefore expresses the slope of the graph of the function.

ACTIVITY 3

Look at the following linear functions:

$$Y = 4 + 2X$$

$$Y = 3 - 2X$$

1. For each function, state the Y intercept and the slope.

2. Use this information to help you sketch the graphs of the functions.

---

1. In the case of $Y = 4 + 2X$, the α constant is equal to 4, meaning that the graph of this function passes through the Y-axis at the point given by the

coordinates (0, 4). The β value is equal to 2, which means that for every 1-unit increase in X there is a 2-unit increase in Y.

In the case of Y = 3 – 2X, the α value is equal to 3, meaning that the graph representing this function passes through the vertical axis at the point given by the coordinates (0, 3). The β value is equal to –2, which means that for every 1-unit increase in X there is a 2-unit decrease in Y.

2. The graphs of the functions are shown in Figures 1 and 2.

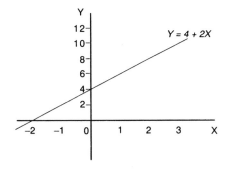

Figure 1: Graph of Y = 4 + 2X

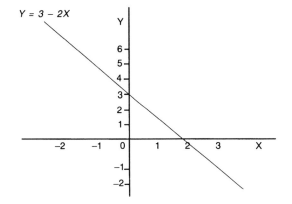

Figure 2: Graph of Y = 3 – 2X

Using these methods, it is easy to characterise the behaviour of any bivariate linear function. This is because such functions are easy to visualise in graphic form. Multivariate linear functions (which we shall be dealing with in Section 7) are rather more complicated.

1.4 Non-linear relationships between variables

Any function whose graph does not have a straight line can be described as non-linear. Quite clearly this could describe a vast multitude of possibilities. However, we will describe just two functions often used in model-building: the exponential function and the logarithmic function.

THE EXPONENTIAL FUNCTION

The word exponential means 'growing at an increasing rate'. To gain a clearer understanding of exactly what this means, we shall look at an example.

ACTIVITY 4

1. Use *Microsoft Excel* to draw a graph of the following set of co-ordinates:

   (0, 0.5), (0.5, 0.70), (1.0, 1.0), (1.5, 1.41), (2.0, 2.0), (2.5, 2.9), (3.0, 4.0), (3.5, 5.7), (4.0, 8.0), (4.5, 11.3), (5.0, 16.0)

   If you don't know how to do this, refer to the instructions in Appendix 1 at the end of this module.

2. What do you observe about the slope of the graph?

---

1. The graph of the data is shown in Figure 3.

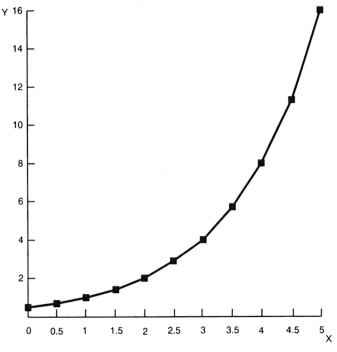

Figure 3: Graph of data in Activity 4

2. You will notice that there is an upward slope: as X increases so Y increases. However, the relationship is not linear. Instead, the slope gets steeper as X increases, showing that Y is increasing **exponentially**. This is very different from linear functions, where the rate of change remains constant.

The graph in Figure 3 is of an **exponential function**. In general, the mathematical form of an exponential function is $Y = \alpha\beta^X$ where α and β are the constants which define the function. Both α and β must be positive numbers. In the case of the function graphed in Activity 4, α equals 0.5 and β equals 2. So this function would be expressed in mathematical language as $Y = 0.5 \times 2^X$.

ACTIVITY 5

1. Use *Microsoft Excel* to calculate values of the exponential function $Y = \alpha\beta^X$, where $\alpha = 0.5$ and $\beta = 2$ for values of X from 0 to 8 inclusive.

In cell A1 enter **0.5** (the value for α) and in cell A2 enter **2** (the value for β). Enter the heading **X** in cell A4 and enter the heading **Y** in cell B4.

Enter the values **0, 1...8** in cells A5 to A13.

In cell B5 enter the formula **=$A$1*$A$2^A5** to calculate $\alpha\beta^X$. Notice the use of the dollar sign for absolute cell references. This formula means 'the value in A1, multiplied by the value in A2 to the power of the value in A5 (or A6 or A7, and so on)'.

Copy this formula into cells B6 to B13. Notice that the absolute references in the formula remain unchanged while the relative cell reference 'A5' changes.

Select cells A5 to B13 and use *Microsoft Excel* to draw the graph of this function. If you don't remember how to do this, refer to Appendix 1.

2. Change the value of β in your spreadsheet (the value contained in cell A2). What happens to the graph?

3. What happens to the graph if the value of β is between 0 and 1?

---

1. The graph of the data is shown in Figure 4.

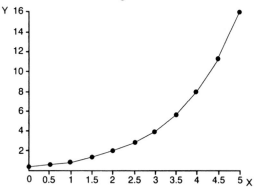

Figure 4: Graph of the function Y = 0.5 × 2^X

2. Increasing the value of β will result in a slope which accelerates at a faster rate. On the chart, this will be expressed in the form of a steeper slope and higher values on the Y-axis.

3. If β takes a value between 0 and 1, the result will be a function which is declining rather than increasing. On the chart, this will be expressed in the form of a downward sloping chart. The nearer to 0 the value of β, the steeper the downward slope of the chart.

Exponential functions can be very useful in the model-building process because there are many economic and business variables which grow or decline at exponential rates. Population is an example of exponential growth. But there are many others. For example, an exponential function can be used to model the growth of money sums at compound interest, as in a savings account, or inflation at a constant rate of growth.

THE LOGARITHMIC FUNCTION

There is another class of mathematical models referred to as **logarithmic functions**. In general, the classic behaviour of the logarithmic function is that of an upwardly increasing trend as with exponential growth. In this case however, the rate of upward increase is gradually slowing down. These functions are also useful in model building. As with the exponential case, we will begin the exploration of these models by referring to an example.

ACTIVITY 6

The following data refers to sales (in £000s) of a product from the first year when it was launched as a new product to the tenth year of its life.

Year	Sales
1	110
2	135
3	153
4	167
5	178
6	188
7	197
8	205
9	213
10	219

1. Enter this data into *Microsoft Excel* and draw a line graph, taking the year to be the X variable and taking sales to be the Y variable.

2. What do you observe about the slope of the line you have drawn?

1. The graph of the data is shown in Figure 5.

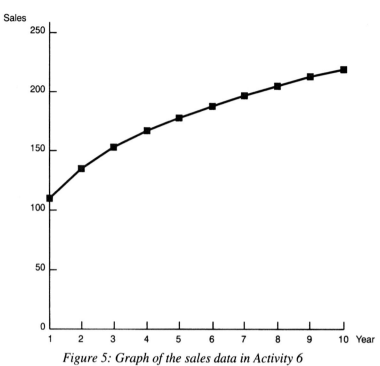

Figure 5: Graph of the sales data in Activity 6

2. Sales are increasing year on year. However, the pattern of increase is not linear: the rate of increase is slowing down. Because of this behaviour, we say that sales are growing at a logarithmic rate, and the function shown in Figure 5 is known as a logarithmic function.

In general, the mathematical form of any logarithmic function is always $Y = \alpha X^\beta$, where α and β are constants which determine how the logarithmic function behaves. For the data in Activity 6, $\alpha = 110$ and $\beta = 0.3$. The function describing sales behaviour would therefore be written in full as:

$$Y = 110X^{0.3}$$

We now need to look at what happens if we change the value of the constants in a logarithmic function.

ACTIVITY 7

1. Use *Microsoft Excel* to draw the graph of the function $Y = 110X^{0.3}$ for values of X from 1 to 10. Enter the values 110 into cell A1 and 0.3 into cell A2; enter values of X from 1 to 10 in cells A5:A14. Take care when entering the formula.

2. What happens to the graph of the function if you alter the value of α?

3. What happens to the graph of the function if you alter the value of β?

---

1. You should have entered the formula =$A$1*A5^$A$2 into cell B5 and copied it down to cell B14. The graph of the function will look very similar to the graph produced in Activity 6 (shown as Figure 5 above).

2. The α value determines the starting point for the series when X = 1. In the sales problem, because α = 110, this would mean that sales in year 1 equal 110.

3. The effect of varying the behaviour of β is more interesting. If β is greater than 0 but less than 1, then the function will have an upward slope, with a gradually declining rate of increase, as with the sales data in Activity 6.

   If β has a value greater than 1, then the logarithmic function will still have an upward slope, as before, but this time the rate of increase will be upward. This will be similar to the exponential function (except that the logarithmic function will not show the same dramatic rates of upward change as the exponential function).

   If β has a negative value, then the logarithmic function will be falling, and the rate of fall will gradually decrease as X increases. This is very similar to the exponential model.

Model-builders are particularly interested in what happens when β is greater than 0 but less than 1. This is because there are many examples where business variables behave in precisely this way. The most common example is probably sales. The life cycle of a new product often begins with sales rising rapidly as the product makes an impact, but then sales begin to level off, as the market begins to mature and becomes more competitive. The logarithmic function is excellent for modelling such situations.

Summary

In Section 1 of this unit we have looked at the nature of functional relationships between variables. We started by introducing functional notation as a means of describing functional relationships. We then distinguished between dependent and independent variables before going on to examine the relationships which can exist between variables. Section 1.3 looked at linear relationships, while Section 1.4 looked at two types of non-linear relationship: those where the relationship is of an exponential nature and those where the relationship is logarithmic. In the next section we will restrict ourselves to one particular kind of functional relationship, that of the linear variety with just one independent variable.

SECTION 2
Bivariate Causal Models

Introduction

In this section we will begin our study of the technique of regression by starting with a model which only involves two variables, one dependent and one independent. For the sake of simplicity, we shall also assume that the relationships between these variables are linear. We use a case study of a mail order firm to introduce the concept of **regression analysis**. We then use **scatterplots** as one method of analysing the data produced by regression analysis before using the **coefficient of correlation** to carry out a more sophisticated analysis of this kind of data.

By the end of this section, you should be able to check for the strength and type of relationship between variables by analysing bivariate data using scatterplots and correlation and to construct a simple linear regression model for bivariate data.

2.1 The relationship between variables

Throughout this section we will use the following case study to illustrate what is meant by a causal model and how it can be used to make forecasts.

Case Study: Celtic Mail Order Ltd

Celtic Mail Order Ltd is a mail order company that deals with children's clothing. Its customers are families living in the United Kingdom. *Celtic Mail Order Ltd*'s reputation is based upon its guarantee to despatch all orders on the same day as they are received in the post. To keep costs down, *Celtic Mail Order Ltd* employs casual labour on a day-to-day basis to deal with orders received: the bigger the volume of orders, the more daily staff are taken on. *Celtic Mail Order Ltd*'s manager is looking for some means of quickly forecasting the number of orders that there are in the incoming mail, so that the correct number of staff can be taken on. She considers that the weight of each day's mail gives a good indication of the number of orders, and has recorded the following data over ten days trading (see Table 1).

Day	Weight (kg)	Orders (00s)
1	23	58
2	17	50
3	24	54
4	35	64
5	10	40
6	16	43
7	15	42
8	24	50
9	18	53
10	30	62

Table 1: Celtic Mail Order Ltd data

You have been given the task of constructing a model that can be used to predict the daily number of orders, given the weight of each day's incoming mail.

ACTIVITY 8

1. What are the two variables in this problem and what is the claimed functional relationship between them?

2. How would we express this in functional notation?

---

1. The two variables are the weight of the incoming mail (in kg) and the number of orders received in the post (in 00s). The claimed functional relationship is that the number of orders depends upon the weight of the mail.

2. This could be written in functional notation as:

$$O = f(W)$$

This states that the number of orders (O) is a function of the weight (W) of the incoming mail.

We have no evidence, as yet, to suppose that such a relationship really exists. Even if we did have such evidence, we still would not know what the nature of that relationship was.

We have two distinct problems here. Before we can construct our model of the relationship between the number of orders and the weight of the incoming mail, we must be able to measure the extent to which the variables depend upon each other.

We do this using scatterplots and through the technique of correlation analysis. If there is no dependency of one variable on another, or if this relationship is weak, then there is little point proceeding with the construction of our model.

If we have evidence that one variable is strongly dependent upon another one, we then need to find out what form this relationship takes. If we cannot do this then we will not be able to predict the behaviour of the dependent variable, which is the real aim of model building. The process of discovering the nature of the underlying relationship between variables is called regression analysis.

2.2 Using scatterplots

Since we have suggested a proposed model where there is a causal relationship between orders and weight of mail, we must be prepared both to substantiate this claim and to offer some explanation of the meaning of the relationship. An essential first step in constructing the model of the *Celtic Mail Order Ltd* problem is to enter the data into a *Microsoft Excel* worksheet.

ACTIVITY 9

Enter the data for the *Celtic Mail Order Ltd* into a new *Microsoft Excel* worksheet. Enter the data in column form. Give column A the title **Weight** and column B the title **Orders**. Save it to file as **Celtic.xls**.

The finished product should look as in Table 2. You should keep this spreadsheet available as you work through the next few sections, as we will be referring to this example.

	A	B
1	Weight	Orders
2	23	58
3	17	50
4	24	54
5	35	64
6	10	40
7	16	43
8	15	42
9	24	50
10	18	53
11	30	62

Table 2: Celtic.xls

Our proposed model suggests that number of orders depends upon the weight of the mail. Correlation analysis is one technique that will help us to see whether there is any evidence for this. One way of doing this is to draw a special chart of the data called a **scatterplot**. A scatterplot is a special kind of graph which shows XY coordinates on the grid but not connected together with the usual line. Scatterplots can be drawn manually but it is much easier to use the chart facility in *Microsoft Excel*.

ACTIVITY 10

Use the **Celtic.xls** spreadsheet you constructed in the last activity as a basis for a scatterplot for the *Celtic Mail Order Ltd* data.

If you don't remember how to use *Microsoft Excel* to draw a graph, refer to Appendix 1 at the end of this unit. You should select the **Chart type** called '(XY) Scatter' and leave the **Chart sub-type** on the default setting (with the description 'Scatter. Compares pairs of values').

The result of drawing the scatterplot of the *Celtic Mail Order Ltd* data is shown in Figure 6. It is conventional to use the Y-axis for the dependent variable, and the X-axis for the independent variable.

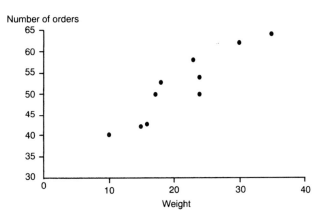

Figure 6: Scatterplot of the Celtic Mail Order data

Now we have drawn a scatterplot, the next step is to interpret it.

ACTIVITY 11

Examine the scatterplot in Figure 6 and consider what it shows about the relationship between number of orders and weight of mail.

1. Describe the distribution of points on the graph.

2. What is the relationship between the two variables?

---

1. The cluster of points on the scatterplot is fairly closely grouped and shows a general upward movement from left to right. A straight line could be drawn through the data points on the scatterplot, and most of these points would lie close to this line.

2. For the mail order data, the scatterplot shows that the two variables are related in that a rise in the weight of the incoming mail is associated with an increase in the number of orders. This relationship appears to be linear. We might, therefore, wish to conclude that, the number of orders depends upon the weight of the incoming mail, but that the relationship is disturbed by a range of other factors (varying number of orders per letter, bills, junk mail and so forth) that vary unpredictably from day to day.

2.3 The coefficient of correlation

Although examination of a scatterplot is a useful start to analysing relationships between variables, it would be helpful to have a more precise way of estimating the degree of association, or **correlation** between variables.

This correlation may be either positive or negative. In the context of correlation analysis, positive correlation means that the two variables change in the same direction and negative correlation means that the two variables change in opposite directions. A good example of positive correlation would be the association between advertising expenditure and sales. We would expect this to be positive in the sense that the higher the advertising budget, the higher the level of sales. A good example of negative correlation would be the relationship between the price of a product and the demand for it. We would expect this to be negative in that we would expect a higher price to result in fewer sales, and a lower price to result in more sales.

Both positive and negative correlation can be expressed by a useful statistic, known as the **Pearson product moment coefficient of correlation**. This is normally abbreviated to r. The value of r is always between -1 and $+1$.

Perfect positive correlation would be described by $r = +1$. This would imply that, as soon as the value of X is known, then the value of Y can be determined with 100 per cent accuracy. Perfect negative correlation would be described by $r = -1$. This would also imply that, as soon as the value of X is known, then the value of Y can be determined with 100 per cent accuracy. A complete absence of correlation would be described by $r = 0$.

Of course, we are unlikely in reality to get these extremes. In so far as r lies close to $+1$ or -1, then we argue that correlation is strong. If r lies close to 0, then we argue that correlation is weak. It is important to state at this point that r is only an effective measure of correlation in those cases where we can assume that any relationship is linear.

ACTIVITY 12

Make sketches showing what the scatterplots would look like for data where:

- $r = +1$
- $r = -1$
- $r = 0$

The scatterplots might look something like the ones shown in Figure 7.

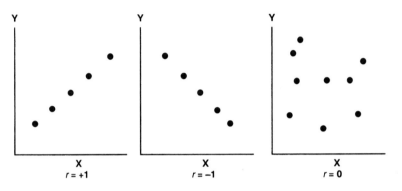

Figure 7: Scatterplots showing three extreme cases of correlation

The scatterplot for positively correlated data slopes upwards to the right, while the plot for negatively correlated data slopes downwards to the right. The more perfectly correlated the data, the closer the points will be to an exact straight line. For more weakly correlated data, the points will have less directional tendency and, in the extreme case of $r = 0$, the plotted points will be scattered randomly over the graph.

We will use *Microsoft Excel* to calculate the value of r.

ACTIVITY 13

1. Return to your **Celtic.xls** spreadsheet containing the mail order data.

- In cell C2 enter the text **Correlation coefficient**.

- In cell C3 enter the formula =**CORREL(A2:A11, B2:B11)**. *Microsoft Excel* then returns the coefficient of correlation. (The general syntax of this formula is =**CORREL(X range, Y range)**.)

2. What do you conclude concerning the relationship between these variables?

---

1. To two decimal places, the value of *r* for the *Celtic Mail Order Ltd* data is +0.92.

2. Remember that +1 is perfect positive correlation. We have a value of +0.92. This confirms what we already know from our analysis of the scatterplot for the data: that is, that correlation is positive and quite strong.

This is a good point in the analysis to stop and reflect on what we have done so far regarding the use and interpretation of scatterplots and *r*. The following activity should help you to absorb the points we have made in this section.

ACTIVITY 14

Many people are concerned with energy, and would like to have reliable methods of forecasting energy use. Suppose you have been asked to develop an energy model where population size is to be used as an explanatory variable. The following data is available. Population is measured in tens of thousands, and energy is measured in thousands of kilowatt-hours (kWh).

Population (0000s)	Energy (000s kWh)
3.7	0.9
12.9	3.1
6.5	2.1
1.0	0.4
11.4	3.5
2.5	1.0
9.3	2.7
5.1	1.5
7.7	2.3
4.9	2.0

1. Which would be the dependent variable and which the independent variable?

2. Enter the data into *Microsoft Excel,* as in the *Celtic Mail Order Ltd* example, using one column for the population data and another for the power use. Save the worksheet as **Energy.xls**. Using *Microsoft Excel*, draw a scatterplot for the data and use it to describe the type of relationship existing between energy use and population.

3. Calculate the coefficient of correlation between the variables. What does it add to your knowledge about the relationship?

---

1. We wish to develop a model for forecasting energy use on the basis of population size. Consequently, energy use is the dependent variable and population is the independent variable.

2. The resulting scatterplot is shown in Figure 8.

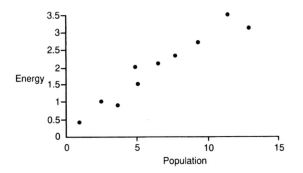

Figure 8: Scatterplot for Energy.xls data

The points seem to lie about an upward sloping line, so we know that positive correlation exists. Further, since the points cluster fairly closely together, we can say that the variables are strongly correlated in a linear relationship.

3. The coefficient of correlation is +0.96. On the evidence of this data, we should be able to develop a successful model of energy use.

Summary

In this section we have looked at models involving only two variables, one dependent and one independent, and we have assumed that the relationships between these variables are linear. We have looked at the concept of regression analysis and we have used two important methods for analysing the relationships between variables: scatterplots and the coefficient of correlation. In the next section, we take a closer look at the technique of regression analysis.

The Technique of Regression Analysis

Introduction

In this section we will discuss the technique of regression analysis. We start, in Section 3.1, by looking at inexact linear relationships and how we can deal with them. Then, in Section 3.2, we introduce the technique of regression analysis by performing manual calculations. Finally, in Section 3.3, we use *Microsoft Excel* to carry out regression analysis. By the end of this section you should be able to make use of *Microsoft Excel* to obtain appropriate regression output.

3.1 Inexact linear relationships

Remember that any two-variable linear function has the form $Y = \alpha + \beta X$. If we can find out the values of α and β then we have solved the problem. Unfortunately, this is not as simple as it may sound. For the *Celtic Mail Order Ltd* data, our scatterpoints do not lie along an exact straight line, and so we cannot write out an algebraic function which exactly predicts the number of orders which will result from a given weight of incoming mail.

ACTIVITY 15

Why doesn't the mail order data lie exactly along a straight line? In other words, why doesn't the weight of the incoming mail exactly determine the number of orders?

The obvious reason why the number of orders is not exactly proportional to the weight of the incoming mail is that the mail will include other items (such as bills and advertising material) that will vary in amount from one day to another. Also there is no fixed ratio of orders to letter: one item of mail might include more orders than another item. Another reason might be inaccuracies in the recording of data.

Suppose we have two variables, X and Y, and we believe that Y depends upon X. We further believe that the relationship is linear but not exact. This might be because other variables may also influence Y or because there may be errors in the measurement of the data. We represent any such disturbances with u (this is called the **disturbance** or **error term**). To allow for this we rewrite the standard form of the two-variable linear function as:

$$Y = \alpha + \beta X + u$$

This covers all the other factors that might affect the variable Y (other than X). So for the mail order problem our model is:

$$\text{Orders} = \alpha + \beta(\text{Weight}) + u$$

To make this model operational we need to establish the values for α and β. Since the error term u varies unpredictably from day to day, the best we can do is to estimate α and β as closely as we can. Let:

a = the estimate of α

b = the estimate of β

Then our estimated model becomes:

$$\hat{\text{Orders}} = a + b(\text{Weight})$$

$\hat{\text{Orders}}$ is the estimated value of orders. (The symbol '∧' over a value indicates that we are using an estimate and not the exact value.) It is because a and b are only estimates of α and β that $a + b(\text{Weight})$ gives the estimated and not the actual value of orders that corresponds to any given value of weight.

For any value of weight in the mail order data, the discrepancy between the actual and estimated value of orders is measured by:

$$\hat{\text{Orders}} - \text{Orders}$$

This discrepancy is called a residual. Clearly it would be desirable, in obtaining values for a and b, for these discrepancies or residuals to be minimised. What this means can best be seen by considering the graph in Figure 9.

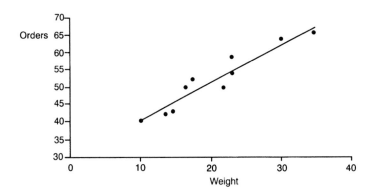

Figure 9: Residuals and Celtic Mail Order Ltd data

Each point on the scatterplot is a pair of values for weight and number of orders. For points which lie above the line, there is a positive residual: for points which lie below the line, there is a negative residual. Choosing the best values of *a* and *b* for the linear model is rather like taking a transparent ruler and drawing a straight line through the scatterplot points in such a way as to best fit the data.

The regression method consists of finding the line which minimises the differences between the actual value of orders and the estimated value. In practice, this means minimising the residuals. However, simply adding residuals together will usually result in a number close to 0. This is because positive and negative residuals, however large, will tend to cancel each other out. This will not help us in our search for the line of best fit. Instead, we add the squares of the residuals and find the line which minimises this value. This is because squaring the negative residuals converts them into positive values.

So we proceed by finding the line which minimises the sum of the squares of the residuals. This value is expressed mathematically as follows:

$$\Sigma(\text{Orders} - \hat{\text{Orders}})^2$$

(The symbol Σ, the Greek capital letter sigma, means 'sum of'.)

3.2 Regression analysis: the procedure

The procedure described above is referred to as **ordinary least squares**. The line of best fit which results from carrying out this procedure is known as a **regression line**. The method is simply called **regression analysis**.

In order to fit a straight line to data, we need to find the intercept (the α value), and the slope (the β value). Since we cannot know the exact values of α and β, we work with estimates *a* and *b*. We start from the premise that the line of best fit minimises the sum of the squared residuals.

The details of how we obtain the values of *a* and *b* are rather complicated. Fortunately, we can use *Microsoft Excel* to do the calculations for us. However, it is worth gaining some understanding of just what these calculations are so that we understand what is happening.

The process is demonstrated using the *Celtic Mail Order Ltd* regression data shown in Table 3.

1	2	3	4
X	Y	X²	XY
23	58	529	1334
17	50	289	850
24	54	576	1296
35	64	1225	2240
10	40	100	400
16	43	256	688
15	42	225	630
24	50	576	1200
18	53	324	954
30	62	900	1860
ΣX	ΣY	ΣX²	ΣXY
212	516	5000	11452

Table 3: Celtic Mail Order Ltd regression data

1. To calculate the value of b, we use X and Y to represent the independent and dependent variables respectively.

2. We sum all of the values of X to give us the total value $\sum X$ (sum of X). This is done in column 1 of the table.

3. We do the same for Y to give us the total value $\sum Y$. This is done in column 2.

4. We calculate all the squares of X and sum these to give us the total value $\sum X^2$. This is done in column 3.

5. We then multiply X by Y to give us the value XY for each pair of variables, and we sum all of the values of XY to give us the total value $\sum XY$ (sum of XY). This is done in column 4.

6. Finally, we calculate the means of the X and Y data (represented by the symbols $\overline{X}$ and $\overline{Y}$. (We use N to represent the number of pairs of XY data.)

   We do this by separately totalling the X and Y data and dividing each by N as follows:

   $$\overline{X} = \frac{1}{N} \times \sum X = \frac{212}{10} = 21.2$$

   $$\overline{Y} = \frac{1}{N} \times \sum Y = \frac{516}{10} = 51.6$$

The value of b is then given by the formula:

$$b = \frac{\sum XY - \overline{X} \sum Y}{\sum X^2 - \overline{X} \sum X}$$

The value of a is then given by the formula:

$$a = \overline{Y} - (b \times \overline{X})$$

These two expressions are the **regression equations**, and solving them will give us the estimates for a and b to fit into the standard linear equation. You should not worry too much about how the formulae for a and b were obtained, as the mathematics are somewhat abstruse!

ACTIVITY 16

Use the regression equations for a and b given above, the data in Table 3, and the values for $\overline{X}$ and $\overline{Y}$. Solve the regression equations to find values for a and b.

$$b = \frac{\sum XY - \overline{X}\sum Y}{\sum X^2 - \overline{X}\sum X}$$

$$= \frac{11452 - (21.2 \times 516)}{5000 - (21.2 \times 212)}$$

$$= 512.8/505.6$$

$$= 1.014240506$$

Do not round off your answer for b at this stage, as we require it to estimate a.

$$a = \overline{Y} - (b \times \overline{X})$$

$$= 51.6 - (1.014240506 \times 21.2)$$

$$= 30.09810$$

So the final line of best fit for the mail order data is obtained as below.

$$Y = a + bx$$

Since b equals 1.014 and a equals 30.098, we have:

$$Y = 30.098 + 1.014X$$

Remember that, for any given weight of incoming mail, this equation gives us the estimated and not the actual number of resulting orders. Now that we have this result, we can try our hand at some prediction.

ACTIVITY 17

The incoming mail weighs 28kg. Use the equation for the line of best fit to predict the number of orders contained in the incoming mail.

The line of best fit is:

$$Y = 30.098 + 1.014X$$

We have a value of X (weight of incoming mail) of 28kg. This gives:

$$Y = 30.098 + (1.014 \times 28) = 58.49$$

We therefore predict that a mailbag weighing 28kg would contain 5,849 orders.

ACTIVITY 18

Take another look at the data you saved as **Energy.xls** in Activity 14.

1. Use the regression equations to calculate values for a and b.
2. Solve the linear equation for the line of best fit for this data.
3. Use this to predict the energy use for a population of 80,000 (X = 8).

---

1. The first task in any regression calculation is to make the correct choice for the X and Y variables. Y is always used to indicate the dependent variable, so we make Y represent energy use.

Population	Energy		
X	Y	X²	XY
3.7	0.9	13.69	3.33
12.9	3.1	166.41	39.99
6.5	2.1	42.25	13.65
1.0	0.4	1.00	0.40
11.4	3.5	129.96	39.90
2.5	1.0	6.25	2.50
9.3	2.7	86.49	25.11
5.1	1.5	26.01	7.65
7.7	2.3	59.29	17.71
4.9	2.0	24.01	9.80
ΣX	ΣY	ΣX²	ΣXY
65.0	19.5	555.36	160.04

Table 4: Regression data for energy use

There are 10 pairs of data (N = 10), so the mean values for X and Y are, therefore, 6.5 and 1.95 respectively.

The value of b, using the regression equation introduced earlier, is:

$$b = \frac{\sum XY - \overline{X} \sum Y}{\sum X^2 - \overline{X} \sum X}$$

$$= \frac{160.04 - (6.5 \times 19.5)}{555.36 - (6.5 \times 65)}$$

$$= 33.29/132.86$$

$$= 0.250564504$$

And the value of a is:

$$a = \overline{Y} - (b \times \overline{X})$$

$$= 1.95 - (0.250564504 \times 6.5)$$

$$= 0.321330724$$

2. We can now solve the linear equation for the line of best fit.

$$Y = a + bX = 0.321331 + 0.250565X$$

3. In making the prediction, it should be noted that population is recorded in tens of thousands, so that 80,000 people would be set as X = 8. Using this value in the linear equation for the line of best fit, we have:

$$Y = 0.321331 + (0.250565 \times 8) = 2.326$$

So 2,326 kwh of energy would be used in a region with a population of 80,000.

3.3 Regression analysis and *Microsoft Excel*

As well as providing the means to produce scatterplots and measure the degree of correlation between variables, *Microsoft Excel* also provides a powerful tool for carrying out regression analysis. We can use the *Celtic Mail Order Ltd* data to show the use of this facility.

In order to see how *Microsoft Excel* deals with regression problems, begin by opening your **Celtic.xls** spreadsheet, containing the *Celtic Mail Order Ltd data*. Click on the **Tools** menu and open up the **Data Analysis** sub-menu. (If you do not have **Data Analysis** installed, refer to the instructions at the start of this unit.) From the sub-menu, select the **Regression** tool (you may have to scroll down the window to do this). Click on **OK**. You will see the dialogue screen shown in Figure 10. A description of the important parts of this dialogue screen follows.

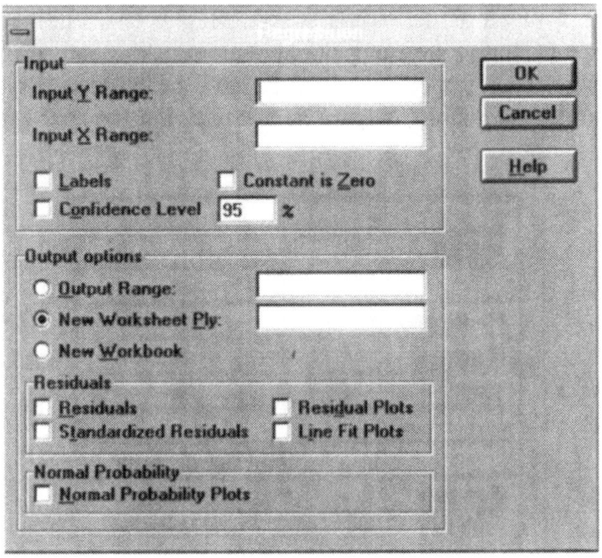

Figure 10: Dialogue screen for regression analysis

The dialogue box may look rather confusing, but fortunately much of the data asked for is optional, and we can afford to ignore it for the moment.

Input Y Range: You must complete this entry. This will be the cell references (for example A2:A11), which contain the Y or dependent variable. You can include the title cell if you have one.

Input X Range: This asks for the references for the cells containing the independent variable(s). As we are performing simple regression analysis, there will only be one variable here for the moment.

Labels: If you have added titles such as **Weight** and **Orders** at the head of the columns containing the variables, you can include the cells which contain them in the **Input Y Range** and **Input X Range** boxes. However, if you do, make sure the **Labels** box is checked so that *Microsoft Excel* knows that the first entry is a title.

Output Range: You need to state the area of the worksheet where you want the output placed. If you leave this blank *Microsoft Excel* will assume that it can place the results starting in cell A1, which may blank out some data you already have stored there! You only need to enter the starting cell. For example, entering **C1** will mean that the output will start at this point.

For the moment leave all of the other boxes blank. Click on **OK** to complete the process.

If you have successfully reached this stage then you will see quite a lot of output. Do not worry if much of the output is confusing at this stage, as we shall be explaining the meaning of most of it during the rest of this unit. Right now we are really only interested in the values of a and b, so we can ignore everything else. A section of the *Microsoft Excel* output screen containing the vital data is shown in Table 5.

ANOVA	
	df
Regression	1
Residual	8
Total	9
	Coefficients
Intercept	30.09810127
Weight	1.014240506

Table 5: Regression output

You will find the a and b values listed in the column headed **Coefficients**. (Regression coefficients is just another name for the two values a and b.) The **Intercept** is the a value of the linear model. The **Weight** variable is the b value in this model.

The only thing that remains to be done is to write down the linear model in its proper form by substituting the values from the computer output into the function $Y = a + bX$ and so obtaining:

$$Y = 30.098 + 1.014X$$

As you will have noticed, this is the same as the solution we obtained in Activity 16. The a and b values have been taken from the *Microsoft Excel* output in Table 5 and rounded to three decimal places.

ACTIVITY 19

We will now revisit the data contained in your spreadsheet **Energy.xls**.

1. Open the spreadsheet and run the *Regression* tool by clicking on **Tools** and **Data Analysis** and completing the dialogue screen as per the instructions given above. Click on **OK** when you have finished.

2. Write down the linear regression model for this data by referring to the output on your screen.

---

1. Output from running the *Microsoft Excel* regression tool is shown in Table 6. When inputting the data into the *Regression* dialogue box, remember that the dependent or Y variable is **Energy**, whilst the independent or X variable is **Population** (abbreviated to **Pop** in Table 6).

   When you obtain this output you will obtain a great amount of detail which will seem rather confusing, and which is of little use to us at the moment. Remember that we only require the regression coefficients (the values of *a* and *b*) in this section. Consequently, the output shown in Table 6 is a much reduced version of that which appears on your screen.

Pop	Energy			
3.7	0.9			Coefficients
12.9	3.1		Intercept	0.321330
6.5	2.1		Pop	0.250564
1.0	0.4			
11.4	3.5			
2.5	1.0			
9.3	2.7			
5.1	1.5			
7.7	2.3			
4.9	2.0			

Table 6: Regression output for the energy problem

2. The intercept is 0.321 and the slope (shown against the independent variable population) is 0.251. Both values are quoted to three decimal places.

   The line of best fit therefore becomes:

   $$Y = 0.321 + 0.251X$$

   You can check this result against your earlier calculation for Activity 18.

Summary

In this section we have examined the technique of regression analysis. We began, in Section 3.1, by looking at those factors which prevent the occurrence of perfect linear relationships between variables and then looked at ways of dealing with this departure from perfect linearity. This entailed drawing a line which minimised the sum of the squares of the residuals or errors: this line is therefore known as the least squares line. In Section 3.2 we introduced the technique of regression analysis by performing manual calculations. It was established that the process of regression involved using the least squares method to find suitable values for a and b, the regression coefficients. Finally, in Section 3.3, we used *Microsoft Excel* to produce regression output. We then used this output to produce a linear regression model for our data. In the next section we look at the predictive accuracy of regression models.

Section 4

Regression Models and Predictive Accuracy

Introduction

So far we have learned how to develop a simple linear regression model and use it to make predictions. Although this is very useful, we also need to know how accurate our predictions are likely to be. We have already started to look at this problem as both the scatterplot and the coefficient of correlation can give us some idea of the strength of the relationship between the dependent and the independent variable. However, to be really certain of our predictions we need to use other techniques as well. In Section 4.1 we use the **coefficient of determination** (also known as **R-Squaredd**) to distinguish between explained and unexplained variation. In Section 4.2 we use the **F test** to measure the significance of R-Squared, thereby providing a means of testing the reliability of our forecasts. By the end of this section you should be able to use R-Squared to analyse the performance of a regression model.

4.1 Explained and unexplained variation

Initially we can approach the matter of predictive accuracy by assessing how well our model explains the data. (Remember that independent variables are often called explanatory variables.) If the model has little explanatory power (that is, if it is a poor fit to the data) then it is of little use for forecasting purposes.

In the case of the *Celtic Mail Order Ltd* model, what we require is a measure of how far the daily variation in the number of orders is explained by the daily variation in the weight of the incoming mail. At one extreme, it could be that the weight of the incoming mail explains none of the variability in the number of orders. At the other extreme, it could be that the weight of the incoming mail explains all of the variability in the number of orders.

ACTIVITY 20

Look back at Figure 6, the scatterplot of the mail order data. Does the weight of the incoming mail fully explain the variability in the number of orders?

Looking at the scatterplot of the data, we notice that the points do not lie along an exact straight line. If weight of mail fully explained the number of orders, we would expect to see a straight line. In other words, not all of the variability in orders is explained by variation in the weight of the mail.

Rather than relying on a graph to tell us how good our predictive model is, we can use a statistic called the coefficient of determination. We shall not give a detailed formula for the calculation of it here, except to remark that it is identical to the square of the Pearson product moment correlation coefficient (see Section 1). However, it is good to have some idea as to what the statistic measures, even if we do not need to involve ourselves in the details of its calculation.

This statistic, usually called R-Squared (or R^2), is a useful measure of the fit of the model to the data. It is a measure of the degree to which variations in the dependent or Y variable are explained by variations in the independent or X variable. It always takes a value between 0 and 1. How should we interpret this statistic?

A value of $R^2 = 0$ means that the independent variable used in the regression explains nothing of the behaviour of the Y variable.

A value of $R^2 = 1$ means that the variation in Y is totally explained by X.

A value of $0 < R^2 < 1$ means that some of the variation in Y is explained by X, while some of it remains unexplained. For example, $R^2 = 0.64$ means that 64 per cent of the variation in the number of orders is explained by the weight of the incoming mail.

Any regression model tries to explain why the dependent variable behaves as it does. While some of the variation in Y is explained by X, some of it is explained by other factors which are not included in our model. Therefore, the following relationship exists. The total variation in Y equals the variation due to X plus the variation due to error or random causes.

In a model with high predictive accuracy, we would expect the variation due to X to be a large proportion of the total variation in Y. Consequently, the ratio of variation due to X to total variation in Y is a good measure of the predictive accuracy of our model. This ratio is called R-Squared. So:

$$R^2 = \frac{\text{Variation in Y due to X}}{\text{Total Variation in Y}}$$

Fortunately, *Microsoft Excel* will produce the value of R-Squared as part of the standard output of the regression. For the *Celtic Mail Order Ltd* data, you can find the value of R-Squared in the upper part of the *Microsoft Excel* output, in the results sheet. You should open your **Celtic.xls** spreadsheet and look for the required output. This is shown in Table 7.

SUMMARY OUTPUT	
Regression Statistics	
Multiple R	0.918571928
R-Squared	0.843774386
Adjusted R-Squared	0.824246184
Standard Error	3.469464446
Observations	10

Table 7: Microsoft Excel R-Squared output

For simple linear regression analysis involving only two variables, the figure you want is the one described as **R-Squared**. The other figures, described as **Multiple R** and **Adjusted R-Squared** relate to multiple regression, a topic we shall address in Sections 7 to 9 of this unit.

The value of R-Squared for the mail order data is therefore 0.8438.

ACTIVITY 21

In Activity 17, you predicted that 28kg of incoming mail would contain 5,849 orders. In the light of the value of R-Squared for this data, how confident are you that this prediction will be correct?

We have a value of R-Squared for this data of 0.84 (or 84 per cent). It tells us that 84 per cent of the daily variation in orders is explained by the weight of the incoming mail. Provided that this relationship continues to hold for values of X (that is, weights of incoming mail) not in the data, this value of R-Squared suggests that we can have a good deal of faith in any prediction based upon the model.

4.2 The significance of R-Squared

So the value of R-Squared gives us an initial measure of confidence for our forecast. A low value would give little confidence, whereas a high value would suggest that we could have a good deal of faith in our forecast. However, there is one important complication. In general when we pass judgement on anything, the more evidence we have, the more comfortable we feel in coming to a decision.

ACTIVITY 22

Suppose we wish to predict the value of some variable Y for a given value of an explanatory variable X. We use available data, perform a regression analysis and look at the value of R-Squared. Which of the following gives you most confidence in making a prediction?

$R^2 = 0.81$, the regression being based on 6 pairs of data

$R^2 = 0.75$, the regression being based on 35 pairs of data

If we are guided by the size of the R-Squared values alone, then they suggest that we should opt for the variable with an R-Squared value of 0.81. However, we should also notice that this is based on a sample size of a mere 6, whereas the R-Squared value for the second variable is based on a sample size of 35. The greater the sample size, the greater the confidence we can have in the value of R-Squared as a diagnostic statistic. Therefore, in spite of the slightly smaller R-Squared value for the second data set, the larger sample size would probably lead us to prefer it.

The number of pairs of data is our sample size. What we are concluding here is that the confidence we have in making a forecast is dependent upon the value of R-Squared **and** the sample size.

Since our data is only a sample, the question arises as to whether the value of R-Squared that we have found could have occurred merely by chance. This possibility is obviously more likely if the sample is small. To resolve this question we conduct a **statistical test of significance**. Remember that the closer the value of R-Squared to 0, the less the independent variable explains about the behaviour of the dependent variable. So another way of asking about the significance of R-Squared is to ask whether we are really sure that R-Squared is greater than 0.

The procedure for deciding this question is known as the **F test**. To carry out the F test, we first need to calculate the **F statistic**, which we can do using the following formula, where n is the sample size:

$$F = \frac{(n-2)R^2}{1-R^2}$$

This formula is only given for information, as the value of F is part of the output given by *Microsoft Excel*. However, you should notice that the appearance of n in the formula indicates that the F statistic depends not only upon the value of R-Squared but upon sample size.

F has been proved to follow a known probability distribution (called the **F distribution**), which means that we know something about its behaviour. Like most significance tests, the F test consists of comparing the F statistic calculated from our data, according to the above formula, with the expected value. We would then ask the question, 'how likely is it that this figure for the F statistic would be obtained if the true picture is that the X variable explains nothing of the variability in the Y variable?'.

It is usual to choose some level of probability and regard the value of R-Squared as being significant so long as the probability of F is less than that level. Although we could choose any reasonably low probability figure, conventionally the probability level chosen is 0.05 (that is, 5 per cent).

You may already know something about the conduct of significance tests. However, if you do not then you need not be too concerned. *Microsoft Excel* provides the output necessary to carry out the F test without the need to formally set it up. So you do not need to know anything about the mathematical theory behind this test and why it works: you simply need to know how to use it.

The results of the F test are provided in the *Microsoft Excel* output. The relevant part of the output for the mail order data is shown in Table 8. To see this output for yourself, take another look at the spreadsheet containing this data, rerunning the regression tool if necessary.

ANOVA					
	df	SS	MS	F	Significance of F
Regression	1	520.1025316	520.1025	43.20799	0.000174178
Residual	8	96.29746835	12.03718		
Total	9	616.4			

Table 8: Excel output for the F statistic

Do not be put off by the sheer quantity of output. **ANOVA** stands for **analysis of variance**, which is the name given to the statistical procedure for analysing the nature of the variation in the Y variable. *Microsoft Excel* needs to use the ANOVA process to establish the F statistic. You will notice that there is a column headed **SS**, which is short for **sum of squares**. (The sum of squares is used in regression analysis as a means of measuring variability.) It is instructive to consider what these SS values mean:

- the total sum of squares for the mail order data is 616.4
- the sum of squares explained by the X variable is 520.1025316
- the sum of squares due to error (**residual variation**) is 96.29746835.

If you divide the sum of squares due to X by the total sum of squares you should see that you obtain the value:

$$\frac{520.1025317}{616.4} \approx 0.8438$$

This is the value for the R-Squared statistic we discussed earlier.

The only other parts of the ANOVA output which are of interest to us are the value of the F statistic and the significance, or probability, of F. As you will see, this statistic and its significance enable us to make a judgement about whether our estimated model and its associated R-Squared is significant or whether it could plausibly have occurred merely by chance.

In the case of the mail order data, the F statistic is 43.20799. The probability of obtaining an F value higher than this is 0.00017. This is minute, so we can safely say that the value of R-Squared is significantly higher than 0.

In general, provided that the probability of F is less than 0.05 we are prepared to take the view that R-Squared is significant: in other words, that the value has not merely occurred by chance.

ACTIVITY 23

Open your worksheet **Energy.xls**, containing the energy use data.

1. Use the *Microsoft Excel* regression tool to obtain appropriate output for this data. (If you do not remember how to do this refer back to Section 3.3 for step-by-step instructions.)

2. Use the output to discuss how well the linear model developed explains the behaviour of energy use.

1. We have already obtained the output stating the regression coefficients (values of a and b) so we can go straight to R-Squared, the F statistic and the significance of F.

   $R^2 = 0.92$

   $F = 94.82679$

   Significance of F= 1.03E–05

   You should note that *Microsoft Excel* uses scientific notation for very small numbers. The number 1.03E–05 is in scientific notation and should be read as 1.035×10^5. Multiplying a number by 10^{-5} involves moving the decimal point five places to the left, thus giving 0.0000103.

2. So we have a value for R-Squared of 0.92. This suggests that the model explains 92 per cent of the variation in energy use (provided we are willing to accept that the figure is significant).

   The probability that we would obtain a value of F as high as 94.82 if the true position is that R-Squared is really 0 is very small (a mere 0.0000103). Consequently, we must assume that R-Squared cannot be 0, but must be really significant. All of this provides evidence that the predictions of energy use obtained from the model may be relied on.

You should now try to consolidate the ideas developed so far by attempting the following activity.

ACTIVITY 24

Dragon Engineering produces quality cast iron baths for the building trade. The company is concerned to improve its cost estimation and to this end has collected the following information on its last 20 orders.

Order size	Cost (£s)	Order size	Cost (£s)
36	2,496	65	4,940
25	5,036	42	5,572
16	3,949	48	5,164
45	3,598	59	5,161
30	2,119	22	3,763
61	5,693	88	8,403
17	2,859	42	3,883
68	4,672	76	4,526
38	4,941	4	1,258
6	1,779	86	7,551

1. What would be the dependent and what the independent variable?

2. Enter the data into a *Microsoft Excel* worksheet in the usual manner (one column for order size and one for costs), and save the worksheet as

Dragon.xls. We intend to model the data by using a linear function. By way of preliminary analysis, draw a scatterplot for the data and calculate the Pearson coefficient of correlation. Does this give you sufficient confidence to proceed with a linear model?

3. Use the *Microsoft Excel* **Regression** tool to obtain output for the *Dragon Engineering* data. Hence construct a model that can be used to forecast cost, given size of order.

4. Use your model to forecast the cost of fulfilling an order for 29 baths.

5. Would you be willing to use your model to forecast the cost of an order for 99 baths? If not, then why not?

---

1. In this case, *Dragon Engineering* wishes to develop a model capable of predicting cost. Consequently, it would be a model where cost is the dependent (Y) variable and order size the independent (X) variable.

2. A scatterplot for the data is shown in Figure 11.

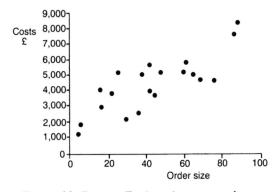

Figure 11: Dragon Engineering scatterplot

The scatter of points is definitely not random: there appears to be some evidence that the data displays a linear relationship between cost and size of order. Further, there appears to be positive correlation, as the trend of the direction of the plot is definitely upward sloping to the right.

The above observations are confirmed when we calculate the coefficient of correlation as +0.81. This is close enough to +1 for us to argue that there is a sufficiently strong relationship to justify proceeding with the construction of a regression model.

3. After running the *Microsoft Excel* regression tool with cost named as the dependent variable, you should obtain output as shown in Table 9.

Regression Statistics					
Multiple R		0.809247933			
R Square		0.654882			
Adjusted R Square		0.635709007			
Standard Error		1078.657497			
Observations		20			
ANOVA					
	df	SS	MS	F	Significance
Regression	1	4E+07	39740699	34.2	1.553E-05
Residual	18	1.1E+07	1163502		
Total	19	6.1E+07			
	Coefficients				
Intercept	1850.823				
Order Size	57.60474				

Table 9: Dragon Engineering Excel output

We are interested in the **R-Squared**, the **Significance**, the **Intercept Coefficient** and the **Order Size Coefficient**.

We start by constructing the linear model itself. The output tells us that the intercept (the a value) is equal to 1850.82, while the coefficient for order size (the b value) is equal to 57.60. The completed model will therefore be:

$$Y = a + bX = 1850.82 + 57.60X$$

4. To predict the cost of fulfilling an order for 29 baths would mean substituting 29 for X in the equation. We would obtain:

$$Y = 1850.82 + (57.60 \times 29) = 1850.82 + 1670.4 = £3,521.22$$

5. Firstly, we can consider the general question about the reliability of any predictions obtained from this model. R-Squared is 0.65 and is significantly higher than 0, because the significance of F (1.55262E–05 or 0.0000155262) is considerably below the significance level of 0.05. This is evidence in support of the explanatory power of our model.

However, we would need to add that the model only explains 65 per cent of the variability of cost (because R-Squared = 0.65). Putting this another way, it would mean that 35 per cent of the variation in cost is not explained by order size. So, although the results are highly significant, predictions derived from the model may display a degree of error.

Proceeding to the prediction of the cost of an order for 99 baths, we would come across an additional problem. The data used to derive our model had order sizes ranging from 4 to 88. An order size of 99 lies well outside this range. If we use the model to predict the cost of such an order size, then we are making the crucial assumption that a model which has some validity for the size range 4 to 88 also has validity outside that range. We would be very unwise to make this assumption unless we have some evidence to justify it.

Summary

In this section, we have investigated the performance of the regression model through the use of two techniques. Firstly, in Section 4.1 we used the coefficient of determination (also known as R-Squared) to distinguish between explained and unexplained variation. Then, in Section 4.2, we measured the significance of R-Squared by using a statistical significance test known as the F test. This provided us with a means of testing the reliability of our forecasts. In the next section we continue with the task of investigating the performance of the regression model.

SECTION 5

The Analysis of Residuals

Introduction

In this section we continue the task of analysing the performance of the regression model. We have already shown that one aspect of this performance – the explanatory power of the model – can be examined by using the coefficient of determination and the associated F statistic. However, another important aspect of regression analysis is concerned with whether the assumptions we made when developing the model were correct or incorrect.

As you will see, we make a number of assumptions when we construct a regression model, most of which we have not yet made explicit. If any of these assumptions are unfounded, then we would have to question whether the particular regression model we have used is the correct one, and sometimes even whether the technique of regression is justified at all. The method of investigating this problem is through a technique called **residuals analysis**. In Section 5.1 we introduce residuals, while Section 5.2 we examine some of the assumptions underlying regression analysis. In Section 5.3 we use *Microsoft Excel* to perform residuals analysis. Finally, in Section 5.4, we look briefly at a further use of residuals analysis: the identification of statistical **outliers**. By the end of this section, you should be able to use residuals analysis to analyse the performance of a regression model.

5.1 What are residuals?

We have mentioned residuals before in this unit (see Section 3.1). A useful way of analysing the behaviour of a regression model is to compare the actual available values of the Y variable with the estimates of them obtained from the regression equation. Taking the example of the *Celtic Mail Order Ltd* data, we would need to compare the estimates of number of orders obtained by using our model with the actual number of orders as recorded in our original data. This is done for the mail order data in Table 10

Case	Weight	Orders		
	X	Y	$\hat{Y}$	$Y - \hat{Y}$
1	23	58	53.42	4.58
2	17	50	47.34	2.66
3	24	54	54.43	−0.43
4	35	64	65.59	−1.59
5	10	40	40.24	−0.24
6	16	43	46.32	−3.32
7	15	42	45.31	−3.31
8	24	50	54.43	−4.43
9	18	53	48.35	4.65
10	30	62	60.52	1.48

Table 10: Residuals for Celtic Mail Order Ltd data

The first column gives the case number of the data. The second column (X) lists the weights. The third column (Y) lists the number of orders which actually resulted from the weight given in the first column.

The fourth column is the weight of orders as predicted by the regression equation. We will denote this with the symbol $\hat{Y}$ (Y estimate).

The fifth column represents the difference between the two, denoted by $Y - \hat{Y}$. These differences are known as the **residuals**. Later in this section you will learn how to use the *Microsoft Excel* **Regression** tool to make the calculation and analysis of the behaviour of residuals a relatively easy matter.

ACTIVITY 25

1. If you totalled all of the residuals together, what would you expect the result to be?

2. Can you explain why this should be the result?

---

1. The residuals will sum to 0, apart from rounding errors.

2. The residuals represent prediction errors made by the regression model and, in so far as some of these errors will be negative and some positive, they will balance out.

ACTIVITY 26

Use the data in Table 10.

1. List the three cases where the prediction error is at its highest.

2. List the two cases where the prediction error is at its lowest.

---

1. The three cases where the prediction error is at its highest are case 1 (error at 4.580), case 8 (error at –4.434) and case 9 (error at 4.650).

2. The two cases where the prediction error is at its lowest are case 3 (error at –0.434) and case 5 (error at –0.238).

   Remember that, orders are estimated in units of 100. An error of 4.5 is, therefore, an error of 450 orders.

When plotting residuals, the value of the residuals is always plotted against the Y-axis. However, the horizontal or X-axis can be used for one of two purposes. It can be used for the independent variable X, or it can be used for the **case number** of the data. (In our mail order data, there are ten weights, and the cases are therefore numbered 1 to 10.) Figure 12 shows residuals plotted by X, while Figure 13 shows residuals plotted by case number.

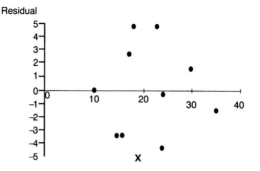

Figure 12: Plot of residuals by X

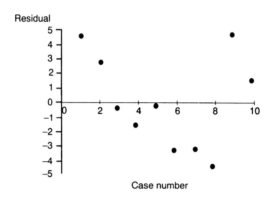

Figure 13: Plot of residuals by case number

5.2 Residuals and the assumptions of the analyst

In addition to telling us the size of prediction errors made by our model, analysis of the residuals can tell us whether our regression model is to be trusted. Together with R-Squared and the F statistic, it is a valuable diagnostic tool in the building of regression models.

In order to understand what analysis of residuals can tell us, it is necessary to consider the basic assumptions which we must make when constructing a linear regression model. You will already be aware of some of these assumptions, but others are more complicated. They are as follows:

- that the data is linearly related
- that the error terms have constant variances
- that the error terms are independent
- that the error terms are normally distributed.

We will deal with each of these situations in turn. In most of the scatterplots used to illustrate these situations, X, the independent variable, has been chosen as the horizontal axis variable. This is because we usually wish to see how the error, or residual, changes as X changes. In brief, the scatterplot of residuals should show a random pattern. If there is any relationship at all between X and the error term, then we must suspect that our regression model is inappropriate for this data.

LINEARITY

It is, of course, essential for there to be a linear relationship between the two variables if we are to use a linear model. We have already seen that one way of spotting non-linearity in the simple bivariate case is to examine the XY scatterplot (see Section 2). In addition, a scatterplot of the residuals can also be used as a check on linearity.

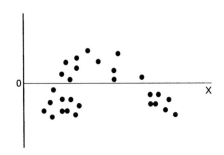

Figure 14: Scatterplot of residuals of non-linear data

If the residual plot appeared as in Figure 14, showing a clear divergence from linearity, then we would have to assume that our assumption of linearity was incorrect. A plot of residuals may be even better than an ordinary XY plot at showing non-linearity. This is because, after carrying out regression analysis, we have removed any linear trend which may exist between X and Y. This means that if our assumption of linearity is untrue, it will show up very starkly in the residuals plot.

ACTIVITY 27

1. Which of the two scatterplots of the residuals for the mail order data – Figure 12 or Figure 13 – should we study in order to test our assumption of linearity?

2. Does the scatterplot support our assumption of linearity?

---

1. We should study Figure 12, as this shows a plot of residuals against the independent variable X.

2. What you should look for here are any signs of a curvilinear pattern in the scatter of residuals. We are a little hampered by the small amount of data available (only 10 residuals). Nevertheless, there is no evidence that such a pattern exists, and therefore no reason to conclude that our assumption of linearity is incorrect.

VARIANCE OF THE RESIDUALS

If a regression model is an appropriate choice for the data, then we would expect the error terms to show no tendency to increase or decrease in size as the value of X changes. This does not mean that all of the errors must be exactly the same: it means that the variability of errors taken as a whole across the range of X is unchanging. This assumption of equal error variance across all values of X is sometimes referred to as **homoskedasticity**.

Any departure from this desirable condition is known as **heteroskedasticity**, and means that our regression model is inappropriate. For example, if the plot of residuals showed the pattern displayed in Figure 15, then our assumption of constant variance of error terms would be incorrect. Clearly, we have a situation here in which errors are growing in variability as X increases.

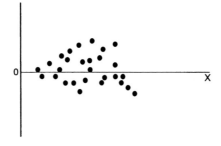

Figure 15: Heteroskedasticity (1)

We could also have the reverse situation, where errors are decreasing in variability as X increases (see Figure 16).

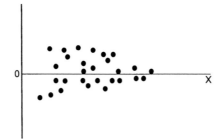

Figure 16: Heteroskedasticity (2)

Both conditions display heteroskedasticity. This is an undesirable condition because it means that we are unable to make trustworthy estimates of the likely errors in predicted Y values.

ACTIVITY 28

Take another look at the scatterplot of the weight data in Figure 12. What does it tell us about the assumption of constant error variance for this data?

We need to look at Figure 12, the plot of residuals against X, for any evidence that errors are either falling or rising as X increases. Again, we are hampered in our conclusions by the small amount of data available, but there is no evidence to assume that the size of errors is anything other than random.

INDEPENDENCE OF ERROR TERMS

If the residuals plot were as in Figure 17 then we would have to assume that the error terms were correlated, and not independent as we would wish.

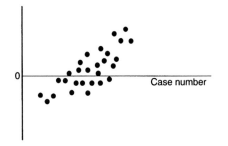

Figure 17: Scatterplot of non-independent data

In this case the slope is upward, but a downward slope would also indicate correlation of error terms. Correlation between error terms is undesirable because it often indicates situations where large errors tend to cluster together.

If using a plot of residuals to check for independence of error terms, it is best to use case number as the horizontal axis variable. This is because the biggest cause of non-independence is the manner in which the data has been collected. For example, in the case of the mail order data, it may be that the first four cases were all collected on Monday, while the other six cases were distributed across the other days of the week.

ACTIVITY 29

1. Which of the two plots of residuals of the mail order data – Figure 12 or Figure 13 – should we study in order to test our assumption that the error terms are independent?

2. Does the scatterplot support this assumption?

---

1. Remember that, for a check on independence, we need to use a scatterplot of residuals against case number, rather than X. We should therefore study Figure 13.

2. We are looking for an upward or downward pattern in such a plot. The plot in Figure 13 is a little more worrying, as there is some evidence that there is a trend in the scatter of points, in this case downwards. While the amount of data available is too small to admit definite conclusions, the existence of such a pattern in the residuals should alert the researcher to possible carelessness in the collection of data. The weight-orders data observations should be independent of each other if regression analysis is to be properly conducted. For example, if the collection of mail order data was biased toward one particular day of the week, then we would no longer be able to maintain the assumption of independence.

NORMALITY OF ERROR TERMS
The best way to test the assumption of normality of the residuals is to group the errors into a frequency distribution and display the results in a bar chart.

ACTIVITY 30

1. Use the residuals of the mail order data to complete the following table:

Size of error	Number of cases
$-5 \leq -3$	
$-3 \leq -1$	
$-1 \leq 1$	
$1 \leq 3$	
$3 \leq 5$	

2. Does this tell you anything about the distribution of errors for this regression model?

1. The completed table is shown in Table 11.

Size of error	Number of cases
−5 ≤ −3	3
−3 ≤ −1	1
−1 ≤ 1	2
1 ≤ 3	2
3 ≤ 5	2

Table 11: Distribution of mail order residuals

2. We would need to construct such a table to check for normality. The table produced above certainly does not look like a normal distribution. A typical normal distribution would have most errors in the range −1 ≤ 1 and fewest in the ranges −5 ≤ −3 and 3 ≤ 5. However, it is difficult to come to any firm conclusions here because of the small amount of data available.

We may conclude by saying that, in a healthy plot, the residuals would look as in Figure 18. There is no curvilinearity, there is constant variability of the residuals across X values, and there is no indication of any correlation between error terms.

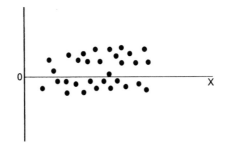

Figure 18: A healthy scatterplot of residuals

RESIDUALS AND STANDARDISED RESIDUALS

We have now addressed four key assumptions which underpin linear regression. Before using *Microsoft Excel* to analyse residuals, you should note that residuals can be obtained in two forms. They can be obtained, as already discussed, by simply calculating the values of $Y - \hat{Y}$ (that is, the difference between the actual value of Y and the estimate for it). Or they can be obtained by converting the values of $Y - \hat{Y}$ to **standard** or **Z values** before using them.

Z values are calculated by subtracting the mean error from the residual and dividing the resulting figure by the standard deviation of errors. Expressed in mathematical notation this is:

$$Z = \frac{(\text{Residual} - \text{Mean of Residuals})}{\text{Standard Deviation of Residuals}}$$

The resulting values are known as **standardised residuals**. This is a useful technique because Z values (also called **standardised normal deviates**) are virtually always between –4 and +4. We will more easily be able to compare plots of residuals for different regression models if they are standardised first. There is no need to worry about the apparent extra work involved in producing standardised residuals since *Microsoft Excel* will calculate them for you.

5.3 Using *Microsoft Excel* to perform analysis of residuals

It is now time to look at some other aspects of *Microsoft Excel* regression output. In order to understand what follows, you should open the *Celtic Mail Order Ltd* worksheet you saved as **Celtic.xls**.

Start the analysis by pulling down the **Tools** menu. Select **Data Analysis** from the sub-menu and select **Regression** from the options listed. Follow the instructions below to complete the **Regression Analysis** dialogue box.

Input: Enter the Y and X data (orders and weight, respectively) in the **Input Y Range:** and **Input X Range:** boxes.

Labels: If you have included the column titles (labels) in the Y and X ranges, you must check this box or *Microsoft Excel* will register an error.

Constant is Zero: Leave this box unchecked. We will discuss this option in the section on multivariate analysis.

Confidence Level: *Microsoft Excel* provides 95 per cent confidence intervals for the intercept and the *b* value as a matter of course. If you want other confidence intervals then you are allowed to check this box and enter the desired interval. Leave the box unchecked for now.

Output Range: You have already encountered this option. If you check this box you must state a starting cell where you wish the regression output to be placed. For example, if you enter **D12** the resulting output will start from this cell. Check the box first, and then enter your chosen cell reference.

New Worksheet Ply: If you prefer the regression output to be placed on a different worksheet, then check this option and enter the name of a new worksheet. For example, if you enter **Results**, then *Microsoft Excel* will create a new worksheet, name it **Results** and proceed to place the requested output on it. Leave this box unchecked for now.

New Workbook: This is useful if you wish to create the output in a completely different *Microsoft Excel* workbook or file. (Remember that a workbook may consist of several different worksheets.) Leave this box unchecked for now.

Residuals: If checked, *Microsoft Excel* produces ordinary residuals. Check this box.

Standardised Residuals: If checked, *Microsoft Excel* produces the residuals in their standard (Z value) form. Also check this box.

Residual Plots: If checked, *Microsoft Excel* will draw a scatterplot of the residuals. Note that *Microsoft Excel* only draws the non-standardised residuals. Check this box.

Line Fit Plots: If this option is checked, *Microsoft Excel* will draw a chart which contains both the original data and the predictions on the same axes. This is a useful check on how well the regression model fits the data. Check this box.

Normal Probability Plots: If selected *Microsoft Excel* will plot the probability distribution of the data. This is of limited use and a grouped frequency distribution of the residuals would be far better. You will, however, have to do this yourself, as *Microsoft Excel* does not currently provide such a plot. Leave this box unchecked.

Now click on **OK** to run the analysis.

The *Microsoft Excel* output relating to the residual analysis of mail order data is shown in Table 12 and Figures 19 and 20.

RESIDUAL OUTPUT			
Observation	Predicted Y	Residuals	Standard Residuals
1	53.42563291	4.574367	1.318464898
2	47.34018987	2.65981	0.766634208
3	54.43987342	−0.43987	−0.126784241
4	65.59651899	−1.59652	−0.460162948
5	40.24050633	−0.24051	−0.06932088
6	46.32594937	−3.32595	−0.958634803
7	45.31170886	−3.31171	−0.954530278
8	54.43987342	−4.43987	−1.279699932
9	48.35443038	4.64557	1.338987527
10	60.52531646	1.474684	0.425046449

Table 12: Microsoft Excel output of residuals and standardised residuals for the mail order data

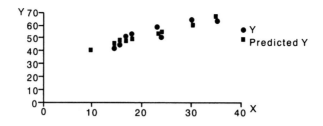

Figure 19: Plot of predictions and original data for mail order data

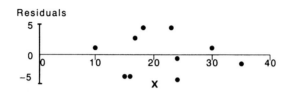

Figure 20: Plot of standardised residuals for mail order data

ACTIVITY 31

Open your spreadsheet **Dragon.xls**.

1. Use the instructions provided above for the mail order data and obtain ordinary and standardised residuals for the *Dragon Engineering* data.

2. Obtain a scatterplot of the ordinary residuals.

3. Analyse the scatterplot with relation to the following:

   (a) linearity of the data

   (b) variance of residuals

   (c) independence of the error terms.

4. Compile a table of the frequency distribution of the residuals broken down into the size groups –2000, –1500, –1000, –500, 0, 500, 1000, 1500 and 2000.

5. Plot the frequency distribution of the residuals on a line chart and say whether they are normally distributed or not.

RESIDUAL OUTPUT			
Observation	Predicted Cost(£s)	Residuals	Standard Residuals
1	3924.593494	−1428.59	−1.324418083
2	3290.941342	1745.059	1.617806082
3	2772.498672	1176.501	1.090708896
4	4443.036163	−845.036	−0.783414722
5	3578.965047	−1459.97	−1.353501971
6	5364.712021	328.288	0.304348675
7	2830.103413	28.89659	0.026789399
8	5767.945208	−1095.95	−1.016027063
9	4039.802976	901.197	0.83548024
10	2196.451262	−417.451	−0.387010022
11	5595.130985	−655.131	−0.607357745
12	4270.22194	1301.778	1.206850241
13	4615.850387	548.1496	0.508177633
14	5249.502538	−88.5025	−0.082048786
15	3118.127119	644.8729	0.597847679
16	6920.040029	1482.96	1.374820066
17	4270.22194	−387.222	−0.358985073
18	6228.783137	−1702.78	−1.578613361
19	2081.24178	−823.242	−0.763209621
20	6804.830547	746.1695	0.691757537

Table 13: Residuals for Dragon Engineering data

1. The *Microsoft Excel* output relating to the residuals is shown in Table 13. Residuals are provided in both their ordinary and standardised forms.

2. The scatterplot of the ordinary residuals should look as in Figure 21. Please note that *Microsoft Excel* does not produce a plot of standardised residuals. If you want such a graph you will have to produce it manually.

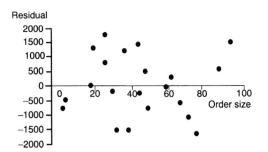

Figure 21: Scatterplot of ordinary residuals for Dragon Engineering data

3. The scatterplot in Figure 21 has 20 data points which should be enough to show any pattern that might be present in the data.

   (a) There does not appear to be any curvilinearity in the data, so the scatterplot confirms our assumption of a linear relationship between order size and cost.

   (b) The variance of the residuals appears to be fairly constant: that is, there is no evidence of heteroskedasticity.

   (c) There does not appear to be any rising or falling trend, so the scatterplot confirms our assumption that the error terms are independent: that is, that they do not cluster together.

4. Your frequency distribution for the *Dragon Engineering* data should look similar to the one in Table 14. (The intervals have been written out in full for ease of understanding.)

Residual	Number
≤ −2000	0
−2000 ≤ −1500	1
−1500 ≤ −1000	3
−1000 ≤ −500	3
−500 ≤ 0	3
0 ≤ 500	2
500 ≤ 1000	4
1000 ≤ 1500	3
1500 ≤ 2000	1

Table 14: Distribution of residuals for Dragon Engineering data

5. Your plot of the frequency distribution of residuals should look as in Figure 22.

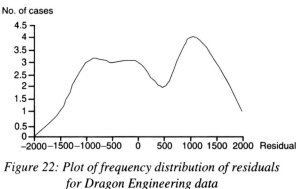

Figure 22: Plot of frequency distribution of residuals for Dragon Engineering data

The purpose of such a plot is to check whether the errors are normally distributed. You should remember that a normal distribution is bell-shaped. The results in Table 14 and Figure 22 could hardly be called a normal distribution, although the evidence is not conclusive. In a proper analytical report on this model, we would have to state our reservations as to whether the errors were normally distributed. Perhaps more data would settle the matter? In cases where statistical results are concerned, we often need more data to come to a firm conclusion.

We can now use the conclusions obtained from the previous activity to assess the reliability of the *Dragon Enginering* model. From Activity 24 we obtained the fitted linear model as Y = 1850.82 + 57.60X. The R-Squared for the model was calculated as 0.65. This value is significant (as shown by the F statistic), meaning that it was not just a chance result. Having carried out an analysis of the residuals, we are able to report that the assumptions of linearity, constant variance and the independence of residuals are valid. We are, however, unable to confirm that the residuals form a normal distribution. We would also have to admit that the model only explains 65 per cent of the variation in costs.

5.4 Using residuals to identify outliers

Residuals can also be used to identify **outliers** or data values at some distance from the rest. Outliers will produce residuals with a large magnitude compared with the others. Why should we take notice of such points? Because all data points are used in the construction of a regression model, outliers can significantly distort our model and make it less explanatory. It may be that the outlier is a result of wrong recording of data and should be removed from the analysis, thus improving the overall model.

The best way to check for the appearance of outliers is to use the standardised residuals, together with the following (approximate) rules concerning their distribution:

- 68 per cent of all standardised residuals should lie in the range ±1
- 95 per cent of all residuals should lie in the range ± 2
- 99 per cent of all residuals should lie in the range ± 2.5.

(The above values are taken from a standard distribution of the normal distribution.)

A useful approach to adopt when looking for outliers is to plot the standardised residuals, and then take special note of points (if any) which lie outside the range ± 2.5. There is little likelihood of such points occurring in the normal course of things, so that if any such outliers are spotted they should be investigated immediately. The process is shown in Figure 23.

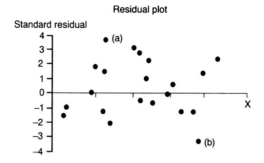

Figure 23: Detecting outliers

The points marked *a* and *b* would immediately be suspect, as they lie outside the expected range. Some other points are also borderline. The next activity will demonstrate the usefulness of conducting residual analysis.

ACTIVITY 32

Open your **Celtic.xls** spreadsheet.

1. The first data pair is recorded as (23, 58). Suppose that this was wrongly recorded as (23, **88**). Change the 58 to 88 in your spreadsheet, and run the *Microsoft Excel* **Regression** tool. (Refer back to Section 5.3 if you need reminding of this procedure.) Ask for standardised residuals. When the output has been produced, draw a scatterplot of the standard residuals. (You will have to do this using *Microsoft Excel* to draw a chart, as the **Regression** tool only produces a plot of the ordinary residuals. See Appendix 1 for a description of how to draw graphs with *Microsoft Excel*.)

2. What difference has this wrong recording of data made to the model?

3. What is the effect of the change on the value of R-Squared?

4. Would analysis of residuals spot the culprit?

1. Your plot of residuals should look as in Figure 24.

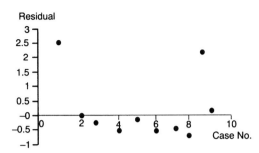

Figure 24: Plot of standard residuals for altered Celtic Mail Order Ltd data

2. After changing the data point (23,58) to (23,88) and rerunning the regression tool the model becomes $Y = 30.83386 + 1.121044X$. (Originally it was $Y = 30.098 + 1.014X$.)

3. However, the most alarming feature of this incorrect recording is that it has resulted in an unsatisfactory model which has an R-Squared value of only 0.350977. (It was 0.84 in the original model.)

4. An examination of the scatterplot would produce useful results. (See Figure 23.) The incorrectly recorded value has a residual which is way apart from the rest. In fact, it has a value in excess of 2.5, which would identify it as an outlier if we used the rule of detection given earlier. This would lead to an immediate investigation of the data point, correction of the error and a much better regression model.

Some analysts advocate the immediate removal of all outliers from the analysis. Others will exercise caution: it is clearly unwise to remove troublesome data from an analysis until we have fully investigated the reason behind the disturbance.

Summary

Residual analysis is a technique based on examining the differences between the observed Y values and the regression model predictions of them. In this section we defined residuals as the difference between the actual values of the Y variable and the estimates of those values as obtained from the regression equation. We then used residual analysis to explore four key assumptions of linear regression models: linearity, constant variance, independence of error terms and normal distribution of error terms. Next we used *Microsoft Excel* to carry out the analysis of residuals. Finally we used residual analysis to detect outliers, which may represent data recording errors. In the next section we will look at a technique for assessing the likely size of any errors in our predictions.

SECTION 6
Confidence Intervals and Regression Analysis

Introduction

In previous sections we have dealt with various methods for checking the integrity of a regression model. R-Squared and the F test are concerned with analysing the explanatory power of a model, while residual analysis is concerned with deciding whether the conditions for a successful regression model are in place. In this section we will return to the question of prediction error by exploring whether there is any way of indicating the possible maximum error there may be in forecasts made by the model. This section will provide some answers to this problem by exploring the concept of **confidence intervals**. We start, in Section 6.1, by defining confidence intervals. In Section 6.2 we look at how to estimate confidence intervals for the regression coefficients. Finally, in Section 6.3, we use confidence intervals to assess the predictions which linear regression models produce. By the end of this section you should be able to use confidence intervals to estimate the likely scale of any errors produced by a regression model.

6.1 What is a confidence interval?

With most statistical processes, the data we produce are the results of sampling exercises and we know that sampling error is therefore an inevitable outcome. Regression analysis is no exception. We can therefore say that both the values of the regression coefficients *a* and *b* and the predictions obtained from the regression model will be subject to sampling error.

In statistics we often distinguish between a **point estimate** and an **interval estimate**. For example, if we were to estimate the average number of orders coming from the daily mailbag received by *Celtic Mail Order Ltd*, a point estimate might consist of a statement like the following: 'the average number of orders per mail delivery is 2,750'. However, since this calculation would have come from a sample of deliveries, we would expect it to be subject to error. Consequently, we might try to allow for this error by quoting an interval rather than a point estimate. An interval estimate might be some statement like the following: 'the average number of orders per mail delivery is in the range 2,500 to 2,800, with 95 per cent confidence'.

So a point estimate is a single value, while an interval estimate consists of two things:

- an interval in which we believe the true value to lie
- a level of probability, which states how confident we are that the stated interval contains the true value.

This level of probability is called a **confidence level**. So the interval estimate stated above is a formal way of saying that we are 95 per cent confident that the average number of orders per delivery is somewhere between 2,500 and 2,800.

A full treatment of the subject of confidence intervals in regression is outside the scope of this unit. Therefore in this section we will avoid a formal development of the subject and restrict ourselves to the use of *Microsoft Excel* output.

6.2 Interval estimates for the regression coefficients

When we are building a simple regression linear model, we first need to estimate the *a* coefficient (or Y intercept as it is often called) and the *b* coefficient, or slope. These are, of course, point estimates of the true values of the intercept and the slope (α and β respectively). How can we provide interval estimates of these values? In order to shed some light on this try the following activity.

ACTIVITY 33

Take another look at the *Microsoft Excel* regression output for the mail order data. (You obtained this in Section 3.3 of this unit.) If necessary, rerun the regression tool to obtain this output. Examine the output carefully. You already know how to find the point estimates *a* and *b*. Can you locate the 95 per cent confidence interval estimates for these coefficients?

The relevant part of the *Microsoft Excel* output is shown in Table15.

	Coefficient	Std Error	t Stat	P-value	Lower 95%	Upper 95%
Intercept	30.0981	3.450197	8.723589	2.33E–05	22.141927	38.054275
Weight	1.014241	0.154298	6.573279	0.000174	0.6584296	1.3700514

Table 15: Microsoft Excel confidence interval output for regression coefficients

The first column, headed 'Coefficient', displays the values of *a* (the intercept) and *b* (the slope). These are the point estimates. The second column is the 'Standard Error', which is required for the process of calculating the confidence intervals. The next two columns, 't Stat' and 'P-value', are not required for simple linear regression. The last two columns, 'lower 95%' and 'upper 95%', are the important ones, as they give us the required interval estimates.

It may seem to you when you examine the computer screen that *Microsoft Excel* produces the upper and lower values twice. This is done so that you can request your own confidence intervals (98 per cent, 99 per cent or whatever) in the regression dialogue box. If you do not select this option, they are left as 95 per cent.

So the output tells us that the point estimate for the intercept or *a* value is 30.0981. The confidence interval columns tell us that we can be 95 per cent confident that the intercept is somewhere in the range 22.1419 to 38.0543. Similarly, the *b* value, or slope, has a point estimate of 1.014, and we can be 95 per cent confident that the true slope lies somewhere in the interval 0.658 to 1.370. This gives us some idea of the amount of possible error in the estimates of intercept and slope.

In working through the last activity, you may have been rather struck by the size of the interval estimates for the regression coefficients. This is largely due to the very small sample size (only 10 data points). You can always improve the precision of the estimates by using larger samples. Even so, we should always be aware of the degree of precision (or lack of it) in the estimates of the regression coefficients.

6.3 Interval estimates for predictions: the standard error of the estimate

Having developed a regression model, the analyst will be interested in how accurate the predictions made from the model will be. One simple way to provide insights into this matter is to use a statistic called the **standard error of the estimate** (henceforth abbreviated to *Se*). This statistic, despite its name, is actually a special case of the standard deviation. Standard deviations are calculated for the special purpose of measuring variability. *Se* measures the variability of the predictions made with the model.

In order to calculate *Se* we must first calculate the sum of squares of the error or SSE for short. (We have already come across this value in dealing with R-Squared.) Table 16 shows the mail order data.

Weight	Orders			
X	Y	$\hat{Y}$	$Y - \hat{Y}$	$(Y - \hat{Y})^2$
23	58	53.42	4.58	20.9764
17	50	47.34	2.664	7.0969
24	54	54.43	−0.434	0.18836
35	64	65.59	−1.588	2.52174
10	40	40.24	−0.238	0.05664
16	43	46.32	−3.322	11.0357
15	42	45.31	−3.308	10.9429
24	50	54.43	−4.434	19.6604
18	53	48.35	4.65	21.6225
30	62	60.52	1.482	2.19632

Table 16: Data for calculating the sum of squares of error

A simple total of the errors is useless because they always total to 0 and therefore tell us nothing about the behaviour of the estimates. We therefore square the errors first and then obtain the total of the squares. This gives us a figure of 96.2978. (In theory, if the regression model never made errors the SSE would be 0.)

Formally, the SSE is calculated as follows:

$$SSE = \Sigma (Y - \hat{Y})^2$$

The symbol Σ stands for 'the sum of', so the formula states that 'the sum of the squares of the errors (SSE) is equal to the sum of the squares of the differences between the real Y values and the estimates of them'.

Using the SSE directly as a measure of prediction error has its difficulties because it is proportional in size to the number of data points used to compute it. We can, however, use it to calculate a more useful statistic, the standard error of the estimate, as follows (where n is the number of data points):

$$Se = \sqrt{\frac{SEE}{n - 2}}$$

In other words, the standard error of the estimate Se is calculated by dividing the sum of squares of the error (SSE) by the number of data points minus 2 ($n - 2$) and calculating the square root of the result.

So for the mail order data the standard error of the estimate is:

$$Se = \sqrt{\left(\frac{96.2978}{8}\right)}$$

$$= \sqrt{12.037225}$$

$$= 3.4695$$

What does this tell us? If the error terms are normally distributed, as they should be, then we can be sure that:

- approximately 68 per cent of all estimates must have errors which lie in the range ± Se (that is, within the range minus one standard error to plus one standard error)

- 95 per cent of estimates will be in error by up to ± $2Se$ (that is, within the range minus two standard errors to plus two standard errors)

- 99 per cent of estimates will have errors which lie in the range ± $2.5Se$.

Since the standard error of the estimate for the mail order data is equal to 3.4695, we can say that:

- 68 per cent of errors will be in the range –3.4695 to +3.4695. The orders data is in 100s, so this means that 68 per cent of predictions will be in error by up to ±347.

- 95 per cent of predictions will have errors in the range –2 × 3.4695 to +2 × 3.4695 or in the range ±694 (after the data has been converted to 100s)

- 99 per cent of predictions will have errors in the range –2.5 × 3.4695 to +2.5 × 3.4695, or in the range ±867 (after the data has been converted into 100s).

This is very useful because (to take the last of the above points as an example) 99 per cent of the time, our estimates will have a maximum error of 867: that is, we could be up to 867 orders out in the predictions. If we relate this to the mail order data, we can calculate what this means as a percentage prediction error. Our minimum order size in the original data is 4,000 orders and our maximum error is 867 orders. We can therefore calculate the percentage prediction error by dividing 867 by 4,000 and then multiplying the resultant figure (0.21675) by 100. Rounded up, this gives us a percentage prediction error of up to 22 per cent. Similarly, if we divide 867 by 6,400 (the maximum order size) and multiply by 100, we obtain a figure of 14 per cent after rounding. In other words, the maximum prediction error is between 14 per cent and 22 per cent, depending on the size of the order. The decision-maker may eventually decide that this is an unacceptable level of error, but at least the method of measuring the degree of error described means that we are able to take such decisions.

Having established that the standard error of the estimate is a useful means of making interval estimates of the amount of prediction error, it only remains to indicate the appropriate output in *Microsoft Excel*.

ACTIVITY 34

Look at the *Microsoft Excel* regression output for the mail order problem (see Activity 33). Locate the standard error of the estimate and check that it is equal to the figure calculated above: that is, 3.4695.

You should be able to find the standard error of the estimate in the same block of output as the R-Squared value. See Table 17.

SUMMARY OUTPUT	
Regression Statistics	
Multiple R	0.918571928
R Square	0.843774386
Adjusted R Square	0.824246184
Standard Error	3.469464446
Observations	10

Table 17: Standard error

You should now try to consolidate what you know about the standard error of the estimate and its use in constructing interval estimates by working through the following activities.

ACTIVITY 35

Return to the energy use problem and open your worksheet **Energy.xls**.

1. Use *Microsoft Excel* to determine the standard error of the estimate for the simple linear model of this data.

2. Use it to comment on the predictive accuracy of the model.

---

1. For the energy use data, the value of *Se* is 0.296586.

2. If we take just one of the interval estimates – 99 per cent – then we would observe that 99 per cent of the predictions obtained from the model of this

data would have errors in the range 2.5 × 0.296586. Remembering that the energy data is in thousands of kilowatt-hours, this would be a maximum error of:

2.5 × 296.586 = 741.465 kwh

The energy usage in the original data has a low of 0.4 (400 kwh) up to a maximum of 3.5 (3,500 kwh). It is very easy to see that, compared with these figures, an error of 741.465 is very sizeable indeed! Clearly, this model would have little predictive accuracy.

ACTIVITY 36

Open your worksheet **Dragon.xls** and re-examine the linear regression model for *Dragon Engineering*.

1. Find the value of *Se* for this data.

2. Comment on the predictive accuracy of the model.

---

1. *Se* is equal to 1078.657 for this data.

2. Considering that the original cost data has a low of 1,258 and a high of 8,403, it can be seen that a standard error as high as 1,078.657 will lead to some potentially very large prediction errors. Whatever other merits this model may have, the accuracy of its predictions is not one of them!

Summary

In this section we have carried out further analysis of the efficiency of a regression model. In particular, we have focused on the problem of making accurate predictions. Estimates made from a regression model incorporate an element of error, and we have used the concept of a confidence interval to estimate the size of this error. Confidence intervals in regression analysis are a complex problem and we have restricted ourselves to two areas: interval estimates for the regression coefficients *a* and *b* and for individual predictions of the Y variable. In the latter case we saw that the standard error of the estimate allowed us to determine outside limits for the size of errors made in regression estimates.

So far in our investigation of causal models we have restricted ourselves to situations in which there are only two variables. The next section of the unit removes this restriction and we examine an approach called **multiple regression**.

SECTION 7
The Multivariate Model

Introduction

The power of regression analysis enables us to use more than one variable for prediction purposes. For example, we may find that both the price of a product and the amount of money spent advertising it are strongly connected with sales. If we wished to construct a regression model for such a situation, there would be one dependent variable (sales) and two independent variables (advertising expenditure and price).

In the example mentioned above, we have a situation which would require a **multivariate regression model**. Any regression model which has more than one independent variable can be described as multivariate: the above example has two independent variables, but it is theoretically possible to have any number.

In Section 7.1 we provide a formal definition of the multivariate model. In Section 7.2 we look at how to analyse the data in a multivariate model and in Section 7.3 we examine the multivariate regression procedure itself. By the end of this section you should be able to construct the general linear multivariate regression model and use this model to make predictions.

7.1 Definition of the multivariate model

The task of multivariate regression is to find a set of independent variables which appear to exert a strong influence on the dependent variable and then build a model which expresses these interrelationships.

Let us suppose that the variable we wish to forecast (Y) is dependent upon a number of explanatory variables. We will label these as X_1, X_2, X_3 and so forth up to X_n where n can be any number, depending on how many independent variables are involved.

So we can write formally that:

$$Y = f[X_1, X_2, X_3 \ldots X_n]$$

This is a formal way of saying that Y is a function of the variables X_1, X_2, X_3 and so on up to X_n. As with the simple bivariate case, it is possible to think of a multivariate model as being either linear or non-linear. It is easy to describe a linear model in the bivariate situation because we can think of it as a straight line drawn on graph paper. The idea of linearity is impossible to visualise in a multivariate model (you cannot draw graphs with more than two variables). Consequently, the definition of a multivariate linear model must be purely mathematical.

The full multivariate linear model is defined as follows:

$$Y = \alpha + \beta_1 X_1 + \beta_2 X_2 + \beta_3 X_3 + \ldots \beta_n X_n + u$$

The term represented by α is equivalent to the intercept in the simple bivariate model. However, we shall not use the expression 'intercept' in what follows because this term implies graphical representation, and it is not possible to display multivariate models graphically. We shall, in future, refer to α as the **constant**. The expression 'constant' in mathematical usage refers to something which does not vary. If the values of all of the independent variables happened to be 0, Y would be equal to the constant term.

The β_1, β_2, β_3... β_n values represent the **regression coefficients**: one for each of the independent variables. The term 'coefficient' in mathematics is used to describe a value which acts as a multiplier for some other quantity, usually a variable.

Finally, the u term at the end represents the error in the estimate.

As with simple linear regression, we have to rely on sample data for our raw material, so using least squares regression gives as the estimated model:

$$Y = a + b_1 X_1 + b_2 X_2 + b_3 X_3 + \ldots + b_n X_n$$

where a, b_1, b_2, b_3...b_n are sample estimates of the regression coefficients α, β_1, β_2, β_3 ... β_n.

Since more than two variables are now involved, the procedure is termed **multiple regression**.

ACTIVITY 37

We have just defined $Y = a + b_1 X_1 + b_2 X_2 + b_3 X_3 + \ldots + b_n X_n$ as the multiple linear regression model with n independent variables.

1. What happens to this expression if $n = 1$?

2. Do you recognise it?

---

1. If $n = 1$ then the multivariate model becomes simply $Y = a + b_1 X_1$.

2. You should recognise this expression as the basic simple linear regression model with only one independent variable.

7.2 Building a multivariate model: analysis of data

In order to illustrate the building of a typical multivariate model we shall use the example of *West Moors Steel*. This firm produces steel pieces to order. For the last

20 orders, data has been collected on the manufacturing time, the order size and the number of operations involved in making each piece. The company wishes to develop a model of the dependency of manufacturing time on the size of the order and the number of operations per piece. The main purpose of the model would be to make predictions of the time required to make up the order.

ACTIVITY 38

Answer the following questions for the *West Moors Steel* case.

1. Identify the dependent or Y variable.

2. Identify the independent or X variables.

3. Use this data to complete the statement 'Manufacturing time is a function of...'.

4. Write out the model using symbols to represent the variables.

---

1. The dependent or Y variable is manufacturing time.

2. There are two independent or X variables: order size and number of operations.

3. We therefore have a multivariate model which could be summarised as follows 'Manufacturing time is a function of order size and number of operations'.

4. As it is usual to use symbols to represent the variables, we could also write:

$$Y = \alpha + \beta_1 X_1 + \beta_2 X_2$$

Y represents manufacturing hours, X_1 represents order size, X_2 represents number of operations, α is the constant term, β_1 is the coefficient of order size and β_2 is the coefficient of number of operations.

As with the simple linear regression model, it is good practice to conduct some preliminary investigation of the data first, in order to assure ourselves that there is a relationship between Y and the X variables and that this relationship is linear.

Here we immediately encounter problems. In the bivariate case we could use scatterplots to analyse the data. As we cannot draw graphs involving more than two variables, this procedure is not applicable to the multivariate model. However, it is still useful to examine pairwise relationships between the variables, meaning that we should examine the relationships between the Y variable and each of the X variables in turn. The data contained in Table 18 will enable us to do this for the *West Moors Steel* data. This table contains observations of the independent and dependent variables for a sample of 20 orders.

Order size	Number of operations	Manufacturing hours
100	6	153
35	11	192
127	7	162
64	12	240
600	5	339
14	16	185
96	11	235
257	13	506
21	9	260
39	8	161
426	14	835
843	6	586
391	8	444
84	13	240
235	9	303
520	12	775
76	8	136
139	11	271
165	14	385
304	10	451

Table 18: West Moors Steel data

ACTIVITY 39

Open up a new *Microsoft Excel* spreadsheet and enter the *West Moors Steel* data from Table 18.

Enter the data with a separate column to represent each variable and give each column an appropriate heading. Enter the X variables first and the Y variable last. Do not leave gaps or empty columns between the variables. Save the spreadsheet as **Westmoor.xls**.

1. Use *Microsoft Excel* to draw a scatterplot to represent the relationship between manufacturing hours and order size.

2. Use *Microsoft Excel* to draw a scatterplot to represent the relationship between manufacturing hours and number of operations.

3. What do these plots tell us about the relationships between manufacturing hours (the dependent variable) and order size and number of operations (the independent variables)?

1. The scatterplot for the relationship between manufacturing hours and order size should be as shown in Figure 25.

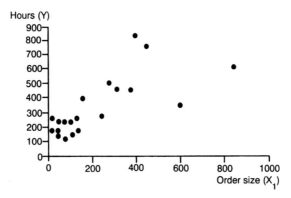

Figure 25: Scatterplot for 'order size-manufacturing hours' for West Moors Steel data

2. The scatterplot for the relationship between number of operations and order size should be as shown in Figure 26.

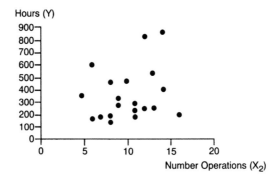

Figure 26: Scatterplot for 'number of operations-manufacturing hours' for West Moors Steel data

3. The relationship between manufacturing hours and each of the variables considered in pairs does not seem to be strong on the visual evidence shown in the scatterplots. That between manufacturing hours and number of operations seems the weakest. Whatever the degree of relationship, there seems to be no evidence to suppose that it is curvilinear. This may suggest that our model may not perform well. However, we shall reserve final judgement until we have seen the correlation evidence.

Another procedure we can use is to examine pairwise correlations between the variables. As before, you could use the *Microsoft Excel* **Correlation function** for each pair of variables. However, if you have a large number of variables, a quicker procedure may be to use the special *Microsoft Excel* **Correlation tool**. This tool is contained in the **Tools** menu under the same **Data Analysis** category we used for regression. After selecting **Data Analysis**, you will see the usual list of options offered to you, one of which is **Correlation**. Select this item and you will see a dialogue screen like the one shown in Figure 27.

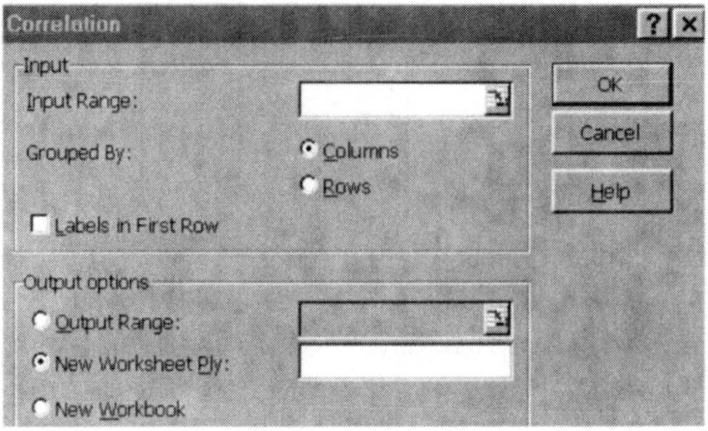

Figure 27: Microsoft Excel correlation matrix dialogue box

This screen is much like the one you saw when using the **Regression** tool, so you should not find it difficult to use. Follow the instructions below to complete the correlation dialogue box for the spreadsheet **Westmoor.xls**.

Input Range: You need to enter the range where all of the Y and X variables are contained. The variables must be in adjacent columns or rows, with no gaps. Column headings should be included.

Grouped By: As you have separate columns for each variable, make sure that **Columns** is selected.

Labels in First Row: As you have entered column headings (titles or labels) in the input range, make sure this option is selected.

Output Range: As you want the output on the same worksheet as the data, select this option and name a cell where you would like the output to be placed: for example, D1, if your data already occupies columns A, B and C.

New Worksheet Ply: This places the output in a separate worksheet within the same file, so do not select this option.

New Workbook: This places the output in a new workbook, so do not select this option.

When you have completed the dialogue box click on **OK** and the required output will be produced.

The output for the *West Moors Steel* data should be as in Table 19. Such a table is called a **correlation matrix**.

	Order size (X_1)	NumOps (X_2)	Hours (Y)
Order size(X_1)	1		
NumOps(X_2)	−0.3216	1	
Hours(Y)	0.738816	0.2343648	1

Table 19: West Moors Steel correlation matrix

The numbers in the body of the table are the coefficient of correlation values for each pair of variables. Simply select a variable name from a row, and another variable name from a column. The point of intersection is the appropriate value of *r* for that pair of variables: for example, in the case of manufacturing hours and number of operations this is 0.2343648.

Notice that the upper right hand side of the correlation matrix is blank: this is because it would only duplicate information already provided. Notice also that the diagonal always contains the value 1, since correlation of a variable with itself is always perfect and positive.

A useful rule for selecting a suitable collection of independent variables for our regression model is to choose those which are strongly correlated with Y and exclude those which are not. We can read from the matrix that correlation between manufacturing hours and order size is equal to +0.739, which is reasonably strong, while correlation between hours and number of operations is quite weak at a mere +0.234. This supports the evidence gained from the plots. However, we need to exercise caution when using scatterplots and a correlation matrix to analyse multivariate data. What we are trying to do is to examine the effect the independent variables have upon Y not just individually but as a whole. It may be that the X_n variables acting together have a joint effect upon Y which is not apparent from a pairwise comparison. For example, the *West Moors Steel* analysis states that correlation between hours and number of operations is quite weak. We should not, however, jump to the conclusion that this is irrefutable evidence for excluding the latter variable from the model. It could be the case that number of operations and order size acting together have a strong influence on manufacturing hours. The lesson here is that we must use the results of a pairwise analysis (scatterplots and correlation matrix) as part of the evidence for assessing the effectiveness of our regression model. We must be careful not to base our decisions solely on such results.

7.3 The multivariate regression procedure

We now turn to the actual regression procedure itself. If we use the *West Moors Steel* data as a continuing example, we note that the model in this case is:

$$Y = \alpha + \beta_1 X_1 + \beta_2 X_2$$

where Y represents manufacturing hours, X_1 represents order size and X_2 represents number of operations. Consequently, we need to find the values of the regression coefficients α, β_1, and β_2 which achieve the best fit to the data. Stated more accurately, since we are using a sample, we must find estimates a, b_1 and b_2 for these coefficients.

Earlier, when discussing the simple linear model, we demonstrated the regression method with a manually calculated example. In practice, the calculations required for multiple regression are cumbersome and become more so as the number of explanatory variables increases. Because of this, all calculations dealt with here will be the result of computer output. In the next activity you will be asked to produce *Microsoft Excel* output for a regression model. We will then use this as the starting point for our discussion of the technique.

ACTIVITY 40

Open your worksheet **Westmoor.xls** and run the regression tool. Remember that there are now two X variables, so you must enter the whole area containing this data. Assuming you have entered order size data into cells A1 to A21 and number of operations into cells B1 to B21, then your range should be entered as **A1:B21**. Remember to check the **Labels** box if your ranges include the column headings. Select a suitable output range, but leave all other options unchecked for now. When you are sure that the dialogue screen is properly completed, click on **OK** and obtain the output.

As output you should have something like that shown in Table 20. The confidence interval data has been left out in order to simplify the results.

Regression Statistics					
Multiple R	0.891236				
R Square	0.794302				
Adjusted R Square	0.770102				
Standard Error	96.96845				
Observations	20				
ANOVA					
	df	*SS*	*MS*	*F*	*Significance F*
Regression	2	617256	308627.989	32.82271	1.45364E–06
Residual	17	159849	9402.88068		
Total	19	777105			
	Coefficients	*Standard Error*	*t Stat*	*P-value*	
Intercept	–196.6	91.3328	–2.1525633	0.046009	
Order size(X_1)	0.815966	0.104383	7.81703008	4.99E–07	
NumOps(X_2)	34.92498	7.707335	4.53139531	0.000295	

Table 20: Microsoft Excel regression output for West Moors Steel

The main difference between the output for the simple bivariate model and the multivariate one is that there are more regression coefficients to calculate, because of the extra variables. Notice that, apart from the intercept, there is a coefficient (0.815966) for the order size and another for the number of operations (34.92498). We can now proceed to complete the model.

ACTIVITY 41

The model for this activity is of the type $Y = \alpha + \beta_1 X_1 + \beta_2 X_2$.

Complete the model by substituting values from the *Microsoft Excel* output for α, β_1 and β_2. You should round figures to four decimal places. Remember that α, β_1 and β_2 are regression coefficients.

If we substitute our estimates of α, β_1 and β_2 obtained from the *Microsoft Excel* output into this equation we obtain

$$Y = -196.6 + 0.8160X_1 + 34.9250X_2$$

where Y represents manufacturing hours, X_1 represents order size and X_2 represents number of operations.

ACTIVITY 42

West Moors Steel has received a rush order for 500 pieces each requiring 7 operations. Use the model to predict the number of manufacturing hours required to set up this order.

The model is:

$$Y = -196.6 + 0.816X_1 + 34.925X_2$$

In this case we have that the number of pieces, X_1, equals 500, while the number of operations, X_2, equals 7. Substituting these values into the regression model gives:

$$Y = -196.6 + 0.816 \times 500 + 34.925 \times 7$$

$$= -196.6 + 408 + 244.475$$

$$= 455.875 \text{ hours}$$

We have successfully constructed a multiple regression model using *Microsoft Excel*. We now need to consider just how good this model is in terms of explanatory power and predictive accuracy. You should try the following activities, which will allow you to review your knowledge of the process of building a multivariate model.

ACTIVITY 43

Orlando plc wishes to develop a model for the sales of a brand of detergent which it produces. The company believes that sales are strongly related to:

- the size of the advertising budget
- the estimated stocks held by retailers
- the price differential with their competitors.

Orlando plc has data for the past 23 months for these variables. Monthly sales, advertising expenditure and current retailer stocks are measured in £000s. Price differential is calculated by subtracting the average competitor price from the *Orlando plc* price. This data is as follows:

Sales (£000s)	Advertising (£000s)	Retailer stocks (£000s)	Price differential (£000s)
825	246.3	5	−0.10
430	160.5	35	0.55
1200	454.0	8	−0.31
590	168.2	28	0.22
597	212.1	14	0.21
539	188.4	25	0.35
639	214.3	6	−0.01
451	248.9	45	0.51
634	247.0	30	0
849	304.8	3	−0.20
568	240.4	32	0.41
645	248.5	9	−0.05
580	310.5	10	0.42
895	271.4	4	−0.25
1080	326.7	6	−0.27
979	476.5	11	−0.25
549	174.8	8	0.42
595	182.0	2	0.35
1010	307.6	7	−0.25
499	155.3	20	0.40
1090	306.9	10	−0.29
579	155.8	14	0.41
760	230.0	19	−0.06

Enter the data into a worksheet as before and save it as **Orlando.xls**.

1. Use *Microsoft Excel* to draw pairwise scatterplots between sales and each of the three independent variables (advertising, stocks and price differential).

2. Use the **Correlation** tool to obtain the correlation matrix for the data (see Section 7.2 for details of how to do this).

1. The three scatterplots (Figures 28, 29 and 30) are shown below.

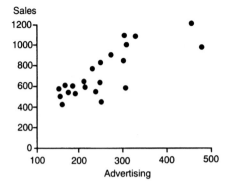

Figure 28: Sales-advertising scatterplot

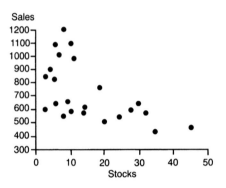

Figure 29: Sales-stocks scatterplot

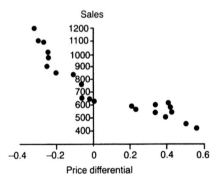

Figure 30: Sales-price differential scatterplot

2. The correlation matrix for the data is shown in Table 21.

	Advtg	Stocks	Price	Sales
Advtg	1			
Stocks	−0.32834	1		
Price	−0.69903	0.583265	1	
Sales	0.794059	−0.57481	−0.91258	1

Table 21: Orlando plc correlation matrix

ACTIVITY 44

For the *Orlando plc* data:

1. Comment on the relationships between sales and the other variables as indicated by the scatterplots.

2. Comment on the relationships between sales and the other variables as indicated by the correlation matrix.

---

1. The scatterplots show a degree of association between sales and the three variables concerned: there is pattern and direction in the plots. Although this is less clear, there does not seem to be very convincing evidence of any non-linearity in the plots. Of course, as with all such evidence, the judgement of the analyst is involved in arriving at such conclusions. Sometimes a degree of risk is involved.

   Notice that in the case of two of the plots, Figures 29 and 30, the slope of the scatterplots is downward to the right. In the case of retail stocks, we might have argued that the higher the stocks, the lower the factory gate demand for the product. In the case of price differential, we should remember that this is calculated by subtracting the industry average from the *Orlando plc* price. Consequently, if this is a negative quantity (because the *Orlando plc* price is lower than the industry average price) then sales will be encouraged. However, if it is positive (because the *Orlando plc* price is higher than the industry average price) then this will discourage sales.

2. The correlation matrix for the four variables is shown in Table 21. To support regression we are looking for evidence of association between sales and the other three variables. High coefficients of correlation are convincing evidence. Notice that in two cases, price differential and advertising, correlation is high (−0.913 and 0.794 respectively). In the remaining case of stocks, correlation, at −0.575, is less convincing but still not negligible. Notice, also, that in two cases correlation with sales is negative (stocks and price differential). This coincides with the evidence of the scatterplots.

In general, the evidence from the plots and the correlation matrix suggests that we have chosen a good package of independent variables and should obtain a good multivariate model.

ACTIVITY 45

Open your worksheet **Orlando.xls**. Use the *Microsoft Excel* **Regression** tool to obtain output for the *Orlando plc* data. Hence construct the multiple regression model of sales.

At this point we are only interested in the model itself, so we proceed directly to the 'Coefficients' section at the bottom of the output (see Table 22). A multiple regression model involving three independent variables would be:

$$Y = \alpha + \beta_1 X_1 + \beta_2 X_2 + \beta_3 X_3$$

where X_1 represents advertising expenditure, X_2 represents stocks and X_3 represents price differential. Substituting our values into the equation, we have:

$$Y = 582.5072 + 0.8392X_1 - 1.9521X_2 - 462.788X_3$$

We have thus developed a multivariate model of sales based on advertising, stocks and price differential. It still remains to analyse the explanatory and predictive power of multivariate models. We will do this in the next section.

SUMMARY OUTPUT					
Regression Statistics					
Multiple R	0.941997				
R Square	0.887358				
Adjusted R Square	0.869573				
Standard Error	80.94099				
Observations	23				
ANOVA					
	df	*SS*	*MS*	*F*	*Significance F*
Regression	3	980596.6	326865.5	49.89214	3.35488E–09
Residual	19	124477.4	6551.444		
Total	22	1105074			
	Coefficients	*Standard Error*	*t Stat*	*P-value*	
Intercept	582.5072	79.73055	7.305948	6.28E–07	
Advtg	0.839197	0.283853	2.956455	0.008106	
Stocks	–1.95208	1.811205	–1.07778	0.294626	
Price	–462.788	93.17464	–4.96689	8.56E–05	

Table 22: Microsoft Excel output for Orlando plc

Summary

We began this section by providing a formal definition of the multivariate model. We then went on to analyse the data in a multivariate model by using scatterplots and correlation data to explore pairwise relationships between the dependent and each of the independent variables. Finally, we focused on the multivariate regression procedure itself, using *Microsoft Excel* to obtain the output. Although much more complex and demanding in terms of arithmetic, this procedure is based on an extension of the least squares method introduced earlier when discussing the simple linear case. In the next section we shall examine the effectiveness of a multivariate model, stressing the similarities to and differences from the procedures used with the simple model.

SECTION 8

The Performance of the Multivariate Model

Introduction

In Section 8 we deal with the important matter of the performance of the multivariate model. We start, in Section 8.1, by using R-Squared as a means of assessing multivariate models. In Section 8.2 we refine the multivariate model by assessing the contribution of the various independent variables. We then go on, in Section 8.3, to address the issue of **multi-collinearity** with relation to multivariate models. Finally, in Section 8.4, we use residuals to analyse the performance of multivariate models. By the end of this unit you should be able to use a battery of diagnostic techniques to analyse the performance of a multivariate regression model.

You will find that some of the material in this section is familiar, in that it involves extending to the multivariate model methods used with the bivariate model. However, the section also contains some new procedures which you will not have come across before.

8.1 R-Squared and the multivariate model

Firstly, we deal with the problem of the explanatory power of the multiple regression model. How well does the group of independent variables we have chosen explain the behaviour of Y, the dependent variable? As we have already seen, one figure shown in the computer output which is of importance is that for R-Squared. As with simple linear regression, the coefficient of determination (R-Squared) is calculated as follows:

$$R^2 = \frac{\text{Variability in Y due to X}}{\text{Total Variability of Y}}$$

However, there are some complications when applying R-Squared to the multivariate case. To illustrate this problem, we should first look at some *Microsoft Excel* output for a multivariate model. As an example, take another look at the regression output for the **Westmoor.xls** worksheet (Table 20). Table 23 summarises the regression statistics for this data.

SUMMARY OUTPUT	
Regression Statistics	
Multiple R	0.891236
R-Squared	0.794302
Adjusted R-Squared	0.770102
Standard Error	96.96845
Observations	20

Table 23: Regression statistics for West Moors Steel data

In previous exercises we have always ignored the fact that there appear to be two values for R-Squared, one simply called 'R-Squared' and the other referred to as 'Adjusted R-Squared'. In bivariate regression analysis, the first of these values is always used. However, there is one difficulty with using R-Squared in situations where there are two or more explanatory variables. Suppose that a forecasting model currently contains one explanatory variable. Suppose further that a second explanatory variable is added to the model. Then the addition of this extra variable cannot reduce the value of R-Squared. The proportion of the variation in Y explained by the previous variable cannot be reduced by the inclusion of a further variable. On the contrary, by adding an additional variable it will always be the case that the value of R-Squared is increased. This effect can be compensated for by using the adjusted R-Squared. This still measures the proportion of the variation in the Y variable accounted for by the explanatory variables, but with a correction to allow for the number of variables. As you can see from the *Microsoft Excel* output in Table 23, the adjusted R-Squared comes out at 77 per cent, not that much smaller (in this example) than the unadjusted figure.

As with the simple linear model we can also use the F test to determine whether the value of R-Squared we have obtained is significantly greater than 0. The procedure is exactly the same: we examine the F statistic and the probability of it being exceeded.

ACTIVITY 46

Look again at the regression output for the *West Moors Steel* data shown in Table 20 in Section 7.3.

1. What is the F statistic and its associated significance? (If you need reminding about the F statistic, take another look at Section 4.2.)

2. Are you satisfied that the adjusted R-Squared of 0.77 is significantly greater than 0?

1. The required information is to be found in the 'ANOVA' section of the *Microsoft Excel* output. The value of adjusted R-Squared is 0.770102. The F value for this data is 32.82271 and has an associated significance or probability of 1.45E–06, which is 1.45×10^{-6} or 0.00000145.

2. Remember that we earlier adopted a probability figure of 0.05 as our yardstick for judging significance. Anything less than 0.05 was a significant result, and indicated that the R-Squared obtained was unlikely to be due to random chance. The figure actually obtained is a very tiny probability, and we would have to conclude that the R-Squared value must be significant.

So the procedure for examining the explanatory power of a multiple regression model is very similar to that for a simple model, except for the necessity to adjust the value of R-Squared to allow for the number of independent variables.

8.2 The contribution of the independent variables

It is now time to turn our attention to the explanatory variables. The value of R-Squared and the accompanying F test are related to how well the model as a whole explains the sample data, and therefore provide a good basis for deciding if the model will make good predictions. However, once the model includes two or more explanatory variables, a further distinct question must also be asked: 'is it the case that each of the variables significantly adds to the explanatory power of the model?'

To answer this, we examine each independent variable in turn and ask if it really tells us anything about the behaviour of the Y variable. For example, in the *West Moors Steel* example, although we know that the model as a whole has good explanatory power ($R^2 = 0.77$), we know nothing, as yet, about the contributions made by the two independent variables, size of order and number of operations.

We continue using the example of *West Moors Steel* and begin by looking at the *Microsoft Excel* output relating to the coefficients. This is shown in Table 24. All other output has been excluded. This was the data from which we constructed our original model.

	Coefficients
Intercept	–196.59964
Order size(X_1)	0.81596593
NumOps(X_2)	34.9249819

Table 24: Regression coefficients for West Moors Steel data

This model was:

$$Y = -196.6 + 0.816X_1 + 34.925X_2$$

The regression coefficient for the X_1 variable (order size) is 0.816, which tells us that, other things remaining equal, the effect of a 1-unit rise in the size of order is to increase the number of hours required to process the order by approximately 0.8. Also, the coefficient for the X_2 variable (number of operations) is 34.95, which tells us that the effect (other things being equal) of a 1-unit rise in this variable is to add almost 35 hours to required manufacturing time. This is quite a useful interpretation of the regression coefficients, but we should be careful about how we use such interpretations. Note the use of the phrase 'other things remaining equal' which, in this context, means 'provided none of the other variables change'. The effect of several variables changing together is not simply the sum of each of the individual variable effects. The effects of changing two or more variables at the same time are much more difficult to analyse than the effects of changing a single variable.

ACTIVITY 47

Look again at the completed model for *Orlando plc* developed in Activity 45. What are the individual effects (other things remaining equal) of the three independent variables:

1. advertising,

2. retail stocks,

3. price?

The relevant Microsoft Excel output for the *Orlando plc* data is shown in Table 25.

	Coefficients
Intercept	582.5072
Advtg	0.839197
Stocks	−1.95208
Price	−462.788

Table 25: Microsoft Excel output for Orlando plc

1. The effect of a 1-unit change in advertising is to change the level of sales in the same direction by 0.839. Remember that these figures are in £000s.

2. The effect of a 1-unit change in the level of retail stocks is to change sales by 1.952 in the opposite direction, as indicated by the minus sign. Again, the figures are in £000s.

3. Finally, a 1-unit change in price has the effect of inducing a 462.788 change in the level of sales in the opposite direction.

In thinking about these changes, you should bear in mind the proviso 'other things remaining equal'.

Apart from this interpretation of the regression coefficients, there is yet another problem. Suppose that the reality of the situation is that a particular independent variable contributes nothing to our knowledge of the behaviour of Y. Perhaps, as a result of sheer chance we have selected a random sample which has misled us into forming the opposite view. Technically, if an independent variable does not contribute to our knowledge of Y then its coefficient should be 0, so the problem can be restated as follows: 'is the regression coefficient of variable X_n significantly greater than 0?'

You may have spotted that we encountered a similar problem with the R-Squared value, where we had to decide whether or not it was a truly significant value or just a chance occurrence. In that case we set up a significance test and used the F test. In the case of the independent variables, we set up a significance test for each of the coefficients β_n. It is also known that the behaviour of b, the sample estimate of β, follows the t **distribution**, which is a special probability distribution. Without getting embroiled in statistical theory, we can describe the procedure of the t test as follows:

- calculate the t statistic for each independent variable
- assuming (for the time being) that the independent variable has no explanatory power, calculate the probability of arriving at that particular value of the t statistic
- if the calculated probability is low (say below 0.05) then we might conclude that the independent variable does in fact have some real explanatory power.

In practice, the conduct of the t test is rather simpler than the theory behind it. *Microsoft Excel* provides output for the t distribution just as it does for the F distribution, so that your task is to carry out the test and apply its results. You should, however, try to get some feel for what is going on, even if you do not need to understand the details.

In order to flesh out the above explanation, we can return to the *West Moors Steel* data. The regression coefficients for the *West Moors Steel* model are shown in Table 26. All output has been obtained from *Microsoft Excel*.

	Coefficients	Standard error	t Stat	P-value
Intercept	−196.59964	91.33280129	−2.1525633	0.046009
Order size(X_1)	0.81596593	0.104383112	7.81703008	4.99E–07
NumOps(X_2)	34.9249819	7.707335039	4.53139531	0.000295

Table 26: Regression coefficients for West Moors Steel data

For the intercept and each of the explanatory variables in the multiple regression, *Microsoft Excel* outputs 't-Stat'. This is the value of t, along with the probability of that value being obtained if the true value of β is in fact 0. *Microsoft Excel* calls this probability the 'P-value'.

ACTIVITY 48

Look at the information contained in Table 26. Is it likely that the coefficient of X_1 is really 0? Why/why not?

Hint: think about how we used probability to decide whether R-Squared was really significant.

Our judgement is based on the use of probability, as it was with the significance of R-Squared. Consider the explanatory variable order size (X_1). The t value for this variable is approximately 7.82, and the probability of getting such a value, if the true picture is that this variable has no explanatory power at all, is only 4.99E–07, or a mere 0.000000499 in ordinary decimals. You can think of this as saying that, if we regard this variable as significant in explaining the behaviour of manufacturing time, then we are running a risk of 0.000000499 of making an incorrect judgement. Since this risk is extremely small, we feel confident in concluding that this variable is significant in explaining the behaviour of Y (manufacturing hours). The same holds for the other variable X_2 (number of operations). The t value is 4.5314 and the probability of getting this is 0.000295, or near enough 0.

We have to establish some kind of criteria for deciding when a t value is significant or not. As with the F test used to judge R-Squared, an arbitrary cut-off point is used. Provided that the probability or significance level of t is less than 0.05 (that is, 5 per cent), then we regard the variable as being significant (in other words, it plays a significant part in explaining the behaviour of Y). If, however, the probability is greater than 0.05 we would usually decide that the variable is not significant. In consequence we might then decide to exclude it from the regression and, hence, from any forecasting model.

In the case of the *West Moors Steel* data, we can conclude on the evidence so far that we have a satisfactory model because:

- the model, as a whole has good explanatory power (because of the high and significant value of R-Squared)

- each of the two independent variables adds to our knowledge of the behaviour of the dependent variable, manufacturing hours, (because of the significant *t* values for each coefficient).

ACTIVITY 49

Study the *Microsoft Excel* regression output for the *Orlando plc* model which you obtained in Section 7.3. The details are shown in Table 22. Answer the following questions. In each case summarise the evidence which led you to answer as you did.

1. Write down the values of the adjusted R-Squared, the F significance, the coefficients of the independent variables, the *t* statistics for each coefficient, and the probabilities associated with these *t* statistics.

2. Does the model have good explanatory power when considered as a whole?

3. Does each of the three independent variables make a contribution to the explanatory power of the model? Would you include all three variables in the regression model?

1. The required *Microsoft Excel* output is summarised in Table 27.

SUMMARY OUTPUT			
Adjusted R-Squared	0.86957275		
Significance of F	3.3549E–09		
	Coefficients	t Stat	P-value
Intercept	582.5072	7.305948	6.28E–07
Advtg	0.839197	2.956455	0.008106
Stocks	–1.9520	–1.07778	0.294626
Price	–462.788	–4.96689	8.56E–05

Table 27: Microsoft Excel output for Orlando plc data

2. The adjusted R-Squared is high at 0.869, which means that the model using all three variables explains nearly 87 per cent of the variation in manufacturing hours. What is more, the probability or significance of the F statistic is 3.3459E–09, or a minuscule 0.000000003459, which is very significant indeed. It is very unlikely that we could have been misled by a sampling error with such a result.

3. We need to look at the probability (P values) for each coefficient. In this case, you might notice that although both advertising and price are significant (because P is less than 0.05), the amount held in retail stocks is not significant (it is 0.294626, which is greater than 0.05). It seems that the retail stocks variable is adding very little, if anything at all, to our knowledge of the behaviour of sales. We would at least have to consider the possibility of removing this variable from the model.

The answer to the last activity has indicated how we might use the results of the t test. If we find that a variable appears to be making no significant contribution to the explanatory power of the model, we should explore what happens to our regression model if we exclude it.

ACTIVITY 50

Open your **Orlando.xls** worksheet containing the *Orlando plc* data. We will now construct a new regression model for sales, but this time omit the retail stocks variable. You will need to remove the stocks variable and close any resulting gaps between columns. The best way to do this is as follows.

- Select the stocks data. (Do this by clicking on the column label.)
- Use the **Cut** facility to remove the column contents and place them in the **Clipboard**. (Do this by clicking on the scissors icon on the standard toolbar or by keying **Ctrl+X**.)
- Select a column in a blank area of your worksheet by clicking on the column label. (For example, select column G.)
- Use the **Paste** facility to insert the stocks data into the selected column. (Do this by clicking on the clipboard icon on the standard toolbar or by keying **Ctrl+V**.)
- Delete the column which originally contained the stocks data. (Do this by clicking on the column label. Then pull down the **Edit** menu and select **Delete**.) All remaining variables should now be in adjacent columns.

1. Rerun the regression tool for the new set of variables and obtain output for adjusted R-Squared, F significance, the regression coefficients and the t statistics and t probabilities.

2. Using the output produced, write down the new regression model.

3. Does the new model seem to be an improvement? If so, how is it improved?

---

1. The output for the new model is shown in Table 28.

SUMMARY OUTPUT				
Adjusted R-Squared	0.8685188			
Significance F	5.953E–10			
	Coefficients	Standard Error	t Stat	P-value
Intercept	568.36941	78.96117357	7.198087	5.73E–07
Advtg	0.7973891	0.282323306	2.824383	0.010476
Price	–515.38111	79.69473384	–6.46694	2.63E–06

Table 28: Summary output for revised orlando plc model

2. So the new model is:

$$Y = 568.36941 + 0.7974X_1 - 515.3811X_2$$

3. To decide whether this is an improvement on the model using all three independent variables, you should look at the output in Table 28 and compare it with the output obtained for the previous *Orlando Plc* model in Table 22.

Notice that the value of R-Squared has not changed. It was 0.8696 for the three-variable model and is 0.8685 for the reduced problem. This is not a real change. However, you may have spotted that the F significance is much lower: 5.953E–10 as opposed to 3.3549E–09. Remember that very small numbers are often expressed in the output as scientific notation, and that 5.953E–10 is, in decimal form, 0.0000000005953, which is much smaller than 3.3549E–09 or 0.0000000033549.

Technically, this means that we can now be even more convinced that we have a significantly high value for R-Squared. You may consider this a fairly marginal improvement and, on this evidence alone, you would be right. However, as we shall see later, there are other ways of assessing the performance of a regression model.

So, using the result of the *t* test, we can examine the contribution of individual independent variables to the model as a whole. If necessary, we can use the information so obtained to remove weak predictors from the model and so improve its performance.

SHOULD THE CONSTANT EVER BE SUPPRESSED?

You may notice that, in many cases, the intercept is also reported as not significant during a *t* test. This would indicate that it should also be left out of the model. This may be sound practice in many instances because the intercept does not always tell us anything useful about the data. Think about the *West Moors Steel* model for instance. The basic model is:

$$Y = -196.6 + 0.8160X_1 + 34.9250X_2$$

This would have the effect of suggesting that an order which had zero size and involved zero operations (in fact, no order at all) would take −196.6 hours to complete!

Therefore, the intercept not only may have nothing useful to tell us about the behaviour of Y, but may even have an absurd interpretation. However, many analysts would still argue in favour of leaving the intercept in the model, because it gives an idea of the general magnitude of the data within which the model was constructed. You should always use good sense when interpreting the intercept. In any case, with some editions of *Microsoft Excel*, there is an error in the program which causes it to give incorrect results if you choose the **constant is zero** option.

8.3 Multi-collinearity

Earlier, when discussing the subject of relationships between variables, we noted that high levels of correlation between the dependent variable and each of the independent variables is a desirable characteristic and will contribute to a successful regression model with high explanatory power. For example, consider the *West Moors Steel* example, first encountered in Section 7.2. This example involved the development of a model where manufacturing hours depended upon size of order and number of operations. A high level of correlation between manufacturing hours and size of order and between manufacturing hours and number of operations would be desirable. However, what about correlation between the two independent variables? Would this be a desirable feature as far as the success of regression analysis is concerned? The answer to this question is 'no'.

This problem, called **multi-collinearity** (or sometimes just simply **collinearity**) is not a matter we had to worry about with simple regression, with only one independent variable to consider. It occurs in multiple regression when two or more of the independent variables in the analysis are significantly correlated. Why do we need to worry about such a problem?

The existence of multi-collinearity might make it next to impossible to properly interpret the regression coefficients for the variables involved as the two variables correlated might interact in a way which is unpredictable. For example, the coefficient of number of operations in the *West Moors Steel* example is 34.92, and we would normally read this as meaning that (other things being equal) a 1-unit change in this variable will increase manufacturing hours by 34.92. If there is significant correlation between this variable and order size, we would not be able to make such assumptions.

Multi-collinearity might even cause a change in sign of the coefficient of some of the variables, from positive to negative, or vice versa. So we would not even be able to say with any certainty whether an increase in the affected variables generally resulted in a rise or fall in the dependent variable.

Multi-collinearity will affect the size of the t values, generally making them smaller. This would make it difficult for us to assess the contribution of each variable to overall explanatory power.

Multi-collinearity will make it very difficult to calculate trustworthy interval estimates for the regression coefficients.

Since it is so important, how do we go about measuring the presence (or otherwise) of multi-collinearity?

One method would be to set up a correlation matrix. As we have already seen, this is easily obtained from *Microsoft Excel*. Such a table would show the pairwise correlations between the independent variables.

ACTIVITY 51

Re-examine the correlation matrices for both the *West Moors Steel* data and the full *Orlando plc* data. (You will find them in Tables 19 and 21.) What do you conclude about the possible presence of multi-collinearity in these regression models?

Remember that multi-collinearity is the presence of correlation between the independent variables. In the case of the *West Moors Steel* problem we have two independent variables, size of order and number of operations. On checking the correlation matrix in Table 19, we find that the value of r between these variables is -0.3216. Although such matters always involve a degree of judgement, this is a low figure and does not seem to indicate the possibility of multi-collinearity. Consequently, there seems to be no problem with the model devised for this data.

There may, however, be a problem with the *Orlando plc* data. In this situation we have three independent variables: retail stocks, price and advertising budget. The correlation between price and advertising is -0.699 and between price and retail stocks, 0.5833. It may be that the degree of multi-collinearity between these variables is high enough to invalidate the information we are obtaining from R-Squared, the F and the t tests. In other words, although the R-Squared for this model (along with other information) may seem to indicate a good model with high explanatory powers, we may not be able to rely on this evidence because it is distorted by the presence of multi-collinearity.

We have seen that multi-collinearity can cause problems with a regression model. In some cases these problems are severe and may lead us to abandon our model. However, most of the problems caused are problems of interpretation: we may still be able to use our model to make estimates, but we will have no idea of the possible error they may contain. Also, we may find it difficult to interpret how each independent variable affects Y if multi-collinearity exists.

It may be possible to eliminate multi-collinearity by removing one of the offending variables. For example, if several variables appear to be highly correlated with each other, then we may be able to make good progress by selecting the one which appears to be most correlated with the dependent variable and eliminating the others from the model.

8.4 The multivariate model and residual analysis

The final topic concerned with the analysis of the performance of the regression model is the behaviour of residuals. The procedure in multiple regression is no different to that used in the simple model: we are looking for exactly the same patterns. Remember that the main use of analysis of residuals is to check that the conditions necessary to support regression analysis are present.

ACTIVITY 52

List the four main conditions necessary to support regression analysis. They were discussed in Section 5.2

The four essential conditions are:

- that the data is linearly related
- that the error terms have constant variances (that is, that across all values of X the error terms should show the same variability)
- that the error terms are independent (that is, that large error terms do not cluster together)
- that the error terms are normally distributed.

Microsoft Excel provides tables and plots of residuals as it does with bivariate models. If you wish to see residuals calculated and plotted, make sure that you select this option when using the **Regression** tool. There is one difference with the *Microsoft Excel* residual plots for simple regression and multivariate regression. For multivariate regression, *Microsoft Excel* provides plots of the residuals against each of the independent variables.

ACTIVITY 53

1. Open your **Westmoor.xls** worksheet. Carry out a residuals analysis check on the *West Moors Steel* model. Remember to check both the 'Residuals'

and the 'Residual plots' options when using the **Regression** tool. As there are two independent variables for the *West Moors Steel* data you will find that *Microsoft Excel* produces two plots.

You will need to test for evidence of non-linearity and heteroskedasticity. (Heteroskedasticity, as you may remember, is when the range within which variation occurs either increases or decreases.)

2. Using *Microsoft Excel,* draw up a distribution table of standardised residuals and use this to produce a frequency plot. To do this, draw up a list of groups – 'less than –2.5', '–2.5 to –2.0', …'2 to 2.5' and count the frequency residuals for each group.

---

1. The *Microsoft Excel* residual plots are shown as Figures 31 and 32. In Figure 31, 'Order Size' is the X-axis variable; in Figure 32 'Number of Operations' is the X-axis variable.

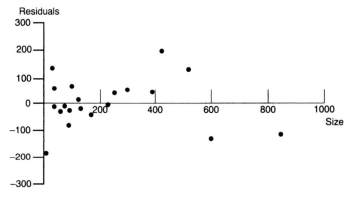

Figure 31: Residual plot Against order size

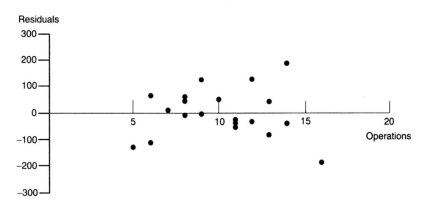

Figure 32: Residual plot against number of operations

We are looking for any evidence of a deviation from a random pattern in the plots. In both plots there seems to be no evidence of non-linearity so we may reasonably assume that this condition has been met.

For heteroskedasticity, we are looking for signs that the spread of residuals about the X-axis is changing dramatically. Although this is not the case in the order size plot, the operations plot seems to suggest that the residuals are becoming larger as order size increases. This does not invalidate our model completely, but it does mean that prediction errors might possibly increase if large order sizes are involved.

2. Remember that the normal distribution curve is bell-shaped. This means that we should have a larger number of points at the centre of the range and gradually lower numbers at either extreme. As usual with such data, we are hindered in our conclusions by the relatively small amount of data (20 observations). However, both Table 29 and Figure 33 suggest that the distribution of residuals is normal.

Z residual	Frequency
Less than −2.5	0
−2.5 ≤ −2	0
−2.0 ≤ −1.5	1
−1.5 ≤ −1.0	1
−1.0 ≤ −0.5	2
−0.5 ≤ 0.0	7
0.0 ≤ 0.5	4
0.5 ≤1.0	2
1.0 ≤ 1.5	2
1.5 ≤ 2.0	0
2.0 ≤ 2.5	1

Table 29: Frequency of standardised residuals

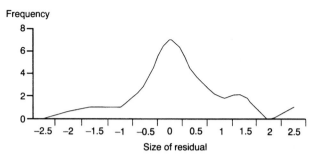

Figure 33: Frequency plot of standardised residuals

Summary

In Section 8 we have dealt with the performance of the model. We started by using R-Squared as a means of assessing multivariate models and we noted that an adjustment needed to be made since R-Squared was often overestimated as a consequence of adding more variables. We then refined the multivariate model by using the *t* test to assess the contribution of the various independent variables. Next, we addressed the issue of multi-collinearity with relation to multivariate models. In particular, we saw how multi-collinearity could badly impair, and even totally invalidate, a multiple regression model. Fortunately, it is possible to remedy this problem by eliminating the offending variables. Finally, we used residuals to analyse the performance of multivariate models.

Now that we have studied the basic methods of constructing and evaluating bivariate and multivariate regression models, we can proceed to make refinements to the process of regression analysis, thereby increasing the power of the method.

Section 9

Refining the Multiple Regression Model

Introduction

In the previous sections we learned how to construct both simple and multivariate regression models. We also discussed how to examine the performance of such models in terms of their explanatory power and predictive accuracy. Now that we have covered the main aspects of regression analysis, we can proceed to examine ways in which we can refine our model. In Section 9.1 we look at how to incorporate **qualitative variables** into a regression model. In Section 9.2 we explore the use of **time-lagged variables**. We also look at ways of improving our model by combining existing variables to form new ones. By the end of this section you should be able to use **dummy variables** to incorporate qualitative variables into a regression model. You should also be able to use lagged variables in regression analysis.

9.1 Making room for qualitative variables

In our analysis so far, all of the variables considered, whether dependent or independent, have been quantitative. However, if a model is to have real explanatory power, it must also be able to account for qualitative variables. For example, in a model where sales is the dependent variable, it seems reasonable to use advertising expenditure (a quantitative variable) as a predictor. However, it is also reasonable to suppose that the type of advertising (a qualitative variable) might be important. Whether the promotion is carried out on the TV, in magazines or through a mixture of both media might have an important influence on sales. An important merit of regression models is that they can incorporate qualitative variables such as the type of advertising used, as well as quantitative variables such as the amount spent on advertising. This is done by defining one or more dummy variables. An example will help to make this clear.

We have already used the *West Moors Steel* example. Suppose that this firm has checked back over its last 20 orders and noticed that some of them were rush orders. For such orders it was decided to monitor their progress, thus reducing the time between operations. It seems reasonable that we should allow for this in the forecasting model.

Now, whether an order is a rush order or a normal order is a piece of qualitative and not quantitative information. To make use of it we define a new variable, which we will call 'Rush'. This is a dummy variable, and is assigned the value 0 if the order is normal and the value 1 if it is a rush order. In essence, all dummy variables are rather like switches: they take the value 1 if a particular characteristic is present and take the value 0 if it is not. The revised *West Moors Steel* data is now as shown in Table 30.

Hours(Y)	Order size	Operations	Rush
153	100	6	0
192	35	11	0
162	127	7	1
240	64	12	0
339	600	5	1
185	14	16	1
235	96	11	1
506	257	13	0
260	21	9	1
161	39	8	0
835	426	14	0
586	843	6	0
444	391	8	0
240	84	13	1
303	235	9	1
775	520	12	0
136	76	8	1
271	139	11	1
385	165	14	1
451	304	10	0

Table 30: West Moors Steel data with dummy variable

So the dummy variable procedure is really a clever trick to give numerical status to data which is not numerical. Once the dummy variable has been set up, it is dealt with in just the same manner as any other variable: it is included in the list of independent variables and the usual output is obtained. The only difference is that a dummy variable is restricted to just two values, 0 or 1. The next activity will give you a chance to follow through the regression procedure using dummy variables.

ACTIVITY 54

Open up the **Westmoor.xls** spreadsheet containing the *West Moors Steel* data. If you have any previous regression output remaining on the sheet, delete it to make room for the new data. Enter the dummy variable 'Rush' into a column adjacent to the existing explanatory variables.

Now rerun the multiple regression model for the data, including the new dummy variable as defined above. When entering the X-range in the **Regression** tool dialogue box remember to include this new variable.

1. Write out, in full, the revised estimated model. What is the effect on the time taken to process an order from making it a rush order?

2. What is the value of R-Squared for the model? Is it significant?

3. Comment on the significance for each of the variables in the model, including the new one.

4. A rush order for 560 pieces is received, each piece requiring 12 operations. What do you predict would be the manufacturing hours needed to produce this order?

Microsoft Excel output for this activity is shown in Table 31.

1. The model incorporating the dummy is now:

$$Y = -129.129 + 0.748X_1 + 34.052X_2 - 86.513X_3$$

where X_1 is order size, X_2 is number of operations and X_3 is the dummy variable.

Since the dummy can only be either 0 (for a normal order) or 1 (for a rush order) it can easily be seen from the above model that a rush order will reduce production time by approximately 87 hours.

SUMMARY OUTPUT			
Adjusted R-Squared	0.806728388		
F	27.43574882		
Significance F	1.52009E–06		
	Coefficients	t Stat	P-value
Intercept	–129.1288548	–1.43556	0.17039
Order size	0.748259414	7.392278	1.5E–06
Operations	34.05223755	4.809963	0.00019
Rush	–86.51318264	–2.05466	0.05662

Table 31: Regression output for West Moors Steel data

2. R-Squared is now 0.8067, which is higher than previously. The F test is highly significant, so that we can place considerable trust in the high value of R-Squared.

3. The two variables order size and number of operations remain highly significant. For the dummy variable the probability of t is 0.057, which is slightly in excess of our cut-off point of 0.05. We could rigorously apply this cut-off point, in which case we would regard the variable as not being significant, and exclude it from our model. However, it would seem a little harsh to be so rigid, especially since the variable has improved the model when considered as a whole. When using any cut-off points or other guides to taking decisions, we should always remember to exercise our judgement. In this case we might argue that the benefits gained from adding the variable outweigh any disadvantages.

4. For a rush order of 560 pieces, involving 12 operations, we would have:

$X_1 = 560$

$X_2 = 12$

$X_3 = 1$

The predicted manufacturing hours would be:

$Y = -129.129 + (0.748 \times 560) + (34.052 \times 12) - (86.513 \times 1)$

$= -129.129 + 418.88 + 408.624 - 86.513$

$= 611.86$ hours

The last activity has demonstrated the ease with which qualitative variables may be added. However, the variable introduced in the previous problem had only two values, normal and rush, and so could easily be modelled by one dummy taking the values 0 and 1. We must now proceed to examine cases where there are more than two values.

Table 32 shows the relationship between the price earnings ratio (P/E), profit margin, annual growth rate and type of business. Firms included in the data are drawn from three sectors: pharmaceutical, information technology (IT) and energy.

Analysts wish to develop a model of how the price/earnings ratio is dependent upon profit margins, growth rate and industrial sector. Since industrial sector is not a numeric variable we must code it.

Unfortunately we cannot use the codes 0 for pharmaceutical firms, 1 for IT firms and 2 for energy firms.

This is because, in doing so, we would be creating a situation where energy firms would have twice the weight of information technology firms. We must use a system of dummy variables where only 0 and 1 are used. This means that we must create more than one dummy variable. The simplest solution is to create two dummy variables: 'Pharm', which is 0 when the business is not in the pharmaceutical sector, and 1 when it is; and 'IT', which is 0 when the business is not in the IT business, and 1 when it is.

Firm	P/E ratio	Profit margin	Growth rate	Sector
Abbot	15.5	15.2	18	Pharmaceutical
AHP	13.3	16.9	11	Pharmaceutical
Amdahl	8.4	11.9	4	IT
Amoco	10.0	9.8	8	Energy
Chevron	10.0	7.0	5	Energy
Digital	10.4	9.8	19	IT
EliLilley	18.9	18.7	11	Pharmaceutical
Exxon	11.3	6.5	10	Energy
HewlettP	14.8	8.1	18	IT
IBM	11.8	9.2	6	IT
Merck	21.0	20.3	16	Pharmaceutical
Meyers	16.2	13.9	14	Pharmaceutical
Mobil	9.7	4.3	7	Energy
NCR	10.1	7.3	6	IT
Pfizer	11.9	14.7	12	Pharmaceutical
Texaco	9.9	3.9	5	Energy
Unisys	7.0	6.9	6	IT
Upjohn	14.6	12.8	10	Pharmaceutical
Warner	16.0	8.7	7	Pharmaceutical

Table 32: Price earnings ratios for firms in pharmaceutical,
IT and energy sectors (Fortune, July 1992)

ACTIVITY 55

What has happened to the energy sector? Why is no extra dummy needed to show membership of this sector?

No third dummy is required to show membership of the energy sector because if 'Pharm' and 'IT' are both 0 then this must mean that, by default, the business is an energy related firm.

This situation is summarised in Table 33.

Variable		
'Pharm'	'IT'	Sector
1	0	Pharmaceutical
0	1	IT
0	0	Energy

Table 33: Dummy variables for industrial sectors

In general, if a qualitative variable has n different possible values, then we will need $n - 1$ different dummy variables to fully represent it.

ACTIVITY 56

1. Enter the company data (Table 32) into a worksheet, add the required dummy variables and save the worksheet as **Company.xls**. Run the *Microsoft Excel* **Regression** tool.

2. Write down the model for the relationship between price/earnings ratio and the independent variables.

3. Comment on the level of R-Squared and its significance.

4. Comment on the explanatory power of each of the regression coefficients.

1. *The Microsoft Excel* output relating to the regression coefficients is produced in Table 34.

SUMMARY OUTPUT			
Regression Statistics			
Adjusted R-Squared	0.607508272		
F	7.965209786		
Significance F	0.001448537		
Variable	Coefficients	t Stat	P-value
Intercept	7.53930776	4.341977	0.000676
Margin	0.182718368	0.873329	0.397216
Growth	0.212795217	1.622668	0.126956
Pharm	2.984168151	1.337628	0.202343
IT	−0.83523026	−0.55346	0.58868

Table 34: Regression output for companies data

2. The required model would be:

$$Y = 7.539 + 0.183X_1 + 0.213X_2 + 2.984X_3 - 0.835X_4$$

where X_1 is profit margin, X_2 is growth rate, X_3 is Pharm and X_4 is IT.

3. Adjusted R-Squared is only 61 per cent, which is not particularly high, although it is significantly greater than 0.

4. When we look at the regression coefficients, we see the most serious problem for this model. None of the regression coefficients are significant, which means that none of the chosen independent variables appear to explain the behaviour of the price-earnings ratio.

9.2 Creating new variables from old

We have now seen how to incorporate qualitative variables into a regression model by using dummy variables. It is also possible to manipulate data in other ways so as to improve the model. For example, in some cases there may be a time lag built into the effect caused by a variable. That is, a change in X in one time period may result in changes to Y in later time periods. A good example might be changes in the advertising variable, which might have an impact in later periods rather than now. It is possible to incorporate this time lag into our regression model.

It is also possible to create entirely new variables by carrying out arithmetic operations on existing ones. For example, we may be supplied with data relating to both sales revenue and costs. Rather than incorporate this data directly into a regression model, we might prefer to subtract costs from sales revenue, resulting in the new variable, profit. We shall consider these operations by examining some data.

The data in Table 35 shows data for *Kleenit Ltd*, an industrial detergent company, from January 1995 to June 1997. The first column contains the month. The second column (InPrice) contains the in-house unit price. The third column contains the average industry price (MeanPrice). The fourth column contains the size of the monthly advertising budget (AdBudget). The fifth column details the type of advertising plan used (AdType), where A represents a campaign using TV only, B represents a campaign using a mix of TV and radio, and C represents a campaign using TV, radio and magazine advertising. The sixth column contains sales data.

The company would like a regression model which would be capable of accurately predicting monthly sales. This would mean developing a model where sales is the dependent variable and in-house price, mean price, advertising budget and advertising plan are possible independent variables.

The company has two requirements for the model. Firstly, it should include not only the amount of advertising expenditure but also the type of advertising used as predictive variables. Secondly, since the company is unlikely to have future knowledge of its competitors' prices, it would prefer to replace the two price variables with a new one showing the differential between its own price and the industry average.

We already know how to meet the first of these requirements, using dummy variables. The second one requires us to create new variables out of old.

Date	InPrice £s	MeanPrice £s	AdBudget £000s	AdType	Sales £m
Jan-95	3.85	3.80	6.75	B	7.38
Feb-95	3.75	4.00	7.25	B	8.51
Mar-95	3.70	4.30	5.50	A	9.52
Apr-95	3.70	3.70	7.00	C	7.50
May-95	3.60	3.85	6.50	A	9.33
Jun-95	3.60	3.80	6.75	C	8.28
Jul-95	3.60	3.75	5.25	C	8.75
Aug-95	3.80	3.85	5.25	B	7.87
Sep-95	3.80	3.65	6.00	C	7.10
Oct-95	3.85	4.00	6.50	A	8.00
Nov-95	3.90	4.10	6.25	C	7.89
Dec-95	3.90	4.00	7.00	C	8.15
Jan-96	3.70	4.10	6.90	A	9.10
Feb-96	3.75	4.20	6.80	B	8.86
Mar-96	3.75	4.10	6.80	B	8.90
Apr-96	3.80	4.10	7.10	B	8.87
May-96	3.70	4.20	7.00	A	9.26
Jun-96	3.80	4.30	6.80	B	9.00
Jul-96	3.70	4.10	6.50	B	8.75
Aug-96	3.80	3.75	6.25	C	7.95
Sep-96	3.80	3.75	6.00	A	7.65
Oct-96	3.75	3.65	6.50	A	7.27
Nov-96	3.70	3.90	7.00	A	8.00
Dec-96	3.55	3.65	6.80	A	8.50
Jan-97	3.60	4.10	6.80	B	8.75
Feb-97	3.65	4.25	6.50	C	9.21
Mar-97	3.70	3.65	5.75	B	8.27
Apr-97	3.75	3.75	5.80	C	7.67
May-97	3.80	3.85	6.80	C	7.93
Jun-97	3.70	4.25	6.50	C	9.26

Table 35: Kleenit Ltd data

ACTIVITY 57

1. Show how you would convert the advertising plan into a numeric variable by using a suitable set of dummies.

2. How would you create a new variable called 'PriceDiff', which will consist of the in-house price minus the industry average price? Assume that you

have a *Microsoft Excel* spreadsheet with in-house price in column B and industry average price in column C.

---

1. In order to convert type of advertising plan into a numeric variable you will need two dummies (to represent three categories). In what follows, two new variables have been chosen: 'TV', which is 0 if the plan is not TV only and 1 if it is, and 'TV/Rad' which is 0 if the plan is not TV and radio and 1 if it is. A mixture of TV, radio and magazine advertising is indicated when both of these variables are set to 0.

2. A new variable 'PriceDiff' is to be used in the place of the existing price variables. It is calculated simply by creating a blank column within the independent variable group and typing in a formula to calculate the difference between prices. For example, if you have 'InPrice' starting in cell B2 and 'MeanPrice' starting in cell C2, then the formula will be simply =B2–C2, copied into as many cells as are required.

This new variable logs the difference between in-house prices and the industry average: it will be negative if in-house prices are lower than the industry average and positive if they are higher.

ACTIVITY 58

1. Open a new worksheet and save it as **Kleenit.xls**. Enter the *Kleenit Ltd* data into it as follows:

- in column A enter the dates
- in column B enter the 'InPrice' data contained in Table 35
- in column C enter the 'MeanPrice' data contained in Table 35
- in column D enter the heading 'PriceDiff', enter the formula =B2–C2 into cell D2 and copy this into the rest of the cells in the column
- in column E enter the 'AdBudget' data contained in Table 35
- in column F enter the dummy variable 'TV' with appropriate values
- in column G do the same for the dummy variable 'TV/Rad'
- in column H enter the 'Sales' data contained in Table 35.

Run the **Regression** tool on the data.

2. Use the output to construct the regression model. How well does this model perform in terms of R-Squared and the explanatory power of its independent variables?

1. Selected *Microsoft Excel* output for the model is shown in Table 36.

SUMMARY OUTPUT			
Adjusted R-Squared	0.779141		
F	26.57632		
Significance F	1.1E–08		
	Coefficients	t Stat	P-value
Intercept	8.536071	11.78908	1.05E–11
Price Diff	–2.69927	–9.81095	4.71E–10
AdBudget	–0.12355	–1.08527	0.288155
TV	0.169335	1.160382	0.256855
TV/Rad	0.064059	0.443371	0.661311

Table 36: Regression output for revised Kleenit Ltd data

2. The model becomes:

$$Y = 8.536 - 2.699X_1 - 0.124X_2 + 0.169X_3 + 0.064X_4$$

where 'X_1' is 'PriceDiff', X_2 is 'AdBudget', X_3 is 'TV' and X_4 is 'TV/Rad'. This model has a significant adjusted R-Squared of 0.779, which seems to indicate a good overall performance. However, the *t* values for the regression coefficients tell another story. Only 'PriceDiff' seems to be significant and the three advertising variables seem to be contributing nothing to the overall predictive power of the model. Output like this is telling us that the model may be improved by removing and/or adjusting the variables in some way.

Clearly there seems to be some problem with the company sales model. A clue as to what might be happening is contained in the regression coefficient for 'AdBudget'. This is given by the output as –0.124, suggesting that (other things being equal), an increase in advertising budget leads to a decrease in sales! This needs closer investigation.

ACTIVITY 59

Using *Microsoft Excel*, calculate the coefficient of correlation between advertising expenditure and sales. Comment on the results.

Hint: the function **=CORREL(X-range, Y-range)** is the appropriate one to use.

The result is 0.1350. For a variable to be a good predictor we would expect a high level of correlation. This result accounts for the poor predictive value of 'AdBudget' and is hardly what we would expect to be the case for advertising. Why would a business spend any money at all on advertising, if correlation were so weak as to be non-existent?

In a situation like the one encountered above, the analyst would use judgement, and start to explore the relationship between advertising and sales. One possibility would be to investigate the possibility of a built-in time lag in the relationship between the variables. This seems likely in the case of advertising: any expenditure on advertising is likely to have its main impact in the future rather than now.

ACTIVITY 60

Using *Microsoft Excel*, calculate the coefficient of correlation between 'AdBudget' and the sales value one month following.

Hint: be very careful about choosing the ranges for the **=CORREL** function, and remember that you will lose the last data pair (because there will be no corresponding sales for the last advertising figure).

You need to exercise some care when entering data. Assuming you have entered 'AdBudget' in cells E2 to E31 and 'Sales' in H2 to H31, if you wish to build a one-month time-lag into the effect of advertising, you will need to enter **=CORREL(E2:E30,H3:H31)**. The resulting coefficient of correlation is 0.865. This is a satisfyingly high correlation value, and suggests to us that we should rerun the regression model with all advertising data lagged by one month.

Very often, in a regression exercise, we may fail to find direct relationships between variables. In such cases, if the data has been recorded over time we might investigate the possibility of the existence of time lags. The existence of such a lag is clearly shown up in the relationship between advertising and sales in the present example. Instead of running the regression model on current advertising, we should replace it with advertising lagged by one period.

ACTIVITY 61

1. Alter the *Microsoft Excel* worksheet for the *Kleenit Ltd* data so that all advertising variables ('AdBudget', 'TV' and 'TV/Rad') are lagged by one month. You can do this either by using the **Drag and Drop** or the **Cut and Paste** functions.

2. Rerun the regression model using 'PriceDiff', 'AdBudget' (lagged), 'TV' (lagged) and 'TV/Rad' (lagged) as the independent variables. What do you observe now about the resulting regression model?

1. The amended data will look as in Table 37. The created variable 'PriceDiff' is shown, as are the time-lagged advertising budget and advertising type variables. You will notice that building in a time lag will always result in loss of data.

Date	In Price	Mean Price	Price Diff	Ad Budget	TV	TV/ Rad	Sales
Jan-95	3.85	3.80	0.05				7.38
Feb-95	3.75	4.00	−0.25	6.75	0	1	8.51
Mar-95	3.70	4.30	−0.60	7.25	0	1	9.52
Apr-95	3.70	3.70	0.00	5.50	1	0	7.50
May-95	3.60	3.85	−0.25	7.00	0	0	9.33
Jun-95	3.60	3.80	−0.20	6.50	1	0	8.28
Jul-95	3.60	3.75	−0.15	6.75	0	0	8.75
Aug-95	3.80	3.85	−0.05	5.25	0	0	7.87
Sep-95	3.80	3.65	0.15	5.25	0	1	7.10
Oct-95	3.85	4.00	−0.15	6.00	0	0	8.00
Nov-95	3.90	4.10	−0.20	6.50	1	0	7.89
Dec-95	3.90	4.00	−0.10	6.25	0	0	8.15
Jan-96	3.70	4.10	−0.40	7.00	0	0	9.10
Feb-96	3.75	4.20	−0.45	6.90	1	0	8.86
Mar-96	3.75	4.10	−0.35	6.80	0	1	8.90
Apr-96	3.80	4.10	−0.30	6.80	0	1	8.87
May-96	3.70	4.20	−0.50	7.10	0	1	9.26
Jun-96	3.80	4.30	−0.50	7.00	1	0	9.00
Jul-96	3.70	4.10	−0.40	6.80	0	1	8.75
Aug-96	3.80	3.75	0.05	6.50	0	1	7.95
Sep-96	3.80	3.75	0.05	6.25	0	0	7.65
Oct-96	3.75	3.65	0.10	6.00	1	0	7.27
Nov-96	3.70	3.90	−0.20	6.50	1	0	8.00
Dec-96	3.55	3.65	−0.10	7.00	1	0	8.50
Jan-97	3.60	4.10	−0.50	6.80	1	0	8.75
Feb-97	3.65	4.25	−0.60	6.80	0	1	9.21
Mar-97	3.70	3.65	0.05	6.50	0	0	8.27
Apr-97	3.75	3.75	0.00	5.75	0	1	7.67
May-97	3.80	3.85	−0.05	5.80	0	0	7.93
Jun-97	3.70	4.25	−0.55	6.80	0	0	9.26

Table 37: Revised data for Kleenit Ltd

2. The selected output from *Microsoft Excel* is shown in Table 38.

SUMMARY OUTPUT			
Adjusted R-Squared	0.92921021		
F	92.8843188		
Significance of F	3.0563E–14		
	Coefficients	t Stat	P-value
Intercept	4.49617667	8.078418	2.65E–08
PriceDiff	–1.6406045	–7.27912	1.61E–07
AdBudget	0.57740985	6.33376	1.51E–06
TV	–0.4080875	–4.96819	4.51E–05
TV/Rad	–0.1809027	–2.22459	0.035768

Table 38: Regression output for revised data for Kleenit Ltd

So the model is:

$$Y = 4.496 - 1.641X_1 + 0.577X_2 - 0.408X_3 - 0.181X_4$$

Notice that for this model, not only do we have a significant R-Squared of 0.93, we also have every regression coefficient with a significant value. This is because the significance of F and t is reported as less than 0.05 in each and every case. So the model is performing well overall with each independent variable making a significant contribution.

Summary

In this section we have investigated how refinements can be made to the regression model. We have seen that it is possible to include qualitative variables via the use of dummy variables. We have also seen that it is possible to incorporate more complex relationships between the variables. For example, it may be possible to create new variables by carrying out arithmetic on the existing ones. It is also possible to take account of time-lagged relationships between variables. These possibilities contribute greatly to the flexibility and power of the multivariate regression model.

In the final section of this unit we look at some ways of extending regression models to take account of non-linear relationships.

SECTION 10

Extending Regression Analysis

Introduction

Throughout this unit we have investigated the construction of both bivariate and multivariate linear regression models. In doing so, we have developed a powerful means of constructing models capable of predicting important business variables. In this final section we explore the possibilities for extending the technique beyond the basic linear model. In Section 10.1 we look at some aids to the process of model building. In Section 10.2 we explore some techniques which allow us to apply linear regression to non-linear relationships. Finally, in Section 10.3, we discuss the role of human judgement in building regression models. By the end of this section you should be able to recode and transform selected non-linear variables in order to use the technique of linear regression on them.

10.1 Aids to building a model

The amount of preparation required to produce and validate a model can be quite exhausting. This next section illustrates some of the difficulties in producing a regression model and examines whether there are any shortcuts we can take. As usual, we illustrate with a case study.

Case Study: Arcturus plc
Arcturus plc wishes to forecast sales in any one of its various sales territories. It has identified four possible explanatory variables and would like some advice as to the most suitable regression model. The four variables are market potential, advertising, market share and number of accounts.

In developing regression forecasting models for business we try to develop the model which accounts for the most variation of the dependent variable. However, we also try to keep the model as simple as possible: the more difficult the model, the less easy it will be for management to understand and implement it.

In carrying out an investigation of the *Arcturus plc* data, there are four possible independent variables. Think of the difficulty of investigating all possible models. There are various possibilities for constructing a bivariate model (with a single independent variable). We could also construct a range of multivariate models (with different combinations of the four independent variables).

ACTIVITY 62

Think about the construction of a regression model for the *Arcturus plc* sales example. There are four possible independent variables.

1. How many possible bivariate models are there?

2. How many possible multivariate models with two independent variables are there?

3. How many possible multivariate models with three independent variables are there?

4. How many possible multivariate models with four independent variables are there?

5. So how many possible models are there in total?

Let us, for the moment, call our four independent variables A, B, C and D.

1. If we restrict ourselves to just one independent variable, there are four possible regression models, because a model could use either A, B, C or D as its independent variable.

2. If we construct a model where there are two independent variables then there are six possibilities, because we could use the following combinations of independent variables: (A, B); (A, C); (A, D); (B, C); (B, D); (C, D).

3. If we construct a model where there are three independent variables then there are four possibilities, because we could use the following combinations of independent variables: (A, B, C); (A, B, D); (A, C, D); (B, C, D).

4. Lastly, there is only one possible model with four independent variables: (A, B, C, D).

5. This means that there are 15 possible models to investigate.

The situation gets worse as the number of possible independent variables grows. For example, in a situation where we have eight independent variables to choose from, there are as many as 255 different models! This indicates something of the labour involved in multiple regression analysis. Fortunately, there are some shortcuts that can be used in building multivariate regression models with a potentially large number of independent variables.

One of these is to build a model incorporating all of the possible variables. Then test the model by looking at the adjusted R-Squared and by analysing the residuals, and eliminate any variables which appear not to be adding anything to the model. Rerun the model, test again and eliminate further variables or add variables which had been excluded, as appropriate. Continue this procedure, removing and adding variables, until you are happy that the adjusted R-Squared and the analysis of the residuals provide evidence of an effective model.

Another shortcut for searching for a predictive regression model is to begin the search for a model by looking for the best possible bivariate model. Then look for the best model with two independent variables. To do this, add and delete variables one step at a time, testing the model after each stage, and stopping when there are no further significant variables left remaining outside the model. Then look for the best model with three independent variables by adding variables to the best of the models with two independent variables.

We shall not explore this matter any further in this module, as *Microsoft Excel* does not provide an algorithm for pursuing either of these shortcuts. However, the student who wishes to make a further study of regression would need to use these methods.

10.2 Non-linear relationships

The models which have been considered so far in this unit have all been linear. In practice, this is not such a limitation as it may seem, since there are many situations which can be modelled quite well using the assumption of linearity. Even if the assumption of linearity is no longer applicable, there are a number of convenient transformations which can be carried out on data which solve this problem and still allow us to use the technique of linear regression.

FIRST AND SECOND ORDER MODELS
First order regression models are those in which the highest power of any variable is 1 and there are no cross products. In other words, there are no squared, cubed or other powers and there are no terms such as X_1X_2, containing one variable multiplied by another. For example, the simple linear regression model $Y = a + bX$ is a first order model with one independent variable. $Y = a_1 + b_1X_1 + b_2X_2$ is a first order model with two independent variables. This process can be carried on for n independent variables, the models all being first order and linear.

However, consider a model such as $Y = a + b_1X + b_2X^2$. In this case we now have a **second order regression model**, so called because the highest power in the equation is a square. (The model is often described as quadratic.) However, there is only one independent variable, X. We can still use the technique of linear regression to fit such a model, even though the resulting data will not be linear. This may seem rather an odd state of affairs, but we should remember that the process of multiple regression presupposes a linear fit of regression coefficients, and not necessarily a linear relationship of the independent variable values. In essence, we can use multiple linear regression to deal with such a model by treating the X^2 term as a second independent variable. The following activity should help to show you what is happening.

ACTIVITY 63

The following data relates to sales over a 9-week period together with the number of times a particular advertisement was shown on television. Enter the data into a new worksheet and save it as **Sales.xls**.

Times	Sales
14	170
9	60
6	29
21	500
17	320
15	250
8	82
5	35
10	90

1. Perform an ordinary simple linear regression of sales on times. Use *Microsoft Excel* to produce the model and R-Squared. How well is this model performing?

2. Could the model be improved by abandoning the assumption of linearity? Use a scatterplot to decide this.

3. Assume that a quadratic model $Y = a + b_1X + b_2 X^2$ is appropriate. To fit such a model, create a second independent variable by squaring the value of 'Times'. You will need to create a blank column next to 'Times'. Call this new column 'Times2' and then use a *Microsoft Excel* formula to create the new variable. Assuming that you have entered 'Times' into column A, and the first data value appears in cell A2, you will need to type the formula =A^2 into cell B2 and then copy it into the rest of the column. When you have created this new variable, carry out a multiple regression of Y on the two variables 'Times' and 'Times2'. Is the new model an improvement?

---

1. Part of the output for the straight linear problem is shown in Table 39. The model would be: $Y = -160.978 + 28.427X$

SUMMARY OUTPUT	
R-Squared	0.92742001
	Coefficients
Intercept	−160.97845
Times	28.4267241

Table 39: Regression Output for sales data

As the R-Squared is a high 0.93, the model seems to be a powerful one.

2. A scatterplot for the data is shown in Figure 34. Although the R-Squared for the linear model is high, the plot shows some evidence of non-linearity, indicating that we can still make improvements on the previous model.

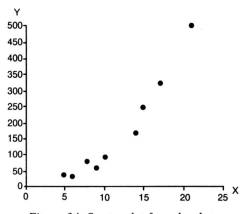

Figure 34: Scatterplot for sales data

The plot appears to resemble the increasing part of a quadratic expression, so that we could possibly improve explanatory power by fitting it to the model $Y = a + b_1X + b_2X^2$.

3. To fit a quadratic model, we square the existing independent variable and treat it as though it were an entirely new variable. The resulting data would look as in Table 40.

Times	Times2	Sales
14	196	170
9	81	60
6	36	29
21	441	500
17	289	320
15	225	250
8	64	82
5	25	35
10	100	90

Table 40: Sales data including squared values of 'times'

We can then fit the model using the method of multiple linear regression. One independent variable would be 'Times' and the second would be 'Times2' Selected output is shown for this model in Table 41.

SUMMARY OUTPUT	
R-Squared	0.98658
	Coefficients
Intercept	53.8438047
Times	−12.293313
Times2	1.60755221

Table 41: Regression output for revised sales data

The model is now $Y = 53.844 - 12.293X + 1.608X^2$. Notice that fitting a quadratic model has improved the value of R-Squared to 0.98658. The model has greater explanatory power because it fits the underlying, quadratic data better.

Activity 63 thus shows that second order models can be fitted by treating the squared term as a second independent variable, and using multiple linear regression.

EXPLORING NON-LINEAR MODELS WITH *MICROSOFT EXCEL*

It is also possible to transform variables in other ways so as to allow the method of linear regression to be used on data which is otherwise not linear. Many of these methods use logarithmic transformations and we shall not pursue them here. However, before leaving the topic of non-linearity we shall illustrate how *Microsoft Excel* can be used to fit curvilinear models providing they have just one independent variable. We can do this via an example.

Allsorts Printers manufactures quality advertising sheets using silk screen-printing. The company is aware that, because of the high set-up costs for each production run, the unit cost (per 100 sheets) for any order decreases with the size of the print run. A random sample of 20 orders has yielded the data shown in Table 42. 'PrintRun' is the number of advertising sheets in the order and 'UnitCost' (in £s) is the cost per 100 sheets. The company is keen to use this data to develop a model to forecast 'UnitCost'.

PrintRun	UnitCost	PrintRun	UnitCost	PrintRun	UnitCost
8,900	6.70	4,200	8.90	5,600	8.11
700	24.62	900	23.78	5,500	8.94
4,700	9.89	2,000	15.57	200	27.68
7,100	6.33	9,700	5.99	5,300	6.81
6,000	7.79	2,400	13.86	300	25.32
7,500	5.70	8,600	5.87	1,700	16.75
1,200	18.57	8,900	6.14		

Table 42: Allsorts Printers data

ACTIVITY 64

Enter the above data into a *Microsoft Excel* worksheet. Use column A for 'PrintRun' and column B for 'UnitCost'. Save the worksheet as **Allsorts.xls**.

Assuming that in an appropriate model 'UnitCost' depends linearly upon 'PrintRun', use the **Regression** tool to estimate this model and forecast the unit cost for an order of 3,000 pages. Comment upon the likely reliability of your forecast by referring to R-Squared and a scatterplot of the data.

The estimated model is:

$$Y = 22.41 - 0.00213X$$

where Y is 'UnitCost' and X is 'PrintRun'.

R-Squared is 0.82 and the F significance is 3.42E–08 or 0.0000000342 in ordinary decimals.

For a print run of 3,000, the forecast unit cost is approximately £16. This looks to be a very reliable forecast. The R-Squared is 0.82 and so 82 per cent of the order by order variability in the unit cost is explained by the variability in the size of the print run. F is extremely significant. However there is one serious problem, as can be seen from Figure 35, which shows a scatter plot of the data.

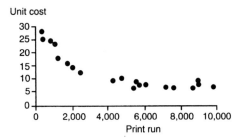

Figure 35: Scatterplot for the Allsorts Printers data

The regression is a poor fit because a linear model has been applied to data which is not linear. This is immediately apparent from the chart, even though the R-Squared that has been obtained is comparatively high. It follows that any forecasts derived from this model are extremely suspect, if not worthless.

Fortunately, there are a number of mathematical transformations that can be used to convert non-linear relationships into linear relationships. Most of them involve the use of logarithms in one way or another. We shall not directly investigate this process of using transformations here, because *Microsoft Excel* allows you to investigate this process using its graphics capabilities.

To see how this is done, open your worksheet **Allsorts.xls.** Click the mouse on the scatterplot of the data. Now double click within the border of the chart to activate it. Then single click on any of the data points to select them. Click on **Chart** on the menu bar and select **Add Trendline.** (If you are using *Microsoft Excel 5.0*, click on **Insert** on the menu bar then on **Trendline.**) You obtain the following dialogue screen.

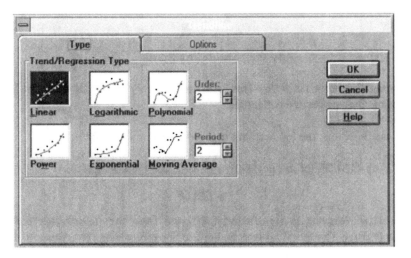

Figure 36: Microsoft Excel Trendline dialogue box

This tool allows you to fit a trendline to a set of data. Choosing **Linear** is equivalent to performing a regression analysis. It is not obvious from the examples shown on screen, but a logarithmic trend is appropriate. If you have forgotten what a logarithmic function is, you may want to reread Section 1.4 of this unit. In any case, even if you cannot visualise a particular model to use, there is nothing wrong with experimenting until you obtain the best result.

Click on **Logarithmic**. Then click the tab labelled **Options** and in its dialogue screen check the boxes for **Display equation on chart** and **Display R-Squaredd value on chart**. Then click **OK**. You should obtain the result displayed in Figure 37.

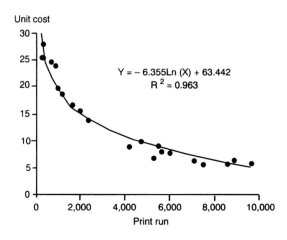

Figure 37: Allsorts Printers scatterplot with trendline

The non-linear trend line obtained has the following equation ('Ln' is short for logarithm):

$$\text{Unit Cost} = 63.442 - (6.355 \times \text{Ln(PrintRun)})$$

R-Squared is shown as 0.96. This is a considerably better fit than the linear regression that you carried out earlier.

Using the trend line, the forecast unit cost for a print run of 3,000 is:

$$63.442 - (6.355 \times \text{Ln}(3,000)) = 63.442 - (6.355 \times 8.0064)$$

$$= £12.56$$

This revised forecast is significantly different from the flawed one that you obtained earlier. The moral is clear: do not use linear regression to estimate a model if there are grounds for suspecting that the data shows evidence of non-linearity.

10.3 Judgement versus technique

In discussing regression you may often have been confused by the sheer number of techniques and devices for constructing models and assessing their performance. It may come as a welcome surprise to discover that human judgement is as important as the mastery of technique in the building of regression models. Suppose we have set ourselves the problem of finding a good regression model to explain and predict the behaviour of a particular variable. How would we go about doing this?

No matter how complex the process might seem to be, there are only two basic reasons for constructing regression models. Firstly, to gain an understanding of how a particular variable behaves, and secondly, to devise a tool which will help us predict the behaviour of this variable.

It does not necessarily follow that a regression equation which is a good explanatory model of the independent variable is a good forecasting tool: people often have different objectives.

The search for a good regression model can often be frustrating. You will very often find that improving a model in one dimension will reduce its quality in other dimensions. For example, we may find that in ridding ourselves of the problem of multi-collinearity in data, we make the model less precise.

There are three stages involved in the conduct of regression analysis:

- preliminary analysis
- the regression itself
- analysis of the performance of the model.

ACTIVITY 65

1. List the activities which can be carried out as part of the preliminary analysis.

2. List the activities which can be carried out as part of the analysis of the performance of the model.

Hint: you may want to check back through earlier sections of this unit.

---

1. Preliminary analysis would involve a preliminary inspection of the variables. Some will be non-numeric, and so of no use in a regression model. (We may later want to look at the possibility of using some non-numeric variables by using dummies.) It is often a good idea during this stage to take a look at scatterplots and a correlation matrix of the numeric variables, in order to examine the strength and direction of the relationships between dependent and

independent variables. We are looking to see if linear correlations between the dependent variable and all the others are strong and significant. We may also be looking for traces of multi-collinearity.

2. In the post-analysis stage we may carry out analysis of R-Squared to check the explanatory power of the model. We would also need to carry out the F test to see if the R-Squared value obtained is really significant; t tests could then be carried out on the independent variable coefficients in order to see what, if any, is their contribution to overall explanatory power. There is also the possibility of using analysis of residuals and carrying out a check on the confidence intervals for the estimates.

Notice how much the use of judgement enters into both the preliminary and post-analysis stages. We may have to make a judgement as to which variables to include in the regression and which to leave out. We have to use judgement when we interpret the scatterplots and the correlation matrix. How do we decide that correlation between dependent and independent variables is high or low? This is especially difficult to do in multiple correlation.

ACTIVITY 66

Suppose that you are attempting to construct a correlation model for sales and have, as possible choices for independent variables, product price, industry average price, promotion budget, type of promotional plan and retailer stocks of the product.

Suppose also that you find that the correlation between sales and industry average price is 0.3, while for sales and product price it is –0.25. Would this be overwhelming evidence in favour of excluding the two variables from the regression procedure?

This is a good example of the need to allow good judgement to bear on the interpretation of quantitative data. Certainly the low correlation figures are good evidence that the variables, considered each on their own, do not seem to exert much influence on sales. However, we should not take too simplistic an approach with the correlation matrix: just because a variable does not have a strong pairwise correlation with the dependent variable, it does not mean to say that it will not be influential in combination with other variables.

It is always a good idea to experiment with data before getting down to the serious task of devising a formal model. It is only by such experimentation that you can hope to get an intuitive feel for the data. For example, try out a number of simple linear regression models of the dependent variable on a selection of some of the independent variables. This will give you valuable insights into the behaviour of the variables and will give you an idea of how this basic model might be improved. It may not be a particularly good model, but spotting the flaws in it is part of the reason for such an exercise.

The post-analysis stage also requires as much judgement as quantitative technique. You may have to decide whether R-Squared is high or significant enough, or whether the *t* test indicates that any of the independent variables should be removed from the model. Analysis of residuals is itself fraught with problems, for you might find that the pattern of residuals indicates that something is amiss, but that the evidence is debatable. This is a common situation for the analyst to be in.

The reason for making these remarks is not to question the validity of the technique of regression, it is merely to underline the fact that the data will not speak for itself, but requires your judgement to interpret it. Remember that the technique will allow you to fit a model to any data consisting of at least two variables, even if it makes no good sense to do so. Even if the technique is applicable to the data, the use of regression will not guarantee that the model delivered will perform well.

Summary

In this final section we have taken a look ahead at some more advanced techniques used in regression. We considered the possibility that the data does not exhibit linear relationships. In such a situation, we cannot use the techniques discussed in previous sections of the unit. However, it was observed that non-linearity of data does not necessarily invalidate the technique. Using mathematical processes of transforming and recoding variables, we can often recast non-linear data in a form which makes the use of linear regression possible. We saw that *Microsoft Excel* provides a limited ability to explore some curvilinear relationships in situations where there is just one independent variable. Finally, we examined the balance between judgement and technique in the conduct of regression analysis.

Unit Summary

This unit has been concerned with explaining the technique of regression analysis and placing it within the context of model building as a whole. Regression analysis is an important technique allowing the analyst to explore relationships between a dependent variable and other independent variables. In doing this, the aim is to build a model which will allow us to understand the behaviour of the dependent variable and make predictions of what values it might assume in various situations.

We began by examining the types of relationships between variables and found that some of them were linear and some non-linear. An important part of the task of the business decisions analyst is to decide on the degree and type of relationship between the variables, because different regression methods need to be used for linear and non-linear cases. We then looked at bivariate causal models (those involving two variables), before examining the technique of regression analysis. We saw that, because *Microsoft Excel* can be effectively used to produce the output needed, the actual physical construction of a regression model is the easiest part of the process.

Most of the difficulty in the use of the technique is concerned with the use of diagnostic techniques to analyse whether the model is effective: we explored some of these in Sections 4 to 6. In Section 4 we used analysis of R-Squared to test the predictive accuracy of regression models, Section 5 introduced a technique known as the analysis of residuals, while in Section 6 we used the concept of confidence intervals to estimate the likely scale of any errors produced by our predictions.

In Section 7, we looked at models with more than two variables: these are known as multivariate models. In Section 8 we looked at ways of assessing the predictions produced by such models and in Section 9 we used this assessment to refine the model. Finally, in Section 10, we took a brief look at some more advanced techniques to allow regression analysis to be applied to non-linear relationships and also considered the role of human judgement in using regression techniques.

Recommended Reading

Books on regression analysis vary enormously in the degree of complexity and the demands they make on the mathematical ability of the reader. The following contain useful chapters.

Anderson, J, Sweeney, D R and Williams, T A (1997) *Quantitative Business Methods*, West Publishing, Minneapolis, USA.

This is a general textbook on statistics which has several chapters on the subjects of regression and correlation. In terms of mathematical understanding, the level of treatment is similar to that contained in this unit. There is, however, a more extensive treatment of the subject of confidence intervals and significance testing.

Black, K (1994) *Business Statistics for Contemporary Decision Making*, West Publishing, Minneapolis, USA.

Chapters 12 and 13 give extensive coverage without requiring too high a level of mathematical understanding. The book comes with a database of problems allowing the student to explore regression models based on a variety of applications.

Flury, B and Riedwyl, H (1988) *Multivariate Statistics, a Practical Approach*, Chapman and Hall, London.

This book places the subject of regression analysis within the wider context of multivariate techniques as a whole. As such, although demanding in parts, it offers a rewarding discussion of the nature of regression and its contribution to modelling.

UNIT 5
TIME SERIES ANALYSIS

Introduction

In many cases the data on which a forecast is based consists of a **time series**. By a time series we mean data on the behaviour of one or more variables over successive time periods. Time series data for sales, output, profits and cash flow are likely to be of particular relevance to the individual firm. In the macro-economy, key time series include those for gross domestic product, unemployment, retail prices and overseas trade.

In this unit we explore how the behaviour of any time series might be analysed, and how such an analysis might be used to forecast future values of the variable or variables concerned. In Section 1 we provide an overview of time series by detailing the component parts of a time series and by distinguishing between two types of time series. In Section 2 we continue our examination of time series by looking at the process known as **decomposition of a time series** (that is, breaking the time series down into its component parts as a prelude to using the time series for forecasting). Section 3 shows how forecasts may be obtained using non-centred moving averages and discusses the interpretation of forecast error. Sections 4 and 5 examine the techniques known as **exponential smoothing** and **autoregression with integrated moving averages (ARIMA)**, respectively.

The techniques discussed in this unit involve the manipulation of often quite substantial quantities of data. Computer software consequently forms an essential part of this unit. **The unit has been written around the assumption that you will be using** *Microsoft Excel*, which is quite adequate for gaining an understanding of time series analysis and for solving simple problems. The analysis of more complex time series would normally require the use of either dedicated software or perhaps a multipurpose statistical package such as *SPSS* or *Minitab*.

Objectives

After working through this unit you should be able to:

- identify the components of a time series
- list the various methods used to forecast a time series
- decompose a time series into its constituent parts
- use the decomposition to obtain a forecast
- use non-centred moving averages to forecast a time series
- use simple exponential smoothing to forecast a time series
- use various methods to assess the degree of forecasting error
- explain the importance of ARIMA as a forecasting method.

SECTION 1
Time Series: an Overview

Introduction

This section of the unit provides an overview of time series. Section 1.1 introduces the various component parts of a time series. Section 1.2 utilises these components to show that a time series can be modelled using either an **additive** or **multiplicative** approach. By the end of this section, you should be able to identify the components of a time series and list the various methods used to forecast a time series.

1.1 The component parts of a time series

In any investigation of time series data it is essential to start by asking what patterns, if any, are present in the series.

ACTIVITY 1

A company keeps a monthly record of sales of its products. The series stretches back over several years. What features do you think might be present in such a series?

Hint: think about why sales might change from month to month and from year to year.

You may have suggested some of the following possibilities.

The sales data may show some long-run trend behaviour. If the market in which the company operates has been rising, then over time its sales will probably have risen. Conversely, if the firm has been operating in a declining market or is facing competition, then its sales may show a decline over time. It is also possible that sales may show a long-run stability.

One point to beware of is that if sales have been recorded in value, rather than volume terms, then there may be a long-term increase, due solely to the presence of price inflation. If sales are recorded in value terms then they may need to be deflated by an appropriate factor to show the underlying real behaviour.

Sales of some goods are responsive to the overall state of the economy. For example, the post-war period in the UK saw a strong long-run growth in the volume of overseas package holidays. However, superimposed upon this long-run trend were fluctuations due to the overall state of the economy. In periods of recession, with rising unemployment and slower growth in real incomes, the volume of package holidays slackened off. The converse happened during boom periods, when unemployment was falling and living standards were rising sharply. So the company's sales may show some correlation with the overall state of the economy. It is important to note that not all products will be affected in the same way.

Sales of products might show some kind of seasonal pattern. For example, some products have a bigger market in winter than summer. Since the data consists of monthly sales, such seasonal fluctuations are quite likely.

There is also a wealth of one-off factors that can affect sales from month to month. For example, the unpredictability of the weather or the short-run effects of promotional campaigns may cause temporary fluctuations.

The last activity has demonstrated that a number of features might be present in our data. It would be useful at this point if we had some actual data to analyse.

ACTIVITY 2

The table below shows *XYZ plc*'s quarterly sales (in tonnes) of a snack food called *Bombay Nutz* for the period 1995 to 1997. 'I' refers to the period January to March, 'II' to the period April to June, and so on.

	I	II	III	IV
1995	11.5	12.2	12.9	15.7
1996	18.9	20.5	21.4	23.4
1997	27.8	28.3	29.1	31.6

1. Open a new *Microsoft Excel* workbook and enter the *Bombay Nutz* data onto it. Use two columns, one headed **Time** and the other headed **Sales**, to contain the data. Save the worksheet as **Bombay.xls**.

   Use *Microsoft Excel* to obtain a graph of this data. (If you don't remember how to do this, refer to Appendix 1.) Select the **Chart sub-type** with the description 'Line with markers displayed at each data value.'. Leave any other settings on default, and place the chart as an object in the existing worksheet. Save your changes.

2. What are the main features of this time series?

---

1. You should have a chart similar to the one in Figure 1, which has been slightly customised.

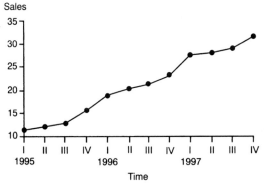

Figure 1: Sales of Bombay Nutz

2. The main features are a pronounced upward trend and a seasonal fluctuation around that upward trend. The upward trend appears to be linear. That is, a straight line is probably representative of the behaviour of the data. In addition to the trend, sales growth in quarter IV is particularly rapid.

Broadly, we might expect to observe four features to be present in any time series, namely:

- a trend component

- a cyclical component

- a seasonal component

- an irregular component.

THE TREND COMPONENT

This is the long-run behaviour of the series, a definite movement in a particular direction irrespective of shorter-term fluctuations. We examine the data to see if the variable is broadly rising or falling in the long run and, if so, whether the increase or decrease is occurring at a constant rate. A trend may be linear or non-linear, highly regular or very complex. It is, of course, possible that there is no trend at all.

Figure 2 shows some examples of different trend behaviour.

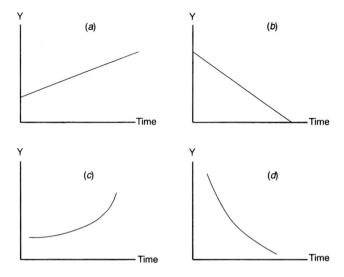

Figure 2: Types of trend behaviour

The variable in question – sales or some other factor of interest to us – is shown on the vertical or Y-axis, while time is shown on the horizontal or X-axis.

In charts *(a)* and *(b)* the variable is respectively growing or declining **linearly** over time. In other words, growth or decline is by a fixed amount in each time period. By contrast, in cases *(c)* and *(d)* the variable is growing or declining **exponentially** over time. In other words, growth or decline is by a fixed proportion in each time period.

THE CYCLICAL COMPONENT
A time series may exhibit medium-term cycles or fluctuations about a long-term trend. The most obvious of these relate to cycles in the level of activity in the macro-economy. A somewhat stylised and exaggerated example would be as shown in Figure 3. Such cycles may be of varying period (or **length**) and of varying degrees of severity (or **amplitude**).

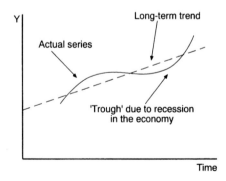

Figure 3: The trade cycle

THE SEASONAL COMPONENT

A more obvious source of fluctuations is that due to seasonal factors. Sales of some consumer goods might be expected to show a marked seasonal fluctuation. Seasonal variation is a periodic and usually short-term (monthly or quarterly) pattern in a time series, compared with the more long-term cyclical fluctuations. Seasonal fluctuations may conveniently be thought of as fluctuations about a trend. Such fluctuations may be constant in amplitude (in which case they are referred to as additive) or they may be subject to a progressive increase or decrease in amplitude (in which case they are referred to as multiplicative).

THE IRREGULAR COMPONENT

This is simply the residual behaviour of the time series, the result of all the other random and irregular factors. Sometimes this residual variation comes from man-made sources such as one-off promotional events, and sometimes it is completely random. The random elements of such variation are considered as **noise** by the forecaster. ('Noise' here refers to 'unwanted interference'.) In general, a time series with a low signal-to-noise ratio (that is, one for which there is a great deal of irregular variation) is likely to prove very difficult to forecast.

1.2 Additive versus multiplicative time series

If a time series is to be the basis of a forecast, then it may be sensible to disaggregate it into its component parts. A forecast can then be built up by considering each of the components in turn. That is, a forecast can be made for trend, seasonality and so forth. However, before we do this we need to consider how the various components of the time series might interact with each other. Basically there are two possibilities: the components of the time series interact **additively**, or the components of the time series interact **multiplicatively**.

Before we explain this in more detail, some notation will be useful. We will let:

Y_t = the value of the variable Y in time period t

T_t = the trend value of variable Y in time period t

C_t = the cyclical component of variable Y in time period t

S_t = the seasonal component of variable Y in time period t

I_t = the irregular component of variable Y in time period t

As is often the case with discussions of time series, we use a capital letter to represent the variable and a subscript t to refer to the time period in which the data is recorded. Thus, in a sales time series:

Y_t would be used to refer to sales in time period t

Y_{t-1} would refer to sales in the period before t

Y_{t+1} would refer to sales in the period following t

The additive model is therefore:

$$Y_t = T_t + C_t + S_t + I_t$$

And the multiplicative model is:

$$Y_t = T_t \times C_t \times S_t \times I_t$$

Unfortunately, identifying and measuring the cyclical component usually proves to be a difficult exercise, and in any initial consideration of a time series this component is usually ignored. We shall adopt this approach in this unit. The additive model then becomes:

$$Y_t = T_t + S_t + I_t$$

And the multiplicative model becomes:

$$Y_t = T_t \times S_t \times I_t$$

All we are really saying here is that some time series (the additive model) can be obtained by simply adding the trend, seasonal variation and irregular variation together, whilst for others (the multiplicative model) we need to multiply these components. The best way of understanding the difference between these two models is to examine some data.

ACTIVITY 3

Consider the following two series of sales data.

Time		SalesA	SalesB
1995	I	8.00	8.00
	II	17.00	18.20
	III	15.00	16.20
	IV	24.00	26.40
1996	I	24.00	23.40
	II	33.00	39.00
	III	31.00	31.60
	IV	40.00	45.60
1997	I	40.00	37.80
	II	49.00	59.80
	III	47.00	45.00
	IV	56.00	64.80

Open a new *Microsoft Excel* workbook and enter the sales data. Use three columns to contain the data, the first headed **Time**, the second headed **SalesA** and the third headed **SalesB**. Save the worksheet as **SalesAB.xls**.

Use *Microsoft Excel* to obtain a single graph showing both sets of data. (If you don't remember how to do this, refer to Appendix 1.) Be careful to select all the data (columns A, B and C).

For each data set, is the seasonal variation roughly constant over time or is the variability increasing over time?

You should have the chart shown in Figure 4.

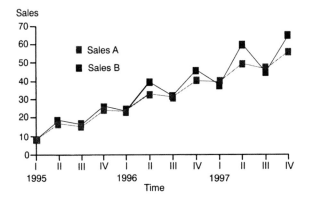

Figure 4: Chart of SalesAB data

For the SalesA data, the seasonal fluctuation is roughly constant over time, while for the SalesB data the seasonal fluctuation is increasing over time.

We should conclude that the additive model seems suitable for analysing the SalesA data while the multiplicative model is more appropriate for analysing the SalesB data.

If the seasonal component appears to be roughly constant in absolute size over time, then the additive model is more appropriate. If the seasonal component is either increasing in absolute size over time (probably as the trend value is increasing), or decreasing in absolute size (again, probably as the trend is decreasing), then the multiplicative model is more appropriate.

Of course, seasonal fluctuations are never completely regular, due to all the other random irregular factors present in any time series, and so it is partly a matter of judgement as to whether the additive or multiplicative model best describes any given data. In the long run, if there were a persistent upward or downward trend to the series then one would expect to find that the seasonal component behaves similarly and the multiplicative model would be more suited to the data.

ACTIVITY 4

Look back at Figure 1. Which model do you think best describes the *Bombay Nutz* data?

Looking at Figure 1, the seasonal fluctuations appear to be roughly constant over time. So the additive model would seem to be suitable.

Summary

In Section 1.1 we showed that a time series can be viewed as the product of four components. **Trend** is the long-run change in the average level of the series. The **cyclical** component is the impact upon a series due to fluctuations in the economy (for example, rising and falling unemployment and differential rates of economic growth). A more short-term **seasonal** component may be present. Finally, there are a myriad of random factors that impact upon any time series. We refer to these as the **irregular** component.

In Section 1.2 we saw that, by utilising these four components, a time series can be represented by either an additive or a multiplicative model. In the former case, a series is the simple result of adding the components together, whereas, in the latter case, the series is formed by multiplying these components. Of course, the choice of model, in any given context, depends upon the judgement of the forecaster. Not all time series will exhibit all four components. Later sections of the unit will consider alternative approaches to time series analysis conditional upon what components are actually present in any particular series.

The next section looks at decomposing time series into their component parts.

SECTION 2
Decomposition of a Time Series

Introduction

If a time series is characterised by the presence of both trend and seasonality, then we can obtain a forecast for the series by forecasting each component separately and then recombining the two. To do this we must start by **decomposing** the series into its separate parts. In Section 2.1 we look at decomposing additive time series. In Section 2.2 we look at decomposing multiplicative time series. Finally, in Section 2.3, we provide further practice of the technique of decomposing time series. By the end of this section you should be able to decompose a time series into its constituent parts and use the decomposition to obtain a forecast.

2.1 The additive model

We start by considering the additive model. We will use the *Bombay Nutz* data first encountered in Activity 2. Suppose that our objective is to forecast sales of *Bombay Nutz* during the four successive quarters of 1998. To do this, we will disaggregate our three-year time series into its component parts.

Firstly we need to estimate the trend component. To do this we employ a **centred moving average**. A centred moving average estimates trend by computing the mean value of the series over a number of time periods. This mean value gives the trend for the middle of the period. The moving average acts to smooth out the data.

To illustrate the procedure we will obtain a three-period centred moving average for the *Bombay Nutz* time series. The data is reproduced in Table 1. We will record the moving average in the column headed '3PMA' ('3PMA' denotes 'three-period moving average').

Sales for the first three periods in the series are respectively 11.5, 12.2 and 12.9. Our first moving average is calculated by adding these three figures together and dividing by the number of periods. This gives us:

$$\frac{\text{Sales for}1995\text{ I} + \text{Sales for 1995 II} + \text{Sales for 1995 III}}{\text{total number of periods}}$$

$$= \frac{11.5 + 12.2 + 12.9}{3}$$

$$= 12.2$$

This is our first moving average, which is centred at the middle point, that is time period 1995 quarter II.

Time		Sales	3PMA
1995	I	11.5	
	II	12.2	12.2
	III	12.9	
	IV	15.7	
1996	I	18.9	
	II	20.5	
	III	21.4	
	IV	23.4	
1997	I	27.8	
	II	28.3	
	III	29.1	
	IV	31.6	

Table 1: Obtaining a three-period moving average

Proceeding in the same way, the next moving average will be centred on 1995 III and will be the outcome of averaging the sales for 1995 II, III and IV. Activity 5 asks you to calculate this and the remainder of the three-period moving average series.

ACTIVITY 5

Complete the three-period moving average for the *Bombay Nutz* data. An accuracy of one decimal place will suffice.

Hint: the last moving average will be centred on 1997 III.

Your calculations should agree with those in Table 2.

Time		Sales	3PMA
1995	I	11.5	
	II	12.2	12.2
	III	12.9	13.6
	IV	15.7	15.8
1996	I	18.9	18.4
	II	20.5	20.3
	III	21.4	21.8
	IV	23.4	24.2
1997	I	27.8	26.5
	II	28.3	28.4
	III	29.1	29.7
	IV	31.6	

Table 2: A three-period centred moving average for the Bombay Nutz data

The second value in the 3PMA series is the average of the three sales values 12.2, 12.9 and 15.7. Calculations proceed similarly up to the final value, centred on 1997 III, which is the average of the sales for 1997 quarters II to IV. Notice that we have no moving average for the first and last time periods in our data set.

We now give a formal definition of a three-period moving average using the notation that was introduced in Section 1.2. Let Y_t be the value of the variable at time period t and let T_t be the moving average. Then:

$$T_t = \frac{Y_{t-1} + Y_t + Y_{t+1}}{3}$$

Formulae such as this are exactly what spreadsheets like *Microsoft Excel* are designed to handle, as you will see by working through the next activity.

ACTIVITY 6

Open your *Microsoft Excel* worksheet **Bombay.xls**. For later use, it is essential to have an additional column with the time period given as 1, 2, 3 and so on. Without this you would be unable to undertake any processing (regression, for example) using time as a variable. Amend the worksheet to correspond with that shown below and save your changes.

	A	B	C	D
1	Time	Time	Sales	3PMA
2	1995 I	1	11.5	
3	II	2	12.2	
4	III	3	12.9	
5	IV	4	15.7	
6	1996 I	5	18.9	
7	II	6	20.5	
8	III	7	21.4	
9	IV	8	23.4	
10	1997 I	9	27.8	
11	II	10	28.3	
12	III	11	29.1	
13	IV	12	31.6	

Use your worksheet to obtain a three-period moving average. You should enter the formula =**AVERAGE(C2:C4)** into cell D3 and copy it down to D12.

The values in cells D3 to D12 should agree with the figures in the '3PMA' column in Table 2.

We are not restricted to using three time periods to calculate a moving average. We can obtain a moving average using any number of time periods we choose. For example, we can calculate a five- or a seven-period centred moving average using the same procedure employed above.

In general, the greater the number of time periods used for the moving average, the more the variation in the original time series (Y) is smoothed out. However, increasing the number of time periods has the adverse consequence that the number of periods at the start and end of the series for which no moving average is obtained increases.

How do we determine the appropriate moving average to employ? The answer is that it depends upon the time series that is being analysed. For the *Bombay Nutz* data the series is quarterly and exhibits a clear seasonal fluctuation during the year: that is, the data shows a four-period fluctuation. The general rule is that if the data shows fluctuation of n periods then we should use an n-period centred moving average. So, for quarterly data showing a four-period fluctuation we require a four-period centred moving average. For monthly data, we require a 12-period centred moving average.

There is an obvious problem here as to how to construct a centred moving average based upon an even number of periods. The solution is to use a slightly more complicated procedure. For the *Bombay Nutz* data we show how the first moving average (centred on 1995 quarter III) is obtained. Look at Table 3 ('4PMA' denotes 'four-period moving average').

Time	Sales	1st 4-period average	2nd 4-period average	4PMA
1995 I	11.5			
II	12.2			
		13.075		
III	12.9			14.00
			14.925	
IV	15.7			
1996 I	18.9			

Table 3: Calculation of a four-period moving average

The average of the first four values in the sales series (for 1995 quarters I to IV) is 13.075. However, this cannot be the first moving average since it is not obvious where it should be centred. Notionally we centre it between quarters II and III. The average of the next four values in the sales series (for 1995 quarters II to IV and 1996 quarter I) is 14.925. This is notionally centred between quarters III and IV. If we then average the two values 13.075 and 14.925 we obtain 14.00. This can be centred at 1995 quarter III and becomes the first value in the four-period moving average.

This procedure is not one of simple averaging. Instead, a four-period moving average (4PMA) is a **weighted** average. To see that this is the case consider how the first value (14.00) is obtained.

$$14.00 = \frac{13.075 + 14.925}{2}$$

$$= \left(\frac{11.5 + 12.2 + 12.9 + 15.7}{4} + \frac{12.2 + 12.9 + 15.7 + 18.9}{4} \right) \div 2$$

$$= \frac{11.5 + (2 \times 12.2) + (2 \times 12.9) + (2 \times 15.7) + 18.9}{4} \div 2$$

$$= \frac{11.5 + (2 \times 12.2) + (2 \times 12.9) + (2 \times 15.7) + 18.9}{8}$$

$$= \frac{11.5 + 24.4 + 25.8 + 31.4 + 18.9}{8}$$

$$= \frac{112}{8}$$

This is a weighted average of the sales values for 1995 quarters I to IV and 1996 quarter 1, the weights being 1, 2, 2, 2 and 1.

Formally, a four-period moving average is defined by the formula:

$$T_t = \frac{Y_{t-2} + 2Y_{t-1} + 2Y_t + 2Y_{t+1} + 2Y_{t+2}}{8}$$

Using a *Microsoft Excel* worksheet, the whole process is quite straightforward, since the moving average can be obtained by entering this formula. Working through Activity 7 will show you how to do this.

ACTIVITY 7

1. We continue with the *Microsoft Excel* worksheet for the *Bombay Nutz* data that you saved as **Bombay.xls**. Before starting, delete the three-period moving average from your worksheet.

   To obtain a four-period centred moving average, enter into cell D4 the formula:

   =(C2+2*(C3+C4+C5)+C6)/8

   Copy the formula down to cell D11. Set the cell formats to two decimal places. Save your changes.

2. Having obtained the moving average, compare it with the original sales data. The best way of doing this is to use *Microsoft Excel* to construct a single chart showing both data sets. To do this, enter the data range as **A1:A13,C1:D13**. Leave any other settings on default, and place the chart as an object in the existing worksheet.

3. What effect does the four-period moving average have on the seasonal fluctuation in the data? Does the moving average appear to be linear?

1. Your worksheet should look as shown in Table 4.

	A		B	C	D
1	**Time**		**Time**	**Sales**	**4PMA**
2	1995	I	1	11.5	
3		II	2	12.2	
4		III	3	12.9	14.00
5		IV	4	15.7	15.96
6	1996	I	5	18.9	18.06
7		II	6	20.5	20.09
8		III	7	21.4	22.16
9		IV	8	23.4	24.25
10	1997	I	9	27.8	26.19
11		II	10	28.3	28.18
12		III	11	29.1	
13		IV	12	31.6	

Table 4: Four-period moving average for Bombay Nutz data

Notice that the formula is copied down only as far as D11. Remember that the last set of cells being averaged are from C9 to C13 and the moving average is centred on the middle of this range (that is, D11). If you incorrectly copy the formula below D11 then the averaging will include cells C14 onwards, which have no sales data in them.

2. The graph of the sales data and the four-period moving average should look like Figure 5.

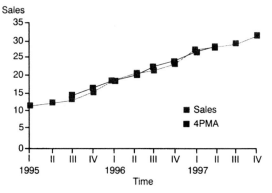

Figure 5: Graph showing sales data and a four-period moving average

3. The four-period moving average has ironed out most of the seasonal fluctuation in the data. Also, notice that the line showing the moving average is virtually straight. We can, therefore, feel confident in assuming that the trend is linear.

Having obtained an estimate for trend we can now proceed to estimate the seasonal component. For each time period – month or quarter – we need to obtain an **index** which describes the magnitude of seasonality. To show how this is done we will continue to use the *Bombay Nutz* data.

ACTIVITY 8

Start with the **Bombay.xls** worksheet you amended in Activity 7. For each time period for which we have a trend estimate, use a formula to calculate the difference between actual sales and the moving average (that is, $Y_t - T_t$). Save your changes.

You should obtain a worksheet like the one shown in Table 5. The formula entered into cell E4 is **=C4–D4**. We start the formula at E4 because it is the first cell for which we have both a sales figure and a moving average. For the same reason, we cannot copy the formula past cell E11.

	A	B	C	D	E
1	Time	Time	Sales	4PMA	$Y_t - T_t$
2	1995 I	1	11.5		
3	II	2	12.2		
4	III	3	12.9	14.00	−1.10
5	IV	4	15.7	15.96	−0.26
6	1996 I	5	18.9	18.06	0.84
7	II	6	20.5	20.09	0.41
8	III	7	21.4	22.16	−0.76
9	IV	8	23.4	24.25	−0.85
10	1997 I	9	27.8	26.19	1.61
11	II	10	28.3	28.18	0.13
12	III	11	29.1		
13	IV	12	31.6		

Table 5: Seasonal variation using Microsoft Excel

To obtain a single-figure estimate of the seasonal component we need to average the $Y_t - T_t$ figures for each quarter. Activity 9 shows how this is done.

ACTIVITY 9

Continue using your **Bombay.xls** worksheet. In cell I2 enter **1995**, in cell I3 enter **1996**, and in cell I4 enter **1997**. In cell J1 enter **I**, in cell K1 enter **II**, in cell L1 enter **III**, and in cell M1 enter **IV**.

Copy and paste the $Y_t - T_t$ figures into cells L2 to M2, cells J3 to M3, and cells J4 to K4. You will need to copy each value separately. To do this, select the cell whose contents you wish to copy, then click on the copy icon on your toolbar. Select the cell where you want to copy the figures to. Click on **Edit** on the menu bar and select **Paste Special**. From the **Paste** options, select **Values**. Click on **OK**. By doing this, only the values are copied and not the formulae that generated them. The cells will require formatting to two decimal places. Cells I1 to M6 of your worksheet should now look as shown in the table below.

	I	J	K	L	M
1		I	II	III	IV
2	1995			−1.10	−0.26
3	1996	0.84	0.41	−0.76	−0.85
4	1997	1.61	0.13		

In cell I6 enter **Average**. Enter appropriate formulae into cells J6, K6, L6 and M6 to obtain the average value for $Y_t - T_t$ for each quarter. Save your changes.

For cell J6 the formula is =**AVERAGE(J3,J4)**. Similar formulae are required in cells K6, L6 and M6. Cells I1 to M6 of your worksheet should now be as shown in Table 6.

	I	J	K	L	M
1		I	II	III	IV
2	1995			−1.10	−0.26
3	1996	0.84	0.41	−0.76	−0.85
4	1997	1.61	0.13		
5					
6	Average	1.23	0.27	−0.93	−0.56

Table 6: The $Y_t - T_t$ values averaged for each quarter

Remember that we are using the additive model to decompose this time series. So we have that $Y_t = T_t + S_t + I_t$. On rearrangement, this gives us $Y_t - T_t = S_t + I_t$. Hence, the average $Y_t - T_t$ value for each quarter is an estimate of the seasonal plus any irregular components of the time series. It is usual to assume that the irregular component is 'well-behaved'. By this we mean that positive values for I are balanced out by negative values so that its average value is 0. It then follows that we can regard the average $Y_t - T_t$ values as an estimate of the seasonal component only. These will be deviations from trend and, therefore, when added should sum to 0. Activity 10 asks you to check that this is the case for the values that you obtained in Activity 9.

ACTIVITY 10

Do the average $Y_t - T_t$ values sum to 0?

Hint: using your **Bombay.xls** worksheet, the easiest way to check is to click in cell N6 and then click the symbol Σ (the icon for **AutoSum**) on the standard toolbar.

Save your changes.

The average $Y_t - T_t$ values in cells J6 to M6 sum to 0.01. Since this is virtually 0 we can conclude that the condition is met.

If the sum of the average $Y_t - T_t$ values departs significantly from 0 then they must be adjusted. For example, suppose that in the present case they had summed to 0.4. Then each average would be adjusted downwards by 0.1 (0.4 divided by 4). Conversely, if they had summed to -0.6 then each would be revised upwards by 0.15.

The four figures that we have obtained are technically called **seasonal indices**. How exactly should we interpret them? The quarter I index is 1.23. This means that, on average, sales are 1.23 million above the trend in the first quarter. Similarly, in quarter II the index is 0.27, which would mean that in this quarter, sales tend to be 0.27 million above trend. Notice that the indices for quarters III and IV are negative, and this we take to mean that in these quarters, sales are below the trend (by 0.93 and 0.56 respectively).

ACTIVITY 11

Continue with your **Bombay.xls** worksheet from the previous activity. Type the label **SComp** into cell F1 ('SComp' stands for 'seasonal component'). Use **Copy** and **Paste Special** to copy the values for the seasonal indices from cells J6 to M6 into cells F2 to F5. (Refer back to Activity 9 if you need a reminder as to how this is done.) Then copy the contents of cells F2 to F5 into cells F6 to F9 and cells F10 to F13. You won't need to use **Paste Special** for this operation as cells F2 to F5 contain numeric values, not formulae.

Save your changes.

Your worksheet should now be as shown in Table 7.

	A	B	C	D	E	F
1	Time	Time	Sales	4PMA	$Y_t - T_t$	SComp
2	1995 I	1	11.5			1.23
3	II	2	12.2			0.27
4	III	3	12.9	14.00	−1.10	−0.93
5	IV	4	15.7	15.96	-0.26	−0.56
6	1996 I	5	18.9	18.06	0.84	1.23
7	II	6	20.5	20.09	0.41	0.27
8	III	7	21.4	22.16	−0.76	−0.93
9	IV	8	23.4	24.25	−0.85	−0.56
10	1997 I	9	27.8	26.19	1.61	1.23
11	II	10	28.3	28.18	0.13	0.27
12	III	11	29.1			−0.93
13	IV	12	31.6			−0.56

Table 7: The estimated seasonal component for the Bombay Nutz data

We can now use the estimate of the seasonal component to obtain a de-seasonalised time series for sales.

ACTIVITY 12

Use your **Bombay.xls** worksheet to obtain a de-seasonalised series for sales of *Bombay Nutz*. You should do this by entering an appropriate formula into cell G2 and copying it down to G13.

Hint: in quarter I of each year, sales are boosted by a favourable seasonal effect. To de-seasonalise the data this effect has to be removed. How do you think this should be done? Bear in mind that we are using the additive model.

Save your changes.

Remember that this is additive data, so that the time series is made up by adding the various components. It follows that to de-seasonalise the series we must take the actual sales figure minus the seasonal component. For example, in quarter I of each year sales exceed the trend value, so taking Sales minus SComp removes the positive seasonal component. On the other hand, in quarter III sales are below trend, in which case the seasonal component is negative. So taking Sales minus SComp (for example, $12.9 - (-0.93)$) removes the negative seasonal effect.

So you should have entered the formula **=C2–F2** into cell G2 and copied it down to G13. Your worksheet should then agree with that shown in Table 8.

	A		B	C	D	E	F	G
1	**Time**		**Time**	**Sales**	**4PMA**	**Y_t - T_t**	**SComp**	**DeSeas**
2	1995	I	1	11.5			1.23	10.27
3		II	2	12.2			0.27	11.93
4		III	3	12.9	14.00	−1.10	−0.93	13.83
5		IV	4	15.7	15.96	−0.26	−0.56	16.26
6	1996	I	5	18.9	18.06	0.84	1.23	17.67
7		II	6	20.5	20.09	0.41	0.27	20.23
8		III	7	21.4	22.16	−0.76	−0.93	22.33
9		IV	8	23.4	24.25	−0.85	−0.56	23.96
10	1997	I	9	27.8	26.19	1.61	1.23	26.57
11		II	10	28.3	28.18	0.13	0.27	28.03
12		III	11	29.1			−0.93	30.03
13		IV	12	31.6			−0.56	32.16

Table 8: De-seasonalised sales data

We can now use the estimates of trend and seasonality to obtain some forecasts, say for the four quarters of 1998. To start we need to forecast the trend. We can do this by using our de-seasonalised series. The simplest method, if the de-seasonalised series is roughly linear, would be to use regression. If the trend is not clearly linear, then we would need to extrapolate it by hand, perhaps using a graph. For the *Bombay Nutz* data the trend is reasonably linear, and so we can use regression.

ACTIVITY 13

Carry out a regression of the de-seasonalised data on time.

If you don't remember how to do this, refer back to Section 3.3 of Unit 4.

The Y Range is the cell references which contain the dependent or Y-variable, including the column labels. For this worksheet, the relevant cells are in columns G so you should enter **G1:G13** as the **Y Range**.

You will need to use the coded time values (1, 2, 3, 4 and so on) as the independent or X-variable. These are in column B of the **Bombay.xls** worksheet so enter **B1:B13** as the **X Range**.

Make sure the **Labels** box is checked so that *Microsoft Excel* knows that the first entry in each range is a title.

Set the **Output Range** as A22 so that the output will start at this point.

For the moment leave all of the other boxes blank. Click on **OK** to complete the process. Save your changes.

Microsoft Excel will output the coefficients and the value of R-Squared.

Write out the regression model obtained. How good would you say this model is for obtaining forecasts?

Regressing the de-seasonalised data on time gives the output shown in Table 9.

	A	B	C	D	E	F
22	SUMMARY OUTPUT					
23						
24	*Regression Statistics*					
25	Multiple R	0.999447				
26	R-squared	0.998893				
27	Adjusted R-squared	0.998783				
28	Standard Error	0.25332				
29	Observations	12				
30						
31	ANOVA					
32		*df*	*SS*	*MS*	*F*	*Significance F*
33	Regression	1	579.2428	579.2428	9026.575	4.08584E–16
34	Residual	10	0.641708	0.064171		
35	Total	11	579.8845			
36						
37		*Coefficients*	*Standard Error*	*t Stat*	*P-value*	*Lower 95 per cent*
38	Intercept	8.023788	0.155907	51.46507	1.86E–13	7.676404382
39	Time	2.012622	0.021184	95.00829	4.09E–16	1.965422255

Table 9: Output for the regression of de-seasonalised sales on time

The bottom of the table gives the coefficients for the regression model. So the model is:

$$\text{estimated trend} = 8.024 + 2.013 \times \text{time}$$

with time taking the values 1, 2, 3 and so on.

Notice that the R-Squared value is 0.999, so virtually all the variation in de-seasonalised sales is explained by the time variable. It could hardly be better than this!

Also, as you can see from the F statistic, the result is very significant. The significance of F is 4.09×10^{-16} and so there is a negligible likelihood that this value for R-Squared has occurred merely by chance.

This means that the model should give very good forecasts.

Now that we have the required regression model, we can prepare the forecasts. We will do this in two stages.

ACTIVITY 14

Add to your **Bombay.xls** worksheet as shown in the table below.

	A	B	C	D	E
15			Trend	Est	Final
16			F/Cast	SComp	F/Cast
17	1998 I	13			
18	II	14			
19	III	15			
20	IV	16			

In order to forecast the four quarters of 1998, we have continued the coded time variable. The four quarters in 1998 become time periods 13, 14, 15 and 16.

Use the regression from the last activity to forecast the trend for each of the quarters of 1998. You will need to enter a formula in cell C17 and copy it down to C20. Remember that estimated trend = 8.024 + 2.013 × time.

The first value for the time variable is in B17, and 8.024 and 2.013 are the values in cells B38 and B39 respectively. Since the formula in C17 is to be copied down, you need to fix the cells B38 and B39 absolutely. You might need reminding that the dollar sign is used to achieve this. For example, when used in a formula, $B$38 would hold the cell reference unchanged wherever you copied the formula to.

Save your changes.

You should have entered the following formula into cell C17 and copied it down to C20.

=$B$38+$B$39*B17

This yields as the forecasts of trend (rounded to two decimal places) the entries shown in cells C17 to C20 in Table 10.

	A	B	C	D	E
15			Trend	Est	Final
16			F/Cast	SComp	F/Cast
17	1998 I	13	34.19		
18	II	14	36.20		
19	III	15	38.21		
20	IV	16	40.23		

Table 10: Trend quarterly forecasts for 1998

In the last activity we obtained forecasts for the trend only. In the next activity we will adjust these figures for seasonality. This process is called **re-seasonalising**.

ACTIVITY 15

Continuing with your **Bombay.xls** worksheet from Activity 14, copy the four seasonal indices in cells F10 to F13 into cells D17 to D20.

To obtain the final forecasts adjust your trend forecasts (in cells C17 to C20) by the estimates for seasonality (in cells D17 to D20).

Hint: remember that this is the additive model.

What are your final forecasts for the four quarters of 1998?

What are they conditional upon?

Because this is the additive model, to re-seasonalise the data we need to add the seasonal component to the trend. Thus, for example, we would need to add 1.23 to the trend estimate for 1998 quarter I. The final re-seasonalised forecast for this quarter would then be:

trend + seasonal component = 34.19 + 1.23 = 35.42

Entering the formula **=C17+D17** into cell E17 and copying it down to E20 yields as the final forecasts the entries shown in cells E17 to E20 in Table 11.

	A	B	C	D	E
15			Trend	Est	Final
16			F/Cast	SComp	F/Cast
17	1998 I	13	34.19	1.23	35.42
18	II	14	36.20	0.27	36.47
19	III	15	38.21	−0.93	37.28
20	IV	16	40.23	−0.56	39.67

Table 11: Final forecasts for Bombay Nutz sales in 1998

These forecasts are conditional upon:

- the additive model remaining appropriate
- the current trend continuing
- the seasonality factor remaining unchanged.

In other words, the assumption is that other things remain the same. Of course, if we know of any reason why all other things will not remain the same then we would be wise to allow for this in the forecast.

2.2 The multiplicative model

So far we have considered the additive model as the basis for decomposing a time series and, hence, forecasting. We now turn our attention to the multiplicative model. With this model, the data is obtained by multiplying together the various components, such as trend and seasonality. You will find that the process of taking a moving average is identical to that used for the additive model: the difference lies in the way in which seasonality is dealt with. We shall begin with some data.

Look at Table 12 which relates to quarterly sales (in £millions) of *Product Z*.

	I	II	III	IV
1992	323	144	474	821
1993	408	248	625	925
1994	434	259	681	1274
1995	831	434	940	1639
1996	1222	592	1054	2001
1997	1278	768	1405	2417

Table 12: Quarterly sales of Product Z

ACTIVITY 16

Open a new *Microsoft Excel* workbook. Enter the information given in Table 12. In order to use the worksheet in further activities, remember to place the calendar time period in column A, the coded value of time (1, 2, 3 and so forth) in column B and sales in column C. Save the workbook as **ProductZ.xls**.

Obtain a line graph of sales against time. The range for the chart will be **A1:A25,C1:C25**.

Is the time series for sales multiplicative?

Your worksheet should look like that in Table 13.

	A		B	C
1	**Time**		**Time**	**Sales**
2	1992	I	1	323
3		II	2	144
4		III	3	474
5		IV	4	821
6	1993	I	5	408
7		II	6	248
8		III	7	625
9		IV	8	925
10	1994	I	9	434
11		II	10	259
12		III	11	681
13		IV	12	1274
14	1995	I	13	831
15		II	14	434
16		III	15	940
17		IV	16	1639
18	1996	I	17	1222
19		II	18	592
20		III	19	1054
21		IV	20	2001
22	1997	I	21	1278
23		II	22	768
24		III	23	1405
25		IV	24	2417

Table 13: Product Z worksheet

Your chart should look like that in Figure 6.

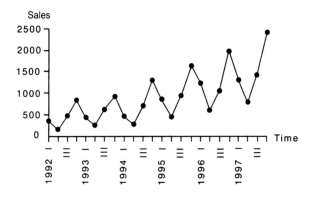

Figure 6: Quarterly sales of Product Z

It seems clear that the data is multiplicative. We can determine this by examining the amplitude of the fluctuations about trend. This is clearly increasing over time.

As with the additive model we estimate the trend by using an appropriate centred moving average.

ACTIVITY 17

What period moving average should we employ for the *Product Z* sales data?

We know that an n-period fluctuation requires an n-period moving average. Look at Figure 6. In quarter II of each of the years, sales are clearly below trend, whereas the opposite applies for sales in quarter IV. So we have a clear quarterly fluctuation and, therefore, need to use a four-period centred moving average to estimate the trend.

You will find that the steps to follow in decomposing a multiplicative time series mirror those that were employed in Section 2.1 for the additive model. However, an essential difference arises when we come to estimate the seasonal component. Remember that this is the multiplicative model: the series is the result of multiplying the seasonal component and the trend together, not of adding them.

We will start by constructing a four-period moving average.

ACTIVITY 18

Continue with your worksheet **ProductZ.xls**. Obtain a four-period moving average for sales and locate it in column D. Two decimal places will suffice.

Your worksheet should agree with that in Table 14. You should have entered the following formula in cell D4 and copied it down to cell D23:

$$=(C2+2*C3+2*C4+2*C5+C6)/8$$

Notice that the last set of data being averaged is in cells C21 to C25.

	A		B	C	D
1	Time		Time	Sales	4PMA
2	1992	I	1	323	
3		II	2	144	
4		III	3	474	451.13
5		IV	4	821	474.75
6	1993	I	5	408	506.63
7		II	6	248	538.50
8		III	7	625	554.75
9		IV	8	925	559.38
10	1994	I	9	434	567.75
11		II	10	259	618.38
12		III	11	681	711.63
13		IV	12	1274	783.13
14	1995	I	13	831	837.38
15		II	14	434	915.38
16		III	15	940	1009.88
17		IV	16	1639	1078.50
18	1996	I	17	1222	1112.50
19		II	18	592	1172.00
20		III	19	1054	1224.25
21		IV	20	2001	1253.25
22	1997	I	21	1278	1319.13
23		II	22	768	1415.00
24		III	23	1405	
25		IV	24	2417	

Table 14: Four-period moving average for sales of Product Z

For each time period (quarter) the seasonal component is estimated as the ratio 'actual sales:moving average'.

For example, in time period 3 (that is, 1992 quarter III) actual sales were 474 whereas the moving average is 451.13. So the ratio of sales over moving average is 1.05 (474 divided by 451.13). Hence, for that time period sales were 5 per cent above the moving average.

ACTIVITY 19

1. Continuing with your worksheet **ProductZ.xls** enter a formula in column E to obtain the ratio of sales to 4PMA for each time period for which a moving average has been calculated.

2. In cell J1 enter the label **I**, in cell K1 enter the label **II**, in cell L1 enter the label **III**, and in cell M1 enter the label **IV**. In cells I2, I3 and so on to I7 enter **1992, 1993** and so on to **1997**.

   Use **Copy** and **Paste Special** (choose **Values**) to arrange the ratios in column E into cells J2 to M7. (See Activity 11 if you need a reminder how to do this.)

---

1. You should have entered the formula =C4/D4 in cell E4 and copied it down to cell E23.

2. The ratios should be in agreement with those shown in Table 15.

	I	J	K	L	M
1		I	II	III	IV
2	1992			1.05	1.73
3	1993	0.81	0.46	1.13	1.65
4	1994	0.76	0.42	0.96	1.63
5	1995	0.99	0.47	0.93	1.52
6	1996	1.10	0.51	0.86	1.60
7	1997	0.97	0.54		

Table 15: Completed ratios array for Product Z data

We now define **seasonal indices** as the average of the ratios for each quarter. For example, for quarter I the average of the ratios in cells J3 to J7 is 0.93 and so this is the seasonal index for this quarter. We conclude that in the first quarter of each year, sales are typically 93 per cent of the trend (as estimated by the moving average).

ACTIVITY 20

Enter an appropriate formula in cell J9 of your **ProductZ.xls** worksheet to obtain the seasonal index for quarter I. Enter formulae into cells K9 to M9 to obtain the seasonal indices for quarters II to IV. Save your changes.

The formula used in cell J9 is =**AVERAGE(J3:J7)**. You should have as the seasonal indices:

	J	K	L	M
9	0.93	0.48	0.99	1.63

Table 16: Seasonal indices for the Product Z data

For the multiplicative model we have that:

$$Y_t = T_t \times S_t \times I_t$$

On rearranging, this gives us:

$$\frac{Y_t}{T_t} = S_t \times I_t$$

So the seasonal indices are estimates of $S_t \times I_t$: that is, the seasonal component multiplied by the irregular component. As with the additive model, we now assume that the irregular component is well behaved: that is, that deviations above and below trend cancel out. It follows that we can then interpret the seasonal indices as estimates of the seasonal component alone.

Since the seasonal indices are deviations from trend (expressed as ratios), then over a year they must cancel out. Therefore they should sum to 4 (or to 400 per cent if you express the ratios as percentages). We need to check that this is the case and Activity 21 asks you to do this.

ACTIVITY 21

Using your **ProductZ.xls** worksheet, determine whether the seasonal indices (in cells J9 to M9) sum to 4.

The seasonal indices sum to 4.02 and so the condition is not satisfied.

We, therefore need to revise the indices. To do this we multiply each index by the ratio 4:4.02. Continuing with the worksheet, this gives as the revised indices those shown in cells J10 to M10 in Table 17.

		J	K	L	M
9	Average	0.93	0.48	0.99	1.63
10	Revised Average	0.92	0.48	0.98	1.62

Table 17: Revised seasonal indices for Product Z data

Using these revised seasonal indices, we can now de-seasonalise the series for sales.

ACTIVITY 22

Continue with your worksheet **ProductZ.xls**. Check that columns A to E record respectively 'Time (calendar)', 'Time (coded values)', 'Sales', '4PMA', 'Sales/4PMA'. In cell F1 enter the label **SComp** and in cell G1 enter the label **SeasAdjust**.

Use **Copy** and **Paste Special** (choose **Values**) to copy the revised seasonal indices from cells J10 to M10 into cells F2 to F5.

Then copy the contents of cells F2 to F5 into cells F6 to F9, cells F10 to F13, cells F14 to F17, cells F18 to F21 and cells F22 to F25.

Enter an appropriate formula in cell G2 and copy it down to G25 to obtain a series for the de-seasonalised sales. Take care with your reasoning here. For example, in quarter I of each year sales typically are 0.92 (that is 92 per cent) of trend.

You should have entered the formula =C2/F2 into cell G2. Sales in this quarter are 92 per cent below trend and we need to remove this effect. De-seasonalised sales are then the actual sales divided by the seasonal index, that is 350.30.

(You should note that, because of the way *Excel* displays figures rounded to (for example) two decimal places while using the unrounded figures to perform calculations, the output of the *Excel* calculations will not necessarily be the same as what you would produce if you performed the calculation using the rounded figures.)

Your worksheet should now look like that shown in Table 18.

	A	B	C	D	E	F	G
1	Time	Time	Sales	4PMA	Sales/ 4PMA	SComp	Seas Adjust
2	1992 I	1	323			0.92	350.30
3	II	2	144			0.48	301.07
4	III	3	474	451.13	1.05	0.98	483.11
5	IV	4	821	474.75	1.73	1.62	507.26
6	1993 I	5	408	506.63	0.81	0.92	442.49
7	II	6	248	538.50	0.46	0.48	518.51
8	III	7	625	554.75	1.13	0.98	637.01
9	IV	8	925	559.38	1.65	1.62	571.51
10	1994 I	9	434	567.75	0.76	0.92	470.69
11	II	10	259	618.38	0.42	0.48	541.51
12	III	11	681	711.63	0.96	0.98	694.09
13	IV	12	1274	783.13	1.63	1.62	787.14
14	1995 I	13	831	837.38	0.99	0.92	901.25
15	II	14	434	915.38	0.47	0.48	907.40
16	III	15	940	1009.88	0.93	0.98	958.07
17	IV	16	1639	1078.50	1.52	1.62	1012.66
18	1996 I	17	1222	1112.50	1.10	0.92	1325.30
19	II	18	592	1172.00	0.51	0.48	1237.74
20	III	19	1054	1224.25	0.86	0.98	1074.26
21	IV	20	2001	1253.25	1.60	1.62	1236.32
22	1997 I	21	1278	1319.13	0.97	0.92	1386.04
23	II	22	768	1415.00	0.54	0.48	1605.71
24	III	23	1405			0.98	1432.01
25	IV	24	2417			1.62	1493.35

Table 18: De-seasonalised multiplicative data for Product Z

Now that we have de-seasonalised the data, we can proceed to obtain forecasts of quarterly sales for 1998. To do this, we need to forecast the trend and then adjust for seasonality. Before doing this, however, we need to check that the seasonally adjusted series is reasonably linear.

ACTIVITY 23

Use *Microsoft Excel* to obtain a scatter graph of de-seasonalised sales on calendar time. The de-seasonalised sales data is contained in column G (headed 'SeasAdjust') and the calendar time data is contained in column A (headed 'Time'). Does the seasonally adjusted series appear reasonably linear?

To forecast the trend, use the **Trend Line** tool in *Microsoft Excel*. If you don't remember how to do this, refer back Activity 64 in Section 10.2 of Unit 4. Select the **Trend/Regression type** with the description **Linear**.

Click on the **Options** tab.

Check the boxes for **Display equation on chart** and **Display R-squared value** on chart.

Figure 7 shows the scatterplot (the data points on the graph), the trendline, the equation for the line of best fit and the value of R-Squared.

The scatterplot suggests that the de-seasonalised data is reasonably linear.

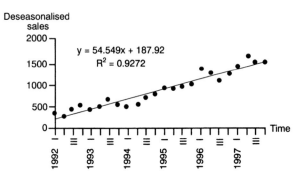

Figure 7: Forecasting the de-seasonalised sales

Replacing y and x with estimated trend and time, the regression equation is:

Estimated Trend = $187.92 + 54.549 \times$ Time

The value of R-Squared is 0.9272.

Unfortunately, the trendline tool does not generate the F statistic, but with this value of R-Squared we can be reasonably sure that the estimated model is significant.

To obtain the final quarterly forecasts for 1998, we must use the above equation to forecast trend and then re-seasonalise.

ACTIVITY 24

Add the following labels and data to cells A27 to E31 of your **ProductZ.xls** worksheet.

	A	B	C	D	E
27	Time	Time	Trend F/Cast	Seasonal Index	Final F/Cast
28	1998 I	25			
29	II	26			
30	III	27			
31	IV	28			

Enter a formula into cell C28 and copy it into cells C29 to C31 to forecast the trend. You will need to use the regression output from the previous activity.

Use **Copy** and **Paste Special** to copy the values of the seasonal indices into cells D28 to D31.

Enter a formula into E28 and copy it into cells E29 to E31 to obtain the final forecasts.

Your worksheet should now be as shown in Table 19. The final quarterly forecasts for 1998 are shown in column E.

	A	B	C	D	E
27	Time	Time	Trend F/Cast	Seasonal Index	Final F/Cast
28	1998 I	25	1551.65	0.92	1430.70
29	II	26	1606.19	0.48	768.23
30	III	27	1660.74	0.98	1629.42
31	IV	28	1715.29	1.62	2776.22

Table 19: Final forecast of Product Z sales for 1998

The trend forecast for quarter I (in cell C28) is given by the formula:

=187.92+54.549*B28

To obtain the final forecast, the trend has to be adjusted for the seasonal component. For quarter I (see column D), sales are typically 0.92 (that is 92 per cent) of trend. So the resulting formula in E28 is =C28*D28.

2.3 Two further forecasting problems

To check your understanding of time series decomposition, you should explore the following forecasting problems before moving on to the next section of the unit.

THE RENT ARREARS PROBLEM

The following data gives the average quarterly rent arrears, owed to a property company *GetRichQuick Ltd*, over a period of three years. All data is in £000s.

	I	II	III	IV
1994	14,200	11,900	16,100	12,800
1995	15,100	13,400	17,300	14,000
1996	16,600	14,200	18,300	15,500

Table 20: Rent arrears 1994 to 1996

At the start of 1997 the method of rent collection was changed. Payment via the Post Office was replaced by door-to-door visits by Mr A. Heavy. Data for 1997 showed the following arrears levels:

	I	II	III	IV
1997	17,200	15,000	19,100	16,300

Table 21: Rent arrears for 1997

GetRichQuick Ltd wishes to establish whether the new method of rent collection is working.

ACTIVITY 25

Open a new *Microsoft Excel* worksheet and save it as **Getrich.xls**. Enter the information given in Table 20. You will need the variables **Time (calendar)** in column A, **Time (coded values)** in column B and **Arrears** in column C.

Obtain a line graph for arrears against time.

In your judgement, is the data additive or multiplicative?

Your chart should be as shown in Figure 8.

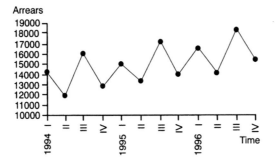

Figure 8: Rent arrears 1994 to 1996

Since the seasonal fluctuation in arrears appears to be of roughly constant amplitude, we can conclude that the data is additive.

To determine whether the new method of rent collection is working, we need to forecast what the quarterly arrears would have been in 1997 if rent collection procedures had remained unchanged, and compare these forecasts with the actual outcome for that year. Let us start by obtaining some forecasts for 1997.

ACTIVITY 26

Using your worksheet **Getrich.xls**, obtain forecasts of rent arrears for 1997 using the following steps:

- calculate a four-period moving average for the 1994 to 1996 rent arrears series, entered in column D
- use the moving average to obtain a series for $Y_t - T_t$ (that is, arrears minus 4PMA), entered in column E
- determine the quarterly averages for $Y_t - T_t$ and revise them if they do not sum to 0
- copy the quarterly averages for $Y_t - T_t$ (the estimated seasonal components) into column F
- obtain a series for the de-seasonalised arrears data entered in column G
- forecast trend arrears for each quarter of 1997 by graphing the de-seasonalised arrears against 'Time (coded values)'

- obtain a trendline
- adjust the trend forecasts by the estimated seasonal components.

Columns A to G of your worksheet should be as shown in Table 22.

	A	B	C	D	E	F	G
1	Time	Time	Arrears	4PMA	Y_t-T_t	SComp	DeSeas
2	1994 I	1	14200			775	13425
3	II	2	11900			−1581	13481
4	III	3	16100	13863	2238	2200	13900
5	IV	4	12800	14163	−1363	−1394	14194
6	1995 I	5	15100	14500	600	775	14325
7	II	6	13400	14800	−1400	−1581	14981
8	III	7	17300	15138	2163	2200	15100
9	IV	8	14000	15425	−1425	−1394	15394
10	1996 I	9	16600	15650	950	775	15825
11	II	10	14200	15963	−1763	−1581	15781
12	III	11	18300			2200	16100
13	IV	12	15500			−1394	16894

Table 22: De-seasonalised rent arrears 1994 to 1996

The four-period moving average is obtained using the following formula entered into cell D4:

$$=(C2+2*C3+2*C4+2*C5+C6)/8$$

The values for $Y_t - T_t$ are calculated by subtracting the four-period moving average from the actual arrears. Table 23 shows the calculation of the quarterly averages for $Y_t - T_t$.

	I	II	III	IV	
1994			2238	−1363	
1995	600	−1400	2163	−1425	
1996	950	−1763			
Average	775	−1581	2200	−1394	0

Table 23: The quarterly averages for Yt – Tt

You should have established that no revisions are required, since they sum to 0. These values should then be copied to column F of your worksheet.

Remember our judgement is that the arrears series is additive and so we obtain the de-seasonalised arrears by subtracting the seasonal component from the actual figures.

Figure 9 shows the chart of the de-seasonalised arrears with the trendline added.

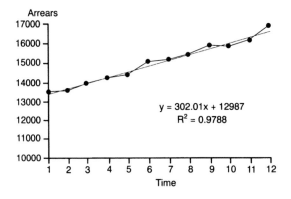

Figure 9: Graph of de-seasonalised rent arrears data with trendline

Replacing y and x with Arrears and Time (coded) respectively, the equation for forecasting trend is:

Estimated Arrears = 12,987 + 302.01 × Time

The value of R-Squared is 0.98.

Table 24 shows the trend forecast.

Time		Time	Trend F/Cast	SComp	F/Cast
1997	I	13	16913	775	17688
	II	14	17215	−1581	15634
	III	15	17517	2200	19717
	IV	16	17819	−1394	16425

Table 24: Rent arrears forecasts for 1997

For example, for 1997 quarter I (that is, time period 13) the trend is forecast to be:

$$12{,}987 + (302.01 \times 13) = 16{,}913$$

To re-seasonalise the data, the estimated seasonal component is added to the trend and this yields the final forecast.

A comparison between the actual arrears for 1997 and the forecasts is shown in Table 25.

Time	Actual arrears	Forecast arrears
1997 I	17,200	17,688
II	15,000	15,634
III	19,100	19,717
IV	16,300	16,425

Table 25: Actual rent arrears compared with forecast arrears

On average, the arrears appear to have been reduced by £466 per quarter. This seems to be a small return for the employment of Mr A. Heavy!

When using time series decomposition to obtain a forecast, it is essential to avoid the danger of overreliance on technique. Judgement is as important as technique. Forecasting is not a purely mechanical process. While carrying out a procedure is mechanical, judgement comes in at three points: deciding what procedure to use; deciding what data set to apply it to; and interpreting the outcome from using the procedure.

Working through the final problem in this section will demonstrate the importance of these points.

Case Study: Megacorp plc

Megacorp plc has collected data on its quarterly sales (in £millions) for the period 1993 to 1998. Table 26 records this information. The company requires forecasts for the remaining two quarters of 1998.

	I	II	III	IV
1993	72	48	61	46
1994	79	53	66	51
1995	80	56	61	51
1996	81	61	73	60
1997	93	70	87	75
1998	117	79		

Table 26: Sales by Megacorp plc 1993 to 1998

ACTIVITY 27

Open a new *Microsoft Excel* workbook and save it as **Megacorp.xls.** Enter the data given in Table 26. Use columns A, B and C and remember to include 'Time' as a coded as well as a calendar variable.

Obtain a line graph of sales.

In your judgement, what features are present in this series?

Your line graph should be as shown in Figure 10.

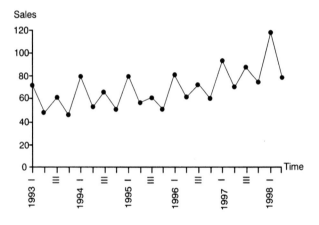

Figure 10: Megacorp plc quarterly sales 1993 to 1998

What does this graph tell us?

Firstly, there is clearly an upward trend, but is it linear?

Secondly, a seasonal pattern is also evident: sales would seem to be above trend in quarters I and III of each year and below trend in the remaining two. However, is the seasonal behaviour additive or multiplicative?

Figure 10 provides insufficient evidence to determine the linearity or otherwise of the trend. Also, it seems unsafe to decide between an additive and multiplicative approach until we have come to some view respecting trend. Perhaps a four-period centred moving average will help to resolve these issues.

ACTIVITY 28

Continuing with your worksheet **Megacorp.xls**, obtain a four-period moving average for sales. You should label this **4PMA** and enter it in column D.

Show sales and the four-period moving average on the same line graph. Take care with the range for the chart. If you have 'Time (calendar)' in column A and 'Sales' and '4PMA' in columns C and D respectively. then the range will be **A1:A23,C1:D23**.

What conclusions do you draw from the chart?

Your chart should agree with that shown in Figure 11.

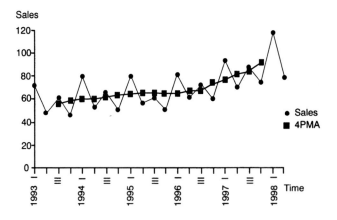

Figure 11: Sales and the four-period moving average

The four-period moving average has smoothed out virtually all the seasonal fluctuation and is, therefore, a good estimator of trend.

However the crucial question is whether the trend is linear. Judging from the chart, the answer is 'no'.

Up to 1995 quarter III, the trend shows some small increase. However, from 1995 quarter IV onwards there is a pronounced upward trend.

You should always extract the maximum information from the data set that you are using. In the present case, the four-period moving average suggests that something happened in the fourth quarter of 1995 which caused trend sales to move markedly upwards. Consequently, rather than basing forecasts upon the complete time series for sales, our judgement is that we should restrict our trend analysis to the period from quarter IV 1995 onwards. In order to obtain a moving average for the final quarter of 1995, this implies that we restrict our use of the time series for sales to the values starting in 1995 quarter II. Figure 12 shows 'Sales' and the '4PMA' for quarter IV 1995 onwards.

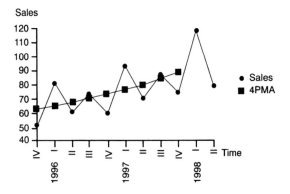

Figure 12: Sales and 4PMA from quarter IV 1995

The fluctuations about the upward trend are clearly multiplicative, though this conclusion is in part dependent upon the particularly high sales figure for quarter I of 1998. As a further complication, the four-period moving average, as well as showing a clear upward trend, also has some indication that the rate of increase is itself rising over time.

Let us summarise our conclusions. In order to forecast sales for quarters III and IV of 1998 our judgement is that:

- only the subset of the sales time series starting in quarter II of 1995 should be used

- for the period 1995 quarter IV to date there is a clear upward trend, though with some indication that it might not be linear

- the multiplicative model would be appropriate.

Having made these judgements we are now in a position to prepare forecasts for quarters III and IV of 1998.

ACTIVITY 29

Continuing with your worksheet **Megacorp.xls,** your objective is to obtain forecasts for the two remaining quarters of 1998. These are to be based on the judgements arrived at above. Assume that the trend is linear. Follow the steps below:

- copy your existing data to **Sheet2** of your workbook (use **Copy** and **Paste Special** and choose **Values**)
- amend your new sheet to conform with that shown in the table below

	A		B	C	D
	Time		**Time**	**Sales**	**4PMA**
1					
2	1995	IV	1	51	62.88
3	1996	I	2	81	65.00
4		II	3	61	67.63
5		III	4	73	70.25
6		IV	5	60	72.88
7	1997	I	6	93	75.75
8		II	7	70	79.38
9		III	8	87	84.25
10		IV	9	75	88.38
11	1998	I	10	117	
12		II	11	79	

- calculate the ratio of sales to 4PMA for 1995 quarter IV to 1997 quarter IV (use column E)
- obtain the seasonal indices for each quarter, check that they sum to 4, and make revisions if necessary
- record the seasonal indices in column F
- obtain a series for de-seasonalised sales in column G
- graph the de-seasonalised sales against time (use the coded version in column B)
- add a trendline to the chart to obtain an equation to forecast trend
- forecast trend sales for quarters III and IV of 1998
- adjust the forecast by the relevant seasonal indices to obtain the final forecasts.

Your worksheet should now agree with that shown in Table 27. The de-seasonalised sales are obtained by dividing 'Sales' by 'SComp' (the seasonal index).

	A	B	C	D	E	F	G
1	Time	Time	Sales	4PMA	Sales/4PMA	SComp	DSeas
2	1995 IV	1	51	62.88	0.811	0.829	61.50
3	1996 I	2	81	65.00	1.246	1.239	65.36
4	II	3	61	67.63	0.902	0.894	68.26
5	III	4	73	70.25	1.039	1.038	70.34
6	IV	5	60	72.88	0.823	0.829	72.35
7	1997 I	6	93	75.75	1.228	1.239	75.04
8	II	7	70	79.38	0.882	0.894	78.33
9	III	8	87	84.25	1.033	1.038	83.83
10	IV	9	75	88.38	0.849	0.829	90.44
11	1998 I	10	117			1.239	94.41
12	II	11	79			0.894	88.40

Table 27: Completed worksheet for Megacorp plc data

Table 28 shows the calculation of the seasonal indices. You should have established that they sum to 3.992 and so require revision. In the table, each index has been multiplied by the ratio 4/3.992. The bottom row shows the revised seasonal indices and these have been copied to column F.

	I	II	III	IV	
1995				0.811	
1996	1.246	0.902	1.039	0.823	
1997	1.228	0.882	1.033	0.849	
Average	1.237	0.892	1.036	0.828	3.992
Revised Average	1.239	0.894	1.038	0.829	

Table 28: Calculation of the seasonal indices for the Megacorp plc data

Graphing the de-seasonalised sales against the coded time variable and adding a trendline yields the result shown in Figure 13. The graph has been slightly customised to reduce the range for the Y-axis.

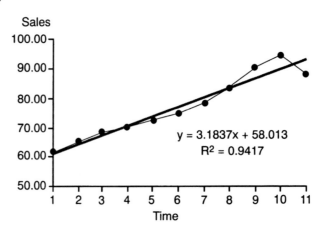

Figure 13: Forecasting the trend for the Megacorp plc data

Substituting sales and time for y and x respectively yields as the equation to forecast trend:

Estimated Sales = (3.1837 × Time) + 58.013

Table 29 shows the final forecasts for quarters III and IV of 1988.

Time		Time	Trend Forecast	SComp	Final Forecast
1998	III	12	96.22	1.038	99.86
	IV	13	99.40	0.829	82.43

Table 29: Final forecasts for quarters III and IV of 1988

For example, the trend forecast for quarter III is:

(3.1837 × 12) + 58.013 = 96.22

The final forecast is then obtained by re-seasonalising the data. The trend forecast is multiplied by 'SComp' (the seasonal index).

So (with some slight rounding) our forecasts for sales by *Megacorp plc* in the remaining quarters of 1998 are that sales in quarter III will be £100 million and in quarter IV will be £82 million.

This problem has required lengthy investigation prior to obtaining the required forecasts. However, analysis of this time series should serve as a salutary lesson. In forecasting, as in other areas of business decision analysis, knowledge of techniques alone is not sufficient. There is no substitute for judgement.

Summary

In this section we examined the process of decomposing a time series into its component parts: trend component, cyclical component, seasonal component and irregular component. We then saw that, having decomposed the series, each component can be forecast separately and the final forecast obtained by reversing the decomposition.

For both the additive and multiplicative models the trend component can be isolated by using an appropriate centred moving average. The number of periods in the moving average must correspond to the seasonality exhibited by the time series. So, for example, if the series exhibits a quarterly variation then a four-period centred moving average is required.

For the additive model an estimate of the seasonal component is obtained by averaging the differences between the series and the moving average. The estimated seasonal component is then used to obtain a de-seasonalised series. Performing a regression on the de-seasonalised series yields a forecast for trend and adjustment by the estimated seasonal component provides the final forecast. The procedure for the multiplicative model is essentially the same except that the estimated seasonal component is obtained as the ratio of the series divided by the moving average.

In the next section we look at non-centred moving averages and the problem of errors in forecasting.

SECTION 3

Non-Centred Moving Averages and Forecasting Error

Introduction

In this section we will be considering situations where a time series does not exhibit any clear trend or seasonal component. We will also be discussing ways in which the idea of **forecast error** can be used to help us select a forecasting method. In Section 3.1 we use **moving averages** to analyse time series which do not exhibit trend or seasonality. In Section 3.2 we look at the problem of forecast error. Finally, in Section 3.3, we look in more detail at how to use *Microsoft Excel* to calculate moving averages.

By the end of this section you should be able to use **non-centred moving averages** to forecast a time series. You should also be able to use **mean absolute differences** and **mean squared errors** as a means of calculating forecasting errors.

3.1 A moving average forecast

Consider the problem of forecasting the next value for a time series that exhibits no clear patterns, whether of trend or seasonality. For example, Table 30 shows monthly sales (in £000s) of *Gargleblaster,* a brand of soft drink.

Month	Sales (1995)	Sales (1996)	Sales (1997)
Jan		138	138
Feb		141	137
Mar		139	136
Apr		142	136
May		147	135
Jun		144	134
Jul		138	141
Aug		140	139
Sep		136	136
Oct	137	138	
Nov	136	144	
Dec	138	135	

Table 30: Monthly sales of Gargleblaster

ACTIVITY 30

Open a new *Microsoft Excel* workbook and save it as **Gargle.xls**. Enter the data from Table 30. You should have **Time (calendar)** in column A, **Time (coded)** in column B and **Sales** in column C.

Obtain a line graph of sales against time (calendar). The range will be **A1:A25,C1:C25**. In your view are there any patterns evident in this series?

Your chart should be in agreement with that in Figure 14.

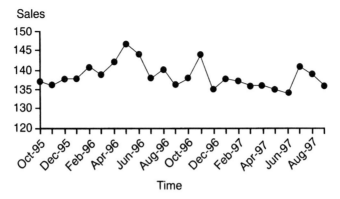

Figure 14: Gargleblaster sales October 1995 to September 1997

There are no obvious patterns in this series.

Faced with the requirement to obtain a sales forecast for October 1997, one simple response would be to use the last actual value of the series as the forecast for the next period. Applied to the data above, the forecast for October 1997 would then be the actual sales for September of that year, namely £136,000.

Let us extend the notation that was introduced in Section 1.2 of this unit. Remember that we use Y_t to represent the value of some variable Y in time period t. Successive time periods are then denoted using the subscripts $t-2$, $t-1$, t, $t+1$, $t+2$ and so on. Conventionally, time period t is held to mean the current period.

We now use F_t to represent the forecast of the variable Y for time period t. Again this notation can be expanded, so that, for example, F_{t-1} would represent the forecast for time period $t-1$ (one period in the past) while F_{t+1} would mean the forecast for time period $t+1$ (one period ahead).

Using this notation, our problem is how to determine F_{t+1} and so on. For the simple response above, we have that $F_{t+1} = Y_t$. In other words, the forecast for the next period is the value of Y in the current period. This rests on the assumption that what has happened today will repeat itself tomorrow.

You might think that such a forecast is unlikely to be adequate, since we are relying on only one observation. For example, if sales of some product are always higher at weekends than on weekdays (judging by past data), it would hardly make sense to use Friday's actual sales as the forecast value for Saturday.

This suggests that the forecast might be obtained by taking the mean value of Y over a specified number of time periods. This is known as forecasting by **non-centred moving averages**. For example, suppose we base the forecast on the mean value of Y over the previous three periods. Then for the *Gargleblaster* data in Table 30 the forecast for October 1997 becomes the average of the sales for the three previous months. Using our notation, this is:

$$F_{t+1} = \frac{Y_{t-2} + Y_{t-1} + Y_t}{3}$$

$$= \frac{141 + 139 + 136}{3}$$

$$= 138.67$$

This is a three-period non-centred moving average. We could also use other numbers of periods so, to proceed, we must decide how many periods to use for the moving average.

ACTIVITY 31

1. Continuing with your worksheet **Gargle.xls**, in cell D1 type **Forecast** and in cell D5 enter the formula =**AVERAGE(C2:C4)**. Our first forecast is for period 4 (that is, January 1996) and is given by the average of sales in the previous three periods. Copy the formula down to cell D26. The outcome in cell D26 is the forecast for October 1997. You should format column D for two decimal places.

2. What is the October 1997 forecast?

1. Your worksheet should be as shown in Table 31.

	A	B	C	D
1	**Time**	**Time**	**Sales**	**Forecast**
2	Oct-95	1	137	
3	Nov-95	2	136	
4	Dec-95	3	138	
5	Jan-96	4	138	137.00
6	Feb-96	5	141	137.33
7	Mar-96	6	139	139.00
8	Apr-96	7	142	139.33
9	May-96	8	147	140.67
10	Jun-96	9	144	142.67
11	Jul-96	10	138	144.33
12	Aug-96	11	140	143.00
13	Sep-96	12	136	140.67
14	Oct-96	13	138	138.00
15	Nov-96	14	144	138.00
16	Dec-96	15	135	139.33
17	Jan-97	16	138	139.00
18	Feb-97	17	137	139.00
19	Mar-97	18	136	136.67
20	Apr-97	19	136	137.00
21	May-97	20	135	136.33
22	Jun-97	21	134	135.67
23	Jul-97	22	141	135.00
24	Aug-97	23	139	136.67
25	Sep-97	24	136	138.00
26	Oct-97			138.67

Table 31: Three-period non-centred moving average for the Gargleblaster data

2. So using a three-period non-centred moving average yields a forecast for sales in October 1997 of 138.67.

However, before accepting this forecast we need to determine whether a three-period non-centred moving average is appropriate for this data. Perhaps a five-period or even a seven-period based forecast would have been better?

3.2 Forecast error

We can approach the problem of what period to choose for the moving average through the notion of **forecast error**.

Look at Table 31 again. The actual value for *Gargleblaster* sales in July 1997 is 141 and the forecast for that month (using the three-period non-centred moving average) is for sales to be 135. The forecast error is calculated as follows:

Forecast Error = Actual Value – Forecast

$$= Y_t - F_t$$

$$= 141 - 135$$

$$= 6$$

As our data gives sales in £000s, the error is £6,000.

Clearly we wish to choose our forecasting method (that is, the number of periods in the non-centred moving average) so as to minimise such forecasting error. The trouble is that there is more than one way of seeking to achieve this objective.

ACTIVITY 32

Consider the two sets of forecasts given in the table below.

Period	Actual value	Method A forecast	Method B forecast
1	11	10	13
2	9	8	12
3	10	9	12
4	11	11	14
5	12	17	15
6	10	9	7

Which forecasting method, Method A or Method B, has the lowest average value for the **absolute difference** between the actual value and the forecast?

Note: the absolute difference is defined as the actual value minus forecast, ignoring the negative sign (if any). So, for example, in period 5 the actual value is 12 and Method A forecasts 17. The absolute difference between the two values is 5.

Your calculations should agree with those in Table 32.

Actual value	Method A forecast	Absolute difference	Method B forecast	Absolute difference
11	10	1	13	2
9	8	1	12	3
10	9	1	12	2
11	11	0	14	3
12	17	5	15	3
10	9	1	7	3
Mean absolute difference		1.5		2.67

Table 32: Absolute forecasting errors

So Method A shows the lowest **mean absolute difference** between actual value and forecast.

This approach lays emphasis on the average discrepancy between forecast and actual value and selects as the best forecasting method that which minimises this discrepancy. Following this approach, in the case of the *Garglebaster* sales data in Table 30, we would:

- obtain forecasts using an n-period non-centred moving average for different values of n
- determine the average absolute forecast error for each value of n employed
- select as the best value of n that which generates the smallest mean absolute difference.

However, calculating the mean absolute deviation is not the only way of assessing the significance of forecast error. Since mean absolute difference measures the average absolute value of the error, it treats large errors pro rata with small errors. For example, forecast errors of 10 and 20 are treated respectively as being two and four times as significant as a forecast error of 5.

Many analysts would argue that large (and perhaps catastrophic) errors should not be treated pro rata, but be given greater weighting. This can be achieved by squaring the forecast errors prior to averaging. Now if we have forecast errors of 5, 10 and 20 then their squares are 25, 100 and 400 respectively. Using the squares, a forecast error of 20 would now be treated as being 16 times more significant that a forecast error of 5.

ACTIVITY 33

1. Look again at the data provided in Activity 32. Determine the average squared forecasting error for Methods A and B. We call the outcome from this calculation the **mean squared error**.

2. Which forecasting method has the least mean squared error?

---

1. Your calculations should agree with those in Table 33.

Actual value	Method A forecast	Squared difference	Method B forecast	Squared difference
11	10	1	13	4
9	8	1	12	9
10	9	1	12	4
11	11	0	14	9
12	17	25	15	9
10	9	1	7	9
Mean squared error		4.83		7.33

Table 33: Squared forecasting errors

2. So Method A has the least mean squared error and on this criterion would be adjudged the best.

Using mean squared error gives larger errors greater weighting than smaller errors. However, Method A is still preferred despite the relatively large squared error of 25 occurring in period 5.

ACTIVITY 34

1. Return to the data in Activity 32. What is the largest forecast error resulting from each of the methods?

2. So, if you are concerned to avoid large errors, which method would you prefer?

---

1. The largest forecast errors are 5 for Method A and 3 for Method B.

2. Clearly given this approach you would prefer Method B, even though on average (whether measured by mean absolute difference or mean squared error) it performs less well than Method A.

Whatever method we choose, we should note that there is no single way of assessing forecast error which is appropriate for all circumstances. Notice that the three approaches above might well give conflicting answers when employed to compare alternative forecasting methods. In other words, however sophisticated the methods we use, there is no substitute for judgement. We must clearly decide which of the error measurement procedures best accords with our requirements in any given circumstances. Some analysts will wish to have a forecasting system which avoids all large errors; others will require a system which achieves a small average error, but at the expense of the occasional large error.

However, given a decision to employ one of the approaches (say mean squared error), we can then choose between different moving averages. Clearly we would choose the one that performs best, in the sense of minimising mean squared error.

ACTIVITY 35

1. Continue with your **Gargle.xls** worksheet:

   - in cell E1 type **MSE**
   - enter the formula =**(C5–D5)^2** into cell E5 (note that '^2' means 'raise to the power of two')
   - copy the formula down to cell E25 (for each forecast, this formula computes the squared error)
   - format the cells in the range E5 to E25 to two decimal places
   - in cell E26 enter the formula =**AVERAGE(E7:E25)** to obtain the mean squared error
   - in column F, use a formula to obtain forecasts (including for October 1996) using a five-period non-centred moving average
   - in column G, obtain the mean squared error for these forecasts.

2. Which has the least mean squared error? So what is your preferred forecast for October 1997?

---

1. Your completed worksheet should look as shown in Table 34.

	A	B	C	D	E	F	G
1	Time	Time	Sales	Forecast	MSE	Forecast	MSE
2	Oct-95	1	137.00				
3	Nov-95	2	136.00				
4	Dec-95	3	138.00				
5	Jan-96	4	138.00	137.00	1.00		
6	Feb-96	5	141.00	137.33	13.44		
7	Mar-96	6	139.00	139.00	0.00	138.00	1.00
8	Apr-96	7	142.00	139.33	7.11	138.40	12.96
9	May-96	8	147.00	140.67	40.11	139.60	54.76
10	Jun-96	9	144.00	142.67	1.78	141.40	6.76
11	Jul-96	10	138.00	144.33	40.11	142.60	21.16
12	Aug-96	11	140.00	143.00	9.00	142.00	4.00
13	Sep-96	12	136.00	140.67	21.78	142.20	38.44
14	Oct-96	13	138.00	138.00	0.00	141.00	9.00
15	Nov-96	14	144.00	138.00	36.00	139.20	23.04
16	Dec-96	15	135.00	139.33	18.78	139.20	17.64
17	Jan-97	16	138.00	139.00	1.00	138.60	0.36
18	Feb-97	17	137.00	139.00	4.00	138.20	1.44
19	Mar-97	18	136.00	136.67	0.44	138.40	5.76
20	Apr-97	19	136.00	137.00	1.00	138.00	4.00
21	May-97	20	135.00	136.33	1.78	136.40	1.96
22	Jun-97	21	134.00	135.67	2.78	136.40	5.76
23	Jul-97	22	141.00	135.00	36.00	135.60	29.16
24	Aug-97	23	139.00	136.67	5.44	136.40	6.76
25	Sep-97	24	136.00	138.00	4.00	137.00	1.00
26	Oct-97	25		138.67	11.69	137.00	12.89

Table 34: Three- and five-period moving average
forecasts for the Gargleblaster data

2. So the mean squared error is 11.69 using three periods and 12.89 using five periods. Of these non-centred moving averages, the three-period one is to be preferred. The forecast for October 1996 is then 138.67.

3.3 Using the *Microsoft Excel* moving average tool

Microsoft Excel has a utility for obtaining non-centred moving averages. A chart can then be obtained comparing the forecasts with the raw data. Working through Activity 36 will show you how the tool is used.

| ACTIVITY 36 |

Continue with your **Gargle.xls** worksheet:

- copy and paste the data contained in cells A1 to C26 to **Sheet2**, keeping the same range

- click on **Tools, Data Analysis** and select **Moving Average**

- set the **Input Range** at **C2:C25**, the **Interval** at **5** and the **Output Range** at **D3** (one row lower than the starting row for the data)

- check the box for **Chart Output** but leave the box for **Standard Errors** unchecked

- click **OK**.

The forecast for October 1997 will be found in cell C26.

You should obtain output similar to that in Table 35 and Figure 15.

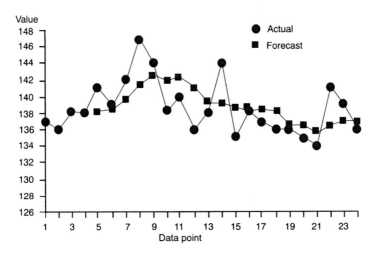

Figure 15: Microsoft Excel moving average tool output for Gargleblaster data

This agrees with the results that you obtained in Activity 35 for a five-period non-centred moving average. You might wish to experiment with other possibilities. Unfortunately *Microsoft Excel* does not output the squared errors and so you cannot immediately determine the optimum number of periods to use in the moving average.

	A	B	C	D
1	**Time**	**Time**	**Sales**	
2	Oct-95	1	137	
3	Nov-95	2	136	#N/A
4	Dec-95	3	138	#N/A
5	Jan-96	4	138	#N/A
6	Feb-96	5	141	#N/A
7	Mar-96	6	139	138
8	Apr-96	7	142	138.4
9	May-96	8	147	139.6
10	Jun-96	9	144	141.4
11	Jul-96	10	138	142.6
12	Aug-96	11	140	142
13	Sep-96	12	136	142.2
14	Oct-96	13	138	141
15	Nov-96	14	144	139.2
16	Dec-96	15	135	139.2
17	Jan-97	16	138	138.6
18	Feb-97	17	137	138.2
19	Mar-97	18	136	138.4
20	Apr-97	19	136	138
21	May-97	20	135	136.4
22	Jun-97	21	134	136.4
23	Jul-97	22	141	135.6
24	Aug-97	23	139	136.4
25	Sep-97	24	136	137
26	Oct-97	25		137

Table 35: Microsoft Excel moving average tool output for Gargleblaster data

Summary

In Section 3.1 we explored the use of non-centred moving averages as a forecasting tool. Using a non-centred moving average the forecast for the next time period is the average value of the series over the immediately preceding n periods. Since the forecast is dependent upon the number of periods used in the moving average, this implies the need for some criterion to determine what value of n is optimal.

In Section 3.2 we addressed this problem by defining forecast error as the difference between the actual and forecast value for a variable and showing that there are a number of different (and possibly conflicting) ways in which such errors can be interpreted. If the forecaster is prepared to treat large and small errors as of equal importance then it would be appropriate to use the average forecast error irrespective of its sign. This is called the mean absolute deviation. However, we could also take the view that larger errors should be afforded a greater weighting in which case use of the mean squared error might be more appropriate. In this approach each forecast error is squared and the resulting squared values are averaged. In most work involving time series, practitioners normally utilise mean squared error as the preferred measure of forecast error.

In Section 3.3 we looked briefly at how *Microsoft Excel* can be used to calculate moving averages.

In the next section of this unit we look at some of the problems associated with forecasting techniques which are based on moving averages, and we explore one solution to these problems.

SECTION 4

Exponential Smoothing

Introduction

The criticisms of moving averages can be addressed by making use of an alternative form of averaging, known as **exponential smoothing**, which is probably the most widely applicable of the time series methods for forecasting business data. In Section 4.1 we introduce the basic principles of exponential smoothing. In Section 4.2 we apply exponential smoothing to some actual data using *Microsoft Excel*. Finally, in Section 4.3, we look in more detail at how to use the exponential smoothing tool available in *Microsoft Excel*. By the end of this section you should be able to use simple exponential smoothing to forecast a time series.

4.1 Exponential smoothing: the basic principles

In Section 3 of this unit we used simple non-centred averages as a basis for forecasting. However, there are a number of problems with basing forecasts upon a simple non-centred moving average:

- within the non-centred moving average each observation is given equal weighting, when perhaps more recent observations should be given greater stress

- a non-centred moving average does not use all observations and, therefore, does not make maximum use of all available information

- if the data shows a clear upward or downward trend, then forecasts will always either lag behind actual values or lead them.

Exponential smoothing provides a way of dealing with these problems. There are several exponential smoothing models available, depending partly on whether the data displays strong trend or seasonal variation. In this unit we will confine our attention to the more straightforward situation where both trend and seasonal variation are absent from the data.

The basic principle of exponential smoothing is that the forecast for the next time period is derived solely from the actual value for the last time period and the forecast for the last time period.

Suppose that this week's sales of a given product amount to 800 units, whereas the forecast was for sales of 900. The forecast error would be 100 (900 – 800). Since sales this week fell short of the forecast it would seem prudent to allow for this when generating a forecast for the coming week. So we would probably decide to lower the forecast in response to this error. This is equivalent to using the current forecast adjusted for the current forecast error as the next period forecast.

There are two extreme possibilities. We might decide to adjust the current forecast to the full extent of the current error. Since sales this week are 100 below forecast, this would generate a sales forecast of 800 for next week (900 – 100). Or we might decide, despite the current error, to leave the forecast unchanged at 900. Between these extremes are a range of alternatives.

ACTIVITY 37

Suppose we decide to adjust the current forecast by 50 per cent of the current error. What is the forecast for sales next week?

The forecast for next week's sales will be the current forecast (900) adjusted downwards by 50 per cent of the current error (100). That is:

$$900 + 0.5(800 - 900) = 900 - 50$$

$$= 850$$

Let us now formalise this procedure: we will use the Y_t and F_t notation defined previously.

The forecast for the next time period is given by:

$$F_{t+1} = F_t + \alpha(Y_t - F_t)$$

where $0 \leq \alpha \leq 1$ is referred to as the **smoothing constant** and is determined by the forecaster.

In words, the formula states that 'next period's forecast consists of the last forecast plus some proportion (α) of the last forecast error'. This is an **adaptive** or **error learning process** for forecasting.

Let us look at another example using this formula.

ACTIVITY 38

Suppose that last period the value of a variable was 76 and the forecast was 80.

If α is 0.8, what will the forecast be for this period?

The last period forecast (F_{t-1}) is 80, while the actual data (Y_{t-1}) was 76. This makes the forecast error:

$$Y_{t-1} - F_{t-1} = 76 - 80$$
$$= -4$$

The smoothing constant is 0.8. Consequently the current period forecast is:

$$F_t = 80 + (0.8 \times -4)$$
$$= 76.8$$

We now show that exponential smoothing has a number of key features. The algebra required to demonstrate these features is less important than the conclusions derived from it. However, it will do no harm to work through the algebra in order to see how the key conclusions have been obtained.

$$F_{t+1} = F_t + \alpha(Y_t - F_t)$$
$$= F_t + \alpha Y_t - \alpha F_t \text{ (on removing the bracket)}$$
$$= \alpha Y_t + (1 - \alpha)F_t \text{ (on rearranging the terms)}$$

All that we have done is to rearrange the formula for exponential smoothing to get:

(1) $\qquad F_{t+1} = \alpha Y_t + (1 - \alpha)F_t$

Now suppose we were to go back one time period and ask how the forecast for period t was determined. Using the same pattern as in equation (1) we would have that:

(2) $\qquad F_t = \alpha Y_{t-1} + (1 - \alpha)F_{t-1}$

Now substitute the expression for F_t from equation (2) into equation (1). This gives:

$$F_{t+1} = \alpha Y_t + (1 - \alpha)\{\alpha Y_{t-1} + (1 - \alpha)F_{t-1}\}$$
$$= \alpha Y_t + \alpha(1 - \alpha)Y_{t-1} + (1 - \alpha)^2 F_{t-1}$$

So we now have that:

(3) $\qquad F_{t+1} = \alpha Y_t + \alpha(1 - \alpha)Y_{t-1} + (1 - \alpha)^2 F_{t-1}$

This process can be continued since again we can ask how F_{t-1} was determined. That is, two periods ago, how was the forecast for the next period determined? Well it must be that:

(4) $\qquad F_{t-1} = \alpha Y_{t-2} + (1 - \alpha)F_{t-2}$

and on substituting for F_{t-1} from equation (4) into equation (3) we get:

(5) $\quad F_{t+1} = \alpha Y_t + \alpha(1-\alpha)Y_{t-1} + \alpha(1-\alpha)^2 Y_{t-2} + (1-\alpha)^3 F_{t-2}$

This process can be continued in the same way, resulting in:

$$F_{t+1} = \alpha Y_t + \alpha(1-\alpha)Y_{t-1} + \alpha(1-\alpha)^2 Y_{t-2} \dots + \alpha(1-\alpha)^n Y_{t-n} + (1-\alpha)^{n+1} F_{t-n}$$

Note: this is not the version of the exponential smoothing formula that you would employ for forecasting. To forecast, the only information required is the actual sales and the forecast for the last period, along with the smoothing factor. However, the version above shows what exponential smoothing is actually doing.

1. All past values of Y are being utilised in the current forecast.
2. The forecast is a weighted average of past values of Y, the weights being $\alpha, \alpha(1-\alpha), \alpha(1-\alpha)^2, \alpha(1-\alpha)^3, \dots \alpha(1-\alpha)^n$.
3. Since α takes a value between 0 and 1, the weights decline exponentially with time. For example, suppose that α equals 0.5. Then the weights are 0.5, 0.25, 0.125 and so on. Hence, more recent values of Y are given a greater weighting when making the current forecast.
4. The weights sum to 1. Here is a brief proof:

$$\alpha + \alpha(1-\alpha) + \alpha(1-\alpha)^2 + \alpha(1-\alpha)^3 + \dots \alpha(1-\alpha)^n$$

$$= \alpha[1 + (1-\alpha) + (1-\alpha)^2 + (1-\alpha)^3 \dots + (1-\alpha)^n]$$

$$\frac{\alpha}{1-(1-\alpha)} \quad \text{(using the formula for the sum of a geometric progression)}$$

$$= 1$$

5. The importance attached to past values of Y depends upon the choice of α. Higher values of α make the forecast more sensitive to current values of Y and lower values make it less sensitive.

ACTIVITY 39

You may have found some of the above mathematics a little unpalatable! Remember that what counts is the conclusion derived from it. To review these conclusions, see if you can fill in the blanks in the following statement.

An exponentially smoothed forecast is a _____ _____ of past values of Y, the weights _____ exponentially over time. The sum of the weights is equal to

_____.

See parts (1) to (4) of the text immediately before this activity.

4.2 Exponential smoothing: the practice

To investigate simple exponential smoothing we will use the following data, which records sales of *Widgets* over the past 11 periods (Table 36).

Period	Sales	Period	Sales
1	489	7	490
2	493	8	487
3	485	9	495
4	482	10	490
5	488	11	492
6	484		

Table 36: Sales of Widgets

Suppose that we have been asked for a forecast for period 12, to be obtained via simple exponential smoothing. Clearly our first problem is to determine what value to use for α, the smoothing constant.

ACTIVITY 40

How should we go about choosing a value for α?

One way of tackling such a problem is to think back to the methods used in Section 3 of this unit, where we were trying to decide how we would select a suitable period for a forecast obtained using a non-centred moving average. In that section, it was decided to select the period which resulted in the best forecasts, in the sense of minimising the forecast error. This would, of course, require us to select a method of appraising forecast error, such as mean squared error or mean absolute difference. Once this had been agreed, we could try out different smoothing constants (different values of α) until we had a result which satisfied us.

So we select that value of α which performs best when used to forecast the value of Y over the past 11 periods. One approach might be to choose that value of α which minimises mean squared error.

In the next series of activities you will experiment with different values of α using *Microsoft Excel*, with minimising mean squared error as the selection criterion.

ACTIVITY 41

Open a new *Microsoft Excel* workbook and save it as **Expsmth.xls**. Enter the following data exactly as contained in the table below. (Note that 'MSE' stands for mean squared error.)

	A	B	C	D	E	F	G	H
1								
2					FORECAST			
3			alpha =		alpha =		alpha =	
4	Period	Sales	0.1	MSE	0.3	MSE	0.5	MSE
5	1	489	489.00		489.00		489.00	
6	2	493						
7	3	485						
8	4	482						
9	5	488						
10	6	484						
11	7	490						
12	8	487						
13	9	495						
14	10	490						
15	11	492						
16	12							

Consider the forecast for period 2 using a value for α of 0.1. It is given by the period 1 forecast 489 (see the note below) plus the forecast error for period 1 multiplied by 0.1. So the formula required in cell C6 is =C5+$C$4*(B5–C5).The formula should then be copied down to cell C16. This generates the forecasts (including period 12) using a smoothing constant of 0.1. Notice that the $ sign is used to keep α fixed at 0.1.

Enter appropriate formulae in column E to obtain a forecast for period 12 using 0.3 as the value of α.

Repeat this for column G, using 0.5 as the value of α.

Note: to undertake exponential smoothing, a starting value is needed. Conventionally, the data for period 1 is used for the first forecast. So the value 489 has been entered into cells C5, E5 and G5.

Your worksheet should now agree with that in Table 37.

	A	B	C	D	E	F	G	H
1								
2					FORECAST			
3			alpha =		alpha =		alpha =	
4	Period	Sales	0.1	MSE	0.3	MSE	0.5	MSE
5	1	489	489.00		489.00		489.00	
6	2	493	489.00		489.00		489.00	
7	3	485	489.40		490.20		491.00	
8	4	482	488.96		488.64		488.00	
9	5	488	488.26		486.65		485.00	
10	6	484	488.24		487.05		486.50	
11	7	490	487.81		486.14		485.25	
12	8	487	488.03		487.30		487.63	
13	9	495	487.93		487.21		487.31	
14	10	490	488.64		489.55		491.16	
15	11	492	488.77		489.68		490.58	
16	12		489.10		490.38		491.29	

Table 37: Forecasts using different smoothing constants

So using 0.1 as the value for α yields a forecast of 489.10 for period 12. An alpha value of 0.3 yields a forecast of 490.38 and an alpha value of 0.5 yields a forecast of 491.29.

We have obtained three different forecasts for period 12, namely 489.10, 490.38 and 491.29. Which of these is the best forecast?

ACTIVITY 42

Continue with your worksheet **Expsmth.xls**. Your objective is to decide which of the three forecasts obtained in the last activity should be adopted. To do this you will calculate the mean squared error for the forecasts generated by each value of α.

Consider the forecasts obtained using an alpha value of 0.1. For period 1 the forecast error is clearly 0. However, for period 2 it is calculated by subtracting the forecast from the actual value. In this case, it is 4 (493 − 489). The square of the error is, therefore, 16. We can obtain the squared error for each of the forecasts by entering the formula =(B5−C5)^2 into cell D5 and copying it down to D15.

The mean squared error is then the average of the squared errors in column D, resulting from the choice of an alpha value of 0.1. You can obtain the mean squared error by using the formula =AVERAGE(D5:D15).

You will require similar formulae in columns F and H.

Your worksheet should agree with Table 38.

	A	B	C	D	E	F	G	H
1								
2					FORECAST			
3			alpha =		alpha =		alpha =	
4	Period	Sales	0.1	MSE	0.3	MSE	0.5	MSE
5	1	489	489.00	0.00	489.00	0.00	489.00	0.00
6	2	493	489.00	16.00	489.00	16.00	489.00	16.00
7	3	485	489.40	19.36	490.20	27.04	491.00	36.00
8	4	482	488.96	48.44	488.64	44.09	488.00	36.00
9	5	488	488.26	0.07	486.65	1.83	485.00	9.00
10	6	484	488.24	17.96	487.05	9.32	486.50	6.25
11	7	490	487.81	4.78	486.14	14.92	485.25	22.56
12	8	487	488.03	1.07	487.30	0.09	487.63	0.39
13	9	495	487.93	50.00	487.21	60.72	487.31	59.10
14	10	490	488.64	1.86	489.55	0.21	491.16	1.34
15	11	492	488.77	10.42	489.68	5.37	490.58	2.02
16	12		489.10		490.38		491.29	
17	Mean squared error =			15.45		16.33		17.15

Table 38: Mean squared errors for forecasts
using different smoothing constants

The forecasting series which has the lowest mean squared error is the one with a smoothing constant of 0.1. So, judged by this criterion, it is the best forecast. The forecast for period 12 is then 489.1.

Using a worksheet, other values for α can also be tried out. Although this is quite straightforward, it is somewhat tedious. Dedicated forecasting software and multi-purpose statistical software (such as *SPSS* or *Minitab*) provide a search option (optimising on mean squared error) to establish the best value for α. In any serious forecasting using exponential smoothing, it would be essential to use such a procedure.

To consolidate what you have learned so far, try the following activity.

ACTIVITY 43

The following data records the number of person-days lost per annum, due to industrial injury, in an engineering firm.

	I	II	III	IV
1994	187	198	311	299
1995	210	257	231	323
1996	201	225	236	318
1997	180			

Open a new *Microsoft Excel* worksheet and save it as **Injury.xls**.

Enter the data and use exponential smoothing to forecast the number of injuries in quarter II of 1997. (You should lay out your worksheet with the same structure as that used in **Expsmth.xls**.)

Try three values of α before you decide on a forecast (as before, assume that the forecast for the first period is the same as the actual data, in this case 187).

You should have a worksheet similar to the one shown in Table 39, although you will almost certainly have selected different values for α.

This does not pretend to be a definitive answer, as all of the possible alpha values have not been tried out. You may have compared different alpha values in your own answer to this problem, and so may have obtained a different (but equally valid) result. Of the models tried in Table 39 the one with an alpha value of 0.2 is the best, because it has the lowest mean squared error. Consequently, the forecast of 238.7 would be the best.

	A	B	C	D	E	F	G	H
1	Forecast for different values of alpha							
2			alpha =		alpha =		alpha =	
3	Time	Days	0.2	MSE	0.4	MSE	0.6	MSE
4	1994 I	187	187.0	0.00	187.0	0.00	187.0	0.00
5	II	198	187.0	121.00	187.0	121.00	187.0	121.00
6	III	311	189.2	14835.24	191.4	14304.16	193.6	13782.76
7	IV	299	213.6	7299.99	239.2	3571.26	264.0	1222.20
8	1995 I	210	230.6	426.34	263.1	2824.28	285.0	5627.40
9	II	257	226.5	929.13	241.9	228.42	240.0	288.78
10	III	231	232.6	2.61	247.9	286.69	250.2	368.74
11	IV	323	232.3	8227.98	241.2	6697.93	238.7	7109.69
12	1996 I	201	250.4	2443.66	273.9	5313.75	289.3	7792.02
13	II	225	240.5	241.70	244.7	389.56	236.3	127.89
14	III	236	237.4	2.07	236.8	0.71	229.5	41.94
15	IV	318	237.1	6536.74	236.5	6641.37	233.4	7155.56
16	1997 I	180	253.3	5375.81	269.1	7939.39	284.2	10850.09
17	II		238.7		233.5		221.7	
18								
19	Mean squared error =			3572.5		3716.8		4191.4

Table 39: Worksheet for injury data

Before leaving this problem, you may have noticed that the forecast for 1997 quarter I is very poor. This shows another feature of exponential smoothing. If there is a sudden major change in the series (in this case from 318 in 1996 quarter IV down to 180 in 1997 quarter I) an exponentially smoothed series takes some time to adjust to the change. Hence the bad forecast for this period.

The basic version of exponential smoothing falls foul of one substantial problem. If the data shows a persistent upward or downward trend, then the forecast will always either lag behind or lead the actual value. To see what this means, try the following activity.

ACTIVITY 44

Sales of *Widgets* (in thousands) are as follows:

Week	Sales	Week	Sales
1	1	6	6
2	2	7	7
3	3	8	8
4	4	9	9
5	5	10	10

Set the forecast for week 1 as 1.

Without using a worksheet or doing any calculations, what is the best value for α?

What do you think of the forecast?

Since sales show a very clear and persistent upward trend then the best value for α is 1. However, this implies that each period's forecast is set equal to the previous period's sales.

Such a forecast leaves a very great deal to be desired. It seems clear that what is happening here is that sales are rising by 1 unit per period, so common sense suggests that the forecast for period 11 should be 11. Simple exponential smoothing fails to pick up the trend. If we selected an alpha value of 1.0 then we would still obtain a forecast of 10 (equal to sales for the previous period).

Clearly, as the last activity shows, simple exponential smoothing cannot cope with a clear trend. Nor (although we have not demonstrated this) can it cope with seasonality. There are procedures for extending the simple model to allow for both trend and seasonality. However, they will not be investigated in this unit.

4.3 The *Microsoft Excel* exponential smoothing tool

This sub-section briefly explores the exponential smoothing utility in *Microsoft Excel*. This can be used to smooth a series and to generate a forecast. It can also output a chart comparing the raw data with the smoothed series. However, the utility doesn't directly generate mean squared errors and neither does it offer a search procedure to optimise on α.

As an example of its use, we return to the sales data shown in Table 36 at the start of Section 4.2. You saved this data as **Expsmth.xls.**

ACTIVITY 45

Open your workbook **Expsmth.xls** and follow the steps below:

- copy the time period and sales data in the range A4 to B16 and paste it into cells A1 to B13 of a new sheet

- with the new sheet active, click on **Tools**, and select **Data Analysis** from the menu options

- select **Exponential Smoothing** and complete the resulting dialogue box as per the figure below (note that *Microsoft Excel* uses the term **damping factor** instead of smoothing factor, and defines this as '1 − α')

- click **OK**

- to obtain a forecast for period 12 select cell C12 and copy the formula it contains down to C13.

Your screen should contain the data shown as Table 40 and the graph shown as Figure 16.

	A	B	C
1	Period	Sales	
2	1	489	#N/A
3	2	493	489.00
4	3	485	489.40
5	4	482	488.96
6	5	488	488.26
7	6	484	488.24
8	7	490	487.81
9	8	487	488.03
10	9	495	487.93
11	10	490	488.64
12	11	492	488.77
13	12		489.10

Table 40: Microsoft Excel exponential smoothing output

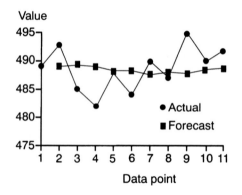

Figure 16: Microsoft Excel exponential smoothing output

A damping factor of 0.9 is equivalent to an alpha value of 0.1. As you can check, the forecasts (for periods 2 to 12) are identical to those that you obtained in Activity 41.

The formula in cell C12 was copied down to C13, to obtain the period 12 forecast. This formula appears somewhat different to the one that you used earlier, though a little algebra shows that it is the same.

Rearranging the formula for exponential smoothing gives:

(1) $F_{t+1} = F_t + \alpha(Y_t - F_t)$

(2) $F_{t+1} = F_t + \alpha Y_t - \alpha F_t$

(3) $F_{t+1} = \alpha Y_t + (1 - \alpha)F_t$

This is the version used in *Microsoft Excel*.

Useful though it is, *Microsoft Excel* has no search procedure allowing you to find the best smoothing constant.

Summary

This section has explored exponential smoothing. This approach provides a simple but powerful method for forecasting a time series. In many cases it is capable of outperforming the more sophisticated models for analysing a time series, and most business forecasting practitioners will have used exponential smoothing in one or more of its guises.

We showed that to obtain a current period forecast, exponential smoothing uses only the actual value for the variable in the last time period along with the forecast value for that period. The current forecast is then determined as the previous period forecast adjusted by some proportion of the previous period forecast error. This adjustment factor is called the smoothing constant. With the aid of some algebraic analysis, we demonstrated that this essentially simple procedure ensures that all past values of the variable contribute to generating a forecast, with more recent values of the variable being given a higher weighting.

A high value for the smoothing constant increases the weighting given to recently occurring values of the variable, whilst the contrary is the case if a low value is chosen. An optimal alpha value would be that which, when employed to forecast past values of the variable, generated the least forecast error.

In the next section we look at another forecasting technique which is based on moving averages. This is a technique known as **autoregression with integrated moving averages** (ARIMA).

Section 5

Introduction to ARIMA

Introduction

Decomposition, moving averages and exponential smoothing are all major techniques within the area of time series analysis. Many other more sophisticated models have been developed which have their starting point in one or other of these approaches. In this concluding section, we will outline one such model, **ARIMA**. ARIMA is an abbreviation for **autoregression with integrated moving averages**.

5.1 What is ARIMA?

ARIMA uses three concepts to obtain its forecasts.

Stationarity

In order to make a forecast, ARIMA requires that the time series data be stationary. So what does a stationary time series look like? A stationary series has a constant mean and a constant variance over time. Visually, the series plot should remain within a level band of constant width. Most time series do not have this desirable condition as the presence of trend and seasonal variation alone would make the data non-stationary. If this is the case, then various mathematical operations must be carried out on the data until it is rendered stationary. The reason for this requirement is that stationary series are easier to forecast than non-stationary ones.

Autocorrelation or Serial Correlation

This is the situation which exists when a variable is correlated with itself. This usually occurs when data in any one period is correlated with values recorded in previous periods. It may be possible to use such relationships to help make forecasts. If we do discover that autocorrelation exists, then we can use the technique of **autoregression**, whereby a variable is regressed upon itself.

Moving Averages

You are already familiar with the use of moving averages as a forecasting tool. ARIMA makes use of such patterns in data as part of the forecasting process.

So ARIMA combines autoregression and a special kind of moving average together in one sophisticated package. Much of the initial groundwork for ARIMA is the product of pioneering work by Box and Jenkins (1976). Their names have become so inextricably linked with ARIMA that the term **Box-Jenkins forecasting** is often used as a synonym of ARIMA. (Strictly speaking Box-Jenkins forecasting refers to one of the actual procedures used to fit models to data, and not to the model itself.

However, this distinction has now become redundant and most analysts use the terms Box-Jenkins forecasting and ARIMA interchangeably.)

5.2 Stationarity of a time series

We first consider the importance of stationarity in forecasting. Look at the plot of the time series in Figure 17. The trend of this series is not constant: instead, it shows a strong upward direction. A changing trend clearly means that the mean level of the series is not constant. Such a series is not stationary. A downward trend would also exhibit non-stationarity.

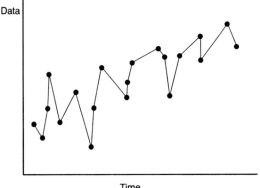

Figure 17: Non-stationary series due to trend

The plot shown in Figure 18, however, does show stationarity. The mean level appears to stay constant and there does not seem to be any reason to suppose that the variance is rising or falling over time.

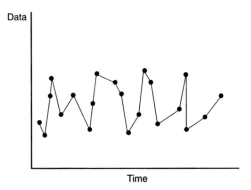

Figure 18: A stationary time series

If the characteristics (mean level and variance) of the time series are changing systematically over time, then we will find it difficult to model the series. By contrast, if the time series is stationary, we will find it relatively easy to model its behaviour.

This might sound like a potentially serious problem, because we are hardly likely to encounter stationary time series in business or economic data. The usual way in which the requirement of stationarity is breached is by the inconvenient appearance of a trend and/or a seasonal variation. Does this mean that attempts to forecast fall at the first hurdle? Fortunately, the answer to this question is "no". As we shall see a little further on, there are mathematical procedures called **differencing** which enable us to turn a non-stationary series into a stationary one.

ACTIVITY 46

Look at the following data.

t	Y_t	$Y_t - Y_{t-1}$
1	0	-
2	2	
3	4	
4	6	
5	8	
6	10	

1. By subtracting each prior Y value from the present one $(Y_t - Y_{t-1})$, fill in the blank column. The first entry, for t equals 1, will remain blank.

2. What do you notice about the resulting data?

1. You should have obtained the following result.

t	Y_t	$Y_t - Y_{t-1}$
1	0	-
2	2	2
3	4	2
4	6	2
5	8	2
6	10	2

Table 41: Stationary data series

2. The resulting data series is completely stationary, in the sense that the value of $Y_t - Y_{t-1}$ is always 2.

The technique used in Activity 46 is called **differencing**. Specifically, it is a first difference, whereby each element in the series is subtracted from the one after. In this case this resulted in a stationary series. Of course, the data in the activity was rather contrived, and it is unlikely that you would meet such a series in real life. This means that you will have to exercise judgement as to when stationarity has been reached. If it has not, then a second difference could be taken, and the results examined for stationarity. It is possible that third, fourth and even fifth differences could be taken, though it is unusual to need to go beyond second differences.

ACTIVITY 47

Take another look at the *Bombay Nutz* data first encountered in Activity 2, at the start of Section 1.1 of this unit.

1. Open your **Bombay.xls** spreadsheet containing this data and examine the graph. (If your saved version of the spreadsheet does not include a graph, you should obtain one now.) Is the data stationary?

2. Enter the label **First Diff** in cell D1 of your worksheet. By entering an appropriate formula in cells D3 to D13, calculate the first differences, and obtain their graph against time.

3. What do you notice about the resulting series?

---

1. Your chart should be as shown in Figure 1 in Section 1.1 of this unit. The data is not stationary.

2. Your worksheet should look as shown in Table 42.

	A	B	C	D
1	**Time**	**Time**	**Sales**	**First Diff**
2	1993 I	1	11.5	
3	II	2	12.2	0.70
4	III	3	12.9	0.70
5	IV	4	15.7	2.80
6	1994 I	5	18.9	3.20
7	II	6	20.5	1.60
8	IIII	7	21.4	0.90
9	IV	8	23.4	2.00
10	1995 I	9	27.8	4.40
11	II	10	28.3	0.50
12	III	11	29.1	0.80
13	IV	12	31.6	2.50

Table 42: Achieving stationarity

The formula in cell D3 is =**C3–C2**. This is then copied down to cell D13.

3. The effect of taking this first difference becomes evident if we examine the graph of the new series along with the original sales. This is shown as Figure 19.

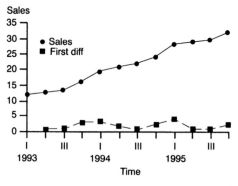

Figure 19: Graph of first differences

Notice that the original trend has now disappeared. The new series is stationary.

You may wonder what the search for a stationary time series actually achieves. A stationary time series is always easier to forecast than a non-stationary one. In brief, the ARIMA process consists of the following steps:

- examine the time series to see if it is stationary
- if it is not already stationary, obtain a first difference
- if the first differences are not stationary, take a second difference (this usually suffices)
- make a forecast of the stationary series (using a combination of autoregression and moving averages)
- finally, reverse the differencing procedure to obtain a forecast of the original series.

5.3 Autocorrelation and autoregression

We now examine the situation which occurs when there is autocorrelation within the data we are trying to forecast. As already described, autocorrelation exists when a variable is correlated with itself. This can easily occur in a time series where, for example, sales in any one period have a marked relationship with sales in the past.

In order to illustrate this, we consider an example. Suppose that we are trying to forecast sales by using a causal model where sales are regressed upon promotional expenditure. Table 43 shows sales of disposable digital watches (in millions) and the amount spent on sales promotion in £10,000s.

Year	Sales	Sales promotion
1982	1.77	211
1983	2.12	152
1984	2.38	226
1985	2.22	278
1986	2.17	268
1987	3.58	412
1988	4.28	553
1989	4.86	508
1990	6.18	707
1991	7.20	868
1992	6.95	664
1993	6.51	647
1994	5.98	693
1995	6.13	804
1996	5.21	796

Table 43: Sales and sales promotion

ACTIVITY 48

Enter the data in Table 43 into a *Microsoft Excel* worksheet and save it as **Watch.xls**.

Obtain a regression model of sales on sales promotion for the digital watch data. Remember that to use the **Regression** utility in *Microsoft Excel* you click **Tools** (from the menu bar), select **Data Analysis** and call up **Regression**. For the data in Table 43 the Y-data is 'Sales' and the X-data is 'Sales Promotion'.

Write out the model in full. Use R-Squared and the F test to comment on its explanatory power.

Microsoft Excel output for the model is given in Table 44.

Regression statistics					
Multiple R	0.940117				
R Squared	0.88382				
Adjusted R	0.874883				
Standard Error	0.699624				
Observations	15				
ANOVA					
	df	SS	MS	F	Significance F
Regression	1	48.40653	48.40653	98.9	1.92E–07
Residual	13	6.363159	0.489474		
Total	14	54.76969			
	Coefficients	Standard Error	t Stat	P-value	
Intercept	0.542888	0.437244	1.241615	0.236	
Promotion	0.007628	0.000767	9.944599	2E–07	

Table 44: Regression output for 'sales'/'sales promotion' model

The model is:

Estimated Sales = 0.542888 + 0.007628(Sales Promotion)

R-Squared is a very respectable 0.88, and the F test tells us that it is significant. This is because the significance of F is only 1.92×10^{-7} (1.92E–07) and so there is a negligible likelihood that this value of R-Squared has occurred merely by chance.

The model developed in Activity 48 seems to have considerable explanatory power. However, perhaps we can do even better.

ACTIVITY 49

On your **Watch.xls** worksheet create two new variables. One variable will be sales lagged by one year, and the other variable will be sales lagged by two years. Call these new variables **Year(1)** and **Year(2)** respectively.

You can easily do this by using **Copy** and **Paste**. Assuming that you have the data for 'Year' in cells A2 to A16, for 'Sales' in cells B2 to B16 and for 'Promotion' in cells C2 to C16, to create a one-year time lag you need to copy and paste the sales data from the cell range B2 to B16 into the cell range D3 to D17.

Similarly, to create a two-year time lag you will need to paste the sales data into cells E4 to E18.

For your revised worksheet, the first year for which you have data on all four variables is 1984, so insert a new row at this point.

In cells A4 to E4 type in the labels **Year, Sales, Promotion, Year(1)** and **Year(2)** respectively.

'Year(1)' and 'Year (2)' are the same as 'Sales', except that they are lagged by one and two years respectively. Notice that creating a variable lagged by one period means losing one whole row of data, while lagging by two periods means losing two rows of data.

Using this revised worksheet, the next activity explains what is meant by autocorrelation.

Your worksheet should now look like the one shown in Table 45.

	A	B	C	D	E
1	Year	Sales	Promotion		
2	1982	1.77	211		
3	1983	2.12	152	1.77	
4	**Year**	**Sales**	**Promotion**	**Year(1)**	**Year(2)**
5	1984	2.38	226	2.12	1.77
6	1985	2.22	278	2.38	2.12
7	1986	2.17	268	2.22	2.38
8	1987	3.58	412	2.17	2.22
9	1988	4.28	553	3.58	2.17
10	1989	4.86	508	4.28	3.58
11	1990	6.18	707	4.86	4.28
12	1991	7.20	868	6.18	4.86
13	1992	6.95	664	7.20	6.18
14	1993	6.51	647	6.95	7.20
15	1994	5.98	693	6.51	6.95
16	1995	6.13	804	5.98	6.51
17	1996	5.21	796	6.13	5.98
18				5.21	6.13
19					5.21

Table 45: Sales lagged by one and two years

ACTIVITY 50

Open your worksheet **Watch.xls**. Use the *Microsoft Excel* **Correlation** tool to calculate correlation figures between 'Sales', 'Year (1)', 'Year (2)' and 'Promotion'. Like the other tools, you find the **Correlation** tool by clicking on **Tools**, selecting **Data Analysis** and then selecting **Correlation**. What do you notice?

Hint: be careful while inputting data ranges. The meaningful range for the above worksheet is **B4:E17**. Notice that this range has labels in the first row.

The correlation matrix is shown in Table 46.

	Sales	**Promotion**	**Year(1)**	**Year(2)**
Sales	1			
Promotion	0.92061	1		
Year(1)	0.92905	0.87167	1	
Year(2)	0.83139	0.79474	0.95082	1

Table 46: Digital watch correlation data

Notice that, as you would expect, correlation between sales and promotion is high at 0.92. What is perhaps less expected is that sales in any one year are correlated with sales in the previous year ($r = 0.929$). Also, sales in any one year are correlated with sales of two years ago ($r = 0.831$). This phenomenon, whereby a variable is correlated with itself, after a time lag, is known as **autocorrelation**. In this case we have discovered autocorrelation for a one- and two-period time lag. It is quite possible that there may be other significant time lags, but you are not asked to investigate this.

ARIMA turns the phenomena of autocorrelation to advantage by using **autoregression**. Autoregression exists where a variable is regressed on itself, time-lagged by one or more periods. In the digital watch sales example, since we have discovered autocorrelation between sales and sales lagged by both one and two periods, it seems reasonable to investigate the possibility of using these time-lagged variables in a multiple regression model.

ACTIVITY 51

1. Use your **Watch.xls** worksheet to create a regression model of sales, regressed on:

   ● 'Promotion'

   ● 'Year(1)' (that is 'Sales' lagged by one year)

   ● 'Year(2)' (that is 'Sales' lagged by two years).

2. Write out the new regression model and identify the new value for the adjusted R-Squared. Is there any improvement on the old model?

---

1. The regression output from *Microsoft Excel* is shown in Table 47.

Regression statistics					
Multiple R	0.963667				
R Squared	0.928654				
Adjusted R	0.904872				
Standard Error	0.560374				
Observations	13				
ANOVA					
	df	SS	MS	F	Significance F
Regression	3	36.78614	12.26205	39.0487	1.74E–05
Residual	9	2.826171	0.314019		
Total	12	39.61231			
	Coefficients	Standard Error	t Stat	P-value	
Intercept	0.372502	0.455077	0.818548	0.4342	
Promotion	0.003383	0.001558	2.171572	0.0580	
Year(1)	0.88111	0.337207	2.612968	0.0281	
Year(2)	–0.34999	0.259443	–1.34899	0.2103	

Table 47: Autoregression model: digital watch sales

2. The model now becomes:

$$Y = 0.3725 + 0.0034X_1 + 0.8811X_2 - 0.3500X_3$$

where X_1 equals 'Promotion', X_2 equals 'Year(1)', X_3 equals 'Year(2)' and Y equals 'Sales'.

Previously the adjusted R-Squared was 0.87 (see Table 44). For the revised model it is 0.93. It is clearly significant.

The significance of F is 1.74×10^{-5} (1.74E–05) and so the likelihood that this result has occurred by chance is again negligible. The revised model is clearly an improvement over the original.

However, inspection of the P-values for the three explanatory variables (see Table 47) shows that only 'Promotion' and 'Year(1)' are significant. The P-value for 'Year(2)' is 0.2103, which is substantially higher than the customary 0.05 cut off point. We would, therefore, drop this variable from any regression model.

ARIMA, therefore, uses autocorrelation as a means of making forecasts. In general, the ARIMA method proceeds by first obtaining a stationary time series and then investigating the existence of moving average patterns and autocorrelation. It requires a considerable amount of skill and experience to identify these patterns within a given time series and, consequently, the practical task of using ARIMA is best left to an expert with specialist computer software. We shall not pursue the technique further.

Summary

In this section we have given a general overview of the important forecasting technique of ARIMA. This approach uses three key procedures to make forecasts:

- differencing techniques are used to obtain stationary time series
- moving averages are employed to detect periodic movements
- finally autocorrelation is checked for.

We started by introducing ARIMA. We then looked at the issue of stationarity before exploring autocorrelation and autoregression.

ARIMA is a powerful forecasting method but requires expert use with the assistance of specialist software.

Unit Summary

This unit has explored some of the main techniques available for the analysis and forecasting of time series. The methods considered were decomposition of a time series, non-centred moving averages, exponential smoothing and ARIMA.

We started by considering the likely components present in any time series. These were identified as trend (the long-run change in the average level of the series), cyclical fluctuations (resulting from the state of the economy), seasonal variation (periodic short-term fluctuations) and irregular changes (due to random factors). We then identified two approaches to modelling a time series: the additive model and the multiplicative model.

Next we looked at how a time series can be decomposed into its constituent parts if it exhibits both trend and seasonal components. We then showed how the trend can be estimated using a centred moving average and how separate forecasts can be prepared for trend and seasonality and the two either added (the additive model) or multiplied (the multiplicative model) to yield the final forecast.

Of course, a time series might not show a clear trend or exhibit a seasonal fluctuation. In such cases decomposition would clearly not be appropriate and other approaches need to be used. One such approach is through the use of non-centred moving averages.

We then introduced the notion of forecast error, a concept which can be interpreted in more than one way depending on the priorities of the forecaster. Another technique which can be used when there is no clear trend or seasonal fluctuation is exponential smoothing. This derives a current forecast using only the immediate past forecast and the related actual value of the variable in question. It takes as the forecast the prior forecast adjusted by some proportion of the prior forecast error. This is a remarkably straightforward procedure for forecasting a time series, yet is also extremely powerful. We showed that forecasts derived using exponential smoothing actually take into account all previous values of the variable, but with greater weighting attaching to those values occurring in the more recent past. Finally, we briefly investigated the more advanced time series analysis technique known as ARIMA.

Having explored these approaches to time series analysis and determined the situations in which they can be used, it is essential to remember that forecasting a series is not a purely mechanical process. You should never let your concern for technique overshadow the need for judgement.

References

Box, G and Jenkins, G (1976) *Time Series Analysis: Forecasting and Control*

Recommended Reading

Most textbooks in the area of operational research and management science include a discussion of time series analysis. However, they rarely include any consideration of advanced techniques such as the Holt-Winters approach to smoothing (which allows for trend and seasonality) and ARIMA.

Dennis, T L and Dennis, L B (1991) *Management Science*, West Publishing, Minneapolis, USA

Section 3 of Chapter 17 covers the same range of approaches to the analysis of time series as are dealt with in this unit.

Anderson, J, Sweeney, D R and Williams, T A (1994) *An Introduction to Management Science*, West Publishing, Minneapolis, USA

See Chapter 16 for a comprehensive discussion of the analysis of time series.

If you wish to explore the extension of exponential smoothing to incorporate trend and seasonality or to investigate ARIMA in more depth then you will need to turn to a specialist text in either business forecasting or time series analysis, such as the following.

Jarrett, J (1991) *Business Forecasting Methods*, Blackwell, Oxford

You would need to start with Part II on time series techniques and then move on to Part IV, which discusses some advanced topics in time series analysis, including ARIMA. Also in Part V, amongst other things, there is some consideration of the related topic of leading indicators.

UNIT 6
SIMULATION

Introduction

In this unit you will be learning about a management science tool which is different in concept to those discussed in earlier units. Most of the techniques you have encountered so far are **analytical** methods, which means that they use **deterministic** mathematical relationships to obtain **optimum** answers to problems. This unit will introduce you to **simulation** methods, in particular to the **Monte Carlo** approach.

In Section 1 we provide an introduction to the subject of simulation. In Section 2 we use a case study to apply the technique of simulation to some data. In Section 3 we look at ways of refining a simulation model. In Sections 4 and 5 we look at two types of simulation problem: scheduling problems and inventory problems respectively. In Section 6 we look in greater detail at the time element of scheduling problems and in Section 7 we briefly discuss some more sophisticated simulation models and some of the computer software which is available for them.

To complete this unit you will need a computer with *Microsoft Excel* (version 5.0 or later) and a pocket calculator capable of generating random numbers. You may also want to refer to the *Microsoft Excel* workbook files supplied in the software pack.

Objectives

After completing this unit you should be able to:

- list the stages of a typical simulation study
- identify the kinds of problems which might benefit from the use of simulation
- identify the important variables in a problem
- use probability distributions to model the behaviour of these variables
- implement a variety of simulation models using spreadsheets.

SECTION 1
What is Simulation?

Introduction

In this section we provide an introduction to the subject of simulation. We start by defining simulation and we then look at some different types of simulation. We go on to examine the basic elements of any simulation problem and to look at the different stages of a simulation study. By the end of this section you should be able to list the stages of a typical simulation study and identify the kinds of problems which might benefit from the use of simulation.

1.1 Defining simulation

This module has been concerned with the body of quantitative techniques collectively described as business decision analysis or BDA. This approach requires us to:

- state a mathematical relationship between certain variables
- form these relationships into a model of the situation
- identify some goal which we want to achieve
- use analytical methods to discover the optimum way to attain this goal.

Analytical techniques always involve searching for a particular solution, whether that solution is a maximum, a minimum, or some other form of optimum. There is a range of methods, tools and formulae to obtain exact solutions to these problems.

Unfortunately, many problems cannot be solved by analytical methods. The reason for this is because such methods require us to have a precise knowledge of the variables involved. Sometimes, it is not possible to decide which variables are important to a problem, and it may be even more difficult to quantify them. Luckily, simulation can be used to provide information where more formal methods may have failed.

We can begin by looking at a definition. In everyday language, 'to simulate' means:

> 'to feign: to have or assume a false appearance of: to mimic' (*Chambers English Dictionary* 7th Edn.).

According to this definition, simulation seems to be an activity we engage in every day of our lives:

- children play at games in which they invent a world that does not exist
- actors assume the role of fictional characters
- job applicants practise being interviewed in front of imaginary interviewers.

It is sometimes useful to build a model of reality and to see what happens to this model under various circumstances. We would be interested in asking questions such as 'if I changed such-and-such a variable, what would be the likely result?'. It is this need to ask 'what if' questions which makes simulation such a necessary human activity. We need a rather more technical approach to simulation than the one contained in the dictionary definition. One definition of 'simulation' is the following:

> '[Simulation is] a way of manipulating a model so that it yields a motion picture of reality' (Ackoff and Sassieni, 1968, p.6).

Simulation models, whether physical, such as a test mock-up of a jet airliner, or logical, such as a computer program, may be used to show how the model changes from one state to another. They show the flow of activities, and how these flows interact with each other. Putting this another way, the real benefit of simulation is that a number of different assumptions can be tried out by making only minor adjustments to the model. This will result in information being obtained about the likely result of a project before it has even started. The simulation approach can help with problems such as:

- how will a jet aircraft, presently at the design stage, respond to stress?
- in a hypermarket planned for an out-of-town shopping area, what would be the optimum number of checkout points to install?
- what would be the optimum number of petrol pumps to install in a new garage?
- what would be the likely flow of profit from a large capital project?
- how should a large manufacturing company choose between different methods of ordering and stocking large numbers of spare parts?

In all of these problems, it is always possible to try the 'wait and see' approach: that is, to actually take the decision and then observe the result. However, this may lead us to make costly errors if we do not get the decision right. There is little point, for example, in building a hypermarket with too few checkout points, and then finding out too late that we cannot adequately manage the flow of customers. What we need is some way of testing out various alternative models of hypermarket design before we actually commit ourselves to expensive decisions. Simulation provides a method for doing this.

SOME TYPES OF SIMULATION

Apart from the use of simulation in physical modelling, such as aircraft design and testing, there are three major areas where the technique is used in a business context.

Operational gaming: competitive business games are an example of this. Teams of participants manage hypothetical organisations in competition with each other. Such games are often used as realistic ways of training new staff.

Financial and corporate modelling: computer programs (such as spreadsheets) can be used to simulate the financial structure of a business.

The Monte Carlo method: this term is used as a way of describing many kinds of simulation. The name comes from the use of gaming devices, such as dice and roulette wheels, to simulate the chance inputs to, and outputs from, a business decision. Although a computer is used nowadays to generate random outcomes in preference to a roulette wheel, the Monte Carlo name has persisted. Monte Carlo methods will be used to simulate business situations in this unit.

1.2 Static and dynamic simulation models

Many types of simulation problem are static. In a static simulation there is no time element: each repetition of the sampling process is independent of the previous result.

Example of a static model: the new product

Consider the case of a business about to launch a new product. The product will sell for £10, but the information concerning costs and the behaviour of demand is sketchy. Unit cost could be any value between £4 and £7, with equal likelihood. Fixed cost could be any value between £2,000 and £3,000. Demand could be any number of units from 5,000 to 10,000 per period.

The firm would like some information about profits. For each simulation of profit we can use random numbers to obtain values for fixed cost, unit cost and demand within the given ranges. Using this method we can obtain many estimates for the profit and come to some conclusions regarding the most likely outcome. However, each run through this model is independent of the previous run, in the same way that each throw of a dice or spin of a roulette wheel is independent of the last one.

In many situations, the process is time dependent. Such problems are known as dynamic simulation problems.

EXAMPLE OF A DYNAMIC MODEL: INVENTORY CONTROL

Consider an inventory control problem in a manufacturing business. Firms often need to make decisions about the amounts of inventory to order and hold in stock using probabilistic data. We cannot always know what stocks are likely to be held at any one time because they are affected by demand, which is likely to be a random variable. The closing stock of one period becomes the opening stock of the next period, so what happens during the Tuesday shift is not independent of what has happened on Monday. We would need to consider the effect of changes in demand over time, and therefore would have to use dynamic methods.

Time dependent or dynamic simulation models are also referred to as **stochastic** models. We will consider an example of just such a model later in this unit.

ACTIVITY 1

Consider the following situation.

A transportation firm has a stock of containers which it is considering hiring to outside customers. It would like to have some information about the usage of this facility. For example, will demand for the containers exceed supply? The likely number of customers in any one day and the length of time they might want each container for is not known with certainty, but the firm has been able to obtain probability figures for these variables. Daily demand and usage is to be simulated.

Would simulation of the above require developing a static or a dynamic model? Write down the reasons for your answer.

This can only be modelled using a dynamic model, since the exact demand and supply position of containers can only be understood by reference to what happened on previous days. We need to know what was hired out previously, and for how long, in order to work out the effect of today's demand and supply.

1.3 The basic elements of simulation

In the following discussion, the term **iteration** is used to describe a single operation of a simulation model. For example, consider the 'new product' simulation mentioned above as an example of a static model. Each time we generate a single random set of cost and demand data and use it to calculate a profit figure, we perform an iteration of the model. The term **run** is used to describe a sample of iterations. Because a single iteration is unlikely to yield valuable results, it is usual to take a sufficiently large sample in a simulation run to establish if there is any pattern in the output data. It is also common practice to have several runs of a simulation model. If a fairly constant pattern emerges, we say the model has achieved a **steady state**.

DEFINING THE PROBLEM AND TESTING ASSUMPTIONS

Before conducting any kind of research, the analyst must define the nature of the problem and make some testable assumptions. Simulation is no exception. For example, in the new product example one of our assumptions might be that modest changes in the probability distributions of costs, prices and sales will not substantially alter the resulting profit distribution. Or, in another example, if we allow for one extra server in a cafeteria, we may assume that this will vastly reduce the probability of a customer having to queue. Whatever our assumptions, we must be able to test them in the resulting simulation run.

DECIDING THE PARAMETERS OF THE PROBLEM

Parameters are factors which stay fixed for the period of one simulation run at least. The analyst may wish to define something as a parameter if it is held to have a potential impact on the way the main variables interact. Parameters are held constant during a simulation run so that we may study this impact.

ACTIVITY 2

Look at the new product example mentioned earlier. Are there any aspects of this problem which you would describe as parameters?

The price of the product is to remain at £10 throughout the simulation and is therefore a parameter.

Care should be taken not to confuse a parameter with a mathematical constant. A **constant** is outside the control of the decision-maker whereas a parameter is within it. If we wished, we could always alter the value of the parameter for a **subsequent** simulation run and observe the impact this change makes. In other words, the parameter is fixed within each simulation run only. We could rerun the new product case with a new price of £12 and observe the impact of this change.

INPUT VARIABLES

Variables are entities which, unlike parameters, change during the course of an actual simulation run.

ACTIVITY 3

What are the factors which should be regarded as input variables in the new product example?

Variable factors in this example would be unit variable cost, demand and fixed cost.

Although there were only three variables in the new product example, simulation is flexible enough to allow for the addition of more variables on subsequent runs. In fact, it is generally a good idea to keep a model simple at first by defining only a very few key variables. You can always improve the realism of the model on subsequent runs by the addition of other variables.

ALGORITHMS

An algorithm is a step-by-step procedure for carrying out a task. In a simulation model, the analyst will have to provide such algorithms in the form of instructions to a computer. In the new product example, there was one algorithm which was used to combine demand, unit cost, price and fixed cost into a profit figure. This algorithm could be written as:

- generate random values for demand, unit cost and fixed cost
- multiply price by demand to obtain revenue
- multiply demand by unit cost to obtain total variable cost
- add total variable cost to fixed cost, obtaining all-cost total
- subtract all-cost total from revenue to obtain profit.

The necessity of such a detailed approach becomes evident when we realise that computers must have such instructions if they are to work successfully.

OUTPUT VARIABLES AND PERFORMANCE MEASURES

The output variables are the visible result from a run of the simulation. Usually they will be in the form of some kind of performance measure, which we have programmed the computer to output. In the case of the new product example, profit is the performance measure for the project, and forms the sole output of the simulation. However, it does not follow that this particular performance measure would be appropriate for another simulation model: the particular output variable(s) chosen would depend upon the subject of the analysis, and the interests of the analyst.

ACTIVITY 4

The following problems have been the subjects of simulation. For each problem area, state one possible **input** variable and one possible **output** performance measure that you think would be appropriate for a simulation run.

1. Air traffic control systems.

2. The scheduling of bank cashiers.

3. Location of distribution warehouses.

4. The planning of parking facilities.

5. Planning a computer network.

There will, of course, be more than one possible answer in each case.

Here are some possible suggestions.

1. It is likely that a study of an air traffic control system would be concerned with the efficiency with which incoming flights are stacked and processed through an orderly queuing system. Consequently, factors such as frequency of incoming flights, number of traffic control staff, number of runways and so on would be input variables.

   There is also a choice of output variables. Air traffic control would be interested in such output performance measures as waiting time, number of flights in the queue and so on.

2. Arrival rates of customers and number of bank cashiers would be two possible input variables.

   Better performance will mean lower waiting times and more rapid processing of queues. Customer waiting times and length of the queue would therefore be two possible output performance measures.

3. Number of customers and their geographical location, and the location of suppliers of the warehouses would be necessary input variables to a study of warehouse location.

   Better performance by a warehouse will involve swift processing of orders at lower costs. Therefore lead time, or the period from receipt of orders to delivery, is an important output performance measure.

4. Number of vehicles attempting to use the car park, capacity of car park and length of time parked would be among the input variables.

   The output performance measures would depend upon what the owners expected from the car park. For example, a commercial enterprise might put number of car-users accommodated and size of revenue as output measures. Other operators of car parks might be more interested in non-financial factors such as the amount of illegal parking, whether the car park played a role in encouraging visitors to a city and so on.

5. Although there may not appear to be much similarity between an air traffic control system and a computer network they do, in fact, have characteristics in common. There will be a stream of customers arriving to use the terminals linked to a network. Some users will have to wait in a queue while others will be lucky enough to obtain a machine immediately. Therefore, user arrival rates, number of machines available, average length of time a network runs before breakdown and so on are all important input variables.

   An efficient network will have to be able to deal with queues of users quickly and deliver fast processing speeds. Therefore, average wait time and processing speeds would be two possible output performance measures.

You should think about the similarities between these apparently different problem areas: good model building depends upon your skills in spotting such connections.

1.4 The stages of a simulation study

No two simulation studies will be alike. However, there are some stages which are common to all such investigations. These are listed here. Each one is then discussed in greater detail below.

1. Define the problem.
2. List the variables and parameters.
3. Construct the simulation model.
4. Assign initial values to variables and parameters.
5. Refine the model.
6. Conduct full analysis.
7. Present final results.

DEFINE THE PROBLEM

At the outset of the process, the analyst should be able to write a clear statement about the objectives of the exercise. This may seem an obvious point to make, but it is vital. Without it, the simulation model will lack clear aims.

LIST THE VARIABLES AND PARAMETERS

What are to be the variables? What performance measures do we wish to see as output? What elements will be parameters rather than variables? It does not necessarily matter if we do not include all possible variables and parameters at this stage, as extra variables and parameters can always be included in subsequent simulation runs.

CONSTRUCT THE SIMULATION MODEL

At this stage we state the relationships between variables and parameters: how do they interact with each other to produce the phenomena we are studying? A good simulation model should be a reasonable reflection of reality. The first model may often be simplistic but, by experimenting, the analyst can gradually refine it so that it becomes more realistic.

ASSIGN INITIAL VALUES TO VARIABLES AND PARAMETERS

We start the simulation run by giving starting valuations to variables and parameters. During the run the variables will change according to some random process, while the parameters will be set by us for the simulation run and will stay constant throughout it. For example, in the new product model, the price is a parameter under the control of the analyst and stays fixed throughout the run.

REFINE THE MODEL

A test simulation run is carried out and the results are analysed and compared with known data about the problem being modelled. As a result of this process, the model may be refined, altered or added to in various ways in order to make it more realistic. This process (which may need to be repeated several times) is known as model validation.

CONDUCT FULL ANALYSIS

Having made the model as sophisticated as we can during stage 5, we are now ready to generate the required final output. This will consist of deciding on a suitable number of iterations to be included in a simulation run, and conducting enough runs to achieve a steady state. The full analysis will consist of detailed output for each variable together with a statistical analysis of these results.

PRESENT FINAL RESULTS

The whole of this process is shown in the flow chart in Figure 1 (over page).

Summary

We started by defining simulation and looking at some different types of simulation. We then distinguished between static and dynamic simulation models. In Section 1.3 we introduced the basic elements of a simulation problem and in Section 1.4 we looked at the various stages of a simulation study.

In the next section we deal with the practical task of constructing working models of business situations.

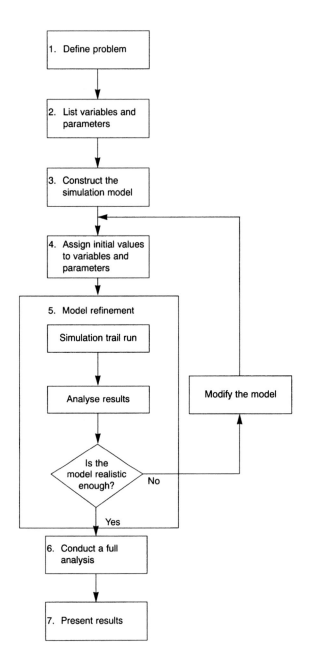

Figure 1: Stages in the simulation process

SECTION 2
The Technique of Simulation

Introduction

This section of the unit introduces the technique of simulation by using a case study. In Section 2.1 we introduce the elements of a simulation problem. In Section 2.2 we explore the problem by using what is known as the roulette wheel approach. In Section 2.3 we look at the data which we need to generate to solve the problem, and in Section 2.4 we look at how to use *Microsoft Excel* to generate this data. By the end of this section you should be able to identify the important variables in a problem and use probability distributions to model the behaviour of these variables.

2.1 The elements of the simulation problem

We start by introducing a case study.

Case Study: **Hertz Plastics plc**

Hertz Plastics plc is a company whose main product is a high impact moulding made especially for the packaging and transit of high value electronic components.

The current production level is 400,000 units per year, at a variable cost of £5 per unit. The market price is £10 per unit and is expected to remain at this level whatever new innovations are made. These figures enable us to calculate that the company earns the following annual contribution from this product (assuming that it can sell all it produces):

$$(\text{Price} - \text{Unit Cost}) \times \text{Production} = (10 - 5) \times 400,000$$

$$= £2,000,000$$

Hertz Plastics plc has the option of introducing a new process for injection moulding, which promises high potential returns but would involve a considerable (and risky) outlay of funds. Naturally, the company would like to have some information concerning the likely returns on the outlay before making a decision about this new process.

The company decides to use a measure called **return on investment** (we will call it ROI for short) to assess the worth of the new process. ROI (which is always expressed as a percentage) is calculated as follows:

$$\text{ROI} = \left\{ \frac{P_1 - P_2}{I} \right\} \times 100$$

where the symbols P_1, P_2 and I are defined as follows:

P_1 = profit and contribution to fixed costs from the **proposed** new process

P_2 = profit and contribution to fixed costs from the **present** process

I = investment cost of installing the new process

So if, for instance, the process were to cost £2,750,000 to install, and 475,000 units were to be produced per year at a variable cost of £4.50, the ROI would be:

$$ROI = \left\{ \frac{P_1 - P_2}{I} \right\} \times 100$$

$$= \left\{ \frac{\left[475,000 \times (10 - 4.5) \right] - \left[400,000 \times (10 - 5) \right]}{2,750,000} \right\} \times 100$$

$$= \left\{ \frac{(475,000 \times 5.5) - (400,000 \times 5)}{2,750,000} \right\} \times 100$$

$$= \frac{612,500}{2,750,000} \times 100$$

$$= 22.3\%$$

In other words, using the project cost as the base for the calculation, the new process would yield 22.3 per cent more than the present process.

Once we understand what the ROI is and we have some data for the main variables involved, it is a very simple matter to calculate it. To check that you understand what the ROI is, try the following activity.

ACTIVITY 5

What would be the ROI on this project if *Hertz Plastics plc* found that:

- it would cost £2,900,000 to install
- it had a production capacity of 480,000 units
- it had a unit cost of £4.50?

Assume that current prices are £10, that production is 400,000 and unit costs are £5.

The contribution from *Hertz Plastics plc*'s present system is £2,000,000 [400,000 × (10 − 5)].

Therefore:

$$ROI = \left\{ \frac{\left[480,000 \times (10 - 4.5) \right] - 2,000,000}{2,900,000} \right\} \times 100$$

$$= \left\{ \frac{(480,000 \times 5.5) - 2,000,000}{2,900,000} \right\} \times 100$$

$$= \frac{640,000}{2,900,000} \times 100$$

$$= 22.07\%$$

In passing, we should note that there are a number of possible ways of measuring the potential return from an investment: the ROI is one method among many. Also, we have chosen to simplify the problem slightly by not discounting the cash flows from the investment.

Unfortunately for *Hertz Plastics plc*, deciding whether or not to go ahead and invest in the new process will not be as easy as was implied by the answer to Activity 5. This is because the company accountants will not be able to predict with certainty what the variable costs and production quantity of the new process will be, and only have a sketchy idea of the amount they will need to spend in order to install it. However, the company is not completely in the dark. The company has available an estimate of the likely range of values for variable costs, production quantity and investment cost. These estimates are shown in Tables 1, 2 and 3.

Variable costs	Probability
£4.30	0.05
£4.40	0.15
£4.50	0.20
£4.60	0.20
£4.70	0.20
£4.80	0.10
£4.90	0.10

Table 1: Variable costs of new process

Hertz Plastics plc believes that the lowest possible value for variable cost is £4.30, and that there is a 5 per cent probability of this minimum occurring. At the other extreme, the company analysts believe a likely maximum for variable costs is £4.90 with a 10 per cent probability. The table also shows the probabilities of variable costs between these minimum and maximum values. These probabilities can only be estimates, as they are management's best guesses from their present knowledge of the situation.

Table 2 shows likely values for production capacity of the new process, and Table 3 shows estimates of final investment cost.

Production capacity	Probability
450,000	0.10
460,000	0.20
470,000	0.30
480,000	0.20
490,000	0.15
500,000	0.05

Table 2: Production capacity of the new process

Installation cost	Probability
£2,500,000	0.05
£2,600,000	0.10
£2,700,000	0.15
£2,800,000	0.30
£2,900,000	0.25
£3,000,000	0.15

Table 3: Investment cost of the new process

How can this data be used to give the company an indication of the likely return on its investment (ROI)? The next two activities will require you to make some calculations concerning the range of possibilities facing *Hertz Plastics plc.*

ACTIVITY 6

Use Tables 1, 2 and 3 to estimate the **minimum** possible ROI for this project.

If you carefully study the formula for calculating ROI, you should see that the minimum possible ROI will occur when unit cost and investment costs are at their highest, and production at its lowest. So we calculate ROI when unit cost is £4.90, investment cost is £3,000,000 and production is 450,000 units.

$$ROI = \left\{ \frac{\left[450,000 \times (10 - 4.9)\right] - 2,000,000}{3,000,000} \right\} \times 100$$

$$= 9.8\%$$

So it is possible that ROI might fall as low as 9.8 per cent.

ACTIVITY 7

Use the same tables to estimate the **maximum** possible ROI for this project.

The maximum possible value of ROI will be attained when unit and investment costs are at their lowest, and production at its highest (assuming that all production can be sold).

So we calculate ROI when variable cost is £4.30, investment cost is £2,500,000 and production is 500,000 units.

$$ROI = \left\{ \frac{\left[500,000 \times (10 - 4.3)\right] - 2,000,000}{2,500,000} \right\} \times 100$$

$$= 34\%$$

So it is possible for ROI to be as high as 34 per cent.

However, it is insufficient just to calculate ROI values. If we are to carry out any useful analysis at all, we must have some idea about how likely it is that these various ROI values will occur. How would we calculate the probability that *Hertz Plastics plc* will attain the maximum ROI?

We have already seen that ROI is at its maximum when project cost is £2,500,000, unit cost is £4.30 and production is 500,000 units. The probability that ROI will achieve this maximum figure is identical to the combined probability that investment cost is 2,500,000 **and** unit cost is £4.30 **and** production is 500,000 units. We can obtain this by multiplying the probabilities of these separate events together. (This is an example of the multiplication rule of probability.) So:

$$\text{Pr(ROI being at a minimum)} = 0.05 \times 0.05 \times 0.05$$

$$= 0.000125$$

So there is slightly more than a 1 in 10,000 chance of the project being fortunate enough to make the maximum possible ROI.

ACTIVITY 8

Using the same tables, what is the probability of the project obtaining the **minimum** possible ROI?

ROI is at its minimum when project cost is £3,000,000, unit cost is £4.90 and production is 450,000 units. Therefore:

$$\text{Pr(ROI being at a minimum)} = 0.15 \times 0.10 \times 0.10$$

$$= 0.0015$$

So there is a 15 in 10,000 chance of the project falling to its minimum ROI.

The answers to Activities 6, 7 and 8 have provided some useful information for the company. The company now has some idea of the maximum and minimum likely values for the ROI, together with the probabilities that these outside values will occur (always assuming that the data in Tables 1, 2 and 3 is accurate).

However, the activities were concerned only with the extreme cases of maximum and minimum ROI and their respective probabilities. As you have seen, there is only a very small probability of these extremes occurring. What about the range of possible returns within these extremes? It will clearly be useful to the company if it can calculate every possible ROI, along with its probabilities.

Suppose, for example, the company decides to set a performance target of 21 per cent for the ROI. *Hertz Plastics plc* needs to know the likelihood of achieving this before deciding whether or not to proceed with the project. What is the risk of the new process not attaining this target?

2.2 The roulette wheel approach

There are three variables in the *Hertz Plastics plc* problem, a situation which is complicated because they are **random** variables. The random element means that it is impossible to predict with certainty what particular values production quantity, unit cost and investment cost will take. However, if we have a knowledge of the underlying probability distribution for the random variable, then we can say how likely it is that certain specific values will occur. This is exactly the position we are in with the *Hertz Plastics plc* problem. We have an (estimated) probability distribution for each of the variables (investment cost, production quantity and unit cost). It would be very useful if we could somehow put these three variables together and produce a probability distribution for ROI. How can this be done?

In brief, the process of simulation consists of treating the decision like a game, which can be played again and again. The result of each game will be a particular value for ROI. What would be the long-term distribution of ROI obtained from playing the game a great many times? Of course, the decision whether or not to go ahead with the project is not a game: *Hertz Plastics plc* can only take the decision once. The company must then live with the consequences (good or bad) arising from that decision. Even so, there is everything to be gained by adopting the gambling approach to the problem, at least on paper.

The gambling approach to the problem implies that we:

- randomly select a value for each of the variables involved
- calculate the return on investment these values would produce
- keep repeating the first two stages of this process until sufficient ROI values have been obtained to establish a pattern.

This process is illustrated in Figure 2.

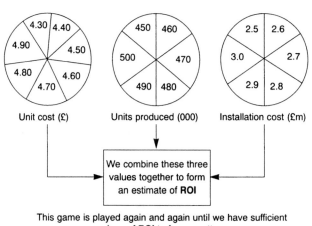

We first spin the roulette wheel, randomly obtaining a value for each of the three key variables

Unit cost (£)   Units produced (000)   Installation cost (£m)

We combine these three values together to form an estimate of **ROI**

This game is played again and again until we have sufficient values of **ROI** to form a pattern

Figure 2: The roulette wheel approach to the Hertz Plastics plc problem

For the sake of simplicity we will assume that the three variables involved in the *Hertz Plastics plc* case study are **discrete** variables. (A discrete variable is one which is restricted to certain values only, and is the opposite of a continuous variable which can take any value.) In the case of the *Hertz Plastics plc* data we will also assume that we are restricted to the values shown in Tables 1, 2 and 3 above.

Random samples are always expected to be representative so, if we are to take true random selections of each of the three main variables, we shall need to ensure that each value is sampled strictly in accordance with its probability. For example, consider the investment costs for the new process shown in Table 3. There is a 0.05

probability that these costs will be £2,500,000. We should therefore ensure that there is also a 0.05 chance that any random sampling procedure selects such a value. Similarly, there is a 0.30 probability that installation costs will be £2,800,000, so there should also be a 0.30 chance that we select this value. If we do not take such precautions, our game will not be a true reflection of *Hertz Plastics plc*'s real-life situation. Now look at Table 4.

Variable costs	Probability	Random number
£4.30	0.05	0 – 4
£4.40	0.15	5 – 19
£4.50	0.20	20 – 39
£4.60	0.20	40 – 59
£4.70	0.20	60 – 79
£4.80	0.10	80 – 89
£4.90	0.10	90 – 99

Table 4: Sampling table for variable costs

Apart from one additional feature, the table is identical to Table 1. The new feature is the final column headed 'Random number'. Each variable cost has been allocated a number range between 0 and 99 inclusive, and the size of this number range is determined by the probability of that particular cost occurring. For example, the variable cost £4.30 has a 0.05 probability of occurring. Accordingly, it has been given the number range 0 to 4 (inclusive). The range 0 to 4 has exactly five digits (0, 1, 2, 3 and 4 of the 100 possible).

Using the same approach, £4.40 has a 0.15 chance of occurring. This will result in it being given the number range 5 to 19, which contains exactly 15 digits. £4.50 occurs with a probability of 0.20, and so is allocated the number range 20 to 39, which has exactly 20 digits. This process continues until the whole table is numbered. On completion, all of the 100 digits from 0 to 99 will have been allocated to variable costs in proportion to the probability of that particular value of variable cost occurring.

ACTIVITY 9

You should now try this for yourself. Rewrite the probability tables for production capacity and investment cost. Add an extra column for random number using the process described above.

The probability tables for production and investment cost are shown as Tables 5 and 6.

Production capacity	Probability	Random number
450,000	0.10	0 – 9
460,000	0.20	10 – 29
470,000	0.30	30 – 59
480,000	0.20	60 – 79
490,000	0.15	80 – 94
500,000	0.05	95 – 99

Table 5: Probability table for production capacity

Installation cost	Probability	Random number
2,500,000	0.05	0 – 4
2,600,000	0.10	5 – 14
2,700,000	0.15	15 – 29
2,800,000	0.30	30 – 59
2,900,000	0.25	60 – 84
3,000,000	0.15	85 – 99

Table 6: Probability table for investment cost

As you will see later, when you are ready to use the computer you will need to write these tables in a way which is slightly different from the above.

2.3 Sampling the data

Now that we have produced random number tables for variable costs, production capacity and installation cost, what do we need to do next? If we wish to treat the *Hertz Plastics plc* problem as a repeatable game, then we must have a method for producing random numbers. For each round of the game we will require three random numbers with values between 0 and 99. Each of these three numbers will represent one of the three decision variables.

A random number generator is a process for producing, or generating, numbers where each of the digits 0 to 9 has an equal chance of appearing. The process of generating streams of random numbers is at the heart of simulation studies, so it is perhaps not surprising that analysts spend a great deal of time developing procedures to deliver satisfactory results.

Producing random numbers is not difficult to do, since all computer programs used in dealing with simulation problems have built-in random number generators. Many pocket calculators have a random number facility and, in the following analysis, the random numbers used have been obtained by this method. If you use your own calculator, remember that most produce a random number between 0 and 1. To handle the activities in this section, simply use the first two digits following the decimal point. So for example, if the calculator produces 0.39506281 in its display window, take this to be the number 39.

FIRST TRIAL RUN

For each iteration of the simulation model we shall generate three random numbers. The first of these numbers will be used to represent variable cost, the second to represent production capacity and the third to represent investment cost.

For the first round of the game, the numbers 47, 87 and 73 were obtained. Looking at the variable cost data in Table 4, you will see that the number 47 lies in the range 40 to 59, which is associated with the variable cost of £4.60. Likewise, examining Table 5 (the production capacity table), the number 87 lies in the range 80 to 94, corresponding to a production of 490,000 units. Finally, looking at Table 6 (the investment cost table), the number 73 lies in the range 60 to 84, which is associated with an installation cost of £2,900,000. These figures would produce an ROI of:

$$
\begin{aligned}
\text{ROI} &= \left\{ \frac{P_1 - P_2}{I} \right\} \times 100 \\
&= \left\{ \frac{\left[490,000 \times (10 - 4.6) \right] - \left[400,000 \times (10 - 5) \right]}{2,900,000} \right\} \times 100 \\
&= 22.3\%
\end{aligned}
$$

SECOND TRIAL RUN

The numbers 43, 19 and 80 were obtained. From Tables 4, 5 and 6, the numbers 43, 19 and 80 are associated with a variable cost of £4.60, a production capacity of 460,000 and an investment cost of £2,900,000. These figures would produce an ROI of:

$$
\begin{aligned}
\text{ROI} &= \left\{ \frac{\left[460,000 \times (10 - 4.6) \right] - \left[400,000 \times (10 - 5) \right]}{2,900,000} \right\} \times 100 \\
&= 16.7\%
\end{aligned}
$$

ACTIVITY 10

Now carry out a third trial run for yourself. Use a pocket calculator or other means to generate three random numbers.

Sample the variables in accordance with the numbers you have produced, and then calculate the resulting ROI.

Remember to calculate ROI according to the formula:

$$ROI = \left\{ \frac{P_1 - P_2}{I} \right\} \times 100$$

The exact value of ROI you obtain will be dependent on the random numbers you have sampled, but you can make a partial check on the validity of your arithmetic by making sure you obtain a result somewhere between the minimum and maximum possible ROI.

THE RESULTS

What have we obtained so far from the calculations just performed? Despite all our efforts, very little. All we have is just three different values for the ROI (the first and second trial runs, and the third trial run from Activity 10). We would have to carry out many more trial runs before the law of large numbers would allow us to identify patterns and trends. The process of carrying out run after run of the *Hertz Plastics plc* decision is a tedious chore which most of us would rather escape if we could. Fortunately, now that we know what is required, we can hand the process over to a computer, which is the ideal tool for carrying out thousands of repetitive operations. This has already been done with the *Hertz Plastics plc* data (see Table 7).

ROI (%)	Frequency
9.00 – 13.00	40
13.00 – 17.00	228
17.00 – 21.00	380
21.00 – 25.00	265
25.00 – 29.00	75
29.00 – 33.00	11
33.00 – 37.00	1
Total Number of Runs	1000

Table 7: 1,000 trial runs of the Hertz Plastics plc problem

Table 7 shows the results obtained from using *Microsoft Excel* to generate 1,000 trial runs, thereby obtaining 1,000 possible ROI results. The resulting values have been grouped into a frequency distribution so that any underlying pattern can be easily discerned. Figure 3 shows the distribution of the resulting ROI results as a bar chart.

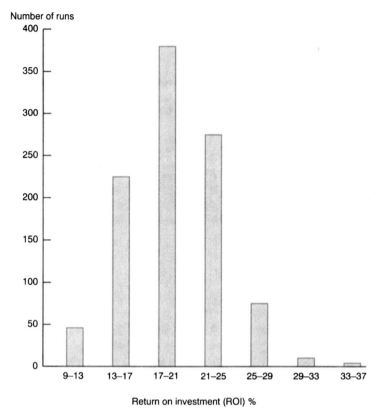

Figure 3: Bar chart of the Hertz Plastics plc simulation

Later on in this section you will have the opportunity to build the worksheet and produce this summary data yourself. However, it is useful to review the results obtained so far in order to gain some insight into what simulation can do. If we accept that 1,000 simulation trials or games is a sufficient basis on which to make conclusions, then what can we say about the project?

One way to proceed might be to calculate the mean of all the 1,000 ROI figures obtained in the *Microsoft Excel* simulation. For the 1,000 figures generated for this exercise, the mean (sometimes known as the expected value) was calculated by *Microsoft Excel* to be 19.6 per cent. It is also useful to have a measure of the variability of ROI as well as its average. For this we can use the standard deviation, which measures variability around the mean. In this case a standard deviation of 4.1 per cent was obtained using *Microsoft Excel*. Total lack of variation in the ROI figure would imply a standard deviation of 0.

How can we use these figures? To answer this, recall that *Hertz Plastics plc* needs to make an ROI of 21 per cent for the project to be viable. If we generated another 1,000 trial runs, we would be likely to obtain a different result because we would be using a different set of random numbers. The mean of 19.6 per cent should be treated like any other sample estimate: in other words, it may be subject to sampling error. Also, 19.6 per cent is the long-run average return which *Hertz Plastics plc* would receive if it had to continually make decisions such as this one. The actual return obtained could be above or below 19.6 per cent depending on chance.

Other things being equal, a larger standard deviation implies greater variability. In this case, we are concerned with the variability of return on investment, which is another way of talking about the degree of risk of an investment. So the standard deviation of a return can be used as a measure of risk. Of two investments with the same mean return, the one with the lower standard deviation is preferable, because it is the less risky of the two.

ACTIVITY 11

Study the results of the simulation of the problem in Table 7 above. Offer some advice to the company as to whether you think the project is worthwhile. What factors would you draw to the company's attention?

As in all cases involving sampling methods, the probabilistic nature of the results should be stressed. However, the simple expedient of treating the decision as a game has produced valuable information:

- we know that (based on this sample of 1,000) the expected return is 19.6 per cent, which is below the company's desired target of 21 per cent
- Table 7 tells us that there is a 64.8 per cent chance that the actual return achieved will be below target (21 per cent) and only a 35.2 per cent chance of the return being on target or better.

Whether the company thinks that these figures justify going ahead depends entirely on management's attitude towards risk.

If any of the estimates of variable costs, production capacity and installation costs change, all we need do is alter the probability distributions of Tables 1, 2 and 3 and repeat the simulation using a computer. This ability to rerun a model with new data makes simulation a very flexible technique.

2.4 Using *Microsoft Excel*

Before leaving the *Hertz Plastics plc* case, it will be useful to see how *Microsoft Excel* can be used to develop a simulation model. A spreadsheet such as *Microsoft Excel* can be used in many kinds of simulation models. A set of computer files is available with this study guide containing a number of workbooks, one of which (**Hertz1.xls**) was used in the analysis of the *Hertz Plastics plc* problem. Although you will be constructing your own spreadsheet for the *Hertz Plastics plc* model, you may wish to use this file for reference purposes, and to assist you during the process of model construction.

LAYOUT OF AN EXCEL WORKBOOK

A *Microsoft Excel* file can also be referred to as a workbook, and each of these workbooks may contain more than one worksheet. It is often a good idea to use these multiple worksheets as a way of organising your work. For example, one worksheet could contain the input data for a simulation, a second could contain the arithmetic workings and a third could contain the output. This procedure will be followed in the implementation of all of the simulation models in this unit. Consequently, each *Microsoft Excel* book will be divided into three connected worksheets.

Sheet1 will contain the probability data representing the random variables, together with the parameters (the data which does not change during a simulation run). In the *Hertz Plastics plc* file that you will construct, the tables of variable costs, production quantity and investment cost along with current price and cost data will appear on **Sheet1**. In the file **Hertz1.xls** supplied with this unit, this sheet has been renamed **Parameters**.

Sheet2 will contain the formulae, procedures, equations or algorithms used to make the repeated calculations required by a simulation. In the *Hertz Plastics plc* file that you will construct, the main procedure appearing on **Sheet2** will be that needed to calculate ROI. In the file **Hertz1.xls** this sheet has been renamed **Workings**.

Sheet3 will contain the output summing up all of the calculations made in **Sheet2**. In the *Hertz Plastics plc* file that you will construct, the summary will contain some statistics, such as the mean and standard deviation of ROI, a frequency distribution of ROI and a bar chart. In the file **Hertz1.xls** this sheet has been renamed **Output**.

Hertz Plastics

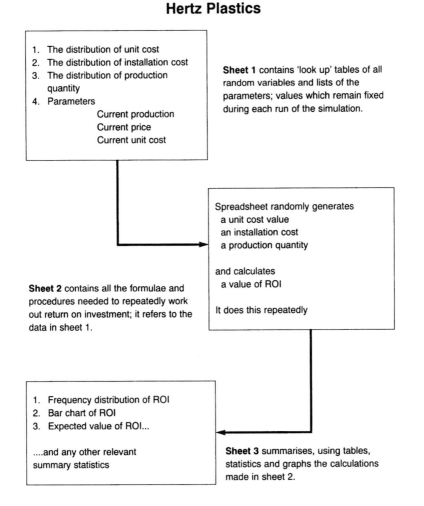

1. The distribution of unit cost
2. The distribution of installation cost
3. The distribution of production quantity
4. Parameters
    Current production
    Current price
    Current unit cost

Sheet 1 contains 'look up' tables of all random variables and lists of the parameters; values which remain fixed during each run of the simulation.

Spreadsheet randomly generates
    a unit cost value
    an installation cost
    a production quantity

and calculates
    a value of ROI

It does this repeatedly

Sheet 2 contains all the formulae and procedures needed to repeatedly work out return on investment; it refers to the data in sheet 1.

1. Frequency distribution of ROI
2. Bar chart of ROI
3. Expected value of ROI...

....and any other relevant summary statistics

Sheet 3 summarises, using tables, statistics and graphs the calculations made in sheet 2.

Figure 4: Structure of Microsoft Excel spreadsheets for Hertz Plastics plc

ENTERING THE INPUT PARAMETERS AND VARIABLES

We shall now illustrate the process of building a model to simulate the *Hertz Plastics plc* problem. As we have already said, we need to start this process by placing all of the input parameters and variables into one spreadsheet. This will have the advantage of organising our data in one place so that it can easily be found and changed if the need arises.

ACTIVITY 12

Open a new workbook in *Microsoft Excel*. You are going to enter the data relating to the input variables (unit cost, production and investment cost) and the fixed parameters (price) into a single worksheet in this new workbook and rename the sheet **Parameters**.

1. Enter the unit cost data first. You need to enter both unit cost and probability as shown in the table below.

	A	B	C	D	E	F	G	H
1	PARAMETERS AND LOOK-UP TABLES							
2								
3	Working and output tables are contained on the next two worksheets							
4								
5	(a) Look-up Tables							
6								
7	UNIT COST							
8	Cum Pr	Cost						
9								
10	0.00	4.30						
11	0.05	4.40						
12	0.20	4.50						
13	0.40	4.60						
14	0.60	4.70						
15	0.80	4.80						
16	0.90	4.90						

Notice that the probability figure is entered first in **cumulative** form ('Cum Pr' is an abbreviation for cumulative probability). For example, the probability of unit cost being below £4.30 is 0.00, so **0.00** will be entered alongside **4.30**. Likewise, the probability that unit cost will be less than £4.40 is 0.05, the probability that it will be less than £4.50 is 0.20, and so on. Notice that the probability column comes first.

2. Enter the production probability data into the cells D10 to E15 in the same way as the unit cost data (probability first, in cumulative form).

3. Enter the investment cost data into cells G10 to H15 in the same way as for unit cost and production.

4. Enter current price (**10**) into cell G22, current production (**400,000**) into cell G23 and current unit cost (**5**) into cell G24. In cell G25 enter a formula

which will enable *Microsoft Excel* to calculate the current contribution. Enter appropriate labels into cells A22, A23, A24 and A25.

5. Finally, change the name of the current worksheet from **Sheet1** to **Parameters**. You can do this by double clicking on the **Sheet1** tab at the bottom of the worksheet. Save your spreadsheet as **Plastic1.xls**.

Your worksheet should look as shown in Table 8.

	A	B	C	D	E	F	G	H
1	PARAMETERS AND LOOKUP TABLES							
2								
3	Working and output tables are contained on the next two worksheets							
4								
5	(a) Look-up Tables							
6								
7	UNIT COST			PRODUCTION			INVESTMENT COST	
8	Cum Pr	Cost		Cum Pr	Units		Cum Pr	Cost
9								
10	0.00	4.30		0.00	450000		0.00	2500000
11	0.05	4.40		0.10	460000		0.05	2600000
12	0.20	4.50		0.30	470000		0.15	2700000
13	0.40	4.60		0.60	480000		0.30	2800000
14	0.60	4.70		0.80	490000		0.60	2900000
15	0.80	4.80		0.95	500000		0.95	3000000
16	0.90	4.90						
17								
18								
19								
20	(b) Fixed Parameters – the following remains constant during a single run							
22	CURRENT PRICE						10	
23	CURRENT PRODUCTION						400000	
24	CURRENT UNIT COST						5	
25	THUS CURRENT CONTRIBUTION						2000000	

Table 8: Completed parameters worksheet for Hertz Plastics plc

The formula entered in cell G25 is =(G22–G24)*G23. This subtracts present unit cost from price and multiplies the result by present production. This produces the current contribution figure of £2,000,000.

You should notice that we have entered every single item of numerical data into the spreadsheet, even if we do not intend to vary it during the run of a simulation. This is always a good practice to follow, for if we ever need to change the data in the future it is possible to do so by altering a single cell in the worksheet. For example, if we need to rerun the simulation with a new price of £12, all we need to do is change the content of cell G22 from 10 to 12. This will automatically cause current contribution in cell G25 to be recalculated and also any other data based on it.

Titles and description of variables and parameters should be written into the parameters worksheet wherever possible, as this allows for easy alteration of data for subsequent simulation runs.

THE SIMULATION WORKSHEET

Now that we have written a parameters worksheet containing the input variables and parameters, we can proceed to construct the main part of the workbook, the sheet which calculates iterations of the model. For each iteration of the model this worksheet will be required to:

- generate random values for variable costs, production capacity and investment cost
- calculate the ROI that these randomly generated values would give rise to.

In order to achieve these aims we will need to use two important *Microsoft Excel* functions.

RAND: *Microsoft Excel* has a built-in function which produces a random number with a value between 0 and 1 (inclusive). To use this function, simply type in =RAND() (remember to include the empty brackets) and press the enter key. The random number will appear in the current cell.

VLOOKUP: the analyst often needs to design a worksheet which will look up a value in a table and then take appropriate action based on this value. For example, a business may offer a series of discounts based on quantity purchased. To calculate customer bills, a spreadsheet would need to multiply price by quantity purchased and then look up a list of quantities to find the appropriate discount offered. Such devices are known as look-up tables, and are useful in many applications. The *Microsoft Excel* command to use with a look-up table has the following syntax:

=VLOOKUP(value,table range,column number)

'Value' is the number that we wish to be checked, 'table range' is the range of cells on the spreadsheet where the table of data is stored, and 'column number' is the column in the table where the relevant information is to be found. So, for example, the following formula will cause *Microsoft Excel* to refer the number 16,000 to a table contained in cells C2 to G11:

=VLOOKUP(16000,C2:G11,2)

The first column of the table will be searched to see if it contains 16,000. If it does, the value in column 2 of the table immediately adjacent to 16,000 will be reported. If 16,000 does not exist, *Microsoft Excel* will stop at the lower number which is closest to it. It is therefore important to sort the first column of the table into ascending order.

These two *Microsoft Excel* functions can be used together in a simulation model. For example, look at Table 8, which shows the parameters worksheet for *Hertz Plastics plc,* and consider the *Microsoft Excel* statement:

=VLOOKUP(RAND(), A10:B16,2)

This statement will generate a random number (which will always be in the range 0 to 1) and then look it up in the first column of the unit cost table in cells A10 to B16. When it finds this value (or the one immediately below it), it will move to column 2 and return the value it finds there. For example, if the random number generated is 0.20, then *VLOOKUP* will search column 1 of the table. It will stop when it comes to 0.20 and return the value adjacent in column 2, which happens to be a unit cost of £4.50. To take a second example, if the random number generated is 0.82 then *VLOOKUP* will search column 1 of the table for this value. As there is no exact value of 0.82 in the table, the search will stop at the value immediately below, which happens to be 0.80. The unit cost immediately adjacent in column 2 – a unit cost of £4.80 – will be returned.

Taken together, the functions *VLOOKUP* and *RAND()* can be used to randomly sample the values contained in a table. This is just the kind of thing we wish to do in a simulation model.

ACTIVITY 13

1. Referring to the **Parameters** worksheet for the *Hertz Plastics plc* problem (see Table 8), write down *Microsoft Excel* statements using *VLOOKUP* and *RAND* to randomly sample:

   - production capacity
   - investment cost.

2. What will the production statement do if the random number generated is 0.36?

3. What will the investment cost statement do if the random number generated is 0.29?

---

1. The statement for production would be:

   VLOOKUP(RAND(),D10:E15,2)

   The statement for investment cost would be:

   VLOOKUP(RAND(),G10:H15,2)

2. If the production *LOOKUP* command generated the number 0.36, then column 1 of the table would be searched for this value. As 0.36 does not occur in the table, the search would cease at the value immediately below, 0.30, and return the value adjacent in column 2, which is 470,000.

3. If the investment cost *LOOKUP* command generated the number 0.29, then column 1 of the table would be searched for this value. As 0.29 does not occur, the search ceases at the value immediately below, 0.15, returning the value adjacent in column 2, an investment cost of £2,700,000.

Now that we have introduced the spreadsheet functions *RAND* and *VLOOKUP*, we can construct the part of the *Microsoft Excel* workbook which carries out the main simulation calculations.

ACTIVITY 14

1. Open your workbook **Plastic1.xls** which you constructed in Activity 12. In this activity you are going to design a second worksheet called **Workings** which will carry out 100 iterations of the *Hertz Plastics plc* simulation model.

   Change to **Sheet2** by clicking your mouse on the tab at the bottom of the screen. Leaving rows 1 to 4 of the sheet free for later notes and descriptions, use rows 5 and 6 for column headings. Row B should be entitled **Unit Cost**, row C **Production**, row D **Investment Cost**, row E **Contribution** and row G **ROI (%)**.

2. In B8 type the following formula:

   =VLOOKUP(RAND(),Parameters!$A$10:$B$16,2)

   This formula refers to the unit cost table on the **Parameters** worksheet. Notice that if you need to refer to another worksheet, you preface the range reference with the title of the sheet followed by a '!' symbol. Notice also the dollar signs in front of row and column. These make the cell references absolute, a necessary procedure, since we will later be copying this formula to other cells.

3. Enter formulae in C8 and D8 to sample the production and investment cost tables.

4. Type in a formula in E8 to calculate contribution using the data in cells B8 to D8.

5. Type in a formula in G8 to calculate the resulting ROI figure. Save your changes.

---

1. The resulting worksheet should look as shown in Table 9.

	A	B	C	D	E	F	G
1							
2	WORKINGS – SEE SHEET 3 FOR OUTPUT						
3							
4							
5		Unit	Production	Investment	Contribution		ROI (%)
6		Cost		Cost			
7							
8		4.3	470000	2600000	2679000		26.1

Table 9: Part of the worksheet used to calculate ROI for Hertz Plastics plc

2. The formula entered into cell B8 is:

=VLOOKUP(RAND(),Parameters!$A$10:$B$16,2)

This command assumes that you already have a sheet called **Parameters** containing a unit variable cost table with the data typed into cells A10 to B16. The command samples a value of unit cost from this table and places it into the current cell. Do not be puzzled if the value of unit cost in Table 9 is different from the one you obtain in your spreadsheet. Remember that the function *RAND* will generate a different random number every time it is used.

3. The formula you should type in cell C8 is:

=VLOOKUP(RAND(),Parameters!$D$10:$E$15,2)

This generates a random number and searches the production table in the **Parameters** sheet. The following formula, in cell D8, achieves the same effect for investment cost:

=VLOOKUP(RAND(),Parameters!$G$10:$H$15,2)

4. Contribution is obtained by calculating total revenue and then subtracting total variable cost. This is done in cell E8 by using the formula:

=(Parameters!$G$22–B8)*C8

Notice that this formula needs to refer to the parameters worksheet in order to obtain the price, hence the use of **Parameters!$G$22**. Currently the price is fixed at £10, but it would not be correct to type in the value **10** in this formula. Putting the price on the **Parameters** sheet and quoting it by cell reference allows us the opportunity to change it with a single keystroke if this should become necessary.

5. The formula in G8 needs to calculate the percentage ROI. We do this by subtracting the current contribution figure (found on the **Parameters** sheet) from the projected one and expressing the result as a percentage of the investment cost. We can do this by using the formula:

= (E8–Parameters!$G$25)*100/D8

In Activity 14 we began the task of simulating the *Hertz Plastics plc* decision. So far we have only carried out one iteration of the model. This is an insufficient basis for an analysis so we must now carry out a run of 100 iterations.

ACTIVITY 15

Open your workbook **Plastic1.xls** and refer to **Sheet2** containing the calculations made in Activity 14.

Copy the contents of cells B8 to G8 down to each row, up to and including row 107 of the sheet, so that you have 100 completed iterations of the model. Each row corresponds to an iteration of the model.

In column A, starting at A8, enter identification numbers, **1, 2, 3, 4** and so on, so that you have a unique reference code for each iteration. Rather than type in all the numbers 1 to 100 manually, use the **AutoFill** facility (or **Edit/Fill/Series**, if you are using *Excel 5*). Give column A the title **Iteration**. Finally, change the worksheet name from **Sheet2** to **Workings** and save your work.

The finished spreadsheet should look as in Table 10. The first ten iterations only are shown.

This activity has provided us with a great deal of information which we now need to organise in a meaningful way.

In Activity 15 we treated the *Hertz Plastics Plc* decision as a game, which we have played 100 times. We now need to summarise the results of the game and analyse what it tells us about the problem.

	A	B	C	D	E	F	G
1							
2	WORKINGS – SEE SHEET 3 FOR OUTPUT						
3							
4							
5	Iteration	Unit	Production	Investment	Contribution		ROI (%)
6		Cost		Cost			
7							
8	1	4.3	470000	2600000	2679000		26.1
9	2	4.5	490000	2800000	2695000		24.8
10	3	4.4	450000	2700000	2520000		19.3
11	4	4.4	470000	2600000	2632000		24.3
12	5	4.8	490000	2600000	2548000		21.1
13	6	4.4	470000	2600000	2632000		24.3
14	7	4.8	480000	2800000	2496000		17.7
15	8	4.8	450000	2900000	2340000		11.7
16	9	4.6	490000	2800000	2646000		23.1
17	10	4.7	490000	3000000	2597000		19.9

Table 10: Part of the Workings sheet for the Hertz Plastics plc model

ACTIVITY 16

In this activity you will construct a third worksheet which will summarise the results in the **Workings** sheet.

We need to estimate minimum and maximum ROI, and the average and standard deviation of ROI.

We will calculate them by using the following functions: *MIN, MAX, AVERAGE, MEDIAN* and *STDEV*. These calculate the **minimum** value in a range, the **maximum** value in a range, the **mean** value of a range, the **median** of a range and the **standard deviation** of a range, respectively.

Each function has the syntax **=FUNCTION(Range)**. The ROI values are contained in cells G8 to G107 of the **Workings** sheet, so for this activity the range will be **(Workings!G8:G107)**. So to calculate the minimum value, you would enter the formula **=MIN(Workings!G8:G107)**.

Open the file **Plastic1.xls** and select **Sheet3** by clicking on the tab at the bottom of the screen. In cell A4 enter the label **Output Statistics**. In cells A6 to A10 enter the labels **Minimum ROI, Maximum ROI, Mean ROI, Median ROI** and **Std Dev**

ROI respectively.

In cell B6 enter the formula =MIN(Workings!G8:G107) to calculate the minimum value for the ROI.

In cells B7 to B10 enter appropriate formulae to calculate the maximum value, the mean value, the median value and the standard deviation respectively.

Hertz Plastics plc has decided that a ROI of 21 per cent or more is viable. We therefore need to know the proportion of ROI figures which are below 21 per cent. We can use the function *PERCENTRANK* to calculate this. The syntax of this function is =PERCENTRANK(range,value) where value is the number whose rank we wish to establish.

In this case, we wish to establish the rank of the viable ROI of 21 per cent, so we would enter the following formula:

=PERCENTRANK(Workings!G8:G107,21)

Enter this formula in cell B12 and enter the label **Below 21%** in cell A12. Rename **Sheet3** as **Output** and save your work.

The **Output** sheet should look as shown in Table 11.

	A	B
1		
2		
3		
4	Output Statistics	
5		
6	Minimum ROI	10.54
7	Maximum ROI	28.33
8	Mean ROI	19.80
9	Median ROI	19.56
10	Std Dev ROI	4.27
11		
12	Below 21%	0.62

Table 11: Output Statistics for Hertz Plastics plc

Remember that the random element in a simulation will mean that the figures shown in Table 11 are the results of one run of 100 iterations only. The figures obtained in your own spreadsheet will be different.

We now have a considerable amount of data about the impact of the decision to be taken by *Hertz Plastics plc*. We can estimate that the ROI will be somewhere in the range 10.5 to 28.3 per cent. The expected (or average) value will be around 19.8 per cent. There is a probability of 0.62 of the return being less than 21 per cent. There is even more information to be obtained from this model, so we will be returning to it in the next section.

Summary

In this section we have used a case study of *Hertz Plastics plc* to introduce the elements of a simulation problem. We then used the roulette wheel approach to assign probabilities to each of the variables in the problem. In Section 2.3 we developed a model to simulate the behaviour of ROI and we generated some of the random data needed to solve the problem. Finally, in Section 2.4, we looked at how to use *Microsoft Excel* to generate sufficient quantities of random data to provide the basis of a more accurate solution to the problem.

In the next section we will look at some ways of refining the simulation model.

SECTION 3

Refining the Simulation Model

Introduction

In the last section we developed a model to simulate a capital investment decision about to be taken by *Hertz Plastics plc*. In this section we will continue analysing this model. In Section 3.1 we will obtain repeat runs from the model in order to determine the existence of a **steady state**. In Section 3.2 we will obtain further output from a simulation run in the form of frequency distributions of results. In Section 3.3 we use 'what if' analysis to show how the parameters of a model can be varied and the resulting output checked to study the effect of this variation. Finally, in Section 3.4, we introduce the *Microsoft Excel* function *RANDBETWEEN* and the use of the logic functions as a means of creating more sophisticated simulation models.

3.1 Obtaining more runs from the simulation model

In Section 2 we examined the output obtained from a single run of the *Hertz Plastics plc* model. In reality, the analysts would not restrict themselves in this way. Instead, they would run the simulation model many times. Every time we run the simulation model we are retaking the decision. The purpose of obtaining output from several runs of a simulation model has two main purposes:

- more data means we can make the estimates we want with greater accuracy

- if the model produces output which varies little from one run to another, then we can have confidence in our results (in technical terms, if the output is like this then we say that the model has reached a **steady state**).

USING MICROSOFT EXCEL FOR REPEAT RUNS

You may already have noticed that each time you change a formula or some data in a *Microsoft Excel* worksheet, all of the cells dependent upon this change will be automatically recalculated. This is the default setting for *Microsoft Excel* and it is usually best to leave it like this. However, in a large complex workbook, such as a simulation model, constant recalculation can be something of a nuisance. This is because *RAND* is a formula and every time you make a change to the sheet, all of the random numbers are recalculated. You can, if you wish, switch off automatic recalculation. To do this click on the **Tools** menu and choose **Options**. When the **Options** dialogue box appears, click on the **Calculation** tab. Under the heading **Calculation** you will be offered the options **Automatic, Automatic except tables** and **Manual**. As already mentioned, *Microsoft Excel* is by default set to automatic recalculation. If you wish to switch this feature off then click on **Manual** and then click on **OK**. The result of this is that the worksheet remains static whilst you are working on it. You can always turn automatic recalculation back on when you have completed the model.

In the meantime, you can use the **F9** key to make *Microsoft Excel* recalculate every formula in the worksheet (and connected worksheets). This is useful if:

- you have switched on to manual calculation and want to see the effect of a changed formula
- you wish to obtain another run of the simulation model.

We will now explore this facility.

ACTIVITY 17

Open your workbook **Plastic1.xls**, which should now consist of three linked worksheets: **Parameters**, **Workings** and **Output**.

1. Switch to the **Output** sheet. Press the **F9** key once. What do you notice?

2. Now press the **F9** key ten times. After each recalculation note down the value of the mean ROI.

3. Examine the results. Do you see any evidence of a steady state emerging?

---

1. You have probably noticed that all of the formulae used on the **Output** sheet automatically change. This is because they are being recalculated, as is every other formula in the workbook. Therefore, those formulae which use random numbers or any cells which are linked to such formulae will change. In a simulation model the **F9** key can therefore be regarded as the rerun key. It will work whether or not you have disabled automatic recalculation.

2. Remember that a simulation model depends upon random numbers, so that every time you press the **F9** key you obtain a different result. The following ten values of mean ROI were obtained after ten presses of the **F9** key.

    19.6, 20.0, 19.6, 19.0, 20.3, 20.0, 20.3, 19.2, 19.3, 20.0

    These numbers have been rounded to one decimal place. You will, of course, obtain different numbers from these.

3. The above results could be regarded as displaying a steady state. The lowest value obtained is 19.2 and the highest 20.3. The results appear to be converging on a value for the mean ROI in the region of 19 to 20 per cent. Carrying out more runs of the model would allow us to confirm this steady state and obtain a more precise estimate of mean ROI.

The result of Activity 17 has shown that rerunning a simulation model is a simple matter.

3.2 Frequency distributions

Statistics such as the mean, the median, the maximum, the minimum and the standard deviation can summarise important aspects of the factors being studied. In addition, it is useful to examine a frequency distribution of a factor such as ROI, since this will show us how variable it is. It would help us to decide whether ROI is highly volatile or very stable. A bar chart to accompany the frequency distribution is a valuable visual indication of this changeability.

If you need to refresh your memory about the nature of a frequency distribution then take another look at Table 7 in Section 2. This was constructed following a run with 1,000 iterations of the *Hertz Plastics plc* model. It states how many times the ROI fell within a given range or class interval. For example, we can see from Table 7, that ROI was between 13 and 17 per cent on 228 occasions. (A bar chart of the frequency distribution of ROI is shown in Figure 3 in Section 2 of this unit.)

There are several ways to obtain frequency distributions of results in *Microsoft Excel*, but the best results are obtained by using the *FREQUENCY* command. The syntax of this command is:

=FREQUENCY(data range,bin range)

'Data range' refers to the cells which contain the variable you wish to be placed in the frequency distribution. 'Bin range' refers to the class intervals into which the variable is to be counted. You need to be aware that *Microsoft Excel* uses the type of frequency distribution where the upper end of the class interval is inclusive. This means that, in a *Microsoft Excel* worksheet, it is only necessary to enter the top end of each class interval for the frequency command to work. For example, rather than enter **15 – 20, 20 – 25, 25 – 30** and so on, one enters **20, 25, 30** and so on. The next activity will help you gain experience with this function.

ACTIVITY 18

Open your workbook **Plastic1.xls**. You are going to construct a frequency distribution and a bar chart of the ROI results and place them on the **Output** sheet.

1. On the **Output** sheet of your spreadsheet type in the values **5, 10, 15, 20, 25, 30, 35, 40** into the cells D9 to D16. This column will represent the ROI classes 'up to 5', 'over 5 and up to 10', 'over 10 and up to 15' and so on. We established in Section 2.1 that the minimum and maximum ROI possible were 9.8 per cent and 34 per cent respectively, so this is sufficient to cover all possibilities and allow for expansion if necessary. Give this column the title **ROI%** in cell D8. The next column, cells E9 to E16, will contain the frequency count, so give this column the title **Frequency** in cell E8.

2. You are now about to enter the *FREQUENCY* command. The frequency command belongs to a special class of *Microsoft Excel* functions, known as array functions, which need to be entered in a special way. To enter the *FREQUENCY* function, follow these steps.

   - Select the cells E9 to E16 by holding the left mouse button down and dragging the mouse downward.

   - With the cells selected in this way, type in the command:

     =FREQUENCY(Workings!G8:G107,D9:D15)

     Do not press the **Enter** key yet. This command will count up the ROI values in cells G8 to G107 of your **Workings** sheet and place the results of the count next to the classes placed in cells G8 to G107.

- Now enter the command by jointly pressing the keys **Ctrl**, **Shift** and **Enter**. To do this press **Ctrl** first, hold it down and then press **Shift** and hold it down. Finally, with both the **Ctrl** and **Shift** keys held down, press **Enter**.

  Because of the rather unusual manner of entering array functions, such as *FREQUENCY*, you may make a few initial mistakes. The usual mistake made is to forget the proper key sequence of **Ctrl**, then **Shift**, then **Enter**. If this happens, just reselect the cells and start again. You should see a count appear in cells E9 to E16 which represents the frequency distribution of possible ROI results.

3. On a blank part of the **Output** sheet use *Microsoft Excel* to draw a bar chart of this frequency distribution. The ROI column will be the X-axis and the frequency will be the Y-axis. Save your changes.

---

1. The situation after entering the classes or **bins** is shown in Table 12.

	A	B	C	D	E
1					
2					
3					
4	Output Statistics				
5					
6	Min	11.33			
7	Max	28.32			
8	Mean	19.72		ROI	Frequency
9	Median	19.21		5	
10	Std Dvn	3.95		10	
11				15	
12	Below 21%	0.62		20	
13				25	
14				30	
15				35	
16				40	

Table 12: Setting up a Table for a Frequency Count

The class values, or bins, are entered into the table. They do not need to be of equal intervals but the table is easier to understand if they are. The classes chosen should cover a sufficient range to include all possible output values.

2. After selecting the cells for the frequency count and typing in the frequency command (but not entering it) the spreadsheet should look as in Table 13. The *FREQUENCY* command appears in the first cell of the frequency column as you type.

	A	B	C	D	E	F
1						
2						
3						
4	Output Statistics					
5						
6	Min	11.33				
7	Max	28.32				
8	Mean	19.72		ROI	Frequency	
9	Median	19.21		5	=FREQUENCY(Workings! G8 :G107,D9:D16)	
10	Std Dvn	3.95		10		
11				15		
12	Below 21%	0.62		20		
13				25		
14				30		
15				35		
16				40		

Table 13: Using the Frequency command

3. The **Ctrl + Shift + Enter** key sequence is now entered and *Microsoft Excel* begins a frequency count and enters it into the selected area as shown in Table 14. Remember that the random element of simulation means that you will have a result similar to that in Table 14, but not exactly the same.

	A	B	C	D	E
1					
2					
3					
4	Output Statistics				
5					
6	Min	11.33			
7	Max	28.32			
8	Mean	19.72		ROI	Frequency
9	Median	19.21		5	0
10	Std Dvn	3.95		10	0
11				15	12
12	Below 21%	0.62		20	43
13				25	37
14				30	8
15				35	0
16				40	0

Table 14: The final result of a frequency count

4. A graph of the frequency data is shown in Figure 5.

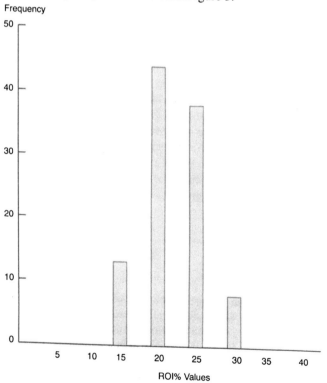

Figure 5: Bar chart showing result of simulation

By using simulation we have been able to obtain a considerable amount of information about the likely outcome of the *Hertz Plastics plc* decision. We know that there is something in the region of a 60 to 70 per cent chance of the ROI being less than the required 21 per cent. The frequency distribution has also given us a fairly clear idea about the degree of variation in the likely result. It should be remembered that a simulation study cannot prove that a given outcome will, or will not, occur: the results merely give the probabilities of various outcomes, and we must therefore base any decision on likelihood rather than certainty. Nevertheless, the information generated by simulation is often of a high quality.

3.3 Altering the model

One of the aspects of simulation which makes it such a useful technique is the flexibility it offers. BDA techniques must be judged on the degree to which they allow us to conduct sensitivity or 'what if' analysis. The difference between 'what if' analysis and sensitivity analysis is usually a matter of degree. 'What if' analysis consists of a general investigation of the way in which the output of a model changes given modifications of any of the inputs. Sensitivity analysis has a similar meaning but is usually concerned with the most sensitive variables only; the ones where slight changes are all that is necessary to cause major changes in the output of a model. Whichever of these activities we are interested in, simulation offers us a useful way of obtaining information.

ALTERING PARAMETERS

As an example of this kind of analysis in combination with simulation, consider the example of *Hertz Plastics plc*. We have already constructed a simulation model which explores the current situation. Suppose, however, that this situation has altered. For example, we constructed the initial model on the assumption that the unit price of £10 would persist. Let us now assume that there is some flexibility here, and that we can raise the price to £12 without serious risk to demand. What would be the effect on ROI of the new price? Clearly it would raise the return from the project, but by how much? This is where the flexibility of a simulation model is helpful. In your workbook for this model you will have entered price as a parameter in the **Parameters** worksheet. It should be possible to make one simple alteration to the model to see the result of the price change.

ACTIVITY 19

Open your workbook **Plastic1.xls**.

On the **Parameters** sheet, change the current price from £10 to £12. You should not need to change it anywhere else as all other formulae should be linked to this one cell. *Microsoft Excel* will automatically recalculate the output if automatic recalculation is switched on. If you have switched automatic recalculation off you will need to press the **F9** key.

What do you notice about the effect of the price change?

Current price is contained in cell G22 of the model. All you need do is alter this from **10** to **12**. There is no need to make any further changes since whenever price is needed, reference is made to this cell. The workbook is fully dynamic across all sheets.

Selected output is shown in Table 15. Remember that the random element means that your own results will be similar, but not identical, to these.

Notice that the price rise has had the effect of raising the expected (mean) ROI to almost 25 per cent. Much more important, the probability of obtaining a return less than the target 21 per cent has now fallen to 0.1. We would, of course, have to rerun the simulation several times to check for the existence of a steady state, but this could easily be done.

	A	B	C	D	E
1					
2					
3					
4	Output Statistics				
5					
6	Min	13.17			
7	Max	38.92			
8	Mean	24.82		ROI	Frequency
9	Median	25.00		5	0
10	Std Dvn	4.55		10	0
11				15	2
12	Below 21	0.1		20	12
13				25	38
14				30	37
15				35	10
16				40	1

Table 15: Rerun of the Hertz Plastics plc model with new price of £12

ADDING OR CHANGING VARIABLES

In the above example we demonstrated the ease with which parameters can be changed in a simulation model. Remember that parameters stay fixed for a single run of the model while variables may change, subject to chance. We may wish to modify the variables used in a simulation model because circumstances have changed. It may also be the case that we wish to add entirely new variables to the model. This latter circumstance usually occurs as a result of a gradual process of making the model more sophisticated.

As an example of the manipulation of new variables, we will return to the *Hertz Plastics plc* model. In our initial model we have assumed that price is a parameter: that is, that it stays fixed during a simulation run. This amounts to an assumption that the price is entirely within the control of the business. This is not always the case, since changing levels of supply and demand must have some effect on price. In response to this, let us suppose that the company's management has thought long and hard about price and is able to suggest likelihoods for various future price levels. The results of their deliberations about price are shown in Table 16.

Price	Probability
£8	0.10
£9	0.30
£10	0.40
£11	0.15
£12	0.05

Table 16: Probabilities of future prices

We are now faced with a situation where we must change future price from a parameter to a variable.

ACTIVITY 20

Open your workbook **Plastic1.xls**. You are going to modify this to allow for the new future price variable. Assume that current price is still £10.

1. Select the **Parameters** worksheet. In cells A19 to B26 enter the new price data as a look-up table. Remember that you need to have the cumulative probability as column 1 and price as column 2.

2. Select the **Workings** sheet. You have to alter this sheet in order to allow for the new variable. Firstly, insert a new column between 'Investment Cost' and 'Contribution'. Give this column the title **Price**. Enter a formula using *RAND* and *LOOKUP* which samples from your price table in the **Parameters** sheet.

3. Rewrite the formula in the 'Contribution' column to allow for the new price variable.

4. Select the **Output** sheet. Under most circumstances, *Microsoft Excel* automatically adjusts formulae to allow for movement of data, new columns and rows and so on, so you should not need to alter your entries for minimum, maximum, mean and so on. Nevertheless, you should check to make sure that the cell references are still correct.

You will need to adjust the frequency table class intervals as ROI has now become much more variable. Delete the old frequency table. Use the new minimum and maximum values as your guide to the range of values to be covered. We suggest that you type in new values in the ROI column starting at –20, and going up in steps of 10 until you have reached 60. You will then need to rerun the *FREQUENCY* command.

Delete the old bar chart and construct a new one showing the new distribution of ROI. Save the new workbook as **Plastic2.xls**.

---

1. The new **Parameters** sheet should look as in Table 17.

	A	B	C	D	E	F	G	H
1	PARAMETERS AND LOOKUP TABLES							
2								
3								
4								
5	(a) Look-up Tables							
6								
7	UNIT COST			PRODUCTION			INVESTMENT COST	
8	Cum Pr	Cost		Cum Pr	Units		Cum Pr	Cost
9								
10	0.00	4.30		0.00	450000		0.00	2500000
11	0.05	4.40		0.10	460000		0.05	2600000
12	0.20	4.50		0.30	470000		0.15	2700000
13	0.40	4.60		0.60	480000		0.30	2800000
14	0.60	4.70		0.80	490000		0.60	2900000
15	0.80	4.80		0.95	500000		0.85	3000000
16	0.90	4.90						
18								
19	PRICE							
20	Cum Pr	Price						
21								
22	0.00	8						
23	0.10	9						
24	0.40	10						
25	0.80	11						
26	0.95	12						
27								
28	(b) Parameters							
29								
30	CURRENT PRICE						10	
31	CURRENT PRODUCTION						400000	
32	CURRENT UNIT COST						5	
33	THUS CURRENT CONTRIBUTION						2000000	

Table 17: Amended Parameters worksheet for Hertz Plastics plc

The actual design of the worksheet is a matter of choice, so you might have made a different but equally valid arrangement. What is of importance is that the new lookup table for price should be typed in as shown.

2. The **Workings** sheet should be laid out in a similar way to Table 18.

	A	B	C	D	E	F	G	H
1								
2								
3								
4								
5	Iteration	Unit	Production	Investment				
6		Cost		Cost	Price	Contribution		ROI%
7	1	4.6	470000	2600000	8	1598000		−15.46
8	2	4.6	490000	2900000	8	1666000		−11.52
9	3	4.8	470000	2800000	10	2444000		15.86
10	4	4.6	460000	3000000	11	2944000		31.47

Table 18: The first ten rows of the amended
Workings sheet for Hertz Plastics plc

A new column has been inserted between 'Investment Cost' and 'Contribution'. This column exists for the purpose of sampling price values. The formula entered into cell E8 is:

=VLOOKUP(RAND(),Parameters!$A$22:$B$26,2)

This takes a random number, looks up the prices table in A22 to B26 of the **Parameters** sheet and reads off the price in column 2 adjacent to the random number.

3. The formula to calculate contribution now needs to use this random number. The formula entered into cell F8 is now **=(E8–B8)*C8**. This subtracts the unit cost from price and multiplies it by the number of production units.

While amending the **Workings** sheet, you will notice that:

- ROI now covers a much wider range of values
- ROI can now be negative, meaning that the new equipment is less profitable than the current arrangements.

4. The new **Output** sheet is shown in Table 19. We have not shown the bar chart.

	A	B	C	D	E	F
1						
2						
3	Summary output				Distribution	
4						
5	Minimum ROI		−17.85		ROI %	Frequency
6	Maximum ROI		66.00		−20.00	0
7	Mean ROI		16.08		−10.00	13
8	Median ROI		17.32		0.00	7
9	Std Dvn ROI		19.27		10.00	18
10					20.00	25
11					30.00	15
12	Below 21%		0.67		40.00	10
13					50.00	6
14					60.00	4

Table 19: Amended Output sheet for Hertz Plastics plc

Notice the frequency table, amended so as to take account of the new wider range of possibilities for ROI. The formula typed into cell F6 is:

=FREQUENCY(Workings!H8:H107,E6:E14)

This is entered in the usual way as an array formula (see Activity 18 for a description of how to enter this formula).

Notice that ROI has become inherently more unstable. The mean ROI is now 16.08 per cent. This is lower than in the previous case where price was a fixed parameter of £10, but not markedly so. The probability of ROI being less than the target figure of 21 per cent is still around 0.67. However, the really significant change is that the standard deviation of ROI has increased dramatically to 19.27, which means that it has become much more variable. This is confirmed by the frequency table, which shows that there are 20 iterations showing a negative ROI. We could use this to argue that there is a 0.2 probability of a negative return. However, at the other end of the scale it should be pointed out that there are 20 iterations with high returns above 30 per cent.

This is therefore a risky project: there are good chances of a very high return (above 30 per cent) combined with a considerable risk of the project making a loss. It would be a managerial decision to weigh up these risks and decide what decision to take.

3.4 The *RANDBETWEEN* function

We will now consider a new problem which will give you extra practice in modelling skills and introduce you to a new *Microsoft Excel* function, *RANDBETWEEN*.

Case Study: Arthur's Tilers

Arthur's Tilers is a builders' merchants which is considering marketing a new roofing tile. The tiles will be sold in lots of 1,000 at a suggested price of £255 per lot. The number of lots sold, the unit cost per lot and the fixed costs will change from week to week. However, the minimum and maximum values for each of these variables is known with some degree of precision as shown in Table 20.

	Minimum	Maximum
Unit cost (per lot)	£155	£195
Fixed cost (weekly)	£5250	£5950
Weekly sales (in lots)	88	132

Table 20: Unit costs, fixed costs and weekly sales

Costs and sales are both thought likely to follow a uniform probability distribution, rounded to the nearest whole pound or lot. A uniform distribution means that all values of the variable occur with equal likelihood. For example, the sales quantities 88, 89, 90, 91 and so on up to and including 132 have the same probability of occurring.

ACTIVITY 21

It has been decided to carry out a study of the cash flow from this new product by simulating 100 weeks of trading.

1. What would be the input variables for such a simulation model?

2. What would be the parameters?

3. What would you suggest as useful output variables for this model?

---

1. Remember that input variables are the factors in a simulation study which vary randomly while the model is running. In *Arthur's Tilers* case, sales, fixed costs and unit costs vary by the week.

2. Parameters stay constant during a single run of the model. Price comes into this category as it stays fixed at £255. Less obvious parameters are the maximum and minimum values of sales and costs for, although the exact

values of these variables changes with each iteration, the variation always occurs within fixed limits.

3. Since we are interested in cash flow, total costs and revenues and profits would be essential output variables. Profits would be the most important output.

Having now decided on the required inputs and outputs for the *Arthur's Tilers* model, we can build a *Microsoft Excel* spreadsheet to implement it.

Note: the software pack which comes with this study guide has a file called **Tilesim.xls** which is a *Microsoft Excel* spreadsheet implementing this model.

ACTIVITY 22

Open a new workbook. Enter the minimum and maximum of fixed cost in cells B6 and C6 respectively. Enter minimum and maximum of unit cost in cells B7 and C7. Likewise, enter the minimum and maximum sales figures in cells B8 and C8. Finally, enter the price of **255** in cell B10.

Give your spreadsheet an appropriate title in cell A1. Type in the labels **Min** and **Max** in cells B5 and C5. Type in the labels **Fixed Cost**, **Unit Cost** and **Sales** in cells A6 to A8. Type in the label **Price** in cell A10.

Rename **Sheet1** as **Parameters** and save it as **Arthur.xls**.

The **Parameters** worksheet should look similar to the one in Table 21.

	A	B	C	D	E	F
1	ARTHUR'S TILERS: PARAMETERS					
2						
3						
4						
5		MIN	MAX			
6	Fixed Cost	5250	5950			
7	Unit Cost	155	195			
8	Sales	88	132			
9						
10	Price	255				

Table 21: Parameters sheet for Arthur's Tilers

As always with spreadsheet model building, the emphasis should be on making the workbook dynamic. Entering every input in just one place on the **Parameters** sheet has the added benefit that we only need to alter one cell if we need to update a value. You may perhaps be puzzled by the fact that no look-up tables appear in Table 21. They are not needed in this case, because we know that each of the variables has a uniform distribution (in other words, each value has an equal probability of occurring).

Having constructed the **Parameters** sheet for *Arthur's Tilers*, we can now go on to construct the **Workings** and **Output** sheets. In order to do this, you will need to have a method for randomly sampling values of cost and sales from their minimum to their maximum values. The *Microsoft Excel* function which accomplishes this is *RANDBETWEEN*. The syntax of this command is:

=RANDBETWEEN(minimum,maximum)

The function randomly returns any whole number between the stated minimum and maximum values. In simulation modelling this is a very useful function, and is clearly exactly what we need to sample from uniform distributions such as cost and sales.

ACTIVITY 23

Open your workbook **Arthur.xls**.

1. Select **Sheet2** of the workbook. In cell B8 you are going to type in a formula to randomly sample unit cost values. To do this, use the *RANDBETWEEN* function. Type in the following formula:

   =RANDBETWEEN(Parameters!$B$7,Parameters$C$7)

   Press the **Enter** key. Notice the use of **Parameters!** before the cell references. This ensures that the maximum and minimum values are taken from the correct sheet. Also, you should note the use of the '$' sign before the row and column for each cell reference. This ensures that the *RANDBETWEEN* formula always refers to the correct cells in the **Parameters** sheet, even when it is copied into other cells.

2. In cells C8 and D8 use the *RANDBETWEEN* function to sample from the fixed cost and sales distributions.

3. In column E8 type in a formula to calculate the profit, given the selected values of costs and sales.

4. Copy the formulae in cells B8 to C8 down to row 107 of the worksheet. This will ensure that your model simulates 100 weeks of sales activity. Give appropriate titles to each column. Finally, rename **Sheet2** as **Workings** and save your changes.

1. The worksheet should look similar to Table 22, showing the first six weeks of the simulation.

	A	B	C	D	E
1	ARTHUR'S TILERS: WORKINGS				
2					
3					
4					
5	Week	Unit	Fixed	Sales	Profit
6		Cost	Cost	(Lots)	
7					
8	1	162	5688	120	5472
9	2	174	5713	102	2549
10	3	182	5572	105	2093
11	4	176	5865	123	3852
12	5	157	5572	119	6090
13	6	192	5704	90	−34

Table 22: Workings sheet for Arthur's Tilers

2. The formula typed into C8 is:

   = RANDBETWEEN(Parameters!$B$6,Parameters!$C$6)

   This randomly samples fixed cost values from between its minimum and maximum values.

   The formula typed into D8 is:

   = RANDBETWEEN(Parameters!$B$8,Parameters!$C$8)

   This samples values from the sales distribution.

3. To calculate profit you need to take total revenue, which is price multiplied by sales, and subtract total cost, which is fixed cost plus unit cost multiplied by sales. The formula typed into cell E8 is:

   = Parameters!$B$10*D8–(B8*D8+C8)

4. See Table 22.

ACTIVITY 24

Add an **Output** sheet to your **Arthur.xls** workbook. If you are unsure how to do this, refer back to earlier activities.

The output should include:

- minimum profit
- maximum profit
- mean profit
- standard deviation of profit
- a frequency distribution of profit over the 100 weeks of the simulation
- a bar chart of the frequency distribution.

What do you conclude about the new tiling product?

The **Output** sheet should look similar to that in Table 23 and Figure 6.

	A	B	C
1			
2	ARTHUR'S TILERS OUTPUT		
3			
4			
5			
6			
7			
8	Minimum Profit		−34
9	Maximum Profit		7614
10	Mean Profit		3469.85
11	Std Dvn		1601.92
12			
13	Profit	Frequency	
14	−500	0	
15	0	1	
16	500	3	
17	1000	3	
18	2000	12	
19	4000	42	
20	6000	31	
21	8000	8	

Table 23: Output sheet for Arthur's Tilers

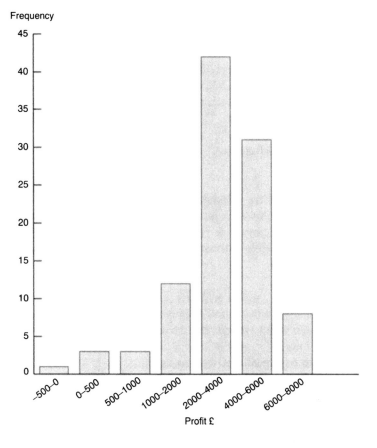

Figure 6: Bar chart of Arthur's Tilers' profits

Notice that it is possible to make a loss: this is indicated by a negative return. However, there is only a single iteration in the class from −£500 to £0, so we may argue that the probability of such an event is low, at only one week in a hundred.

The profit could be as high as £7,614. We can't put a precise figure on the probability of this although we can note that there is an 8 per cent chance of profits being between £6,001 and £7,614.

The average return is £3,469.85 per week. Notice the high variability of the return, as evidenced by the standard deviation. At £1,601.92 this is high compared with the mean profit.

The bar chart suggests the possibility of a negative skew in the distribution of profits. A possible next step in the simulation study might be to investigate this further.

3.5 Using logic functions

So far you have used a battery of techniques to assist you in the building of simulation models. You know something about the use of look-up tables and the two random number functions *RAND*, which generates a random number between 0 and 1, and *RANDBETWEEN*, which generates a random whole number between a specified minimum and maximum. These methods alone allow the development of some quite sophisticated models. In the final part of this section we consider some additional *Microsoft Excel* functions.

Case Study: the Sizzling Gastropod bistro

The *Sizzling Gastropod* bistro has just acquired a source of sturgeon from a Black Sea port, and will be placing these on the menu as *Volga Sturgeon Steaks*. The purchase cost of these steaks will be £15 and the bistro reckons to offer them to gourmets at £22 each.

The two variable factors which will affect its profits are demand and supply. Because of factors beyond its control, supply might be anything from 0 to 5 steaks per night. Discussion with suppliers, and the managers' own business skills suggest a probable distribution of supply as shown in Table 24. Whatever the supply, the bistro guarantees to buy up all available stocks.

Supply	Probability
0	0.02
1	0.08
2	0.20
3	0.30
4	0.25
5	0.15

Table 24: Supply of sturgeon steaks

Based upon the demand for lobster, the nightly demand is projected as shown in Table 25.

Demand	Probability
0	0.01
1	0.14
2	0.25
3	0.30
4	0.20
5	0.07
6	0.03

Table 25: Demand for sturgeon steaks

The bistro will treat the sturgeon steaks as perishable, to be sold on the day of purchase or fed to the house cat (who is used to gourmet seafood). The bistro also knows from experience that a proportion of customers who order a particular dish when it is not available will not patronise the restaurant again. The bistro sets a value of £2 lost goodwill for every unsatisfied customer.

The bistro's management would like some idea of the likely cash flows from this new venture before they place surgeon steak on the menu. As is always advisable, before we attempt to start building a model to simulate this problem, we should list the inputs to the problem and decide on the output we would like from a completed model.

ACTIVITY 25

1. Make a list of the inputs to the bistro problem and say whether they are parameters or variables.

2. What output do you think might be useful from a simulation of the problem?

---

1. Supply and demand are variables, as they change randomly from night to night. Cost price, the valuation of lost goodwill and selling price are not subject to random variation, and so are parameters.

2. The nightly profit from sturgeon steaks would be one of the required outputs from a simulation model. The bistro might also like to have some statistics about the number of steaks which are thrown away due to excess supply, and the number of times customers fail to obtain the item.

Now that we have compiled a list of the input variables and parameters for the bistro problem it is possible to begin the construction of a spreadsheet model. We will do this in the next few activities.

(**Note**: in the software pack which is supplied with this study guide there is a file **Gpodsim.xls** which is an implementation of this model.)

Firstly, as in the case of the previous models we need to construct a parameters worksheet. Notice that the probability distributions of the variables supply and demand are given in table form, so we will need to use look-up tables.

ACTIVITY 26

Open a new workbook.

In cells B9 to C14 enter a look-up table for the supply variable. Remember that the cumulative probability must precede the variable so that it will be entered in column B from B9 to B14. The supply values **0**, **1**, **2**, **3**, **4** and **5** will be entered in column C from C9 to C14. Enter a look-up table for the demand variable in a similar manner in cells E9 to E15.

Now enter the fixed parameters, cost price (**15**) in cell D18, lost goodwill (**2**) in cell D19 and selling price (**22**) in cell D20. Enter appropriate descriptions and titles for these inputs, rename **Sheet1** as **Parameters** and save the spreadsheet as **Bistro.xls**.

Your spreadsheet should look something like the one shown as Table 26. As before, the **Workings** sheet will use this data in order to make its calculations.

The next step we need to take in developing the model is to construct a worksheet which will carry out the necessary calculations of cash flow. To do this, we need to randomly sample supply and demand figures and then calculate the costs and revenues which result. However, there are some complications arising here which did not occur in the case of *Hertz Plastics plc* and *Arthur's Tilers*. Some of these are explored in the next activity.

	A	B	C	D	E	F
1						
2	THE 'SIZZLING GASTROPOD' PARAMETERS					
3						
4						
5						
6						
7						
8		Cum Pr	Supply		Cum Pr	Demand
9		0.00	0		0.00	0
10		0.02	1		0.01	1
11		0.10	2		0.15	2
12		0.30	3		0.40	3
13		0.60	4		0.70	4
14		0.85	5		0.90	5
15					0.97	6
16						
17						
18		Cost Price		15		
19		Lost Goodwill		2		
20		Selling Price		22		

Table 26: Parameters sheet for the bistro model

ACTIVITY 27

1. Suppose that on one evening in the *Sizzling Gastropod* demand for sturgeon steaks happens to be greater than supply. How would you calculate revenue earned on that night?

2. Suppose that supply happens to be greater than demand. How would you calculate revenue earned?

3. How would you calculate the amount of lost goodwill incurred on any night?

---

1. Revenue is earned on what is sold, not what is demanded. If the demand for steaks is greater than the supply then this means that some custom will have to be refused. Revenue will be calculated by multiplying the supply figure by price. To test this, suppose that on one evening demand happened to be for five steaks, but only three were supplied. Only three can be sold, so revenue will be:

   $3 \times 22 = £66$

2. If supply is greater than demand then revenue is earned on the amount demanded, not on what is supplied. For example, if five steaks are supplied and only four are demanded then revenue will be:

$$4 \times 22 = \text{£}88$$

One of the steaks will be wasted.

3. This needs to be done in two stages:

- firstly, we need to determine whether any customers have been refused a steak

- if the answer to the above question is 'yes', then we calculate how many customers have been refused.

These problems may seem small, but they need to be dealt with carefully in a spreadsheet. They constitute problems of a kind which occur frequently in simulation modelling. We often require a computer program like *Microsoft Excel* to take one action if a particular set of circumstances occurs and another action in different circumstances. For example, consider the revenue calculation example. If supply exceeds demand then revenue will be calculated as demand times price, but if this is not true then we calculate it as supply times price.

Fortunately, a useful *Microsoft Excel* function exists to assist us in circumstances such as this. It is known as the *IF* function, and its syntax is as follows:

=IF(condition,action if condition true,action if condition false)

'Condition' is some test or calculation, the result of which may be true or false. *Microsoft Excel* will execute one course if the condition is true and another if it is false. For example, consider the expression:

=IF(A2<0,"negative","zero or greater")

This examines the contents of cell A2. If the contents are less than 0 (A2<0) then *Microsoft Excel* will write 'negative' in the current cell. If the contents are not less than 0, *Microsoft Excel* will write 'zero or greater'. The actions can also be mathematical expressions rather than text messages, in which case the speech marks ("") must be omitted.

This is exactly the kind of function we require in the bistro model, for we require *Microsoft Excel* to test which is greater, supply or demand. If demand is greater, then *Microsoft Excel* must multiply supply by price, otherwise it must multiply demand by price.

ACTIVITY 28

Open your **Bistro.xls** workbook and select **Sheet2**.

1. In cell B10 enter a formula to randomly sample a demand figure from the look-up table in the parameters sheet.

2. In cell C10 enter a formula to randomly sample a supply figure.

3. In cell D10 enter a formula which calculates revenue. Remember that you first need to test whether supply is greater than demand. If it is, then revenue will be calculated as demand times price. If not, then revenue will be calculated as supply times price. You will need to use the *IF* function.

4. In cell E10 enter a formula to calculate the total purchase cost of the sturgeon steaks.

5. In cell F10 enter a formula which calculates the monetary consequences of lost goodwill. If demand is greater than supply then there will be a loss. Use the *IF* function to test whether demand is greater than supply. If it is, the command will calculate the amount lost, otherwise it will write in a '0'.

6. In cell G10 enter a formula to calculate the night's profit on sturgeon steaks. This will be revenue minus cost minus lost goodwill.

7. In cell H10 enter a formula which calculates the number of customers who have been turned down when requesting a sturgeon steak. You will not need to use the *IF* function to achieve this.

8. In cell I10 enter a formula to calculate the number of sturgeon steaks thrown away. It is best to use the *IF* function to achieve this.

In order to simulate 100 nights of restaurant business, copy down all formulae up to and including row 109. Finally, give all columns appropriate titles, rename **Sheet2** as **Workings** and save your changes.

The completed **Workings** sheet should look similar to the one in Table 27. Remember that the use of random numbers will mean that the numbers in the columns on your own sheet will be different. Only the first six nights of business are shown.

	A	B	C	D	E	F	G	H	I
1									
2									
3									
4									
5									
6									
7									
8						Lost		Lost	Over
9	Day	Demand	Supply	Revenue	Cost	Goodwill	Profit	Custom	Stock
10	1	4	0	0	0	8	−8	4	0
11	2	4	2	44	30	4	10	2	0
12	3	1	3	22	45	0	−23	0	2
13	4	3	3	66	45	0	21	0	0
14	5	1	4	22	60	0	−38	0	3
15	6	3	5	66	75	0	−9	0	2

Table 27: Workings sheet for bistro model

1. The formula in cell B10 will be:

   VLOOKUP(RAND(),Parameters!$E$9:$F$15,2)

   This formula samples a demand figure from the **Parameters** worksheet.

2. The formula in cell C10 should sample the supply data from the **Parameters** worksheet and should be written as:

   VLOOKUP(RAND(),Parameters!$B$9:$C$14,2)

3. To calculate revenue we need the *IF* function. The formula should be:

   =IF(C10>B10, B10*Parameters!$D$20,C10*Parameters!$D$20)

   In ordinary language this means: 'test whether supply (C10) is greater than demand (B10): if it is, multiply demand by price: if not, multiply supply by price.'

   Notice that the price is contained on the **Parameters** worksheet, so the cell references should recognise this fact.

4. Calculation of cost of purchase is a straightforward matter, and is always equal to supply times purchase price. The formula to be entered in cell E10 is:

   =C10*Parameters!$D$18

5. We need to calculate the consequences of lost goodwill in cell F10. Although there are several ways of accomplishing this, one of the easiest ways (using the *IF* function) is:

   =IF(B10>C10,Parameters!$D$19*(B10–C10),0)

   In ordinary language this means: 'test whether demand (B10) is greater than supply (C10): if it is, then there are some unsatisfied customers, calculate how many there are (B10-C10), and multiply this number by the lost goodwill value; otherwise write '0.'

6. Cell G10 should contain a profit calculation. The formula to be written here is:

   =D10–E10–F10

   This calculates revenue minus cost minus lost goodwill.

7. Lost custom is the number of customers turned away unsatisfied. Each lost customer costs £2 in lost goodwill. As a consequence, we can easily calculate this number by dividing the monetary consequence of lost goodwill by £2. The formula to be written into cell H10 should be:

   =F10/Parameters!$D$19

   Parameters!$D$19 refers to the current estimate of lost goodwill per customer.

8. The wasted sturgeon steaks is best calculated using the *IF* function as follows:

   =IF(C10>B10,C10–B10,0)

   In ordinary language this means: 'test whether supply (C10) is greater than demand (B10): if it is then calculate supply minus demand (C10–B10) and write it into cell I10; otherwise write '0'.

You may have found the construction of the **Workings** sheet for the bistro problem significantly more difficult than for the *Hertz Plastics plc* or *Arthur's Tilers* problems. This is because the use of the *IF* function requires a little more thought than many other functions. However, a study of its use will pay great dividends because it greatly increases the power of spreadsheet programming, not just in simulation modelling but in other areas too.

We are now in a position to finalise the bistro model with the construction of an output sheet.

ACTIVITY 29

Open your **Bistro.xls** workbook and select **Sheet3**.

In a suitable position on **Sheet3** calculate statistics to summarise the results of the simulation of 100 nights trading in sturgeon steaks at the bistro. Your summary should include:

- mean profit
- standard deviation of profit
- mean cost
- standard deviation of cost

- a frequency distribution of excess supply (how often excess supply of 0, 1, 2, 3, 4 or 5 steaks occurs: use the *FREQUENCY* function for this, and enter in the values 0 to 5 as classes or bins)
- a frequency distribution of excess demand (how often is there an excess demand for 0, 1, 2, 3, 4, 5 or 6 steaks?).

Type in appropriate descriptions for your output, rename **Sheet3** as **Output** and save your changes.

Allowing for design and the random element, your Output sheet should look something like the one in Table 28.

	A	B	C	D	E	F	G
1							
2	THE 'SIZZLING GASTROPOD' - ANALYSIS						
3							
4							
5	£ Profit			Excess	Number of	Excess	Number of
6	Mean	5.6		Supply	Nights	Demand	Nights
7	Std Dvn	16.40		0	60	0	65
8				1	21	1	14
9				2	15	2	8
10	£ Cost			3	2	3	7
11	Mean	45.45		4	2	4	5
12	Std Dvn	19.17		5	0	5	1
13						6	0

Table 28: Output sheet for the bistro model

Notice the low nightly average profit, which suggests that the new venture will not be very successful. There would need to be many nights of negative profit to obtain an average this low. Notice, also, the great variability in profit, as evidenced by a standard deviation of 16.40 (much higher than the mean). There are also 40 nights on which at least one sturgeon steak had to be thrown away. We could have obtained more output (for example, a distribution of profit), but the statistics we have do not suggest a viable project, given current supply and demand figures.

Summary

In this section you have refined your existing model building skills and significantly added to your ability to construct *Microsoft Excel* worksheets. We started by exploring the possibility of obtaining repeat runs from a simulation model. This allowed us to determine the existence of a steady state. We then obtained further output from the model in the form of frequency distributions of results. Next we used the spreadsheet to carry out 'what if' analysis, in particular by altering the parameters of a model and studying the effect of such variation. Finally, we used the *Microsoft Excel* function *RANDBETWEEN* to sample from uniform probability distributions. We then used the *IF* function to choose between two courses of action.

In the next section we will be looking at a class of problems known as scheduling problems.

SECTION 4

Waiting Lines and Scheduling Problems

Introduction

A large class of business problems is concerned with examining the behaviour of queues and waiting lines. When we think of the everyday meaning of a queue, we normally expect it to consist of a line of people waiting for some kind of service. In BDA we may quite possibly be interested in human queues, but this is not always the case. In this section we will be studying the construction of models in which queues (or waiting lines) are a major factor. In Section 4.1 we use a case study to introduce a simple waiting line problem. In Section 4.2 we identify the various components of the waiting line problem and in Section 4.3 we explore the variables in the problem. We then go on, in Section 4.4, to use *Microsoft Excel* to analyse the problem. Finally, in Section 4.5, we look at some extra complications to waiting line problems.

4.1 A waiting line problem

The essential parts of any waiting line are:

- a queue, which may consist of people or of objects
- a service point, where the people or objects receive some kind of service or processing.

As an example of a simple waiting line we consider the case of *Torch plc*, a factory making battery chargers.

Case Study: **Torch Plc**

Torch plc has been experiencing difficulties with its battery charger assembly plant. The layout of the plant is about to be redesigned as a continuous assembly line. Management would like to have some prior knowledge of the efficiency of the proposed design.

The firm normally uses sets of component parts bought from outside suppliers in kit form. These sets of parts arrive at the beginning of a shift. The actual number of sets of parts arriving at the beginning of any one shift is a variable, which is beyond the control of management as it is affected by the suppliers' capacity and by the availability of transport. The battery charger assembly line will have a variable capacity to assemble: that is, the actual number of sets of parts assembled may not be equal to the number delivered. This may occur for any of a number of reasons including staff absenteeism, variable performance of staff, mechanical problems and so on.

If the assembly line cannot assemble all of the kits delivered during a shift, then the remainder will have to wait in a work-in-progress (WIP) area until the next shift. It is also possible that the assembly line capacity will exceed the available parts to be assembled, in which case there will be a degree of spare capacity or enforced idleness.

After a kit of parts has been assembled, it is passed on to the inspection division. This division also has a variable capacity to deal with the day's output. Any battery chargers left untested as a result of lack of capacity will have to wait in another WIP holding area until the next shift.

In this case study we have two queuing situations. One queue consists of kits of parts waiting for service at the assembly point, while the other queue is of completed goods waiting for inspection. The firm would like to see the result of a simulation of the proposed assembly line design over a period of 100 shifts.

ACTIVITY 30

For the *Torch plc* assembly line problem, describe suitable performance measures or output variables that you think should be provided by a simulation study.

Hint: what do you think management would want to know about the proposed system?

Just as there a number of possible choices of performance measures for an assembly line, so also will there be a number of different possible answers to Activity 30.

It is possible that sets of parts may arrive which cannot be dealt with during a shift, because of reduced capacity of the production line. While this is not necessarily a problem, it would become so if there were a prolonged tendency for production capacity to be below the number of sets of parts available for assembly. Such a situation would create bottlenecks, since the production line would be unable to cope.

Similarly, assembly line capacity may be considerably greater than part delivery. This is also a problem which management will wish to avoid, since it involves idle resources (unused capacity on the production line), and therefore lost profits.

Therefore, suitable performance measures might include:

- number of parts waiting to be assembled
- length of time a set of parts spends in the queue
- proportion of time the production line is over capacity
- proportion of time the production line is under capacity.

A similar set of performance measures would be suitable for studying the efficiency of the test or inspection centre:

- number of completed goods awaiting inspection at any one time
- length of time completed goods wait to be inspected
- proportion of time the test bench is over capacity
- proportion of time the test bench is under capacity.

4.2 The components of a waiting line problem

The *Torch plc* case study illustrates the classic aspects of any waiting line problem:

- there are one or more queues or waiting lines waiting for service
- there are one or more service points
- the situation is **dynamic**: what happens in any one work shift is dependent on what happened in the previous shift.

It is often useful to start the analysis of a new problem by trying to draw a flow chart of it. This forces us to consider the logical relationships between the various parts of a model. See Figure 7 for a flowchart illustration of this problem.

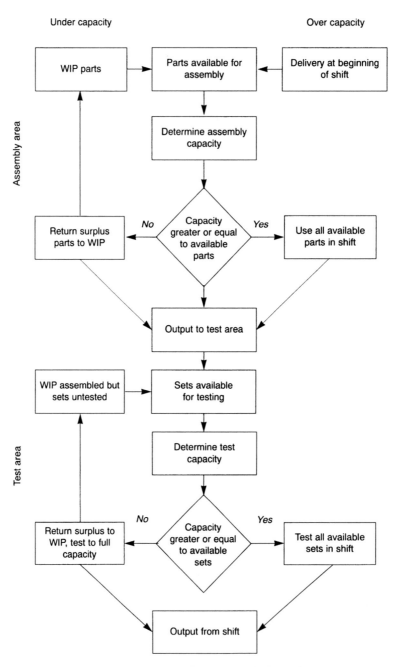

Under capacity   Over capacity

Figure 7: Flow chart for the Torch plc problem

4.3 The variables

We will now start to add some detail concerning the behaviour of the main variables in the problem. After a little research, the management of *Torch plc* believes that:

- the number of sets of parts delivered may be any value between 29 and 35
- the assembly line will have a variable capacity and may be able to assemble as many as 37 sets or as few as 32 sets
- the test centre will have a variable inspection capacity and may be able to deal with between 33 and 36 finished goods.

Management would like to test the proposed system under varying conditions and in order to start this process has asked the following 'what if' questions.

What if, at the start of the next shift:

- three sets of parts are waiting in the work in progress area
- 34 sets of parts have been delivered at the beginning of the current shift
- one product was finished but uninspected at the close of the last shift
- the assembly line has a capacity of 35 for the current shift
- the test centre can inspect up to 34 finished goods in the current shift.

Of course, in order to really test the system, *Torch plc* would need to have the answer to many such questions. Nevertheless, the above example will suffice as a starting point for analysis of the model.

How will the assembly line perform, given this data? Will there be over or under capacity in the assembly line and test centre? Will there be a queue of parts waiting for assembly or of finished goods waiting for inspection?

We may write down the results of a simulation run in the form shown in Table 29.

Shift	Assembly area					Inspection area				
	Parts Delvd	WIP	Total	Cap	Sl/Qu	Assd Parts	WIP	Total	Cap	Sl/Qu
1	34	3	37	35	−2	35	1	36	34	−2

Table 29: The assembly line and test area of Torch plc

Note: 'Parts Delvd' = parts delivered, 'WIP' = work in progress, 'Cap' = capacity, 'Sl/Qu' = slack/queue. A positive number in the Sl/Qu column indicates slack and a negative number indicates a queue.

The assembly line is unable to cope with the sets of parts available during this particular shift. It can deal with only 35 whereas 37 sets are actually available for assembly (34 delivered plus 3 already in WIP). The two unassembled sets will have to wait in the assembly line WIP area until the next shift, where they will be added to the total to be assembled.

Likewise, there are 36 finished goods to be inspected during this shift (35 assembled during this shift plus 1 from WIP), whereas the test centre can only deal with 34. The two finished but uninspected goods must wait in the test area WIP until the next shift.

ACTIVITY 31

Assume that all of the three variables in the *Torch plc* problem (parts delivery, assembly capacity and inspection capacity) are **uniformly distributed** (that is, that all possible values are equally likely to occur). In this activity you will be simulating the next five shifts so you will need to generate 15 random numbers (three numbers for each shift).

1. Use either a pocket calculator or *Microsoft Excel* to generate the 15 random numbers. Divide them into five groups of three numbers, one number for each of the three variables.

   Note: there are a variety of ways in which you may generate random numbers. If you use the random number function on a pocket calculator you will obtain values between 0 and 1. This activity specifies that each variable is uniformly distributed so simply use the first two digits following the decimal point and ignore any numbers which fall outside the ranges required. You could also use the *Microsoft Excel* function *RANDBETWEEN*, described in Section 3 of this unit.

2. Assume that the starting position for this small simulation begins where the shift shown in Table 29 leaves off (that is, with two sets of parts in the assembly line WIP and two finished but uninspected goods in the test area WIP). Use your random numbers to simulate activity in the next five shifts.

---

1. So in order to carry out this simulation we require, for each shift:
   - a random number between 29 and 35 for the number of parts arriving at the beginning of the shift
   - a random number between 32 and 37 to simulate the variable capacity of the assembly line
   - a random number between 33 and 36 to simulate the capacity of the inspection centre.

   The numbers obtained have been divided into five groups of three (one group per shift). These are shown in Table 30.

Shift	Delivery of parts	Production capacity	Inspection capacity
2	32	36	34
3	35	33	34
4	32	36	35
5	35	32	34
6	32	32	35

Table 30: Random numbers used in Activity 31

2. Table 30 uses these figures to simulate activity up to and including shift 6. (Remember that shift 1 is the position as shown in Table 29.)

	Assembly area					Inspection area				
Shift	Parts Delvd	WIP	Total	Cap	SI/Qu	Assd Parts	WIP	Total	Cap	SI/Qu
1	34	3	37	35	−2	35	1	36	34	−2
2	32	2	34	36	+2	34	2	36	34	−2
3	35	0	35	33	−2	33	2	35	34	−1
4	32	2	33	36	+3	33	1	34	35	+1
5	35	0	35	32	−3	32	0	32	34	+2
6	32	3	35	32	−3	32	0	32	35	+3

Table 31: Simulation of first six shifts at Torch plc

It should be remembered that your own figures will differ from those in Tables 30 and 31, as you will have obtained different random numbers.

Each line in Table 31 represents a single shift. Shift 1 shows the position at the start of the simulation, with two sets of parts still unassembled, and two finished goods still awaiting inspection. You should be careful to ensure that any unassembled or uninspected goods left in the WIP area are carried forward to the next shift. As an illustration of this model, shift 2 is described below.

SHIFT 2

32 sets of parts are delivered and, together with the two from the previous shift's WIP, there is a total of 34 to assemble. Assembly capacity during that shift is equal to 36, which means that there is no unfinished business: on the contrary, there is idle capacity. The assembly line could have managed two more sets of parts.

So there are 34 finished goods to proceed to inspection. Together with the two from the WIP area from shift 1, this means a total of 36 to inspect. Since inspection capacity during this shift is only 34, there will be a queue or waiting line of two finished but untested goods in WIP, which must be dealt with in shift 3. Shifts 3 to 6 will proceed in the same manner.

From the point of view of production management, the important columns to watch for are:

- assembly (slack or queue)
- inspection (slack or queue).

The management will be interested in whether there is any evidence to suggest that bottlenecks in production will frequently occur, because of insufficient capacity in the assembly line or test centre. Or is there slack in the process because assembly and testing capacity exceeds the supply of parts and finished goods?

Of course, a simulation run of just six shifts cannot yield reliable information: the model needs a much longer run. Having set up the model and carried out a small manual test, you should be able to see that the next stage in analysing the performance of the assembly line is to generate data for many shifts. We want to see if a pattern emerges. As with previous models, we turn to the computer for help.

4.4 Using *Microsoft Excel* to analyse a waiting line problem

You will now begin the task of constructing a spreadsheet model to simulate the *Torch plc* problem. As with the other models, there is a spreadsheet file available in your software pack called **Prodline.xls**, which you may use for reference if you wish.

Torch plc has produced some probability data for delivery of parts and assembly line capacity. This data is shown in Tables 32 and 33.

Sets of parts delivered	Probability
29	0.03
30	0.09
31	0.21
32	0.24
33	0.29
34	0.10
35	0.04

Table 32: Parts delivery

Capacity to assemble	Probability
32	0.26
33	0.31
34	0.21
35	0.10
36	0.10
37	0.02

Table 33: Assembly capacity

Torch plc also believes that minimum inspection capacity is 33 and maximum capacity is 36 with the probabilities being equally distributed within these limits.

Taking just two figures for the sake of illustration, there is a 21 per cent chance that 31 sets of parts will be delivered at the beginning of any one shift and a 10 per cent chance that the assembly line will have the capacity to deal with exactly 35 sets. Inspection centre capacity varies from 33 to 36 and has a uniform distribution: in other words, there is an equal probability of each of the values occurring.

As with all simulation studies, the assumptions relating to the probabilities of different delivery and capacity figures need only be tentative, the technique being flexible enough to incorporate changes made by the decision-makers as they acquire more knowledge during the development of the project. The checking of probability distributions for how well they approximate to reality is an important part of the validation procedure for simulation models.

ACTIVITY 32

Open a new workbook. On **Sheet1** you will enter the variables and parameters for the *Torch plc* problem in the same way as for previous models.

Enter the parts delivery data (Table 32) as a look-up table into **Sheet1** in cells B6 to C12. Use column B for cumulative probabilities and column C for the number of sets of parts delivered.

Enter the assembly capacity data (Table 33) into cells E6 to F11.

Inspection capacity is a uniform distribution so only the minimum and maximum values need be entered. Enter the minimum value into cell I5 and the maximum value into cell I6.

The starting position of the simulation now needs to be entered as parameters. We will assume for the time being that there are two unassembled sets of parts in the assembly WIP area and one assembled uninspected product in the inspection area. Enter the assembly area WIP figure of **2** into cell F14 and the inspection area WIP figure of **1** into cell F15.

Finally, provide appropriate titles for the input, rename **Sheet1** as **Parameters** and save the worksheet as **Torch.xls**.

Your completed **Parameters** sheet for the *Torch plc* model should look similar to the one in Table 34.

	A	B	C	D	E	F	G	H	I
1	TORCH PLC: ASSEMBLY LINE PARAMETERS AND LOOK-UP TABLES								
2									
3									
4		Delivery			Assembly Capacity			Inspedion Capadty	
5		Cum Pr	Sets		Cum Pr	Sets		Minimum	33
6		0.00	29		0.00	32		Maximum	36
7		0.03	30		0.26	33			
8		0.12	31		0.57	34			
9		0.33	32		0.78	35			
10		0.57	33		0.88	36			
11		0.86	34		0.98	37			
12		0.96	35						
13									
14		Starting WIP of Unassembled Sets				2			
15		Waiting For Inspection				1			

Table 34: The Parameters sheet for the Torch plc problem

Up to this point, the building of the simulation model has been very similar to the *Hertz Plastics plc*, the *Arthur's Tilers* and the *Sizzling Gastropod* models. The next stage will differ, however, because the *Torch plc* problem is dynamic and not static. We need to allow for the fact that the end position of one iteration of the model will constitute the starting point of the next, in the sense that there may be unassembled or untested goods in the WIP area at the end of the shift.

The main difference this will cause in our model building will be that each iteration, or line, of the **Workings** sheet will need to refer back to the previous line. For example, line 5 will need to refer back to line 4 of the sheet in order to establish what the WIP situation was at the end of that shift. This is quite different from our previous cases where each line of *Microsoft Excel* instructions was self-contained. A consequence of this, as you will see later, is that line 1 will need to contain slightly different formulae from all subsequent lines. This is because we need to set up the initial starting position of the model before we begin. In other words, we must tell *Microsoft Excel* what the initial WIP situation is.

ACTIVITY 33

In this activity you will write a line of *Microsoft Excel* instructions to simulate shift 1 of the proposed assembly line. Open your workbook **Torch.xls** and select **Sheet2**.

In cell **B9** enter a formula which displays the number of sets of parts delivered at the beginning of the current shift. It will be a value randomly sampled from the delivery distribution in the **Parameters** sheet.

In cell **C9** enter a formula which shows the starting WIP situation in the assembly area. This is stated in the **Parameters** sheet.

In cell **D9** enter a formula to calculate the total number of sets of parts which are to be assembled during the shift (it will be the sum of columns B and C).

In cell **E9** enter a formula which displays assembly capacity in the current shift, randomly selected from **Parameters**.

In cell **F9** enter a formula which calculates the amount of slack in the assembly area. You will need the *IF* command for this. If assembly capacity is greater than the delivery of parts plus WIP, then this column will show slack as column D minus column C, otherwise it will return a '0'.

In cell **G 9** enter a formula which calculates the size of the queue (that is, the number of parts left unassembled which will have to wait until the next shift). If assembly capacity is less than the parts awaiting assembly, then this column will show the unassembled parts which must wait in the queue in WIP. The *IF* command is required.

In cell **H9** enter a formula which displays the number of parts assembled during the shift which go forward to inspection.

In cell **I9** enter a formula which displays the starting WIP position in the inspection area. It will refer to the **Parameters** sheet.

In cell **J9** enter a formula which calculates the total number to be inspected in the current shift. It will be the total of columns H and I.

In cell **K9** enter a formula which calculates inspection centre capacity during the current shift. It will be a number randomly selected from the **Parameters** sheet.

In cell **L9** enter a formula which calculates the amount of slack in the inspection centre. You will need the *IF* command to achieve this. If inspection capacity is greater than the number of finished goods available to inspect, then this slack will show up in this column as column J minus column K: otherwise a '0' should be displayed.

In cell **M9** enter a formula which calculates the number of completed but uninspected goods having to queue in the inspection WIP area. You will need to use the *IF* command.

In cell **N9** enter a formula which calculates the number of finished goods inspected by the test area. You will need to use the *IF* command.

Do not copy these formulae down into other rows for the time being. Add suitable labels to the worksheet, rename **Sheet2** as **Workings** and save your changes.

Your spreadsheet should look similar to the one in Table 35.

	A	B	C	D	E	F	G	H	I	J	K	L	M	N
1														
2														
3														
4														
5														
6			ASSEMBLY AREA							INSPECTION AREA				
7				Total				Total		Total				Total
8	Shift	Delvd	WIP	In	Cap	SI	Qu	Out	WIP	In	Cap	SI	Qu	Out
9	1	31	2	33	34	1	0	33	1	34	35	1	0	34

Table 35: First line of the Workings sheet for Torch plc

A detailed description of each cell follows.

Cell **B9** states the number of sets of parts delivered this shift. It will randomly sample this number from the look-up table in the **Parameters** sheet. The required formula is:

$$=VLOOKUP(RAND(),Parameters!\$B\$6:\$C\$12,2)$$

Cell **C9** contains the formula **=Parameters!F14**.This refers to the initial WIP position in the assembly area.

Cell **D9** states the total amount of sets of parts waiting to be assembled during this shift, which will be the sum of the amount delivered and the amount waiting in WIP. The formula which achieves this is **=B9+C9**.

Cell **E9** calculates the assembly line capacity during the current shift. This number will need to be randomly sampled from the look-up table in the **Parameters** sheet using the following formula:

=LOOKUP(RAND(),Parameters!$E$6:$F$11,2)

Cell **F9** calculates the amount of slack (if any) in assembly line capacity. This is the excess of capacity over parts to be assembled. Using the *IF* command the formula which achieves this is:

=IF(E9>D9,E9–D9,0)

This formula tests whether there is any slack by checking whether E9 (capacity) is greater than D9 (parts to be assembled). If capacity is greater than parts then the excess is calculated, otherwise a '0' is displayed.

Cell **G9** performs a similar test and calculation for the queue or undercapacity. The formula is

=IF(D9>E9,D9–E9,0)

Cell **H9** displays the total output from assembly. This will need an *IF* statement because if capacity is greater than the sets of parts waiting to be assembled, then total output will be equal to the latter. However, if capacity is less than sets awaiting assembly, the total output will be equal to the former. The formula which achieves this is:

=IF(D9>E9,E9,D9)

Cell **I9** displays the starting test area WIP level. The formula will be:

=Parameters!F15

Cell **J9** calculates the total quantity of completed goods waiting to be assembled, and will be equal to the output from assembly plus the amount waiting in test area WIP. The formula required is **=H9+I9**.

Cell **K9** displays the capacity of the inspection centre for this shift. This number will be randomly sampled from a uniform distribution with a minimum and maximum value to be found on the **Parameters** sheet. The *RANDBETWEEN* function accomplishes this action. The required formula is:

=RANDBETWEEN(Parameters!$I$5,Parameters!$I$6)

Cell **L9** calculates the amount of slack (if any) in inspection capacity. This is the excess of test area capacity over goods to be tested. Using the *IF* command, the formula which achieves this is:

=IF(K9>J9,K9–J9,0)

This formula tests whether there is any slack by checking whether K9 (test area capacity) is greater than J9 (goods to be tested). If test capacity is greater than goods to be tested then the excess is calculated, otherwise a '0' is displayed.

Cell **M9** performs a similar test and calculation for the queue or undercapacity in the test area. The formula is:

=IF(J9>K9,J9–K9,0)

Cell **N9** calculates the amount of finished goods passed by the test area. As with output from the assembly area, this will need an *IF* statement because, if test capacity is greater than finished goods waiting to be tested, then total output will be equal to the latter. However, if test capacity is less than the quantity of goods awaiting inspection, the total output from the test area will be equal to the former. The formula which achieves this is:

=IF(J9>K9,K9,J9)

Although we have made a start on the **Workings** sheet of the *Torch plc* problem we still have some way to go. So far we have only entered the instructions to simulate the first shift. As this is a dynamic model the situation at the end of shift 1 will constitute the starting position for shift 2. In general, the final position at the end of shift *n* becomes the starting position at the start of shift *n* + 1. In practical terms, the WIP in both assembly and test areas in shift 2 will be equal to what is left in the queues of these areas during shift 1. We must find some way of carrying forward this data.

ACTIVITY 34

Open your workbook **Torch.xls** and select the **Workings** sheet. In this activity you will complete the **Workings** sheet to produce a simulation of 100 shifts.

Cells C10 and I10 contain the WIP position for the second shift. Remembering that starting WIP in any one shift is the same as the ending queue position in the previous shift, enter formulae in cells C10 and I10 which update WIP.

Apart from these two cells, the remaining formulae in row 10 will be the same as in row 9. Copy these formulae into row 10 so that you now have a complete simulation of shift 2. Copy the whole of A10 to N10 down as far as row 108. You will now have simulated 100 work shifts. Save your changes.

C10 displays the WIP for the assembly area at the beginning of shift 2. This figure will be the same as that in the queue of the assembly area for shift 1. The required formula to be entered into cell C10 is a single cell reference =G9. G9 is the cell which contains the queue data for shift 1. Likewise, the formula to be typed into I10 (which displays the WIP data for shift 1) is the single cell reference =M9. Cell M9 contains the queue position in the inspection area for shift 1.

If the remainder of the formulae are copied from the shift 1 row, then a complete simulation of shift 2 has been completed. After copying all shift 2 formulae down to row 108, a complete simulation of 100 shifts will have been achieved. You should have a worksheet which looks similar to the one in Table 36. The first five shifts only are shown.

	A	B	C	D	E	F	G	H	I	J	K	L	M	N
1														
2														
3														
4														
5														
6			ASSEMBLY AREA								INSPECTION AREA			
7				Total				Total		Total				Total
8	Shift	Delvd	WIP	In	Cap	SI	Qu	Out	WIP	In	Cap	SI	Qu	Out
9	1	31	2	33	34	1	0	33	1	34	35	1	0	34
10	2	33	0	33	32	0	1	32	0	32	36	4	0	32
11	3	33	1	34	33	0	1	33	0	33	33	0	0	33
12	4	32	1	33	33	0	0	33	0	33	36	3	0	33
13	5	33	0	33	32	0	1	32	0	32	35	3	0	32

Table 36: First five shifts of the Torch plc model

We have now completed the dynamic simulation model for *Torch plc* and it only remains to obtain some useful output. The complexity of the output from dynamic models such as *Torch plc* is much greater than that from static models such as *Hertz Plastics plc*. To obtain some of this output you will need to use a new *Microsoft Excel* function, *COUNTIF*, which performs a conditional count of data within a specified range. The syntax of this command is:

=COUNTIF(data range,criteria)

This examines the data within the range specified by the user and counts how many times it satisfies a given criteria.

For example, the command **=COUNTIF(A1:A100,">10")** will examine the contents in cells A1 to A100 and count the number of times a value greater than 10 occurred. Notice that the criterion >10 must be placed inside speech marks.

In determining how to design the output sheet for the simulation model, it is useful to think about what a production manager might want to know about the performance of the proposed assembly. The output would fall into three categories:

- output relating to the performance of the assembly area
- output relating to the inspection area
- output relating to the plant as a whole.

This particular simulation model differs from the previous cases in the sheer quantity of possible output which could be generated. Because of this, we will restrict ourselves to just the first category of output, that relating to the assembly area. The next activity will provide you with some insights into the analysis of dynamic models.

ACTIVITY 35

Open your workbook **Torch.xls** and select **Sheet3**.

1. In cell A6 type in the description **Average assembly capacity**. Next to it, in cell E6, enter the formula:

   =AVERAGE(Workings!E9:E108)

   Since column E contains the assembly line capacity data, this function will display its average capacity.

   We now need to find the average length of the queue of parts waiting in the assembly test area. However, it would be useful to have two versions of this average, one for all iterations and the other which ignores times when a queue did not exist. So enter the description **Average assembly queue** in A8. In A9 enter **(a) for all iterations** and in E9 enter the formula:

   =AVERAGE(Workings!G9:G108)

   Column G of the **Workings** sheet contains the queue data for the assembly area. In cell A10 enter the description **(b) only when queue exists**, and in cell E10 type in the formula:

   =SUM(Workings!G9:G108)/COUNTIF(Workings!G9:G108,">0")

   This formula uses the *COUNTIF* command to calculate the average queue length only for those times when there was a queue. It does this by totalling up all of the assembly queue values in column G and dividing by the number of occasions when a queue existed (when the value in column G is greater than 0).

2. Now do the same thing for the spare capacity in the assembly area. Enter formulae into cells E13 and E14 which calculate the average spare capacity for all iterations and the average spare capacity only for those occasions when there was spare capacity.

3. We will now use *Microsoft Excel* to obtain a cumulative frequency distribution for queue sizes. In cell A16 type the description **Number of iterations with queue**. In cell E16 enter the formula:

   =COUNTIF(Workings!G9:G108,">0")

This formula uses *COUNTIF* to count the number of times there was a queue in the assembly area ("**>0**").

In cell A17 enter the description (**a**) **queue = 1**, and in cell E17 use *COUNTIF* to enter a formula which calculates the number of times there was a queue of exactly 1.

Now finish the distribution. In cells A18 to A21 enter the descriptions (**b**) **Queue more than 1**, (**c**) **queue more than 2** and so on up to a queue length of more than four. In cells E18 to E21 enter formulae which calculate the number of times there were queue lengths greater than the specified size.

4. Now do the same for slack or spare capacity. Use A23 to A28 to enter the descriptions **Number of iterations with slack**, (**a**) **slack = 1**, (**b**) **slack more than 1** and so on up to (**e**) **slack of more than 4**. In cells E23 to E28 enter formulae which calculate the number of times these events occur.

5. In cell A30 type the description **Mean no. output from assembly area**, and in cell E30 enter a formula to calculate this value. Finally, rename **Sheet3** as **Output** and save your changes.

---

1. As you have seen from Activity 35, the amount of output which can result from a dynamic simulation of this type can be considerable. We have deliberately restricted ourselves to the assembly, but you can easily see that we would require the same statistics about queues and slack for the inspection area. Table 37 shows the output asked for in the activity. As before, you should remember that the random principle in operation throughout simulation modelling will mean that your own **Output** sheet will be similar to Table 37 but not exactly the same.

	A	B	C	D	E
1	TORCH PLC: PRODUCTION LINE OUTPUT				
2					
3					
4	ASSEMBLY LINE CAPACITY				
5					
6	Average assembly capacity				33.45
7					
8	Average assembly queue				
9	(a) for all iterations				0.74
10	(b) only when queue exists				2.00
11					
12	Average spare capacity (slack)				
13	(a) for all iterations				1.07
14	(b) only when slack exists				2.28
15					
16	Number of iterations with queue				37
17	(a) queue = 1				15
18	(b) queue more than 1				22
19	(c) queue more than 2				10
20	(d) queue more than 3				5
21	(e) queue more than 4				0
22					
23	Number of iterations with slack				47
24	(a) slack = 1				15
25	(b) slack more than 1				32
26	(c) slack more than 2				17
27	(d) slack more than 3				7
28	(e) slack more than 4				3
29					
30	Mean output from assembly area				32.38

Table 37: Output sheet for Torch plc

2. The formula in cell E13 is:

=AVERAGE(Workings!F9:F108)

This calculates the average spare capacity, or slack for all iterations. However, the formula in cell E14 is:

=SUM(Workings!F9:F108)/COUNTIF(Workings!F9:F108,">0")

This calculates the mean queue length only for those occasions when there actually was a queue. It does this by using *COUNTIF* to find out how many times the queue was above 0, and then dividing this number into the total of all queues over the 100 iterations.

3. Cell E17 needs to report the number of times that the queue was equal to 1. This can be done with the *COUNTIF* command by entering the formula:

> **=COUNTIF(Workings!G9:G108,"=1")**

Likewise, cell E18 reports the number of times a queue greater than 1 occurred by using the formula:

> **=COUNTIF(Workings!G9:G108,">1")**

Cells E19, E20 and E21 have similar formulae, with the final part of the bracketed expression changed accordingly.

4. A similar operation needs to be carried out to construct a cumulative distribution of slack, or spare capacity. This begins in cell E23 with the formula:

> **=COUNTIF(Workings!F9:F108,">0")**

This counts up the number of times that there was spare capacity in the assembly area. Cell E24 reports the number of times that the amount of spare capacity was equal to 1. This can be done with the *COUNTIF* command by entering:

> **=COUNTIF(Workings!F9:F108,"=1")**

Likewise, cell E25 reports the number of times there was spare capacity greater than 1, using the formula:

> **=COUNTIF(Workings!F9:F108,">1")**

Cells E26, E27 and E28 have similar formulae, with the final part of the bracketed expression changed accordingly.

5. The formula in cell E30 reports the average output per shift from the assembly area, and uses the formula:

> **=AVERAGE(Workings!H9:H108)**

So we have already obtained a considerable amount of information regarding the behaviour of the assembly area. We know, for example, that the average queue for any one shift is 0.74, while the average slack is 1.07. Clearly, this assembly line is idle more often than it is overworked. This is not necessarily a condemnation, since a certain degree of spare capacity is always a good safety valve in a productive enterprise. It would be up to management to decide whether the position was tolerable. In this case, whilst there were 22 shifts with an assembly queue of more than 1, there were 32 shifts with spare capacity of more than 1. We would, of course, also need to obtain some output for the inspection area before we passed judgement. This could be obtained in exactly the same way as the assembly output.

One aspect of queues and spare capacity which can only be analysed by looking at the output on a shift-to-shift basis is the degree to which a queue persists. Queues are not in themselves to be dreaded: what is important is whether they grow longer or shorter and how long they take to disappear.

4.5 Waiting line problems: some extra complications

In many waiting line problems, especially where the queue is made up of human beings rather than inanimate goods or services, there will be additional difficulties not encountered in the *Torch plc* assembly line example. We consider some of these complications below.

BALKING

Consider a petrol station waiting line. If the user of the service arrives and finds the service occupied, he or she may leave immediately and not wait for service. This is known as **balking**. In many simulation problems we may well have to allow for the fact that users arriving at the queue for a service will have variable levels of tolerance to waiting lines before they balk. Some users may balk at a queue of any length. Others may be willing to queue provided the waiting line does not exceed a particular length.

RENEGING

In many cases, users of a service will be more concerned with waiting time than with length of queue. A user may be prepared to wait for a given length of time in a queue. If this length of time is exceeded, then they will leave the queue. This is known as **reneging**.

QUEUE DISCIPLINE

How is the queue of people or objects dealt with? There will presumably be some kind of procedure, known as **queue discipline**, for dealing with arrivals. Usually, in the case of human queues, the servicing is on a 'first come, first served basis', but this is not always the case. A hospital accident and emergency department, for instance, normally works on this basis, but would have to vary this for emergency admissions.

NUMBER OF SERVICE POINTS

In the *Torch plc* example there was only one service point for assembly and only one point for inspection. We may have to design a simulation model to cope with cases where more than one such point exists.

Making assumptions concerning the tendency to balk or renege in queuing situations presents difficult problems for the analyst. You should be aware of these problems but a detailed consideration of their solution lies outside the scope of this course.

Summary

In this section we studied the construction of dynamic simulation models by looking at the problem of waiting lines, and considered the method for developing a model to describe their behaviour. We used a case study to analyse the components and variables in a waiting line problem and to explore the behaviour of a proposed solution to the problem. We then made use of the logic statement *IF* and the command *COUNTIF* to allow us to simulate the problem with *Microsoft Excel*. Finally, we discussed some general considerations which can effect any waiting line problem.

In the next section we look at a class of problems known as inventory problems.

SECTION 5

Inventory Problems

Introduction

In this section we will be examining how simulation can help the decision-maker to plan ahead so that costs due to ordering and stockholding can be minimised. In Section 5.1 we define some of the key concepts used when discussing inventory control, in Section 5.2 we use a case study to introduce the elements of an inventory control problem and in Section 5.3 we use *Microsoft Excel* to run a simulation of the problem. Finally, in Section 5.4, we look at some of the factors which may complicate inventory problems.

5.1 The background to inventory control

A common problem encountered by manufacturing businesses is the management of stock. It costs money to hold stock (warehousing, security and so on), so the business will not wish to hold more stock than is necessary. On the other hand, each time that stock runs out, new stock has to be ordered. There are costs associated with reordering, so the business will wish to minimise the number of times it has to do this. In addition, orders have variable **lead times** (the time taken between placing an order and its delivery), and the business will wish to minimise the disruption caused by this fact.

Before we take a look at the case study, it is important to define some common terms used in inventory control.

Inventory or stock is the number of units of stock held by the business.

Opening inventory or opening stock is the number of units of stock held by a business at the opening of a period of trading.

Closing inventory or closing stock is the number of units of stock held at the close of a period of trading.

Stockout is the state of being out of stock of a particular item.

A **backorder** has to be placed if a customer order cannot be met from inventory. The customer must then wait until the goods arrive in stock. The number of units which the customer is waiting for is known as the backorder quantity. The customer may not tolerate this waiting and may go somewhere else, in which case the business will lose sales.

Lead time is the delay period between the placing of an order and receipt of the goods.

Reorder quantity is the number of stock units which the firm orders, whenever it experiences a stockout or reaches the reorder point (see below). The firm may decide to have a fixed reorder quantity each time this situation occurs.

Reorder point. A firm will rarely wait until it is completely out of stock before it reorders. Instead, it will usually place an order when stock falls below a certain level. This level is known as the reorder point.

Average inventory. Over a period of time, the inventory changes constantly. We need to find the average inventory being carried, because this will allow us to determine the cost of holding stock. There are various analytical methods for determining average inventory, but in this unit we will take it to mean the average of all the closing stock figures over a representative number of trading periods.

Fixed inventory cost. Most of the costs incurred by the act of ordering goods are fixed. The actual jobs of sourcing, negotiating, ordering and clerical work are the same whatever the size of the order.

Variable inventory cost. Each unit of stock held will incur a holding charge (security, warehousing and so on). Total inventory carrying cost over a period is calculated by multiplying unit holding cost by average inventory. In addition, most managers agree that there is an extra cost incurred if there are backorders to be met. This is because of the loss of goodwill, extra clerical and shipping costs and so on which backorders usually create. In practice, the backorder cost for a period will be calculated by multiplying unit backordering cost by average backorder quantity over a period. The total variable inventory cost is the sum of inventory carrying costs and average backorder costs.

We are now ready to look at a stock control case study.

5.2 The components of an inventory problem

Case Study: Packard Chemicals plc

Packard Chemicals plc is concerned about developing a viable inventory policy for one particular product which is bought in and refined by the company and then reshipped to its own customers. At the moment, the company has a fixed reorder quantity of 120 units, but wishes to determine the optimum reorder point. The company would like to see some costings for various reorder quantities and reorder points.

Packard Chemicals plc calculates that inventory holding cost is £10 per unit per year. Backorder cost is £100 per unit per year. For the moment, the company wishes to keep the reorder quantity fixed at 120 units, so we can initially disregard the actual ordering cost, since this will be the same whatever variations we make to the reorder point. However, the company has stated that the analysis might persuade it to vary its practice on this point, so that any simulation model would need to be flexible.

Using this data, total variable cost of inventory per year is:

- £10 multiplied by average inventory, plus
- £100 multiplied by average backorder.

Packard Chemicals plc has established from records that daily customer demand for the product could be any figure in the region of 17 to 23 units. The company has reliable data from its ordering records which states that lead time could be as little as one day, but has never been more then five days. The company has established a tentative probability distribution for both of these variables. These are shown as Tables 38 and 39.

Daily demand (units)	Probability
17	0.05
18	0.10
19	0.20
20	0.30
21	0.20
22	0.10
23	0.05

Table 38: Distribution of daily demand

Lead time period (days)	Probability
1	0.10
2	0.20
3	0.40
4	0.20
5	0.10

Table 39: Distribution of lead times

Various reorder points need to be tested as to their effect on total inventory cost. For each day of the simulation model:

- a demand figure is randomly generated
- the demand figure is subtracted from the opening inventory
- this results in a closing inventory figure.

If closing inventory reaches the test minimum reorder point, then the reorder quantity is called for and a random lead-time figure is generated. Backorders must be kept carefully tracked. Inventory cannot fall below 0, but any orders which cannot be met from stock will add to the quantity of backorders.

For the purposes of this simulation model we will assume that goods reordered are available to meet customers' requirements on the day following their arrival at *Packard Chemicals plc*. We will assume that the current reorder point is 80 units, and the reorder quantity is 120 units.

In order to visualise what is happening in this model, we can take an example of three days of business. We will need to randomly select demand figures for each day of business together with lead times whenever an order needs to be placed. The result is shown in Table 40. Remember that the reorder point is a stock level of 80 units and reorder quantity is 120 units. In other words, if stock falls **below** 80 units, then an order for 120 units is placed.

A	B	C	D	E	F	G	H	I	J	K	L
0		120	0	0	120	0				N	
1	N	120	0	21	99	0	N			N	
2	N	99	0	19	80	0	N			N	
3	N	80	0	22	58	0	Y	3	7	Y	7

Table 40: Three days of business for Packard Chemicals plc

Each of the rows in Table 40 represents one day of business for the company. The columns of Table 40 are as follows:

Column A contains a day code

Column B specifies whether an order is due to arrive on that day

Column C gives the quantity of opening stock

Column D gives the opening backorder

Column E gives the level of demand

Column F gives the closing stock

Column G gives the closing backorder

Column H specifies whether an order needs to be placed

Column I gives the lead time for the order

Column J specifies the day on which the order will arrive

Column K specifies whether there is an order pending

Column L specifies the day on which the pending order will arrive.

Notice that, as well as opening and closing stock columns, the model also contains opening and closing backorder columns. It is very important to keep careful separate track of this, since any newly delivered inventory must have backorders deducted from it (remember that backorders represent waiting customers, who must be supplied before any new customers). The resulting figure will be the opening stock for that day.

Day 0 in Table 40 represents the starting position before the simulation commences, with opening stock at 120 and no backorders.

Day 1 Opening stock is the same as the closing stock for day 0, 120 units. A randomly sampled demand figure of 21 was obtained, leaving closing stock at 99 units (120 – 21). There are no backorders to be dealt with and no reorder needs to be placed, because stock has not fallen below 80. Consequently, we do not need to worry about lead time and do not need to track the progress of pending orders.

Day 2 Opening stock is 99 units, and there is no backorder to be given priority. Demand on day 2 is 19 units, leaving a closing stock of 80 units (99 – 19). Closing backorder is 0. As the stock level is 80 no reorder is placed yet.

Day 3 Opening stock is 80 units. Demand on that day is 22 units and there is no backorder to deal with. Closing stock has therefore fallen to 58 (80 – 22), which is below the reorder point of 80. This triggers a new order for 120 stock units, which (in this instance) has a lead time of three days. Thus it will replenish opening stock on day 7. In reality, it arrives on day 6, but incoming stock is only available the day after arrival.

ACTIVITY 36

Continue the simulation of the *Packard Chemicals plc* inventory control problem until the end of day 12. Start on day 4, with the situation at the end of day 3 as shown in Table 40.

Use the following values for demand and lead times. They have been randomly taken from the distributions for these variables in Tables 38 and 39. Continue to make the assumption that 120 is the reorder quantity and that a stock of 80 is the reorder point. The lead times will only be needed on the occasions when an order is placed.

Day	4	5	6	7	8	9	10	11	12
Demand	19	20	21	20	21	18	19	19	20
Lead time	3	4	2	3	2	2	5	2	3

Using the demand and lead time values in Activity 36, the continued simulation would look as in Table 41. The columns are as in Table 40, the minimum reorder point is a stock level of 80 units, and reorder quantity is 120 units.

A	B	C	D	E	F	G	H	I	J	K	L
0		120	0	0	120	0				N	
1	N	120	0	21	99	0	N			N	
2	N	99	0	19	80	0	N			N	
3	N	80	0	22	58	0	Y	3	7	Y	7
4	N	58	0	19	39	0	N			Y	7
5	N	39	0	20	19	0	N			Y	7
6	N	19	0	21	0	2	N			Y	7
7	Y	118	0	20	98	0	N			N	
8	N	98	0	21	77	0	Y	2	11	Y	11
9	N	77	0	18	59	0	N			Y	11
10	N	59	0	19	40	0	N			Y	11
11	Y	160	0	19	141	0	N			N	
12	N	141	0	20	121	0	N			N	

Table 41: Simulation of 12 days' business for Packard Chemicals plc

It may seem to you that displaying the data as shown in Table 41 duplicates some of the information. For example, columns J and L say essentially the same thing. This duplication is necessary in order to make the spreadsheet model work.

It should not be necessary to remind you that a simulation run of the size undertaken in Activity 36 (12 days only) is insufficient to show how the current reorder policy is working. The larger the sample, the more we can start to identify a pattern in the run of results.

ACTIVITY 37

Use the data generated by your answer to Activity 36 to calculate the average inventory and average backorder for the period involved. Hence estimate the annual total variable cost of inventory.

In working through this activity remember that for this company:

inventory cost = (avge daily inventory × 10) + (avge daily backorder × 100)

avge inventory = avge of all closing inventory figures for the period

Exclude day 0 from the calculation.

Using the data from Table 41 and the answer to Activity 36, we have that:

$$\text{avge daily inventory} = \frac{(99 + 80 + 58 + 39 + 19 + 0 + 98 + 77 + 59 + 40 + 141 + 121)}{12}$$

$$= 69.25$$

avge daily backorder = 0.17

In each case, the **closing** figure for each day has been averaged.

Thus average inventory cost for a reorder level of 80 is:

(69.25 × 10) + (0.17 × 100) = £709.50 per year

Remember that this cost figure does not include ordering cost and is based on a sample of only 12 days.

In working through this simple manual simulation of the *Packard Chemicals plc* model we have established that the random input variables are demand and lead time, and that reorder point, reorder quantity, initial opening stock, initial backorders, order cost and backorder cost are parameters. We have also established that the most important algorithms we need to formulate will calculate:

- average closing stock
- average closing backorder
- average inventory cost.

5.3 Developing a spreadsheet model to solve an inventory problem

Implementing the *Packard Chemicals Plc* inventory problem on a spreadsheet results in a far more complex model than those you have had to deal with in previous sections. The case study is a good illustration of the complexities involved in model construction. Among the *Microsoft Excel* files on the software pack is a full implementation of the problem. This file is called **Stockcon.xls**. You may wish to study this file if you encounter difficulties while constructing your own model in the following activities.

ACTIVITY 38

In this activity we design the **Parameters** sheet for *Packard Chemicals plc*. Open a new workbook.

Enter the demand data (see Table 38) in cells A6 to B12. Remember to use the standard *Microsoft Excel* look-up table form, with cumulative probabilities in cells A6 to A12 and demand in cells B6 to B12.

Enter the lead time data (see Table 39) in cells D6 to E10 in the same way.

Enter the fixed parameters in cells D16 to D21 as follows:

in D16 enter the initial opening stock **(120)**

in D17 enter initial opening backorders **(0)**

in D18 enter order cost **(10)**

in D19 enter backorder cost **(100)**

in D20 enter reorder quantity **(120)**

in D21 enter reorder point **(80)**

Give suitable descriptive titles to these items, rename **Sheet1** as **Parameters** and save the file as **Packard.xls**.

Your **Parameters** sheet should look similar to the one in Table 42.

	A	B	C	D	E
1	Stock Control: Packard Chemicals plc				
2					
3	(a) Look-up Tables				
4	Daily Customer Demand			Order Lead Times	
5	Cum Pr	Amount		Cum Pr	Days
6	0.00	17		0.00	1
7	0.05	18		0.10	2
8	0.15	19		0.30	3
9	0.35	20		0.70	4
10	0.65	21		0.90	5
11	0.85	22			
12	0.95	23			
13					
14					
15					
16	Initial Opening Stock			120	
17	Initial Opening Backorders			0	
18	Ordering Costs (per order)			10	
19	Backorder Costs (per order)			100	
20	Reorder Quantity			120	
21	Reorder Point			80	

Table 42: Parameters sheet for Packard Chemicals plc

The construction of the **Parameters** sheet for *Packard Chemicals plc* does not differ in any significant way from that for any other model. The real sophistication of this model is to be found in the **Workings** sheet. This is a dynamic model, so that any single day of the simulation will need to refer back to the previous day. The *IF* statement will be used extensively and you will also need to use several other *Microsoft Excel* formulae which you may not have met before.

THE AND STATEMENT

This function is used in conjunction with *IF*. In some circumstances you may need to test whether more than one condition is true when using the *IF* statement. You accomplish this by using the *AND* statement. The syntax is as follows:

IF(AND(condition 1,condition 2),action,alternative action)

The *IF* statement will now check to see that both conditions are true. If they are, then 'action' is taken. If one or both are false then 'alternative action' is taken. For example, the following statement will check to see if the number in cell A5 is more than 10 and less than 20:

IF(AND(A5>10,A5<20,"In range","Out of range")

If it is, the message 'In range' will be written; otherwise the message 'Out of range' will be displayed. In this example the actions involve displaying text, but they can also perform arithmetic, in which case no speech marks are required.

THE OR STATEMENT

This function is also used in conjunction with *IF,* and also checks whether more than one condition is true. However, while *AND* ensures that both conditions must be true if the action is to be taken, *OR* means that the action is performed if one or more condition is true. The syntax is identical to *AND.* For example, the following formula will test whether cell A5 contains a number which is either less than 0 or more than 1,000,000:

IF(OR(A5<0,A5>1000000,"Out of range","In range")

If either of these conditions is true, then the message 'Out of range' gets displayed, otherwise 'In range' is shown.

With these extra functions it is now possible to construct the main **Workings** sheet for this model. It will be useful to have Table 41 in front of you as you work, as the construction of the spreadsheet model will closely follow the layout to be found there. The first row of the **Workings** sheet will be substantially different from the rest of the model, as it will need to contain the initial set-up information.

ACTIVITY 39

Open your workbook **Packard.xls** and select **Sheet2**.

In column A, from A9 to A109 enter the numbers 0 to 100. This column should be titled **Day**, and identifies each business day with a code number. Day 0 will contain the initial set-up information.

Column B will display whether an order is due to arrive on that day. It is better if a numeric code is used for this data rather than alphabetic characters. The number '1' will indicate that an order is arriving while a '0' will indicate the contrary. As the first row is day 0, enter a **0** in cell **B9**.

Column C will contain the opening stock for the day. Enter a formula in cell **C9** which shows the opening stock at day 0. This is stated in the **Parameters** sheet.

Similarly, column D will display the opening backorders for the day (the orders which must be dealt with before any other business). Enter a formula into cell **D9** showing the opening backorders. This is stated in the **Parameters** sheet.

Column E will display the daily demand. As day 0 only contains set-up information, this should initially read 0. Enter this figure into cell **E7**.

Column F will display the closing stock for the day. As this is day 0 and no business has yet been done, closing stock will be the same as opening stock, so enter an appropriate formula into cell **F9**.

Column G will display the closing backorders. On day 0 this will be the same as opening backorders. Enter a formula into cell **G9**.

Column H will show whether an order for more stock is being placed on that day. Leave this column blank for the moment.

Column I will show the lead time for any order placed. Leave this blank for the moment.

Column J displays the day a pending order is due to arrive at the plant. Leave this blank for the moment.

Column K will display whether or not an order is pending. In the completed worksheet a numeric code will be used here: 0 means 'no' and 1 means 'yes'. As this is day 0, enter a **0** into cell **K9**.

Column L will contain a number representing the day that a pending order will arrive at the plant: otherwise it will contain a 0. This duplicates information that is already contained in column J but, as you will see later, is needed for the spreadsheet to work correctly. Enter a 0 into cell **L9**. Finally, give proper titles to each column, rename **Sheet2** as **Workings** and save your changes.

	A	B	C	D	E	F	G	H	I	J	K	L
1	Packard Chemicals plc: Main Workings Area *0 = No, 1= Yes											
2												
3												
4		*						*			*	
5				Open			Close				Ord	
6		Ord	Open	Back		Close	Back	Place		Arr	Ord	Arr
7	Day	Arr	Stock	Ord	Dem	Stock	Ord	Ord	Lead	Day	Pend	Day
8												
9	0	0	120	0	0	120	0				0	0

Table 43: Initial set-up data for the Packard Chemicals plc Workings sheet

The initial layout of the spreadsheet is shown in Table 43.

In cell C9 the initial opening stock figure (120) should be obtained from the **Parameters** sheet by entering the formula:

=Parameters!$D$16

In cell D9 the initial opening backorders are obtained by the formula:

=**Parameters!$D$17**

In cell F9 the initial closing stock is the same as opening stock and is obtained by the formula =**C9**.

In G9 the initial closing backorders is the same as opening backorders and is obtained by the formula =**D9**.

Having entered the initial set-up information in day 0, we can now proceed to start the simulation proper. For this you will need to make extensive use of the IF statement together with *AND* and *OR*. You will find this model a challenging one to construct.

ACTIVITY 40

This activity continues with the **Packard.xls** file.

1. Column B should contain a '1' if a delivery of stock has been received that day and a '0' otherwise. You can best do this by comparing the current day (recorded in column A) with column K (which shows the day on which a pending order is due and a '0' if no order is due). Enter a formula in cell **B10** which checks whether a pending order has arrived and then takes the appropriate action.

2. Column C will contain the opening stock which will be the previous day's closing stock plus newly arrived inventory (if any), minus the previous day's closing backorders (if any). Enter a formula into **C10** which calculates this amount. You will need to exercise care because the calculation might produce a negative figure, and stock cannot be less than 0. Your formula will need to produce either a positive stock figure, or a 0 in those cases where demand is greater than stock.

3. Column D states whether there are any backorders to fill, and how many. Enter a formula into cell **D10** which calculates this.

4. Column E displays daily demand sampled from the demand look-up table on the **Parameters** sheet. Enter a formula into cell **E10** which does this.

5. Column F displays closing stock, which is opening stock (column C) minus demand (column E). If demand is greater than opening stock, this figure will be negative, in which case the closing stock will be reported as 0. Enter a formula into cell **F10** which does this.

6. Column G displays closing backorders. This figure will either be the same as opening backorders or opening backorders plus unfulfilled demand. Enter a formula into cell **G10** which calculates the appropriate amount.

7. Column H states whether an order needs to be placed on that day. Enter a formula in cell **H10** which writes 1 if an order needs to be placed, but otherwise leaves the cell blank. In this cell you will need to check whether

stock has fallen below the reorder point and whether there is already an order pending.

(**Note**: in *Microsoft Excel*, the correct way to leave a cell blank is to use the expression ""; that is, speech marks with nothing between them.)

8. Column I displays the lead time for an order (if one has been placed). Enter a formula in cell **I10** which samples lead times from the look-up table on the **Parameters** sheet if an order has been placed, but otherwise does nothing.

9. Column J displays the day on which an order will arrive. Enter a formula into cell **J10** which does this if an order has been placed on that day, but does nothing otherwise.

10. Column K will display a 1 if an order is pending and a 0 if not. Write a formula into cell **K10** which achieves this. An order is pending if one has been placed on that day or if the arrival day data in column L is greater than 0.

11. Column L displays the day on which a pending order will arrive or a 0 if there is none pending. Enter a formula into cell **L10** which performs this action. Although this column seems to duplicate some information, it is necessary because it is used by column B to check whether an order is being delivered that day.

12. Copy all formulae down to row 109 and save your changes.

The **Workings** sheet should look similar to the one in Table 44. Only the first three days are shown.

	A	B	C	D	E	F	G	H	I	J	K	L
1					Packard Chemicals plc: Main Workings Area *0 = No, 1= Yes							
2												
3												
4		*						*			*	
5				Open			Close			Ord		
6		Ord	Open	Back		Close	Back	Place		Arr	Ord	Arr
7	Day	Arr	Stock	Ord	Dem	Stock	Ord	Ord	Lead	Day	Pend	Day
8												
9	0	0	120	0	0	120	0				0	0
10	1	0	120	0	20	100	0				0	0
11	2	0	100	0	21	79	0	1	3	6	1	6
12	3	0	79	0	21	58	0				1	6

Table 44: The completed Workings sheet for Packard Chemicals plc

Because of the degree of complexity of the model, detailed notes on the formulae used are given below. It is also important to point out that, because of the range of formulae provided by *Microsoft Excel*, it is possible to achieve the same result with different methods. For this reason the solutions below should not be regarded as definitive.

1. Column B states whether an order has arrived (0 means 'no', 1 means 'yes'). This can be achieved by using the following formula:

    =IF(L9=A10,1,0)

    This works by comparing columns A and L and taking appropriate action. Column L contains a record of when a pending order is due for each day's business. If no order is pending a 0 is shown. Column A shows the number for the current day. If an order has arrived, then the day shown in column A will be equal to the day shown in column L.

2. Column C records opening stock, which will be the previous day's closing stock plus newly arrived inventory (if any), minus the previous day's closing backorders (if any). A factor which complicates matters here is that a straightforward deduction of backorders might result in a negative number. This may be a rare occurrence but the simulation model should allow for it. The following formula will achieve the required result:

    =IF(B10=0,F9,MAX(Parameters!$D$20+F9–G9,0))

    This command first checks B10, to see whether stock has just been delivered. If it has not (B10=0) then opening stock will be the same as yesterday's closing stock. If a delivery has been made, then the delivery quantity is added to yesterday's closing stock and backorders subtracted. Notice the use of the *MAX* command. This selects which of the two values (0 or adjusted stock) is greatest, and rules out the possibility of negative opening stock.

3. Column D states whether there are any backorders still to fulfil at the opening of the day's business. This can easily be checked: if opening stock is greater than 0 then there can be no backorders. However, if opening stock is 0 then opening backorders will be equal to yesterday's closing backorders less backorders cleared by a new delivery of stock. The following formula calculates this:

    IF(C10>0,0,G9–(B10*Parameters!$D$20))

4. Column E records the daily demand figure. A combination of *VLOOKUP* and *RAND* can be used here. The following formula samples demand from the look-up table in the **Parameters** sheet:

    =VLOOKUP(RAND(),Parameters!$A$6:$B$12,2)

5. Column F keeps track of closing stock, which is calculated by subtracting demand from opening stock. As before, the possibility of a negative result arises on those days when demand is higher than the stock level. When this happens the negative should be adjusted to 0. The following formula will place the correct amount into the cell:

    =IF((C10–E10)>0,C10–E10,0)

6. Column G keeps a record of closing backorders. The following formula checks to see whether opening stock is greater than demand:

=IF(C10>E10,D10,D10+(E10–C10)

If it is, then there will be no new backorders, so that closing backorders is the same as the opening figure. If, however, demand exceeds stock, then the amount of the shortfall (E10–C10) is added to opening backorders.

7. Column H will cause a 1 to be displayed if a new order for stock has to be placed on that day. This can easily be tested by comparing the closing stock figure with the reorder point.

Any outstanding orders pending must also be checked or duplicate orders will result. The following formula uses the *AND* and *OR* statements in combination with *IF* to accomplish this:

=IF(AND((OR(K9=0,A10=L9)),(F9<Parameters!$D$21)),1,"")

This is quite a complicated formula. First, it checks to see whether a delivery was pending. It checks if column K had a 0 in it the previous day, Column K displays whether an order is pending with a 1. If a 0 appears, then there is no pending order. Second, it checks to see whether an order was made that day (L9=A10). If either these conditions is satisfied then a new order can be placed without creating a duplicate order. Third, the command checks whether closing stock is less than the reorder point. If closing stock is less than the reorder point and a new order can be placed without creating a duplicate order, a 1 will be placed in column H. Otherwise, nothing will be done ("").

8. Column I checks to see if an order has been placed that day. If it has, a lead time will be sampled from the look-up table in the **Parameters** sheet. Otherwise nothing happens. This is done using the following formula:

=IF(H10=1,VLOOKUP(RAND(),Parameters!$D$6:$E$10,2),"")

9. Column J checks to see whether an order has been placed on that day. If it has, then a calculation of the day of arrival is made. It should be remembered that the stock is available for use on the day after it arrives, so that 1 should always be added to the result. The following formula will calculate the correct figure by adding the lead time of the order to the serial number of the current day and then adding 1:

=IF(H10=1,A10+I10+1,"")

If no order has been placed then no action will be taken.

10. Column K shows for each day of business whether an order is pending (1) or not (0). This information is required by the formula in column H to avoid duplicating orders. The following formula combines the *IF* and *OR* statements to achieve this:

=IF(OR(L9>A10,H10=1),1,0)

Two checks are needed. Has an order been placed in the recent past and is still pending? Or has an order been placed on the current day? If the current day (column A) is less than the figure in the previous day's 'day of arrival' column (L), then an order is pending. If the number in column H for the current day is 1, then an order has just been placed.

11. This column keeps a record for each day of when a pending order is due. If no order is pending, a 0 is shown. The information is required by the formula in column B as a means of checking whether an order has been delivered on the current day. The following formula checks column 10 to see if an order is pending:

   =IF(K10=1,MAX(L9,J10),0)

   If it is, then column J for the current day will be compared with the column L value for yesterday. The maximum of these figures will be chosen. This ensures that the correct day of delivery will be placed in column L.

As this particular model is more sophisticated than the previous examples, it may be necessary for you to study it in some detail to understand it. Check that you understand what each formula is doing, especially those using the logic statements, such as *IF*, *AND* and *OR*.

Now that the model has been implemented we can turn to the task of obtaining useful summary output concerning the current restocking policy.

ACTIVITY 41

Open your workbook **Packard.xls** and select **Sheet3**. Write formulae to calculate the following:

1. The average closing stock over the period of the simulation.

2. The standard deviation of closing stock.

3. Average closing backorders over the period.

4. The standard deviation of closing backorders.

5. The yearly cost of ordering stock.

6. The number of times an order for stock was placed during the simulation period.

7. The number of days a stockout occurred during the year.

Give suitable labels to the information, rename **Sheet3** as **Output** and save your changes.

Your worksheet should look similar to Table 45.

	A	B	C
1			
2			
3			
4			
5	Average Closing Stock		72.51
6	Standard Deviation Closing Stock		37.48
7	Average Closing Backorder		0.08
8	Standard Deviation Backorder		0.50
9	Cost (Year)		£733.10
10	Number of times order was placed		17
11	Number of times stockout occurred		3
12			

Table 45: Output sheet for Packard Chemicals plc

1. Average closing stock is calculated by the formula:

   =AVERAGE(Workings!F10:F109)

2. The standard deviation of closing stock is calculated by the formula:

   =STDEVP(Workings!F10:F109)

3. Average closing backorders is calculated by the formula:

   =AVERAGE(Workings!G10:G109)

4. The standard deviation of closing backorders is calculated by the formula:

   =STDEVP(Workings!G10:G109)

5. Remember that the cost of keeping a unit of stock for a year is £10 while for a backorder the cost is £100. We can calculate that yearly cost is £100 multiplied by average backorders, plus £10 multiplied by average stock. Thus the formula to enter is:

   =Parameters!D18*D5+Parameters!D19*D7

6. The easiest way to calculate the number of times an order for stock is placed is to use the conditional *COUNTIF* statement. The following formula will examine the H column, which records a 1 if an order has been placed, and the number of times a 1 occurs will be calculated:

   =COUNTIF(Workings!H10:H109,"=1")

7. A similar formula can be used to calculate the number of times a stockout occurred:

   =COUNTIF(Workings!G10:G109,">0")

This formula examines column G of **Workings** and counts the number of days it is greater than 0. As this column records closing backorders, the formula will calculate the desired value.

We can now use this model to explore the effect of changing some of the main parameters. For example, how would cost be affected if the reorder level or the reorder quantity were altered?

ACTIVITY 42

At the moment *Packard Chemicals plc* has a minimum reorder point of 80 units. By altering the appropriate part of the worksheet, compare the estimated inventory costs of the following minimum reorder points for the period of the simulation.

1. 60 units.
2. 70 units.
3. 80 units.
4. 90 units.

What is your advice to the company?

The following figures were obtained from a single run of the model. Normally, as has already been discussed previously, the procedure would be to make several runs to check for the existence of a steady state. As always, the use of random numbers will mean that your own results are unlikely to be exactly the same as those below.

1. If the reorder level is 60 units then the estimated inventory cost is £1,300.10.

2. If the reorder level is 70 units then the estimated inventory cost is £712.08.

3. If the reorder level is 80 units then the estimated inventory cost is £692.87.

4. If the reorder level is 90 units then the estimated inventory cost is £677.52.

In this case, other things remaining equal, a reorder point of 90 units is preferable as this is associated with the lowest estimated inventory cost. However, it is usual to postpone definitive conclusions until the results of several runs are available.

The analyst would also be wise to study the effect of such changes on other aspects of the inventory policy. Increasing the minimum reorder point, although it decreases the risks of backorders, might result in *Packard Chemicals plc* having to place more frequent orders.

5.4 Some complications in the simulation of inventory problems

The model of *Packard Chemicals plc* which we have developed in this section provides a starting point for a thorough analysis of inventory problems. In practice, we would need to refine the model to make it approximate more closely to real life situations.

ORDERING COST VERSUS HOLDING COST

In the *Packard Chemicals plc* model we have only considered two types of inventory cost: backorder cost, which is an emergency cost element caused by excess of demand over supply, and stock holding cost. There would also be a cost incurred as a result of placing an order. While the holding cost is variable, depending upon the size of the stock, the ordering cost is fixed, being the same whether an order is for 5 or 500 units. The larger the order size, the less frequently orders need to be placed. This consequently reduces order cost, but increases holding cost because the average stock held is higher. These costs therefore tend to be inversely related, which complicates the task of establishing an optimal inventory policy.

QUEUE BEHAVIOUR

Customers placing an order with *Packard Chemicals plc* will constitute a queue and, like all queues, will have certain behaviour patterns. For example, if there is insufficient stock to satisfy an order backordering has to take place. Will customers wait for their goods, or will they go elsewhere? If they do decide to wait, how long will they remain as patient customers before reneging?

In the *Packard Chemicals plc* model we assumed that customers would wait until their orders arrived. This is almost certainly an over-simplification of the process and the next step forward would probably involve exploring queue behaviour and incorporating it into the model.

DEPENDENT AND INDEPENDENT DEMAND

Inventory can be classed as either dependent or independent, according to where the demand for the stock items comes from. If the demand for the stock comes from outside the organisation then it is described as **demand independent**. The *Packard Chemicals plc* model was developed for such a situation, for the demand for these stock items originated with customers outside the business. In the **demand dependent** case, the demand for the inventory comes from inside the organisation. For example, a manufacturer assembles components into some finished product or products. Stocks of these components are held to meet an internally set demand for the final products. A distinction between these two types of inventory is necessary because they require very different control systems. Tailor-made systems exist to facilitate inventory control in the demand dependent situation, these methods being generally known as **materials requirements planning** or MRP.

Summary

In this section we examined the contribution that simulation could make to the exploration of inventory problems. We started by introducing some of the key concepts used in inventory control. We then used a case study to identify the elements of an inventory problem. In Section 5.3 we used *Microsoft Excel* to run a simulation of the problem and explore the impact of varying the reorder point. Finally we briefly discussed some factors which need to be considered in the development of a more sophisticated model.

In the next section we look at the time element in waiting line problems.

Section 6

Waiting Lines: the Time Element

Introduction

Both the *Torch plc* model in Section 4 and the *Packard Chemicals plc* model in Section 5 were dynamic models involving queues and service points. We now introduce another element into the waiting line problem, the problem of time. In Sections 6.1 and 6.2 we use a case study to introduce the elements of a waiting line problem in which the time element is paramount. In Section 6.3 we use *Microsoft Excel* to produce a model of the problem. Finally, in Section 6.4, we look at some complicating factors in the simulation of such problems.

6.1 A waiting line problem with a time element

We are already familiar with the concept of queues of variable amounts of people or products waiting for a service from a centre with limited resources. We may now add the following observations.

1. The people or products arriving for service do so at irregular intervals. There may be bunching of arrival, with many arriving within very short intervals of time. Or there may be long periods when there are no arrivals. We shall refer to the time period between the arrival of customers or products as the **inter-arrival time.**
2. When a person or product enters the service area, there is no guarantee that they will all spend equal amounts of time in service. In fact, we know from our own experience that service times differ, even for customers apparently requiring the same degree of attention.

Simulation can help us build a model of such a system which has limited service facilities catering for customers who arrive at irregular intervals and who spend variable periods of time in service.

Case Study: the cafeteria problem

In order to illustrate the difficulties that time causes in simulation models we will consider the case of a university cafeteria which has just one service point. Customers take their goods and queue up to pay at this point. (Of course, many cafeterias have multiple service points and simulation models can be constructed which will deal with such situations. Nevertheless, for simplicity's sake, we will develop a model with only one service point.)

Students seem to arrive at random intervals at the cafeteria but, after a little research, a probability distribution can be constructed. This is shown as Table 46.

Inter-arrival times (seconds)	Probability
10	0.10
15	0.25
20	0.30
25	0.25
30	0.10

Table 46: Inter-arrival time probabilities

This table shows inter-arrival times. For example, the probability that there is a 15-second interval between the appearance of customers is 0.25. The expected (or mean) inter-arrival time (μ) is calculated from the following formula:

$$\mu = \sum X.pr(X)$$

X stands for the inter-arrival time, and $pr(X)$ is the probability that inter-arrival time is X. In ordinary language this means that we multiply all arrival times by their respective probabilities and add the results. In the case of the cafeteria:

$$\mu = \sum X.pr(X)$$

$$= (10 \times 0.1) + (15 \times 0.25) + (20 \times 0.30) + (25 \times 0.25) + (30 \times 0.10)$$

$$= 20 \text{ seconds}$$

Note: time is, in theory, a **continuous** variable, which means that it can take any value. In this model we are treating it as **discrete**. A discrete variable can only take certain fixed values. In the case of the cafeteria we treat customers as arriving at either 10, 15, 20, 25 or 30 second intervals. This assumption of discreteness is made for the sake of simplicity and will make our model less realistic but will not invalidate it.

Also, when a customer arrives at the cafeteria, they may have to wait in the queue for service (remember that there is only one service point). Even when they leave the queue and enter service, they do not leave the system until the cashier has finished the transaction. Time taken in a cafeteria service area is variable. It has been established that a likely distribution of service times is as shown in Table 47.

Service times (seconds)	Probability
5	0.08
10	0.14
15	0.18
20	0.24
25	0.22
30	0.14

Table 47: Service times

From Table 47 we see, for example, that a customer who is currently in service has a 24 per cent chance of being there for 20 seconds. The **expected waiting time** in service can be calculated as:

$$\mu = \sum X.pr(X)$$

$$= (5 \times 0.08) + (10 \times 0.14) + (15 \times 0.18) + (20 \times 0.24) + (25 \times 0.22) + (30 \times 0.14)$$

$$= 19 \text{ seconds}$$

We make the same simplification of discreteness for waiting times as we do for inter-arrival times, so customers either spend 5, 10, 15, 20, 25 or 30 seconds in service.

So, on average, customers of this cafeteria arrive every 20 seconds, spending 19 seconds in service. Of course, these figures are averages and it would be much more useful to have some more detailed information, such as a probability distribution for time spent in the queuing and serving system.

6.2 Basic elements of the model

The university cafeteria problem has the following basic elements:

- there is only one waiting line (inter-arrival times are as shown in Table 46)
- the waiting line is treated on a first come, first served basis
- we shall assume no balking or reneging
- there is only one service point (service times are as shown in Table 47).

Some of these assumptions (such as no balking or reneging) may seem unrealistic. This would be a fair criticism of the model but, as we have remarked before, it is customary practice in building simulation models to start by constructing a simple model first. When the simple model works we may then begin to make it more realistic by introducing extra variables and parameters, or other more complex features.

ACTIVITY 43

Think about how you would build a simulation model of a 'single queue, single server' system, such as the cafeteria model.

1. What are the main parameters and variables in the cafeteria model?

2. Write down the most important output measures you would expect from such a simulation. In other words, what would the builder of such a service system wish to know?

---

1. In the cafeteria problem the variables are:
   - the inter-arrival times
   - the service times.

   There are no fixed parameters specifically referred to, but the analyst may wish to make the number of people in the queue at the start of the simulation a part of the analysis. Customers do not always come to a cafeteria servery and find no queue. The analyst may wish to explore how well the system copes with starting queues of varying sizes.

2. The planner of a cafeteria might be concerned with the following factors.

- Is there a tendency for a queue of customers to build up over time, or is the system able to cope with the rate at which people turn up?

- Is the single service point over-stretched or are there many long periods when the server is idle?

- How long do people spend in the queue waiting for service and what is the distribution of these times?

- How long do people spend in the system as a whole (queuing time plus service time) and what is the distribution of these times?

You may well have thought of other factors in answer to this activity, but the above are probably the most important.

In passing, you should compare this cafeteria model with the *Torch plc* assembly line model developed earlier in the unit. Both models involve queues waiting for service, and in both cases an important reason for carrying out the simulation would be to analyse the degree of under or over-utilisation of the system. The differences between the two revolve around the fact that the cafeteria queue is human, and so the question of queue discipline may arise. Also, unlike *Torch plc*, we have made the question of time a crucial feature of the cafeteria problem. A flow diagram of the cafeteria model is shown in Figure 8.

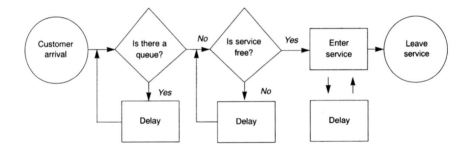

Figure 8: Flow chart of cafeteria model

6.3 Developing a computer model

As with the development of most simulation models, it is of great help if we begin by thinking about the kinds of information we want the model to produce. It is also useful to carry out a very small manual simulation, as this often produces valuable insight on the building of a spreadsheet model.

The first question which arises is how we are to record events in the cafeteria. Should we record activity in the cafeteria on a minute-by-minute basis, or should we record events by observing what happens to each customer? It is at this point that we come up against the limitations of the spreadsheet in simulation modelling. Versatile as it is, *Microsoft Excel* is not a purpose-designed simulation program and will have difficulties in coping with models where the passing of time is the key event. Consequently, we will regard the appearance of customers as the main event. The major effect of designing the model this way will mean that each line of the **Workings** sheet of a *Microsoft Excel* model will correspond to a single customer and will record when they come into the system and when they leave the system. If we based the model on the passing of time, each row of the worksheet would correspond to a particular point of chronological time, say a minute.

Having decided on the particular method to follow, we need to decide how data is to be recorded. The scheme shown in Table 48 will be used as a basic framework for developing a computer model of the cafeteria problem. The meaning of each of the columns in the table is described below.

Customer number	Inter-arrival time	Clock arrival time	Time entering service	Time in service	Time exit service	Wait time	Total time spent
1							
2							

Table 48: Suggested scheme for the cafeteria problem

Customer number

This column identifies each new arrival in the cafeteria by a number. Each customer will occupy one row in the spreadsheet.

Inter-arrival time

Inter arrival time records the time elapsed (in seconds) between the arrival of the current customer and the previous one. It will be a random variable sampled from the distribution of inter-arrival times.

Clock arrival time

This is chronological time which, starting from a clock time of 0 seconds, keeps a track of the time of arrival.

Time entering service

This column records the clock time when the customer enters service. It is not the same as the time of arrival because some customers may not be able to enter service straight away but may have to wait until the service area becomes free.

Time in service

This records the time a customer spends in service. It will be a random variable sampled from the distribution of service times.

Time exit service
This column records the time the customer leaves service, and will be the result of adding the time spent in service to the time of entering service.

Wait time
Wait time is the amount of time the customer spends waiting for service and will be the result of calculating the difference between the time of entering service and the time that the customer arrived in the cafeteria. Sometimes it will be 0 (when the customer does not have to wait).

Total time spent
The final column records the total time spent in the whole system: that is, wait time plus service time.

Figure 9 may help to clarify this process.

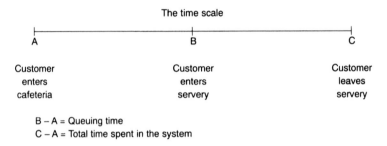

The time scale

A
Customer enters cafeteria

B
Customer enters servery

C
Customer leaves servery

B – A = Queuing time
C – A = Total time spent in the system

Figure 9: The customer's progress through the system

ACTIVITY 44

In this activity you will simulate the activity in the cafeteria during the arrival of the first five customers. Assume that the customers have the following inter-arrival and service times.

Customer	1	2	3	4	5
Inter-arrival time	20	25	10	20	25
Service time	25	20	25	25	15

All times are in seconds. Start the recording of time at 0 seconds with no customers in the queue. Remember that inter-arrival time refers to the gap between the arrival of the current customer and the previous one.

The first customer has an inter-arrival time of 20 seconds and a service time of 25 seconds, so he or she will arrive 20 seconds after the start of the simulation, and will require 25 seconds in the service point.

The second customer arrives 25 seconds after the first one and needs 20 seconds of service time. The process continues in this manner. Table 49 shows how the five customers should be recorded.

Customer number	Inter-arrival time	Clock arrival time	Time entering service	Time in service	Time exit service	Wait time	Total time spent
1	20	20	20	25	45	0	25
2	25	45	45	20	65	0	20
3	10	55	65	25	90	10	35
4	20	75	90	25	115	15	40
5	25	100	115	15	130	15	30

Table 49: Data for the first five customers at the cafeteria

Customer 1 enters the cafeteria 20 seconds from the start, enters service immediately (since there are no customers already waiting), and spends 25 seconds in service. Thus customer 1 leaves service 45 seconds into the simulation (arrival time plus waiting time plus service time equals 20 + 0 + 25 = 45). Total time spent in the system is composed of waiting time plus service time, which is 25 seconds (0 + 25).

Customer 2 arrives 25 seconds after customer 1, which means an arrival time of 45 seconds from the start of simulation (20 + 25). Luckily for this customer, the previous customer is just leaving, so an immediate entry into service is possible. This customer requires 20 seconds in service, and so will exit the system at 65 seconds clock time (45 + 20).

Customer 3 is not so lucky. He or she arrives 10 seconds after customer 2 (clock time is 55 seconds) to find that the service point is occupied and will not be vacant until clock time 65 seconds. This customer will therefore have to wait for service. Service time is 25 seconds, so the customer leaves at clock time 90 seconds (65 + 25), after having spent a total time of 35 seconds in the system (10 seconds waiting time plus 25 seconds actual service).

The process will carry on in this manner for each of the first five arrivals. You should be able to see that (in this solution) customers 3, 4 and 5 have all had to wait for varying periods. Of course, in a full simulation we would carry out more iterations than this and also produce the arrival and wait times by random sampling.

We can now begin the process of building a *Microsoft Excel* model for the cafeteria problem. The scheme developed in Table 49 will be used as the template for the worksheet.

Note: there is an implementation of this model supplied with the software pack accompanying this study guide. The file is titled **Waitline.xls** and you may refer to it if you experience any difficulty.

ACTIVITY 45

Open a new *Microsoft Excel* workbook and enter the inter-arrival and service time distributions into **Sheet1** as look-up tables. Enter inter-arrival time into cells A5 to B9 and service time into cells D5 to E10. Make sure that cumulative probability is the first column for each table. There are no fixed parameters for this model.

Rename **Sheet1** as **Parameters** and save the file as **Cafe.xls**.

Your completed **Parameters** sheet should look like the one in Table 50.

	A	B	C	D	E
1	THE CAFETERIA MODEL: LOOKUP TABLES				
2					
3	INTER-ARRIVAL TIMES			SERVICE TIMES	
4	Cum Pr	Time		Cum Pr	Time
5	0.00	10		0.00	5
6	0.10	15		0.08	10
7	0.35	20		0.22	15
8	0.65	25		0.40	20
9	0.90	30		0.64	25
10				0.86	30

Table 50: Parameters Sheet for the Cafeteria Problem

Notice that this model is in stark contrast to the others encountered in this unit in that there are no fixed parameters. All of the inputs are random variables. This does not rule out the possibility that, as we refine the model, we might wish to define such values. For example, we are assuming that the simulation is starting with no one already in the queue: in other words, we are starting the model with a 'blank sheet'. We might later want to explore the situation by assuming a pre-existing queue. However, as with all simulation models, we begin with a simple position which we can refine later, should we so wish.

A completed parameters sheet is now in place, so we can begin the design of the model. As already stated, we are using Table 49 as the template for the design, so you may find it useful to have this to hand as you work. Each row of this worksheet will refer to one customer. There will be a simulation of 100 customers. This is a dynamic simulation, because the progress made by any customer will depend upon whether the previous customer is still in the system. The effect of this will be to make the formulae in the first row slightly different from the remainder. This first row will contain the information necessary to set up the model.

ACTIVITY 46

Open your **Cafe.xls** workbook and select **Sheet2**. In this activity you will complete the first row of the **Workings** sheet.

1. Column A will contain a number identifying each customer. Fill the column from A7 to A106 with numbers from 1 to 100.

2. Column B will show the inter-arrival time for each customer. In cell B7 enter a formula which samples the inter-arrival look-up table in the **Parameters** sheet.

3. Column C will show the arrival time of the customer, assuming that time begins at 0 seconds. Enter a formula into cell C7 which calculates this time.

4. Column D shows the time when the customer enters the service area. For the first customer, with no one in the queue, this will be the same as the arrival time because the customer can be dealt with immediately. Enter a formula into cell D7 which calculates this time.

5. Column E displays the amount of time the customer spends in service. This will be a time sampled from the service look-up table in the **Parameters** sheet. Enter the appropriate formula into cell E7.

6. Column F shows the time that the customer leaves service and emerges from the system. Enter a formula into cell F7 which calculates this time.

7. Column G calculates how long the customer has had to wait for service. Enter a formula into cell G7 to achieve this.

8. Column H keeps a record of the total time (queue plus waiting) that a customer spends in the system. Enter the appropriate formula into cell H7.

Enter appropriate titles for each column, rename **Sheet2** as **Workings** and save your changes.

Your **Workings** sheet should look similar to the one in Table 51.

	A	B	C	D	E	F	G	H
1	CAFETERIA MODEL MAIN WORKINGS							
2								
3								
4		Inter	Clock	Time		Time		Total
5		arrival	arrival	enter	Time in	exit	Wait	time
6	User	time	time	service	service	service	time	spent
7	1	25	25	25	15	40	0	15

Table 51: First row of the Workings sheet for the cafeteria problem

1. The quickest way to fill a column with a series of numbers is to manually enter the first two numbers and then use the **Fill** command.

2. The formula to be entered here is:

    =VLOOKUP(RAND(),Parameters!$A$5:$B$9,2)

    This will sample a value for inter-arrival time from the look-up table in the **Parameters** worksheet.

3. Clock arrival time for the first customer will be the same as the inter-arrival time (because the clock starts at 0 seconds). Consequently, all you need to enter into cell C7 is the formula **=B7**, which copies the time from B7 into C7.

4. The time that the customer enters service is the same as the clock arrival time, because there are no existing customers in the queue. Therefore, the formula **=C7** should be entered into cell D7.

5. Column E displays the service time for the current customer. Enter the following formula:

    =VLOOKUP(RAND(),Parameters!$D$5:$E$10,2)

    This samples a value from the appropriate **Parameters** sheet look-up table, and inserts this value into cell E7.

6. Column F displays the time when the customer leaves the service. This is calculated by taking the service time and adding it to the time the customer comes into the system. The formula **=D7+E7** should be entered into cell F7.

7. Wait time is the time the customer spends in the queue waiting for service. It will be calculated by taking the time of actual entry to the service area minus the clock arrival time. Consequently, the formula **=D7–C7** should be entered into G7. Of course, as this is the first customer, the wait time will be 0.

8. Column H is the total time (queuing plus waiting) spent in the system. The formula **=F7–C7** should be entered into H7.

Entering the formulae for the second and subsequent customers is less easy, because the arrivals may have to wait for the servery to clear if the previous customer is still there. Nevertheless, only two formulae will be different:

- the clock arrival time in C8 to C106 will now be the last customer's arrival time plus the new customer's inter-arrival time
- the time of entering service in D8 to D106 will now be the same as the clock arrival time (if there are no customers in the queue) or the time of the last customer's exit from the system.

ACTIVITY 47

Open your worksheet **Cafe.xls.** In this activity you will complete the **Workings** sheet for the cafeteria model.

Enter formulae in cells C8 and D8 to calculate clock arrival time and time of entering service respectively. The other formulae in cells A8, B8 and E8 to H8 will be the same as in row 7.

Copy all the formulae down to row 106 to obtain a simulation model for 100 customers. Save your changes.

In cell C8 you need to enter a formula which calculates the clock arrival time for the current customer. This can be done by adding this customer's inter-arrival time to the previous customer's clock arrival time. The formula =C7+B8 will achieve this.

In D8 a formula is needed to calculate the time when the current customer enters the servery. This could be the same as the clock arrival time (C8) if the customer is lucky to have no one in front. However, the customer might find that the previous one is still there and so will be unable to enter service until he or she leaves (F7). The formula which will make the correct selection of times is =MAX(C8,F7). This will choose whatever is the greatest of the clock times.

Now that we have constructed a worksheet which simulates the arrival of 100 customers we can proceed to the final stage, which involves obtaining output from the model. There is a considerable amount of output which could be obtained from a queuing simulation model.

- How long does the customer spend in the queue on average?
- How long does the customer spend in the whole system on average?
- What is the maximum time a customer spends in the queue?
- What is the maximum time a customer spends in the system?
- How variable is waiting time?

ACTIVITY 48

In this activity you will construct an output sheet for the cafeteria model. Select **Sheet3** of your workbook **Cafe.xls**. In convenient cells on the worksheet:

1. Obtain the mean, maximum and standard deviation of the time a customer spends in the queue.

2. Obtain the mean, maximum and standard deviation for the time the customer spends in the whole system.

3. Obtain two frequency distributions, one for the time the customer spends in the queue and the other for the time spent in the system as a whole. You should cover the time range from 0 seconds to 100 seconds. Give appropriate labels to this information, rename **Sheet3** as **Output** and save your changes.

Your **Output** sheet should resemble Table 52. The actual figures recorded in your sheet will differ from those shown in Table 52 because of the random element.

	A	B	C	D	E	F	G	H	I
1	The Cafeteria: Statistical Output								
2						Distribution of time in queue/system			
3	Maximum time spent in the system				95	Time	Queue	System	
4	Maximum time spent in the queue				80	10	43	4	
5						20	18	11	
6	Mean time spent in the system				44.90	30	10	28	
7	Mean time spent in the queue				25.65	40	3	19	
8						50	3	8	
9	Standard deviation of system time				25.95	60	8	4	
10	Standard deviation of queue time				2.50	70	9	3	
11						80	6	8	
12						90	0	7	
13						100	0	8	

Table 52: Output sheet for the cafeteria problem

1. Data relating to the time spent in the queue is contained in column G on the **Workings** sheet. Consequently the correct formulae to type in are:

   =MAX(Workings!G7:G106)

   =AVERAGE(Workings!G7:G106)

   =STDEVP(Workings!G7:G106)

   These will calculate the maximum, the mean and the standard deviation respectively.

2. The data relating to time spent in the system as a whole is contained in column H on the **Workings** sheet. Use the same formulae as above but alter the cell references so that the formulae refer to column H.

3. Obtain the two frequency distributions in the usual way, using the *FREQUENCY* command. In the example in Table 52, a class interval of 10 has been chosen as convenient. Thus, 43 customers spend from 0 to 10 seconds in the queue, 18 spend from 11 to 20 seconds and so on.

   It can be seen from the above output that no customer spends more than 95 seconds in the system and 80 seconds in the queue. The frequency distributions show that 71 per cent of customers spend 30 seconds or less in the queue. However, it cannot be stressed too strongly that, because of the variability of arrival and waiting times, several reruns of the model must be obtained before any firm conclusions can be drawn.

6.4 Complicating factors in the simulation of waiting lines with a time element

In the implementation of the cafeteria model we have made several assumptions which need to be clarified.

NEXT EVENT AND FIXED TIME SIMULATION MODELS

We have chosen to log the activities at the cafeteria by proceeding from one customer to another. In effect, each row on the **Workings** sheet of the model refers to a single customer. Such models are referred to as being of the **next event** type. Other models involving time are of the **fixed time** type. This means that time is divided into a number of discrete periods (for example, seconds) and the simulation proceeds by logging activities from second to second, rather than from customer to customer. Both of these are valid types of model, but they yield different kinds of information. In practice, the analyst would first need to make a decision as to whether to use next event or fixed time. It is not uncommon for both approaches to be used simulataneously.

QUEUE BEHAVIOUR

Whenever the simulation is of a human queue rather than of a queue of objects, the question of queue behaviour naturally arises. Some people will not wait at all if they see a queue (balking), whilst others will wait for what they consider to be a tolerable period before giving up (reneging). In a sophisticated model, the analyst would need to investigate whether this behaviour existed. In practice, having constructed the basic model, it would not be too diffiult to incorporate balking and reneging. This could be done by including data giving probabilities of a customer balking and a look-up table incorporating a probability distribution of length of time before reneging.

MULTIPLE SERVICE POINTS

The cafeteria model was simplistic bcause it only allowed for one service point and one queue for this point. A sophisticated model would need to be flexible enough to cope with situations where there were multiple service points. This immediately increases the complexity of programming required, because the model would need to cope with the possibility that there might be one queue for each servery, or a single queue for both serveries. In addition, the existence of multiple serveries and multiple queues raises the possibility of customers changing from one queue to another. A spreadsheet is unable to cope with such complications, and the analyst would need to use special purpose-designed simulation software.

Summary

This section introduced a further complication into building a simulation model: the time element. We used a case study to explore a waiting line problem with a time element. We then used *Microsoft Excel* to produce a model of this problem. We saw that this involved treating the time taken between the arrival of different people or products as a variable. Furthermore, the time taken to serve customers or process products also needs to be treated as a variable. This has profound implications for the management of such service points. There could be problems if customers or products have to wait too long in a queue. There could also be problems if the service point is under-utilised.

In the final section of this unit we look briefly at some approaches to simulation which go beyond the use of spreadsheet models.

SECTION 7
Additional Topics in Simulation

Introduction

In Sections 1 to 6 we have developed a number of simulation models, some of them quite sophisticated. The technique of simulation is highly flexible and is likely to become more widely used as developments in computers proceed. This final section briefly describes some further topics for students interested in continuing their studies in the subject.

7.1 More sophisticated simulation models

You have already gained some experience in modelling such situations as:

- cash flows from new products
- returns from projected new investments
- maintenance of inventory
- queues of components and goods waiting for assembly and inspection
- queues of customers waiting for service.

The best way to develop a simulation model is to begin with a relatively simple formulation of the problem. There is no need to feel that such a procedure is second best, for once a simple model has been successfully developed modifications can be made to it to make it approximate more closely to reality. From this point of view, the models developed in this unit should be seen as starting points for the creation of more sophisticated versions.

However, the types of problems which can be modelled using simulation depend very much on the limitations of the computer software available to us. *Microsoft Excel* is capable of producing some sophisticated and useful models but has some limitations. There are many circumstances in which physical location is a key variable in a model. For example, a manager may wish to explore the effect of different locations of loading bays, despatch points and assembly lines on the flow of activity in a projected new factory building. In another example, a road traffic analyst may wish to examine the effect of different signalling and road access systems given certain assumptions about traffic flows and other similar variables. A spreadsheet is not powerful enough to handle such situations.

There are also many occasions on which we would need to make time a central element in the simulation. Most simulation models incorporating time are of the **fixed time** type. This means that time is divided into a number of equal interval periods, and the simulation proceeds by moving from one time period to another, logging what happens during each second or minute. By contrast, all of the simulation models developed in this unit are of the **next event** type. That is, the simulation proceeds by moving from one customer or product to another, rather than one time period to another. Simulation models incorporating time, especially as a continuous variable rather than a discrete one, require a higher level of developmental skills than next event models.

7.2 Computer packages commonly used in simulation

The development of simulation as a BDA technique is closely tied to the power of computers and computer software. More sophisticated computer software will increase the ability of the technique to cope with more complex models. Both the specialist user and the general manager are now well served by the range of simulation software currently available.

TEMPLATE PACKAGES

If the analyst tends to design models which are very closely related to previous models, there are fewer decisions to be made. A template can be used which has a basic structure. After a few parameters are changed, the software is ready to run the simulation. It is unnecessary for the analyst to write a program to simulate the problem because the template software already incorporates the basic model structure. However, it must be remarked that such software is not very flexible: if a problem does not have the characteristics contained in the template, then it will have to be dealt with by other methods.

SPREADSHEETS

Many simulations (such as the models described in this unit) lend themselves to implementation using spreadsheets. All spreadsheets have facilities for generating random numbers and for copying formulae into as many rows as are required by the sample size. However, they cannot handle large complex simulations without recourse to fairly elaborate macros. (Macros are pre-programmed blocks of computer code, used by spreadsheet analysts to perform elaborate tasks.) Nor can they handle problems which require the simulation of such situations as the layout and design of factory or office premises. Nevertheless, as you have seen, a program such as *Microsoft Excel* can handle many types of simulation and is able to perform all of the simulation exercises in this unit.

SPECIAL-PURPOSE SIMULATION LANGUAGES

A number of special-purpose simulation programming languages are now available. These are more flexible than template packages or spreadsheets and allow the analyst (who will need some programming skills) more control over the environment of the simulation problem. A good example of such a simulation package is *GPSS* (**General Purpose Simulation System**). Many of these simulation languages are linked to graphics or animation programs which allow the user to show in animated form the links between the parts of the model. *WITNESS* is a good example of such software. For example, a simulation model of the workings of a factory production line might graphically illustrate the flows, stoppages, queues and bottlenecks of production by showing symbols moving on an animated screen. The student who wishes to continue his or her studies in simulation will inevitably encounter such software, and will consequently need to develop programming skills.

GENERAL-PURPOSE PROGRAMMING LANGUAGES

Some problems are so singular that they cannot be modelled by using a template package, or even a special purpose simulation language. New classes of problems may arise which were never anticipated by such software. In these cases, a general purpose language may be necessary. General purpose languages are powerful tools for simulation purposes, but are also the most time-consuming, since each model must be constructed from scratch. In addition, such programming languages (for example, *Fortran* and *ALGOL*) require considerably more programming skill than template packages, spreadsheets and special-purpose simulation languages.

7.3 Simulation: some pros and cons

The greatest single advantage of simulation is that it can be used where analytical methods cannot. Analytical methods use exact mathematical techniques to achieve a result (linear programming is an example of this): many situations are too complex to use such methods. This may be because of the large number of variables or because the variables do not appear to conform to any known pattern of behaviour. In such cases, a computer simulation would be preferable to analytical techniques. Computer simulation models are also powerful because it is relatively easy to make experimental changes to them, and carry out 'what if' analysis.

However, the use of simulation does have dangers. The first of these problems is that the development of a model represents a considerable task for the analyst entrusted with it. The combined activities of development, validation, running and analysis of the model can be lengthy. It is also important for the analyst to realise that simulation does not guarantee that an optimal solution has been achieved. If the decision-maker has a good idea of what are, and what are not, reasonable values of the decision variables, then the model can be run with appropriate choices, making the likelihood of a good solution high. However, if the decision-maker is unclear as to what constitute likely values for the decision variables, then there is less likelihood of a good solution.

Summary

In this section we have briefly looked at some further topics which are of interest to anyone who wishes to move beyond the restrictions of spreadsheet-based simulation.

Unit Summary

In this unit you have studied some of the methods used in simulation. We began by comparing simulation with other methods used in BDA and noted that while the latter often use deterministic analytical methods, the former is more concerned with randomness. Consequently, simulation requires a good working knowledge of the laws of probability and especially of the behaviour of probability distributions. Next, the major components of a simulation model were examined and the terms **variable**, **parameter** and **output variable** were defined and differentiated.

Using an essentially practical approach, we examined the way in which a spreadsheet such as *Microsoft Excel* could be used to build a working model of the dynamics behind many everyday business situations, such as inventory control, cash flow analysis, queuing and waiting lines, and scheduling. We pointed out that a spreadsheet model may initially be very simple and unsophisticated. (In fact, such simplicity is usually a desirable feature in the early stages of model building, since extra refinements can always be added later.) The output variables from a run of the simulation model can then be examined using statistical analysis, and any emerging patterns identified. If necessary, additional runs of the model can be made to check for the existence of a steady state.

Although spreadsheets can be powerful tools for model construction, it should be pointed out that they can only handle a subset of problems. For example, they cannot handle problems which involve the design and layout of office and industrial premises. Situations where time is a key variable are also difficult to deal with using a spreadsheet. For such models, more specialised simulation software is required which can use computer animation to model flows and patterns of activity.

References

Ackoff, R L and Sassieni, M W (1968) *Fundamentals of Operational Research*, John Wiley, New York, USA.

Recommended Reading

Books on simulation vary greatly in the amount of mathematical knowledge they assume the reader to have. The following books treat the subject in a manner suitable for business studies students.

Daellenbach, H G (1994) *Systems and Decision Making: A Management Science Approach*, John Wiley, New York, USA

Kleijnen, J and Groenendaal, WV (1992) *Simulation – A Statistical Approach*, John Wiley, New York, USA

Vose, D (1992) *Quantitative Risk Analysis: A Guide to Monte Carlo Simulation Modelling*, John Wiley, New York, USA

APPENDIX 1
DRAWING CHARTS WITH
Microsoft Excel

1.1: Drawing Charts with *Microsoft Excel 97*

DRAWING LINE CHARTS WITH *MICROSOFT EXCEL 97*

We will illustrate the process of drawing graphs using the following data, entered into a *Microsoft Excel* worksheet exactly as shown. **Sales** and **Sales Cost** are in £000s.

	A	B	C
1			Sales
2	Year	Sales	Cost
3	1988	23.2	10.1
4	1989	20.5	9.5
5	1990	21.7	11.2
6	1991	25.8	12.0
7	1992	26.2	13.5
8	1993	30.1	15.5
9	1994	28.0	16.0
10	1995	22.6	13.3
11	1996	18.3	11.1
12	1997	25.9	13.1

Table 1: Sales data

Note: data for graphing can be entered in rows as well as columns. Also, although variables may be separated by blank columns or rows, it is best to avoid this if possible, because data cannot then be entered as a single range.

Graphs can be drawn by:

- clicking on **Insert/Chart** in the menu bar
- clicking on the *ChartWizard* icon (see Figure 1).

Figure 1: The *ChartWizard* icon

Whichever of these you choose, you will see the dialogue box shown in Figure 2. This is the first of four screens provided by *ChartWizard* to help you achieve the kind of graph that you want. Step 1 allows you to choose the type of graph you require. See Figure 2.

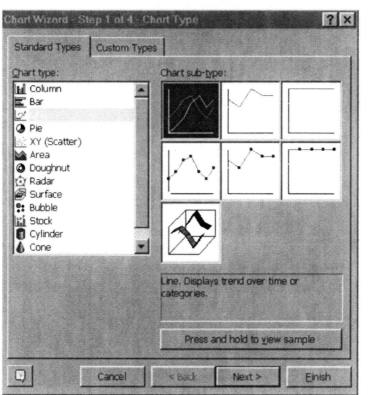

Figure 2: Microsoft Excel 97 Chart Wizard Step 1

It is best to stay with the **Standard Types** selection, as this usually offers a sufficient variety of graphs. The **Custom Types** selection offers more possibilities of customisation, but is consequently more difficult to handle.

Firstly choose the type of graph you want: this will depend on what data you have. The graphs most often encountered in this book are **Column/Bar charts, Line graphs** or **XY scatterplots**.

We will use the **Line graph** as an illustration of the *ChartWizard* process. Line graphs are particularly useful for showing sales or similar data over time. *Microsoft Excel* will allow you to draw simple line graphs with only one data item, or multiple line graphs showing several variables.

Select **Line** from the options listed under **Chart type** and you will be shown a selection of different kinds of line graph (**Chart sub-type**). A brief description of each type of chart appears below the illustrations of the various chart sub-types. We will pick the first type, so click on this graph and then press **Next**.

You will now see the second screen of the *ChartWizard*: this enables you to declare the variable(s) you wish to graph and the labels for the X-axis. See Figure 3.

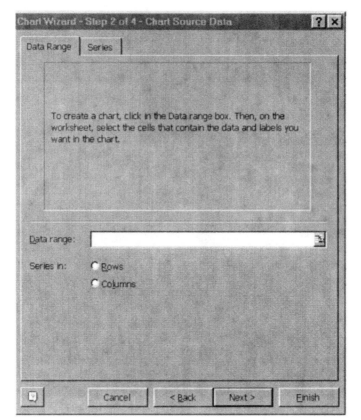

Figure 3: Microsoft Excel 97 Chart Wizard Step 2

In the **Data Range** selection you are invited to state the range in which the data lies. For this illustration we will draw a line graph of sales over time. The sales data lies in cells B3 to B12. There are two ways to enter data.

You can enter the range containing the data into the box labelled **Data Range**. In this case you would enter **B3:B12**.

Or you can click on the button at the end of the box labelled **Data Range**. The *ChartWizard* dialogue box will temporarily disappear, except for the **Data Range** box. You can then see the worksheet screen and use your mouse to select the required data range. Click on the button at the end of the data range box to return to the *ChartWizard*.

Note: you may, if you wish, include a title cell in the data range, but it is far easier to allot titles and labels later.

Make sure that **Rows** or **Columns** is selected as appropriate. In the case of the sample data, **Columns** is the correct choice.

You should click on the **Series** tab before leaving screen 2 of the *ChartWizard*. The purpose of this selection is to allocate the X-axis variable and also choose names if you wish. Now look at Figure 4.

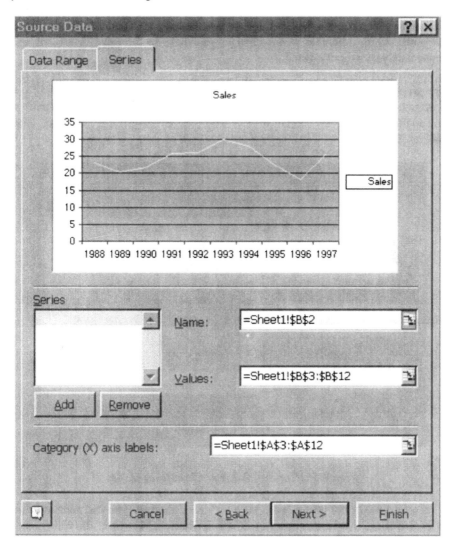

Figure 4: Microsoft Excel 97 Chart Wizard – the X-axis labels

Choose the X-axis labels either by entering the worksheet range that contains them, or by using the mouse as explained above. In the case of this line chart, we are graphing sales against year. The X-axis would represent year, so we would need to select A3 to A12.

You may also name the variable shown in the line chart if you wish. You do not have to do this, but it is particularly useful if you have more than one variable, as it will immediately supply a key with the names you have provided. If you only have one variable the graph will also be given the name of this variable.

For each variable listed in the **Series**, a **Name** box and a **Values** box appear to the right. The **Values** box simply states the worksheet range of the variable (in this case B3 to B12). The **Name** box is where you title the variable. You can do this by either typing in **Sales** (or some other suitable description), or by selecting the cell(s) which contain the label. In this case the label is in cell B2. The second of these methods is preferable, as any changes you make to the name in the cell will immediately show in the graph.

The graph is now complete in its basic form, and you can click on **Finish** if you wish to obtain the result. However, the next screen allows you to make alterations and additions to the basic format, so it is worth persevering. Click on **Next**. Now look at Figure 5.

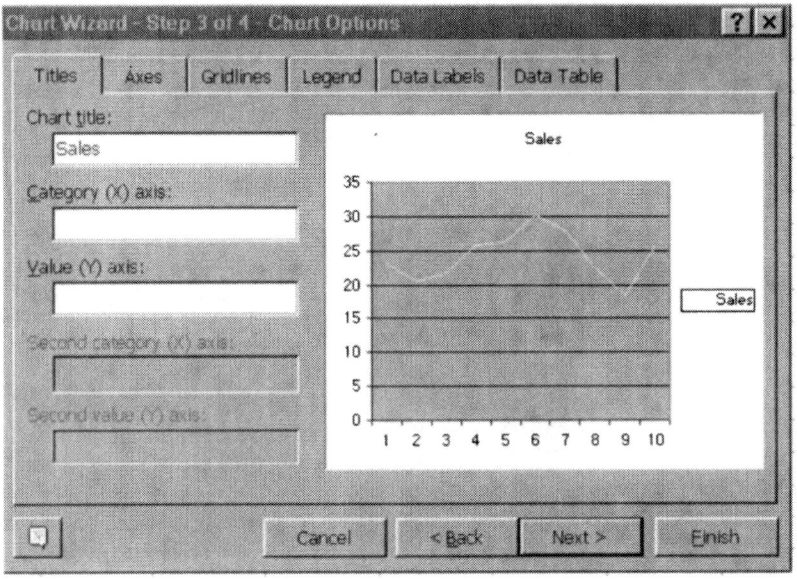

Figure 5: Microsoft Excel 97 Chart Wizard Step 3

This screen performs various functions which are important from the point of view of presentation. It is best to experiment with it yourself. However, the following is a summary of what it will do.

Titles allows you to provide labels for the chart as a whole, and for the X and Y-axes in particular.

Axes allows you to make changes to the way in which the X and Y-axes are displayed. It is usually best left in the default state.

Gridlines allows you to decide whether to show horizontal and/or vertical gridlines, or no gridlines at all. Gridlines can be useful for reading graphs which have detailed scaling.

Legend allows you to decide how to display the series label.

Data Labels allows you to label each point on the graph. This is of limited use.

Data Table allows you the option of including a table of the values used to draw the graph within the presentation. This is of limited use.

After completing Step 3 of the ChartWizard, click on **Next**. You will see the final screen, shown here as Figure 6.

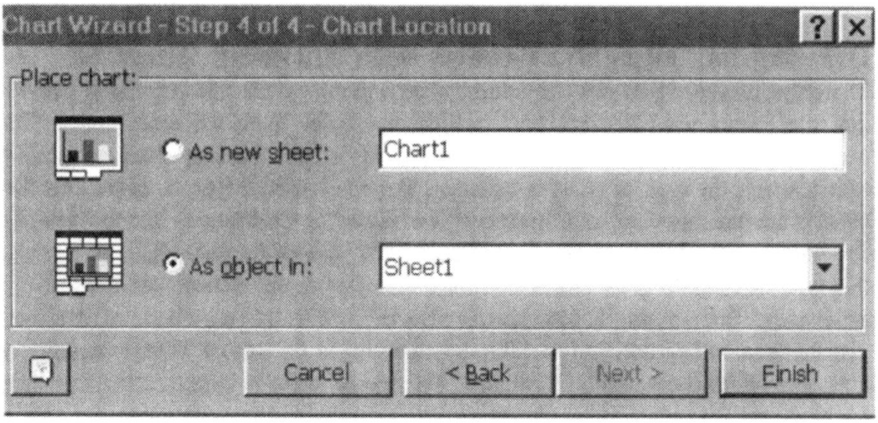

Figure 6: Microsoft Excel 97 Chart Wizard Step 4

This last screen allows you to decide where the graph will be placed.

As new sheet: if you select this option, the chart will be placed in a newly created worksheet of its own called **Chart1**. (You may change this name if you wish.)

As object in: unless you decide otherwise, the graph will be placed within the current worksheet. If you wish, you may place it in another already-created worksheet by altering the description from **Sheet1** to **Sheet2** (or whatever you have called the sheet).

Click on **Finish** and you will see the graph. You may select and move, resize or delete this chart as you would with any other *Microsoft Windows* graphic. If you wish to reformat a particular part of the graph, such as the X-axis or the title, do this by clicking on the item to select it, and then clicking the right mouse button to obtain a specialised menu. You should experiment with this facility.

Drawing XY scatterplots with *Microsoft Excel 97*

Select the *ChartWizard* in the usual way. Select the category **XY scatterplot**, and you will see a list of possible XY plots. A scatterplot consists of two variables, one selected as X and the other as Y with no lines connecting the graph coordinates. Consequently, the correct category to choose is the first in the list.

After clicking on **Next**, you will be asked to complete the range in the way described for the line graph. The difference in entering data for the XY plot is that you are graphing two variables, so the range will reflect this. For example, suppose that we were drawing a scatterplot of the sales and sales cost data shown in Table 1. We would enter the range as **B3:C12**. *Microsoft Excel* will treat the first column of data as the X variable. After clicking on **Next**, the process continues as for the line graph.

Drawing bar or column charts with *Microsoft Excel 97*

The only difference between the column chart and the bar chart in *Microsoft Excel* is that the former uses vertical bars, whilst the latter uses horizontal ones. The procedure for drawing such charts is identical to that for the line chart, except for step 1, where the type of chart is selected. The most useful type of column or bar chart is the one described as **Clustered column** (or **Clustered bar**), where the height or length of the bars is proportionate to the size of the variable. You can use this type of chart to draw charts of single variables or for several variables on the same axes. The column or bar chart is also useful for drawing charts of frequency distributions, where the first variable (or column) is the set of class intervals, or bins, into which the variable is counted. The second column contains the frequency count.

1.2: Drawing Charts with *Microsoft Excel Version 5*

If you are using an earlier version of *Microsoft Excel*, there are some differences as to how to draw charts. The following gives the major differences between version 5 and *Excel 97*.

Click on the **ChartWizard** or on **Insert/Chart**. The first thing that happens is that the cursor changes to a cross-shaped icon. Position the icon in a convenient area of a blank part of the worksheet and draw a rectangular area on the screen by holding the left mouse button down and dragging. The graph will be placed in the resulting rectangle. Do not worry if you are not sure about what size to make it: you can always alter this later. The first screen (of five) of the *ChartWizard* now appears. This is shown as Figure 7.

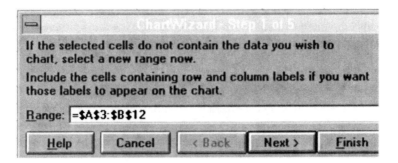

Figure 7: Microsoft Excel Version 5 ChartWizard Step 1

This screen requires you to enter the data that you require to be graphed. Whether you are drawing a line chart, a scatterplot or a column/bar chart, you should enter the range containing **all** the variables, both X and Y-axis. For example, in the sales-year line chart drawn earlier, you would need to enter the range **A3:B12**. Enter the range either by typing it in or by using the mouse. You may include titles in this range. If you do, they will be used as labels (see step 4). Click on **Next**. Screen 2 for the *ChartWizard* now appears.

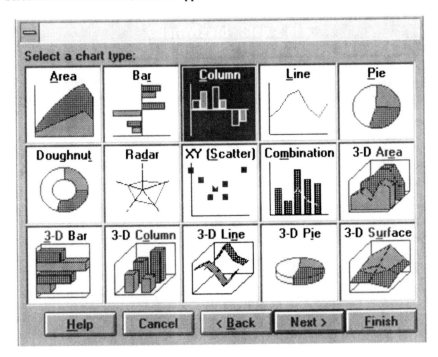

Figure 8: Microsoft Excel 5 ChartWizard Step 2

Select the type of chart you require, for example **Line**. Click on **Next**. You will now see a list of chart categories. Select the one required. For example, for the line chart the most useful are either number 1 (connecting the points with straight lines) or number 12 (connecting the points with smooth curves). See Figure 9.

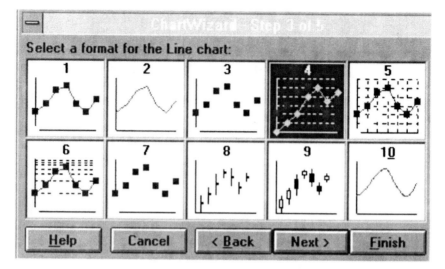

Figure 9: Microsoft Excel 5 ChartWizard Step 3

Click on **Next**. It is important that the next screen is checked carefully, as it is used to tell *Microsoft Excel* which column (variable) to use as the X-axis data.

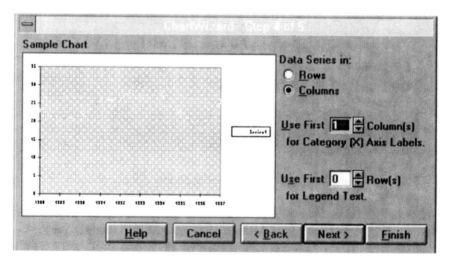

Figure 10: Microsoft Excel 5 ChartWizard Step 4

Click on **Rows** or **Columns**, depending on how you have typed in the data. Where the screen says Use **First __ Columns for Category (X) Axis Labels**, this is asking for the number of the column (or row) where you have entered the X-axis data. In most cases, this will be the first column, so make sure that 1 is selected in this box. If you have included column (or row) headings in the data range in step 1, then you need to make sure that the box entitled **Use First __ Row(s) for Legend Text** has 1 selected in it. Otherwise leave it as **0**. Click on **Next**. You will now see the final screen of the *ChartWizard*. This is shown as Figure 11.

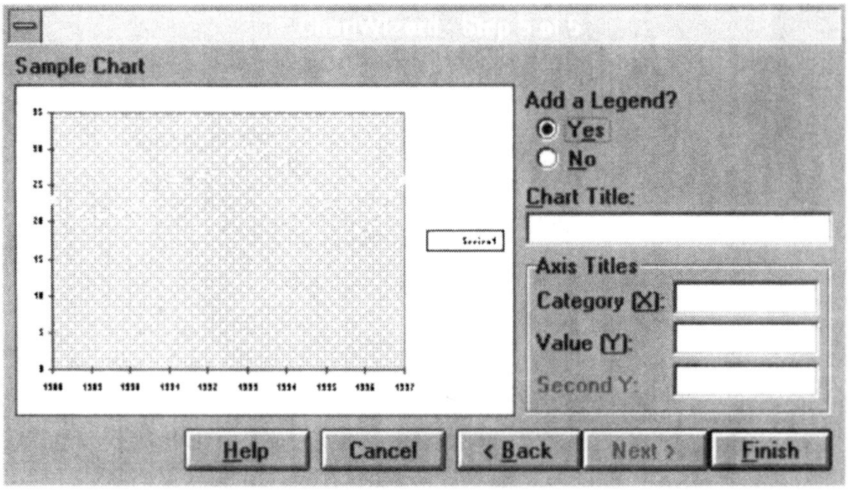

Figure 11: Microsoft Excel 5 ChartWizard Step 5

Although the chart is now basically complete, screen 5 is useful for formatting. A graph legend (or key) may be added if wished: click on **Yes** or **No** accordingly. Legends are useful where you have multiple line curves or bar charts. You can also enter in text which will be used for X-axis, Y-axis and overall chart titles. Click on **Finish** and the chart is complete.

The resulting chart may be resized, deleted or reformatted after completion. Clicking on a feature of the graph, such as the X-axis, chart title or legend, and then on the right mouse button will display a formatting menu relating particularly to the selected feature.

APPENDIX 2
INSTALLING THE REGRESSION TOOL

Both *Excel 97* and version 5 provide a facility called **Data Analysis** to be found in the **Tools** menu on the menu bar. It must be stressed that this function is an *Add-in*. Although provided with the *Microsoft Excel* software, the user must install the *Data Analysis ToolPak* before it can be used. To do this, click on the **Tools** menu, and then on **Add-ins**. A dialogue box like the one shown in Figure 1 will appear.

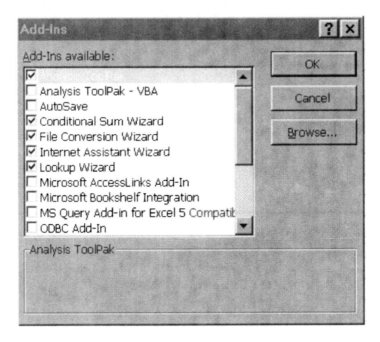

Figure 1: Add-ins dialogue box

The box shows a list of the add-ins which can be used with *Microsoft Excel*. The one required for regression analysis is called **Analysis ToolPak**. (**Note:** not **Analysis ToolPak VBA**.) To install it simply click on the box next to the name, and then on **OK**. After a short pause the routine will be installed. If it has been successful, you should find that an item called **Data Analysis** will appear on the **Tools** menu.

Regression analysis is a function within the data analysis pack. There are no material differences between the regression tool for *Excel 97* and version 5, except for the way in which data may be input. In version 5, the data ranges for dependent and independent variables must be typed in. In *Excel 97*, the user may either type in a range (as with version 5) or use the mouse to select a range.

Printed in the United Kingdom
by Lightning Source UK Ltd.
136513UK00001B/11/P